BERLIN

Also by Barney White-Spunner

Horse Guards
Of Living Valour
Partition

BERLIN

The Story of a City

BARNEY WHITE-SPUNNER

PEGASUS BOOKS
NEW YORK LONDON

BERLIN

Pegasus Books, Ltd.
148 West 37th Street, 13th Floor
New York, NY 10018

First Pegasus Books cloth edition May 2021

ISBN: 978-1-64313-722-3

10 9 8 7 6 5 4 3 2 1

Printed in the United States of America
Distributed by Simon & Schuster
www.pegasusbooks.com

In memory of Michael Sissons –
mentor, inspiration and friend

Contents

LIST OF MAPS AND ILLUSTRATIONS

All maps and artwork © ML Design

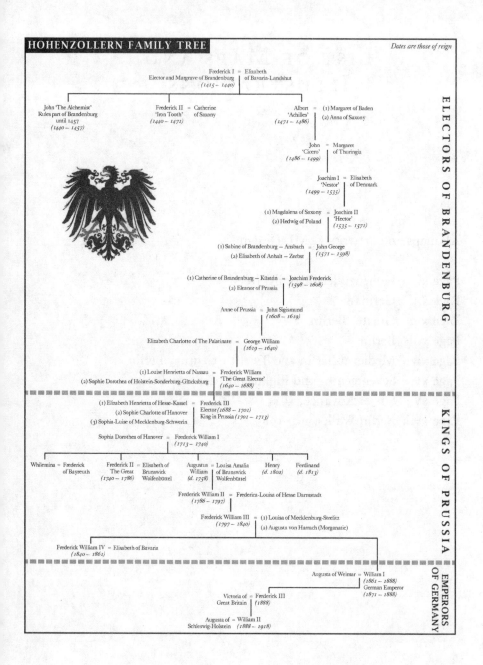

HOHENZOLLERN FAMILY TREE

Dates are those of reign

ELECTORS OF BRANDENBURG

Frederick I = Elizabeth
Elector and Margrave of Brandenburg | of Bavaria-Landshut
(1415 – 1440)

John 'The Alchemist'
Rules part of Brandenburg
until 1457
(1440 – 1457)

Frederick II = Catherine
'Iron Tooth' | of Saxony
(1440 – 1471)

Albert = (1) Margaret of Baden
'Achilles' | (2) Anna of Saxony
(1471 – 1486)

John = Margaret
'Cicero' | of Thuringia
(1486 – 1499)

Joachim I = Elisabeth
'Nestor' | of Denmark
(1499 – 1535)

(1) Magdalena of Saxony | Joachim II
(2) Hedwig of Poland | 'Hector'
(1535 – 1571)

(1) Sabine of Brandenburg – Ansbach = John George
(2) Elisabeth of Anhalt – Zerbst | *(1571 – 1598)*

(1) Catherine of Brandenburg – Küstrin = Joachim Frederick
(2) Eleanor of Prussia | *(1598 – 1608)*

Anne of Prussia = John Sigismund
(1608 – 1619)

Elizabeth Charlotte of The Palatinate = George William
(1619 – 1640)

(1) Louise Henrietta of Nassau = Frederick William
(2) Sophie Dorothea of Holstein-Sonderburg-Glücksburg | 'The Great Elector'
(1640 – 1688)

KINGS OF PRUSSIA

(1) Elizabeth Henrietta of Hesse-Kassel = Frederick III
(2) Sophie Charlotte of Hanover | Elector *(1688 – 1701)*
(3) Sophia-Luise of Mecklenburg-Schwerin | King in Prussia *(1701 – 1713)*

Sophia Dorothea of Hanover = Frederick William I
(1713 – 1740)

Whilemina = Frederick
of Bayreuth

Frederick II = Elisabeth of
The Great | Brunswick
(1740 – 1786) | Wolfenbüttel

Augustus = Louisa Amalia
William | of Brunswick
(d. 1758) | Wolfenbüttel

Henry
(d. 1802)

Ferdinand
(d. 1813)

Frederick William II = Frederica-Louisa of Hesse Darmstadt
(1786 – 1797)

Frederick William III = (1) Louisa of Mecklenburg-Strelitz
(1797 – 1840) | (2) Augusta von Harrach (Morganatic)

Frederick William IV = Elisabeth of Bavaria
(1840 – 1861)

EMPERORS OF GERMANY

Augusta of Weimar = William I
(1861 – 1888)
German Emperor
(1871 – 1888)

Victoria of = Frederick III
Great Britain | *(1888)*

Augusta of = William II
Schleswig-Holstein | *(1888 – 1918)*

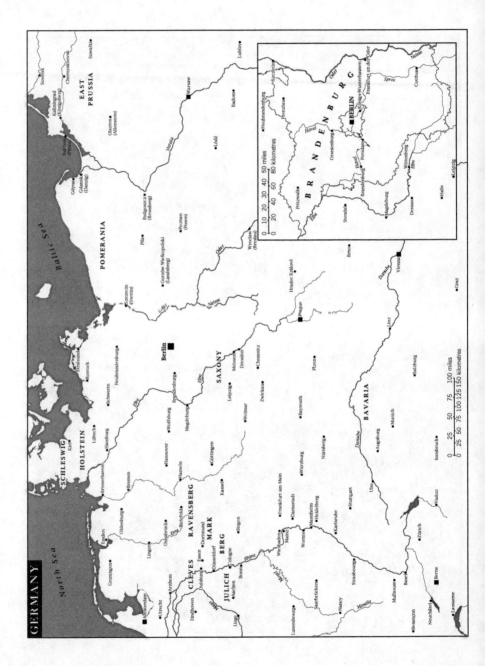

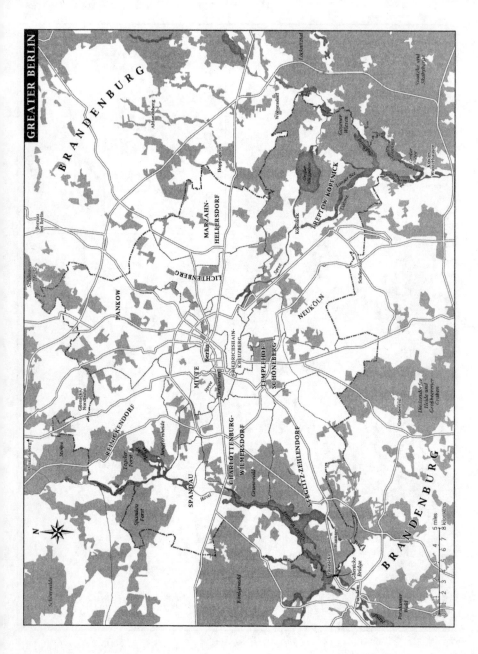

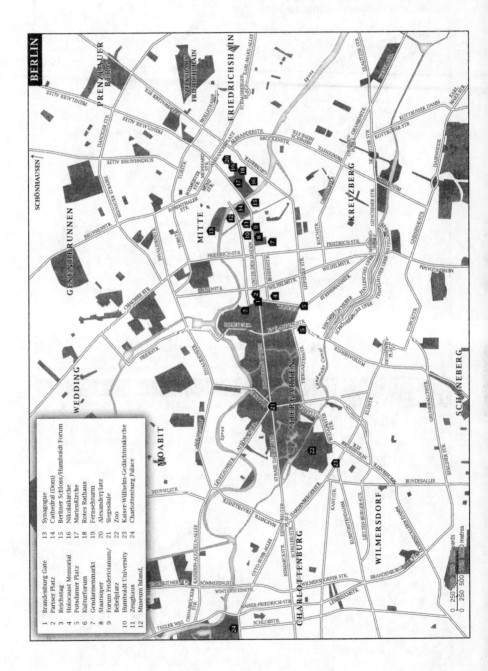

BERLIN

1	Brandenburg Gate
2	Pariser Platz
3	Reichstag
4	Holocaust Memorial
5	Potsdamer Platz
6	Kulturforum
7	Gendarmenmarkt
8	Staatsoper
9	Forum Fridericianum/ Bebelplatz
10	Humboldt University
11	Zeughaus
12	Museum Island
13	Synagogue
14	Cathedral (Dom)
15	Berliner Schloss/Humboldt Forum
16	Nikolaikirche
17	Marienkirche
18	Rotes Rathaus
19	Fernsehturm
20	Alexanderplatz
21	Siegessäule
22	Zoo
23	Kaiser-Wilhelm-Gedächtniskirche
24	Charlottenburg Palace

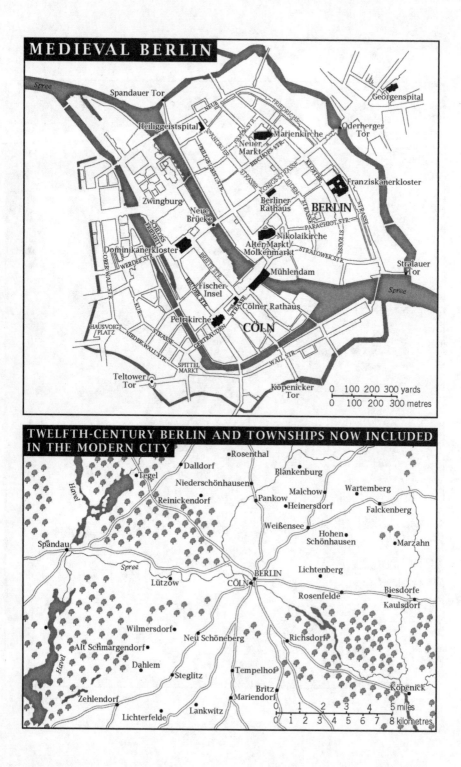

MEDIEVAL BERLIN

Spree

Spandauer Tor

Georgenspital

Heiliggeistspital

NEUE

FRIEDRICHS

Oderherger
Tor

SPANDAUER

Marienkirche

Neuer
Markt

BISCHOFS STR.

Franziskanerkloster

HEILIGE GEIST STR.

STRASSE

KÖNIGS STR.

JUDEN STR.

KLOSTER STR.

BERLIN

STRASSE

Zwingburg

Berliner
Rathaus

Neue
Brücke

PARACHIOT STR.

SCHLOSS FREIHEIT

Nikolaikirche

Dominikanerkloster

Alter Markt/
Molkenmarkt

STRALOWER STR.

OBER WALL STR.

WERDER STR.

Mühlendam

Stralauer
Tor

Spree

KUR STR.

BREITE STR.

WINDER STR.

Fischer
Insel

Cölner Rathaus

HAUSVOIGT
PLATZ

Petrikirche

STRASSE

CÖLN

NIEDER-WALL STR.

STRASSE

GERTRAUDEN

WAL. STR.

Teltower
Tor

SPITTEL
MARKT

Köpenicker
Tor

| 0 | 100 | 200 | 300 yards |
| 0 | 100 | 200 | 300 metres |

TWELFTH-CENTURY BERLIN AND TOWNSHIPS NOW INCLUDED
IN THE MODERN CITY

Rosenthal

Havel

Tegel

Dalldorf

Blankenburg

Niederschönhausen

Malchow

Wartemberg

Reinickendorf

Pankow

Heinersdorf

Falckenberg

Spandau

Weißensee

Hohen
Schönhausen

Marzahn

Spree

Lichtenberg

Lützow

BERLIN

CÖLN

Biesdorfe

Rosenfelde

Kaulsdorf

Wilmersdorf

Neu Schöneberg

Richsdorf

Havel

Alt Schmargendorf

Dahlem

Steglitz

Tempelhof

Köpenick

Zehlendorf

Britz

Mariendorf

Lichterfelde

Lankwitz

| 0 | 1 | 2 | 3 | 4 | 5 miles |
| 0 | 1 | 2 | 3 | 4 | 5 | 6 | 7 | 8 kilometres |

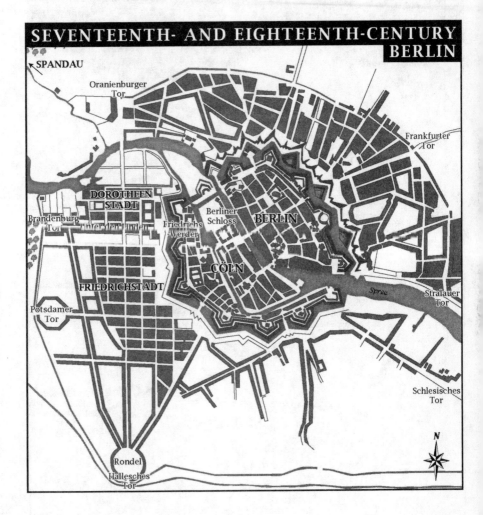

SEVENTEENTH- AND EIGHTEENTH-CENTURY BERLIN

SPANDAU

Oranienburger Tor

Frankfurter Tor

DOROTHEEN STADT

Brandenburg Tor

Unter den Linden

Berliner Schloss

Friedrichs-Werder

BERLIN

CÖLN

FRIEDRICHSTADT

Potsdamer Tor

Spree

Stralauer Tor

Schlesisches Tor

Rondel

Hallesches Tor

N

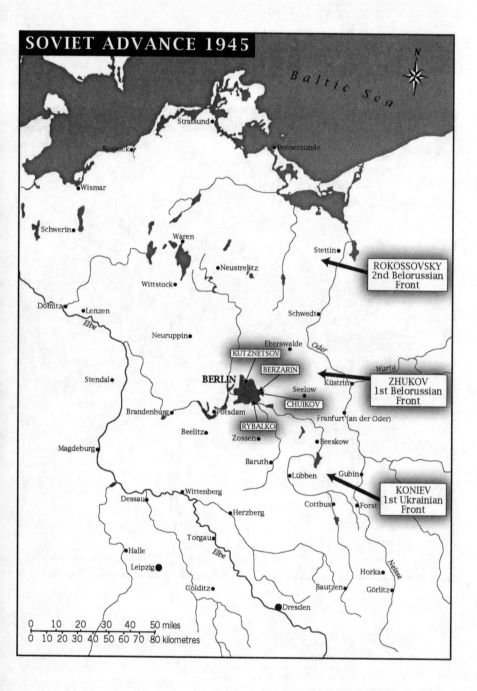

SOVIET ADVANCE 1945

Baltic Sea

N

Stralsund

Rostock

Peenemünde

Wismar

Schwerin

Waren

Neustrelitz

Wittstock

Stettin

ROKOSSOVSKY
2nd Belorussian
Front

Dömitz

Lenzen

Elbe

Neuruppin

Schwedt

Oder

Eberswalde

KUTZNETSOV

BERZARIN

BERLIN

Seelow

CHUIKOV

Küstrin

Warta

ZHUKOV
1st Belorussian
Front

Stendal

Brandenburg

Potsdam

Beelitz

RYBALKO

Zossen

Franfurt (an der Oder)

Magdeburg

Baruth

Beeskow

Lübben

Gubin

KONIEV
1st Ukrainian
Front

Dessau

Wittenberg

Herzberg

Cottbus

Forst

Torgau

Elbe

Halle

Leipzig

Colditz

Dresden

Bautzen

Horka

Görlitz

Neisse

| 0 | 10 | 20 | 30 | 40 | 50 miles |

| 0 | 10 | 20 | 30 | 40 | 50 | 60 | 70 | 80 kilometres |

BERLIN WALL 1961-1989

N

FRENCH ZONE

Tegel

Chausseestraße

Bornholmer
Straße

SOVIET ZONE

Staaken — Heerstraße

BRITISH ZONE

Invalidenstraße

Prinzenstraße

Oberbaumbrücke

Friedrichstraße
Checkpoint Charlie

Gatow

AMERICAN ZONE

Tempelhof

Sonnenallee

Dreilinden
(Checkpoint Bravo)

Drewitz

Waltersdorfer
Chaussee

EAST GERMANY
(RUSSIAN ZONE)

✈ Airports

✕ Checkpoints open to Germans only

⊗ Checkpoints open to Germans and non-Germans

West Berlin

Viewing platform for
West Berliners and tourists

3.6-meter-high Grenzwall
75 L-shaped wall

Floodlight
poles

BT-11 guard tower, manned 24/7
by teams of 2-5 with clear fields of fire

East Berlin

("Restricted Zone")
off-limits to ordinary citizens
and buildings cleared away

Inner 2-meter-high signal
fence with signal equipment
linked to fence

Older 3-meter-high
inner concrete wall,
topped with barbed
wire

Guard
hut

Dog
run

Hedgehog anti-vehicle obstacles

Vehicle ditches

Asphalt road for border patrols to move quickly
between guard towers

Notes on the Text

Names. My approach to names has been to make them as approachable as possible to an English-speaking readership. Consequently, I have generally used the English version of the Hohenzollerns' names, hence The Great Elector instead of the correct German *Große Kurfürst*, Frederick the Great (or just Frederick) for Friedrich II, and William II for Kaiser Wilhelm II. Other names I have mostly left in their German form and I have tried, where possible, to give people's full name as the Germans so correctly do. Place names have similarly nearly all been left in German but there are again exceptions where it makes the text easier to understand. So, for example, I use Saxony rather than Sachsen, Silesia as opposed to Schlesien.

For those unfamiliar with German, the letter *ß*, called an *Eszett*, is sometimes confusing. It replicates a double *s* but is only used where the preceding vowel sound is long, as in *Straße*, or a diphthong, as in *Schultheiß*. If the preceding vowel is short then *ss* is used, as in *Schloss*. It is muddling, and there are, as always, exceptions that don't follow the rule, but if you read each *ß* simply as an English *s* then you will not go far wrong.

Currency. The various different currencies that Berlin has used over its life are also confusing, and converting them into sensible modern equivalents is challenging. This is a simplified guide, as to cover all the various ramifications would only serve to confuse further and is unnecessary to enjoy this story.

Prior to 1566 a wide variety of European currencies were in use across the Holy Roman Empire. Berlin's permission to mint its own coinage in 1396 was a major step in the development of its economy, but Imperial groschen and guilders remained the preferred coinage across North Germany over Berlin pfennig, or pennies. From 1566 the Hapsburgs minted Imperial Reichsthalers and the thaler became the accepted North Germany currency until 1750 when Frederick the Great, desperate for funds to fight his wars and unwilling to be slave to Austrian currency, issued Prussia's own Reichsthaler. Thalers were divided into 24 groschen (later 30) and each groschen was worth 12 pfennig; it's easiest to think of them as pounds, shillings and pence, and the terms schilling and groschen were often used together. I have tried to calculate rough equivalent modern values at various points in the text.

Reichsthalers lasted, in various forms, until the creation of Germany in 1871. In 1873 German Imperial Reichsmarks were issued, usually just called marks. These were in use until the great inflation of the early 1920s when they were supplemented, but not actually replaced, by the Rentenmark, the currency that is credited with restoring some confidence in the economy. Its initial valuation was 1 billion Reichsmarks and it was decimal, being divided into 100 pfennig. Both currencies were written as 'RM' and remained until after the Second World War. The Allied Powers briefly issued a temporary currency post-war but in June 1948 the new Deutschmark, written as DM, was first issued, one of the factors that caused Stalin to seal off Berlin and which led to the Berlin Airlift. There were, again, 100 pfennig to one Deutschmark. East Germany issued its own marks in retaliation, usually referred to as Ostmarks. After reunification in 1989 Germany used the Deutschmark until 1 January 1999 when it went over to the Euro. Older Berliners would still refer to a 10-pfennig coin as a groschen, although that is now dying out with the Euro.

PROLOGUE

Berliners started knocking down the Berlin Wall, block by block, on 9 November 1989. That monstrous barrier of concrete and barbed wire, with its watchtowers, death strips, machine guns and officious border guards, which had divided both Berlin and Europe for twenty-eight years, was demolished over the following weeks so that nothing remained apart from small sections preserved as a reminder of what had once been and the suffering it had caused. Reunification of East Germany – the German Democratic Republic, or GDR – and West Germany – the Federal Republic of Germany, the FRG – followed just under a year later. Surely, many assumed, the reunited country would logically decide to restore Berlin as its capital? Berlin was the natural *Hauptstadt*, the capital of Prussia and of Germany in that brief period between 1870 and 1945 when Germany was a united nation. The kaisers had ruled from the Berliner Schloss, the Reichstag was in Berlin and so much of the history of what made Germany was surely in

Berlin's streets, its institutions, its museums and in its people? But many disagreed.

A lot of Germans thought Berlin was associated with first Prussian and then Nazi militarism. These were people who saw the border between the GDR and FRG as more than just a communist-designed plot to divide Europe. For them it was the border between two Germanies, between the flat, sandy plains of Brandenburg and Mecklenburg and the western-looking areas along the Rhine, areas the more historically minded argued had been colonised by the Romans and looked towards Europe while Berlin looked out east towards Russia and the steppes. Berlin did not represent what the FRG had strived so hard to achieve since 1945 and it was certainly not symbolic of what they hoped the reunited Germany would now become.

The national debate, which lasted for a year and a half, was difficult and emotional. Eventually the vote was taken in the Bundestag, the German parliament sitting in the small and rather undistinguished Rhineland city of Bonn, which summarised so nicely the values that had allowed the FRG to rebuild itself. The result was close. By a narrow majority of eighteen, on 20 June 1991 German politicians decided that the national capital would be in Berlin, although even then several important government offices were to remain in Bonn.

What made this intense debate seem rather strange to Berliners was that they saw themselves as anything but representatives of the old Prussia. Not only, they argued, was Berlin not the true capital of Prussia (which was instead Königsberg, now Kaliningrad, a small Russian enclave sandwiched between Poland and Lithuania, and 500 miles away to the east), but the character, history and people of Berlin had, almost since its foundation, been the very antithesis of the Prussian military cult that so alarmed the Rhineland deputies. Berlin may have been the administrative capital of Prussia for nearly five hundred years but it has always retained its own distinctive, rebellious, irreverent character; it was never a 'Prussian' city.

Berlin is in Brandenburg, hundreds of miles west of what was originally Prussia. It would eventually become the capital of

Brandenburg in 1486, but only of Prussia in 1701. It was not until 1871 that Berlin became capital of Germany, which did not exist as a state until Bismarck created it. Berlin is, coincidentally, exactly the same distance east of the River Rhine and Germany's western border as it is west of Kaliningrad. Today it is very close, barely 30 miles, to modern Germany's eastern border with Poland on the River Oder. It has therefore always been as much an eastern European city as it has a western one, shaped and subject to the winds and moods of the great plains reaching towards the steppes, as it has to the very different but no less damaging pressures from the west. It has always been a city on the edge.

The story of the city is also the story of the Hohenzollerns – electors of Brandenburg, dukes then kings in, and later of, Prussia and finally German kaisers. For much of their joint history the fate of Berlin and its dynasty are intertwined. This book is not a history of Prussia but it is the joint story of electors and kings and their capital, which variously supported and opposed them, gradually came to resent them and finally exiled them.

There is a particular frisson about Berlin, a combination of excitement, anticipation, nervousness and the unexpected. Through all its life it has been a city of tensions. Its position – on the frontier of Europe, on the 'Mark', where Christianity met paganism, where the Huns met the Slavs, where Europe met Russia and where fertile land met the sands, swamps and forests of Pomerania and Prussia – gives it a geographical tension. It was also long a city of religious tension, between a largely Lutheran people and a Calvinist government, and later becoming pretty irreligious altogether. In the nineteenth century political tension became acute between a city that was increasingly democratic, home to Marx and Hegel, and one of the most autocratic regimes in Europe. In 1918 that tension resulted in revolution, the *Dolchstoß*, the stab in the back, which allowed the German army to claim that it had never been defeated and which, with the economic chaos in the 1920s, paved the way for the Nazis. Between 1945 and 1989 the political tension between the GDR and West Berlin, the western city trapped in a communist state, took that tension to the extreme. From the mid-eighteenth century there was artistic tension as free thinking and liberal movements, championed by monarchs like Frederick the Great, started to find themselves in direct contention with the formal – some would say stultifying – official culture while in the 1920s, and in the last few decades, Berlin has challenged the rest of Europe with the diversity of its free thinking.

Underlying all this was the ethnic tension between multi-racial Berliners and the Prussians. Berlin has long been a city of immigrants. Many European capitals have historically had large immigrant populations but few have been as diverse as Berlin, possibly because few European cities have suffered such catastrophic destruction twice as Berlin has; nor have many been as successful at incorporating new identities into their own distinctive character. Berliners make great play of the idea of the 'traditional Berliner' but there is no such person. A typical Berliner is instead someone who comes to Berlin and adopts the casual, slightly grumpy, sharp yet warm, hedonistic and vibrant character that has come from waves of settlers. Burgundians, Huns, Wends, Dutch, Flemish, Poles, Jews, Huguenots, French, Austrians, Silesians, Russians, Turks, Africans, Vietnamese and many, many more are all as typical Berliners as the descendants of the now very few families who can trace their ancestry back to the city's founding. 'Perhaps the absolutely typical Berliner is the one who has just arrived,' noted Christoph Stölzl, a Bavarian, who recalled:

'on 1 October 1987 I took up my duties as the founding director of the German Historical Museum. On my desk was an invitation, from a Senate Office of the State of Berlin as I recall, to participate in a podium discussion "Problems of Urban Planning Today". I gave those who had invited me a call, and politely explained that I had only been in office for a day and that I had no wish to presume to have an opinion already on such intricate topics. But the voice on the other end of the telephone decreed in a sharp Berlin tone; "You are here now, so you have an opinion!" In Hamburg it takes two years to have an opinion; even in Munich it takes at least one but in Berlin you are a Berliner as soon as you arrive.'[1]

Berlin's character has also been defined, more tragically, by those who have left. It is as much a city of emigrants as it is of immigrants, although that is a characteristic most brutally evident in the twentieth century.

Evidence of Berliners' independence and resistance to authority is that no Prussian or German ruler has ever really felt welcome there. From the earliest Hohenzollerns to post-1945 Germany, rulers have found ways of living outside the city from which they had to run their governments. Generations of Hohenzollerns built country retreats outside Berlin, which, comfortable and agreeable as they may have been, chiefly served to remove them from the city itself. Berlin was never as supportive of the Kaiser in 1914 as the rest of Germany; it was the revolution in Berlin in 1918 that led to his abdication and Germany suing for peace. Hitler, greatly to Berlin's credit, loathed the place. Goebbels, the Nazi gauleiter, described it as 'a melting pot of everything that is evil – prostitution, drinking houses, cinemas, Marxism, Jews, Strippers, Negroes dancing, and all the vile offshoots of so-called modern art'.[2] The city was home to much of the opposition to the Nazis, although paradoxically it suffered more than any other German city from Hitler's war. Konrad Adenauer, the great West German Chancellor from 1949 to 1963, called it 'a Babylon amidst the Northern Steppes'[3] and wanted to trade it for parts of East Germany. Berliners never liked him much either.

Berlin is also so absorbing because its distinctive independence of character allows it to keep and cherish its memories, however painful they may be to confront. Whereas some cities, particularly those in eastern Europe that have suffered so much, practise a sort of 'heroic denial' by rebuilding themselves as they imagined they once were, Berlin refuses to hide its past. Its buildings, such as the Reichstag and the Berliner Schloss, must pull together the different strands of its story so that it remembers through its architecture. 'Memories,' said Neil MacGregor, 'shape Berlin. It doesn't use the past to escape; rather it confronts it and tries to live with it.'[4]

Berlin's attitude is best described as liberalism but with a certain degree of order. Like many Germans, Berliners are law-abiding; it is still unusual to see a pedestrian cross an entirely empty street until the iconic Ampelmann signal goes green. Yet Berlin has revolted five times and has long been one of the most socially and culturally innovative cities in Europe. The reason that so many people, especially young people, love it is that no one will ever judge you there. It is, though, a hard city, a city of live and let live. It can also, as this story will show, be a brutal city. Berliners are famously direct, even rude, a characteristic that is more a tradition than a true reflection of their character and that does not mean the city is not an increasingly nice place to live. With so much space, so many parks, a huge variety of entertainment, endless restaurants and cafes, with its political life, its cultural life, its seemingly thousands of dogs, mad cyclists, its marches, its history, its waterways, its new housing and, airports excepted, its excellent transport, it is small wonder that people from across Germany are now making their home there as well as a steady stream of immigrants who, in the best Berlin tradition, keep coming. Reunification has taken longer than perhaps people thought it would; there is still a strong element of the divided city, of East versus West, but that is now beginning to disappear. The question is how will Berlin develop in this century? Will it retain its rough-around-the-edges feeling that alarmed Goethe, welcoming immigrants and home to every diverse culture? Or will the fact that it has become such an agreeable place to live change its character? Many see the gentrification of the city as a greater threat to its traditional character than continued immigration, something that is explored in the concluding chapter.

For me Berlin was a formative experience. It was a city I first knew in the 1970s, long before the Wall came down, and it has fascinated me ever since. I still get that same sense of excitement, dread even, when I arrive now as I did when I was travelling through the GDR and across the Wall forty years ago. The city has ghosts everywhere – medieval ghosts, Hohenzollern spirits, Nazi devils and communist shadows. When I started to write this book, many Berliners said to me, 'Please, not another book about the Nazis and the Second World War. Our history did actually start before 1933.' What is so frustrating for Germans in general, and Berliners in particular, is that they still feel defined by the Nazi era, by those twelve terrible years until 1945 and, to a lesser extent, by the Iron Curtain and the Wall. Yet, as they point out, those years were an aberration, an interruption, admittedly a terrible one, but an interruption nonetheless in a story that starts a very long time ago. Berlin's story, its traits and habits, its character and spirit, did not begin when the Wall went up in 1961 nor when it came down in 1989; neither did they start with Hitler, nor with the foundation of the German Reich in 1871; they did not start in 1848 nor in 1815 with the expulsion of the French invader, nor in 1648 as the city recovered from its first crucifixion. They started, as this book does, with written history.

CHAPTER ONE

1237–1500

*'How on earth did someone come up with
the idea of founding a city in the middle of all
that sand?'*

STENDHAL, 1808

Berlin lies in the very flat and sandy Brandenburg plain between the Elbe and the Oder rivers. Standing on the top of the Fernsehturm, the former broadcasting tower in the centre of the city near Alexanderplatz, you can gaze for many miles to the north without even an undulation to interrupt your view. To the south-east you can see some low hills, the Müggelberge, above the Müggelsee, but they only rise to 300 feet. You may also just be able to make out a slight rise above the Oder, known optimistically as the Seelow Heights and from where the Soviets launched their final assault on the city in 1945. To your south there is a bit of a bump at the old Tempelhof airport, but it is hardly worth dignifying as a hill. To the west there is a sizeable mound, the Teufelsberg, but this is man-made from much of the hundred million tons of debris from the destruction of the city in the Second World War. Otherwise all around is very, very flat so that Berlin has no natural defences.

Brandenburg was known derisively as 'the sandbox' because of its poor soil. It is not even German soil. During the Ice Age three huge glaciers from Scandinavia flowed south and terminated where Berlin now stands, allowing Berlin's wits to argue that this is why it is such an atypical German city. In early modern Europe Brandenburg had few towns of much importance and certainly could not compete in terms of population and wealth with Saxony's flourishing cities of Dresden and Leipzig to the south, nor with Poland to its east. West of the Elbe lay the successful imperial city of Magdeburg, and the rich farmland of the Hanover plains. Brandenburg's major settlements were at Frankfurt an der Oder (not to be confused with the much larger Frankfurt am Main) and Brandenburg itself, a town that might plausibly have emerged as the capital, as indeed it briefly had been. There is little in Brandenburg's geography to suggest it might become the centre of an empire and even less physically to recommend Berlin as its capital.

Berlin stands, however, where the River Spree flows into the River Havel, which in turn winds its lazy and pretty course through the plain to join the Elbe at Havelberg. The Spree is not much of a river, a mere stream when compared to the great rivers of Germany, but it was navigable to the boats used for transport in early modern Europe and full of fish, both of which would mean that it supported settlement. It was logical that a settlement would be near the confluence with the Havel, as goods could then travel down the Elbe to Hamburg and the ports that would form the Hanseatic League. A few miles upstream from that junction, as the Spree bent north, it divided around an island, creating a channel useful for trapping fish and wharfing boats. Variously called *Fischerinsel* (Fisherman's Island) and much later *Museumsinsel* (Museum Island), this island would become the centre of the city.

The Brandenburg plain has been populated for millennia, at least as early as 4000 BC, with a settlement on the island traceable back to 2000 BC. The original people were probably what the Romans called the Semnones, famously described by Tacitus as warlike people with strange top knots who worshipped trees and horses. By 3 BC Tiberius and his Roman legions had reached the Elbe and, although he made treaties with the Semnones, he did not attempt to colonise to the east, a decision that would arguably have a fundamental impact on later German history, though Frederick the Great, the famous King of Prussia from 1740, would later claim in his witty if historically doubtful *Memoirs of the House of Brandenburg* that major Roman remains had been found at Zossen near Berlin.[1] Others have tried to link Berlin's founding with Arminius, or Herman, the German prince who famously massacred three Roman legions commanded by Varus in the Teutoburger Wald in 9 AD, but there is no evidence for that.

The Roman border on the Elbe held until the late fourth century AD, despite the Semnones being pushed south by Burgundian immigrants from the area of what is now Denmark, but both Burgundians and Semnones were from around 400 AD to be pushed west by waves of Huns migrating from the east. The Huns, demonised as the worst sort of savages in European history and who gave their name to the derogatory term for the Germans, settled around what would become Berlin. The grave of a Hun warrior buried with his horse has been found in Neukölln, now a district in south Berlin. The Huns were, however, a migratory people and habitually pushed on westwards, led by Attila whose name has been used to terrify generations of western children. Attila pursued the fleeing Burgundians, as devotees of Wagner will know, until he collapsed and died after a drinking bout in 453 AD. It was now the turn of the Huns to be pushed westwards as, from around 500 AD, waves of Slavs from Russia and the Carpathians settled the area of Poland and up to the Elbe. It was with the arrival of these Southern or Western Slavs, called Wends, that the story of Berlin begins to take on a more definite shape.

The Wends, unlike their Christianised Eastern Slav brothers, did not write anything down much before 1000 AD so their early history is a bit murky, but we know that they developed twin settlements at Berlin and Cölln, either side of the Spree opposite Fischerinsel, where they cohabited peacefully with the remaining Huns, in an early example of Berliners absorbing immigrants, and adopted their religious practices. There was also very possibly a Jewish population

in the area, and it was certainly well established by 1000 AD. The
Wendish legacy remains strong in Berlin today; places names that
end in -ow, -itz or -ick mostly have Wendish origins; Pankow,
Treptow, Steglitz, Beelitz, Köpenick and Spandau, which was originally spelled Spandow, are all Wendish names. Wendish – or, more
correctly, Polabian – was allegedly still spoken in the more remote
parts of Brandenburg until the Second World War, when such
uncomfortable reminders of Slavic origin were quickly eliminated.
There is a rather nice story that Berlin takes its name from the bear,
which has long been the city's symbol, but it is more likely it comes
from the Wendish *berl*, which means a marsh, while Cölln probably
comes from the word for a settlement or colony, much as the other
Köln on the Rhine.

Berlin and Cölln were not initially that important, with the
major Wendish settlements and fortifications being at Spandau
and Brandenburg. From the tenth century onwards Berlin's history
becomes part of the wider struggle between the Frankish Christian
kings ruling west of the Elbe, who were heirs of Charlemagne and
predecessors of the Holy Roman Emperors, and the pagan Wends. In
781 AD the country between the Elbe and the Oder had been taken
by Charlemagne but it was too much for his dynasty to hold. In 843
at the Treaty of Verdun the Wendish–German border was reaffirmed
along the Elbe. It was not until 928 that the attractively named
Henry the Fowler – both King of the Franks and Duke of Saxony –
firmly consolidated German rule and established the 'Mark' (literally
the 'frontier' or 'march' in English) to be governed by a mark grave
or margrave. He had an initial and unsuccessful attempt to stop the
Wends from worshipping trees or watering them with the blood of
their victims. In 946 or thereabouts his successor, Otto I, founded a
bishopric at Brandenburg but in 983 there was a major Wend revolt
while the attention of his son, another Otto, was diverted to southern Europe. It was a major setback, driven by insensitive German
colonisation and forcing Christianity on a reluctant population.

This reluctance to accept organised and hierarchical religion is a
theme that would become part of Berlin's character. It was not until

over a century later that the Mark was re-established, by the last of the Ottonian kings, Lothair III who ruled from 1125 until 1137. He did two things that would make it hard for the Wends to continue in their pagan ways. First, he made peace with Poland, now converted to Christianity, which exerted pressure on Brandenburg from the east. Secondly, in 1137 he appointed Albert the Bear as margrave. Albert, probably because of his name and because he was known as a handsome man, seems to have acquired a historical reputation as something of a Berlin hero. There is a statue of him in Spandau looking suitably strong, and Carlyle described him as 'restless, much-managing, wide-warring'. In reality he was an ambitious Saxon noble who saw an opportunity to enrich himself.

Between 1137 and 1157 Brandenburg was subject to vicious fighting as the Wends fought to maintain their independence against Albert's campaign of *Tod oder Taufe* ('conversion or death'). They were for a time successful and, led by Jaxa of Köpenick, a village now in Berlin's outskirts, they initially succeeded in defeating Albert and sending him back across the Elbe; there was even a coin minted in Berlin with Jaxa's head. But by 1157 it was all over. Jaxa had been deserted by his Polish allies and his last surviving stronghold had submitted. Albert reigned unchallenged as margrave under the Holy Roman Emperor, now Frederick Barbarossa whose Hohenstaufen dynasty had succeeded from the Ottonians. The *Drang nach Osten*, the German desire to drive to the east at the expense of the Slavs, had started.

Christianity was initially slow to take root in Berlin. The Wends worshipped a supreme being called Sventovit, to whom many Berliners today owe their name. He was usually represented with four faces and carved into a tree as trees continued to have a special significance for them. They found Christianity difficult to comprehend. Attempts to translate the Lord's Prayer into Polabian were not particularly successful as the Wends, revealingly, had no word for temptation, so it had to be borrowed from German thus confusing them further. Boso, a missionary bishop, also helpfully translated the Kyrie Eleison into Wendish, thinking this might encourage people

to convert, but was incensed when he discovered that the words had
been changed by the locals so that they read 'There is an alder tree
in the copse'.[2]

Yet, with Poland now Christian, the Teutonic Knights crusading to convert Prussia, the Danes forcibly converting their
northern kinsmen, and the Germans now firmly in the ascendant,
Berliners realised they had little option. By the mid-twelfth century Christianity was well established. Berlin's first church, the
Nikolaikirche, was dedicated to St Nicholas and was started around
1232. St Nicholas was, of course, the patron saint of tradesmen. It
was a late-Romanesque-style basilica with a pillared aisle and three
apses. It has been destroyed twice, in the fire of 1380 and again due
to bombing in the Second World War. Despite being turned into a
museum in 1938, it has remained at the centre of Berlin life. It was,
in the absence of any cathedral, for many years the spiritual centre
of Berlin. It was where the Provost, the head of the Christian church
in the city, had his office and it was very much the fashionable place
to be buried, its walls covered in memorials to the great and the
good. It was in its simple and effective nave that the twin councils
of Berlin and Cölln would decide to join forces in 1307; it was where
the first elected Berlin council met in 1809 and the Berlin House of
Representatives held its constituent meeting in 1991 after reunification. The Nikolaiviertel, the St Nicholas' Quarter, that developed
around it became an important commercial area, the site of the *Alter
Markt* (the old market), which later became the *Molkenmarkt* (the
whey or dairy market). This is now the oldest and one of the most
attractive if substantially rebuilt parts of the city, still dominated by
the twin towers of the church rebuilt on their original thirteenth-
century foundations.

Not to be outdone, about the same time Cölln started a church
sensibly dedicated to St Peter, the patron saint of fishermen, so he
could protect the valuable fishing industry along the Spree. By 1237
its priest was a certain Symeon and the first mention of Berlin or
Cölln in a document was when he witnessed a legal dispute between
the Margrave and the Bishop of Brandenburg. 1237 has consequently

been taken as the year the city was founded. The Petrikirche would fare worse than its neighbouring Nikolaikirche, being rebuilt five times until it was finally damaged beyond repair in 1945 and its remains flattened by the GDR.

Reluctant Christians as they were – and have remained – Berlin and Cölln took the opportunity offered by Albert's control to expand commercially, thus establishing the second part of the city's distinctive character: that of an important trading centre. Albert had a house in Berlin, the Aulahof Berlin, but the city having no natural defences, the main centres of power remained at the fortresses Spandau and Köpenick and in Brandenburg. Berlin and Cölln's early development was therefore not the result of them being administrative centres but rather of them establishing themselves as trading towns. They were helped in this by Albert and his successors' policy of inviting settlers into Brandenburg, more immigrants, especially Flemish and Saxons, the fighting having left the Mark badly depopulated. The Flemish and Dutch settlers were particularly welcome as they understood rivers and drainage, for it was the Spree and the Havel that made the twin towns an increasingly important traffic hub.

Two long-distance trade routes met where the rivers joined. One was an east–west route from Magdeburg on the Elbe, still very much the better-established city, via Brandenburg thence by Berlin and Cölln to Frankfurt on the Oder and on to Poland. Berlin would always maintain this east–west axis that would become an important feature as it developed. There were two north–south routes. One ran from Stettin, the port where the Oder flows into the Baltic, via the twin towns and then south to Halle, Leipzig and Meissen in the densely populated and important markets of Saxony. The second route ran south from Hamburg near the North Sea, along the Elbe and then the Havel to Spandau and then on to Berlin and Cölln.

The twin towns also benefited from being situated in the middle of the Brandenburg plain, which, although sandy, was still relatively fertile and blessed with substantial forests. Timber was one of the main exports, shaped into planks for which there was a considerable demand in cities like Hamburg for both ship- and house-building and also for barrels, which were the containers of choice in thirteenth-century Europe. One of the earliest recorded Berlin transactions was in 1290 when Tippo from Cölln, who was nicknamed Clubfoot, delivered 18,000 wooden boards to Hamburg; not to be outdone, Johannes Rode from Berlin sold 27,500. Both of these are quite substantial transactions. In 1274 Berlin oak was exported to England and used in building Norwich Cathedral. Rye – or Berliner *Roggen*, the traditional Berlin corn – was also exported in large quantities, as was freshwater fish from the Spree, and woollen cloth gathered from the farms and villages of Brandenburg, worked up in Berlin and then sold as a finished product. Berlin was an early member of the Hanseatic League, the organisation of northern trading cities that started with agreements to protect their common interest but became formalised in the late thirteenth century. By 1290 Berlin and Cölln were exporting double the goods in terms of value to Hamburg than any other town in Brandenburg.[3]

Konrad von Beelitz, one of the first Berliners whom we know something about, made his fortune as a cloth merchant. He was one of the founders of the Berlin tailors' guild and sold 343 silver marks' worth of cloth bales in Hamburg in 1295, quite enough for him to be able to afford a handsome tomb when he died in 1308. Alongside the tailors were the 'Cloth Miners', journeymen who bought the raw product and then sold it on to be finished. They aroused considerable suspicion among the more respectable class in Berlin, who thought they had far too much contact with the women who weaved the cloth on hand looms, and they were known for their casual dress and their association with passing minstrels and prostitutes. In an attempt to improve their morals, they too were formed into a guild. Other guilds were established for the river skippers, and later for bone carvers, butchers and bakers, but the most famous was for the shoemakers who by the 1300s had established links to many European cities including London and Rome.

The twin towns' development was rapid. By 1230 they were a key part of the Brandenburg economy, and in 1237 the Margrave gave them the same town charter as Magdeburg enjoyed, guaranteeing citizens protection within the walls and right of ownership and also starting commercial regulation. More importantly, in 1260 Berlin and Cölln were granted a *stapelrecht* (a staple right), which meant that all goods passing through the towns had to be offered for sale in their markets, leading to a huge increase in business. There were four markets. Goods entering Cölln from the south-west first stopped at the *Fischmarkt* (fish market) outside the Petrikirche. They could then progress via the *Mühlendamm* (a damn on the Spree that drove mills, regulated the water level and acted as a bridge), to the *Alter Markt* in the Nikolaiviertel. A *Neumarkt* (new market) had also grown up, on what is now the Alexanderplatz, which was approached by the *Lange Brücke* (long bridge). Berlin and Cölln also pioneered the idea of trade fairs; Berlin had three, on May Day, the Feast of the Holy Cross on 14 September and on St Martin's Day (11 November).

Inevitably, with their increasing wealth, and with tree worship now restricted to the more remote villages, Berliners built more churches as church attendance became compulsory. Around 1250 a Franciscan monastery was established on land given by the Margrave Otto V alongside the Aulahof. It would survive in various different guises – most notably after the Reformation as an upmarket school, the *Gymnasium zum Grauen Kloster* – despite serious fires in 1380 and 1712, until 1945 when it finally succumbed to Allied bombing, although the skeleton of the church itself still stands. Its most famous pupil was Bismarck. Albert the Bear's descendants, the Ascanian margraves, were mostly buried there, as were many other notable Berliners. The Dominicans had also established a foundation in Cölln but this did not survive the Reformation, its land being appropriated by the Margrave, and the monks dispersed.

Two other important churches were started around the same time. The Marienkirche (St Mary) was started about 1270, dominating the Neumarkt and the northern part of Berlin. Built of brick in the North German Gothic style, it was a hall church with nave and side aisles that, though extensively rebuilt due to fire and war, still preserves much of its original structure and, perhaps more importantly, its feel. It is still in use as a church today and, as its Pastor writes, the Marienkirche 'may be read as a book of Christian faith and history as well as a memorial to the city of Berlin'.[4] Later its murals would contribute significantly to Berlin's story – as does its library, which incorporates the surviving archive from the Nikolaikirche.[5] The second was the *Heilig-Geist-Kapelle* (the Chapel of the Holy Ghost), built as the chapel for a monastic hospital. It is one of the most beautiful and simple early buildings in the city. It has a vaulted roof, actually added later, and it has miraculously survived war and the attentions of the GDR government who decided to demolish it but then used it as a school cafeteria. It is now, mercifully, part of Humboldt University. Lastly, the Templars, the crusading monastic order founded to assist pilgrims journeying to Jerusalem, established a church at Tempelhof in 1237 on land given by the Margrave to help finance their mission. After the order was abolished in 1312 the Margrave took his land back, granting it briefly to the Templars rivals, the Knights of St John, but in 1435 it was sold back to the Berliners, who would much later have cause to be very grateful for it.

The Jewish community was also well established by the mid-thirteenth century. The oldest graves found so far around Berlin are Jewish, most notably at Spandau, from 1244, something the Nazis found uncomfortable. Jews were persecuted – as they were all over medieval Europe – and tended to live and work in separate areas to non-Jews and were frequently prohibited from trading or socialising with Christians. Yet they seem to have been better treated in Berlin than in other German cities and to have formed a substantial community. In the city's early years they were butchers, wool merchants and weavers; a document from 1295 forbids non-Jews from buying cloth from Jews, suggesting they had been offering advantageous terms. They were also money lenders, a trade unattractive to Christians as they were not allowed to charge interest, and pawnbrokers. By the 1350s there were eleven registered *Judenbuden* (Jews' booths) where pawned goods could be sold.[6]

~

By the end of the thirteenth century the twin rough fishing villages
on the Spree had become rich and well-established commercial
towns, Christian communities inhabited by Huns, Germans, Wends,
Dutch and Jews. Neither Berlin nor Cölln were the equal of the
great medieval German cities like Munich, Magdeburg or Cologne,
and they lacked any really important buildings such as a cathedral. However, for the last 150 years life for many of their citizens
had been relatively safe and prosperous, but more so if you were a
German rather than a Wend. Albert and Otto's followers, German
knights, had been granted land in return for their service, leaving
the Wendish population grouped in the villages; in Berlin itself the
Wends tended to be weavers or employed as labourers. Many of the
villages spoke only Polabian rather than German, which was now the
accepted language in Brandenburg, and were administered by agents,
Schultheiß, acting for either the Margrave or his barons. Berlin and
Cölln had expanded so much that a new wall had been built out of
sharpened wooden stakes, the first of many that would encircle or
divide Berlin. Their population is estimated to have been around
1,200, ruled by a city council of twelve with two elected mayors.
There was an effective judicial system, administered by the council
on behalf of the Margrave.[7] Food appears to have been plentiful and
meat cheap, and the staples of bread, sausage and cheese all washed
down with home-brewed beer and dry white wine would have been
very familiar to Berliners today.

Yet the tension that would soon arise in Berlin was not now
between the Germans and the Wends but more between a rich and
powerful emerging group of merchants and a margrave who was
both keen to exploit the towns' wealth and anxious that his authority was not undermined. Those Germans who had gone into trade
were clearly now doing very well. About half the population had
the Bürgerrecht, which meant they enjoyed full rights as citizens,
and which could be bought by successful merchants; interestingly
women were eligible as well as men. Non-honourable professions
such as shepherds and millers were excluded, as 'were the children
of knackers, barbers ... the descendants of gravediggers and the

children of convicts or the illegitimate offspring of priests'.[8] Berlin was minting its own coinage and citizens also enjoyed grazing rights on land the city owned in the surrounding countryside.

Several prominent families were coming to dominate the council, families like the von Beelitz, Ryke, Rathenow and Blankenfelde – names that will recur constantly in this story and are still very much present in the city today. They were very conscious of the idea that *Stadt Luft macht frei* – that if you lived in a town like Berlin you enjoyed these privileges as a free man and were independent of the temporal authority of the local prince – something that was already well established in other German cities. In 1307 Berlin and Cölln merged their administrations and established a joint council in a shared town hall situated, symbolically, on the Lange Brücke so it was between the twin towns, and painted red. Berlin's dominance was demonstrated by them having two mayors and ten councillors whereas Cölln had a single mayor and five councillors. This is when the bear became the official symbol of the joint towns, with the eagle (the symbol of both Cölln and Brandenburg) beneath him. From then the twin towns would be referred to as simply as Berlin. The Margrave appointed a *Schultheiß* (after which one of Berlin's more famous beers is named) to represent him in Berlin but he was clearly inferior in influence to the council. Berlin's third continuing characteristic, its long history of resistance to outside authority, was beginning to stir.

The thirteenth century had been good to Berlin but the fourteenth was to turn out very differently, as it was for so much of Europe. First Albert the Bear's Ascanian line died out with the death of Margrave Waldemar in 1319, leading to a period of turmoil. The Saxons tried to seize the Mark but were opposed by the Wittelsbach dynasty from southern Germany, who argued they had a superior claim. The Berliners strongly preferred the Wittelsbachs and in the fighting the Provost of Berlin – Nikolaus von Bernau, the churchman responsible to the bishop for all the city's churches and a keen Saxon supporter – was beaten to death by a mob in the Neumarkt and his body burned. As a punishment Berlin was placed under a papal interdict for twenty years; there was no celebration of Holy Mass, no granting of Sacraments and no Christian burials. The Pope was, it should be said, strongly anti-Wittelsbach.

It does not seem to have bothered the Berliners unduly, as it might other German cities, and they took their time meeting the requirements to have the ban lifted: the donation of an altar to the Marienkirche, a hefty fine payable to the Bishop of Brandenburg and the erection of a stone cross to mark where the crime had been committed, which now stands immediately to the left of the west door of the Marienkirche as you face it, although there is no sign to say what it is. The Wittelsbachs did not, however, prove a particularly good choice. Like their Ascanian forebears, they found the Berlin Council too mighty, and they supported an insurrection by the city's tradesmen in 1346. The last Wittelsbach margrave was Otto VII, tellingly known as The Lazy, who abdicated in 1373. He sold the Mark to Charles IV, of the House of Luxembourg, for 2,000 florins but never actually got paid – evidence of how problematic he had been finding ruling this troublesome frontier territory. The emperors equally took little interest despite Charles IV being the single emperor who actually visited the city in 1373.

The 1346 revolt was, however, quickly overshadowed in 1347 when Berlin was very badly hit by the Black Death. It would be the first of several devastating outbreaks from which Berlin, given the number of traders and visitors who passed through, suffered particularly badly. It is estimated that 10 per cent of the city's population died, which was actually less than in many German towns. Predictably, the Jews were blamed, as they were in several European cities. Several were publicly burned in expiation and many others emigrated to Poland. Those who remained crowded together in a fortified area near the Klosterstraße and in 1354 the Margrave guaranteed their protection. It would not, sadly, be the last time the Jews were blamed for the city's misfortunes. As the plague subsided, so the next catastrophe struck: the great fires of 1376 in Cölln and then in 1380 in Berlin, which destroyed much of the wooden city. An unfortunate knight, Erich von Falke, was executed as an arsonist and his head put on a pike outside the Oderberger Tor. Public order seems to have suffered during this turbulent period. 'The married men of Berlin passed at the time for honest but jealous husbands,' Frederick the Great tells us, and that 'when a secretary of the bishop of Magdeburg went to bathe at the public bath in Berlin; where happening to meet a young woman, who was a burgher's wife, he proposed to her in joke to go and bathe with him. The woman was affronted at the proposal; upon which a crowd of people got about him; and the burghers of Berlin, who understood no raillery, dragged the poor secretary into a public marketplace, where they beheaded him without any form of trial.'[9]

There were, however, two relatively positive developments among all this wretchedness. The margraves had maintained a mint in Berlin, but in 1369 the city acquired the right to mint its own coins, and the Berlin pfennig – though still in competition with emperors' Bohemian groschen – rapidly became accepted currency, establishing Berlin as an important financial centre as well as a commercial one. Secondly, in 1391 Berlin became a self-governing city within the Holy Roman Empire. Berliners now controlled their own legal system, and could become officially members of the Hanseatic League, although they had participated unofficially for years.

Yet, by the early 1400s, Brandenburg was in even more chaos. The Luxembourg rule was ineffective and, as Frederick the Great noted with some relish given what was about to happen, 'the highways were infested with robbers, all civil polity was banished, and the proceedings of the courts of justice suspended'.[10] In 1402 the Mark passed briefly to the Teutonic Knights, the military order who had established themselves as rulers of Prussia in 1283, but by 1415 it had been redeemed by the Emperor Sigismund who realised that he must now sort out its government. The plague had led to severe rural depopulation, which had in turn led to agricultural depression and extreme poverty. Powerful local landlords took advantage of this increasingly chaotic situation and the lack of effective central authority to establish their own military bands. These *Raubritter* (robber barons) were marauding across the Mark, taking what they wanted. Berlin, self-governing and still relatively wealthy as it was, suffered considerably from the resulting disruption, being threatened in particular by the von Quitzow family.

~

The Emperor Sigismund's solution to restoring order in the Mark of Brandenburg was, in 1411, to 'grant' it to Frederick von Hohenzollern, the wealthy Burgrave of Nuremberg in southern Germany, in exchange for 400,000 Hungarian gold guilders. He also bestowed on him the dignity of 'Elector', making him one of the seven potentates across the Empire entitled to elect his successors. The Hohenzollerns were parvenus to the world of fifteenth-century power politics and, like similar families who had found riches, they would later go to rather ridiculous lengths to prove their descent from great classical figures. They had, however, grown very rich from accumulating land in southern Germany and Sigismund was, like most emperors, broke. Frederick would spend four years sub-duing the *Raubritter*.

Later, when the Berliners were not quite as enthusiastic about Hohenzollern rule, they would romanticise the robber barons as some sort of freedom fighters, but the reality in the first decade of the fifteenth century was that Berlin's very survival was threatened as lawlessness made trade impossible. In 1402 the Berlin councillors complained to the Margrave that von Lindow and von Quitzow had burned twenty-two villages in a week, and a letter survives from Dietrich von Quitzow in which he threatens to take everything that Berlin and Cölln possess unless he receives 600 'good Bohemian Groschen'.[11] It was therefore the Berliners who welcomed the Hohenzollerns and the barons who opposed them. 'And should it rain burgraves from heaven for the space of a whole year, yet shall they not take root in this March of Brandenburg,' boasted one baron, but it rained burgraves for four years and by 1415 Frederick had restored order – largely because he possessed a strong and dis-ciplined military force and used cannon to destroy the von Quitzow strongholds.[12]

In 1415 Frederick made his formal entry into Berlin and on 18

October was sworn in as Margrave. In common with his predecessors, he chose to live at Spandau, no doubt feeling safer in its moated
fortress on the Havel than in the more open Berlin. His brother John
(known as the Alchemist), to whom he abdicated his responsibilities
in the Mark in 1426, did the same but John's brother, the Elector
Frederick II (always known as *Eisenzahn,* Iron Tooth), had very
different ideas. In 1443 Iron Tooth occupied a site on Fischerinsel
where he started building a palace, which Berliners nicknamed
the *Zwingburg* (the stronghold), on the site today occupied by the
Berliner Schloss. Had Iron Tooth not chosen Berlin, the city would
probably have developed as many other free German cities did
within the Holy Roman Empire, like Frankfurt, Augsburg, and
the Hanseatic towns such as Hamburg or Lübeck. Instead, as the
Hohenzollern capital, its life was now fated to become inseparable
from the fortunes of a dynasty that would last until 1918. This biography will not become a history of Brandenburg – nor later of Prussia
or indeed Germany – but it must tell the story of the Hohenzollerns
alongside that of Berlin in so far as Berliners first opposed them,
then supported them, gradually came to resent them and finally got
rid of them.

It was not long before the Berliners realised that Iron Tooth
intended to treat them in much the same way as he had the *Raubritter,*
and that their previous privileges were slowly to be eroded. The city's
council and its law courts were disbanded and replaced with Iron
Tooth's own administration and he interfered with Berlin's lucrative
trading arrangements, forcibly withdrawing not only Berlin but all
Brandenburg's cities from the Hanseatic League in 1442. In 1447
the burghers decided they had had enough. They reopened the old
town hall and revolted. The sluice gates on the Spree were opened
to flood the Zwingburg's foundations and Iron Tooth's walls torn
down. Yet they were no match for Iron Tooth's military, based on the
knights who had benefited from the Hohenzollern conquest and his
well-supplied arsenal at Spandau. He moved into Berlin with a force
of reputedly 600 knights, re-established control, exiled the most
troublesome burghers and threw a statue of Roland, which had stood

in the marketplace in Cölln, into the Spree. (Throwing unwanted statues into the Spree would become another well-established Berlin tradition.) Frederick the Great put it rather differently, and Hohenzollern propaganda had it that Berliners 'long accustomed to cruel masters, with difficulty submitted to his mild and legitimate government.' Iron Tooth 'appeased their commotions with prudence and lenity', he continued, but that does not explain why it took such a sizeable military force to restore order.[13] Berlin has never managed to stage a successful violent revolution; attempts in 1447, 1848, 1918 and 1953 all failed. It was not until 1989, when they tried peacefully, that they succeeded.

Berliners later tried to make rather more of Roland than perhaps they should have done. This Roland was the same one who had sounded his horn at Roncevaux, thus saving his sovereign Charlemagne from the rebellious Basques, but he was governor of the Breton March in France and had nothing to do with Brandenburg. In the eleventh century his deeds were immortalised in the poem 'The Song of Roland', which led to him being adopted as a sort of inspirational freedom fighter across Europe, including Berlin. His Berlin legacy might have remained in the mud of the Spree had a resourceful Berlin author, Willibald Alexis, not written a historical novel about a *Roland of Berlin* in that period after the Napoleonic Wars when traditional German heroes were at a premium. His story, in which the *Bürgermeisters* Johannes Rathenow of Berlin and Matthäus Blankenfelde of Cölln lead the city in resisting the evil Margrave Frederick, became even more popular when it was made into an opera by Leoncavallo in 1904, but it has scant historical basis. There is a rather tall and angular reconstruction of this Roland statue that stands outside the Märkische Museum but there is no way of knowing whether it actually looks anything like the original.

Yet the 1447 uprising did give rise to the idea of *Berlin Unwille*, a legacy that Berlin would not allow itself to be subject to arbitrary acts such as Iron Tooth's, and this became an important part of the city's self-belief. Berliners were not alone in being supressed, and early modern Germany history has many similar incidents as 'free' cities tried to protect their rights against powerful rulers who possessed a monopoly of force. Arguably Berlin fared rather better than Stettin, where the ruler of Pomerania massacred the ringleaders and encased their bones in the foundations of his new castle after they rebelled in 1428.[14]

Berlin underwent a fairly miserable decade in the 1450s, as the Zwingburg's walls rose and they had to subject themselves to Iron Tooth's dictatorial rule. By then the city had a population of about 7,000, about 500 of which were Iron Tooth's soldiers; yet another Berlin custom – that of living with a sizeable military garrison – had been established. Apart from a brief period in the 1920s, Berliners would live alongside their oppressors or protectors, depending on their perspective, until 1989. Living alongside really did mean exactly that, with the soldiers billeted on families, since the concept of a barracks, where the military all lived together, was still distant. Berliners were also introduced to another novel and contentious custom when in 1450 Iron Tooth demanded 1,000 conscripts for his war against Saxony. Conscription would eventually become part of their lives, although (unlike rural Brandenburg) they would later manage to avoid its worst excesses.

However, despite the grumbling, Iron Tooth's rule did re-establish stability. Rebuilding continued after the two disastrous fires of the 1380s. Iron Tooth, who felt confident enough to go on pilgrimage to Jerusalem in 1453, built a chapel alongside the Zwingburg, which the Pope elevated to the status of a parish church, complete with saints' relics. It was dedicated to Saint Erasmus of Formia, the patron saint of sailors (which is understandable given Berlin's dependence on the water) but also of stomach pain, which may point to some affliction that had hit Iron Tooth on his travels. By 1470 the rebuild of the Nikolaikirche was complete, as were both the Klosterkirche, the Franciscan community's monastery in Berlin, and the Dominicans' establishment across the river on Bruderstraße in Cölln. The Heiliggergesitspital, the hospital just inside the Spandau gate, was also functioning again.

Plague hit the city very badly again in 1484, which, horrendous as it was, at least gave rise to one of the most vivid and effective art-works of medieval Berlin. The 'Totentanz' (the Dance of Death) is a mural painted in the narthex of the Marienkirche, remarkable for its commentary on contemporary Berlin and for its survival perhaps more than for its artistic merit. The 22-metre painting shows, on one side, a series of church dignitaries each being led by a skeletal figure in a shroud, representing Death, towards a central figure of the crucified Christ. On the other side Death leads figures representing temporal society. Underneath is a harsh, witty dialogue as Death explains that he is inevitable and comes to everyone regardless of their earthly estate. It was a common theme across Europe at the time, but the Marienkirche dialogue is sharp – the forerunner of the Berliner *Schnauze* (sharp tongue) or their *Schnoddrigkeit* (lip), which has become such a Berlin tradition.

The church figures range upwards in seniority from a lowly Franciscan monk to the Pope. The monks, of which there are several, generally get treated quite well (it is possible the monastic communities paid for the painting), whereas the dean gets told he should have thought about what would eventually happen while he was enjoying his 'high estate', and the doctor is told he has annoyed Death by attempting to prolong his patients' lives. The temporal characters fare rather worse. The lowest figure is a fool, who tells Death he is a 'foul rascal' and that he will prepare a skit for him. Next comes an innkeeper, who is told she has been 'tapping and billing deceitfully' and who bitterly regrets not having time to get rid of her forged measuring jug. The squire is criticised for being busy with hunting and courtship, and he is outranked – an interesting comment in itself – by the money lender who, predictably, gets told he is now to suffer 'great woe' for 'having returned to the poor one shock for two'. The duke is told he suppressed the 'poor with violence and let the rich go free', whereas the emperor, who tops the temporal order, is actually treated quite respectfully, though Death can only compliment him on his beautiful wife and pretty horses rather than his government. He is told he has enjoyed 'heaven on earth' and that he must now follow Death 'whether you like it or not'.[15]

It is remarkable that the 'Totentanz' has survived. It is probable that it was altered in the sixteenth century, with the characters' legs being bent so that they seemed to be dancing more energetically, and it was subsequently whitewashed over in 1614 as Calvinism took hold in Berlin. It was rediscovered in 1860 and cleaned but was damaged when the Marienkirche was bombed in the Second World War. Originally neglected by the GDR, it was eventually restored by the East Berlin authorities in time for the city's 750th birthday celebrations in 1987, the Communist authorities having appreciated that there was perhaps something in a religious artwork that showed everyone was equal.

In 1471 Iron Tooth, then aged fifty-eight, abdicated the electorate in favour of his brother Albert, known as Achilles. The electors would maintain what Frederick the Great called the 'ridiculous custom of giving surnames to princes' until 1539.[16] Iron Tooth retired to his Hohenzollern lands in southern Germany and died the next year. Albert's main achievement was to decide that in future the eldest Hohenzollern son would inherit the electorship and Brandenburg, while the younger sons would get the other family lands in southern Germany, a decision that gave rise to the bewildering web of titles and principalities that would make life so fascinating for German genealogists and so confusing for historians. When his eldest son John, known as Cicero because he was supposedly a great orator, inherited in early 1486 he announced that his main residence would now be the Zwingburg and that Berlin was to be the capital of both Brandenburg and the Hohenzollerns. Berlin, having achieved prosperity as a trading city, now had 'greatness thrust upon it' as a *Residenzstadt*, the centre of government for a dynasty that, while relatively unimportant in the late fifteenth century, would become both one of Europe's leading royal houses and her nemesis.

The Hohenzollern standard now flew over the Zwingburg. What exactly was on it is a matter of conjecture. Since the thirteenth century Berlin had adopted the bear as its symbol. It is not clear where this came from. There would certainly have been lots of European brown bears in Brandenburg's forests, or possibly it was the heraldic device of Albert (hence his nickname). Although the Romans had imported wild animals for their circuses, subtropical Africa was largely unknown to medieval Europe and fierce animals were at something of a premium when it came to designing coats of arms. Bears and eagles proliferated. The symbol of Brandenburg was rather an angular and angry red eagle, later turned into a black eagle that forms the basis of modern Germany's crest today. The earliest surviving seal of Berlin, from around 1300, shows a Brandenburg eagle supported by two bears. There is a nice but unsubstantiated story that the Berliners maintained a bear with a chain around its neck as a symbol of their subjugation to the Hohenzollerns, and that it had an eagle riding on its back, but the original Hohenzollern crest was a rampant lion and the eagle that has since become so associated with Prussian militarism was in fact the original Brandenburg one. Whatever its origins, since the late fifteenth century a bear in its various postures and moods – whether subdued, angry, friendly or just confused – has come to be the symbol of Berlin and its spirit, while the Hohenzollerns made wholesale use of the eagle. The eagle is always said to have had a double face because it was 'at once a symbol of despotism at home and of protection against the fury of the world outside'.[17]

Life in Berlin was at least well regulated, if a little less free. One of the earliest records in existence is the *Stadtbuch* (town book), a detailed bureaucratic record of almost everything that concerned the city's administration from 1272 until 1489. After many important documents were destroyed in the fire of 1380, the council engaged the 'Notarius' Heinrich Schönfließ to collect and copy what was left and to organise a proper register. He started work in 1397 and the *Stadtbuch* is the result of his labours.[18] It is, in common with most records that bureaucrats keep, rather dull but invaluable as a historical source. It lists the city's revenues and where they came from, the income of city officials, the city's rights and privileges, debts and inheritance, bonds and debentures as well as listing all those who enjoyed the *Bürgerrecht*. Interestingly, it has specific sections on both women's and Jewish rights. It also lists the quite horrific

judicial punishments, which had been as severe under the free city
as they were under the Hohenzollerns. The *Stadtbuch* records that
a young man is burned for stealing herrings; a man is beheaded for
starting a fire in the forest; a young girl is flogged for stealing salt;
three men are burned for selling zinc as silver; a woman is buried
alive for trespassing; two men are broken on the wheel for stealing
from a church; a shoemaker is beheaded for harassing a woman,
and the wife of a Cölln man has her ears cut off for stealing a coat.[19]

Minor punishments, such as floggings and amputations, were
carried out on Mondays and Saturdays, while public executions were
staged by the Olderburg Gate every second Wednesday. Between
1391 and 1448, out of a population somewhere around 7,000, forty-
six people were hanged, twenty burned at the stake, twenty-two
beheaded, eleven broken on the wheel and seventeen buried alive,
nine of whom were women. Breaking on the wheel was a particularly unpleasant form of execution, in which the victim's limbs were
smashed with a hammer so that his body could be threaded through
the spokes of a wheel and left on public display.[20]

But, if you behaved yourself, life could be good. Thomas von
Blankenfelde, whose name Willibald used in his novel, was mayor
seven times between from 1481 until 1493. Described as a 'merchant
of not inconsiderable style',[21] he worked closely with Iron Tooth,
commanding the right wing of his army when he was pressing his
case to the Stettin inheritance. He traded from Danzig on the Baltic
to Munich in Bavaria. Educated in Leipzig, he was the first man to
become mayor who had been to university. He married twice, his
wives coming from equally well-established Berlin families, and had
twenty-one children. His house, at 49 Spandauer Straße, had his
coat of arms emblazoned above its entrance. He also acquired considerable property in the villages around Berlin, something that was
becoming popular with successful merchants. He had himself and
his family painted at the foot of the cross in a crucifixion scene, and
his many descendants would remain prominent in Berlin for generations; the painting still hangs in the Marienkirche, with Blankenfelde
and his sons to the right of the cross, and his long-suffering wife to

the left. He was not alone in his success and evidence remains of a number of very fine fifteenth-century houses, although sadly this is now largely in pieces rather than whole buildings.

Poorer families generally lived in just one room, and daily life was played out on the streets. Although the more important public buildings and private houses had been rebuilt in stone, this was too expensive for most people, who had to make do with wood. Many people were employed in villages outside the city, and the gates were opened half an hour before sunrise and closed half an hour before sunset on the sound of a bell. Life was strictly regulated, as the punishments inflicted on transgressors makes clear, as were trading standards through the guilds. From 1334 there were also, as was common across Europe, regulations in force to protect the privileges of the burghers. These laid down what clothing was permissible and how much jewellery could be worn in public, prohibited dancing on the street after the city gates were closed and even limited the number of guests permitted at a wedding.[22] Within Berlin's already cosmopolitan society, the rules by which people could live were strict, a trait that has remained typical of the city ever since. Even beggars were licensed, wearing a patch on their clothes declaring their poverty.[23] Berliners have an enviable tradition of challenging major issues but are, ironically, careful observers of regulation in their everyday lives.

The Jewish community had also recovered from being blamed for the Black Death. There were periodic pogroms across Brandenburg, including a particularly unpleasant persecution in 1446, but the Berlin community survived this. They lived under strict and restrictive rules so that no Jew could employ a Christian servant and marriages between Jews and Christians were banned. Jews were identified in public by wearing a *Judenhut* (Jew's hat), they were forbidden to proselytise and would suffer more severe punishment than a Christian convicted of the same crime. However, they could now also practise as doctors, which many started to do, as well as money lenders and pawnbrokers. They could also be citizens but they were banned from holding public office. In 1472 the Elector Albert spoke out publicly about the need to integrate the Jewish community more closely, possibly because by that stage it is estimated that they were contributing annual tax revenue of 4,000 gold guilders, evidence of a sizeable and relatively affluent community.[24]

Berlin in 300 years had developed from twin fishing villages on the Spree to being the established capital of an elector of the Holy Roman Empire with its churches, its palace and an active trading community. It had eclipsed the town of Brandenburg itself, some-time capital of the early margraves, and come to dominate both Spandau and Köpenick with their impressive fortifications. It had done this by making itself an important financial and trading centre, by developing a sophisticated administration and by emancipating within its walls the many diverse people who had come to live there. The Berliners had established the particular individual character and atmosphere that seems to go with the place – the *Berliner Luft*, which they have maintained ever since. *Berliner Luft* has been inter-preted as many things over the centuries and has become famous as a song that is now the unofficial anthem for the city; it also is a cocktail and a very popular liqueur. It is probably best translated into English as the Berlin equivalent of London Pride.

Medieval Berlin has survived not just in that *Berliner Luft* but also in its buildings and in its centre clearly defined by the Spree and Fischerinsel. It is quite remarkable that in a city that has suffered so much destruction, you can see so clearly today what it was like in its early years (see map on p. xiv). Admittedly Cölln has fared worse than Berlin, but you can walk across the Mühlendamm – today a bridge carrying a dual carriageway – via Fischerinsel, along Scharrenstraße (literally Market Stall Street), into the Nikolaiviertel, originally home to the *Alter Markt*. Despite the tourist shops and pubs that have infected the area, as they have the centres of so many medieval European cities, you still get a feeling of what it was like. All this area was in East Berlin between 1945 and 1989, and left derelict for many years until the government of the GDR undertook an ambitious and not unsympathetic renovation programme for the city's 750th birthday celebrations in 1987. Beyond you is the *Rote Rathaus* (the red town hall), which occupies almost exactly the same site as Berlin's original town hall before it was moved to the Lange Brücke. You can continue via the Klosterkirche (skeletal after Second World War bombing but still impressive) to the Neumarkt – now in effect the Alexanderplatz, still dominated by the Marienkirche where the 'Totentanz' is being restored. You have to ignore the Fernsehturm and the slightly brutalist shopping centres on the Alexanderplatz itself, which is not impossible if you are disciplined in concentrating on the medieval. Nearby is the Heilig-Geist-Kapelle. You can see its much-restored exterior that abuts Spandauer Straße, although you need to negotiate access with Berlin University. You can then cross the Lange Brücke, where the town hall stood, and see the Humboldt Forum, which is the recently renovated Berliner Schloss, on the same site as Iron Tooth's Zwingburg, of which rather more in due course.

It would be another 150 years until Berliners began to benefit substantially from Hohenzollern rule, and before they did so they had to live through the Reformation and then suffer the Thirty Years War, the two events that would shape modern Europe.

CHAPTER TWO

1500–1640

*'Even the strongest minds cannot, with
impunity, defy the prejudices of the age'*

FRIEDRICH SCHILLER

With its population of about 8,000 in the closing years of the fifteenth century, Berlin was certainly not a match for the great cities of Germany. Augsburg had a population of 30,000, as did Danzig and Magdeburg on the Elbe. Even the Hohenzollerns' home city of Nuremberg had 20,000 and Hamburg 15,000, while Paris, the biggest city in Europe, had over 200,000 and London 75,000.[1] To the east Berlin was dwarfed by Kraków and Breslau, both more than twice its size. It had no cathedral, unlike Magdeburg, and no university, unlike Leipzig, and when the Elector Joachim founded one he showed his dislike of Berlin by doing so in Frankfurt an der Oder rather than in his capital.

John 'Cicero', the orator Elector, had died in 1499. His successor was Joachim I, or 'Nestor', named after the mythical Greek king known for his 'wise counsel'. He was the first Hohenzollern to have been born in Berlin and who saw himself, if not actually as a Berliner, as a Brandenburger first. He was well educated and interested in the humanities, so perhaps taking 'Nestor' as a name was at

least partially justified. Frederick the Great gave him the credit for
being the first 'modern' Hohenzollern monarch and for 'civilising a
nation that had been in a state of barbarousness'. He was 'master
of mathematics, astronomy and history; he spoke French, Italian
and Latin with ease; he was fond of polite learning' and the university at Frankfurt an der Oder soon had 900 students from all over
Germany and from Poland.[2] However, Johannes Trithemius, Abbot
of Sponheim in the Rhineland, visiting Berlin in 1505, thought his
court 'good natured but ignorant and uncouth', and that the courtiers took 'more pleasure in feasting and carousing than in acquiring
knowledge'.[3] Berlin was certainly still a fairly unsophisticated city,
a frontier town outside which 'the nobility continued to rob on the
highways'[4] but, despite the good abbot's reservations, things were
slowly changing.

During the coming century Berlin would establish its own distinctive language, the Reformation would allow Berliners to find a
formula for organised religion that they found acceptable and they
would enjoy the beginnings of a cultural renaissance that came
to them rather late compared to southern and western German-
speaking lands. They would, however, also experience commercial
decline as international trade moved from the Hanseatic cities
to northern and western Europe and they would reluctantly find
themselves increasingly dependent on the Hohenzollern electors for
their economic survival. For the next 130 or so years it was said
that the Palace, the Zwingburg, 'did not stand in Berlin, Berlin was
the Palace'.[5] Consequently, much of the next part of this story must
follow the fortunes and the intrigues of the Hohenzollerns, whose
decisions would have such an impact on how Berlin developed.

In 1502 Joachim married Elizabeth of Denmark. It was initially
a happy marriage that produced five children. Living in the gloomy,
fortified Zwingburg was not really to either of their taste and they
started what became a Hohenzollern tradition of building houses
in the outlying villages. Joachim chose Potsdam, a beautiful setting
where the River Havel charts an even more indecisive course than
normal through the woods and meadows 20 miles south-west of

Berlin, creating a series of lakes and islands. Potsdam is still beautiful today, despite having grown into a substantial town, becoming a garrison and then being flattened by British and American bombers towards the end of the Second World War. In the early decades of the sixteenth century it must have seemed like heaven on earth after the pressures of Berlin, which was hit by the plague yet again in 1501. Potsdam also offered opportunities for hunting in the sprawling *Grunewald*, the magnificent forest that still makes Berlin today the most sparsely inhabited European capital. It was common practice for contemporary European royal families to build retreats outside their capital cities. The Hohenzollerns always had a slightly jealous eye on their wealthier southern neighbours, the Saxon Royal court in Dresden. The Wettin dynasty already enjoyed Albrechtsburg and would soon start work on the magnificent Moritzburg, just outside Dresden itself. Hampton Court and Fontainebleau were similar examples in London and Paris respectively, but Joachim started a Hohenzollern habit that would see many of his successors live almost permanently in Berlin's outskirts. He did not, however, have the money to build anything very substantial, and it would be his seventeenth- and eighteenth-century successors who would turn Potsdam into a major royal town.

Events in Berlin would, however, soon conspire both to challenge Joachim's authority and to destroy his marriage. Joachim saw Brandenburg's and Berlin's future – and hence that of his family – as being loyal subjects of the Emperor and thus strongly Roman Catholic. Konrad Wimpina, whom he had appointed to head his new university, was known for his narrow, traditional theology and the Abbot of Sponheim commented on how religious Joachim's court was, noting – perhaps hopefully as far as the Berliners themselves were concerned – that 'their attendance at Mass is all the more devout for the fact that they were the last of the German people to be converted to the Christian faith'.[6] In the early part of his reign, Joachim found his Catholicism relatively straightforward to maintain, through renewed persecution of the Jews – always seen as a good way of proving one's faith and appealing to public prejudice. In

1510 Berlin was racked by the scandal of the Desecration of the Host. In February 1510 a Catholic coppersmith stole a golden monstrance and two hosts from a church in Knobloch, a small town west of Berlin. Trying to extricate himself, he blamed a Jew from Spandau whom he said had wanted the hosts. In the ensuing hysteria, fifty-one Jews were rounded up and accused of both desecrating the host and of abducting Christian children, despite there being no evidence that any children were actually missing. The trials were held in public and show contemporary Berlin at its least edifying. Thirty-eight of the unfortunate Jews were burned at the stake on the Neumarkt in front of the Marienkirche, while three who accepted conversion to Christianity at the last minute were beheaded along with the coppersmith. The remaining thirteen either died under torture or managed to flee. The executions were followed by a more general persecution across Brandenburg that, typically of contemporary Jewish persecutions, was short lived as it became clear that the money markets did not function without the Jews. Neither were there any good doctors.[7]

Soon after the Desecration scandal, a portly Dominican friar called Johann Tetzel came to Berlin to sell 'indulgences'. The theory of an indulgence is that a priest, acting as an instrument of God, has the authority to forgive sin providing the sinner is truly repentant, but more is required if the guilty person was actually to be absolved from the punishment that God would impose for that sin in purgatory. The indulgence was money paid to the church in mitigation. The concept sounds extraordinary today but in early sixteenth-century Europe the idea of heaven and hell was powerful and immediate, and Tetzel did good business. The money raised was said to be going to pay for St Peter's in Rome, but the reality was more dishonest. The Elector Joachim's younger brother, Albert, who had been made a cardinal aged just twenty-eight, was Archbishop of both Magdeburg and of Mainz – two lucrative posts that he was not supposed to hold jointly ('pluralism' being an offence the Church was meant to be stamping out). However, Albert had made a financial arrangement with the Pope, Leo X, outpricing a rival candidate fielded by the Elector of Saxony, so that half the money

Tetzel raised found its way via a complicated deal into the papal coffers. The deal had been arranged by Johann Blankenfelde, son of Thomas, who had borrowed the money from the Fugger banking house in Augsburg. Tetzel would have a free hand to sell indulgences in Brandenburg, Blankenfelde would take a cut to repay the Fuggers, making a healthy profit on the way, and Albert Hohenzollern could keep both his archbishoprics. To make matters worse, Tetzel did not actually bother ensuring the person paying for the indulgence had properly repented, providing the money was forthcoming and, worse still, he sold indulgences against sins not yet committed, giving the indulgee free licence to misbehave.

It all seemed beautifully simple until, on 31 October 1517, Martin Luther, an Augustinian friar in Saxony, famously nailed his *Ninety-Five Theses* to the door of the church in Wittenberg. Luther, who was teaching at Wittenberg University, had spent time in Rome and, although critical of the practices of the Church, he remained a devout Catholic. It was the actions of 'this ignorant and impudent friar', as he called Tetzel, that pushed him over the edge. Thesis 27 said, 'They preach mad who say that the soul flies out of purgatory as soon as the money thrown into the chest rattles'; Thesis 28 read, 'It is certain that when the money rattles in the chest, avarice and gain may be increased, but the suffrage of the Church depends on the will of God alone' and Thesis 86 said, 'Why does the Pope, whose riches are at this day more ample than those of Croesus, not build the basilica of St Peter with his own money rather than that of poor believers?'[8] There was a popular bit of doggerel based on these lines that went 'As soon as the gold in the casket rings, the rescued soul to Heaven springs'.[9]

Luther's actions caused uproar, and what started as a simple protest against an inexcusable abuse began the Reformation and the great schism in the Church. Tetzel himself was required to answer Luther's accusations and did so – unsatisfactorily – twice in Joachim's new university, and he died in 1519, largely forgotten but for the storm that he had caused. Joachim, however, remained staunchly loyal to the Pope. Given the position of his brother it would have been difficult for him to do otherwise, but Luther's actions had articulated a feeling of dissatisfaction within the Church that was particularly prevalent in northern Europe and especially so in Berlin with its cosmopolitan population and scepticism of Catholicism. Luther began to develop his ideas and became the leader of a movement that demanded fundamental reform of the Church. In 1521 the Emperor Charles V called an Imperial Diet (or conference) at Worms, which issued an edict condemning Luther as a heretic. His writings were to be burned and anyone who followed him was similarly declared to be a heretic. Joachim faithfully had Luther's books burned in Berlin, but it was too late to contain what was now becoming a widespread movement not just in Germany but across Europe.

Matters were complicated by the fact that Joachim had been having an open affair for some time with Katharina Hornung, the very beautiful twenty-first child of the prolific Thomas Blankenfelde and sister of the indulgence-fixing Johann. She appears towards the rear of the kneeling line of Blankenfeldes in the Marienkirche Crucifixion painting. In 1524 she married a wealthy Cölln merchant called Wolf Hornung who was a close friend of Joachim's, and the Elector paid for their sumptuous house. However, Joachim seems to have assumed that purchasing the house gave him rather more rights with the young Frau Hornung than perhaps he should have done. Hornung put up with their affair for a year but, after hearing a sermon by Martin Luther in 1525 condemning adultery, he flew into a rage and stabbed his wife in the stomach. Hornung, terrified of the Elector's reaction, fled and found his way to Saxony where Luther, who already thought Joachim a religious reactionary, took up his case.

Joachim's problems were compounded when his wife, Elisabeth of Denmark, not unnaturally objected to his affair. Things had been deteriorating between them for some years. Elisabeth had been sick and remained confined in the Zwingburg when Joachim travelled to Potsdam and around Brandenburg. In 1527 he had even taken Katharina on an official visit to Warsaw. Elisabeth was also supporting her spendthrift younger brother, who had installed himself in Berlin and had a marked aversion to paying her back for his keep. But she was more influenced by her older brother, Christian, the Danish king. He had been an early follower of Luther, and in 1527 Elisabeth bravely told Joachim she was now following his example and professing Lutheranism. Joachim demanded that she recant but she refused and when he was away from Berlin she escaped to Saxony and took refuge with her uncle, the Elector Johann, known as *Beständige* (the Steadfast), who had succeeded his brother Frederick as Luther's protector.

Dresden was now becoming something of a Lutheran centre of resistance to Catholic Berlin. Hornung petitioned the Emperor at the next Imperial Diet, at Speyer, but predictably received little satisfaction. The argument became potentially more serious after the Diet of Augsburg the following year, which produced the Augsburg Confession, a document summarising what Lutheranism meant and giving the reformed religion a definite structure and doctrine. It led in 1531 to the formation of a military alliance of the reformist states in north Germany, the Schmalkaldic League, who were now in a position to challenge the Empire and Catholic monarchs like Joachim. Luther himself spent an extraordinary amount of time pressing Hornung's case, writing a 150-page case against Joachim intended for delivery to the Imperial Court, which seems a curious use of time when he was shepherding a new religion.[10] Berlin had been more instrumental in prompting the Reformation than perhaps the city realised.

Elisabeth and Joachim remained unreconciled. Katharina, who had three children by Joachim, found life with him had become fairly miserable but on 11 July 1535 Joachim died at the young age of fifty-one. Katharina did not long outlive him, and her three children – all of who Joachim provided for generously – were brought up by Katharina's nephew, yet another Johann Blankenfelde mayor of Berlin.

In the event Luther's efforts proved unnecessary as Joachim's son – Joachim II, known as Hector and destined to be the last Hohenzollern with a classical patronymic – succeeded. As his father was dying, he made Hector promise to remain Catholic and initially it looked as if he might follow his father's advice. An approach by the joint Berlin and Cölln councils on 13 February 1539 said that Berliners 'graciously wanted to allow and yield that they would enjoy and receive the holy sacrament according to the Christian rites and institution under both forms at Easter time'.[11] Joachim refused. He was, however, by conviction a reformer and more under the influence of his mother. The early Hohenzollerns made, on the whole, good marriages. Both Protestantism and Prussia would come to Brandenburg through marriages to capable and powerful women, and Elisabeth stands out in German history as someone whose morals and courage were of particular and far-reaching consequence.

Joachim II had to wait until he felt secure enough, given the ongoing fighting between the Emperor and the Reformers, to begin his 'Christian Reformation'. His opportunity to adopt the reformed religion came very soon after he rejected the council's approach in April 1539 with the Treaty of Frankfurt. Although the principle of 'cuius regio eius religio' (in other words, individual rulers could decide on what their state religion would be) was not formalised until 1555, its application was already becoming apparent. In the summer of 1539, he summoned reformist theologians to Berlin. On 1 November the Protestant Communion was celebrated for the first time in Brandenburg at the church of St Nikolai in Spandau. The next day it took place for the first time in Cölln, rather than the Nikolaikirche in Berlin, led by the Provost of Berlin, Georg Buchholzer. Buchholzer, a Berliner who had been a priest in the Neumark, part of Brandenburg east of the River Oder, had been working quietly on Protestant sermons with Joachim for some months. He had only arrived in Berlin in September, and throughout the winter of 1539–40 his sermons were distributed to all parts of Brandenburg. Berlin and the Mark were now firmly Lutheran. Elisabeth did not return from Dresden until 1545, at the age of sixty. She disapproved of Joachim's second wife, the Catholic Hedwig of Poland, who still heard Mass and refused to learn German, although Elisabeth helped her younger son John in his conversion of Brandenburg-Küstrin, the part of the

Mark that Joachim I had left him. She spent her remaining days in Spandau.[12]

Berlin has always taken a pragmatic approach to its faiths. The reformed religion that Berliners adopted during the 1540s and formalised after the Peace of Augsburg in 1555 when the Emperor officially recognised *cuius regio eius religio* was generally quite relaxed. Bishops were retained, as were saints and their feast days, and Mass was still said in Latin. It was a formula that suited Berliners well, being liberal and remarkably tolerant by the standards of mid-sixteenth-century Germany. They would defend it fiercely when they felt it threatened as subsequent Hohenzollerns became more radical.

The man credited with making the Reformation work for Berlin was Buchholzer, who sensed that Berliners needed this light touch. Remarkably he 'diligently and faithfully presided over the preaching, sacrament giving and maintenance of other Christian ceremonies'[13] to the major congregations in Berlin, the Nikolaikirche and the Marienkirche, for twenty-six years and was known as the 'Reformer of Berlin'. He was, in many ways, a man ahead of his time. A close friend and correspondent of Luther, and strongly influenced by him, he was also a follower of the humanist Melanchthon, from whom he drew his interest in the church leading on humanistic education and the need to perform good works. He also ran all three of the city's hospitals. Although he was not above entering into what today seem like rather idiosyncratic theological disputes – such as one that went on for years with Joachim's chaplain, Johannes Agricola, who was jealous of his influence, about whether he had preached that the Virgin Mary acted as a mediator between God and man – Buchholzer was essentially a pragmatist who made the Church relevant to Berliners. Ultimately Joachim became suspicious that Buchholzer's social-reforming tendencies were going too far and dismissed him in 1564, but it was the tolerant, humanist religious practice Buchholzer championed that Berliners would defend so fiercely in the coming decades. It also led to the strong, quiet, socially conscious Christianity that has since been typical of many Berliners and would contribute strongly to the Pietist movement that was so important in eighteenth-century Berlin.

Agricola was himself an enlightened cleric who had studied under Luther in Wittenberg and been appointed by Joachim when the Saxon court found his preaching too reformist. In many ways he was a surprising choice, his social views being fairly extreme. He had written a dialogue between a devout protestant and a social revolutionary, which concluded with the line 'What shall we do to get rid of tyrants?' This was inflammatory stuff, not least because it preceded the 1525 peasants' revolt that spread across German-speaking lands (although not in Brandenburg). In 1537 he had then written a play about Jan Hus, the Czech reformer burned in Prague in 1415. However, towards the end of his life – he died of plague in Berlin in 1566 – he became more conservative, seeking some sort of reconciliation with the Catholic Church. Possibly his greatest legacy, however, was secular in his original work *Dreihundert gemeine Sprichwörter, der die Deutsche nuns gebrauchen und doch nicht wissen, woher sie kommen,* which translates as '300 Common Proverbs that we use in German but we don't know where they come from'. Here was a leading intellectual and well-respected man taking an interest not in church Latin but in everyday language. Many of the proverbs he lists are still in common use in Berlin today, such as 'Barking dogs seldom bite' while others such as like 'Long hair, short wit' have more or less disappeared. His old revolutionary spirit was in evidence in one of his more famous: 'At court the hand is often given, the heart rarely.'[14]

In 1539 Joachim II also allowed Jews – still technically banned since 1510 – back into Berlin, and in 1556 he appointed his 'dear and true Lippold' to be the leader of the Jewish community through-out the Mark.[15] Lippold wasn't especially popular with the Jewish community, partly because he was thought to be too strict in his insistence on religious observance and partly because the basis of his appointment was that he was Joachim's banker. But in 1564 the Jewish community paid 8,000 guilder to build a synagogue and to purchase land for the first Jewish cemetery in the city.

Berlin under Joachim II could not honestly be described as a city enjoying a renaissance, but it was certainly a city that was changing and one where the arts were beginning to take root. Joachim himself was a determined builder. He started with the gloomy Zwingburg itself, and employed a Saxon stonemason, Konrad Krebs, to draw up plans. He created an L-shaped palace with two distinct corner towers and a large internal courtyard that could be used for ceremonial parades. Krebs used sandstone rather than the normal Brandenburg brick, and he created what was perhaps optimistically called Berlin Cathedral on the site of the old Dominican monastery connected to the Schloss by a walkway. However, Krebs died before the work was finished, and Joachim had already run out of money. This was not altogether surprising as at the same time he was building a waterside hunting lodge at Köpenick, then a day's ride to the east of Berlin, in a glorious setting where the River Dahme joins the Spree. There is nothing of the original building left, a new baroque palace having been built on the site for Frederick I, and even that is now scarcely recognisable after various iterations as barracks, prison and school. Yet Joachim started a popular Berlin habit in escaping from the city to the delights of Köpenick. Today thousands of Berliners flock to swim in and picnic beside the nearby Müggelsee, one of a series of lakes through which the upper Spree meanders. For the next two centuries Köpenick would remain a charming village surrounded by forest.

Joachim II was also building another hunting lodge in the Grunewald, which remains today almost as he would have known it. The *Jagdschloß Grunewald,* which was finished in 1542, is a simple and unpretentious large country house rather than a proper *schloss* and it remains one of the best-preserved and atmospheric buildings of sixteenth-century Berlin. It still feels as if it is hidden deep in the forest, on a clearing beside a small lake, the *Grunewaldsee,* despite being only a short bus ride and walk from Berlin's main shopping street, the Kurfürstendamm. Hunting ran deep in the Hohenzollern blood, as it did with so many European royal families, and Joachim would spend increasing amounts of time in the Grunewald. Yet pursuing the Grunewald's stags was not his only reason for being there. His second wife, the very Catholic and non-German-speaking

Hedwig of Poland, had suffered an unfortunate accident when she
had fallen through the floor of one of Joachim's other hunting lodges
and impaled herself on a stag's antler displayed in the room below.
This left her crippled and she found her place increasingly taken by
Anna Sydow, Joachim's mistress and wife of the owner of an important Berlin iron foundry. Joachim installed Anna in the Jagdschloss,
where she lived until his death in 1571. He made his heir, John
George, promise to ensure she was well cared for, but no sooner had
his father died than John George had her variously imprisoned in
Spandau or walled up in the stairwell of the Jagdschloss (depending
which story one believes, though it is perhaps more than coincidence that recent research has shown one of the stairwells in the
Jagdschloss was bricked up the year Joachim died).

The Jagdschloss is also now home to the fruits of another of
Joachim's and his father's glorious extravagances: the art of both
Lucas Cranach the Elder (1473–1553) and his son, Lucas Cranach the
Younger (1515–1586). The Cranachs came from southern Germany
but were employed as court painters at the Saxon court. Joachim II
became a friend and extensive patron of both father and son, and
the first floor of the Jagdschloss is now devoted to their work. The
Cranachs' workshop was large and produced official portraits to
order, including many of Joachim as a young man looking imposingly
martial for distribution around Brandenburg. Cranach the Elder also
painted Joachim I at least twice – famous portraits that show him in
all his electoral splendour but otherwise seem very direct (with beady
eyes and a mean mouth). The later portraits of Joachim II also seem
harsh, but an image of uncompromising majesty is probably what
was wanted. The Cranach workshop also produced much more for
Berlin. There is a stunning series of the Passion, which – unusually
for religious scenes in Germany at the time – shows a lot of nudity.
Then there is a series of historic and mythical 'Judgements' commissioned by Joachim II for the Zwingburg – or the *Berliner Schloss*, as
we should more accurately refer to it after his renovation work. They
were intended for Joachim's private quarters and are particularly
interesting because they minimise the use of red and blue (expensive

colours in a contemporary painting as the materials to make those paints were difficult to come by), which perhaps indicates just how short of funds the Elector had become.

Jagdschloss Grunewald continued to provide a welcome retreat from Berlin for the Hohenzollerns for many years, evidence of how rural west Berlin would remain until the twentieth century. There is a wonderful painting of Kaiser Wilhelm I arriving for an informal day's hunting in 1887, with ranks of red-coated riders and a military band playing outside the front door. Yet there is another twist to the story of the Jagdschloss's art collection. One of the paintings in the collection is a rather gory, almost sadistic 'Flagellation' by a fourteenth-century Cologne Master. It was originally owned by an English merchant in Berlin, Edward Solly, who sold his entire gallery to Frederick William III in 1821 as the Hohenzollerns were establishing a national art collection. The 'Flagellation' hung at the Jagdschloss until it mysteriously went missing sometime around 1945, that year of chaos in Germany. Recently Berlin authorities were able to search for it online and finally locate it, surprisingly, in the collection of the University of Indiana. The American officer responsible for cultural affairs in Berlin in the years after the Second World War was a certain Herman B. Wells, who coincidentally ended up as Professor of Fine Art at Indiana University. The 'Flagellation' is now safely back where it belongs, alongside the many Cranachs overlooking the Grunewald.

Joachim also founded the first formal group of musicians in Berlin. There had, of course, been choirboys in the Nikolaikirche and the Marienkirche, but in 1540 Joachim recruited a dozen trumpeters and drummers, together with a singing master, and later added strings so that by 1570 he had a small orchestra under a *kapellmesiter*. The musicians were recruited internationally, and a record of their work shows that their repertoire was drawn from across Europe. When not engaged in the cathedral or palace, they were free to play for the congregations of other churches. From this small group came two significant Berlin traditions. First, they allowed Berliners to enjoy sung Lutheran church services, initially in Latin but increasingly in German so they could participate in the singing. Hymns rapidly became a popular part of churchgoing and being able to join in what had previously been rather dry Latin services, a significant factor in the appeal of Lutheranism. Secondly, Joachim's small group started the concept of the public concert, something that has been a key part of Berlin's life ever since. Berlin may not have given birth to many of Germany's great composers but it has most certainly been the place so many of them – from Bach to Beethoven – wanted to perform, not just for the kudos of playing in front of the royal court but for the enthusiasm and appreciation of Berlin audiences.

Another Berlin innovation post the Reformation was the Berlin theatre. It could not be said to compare in any way with what Shakespeare was staging in London, but the first recorded public play was put on in 1541. It had the catchy title of *Ein seer schön und nützlich Spiel von der lieblichen Geburt Unseres Herrn Jesu Christi* ('A very beautiful and beneficial play about the gracious birth of Our Lord Jesus Christ') and was written by Heinrich Klaust, the headmaster of a school in Cölln. Some of the parts were taken by his pupils and much of the play was sung. Public reaction to its first night is sadly not available, but this relatively modest beginning started one of Europe's most celebrated theatre traditions and one that would be quickly developed.[16] There was, in particular, a growing cultural exchange with England, facilitated partly by England's growing trading interests and partly from the English soldiers who sold their services in the profusion of armies that plagued Europe in the latter part of the sixteenth century. English players brought comic theatre, *Englische Komödianten*, which was soon adapted to produce typically German comic characters like Hans Wurst, and a form of jocular popular comedy that would be played out in Berlin's *kneipen* (inns or pubs) for centuries. They also brought William Shakespeare's plays to Berlin, starting a long-lasting love affair with his work that is as strong today as it was then. Volumes of both his comedies and tragedies were published in German in the early decades of the seventeenth century when the Electors maintained a Berlin troupe of nineteen actors and sixteen musicians

under John Spencer, and when he retired they advertised in London
for a replacement.[17]

An important development was in the language that Berliners
spoke. For centuries this had been a form of rough *plattdeutsch* (Low
German) with many phrases and expressions from the Hanseatic
ports that was difficult for other Germans to understand. Now, as
trade links with central Germany predominated, and merchants
tended to look south to Leipzig and Dresden as opposed to north to
the Baltic and the North Sea, this began to change. Luther's writings
made the German spoken in Saxony – *hochdeutsch*, referred to as
Meissenisch (literally 'of Meissen') – widely known, and it became
the preferred language of government and the law across large areas
of Germany, including Berlin. The 1510 Desecration of the Host
trial was conducted in this high German, probably of scant interest
to the poor Jews in the dock but evidence that the city's speech was
changing. The leading merchant families changed the spelling of
their names so as to appear more educated; for example, the Ryke
family become Reiche, and the Schum family change to Schaum. The
change was quick but inevitably Berlin interpreted it in its own way
so that, although Berliners were nearly all speaking this Meissenisch
by the mid-sixteenth century, they kept their traditional accents and
style. Berliners 'took over the Upper Saxon language (Meissenisch),
but they spoke it as if it were Low German' and, when later combined
with all the various languages and expressions brought by successive
waves of immigrants, this would give Berlin its very individual accent
and dialect, *Berlinerisch*, which it has kept ever since.[18]

Berlinerisch is an evolving dialect, and it is difficult to be certain
when exact words and customs were adopted. From the beginning,
though, being a language of the street, it seems to have followed
various traits rather than any rules. Vowels are flattened so that
whereas someone speaking *hochdeutsch* would say *auch*, pronounced 'owch' (meaning 'also'), or *auf*, pronounced 'owf' (meaning
'on'), a Berliner would say 'ooch' and 'uff', with the u pronounced
as in 'push'. They also pronounce *klein* (meaning 'small') as 'kleen'
while a proper German speaker says 'kline'. Perhaps the best-known

Berlinerisch habit is to say *Ick* (German for 'I' and pronounced 'ick') instead of '*ich*' with the 'ch' pronounced as in 'China'. The letter *g* is pronounced as 'j', so 'jut' for *gut* (good), and *s* has become 't', so 'wat' instead of *was* or 'dit' or 'det' instead of *das*. Plurals used to acquire an additional *s*, so *Klopse* (meatballs) became 'Klopses'. Nouns have an extra 'the' in front, such as *dem sein Haus* (literally 'the his house') instead of the conventional *sein Haus* (his house). Grammar can be occasional, and proper nouns and names are taken and used as expressions. '*Nachtijall ick hör dir trapsen*', which in German should be '*Nachtigall ich höre Dich kommen*' (in English literally 'nightingale, I hear you coming', or 'I have a suspicion of something'), is a famous line used in German literature. A five-pfennig coin was a *Sechser* and there is still a bridge in Tegel called 'Sechserbrücke' because the toll used to be five pfennigs. There is something purposefully disrespectful – almost rebellious – about *Berlinerisch*, as if it encapsulates that spirit of *Berlin Unwille*. A classic example is that a polite German might finish a sentence with *Nicht wahr?* ('Is it not?') but a Berliner will simply say '*Huh?*'

The relationship with the Cranachs, and Krebs's work on the Berliner Schloss, and this linguistic change all show how strong the cultural influence of Saxony was in Berlin. The rows over religion and Joachim I's affair do not seem to have prevented the development of close personal and cultural links. Berlin would remain in awe of Dresden – slightly jealous, in fact, culminating in one of Frederick the Great's most inexcusable acts in the eighteenth century; the bombardment of Dresden. An incident that shows Berlin still had some way to go to match Saxon sophistication is the curious story of Michael Kohlhaas, a merchant from Cölln who went on a commercial trip to Leipzig in 1532. As he rode through Saxony, a local Saxon lord took two of Kohlhaas's horses, supposedly as a fee for his passage. Kohlhaas tried to obtain redress through the Saxon courts but failed. Outraged, he then took it upon himself to burn down several houses in Wittenberg. Gathering a group of outlaws around him, he continued to commit acts of terror throughout Saxony, eventually returning to Berlin where he set himself up as a highwayman.

There is still an area called Kohlhasenbrück in Zehlendorf where he allegedly tried to rob a convoy carrying the Elector's silver as it was crossing the Bäke, a tributary of the Havel, and subsequently hid the silver ingots in the riverbank. He was captured shortly thereafter and in 1540 sentenced to be broken on the wheel. Kohlhaas might well have disappeared from historical view had Heinrich von Kleist (of whom much more later) not turned him into a popular hero in his 1810 *Erzählungen* novellas, making him a sort of Robin Hood character who defended ordinary people and stood up for his rights against an over-mighty Saxon Elector – useful propaganda when Prussia was occupied by Napoleon. Berlin would take many years before it felt confident in dealing with Dresden.

The main problem for Berlin was that Saxony was much richer than Brandenburg, and during the second half of the sixteenth century that position worsened as the Hanseatic ports started to lose their trading advantages to the Dutch and British fleets operating along the Channel. This resulted in the richer merchant families who had land around Berlin tending to leave the city and work their estates, which had two effects. First, it meant there was less money in the city, leaving the court as the major consumer but with less tax revenue. Joachim II, always short of money, was not averse to conducting sudden 'wealth' taxes on the richer citizens. On 4 August 1567 he had all gold, jewellery and coin valued and helped himself to a share. Unsurprisingly, this was unpopular – not least because so much of Joachim's expense was caused by his various building projects – and Lippold, his Jewish banker, was predictably blamed.

Joachim's financial problems also perhaps reveal another side to his developing enthusiasm for the Reformation as he and Lippold came to realise just how rich the Church was in Berlin. Jagdschloss Grunewald was built with the proceeds of the sale of church land, and the Hohenzollerns' reforming zeal seems to have increased as it became apparent just how much ecclesiastical property could be available. The problem was more finding a market for it. Much of it went to these richer Berlin merchant families establishing themselves in wider Brandenburg. Schloss Tegel (famous when it much later became the home of the von Humboldt family), for example, was built in 1550 for Brettschneider, one of Joachim's officials, on land once owned by a convent. Tactfully he used the same architect, another Saxon called Caspar Theyss, as Joachim had for Grunewald. Secondly, this exodus of the wealthier merchant families weakened Berliners politically; as the power of the rural landlords – the *Junkers* as they became known (though the term Junker derives from Prussia) – increased, so that of Berlin was correspondingly reduced.

Joachim II died in 1571. Despite his chronic shortage of money, he had increasingly come to see himself as an important northern European ruler. In 1562 he had gone to the Diet summoned by the Emperor Ferdinand to elect a successor with 'sixty-eight gentlemen in his retinue and an equipage of 452 horses'.[19] His funeral was no less lavish, with his successor, John George, making a 'superb internment for his father' despite entombing his mistress in the stairwell of Schloss Grunewald.[20] Neither did it save the wretched Lippold, who was arrested and subject to a particularly grisly execution soon afterwards, accompanied by the now-traditional pogrom. Jews were banned from Berlin 'for all time'; it would take nearly a hundred years before they returned. Lack of money did not stop John George either, who had a particular love of display. 'There was a mixture of ferocity and magnificence in the customs of those days,' thought Frederick the Great. 'The cause of this singularity was the desire the nation had to emerge from its barbarousness ... they were so stupid as to confuse ceremonies with politeness, magnificence with dignity, debauchery with pleasure, pedantry with learning'.[21] John George celebrated the birth of his eldest son with four days of games in Berlin, which took place on the *Lustgarten* (the pleasure ground), an open space north of the Berliner Schloss on the island that would undergo many different iterations in its long association with the city and its rulers. There were tournaments with jousting, naval battles on the Spree and – John George's particular favourite – fireworks. He supervised the firework display personally, sitting in a window of the Schloss and giving signals to the firers.

He also brought Leonhard Thurneysser to Berlin. Thurneysser

described himself as an alchemist, a metallurgist and a doctor. He dwelled in the netherworld between realism and fantasy at a time when scientific knowledge was insufficient to disprove his wilder theories. Originally from Basel, he had tried his luck in several European countries and (if he is to be believed) North Africa before healing John George's wife in Frankfurt an der Oder. The grateful elector brought him back to Berlin on an enormous salary and set him up in the Grauen Kloster, where he established a laboratory and became a local Berlin celebrity. He produced a major book in 1575 entitled *Archidoxa* that purported to interpret the movements of the planets, thus allowing him to predict the course of natural events and – perhaps more profitably – to tell his customers' horoscopes. He claimed there was gold under the Spree and that the Mark was rich in precious metals, thereby endearing him further to the impoverished Elector. Inevitably he also thought he could turn base metal into gold. The charade lasted until 1584 when his various marital complications forced him to return to Basel. Although he did later come back to Berlin, by that stage his spell had been broken, no gold had materialised and he died, having converted to Catholicism, in poverty. Thurneysser did, however, give Berlin one very helpful legacy in that he established a printing press. In 1600 Berliners were treated to their first regular newspaper, a weekly sheet published by the Elector's Postmaster, Christoph Frischmann, and in 1614 two brothers, Johann and Samuel Kalle, founded a book-publishing house with accompanying shop.

Despite this love of ostentatious display, this celebrating of charlatans like Thurneysser, and the mob violence that led to Lippold's execution, all of which show the 'barbarousness' Frederick the Great so lamented, John George did oversee a gradual tightening of the religious practice from the loose, pragmatic Lutheranism that had characterised his father's reign. Buchholzer and Agricola were dead, and Berlin noticed a more structured interpretation of the Reformation. John George adopted the 1548 Augsburg Interim – which meant that the Church in Berlin and the Mark now adhered to the Lutheran pattern common in other parts of the German-speaking world, with sacraments, bishops and saints – and, although a firm Lutheran, he allowed Calvinist refugees to settle in Berlin. Johannes Calvin, from whom Calvinism takes its name, was a French reformer from Geneva. Much younger than Luther, and a Catholic in his early life, he began to think that Luther had not taken the Reformation to its logical conclusion. The essence of Calvin's teaching was that man did not need any intermediaries in his communication with God. Christians had the scriptures, which people needed help in interpreting, but there was no requirement for bishops or any of the church ritual that Luther had kept from Catholicism. Calvin articulated his views in his *Institutes of the Christian Religion*, first published in 1536 but constantly updated until his death in 1564. Calvinism was considered too extreme to be allowed as an accepted religion under the *cuius regio eius religio* principle agreed at Augsburg and was seen by some rulers as dangerously radical, since it could be interpreted as empowering the people against the accepted hierarchy. This was a misconception and, as some princes realised, if they did not have to deal with a hierarchy of bishops, they could assume the episcopal role themselves. Berliners would soon realise just what this meant.

~

As the sixteenth century drew to a close, the Hohenzollerns were still fairly minor players in the politics of Europe. Joachim II may have gone in state to the Imperial Diet – and on his death the Mark (which had been divided by his father into two parts, his brother John ruling the eastern part from Küstrin) may have been reunited – but Brandenburg was still economically and culturally seen as something of a backwater, especially when compared to Saxony. Berlin was not much bigger than it had been a century before. Physically it still occupied roughly the same area: Cölln, the Island and Berlin itself. Despite all Joachim's work on the Berliner Schloss, which now boasted Berlin's first tennis court and indoor riding school, there had been little other building and it still had the feel of an agricultural market town, with many people leaving daily to work on the surrounding farms. The population hovered around 12,000, having been savagely reduced by further plague epidemics in 1566 and a particularly terrible outbreak in 1576 (allegedly caused by a woman stealing the coat of a plague victim and spreading the epidemic around the city), which killed about 4,000 people.[22] London, by way of comparison, had a population of 130,000 in 1618.[23] The plague was a curse that would take the city many years to rid itself of; its effects, coupled with the economic downturn and a run of poor harvests that caused local famines, meant that growth was minimal.

The last two decades of the sixteenth century were consequently a fairly miserable time for Berliners. Poverty became more widespread. Those who were lucky enough to be members of one of the guilds were looked after by their fellows; those outside were less fortunate, although they were helped by a comprehensive Poverty Law of 1596. This was remarkably forward-leaning at a time when welfare arrangements across Europe were basic. The sick were to be cared for in one of the city's four hospitals, with the city carrying the costs. Poor children received support and were allowed to sing in choirs outside people's doors to earn money. Those artisans who could no longer work and had descended into poverty, the so-called *Hausarmen*, received alms every fortnight. Beggars were checked; if they were judged genuinely unable to work, they were given an official badge and allowed to beg three days a week between 10 a.m. and noon. There were several laws passed in an attempt to reduce prostitution. This was a particularly popular profession that flourished in the economic downturn due to the number of visiting merchants who still came to the city. It had been variously legislated against – the first law banning it was in 1486 – or tolerated, but the spread of syphilis across Europe in the middle of the century made it a more serious issue. In 1583 the Elector promulgated an order for 'Clean Living' in an attempt to regulate its proliferation.[24]

There was, though, still the opportunity for the rich to enjoy the finer things in life. The guilds each held an annual festival with processions, and a feast where wine made from grapes grown in Berlin, as well as large quantities of beer, was drunk. By 1565 there were seventy vineyards around the city and twenty-six producers.

In 1580 the council found it necessary to issue an edict on 'luxury', which divided the city's population into four 'classes'; which class you were judged to belong to by income dictated how you were permitted to dress and to entertain. Bizarre as this sounds, it was not an uncommon form of regulation across sixteenth-century Europe and would still form part of Berlin's electoral franchise in the mid-nineteenth century. Tailors were forbidden from making clothes for customers who did not belong to the correct class for each type of material. Weddings, which had become a major festive occasion, were equally strictly controlled with the edict detailing the number of guests, tables, servants, musicians and torch-bearers each class was permitted to lay on. They tended to be three-day affairs, with the actual church marriage on Sunday followed by a major party that evening. On the Monday there was a service of blessing followed by more feasting; on the Tuesday (now without the bride and groom) the relations and friends gathered for yet another party.[25]

Despite the economic downturn, immigration continued. This was now mostly from the south, from other parts of the German-speaking world where economic conditions were equally difficult – and, in an interesting historical twist, particularly from Saxony – but also from Thuringia, the area immediately west of Dresden and Leipzig, and from Franconia, the southern part of Germany north of Bavaria. Although the numbers were not as significant as they had been in medieval Berlin, nor as significant as they would be later, sixteenth-century Berlin was still an immigrant city. With the new settlers came linguistic and cultural changes that the city quickly assimilated. However, three things were to happen in the first decades of the seventeenth century that would change fundamentally the fortunes of both the city and the dynasty. First, the Hohenzollerns would become the rulers of Prussia. Secondly, they would adopt Calvinism. Thirdly, in 1618, the ambassadors of the Holy Roman Emperor were unceremoniously thrown from a window by the Protestant burghers of Prague, the 'Defenestration', thus starting the Thirty Years War.

The Prussian inheritance is perhaps the occasion when the fortunes of the Hohenzollerns and of Berliners are at their most intermingled and the dynastic events that led to the one becoming rulers of Prussia and the other to live in its capital need some explanation. Prussia lay well to the east of Brandenburg, beyond Poland and south and west of Lithuania, a flat, marshy land bordering the Baltic with its capital in Königsberg. One of the last pagan parts of Europe, it had been subjugated fairly brutally by a crusading order, the Teutonic Knights, who had forcibly converted its inhabitants to Christianity in the thirteenth and fourteenth centuries. Many of the Teutonic Knights were German but by no means all and, as with much of the crusading movement, they offered an opportunity to land-hungry warriors from across Europe. By 1283 they had more or less established control and ruled their new territory from a series of powerful castles, the principal one being Marienburg where the order had its headquarters. Yet by the early fifteenth century the Poles and Lithuanians had tired of the knights' habit of raiding across Prussia's borders, while the Prussians themselves chafed at the high-handed regime the knights imposed. In 1410 a combined Polish and Lithuanian force decisively defeated the knights at Tannenberg. Over the course of the next century the knights gradually lost control of their territory so that by 1525 their Grand Master, Albrecht (another Hohenzollern from the Ansbach branch of the family), decided that the only course left was to submit to the King of Poland and incorporate Prussia as a duchy within the Polish kingdom. He was also one of the first rulers enthusiastically to embrace Lutheranism despite Poland remaining solidly Catholic.

The Brandenburg Hohenzollerns were, as has been noted, good at marrying. Joachim II's second wife, Hedwig, she who so unfortunately fell through the floor impaling herself on an antler, was the sister of the Polish king, Sigismund Augustus. Joachim made a deal with his brother-in-law in 1564 that should Albert Frederick – then Duke of Prussia and Sigismund Augustus's vassal – die without male heirs, his sons would be his nominated successors. In return he promised to provide troops if Poland was attacked, something of a one-sided deal as Brandenburg had no standing army and any troops would inevitably have come from a forced recruitment drive in Berlin. Albert Frederick duly married Marie Eleanor of Cleves, but only had daughters, Ann and Eleanor.

John George died in 1598. His successor, Joachim Frederick, was determined to ensure that his grandfather's plans worked out. Consequently he matched his son, John Sigismund, in marriage to Ann in 1599, despite his mother telling the boy that Ann was rather ugly. Albert Frederick struggled on, increasingly imbecilic, and in 1603 Joachim Frederick started to assume regency powers in Königsberg, helped by the fact that in 1603 he had married Ann's younger sister Eleanor as his second wife. When he died in 1608 his son – and, bizarrely, now brother-in-law – John Sigismund continued to act as regent until the aged Duke Albert Frederick finally died in 1618.

Ann of Prussia was in fact quite a catch for she brought with her not just Prussia but also, through her mother, the inheritance of John William of Jülich-Cleves-Berg and his extensive lands on the Rhine, in what is now the German province of North Rhine Westphalia and its neighbouring Dutch province of Gelderland. The law in Jülich-Cleves allowed for female succession, and Ann found herself at least the titular holder of not only Jülich-Cleves itself but also of Berg, Mark and Ravensberg. The problem was that the population of Jülich itself and Berg were Catholic and disliked the idea of being ruled by Lutheran Prussians. Fighting broke out, settled at the Treaty of Xanten in 1609, which saw these two states going to the Catholic Duke of Palatinate-Neuberg (not to be confused with the Protestant Elector Palatine) while the Hohenzollerns ended up with Cleves, Mark and Ravensberg (which were all Protestant). Ravensberg was a rich farming county between the Rhine and the Elbe, centred on the city of Bielefeld, whereas Cleves was a developed industrial province astride the Rhine, and strongly Calvinist. Mark was an equally rich province, roughly equivalent to the modern German industrialised area on the River Ruhr, and was also Calvinist. It would take most of the next century for all these territories to be fully integrated into Brandenburg, but their incorporation would mean that Berlin would now look not just east to the Baltic and Prussia but also west to the

Rhine. It was no longer just the city in the sandbox, but Berliners' reaction to this potentially vast increase in Hohenzollern territory was overshadowed by events in the city itself.

John Sigismund's second move was to convert to Calvinism. He seems to have done this partly from conviction. He had been sent by his father to Strasbourg University, where he had been impressed by Calvin's intellectually capable and persuasive followers. He also took exception to the bombastic Provost of Berlin, Simon Gedicke, who had none of Buchholzer's subtle charm. In 1610 his younger brother Ernst converted and at Christmas 1613 John Sigismund made a public declaration of his own conversion. It did not go down well in Berlin. However deep his personal conviction may have been, Berliners objected strongly. Events came to a head at Easter 1615 when John Sigismund invited the Reformist preacher Martin Füssel to preach in the Schloss Chapel. Although what happened in April 1615 cannot be described as a revolution, it came close to it and was a rare example of Berliners prevailing over the dynasty. They saw John Sigismund's conversion as being politically expedient given the Jülich-Cleves inheritance. 'If you want to reform, move to Jülich! There you can have reform enough,' shouted the Lutheran cleric Peter Stuler from the pulpit of Cölln's Petrikirche on Palm Sunday.[26] Berliners also valued the rather loose Lutheran structure that Joachim II had initiated and that they felt gave them some protection. They saw, as did John Sigismund, that under a Calvinist system the Elector could control the church directly and that Calvin himself had emphasised the need for national conformity to the religion of the ruler.

John Sigismund had been away from Berlin and his brother had ordered the removal of pictures, altars, statues and crucifixes from the Schloss Chapel before Easter week began. Stuler's outcry prompted serious rioting. The houses of Calvinist preachers were ransacked, and order was only restored by the Elector's guard. Füssel was reduced to preaching the Sunday sermon 'in a bright green undergarment, which was all the rioters had left him'.[27] The confrontation ended in an uneasy truce. Stuler was thought to have gone too far and fled to Wittenberg but the council distanced themselves from John Sigismund. He was forced to acknowledge Lutheranism and to allow the Berlin churches to keep their services but he himself remained Calvinist, despite his devoutly Lutheran wife objecting strongly. Poor Ann! Her destiny was to be something of a dynastic pawn and, in spite of an initially happy marriage, she and John Sigismund became badly estranged, with him never bothering to reply to the numerous letters she wrote him.[28] The dispute between the Hohenzollerns' Calvinism and Berlin's Lutheranism would come to dominate the city for the next hundred years.

Yet both the Hohenzollerns' acquisition of Prussia and their Rhineland territories, and the dispute over religious observance, would be overshadowed by the third and most terrible event that dominated the first half of seventeenth-century Berlin and the history of the city for centuries afterwards: the Thirty Years War. Berlin has been crucified twice in its life; first by the Thirty Years War, then by the combined Second World War bombing and Soviet invasion of 1945. Both wars not only killed or displaced about half the population, but they also left the city in ruins and morally shattered. The effects of what happened in 1945 are still well known to many people alive today. The Thirty Years War, by contrast, now seems like forgotten history and is neither well known nor well understood, despite generations of schoolchildren being asked in history exams whether it was a war of religion. However, the Thirty Years War shaped Berlin, Brandenburg, Prussia and Germany as profoundly as the Second World War. It killed about 5 million people across Europe, so 20 per cent of the pre-war population. Comparable figures for Europe in the First World War are 5.5 per cent and in the Second World War about 6 per cent. A large part of the German sense of victimhood derives from what the German-speaking world suffered during those terrible years, whereas Berlin derives much of its spirit of phlegmatic resilience from what it endured. By the time the war finally ended in 1648, Berlin had lost half its people.

Like other terrible European wars, while the origins of its outbreak are clear, the actual causes are less easy to define. Berlin was not alone in suffering from an economic downturn in the last decades of the fifteenth and early decades of the sixteenth centuries. Inflation was high, banks were failing and even the venerable House of Fugger, which had bankrolled Joachim I's speculation in Indulgences, went into liquidation in 1614 owing 8 million gulden.[29] There was also widespread fighting across Europe, as societies struggled to overthrow alien governments, particularly in the Spanish Netherlands, in Ireland and with civil war in France. Armed rebellion was seen as a necessary and effective means of achieving political aims, and the agricultural conditions that had caused the Peasants' War in Germany persisted so that rural unrest was widespread. Against this depressed economic and social background, the pressures caused by the Reformation and the challenges posed to the power of the Hapsburg Emperor by the German states, meant that when war erupted in Prague in 1618 it was difficult to control.

The war can be roughly divided into three parts. From the 'Defenestration' of Prague in 1618 until 1629, the Hapsburgs were generally successful in defeating threats to their power so that they felt confident enough to issue an Edict of Restitution that outlawed Calvinism and demanded the return of all confiscated Catholic Church property. It was an unwise move, as proved the next year when the Swedes invaded North Germany and the war entered its bloodiest period. In 1635 there was another pause, with the Hapsburgs acknowledging in the Peace of Prague that they could not stop the spread of Lutheranism and Calvinism. But from 1635 until 1648 the war effectively stopped having much religious purpose at all and became a European war of dynastic rivalry as Catholic France struggled with the Hapsburgs, Catholic Spain and the Holy Roman Emperor. It finally ended in 1648 at the Peace of Westphalia.

Berlin was not well served by its rulers as war broke out. George William had succeeded his father as Elector in 1619 but was a weak man who had a 'most unfortunate reign', thought Frederick the Great. He was 'a sovereign incapable of governing', spent much of the war in Königsberg, and he chose in his chief minister in Berlin (the pro-Hapsburg Schwarzenberg) a man who was 'a traitor to his country'.[30] Although George William was an elector and married to the sister of the Elector Palatine, whose assumption of the crown of Bohemia had been a major factor in the war's outbreak, he had no army as such and was effectively sidelined. The Spanish and the Dutch fought over Cleves, the Swedes invaded Prussia, and George William himself reckoned he was so poor that he could not afford to attend the Imperial Diet called at Ratisbon in 1630, the Mark by this stage being 'so greatly exhausted, as to be incapable of supplying my ordinary expenses, much less those of a journey of that kind'.[31] However, wisely, he did appreciate the weakness of his situation and how poorly the Mark was defended. He attempted for as long as he could to remain both a supporter of the Protestant cause and also loyal to the Emperor.

Consequently, Berlin suffered relatively little in the early years, with the fighting more in Bohemia and southern Germany. There were regular protests about rising prices and inflation caused by the war, including a major demonstration in Berlin in 1622 where several people were killed. Due to what is known as *Kipper und Wipper* (the twin processes of clipping and debasing coinage common across the German states as governments struggled to meet the war's cost), people lost confidence in the value of currency. Prices in Berlin rose approximately eight times between 1621 and 1623.[32] However, Hans Georg von Ribbeck, one of the Elector's council, felt confident enough in 1624 to commission a very fine renaissance mansion on Breite Straße that, with some imagination, you can still make out today beneath its various rebuilds. But in 1627 Brandenburg found itself sandwiched between an invading Danish army to its north and a Protestant army under Mansfeld to its south. To prevent these two forces joining up, Wallenstein, the Emperor's mercenary general, invaded the Mark and occupied it. An Imperial army commanded, unusually, by a Lutheran Brandenburger, Hans Georg von Arnim, occupied Berlin on 15 November 1627. George William had attempted to forestall them by sending a rather pathetic force of sixty of his Royal Guard, but the Berliners pelted them with paving stones, thinking they were making a renewed attempt to enforce Calvinism. There was little the city could do but submit. A worse

Imperial occupation came in 1630 when a much larger Imperial force
of 40,000 troops occupied the city and stayed for a year.

The issue with these armies was that they were largely mercenaries, that is engaged by recruiters acting for generals – men like
Wallenstein and Tilly, who sold their services to the Emperor, or
Mansfeld who did the same for the Protestant princes. Consequently,
their loyalty was to themselves and many saw military service as
either a method of feeding themselves and their families or, particularly in the case of officers, simply profiteering. The wages they
had to pay their soldiers came as often from plunder as from their
employer's coffers. While Berlin avoided a massacre – unlike its
unfortunate neighbour Magdeburg, which was sacked by Imperial
troops in May 1631 with 30,000 killed – it was inevitable that
a population of about 10,000 could not support four times that
number of soldiers. The demand for food, the looting, the lack of
discipline leading to widespread rape and murder, condemned the
poor Berliners to a year of misery. Armies also carried disease with
them, so that plague returned yet again, accounting for an estimated
2,000 lives between 1630 and 1631.

Life as a soldier could be as rough as it was for the unfortunate
people whose land they occupied, and many who signed up did so
because their own homes and livelihood had been destroyed earlier
in the war, thus leaving them with little option. Peter Hagendorf
joined Wallenstein's army that would invade Brandenburg in 1627
because he 'was totally destitute'. His diary is as interesting for its
concentration on his and his family's battles for survival as for the
fact that it hardly mentions actual combat. He married twice during
the war, his wives becoming camp followers, and of their nine children only two survived. He describes marching from Neustettin to
Spandau through a Brandenburg countryside that was well supplied
but that apparent prosperity would not last.[33]

Berlin's nemesis, however, came not with the Emperor's Catholic
armies but from the Protestant Swedish army under its able if ruthless
king, Gustavus Adolphus. He was also married to George William's
sister, but Swedish national ambition seems to have taken precedence

over family loyalty. Gustavus Adolphus, having already invaded Poland, marched into Brandenburg and arrived in front of Berlin in June 1631. George William, having just got rid of Wallenstein's men, tried his best to deter him. Gustavus Adolphus claimed that his brother-in-law had promised to cede Spandau to him and that he had reneged on his promise. He now trained his guns on Berlin while George William first sent out his wife and mother-in-law to negotiate. They had little success. Gustavus Adolphus argued – falsely but convincingly – that Berlin had been opened to Imperial troops so why should it not now be open to him? 'All that I require,' he said, 'is security, a moderate sum of money, and provisions for my troops; in return I shall promise to protect [this] country.'[34] It was one of the great lies in Berlin's history. George William was forced to ride out to meet his brother-in-law at Köpenick, where in happier times Joachim II had built one of his several hunting lodges. Overawed by Gustavus Adolphus, and with no troops of his own (a lesson that would affect his successors for generations to come), George William could do little but place the resources of Brandenburg and the fortresses of Spandau and Küstrin at Gustavus Adolphus's disposal, guarantee him a subsidy of 30,000 Reichsthalers a month and then proceed to get horribly drunk with him.[35] What was given away so easily would result in a period of purgatory for Berlin: the Swedes occupied Berlin for three years, then between 1635 and 1638 the city was fought over almost constantly as the Swedes and the Imperial forces campaigned across the Mark.

Already wrecked from its occupation by the Imperial armies, the Swedes used Berlin as a campsite, extracting what little was left of value from a rapidly shrinking population. Gustavus Adolphus is usually judged as a great general but his control over his troops was wanting. Their favoured methods of extracting money from Berliners was either to sprinkle a child with gunpowder and then set light to them in front of their parents or to pour raw sewage down their throats; to this day, raw sewage is known in Berlin as the Swedish Drink. 'For this,' wrote Peter Thiele, an official from Beelitz, then a village just outside Berlin, 'the robbers and murderers took a piece of wood and stuck it down a poor soul's throat, stirring and pouring in water, to which they added sand and human excrement thus pitifully torturing the victims for their money. This befell a citizen of Beelitz, David Örttel ... who died soon afterwards as a result.'[36] A contemporary woodcut shows a variety of similar tortures being visited on a poor victim by a laughing Swedish soldier including twisting their eyes out, skinning them alive, hanging them in smoke and planing off their faces.[37] Jürgen Weber, a Berlin baker, testified that soldiers had 'stuck a piece of wood half a finger's length into his fistula to make him confess where his money was'.[38]

A Swedish soldier, went a contemporary saying, needed three peasants – one to give up his lodging, one to provide his wife and one to take his place in hell.[39] Young women had long ago vanished from Berlin's streets – raped, carried off as a wife or simply having fled to avoid such a fate. Thiele thought it 'indescribable. They [Swedish soldiers] behaved barbarically in Beelitz, despoiling old women, not a few of them 60 years old, to say nothing of the young ones'.

While these atrocities were occasional, the threat of having soldiers billeted on them in their homes and the official extraction of money and food to support them was constant. 'We were up to our necks with the collection enforcers they set upon us,' Thiele complained, 'as numerous as locusts – at times over 40' in the village of Beelitz alone. 'And we had to give them their rations and subsistence money too, not to mention what they pinched and pilfered from people – cattle, sheep, bread, grains, everything from their farms. The field chaplain and the regimental hangman haven't come to extort from us yet, but apart from them practically everyone has been here to enforce contributions.'[40] Sir Thomas Roe, an Englishman travelling through the area, wrote, 'I hear nothing but lamentations nor see variety but of dead bodies. In 80 English miles not a house safe to sleep in; no inhabitants save a few poor women and children' desperately searching for food. Starvation inevitably followed, 'the much used gallows were regularly plundered and even graves were found emptied. In one case fresh human bones were discovered in a pit with their marrow sucked dry.'[41]

Starvation got worse as the war progressed. Peter Thiele noted that 'the poor people ate outlandish things ... They ground up beechnuts, linseed residues, cabbage stalks and especially nettles ... many died because of these unnatural foods. In Beelitz there were often more than a hundred poor souls on the streets.' Depopulation meant that 'the best farms lay desolate and around a thousand acres, without counting other outlying fields, were left unplanted'. The soldiers ended up being as hungry as their victims. As one regiment reached Beelitz they 'ate dogs, cats and rotting dead horses. Everything they found in the barns outside they either consumed or destroyed.'[42]

Berlin's crucifixion seemed to go on and on. People gave up trying to remember when life had seemed more or less normal, and the arguments between Lutheranism and Calvinism seemed like a luxury from a vanished age. Fighting was still continuing in 1641, fourteen years after the initial Imperial occupation. George William had permanently moved to Königsberg in 1638, leaving Berlin to the strongly Imperialist Schwarzenberg who burned what little was left of Cölln in 1641 in an attempt to frustrate yet another approaching Swedish army. In the event it turned out to be little more than a disorganised rabble but, by the time the fighting around Berlin (if not the war itself) finished in March 1641, Berlin's population was a starving, dispirited, sick group of about 4,000 souls, less than half what it had been in 1627 and with only 850 houses left standing – 200 of which were uninhabitable.

The spiritual damage to Berlin was perhaps even deeper than the physical. Writing over a century later, Frederick the Great thought that 'the traces' of the war 'are to this day very discernible in Germany'.[43] Berlin was not alone in its suffering, and the psychological effect of the war would scar Germany for generations – and arguably still does. A relatively rich, prosperous and beautiful part of Europe, the German states had been invaded from the south by the Hapsburg armies, then drawn as much from the Balkans as from Austria. The Croats would be among the most feared Imperial troops, as they were so often in succeeding centuries. It was noted that, when taking a town, the Croats would amuse themselves by throwing children into the flames.[44] Germany had been invaded from the north by the Danes and then the Swedes, and from the west across the Rhine, from France. She had not been invaded from the east.

The war 'nurtured' in the German states and particularly Berlin 'what became by the 19th century a strong sense of victimhood,'[45] thought Stephen Green. As Berliners surveyed the wreck of their lives and homes in 1648, as the Peace of Westphalia finally stopped the fighting, they would feel not only regret but bitterness. The poet Andreas Gryphius, who lived between Brandenburg and Silesia, articulated their feelings well in his poem '*Tränen des Vaterlandes*' (Tears of the Fatherland) in which he writes

'Now our devastation is complete – indeed more than complete!
The brazen hordes of foreigners, the blaring bugles of war,
the blood-slaked sword, the thundering siege gun –
they have consumed everything we worked so hard for.'[46]

Why had they been singled out for this persecution? Thiele summed up the view of many Berliners when he wrote, 'This whole war has been a veritable robbers' and thieves' campaign. The generals and colonels have lined their pockets while princes and lords have been led by the nose. But whenever there has been talk of wanting to make peace they have always looked to their reputations. That is what the land and the people have been devastated for.'[47]

Friedrich Schiller, one of the great thinkers and writers of eighteenth-century Germany, would write a detailed history of the war – almost as if to do so was necessary in order to write about contemporary Germany. 'For half a century,' thought Schiller, the war 'smothered the glimmering sparks of civilisation in Germany, and threw back the improving manners of the country into their pristine barbarity and wildness'.[48] Even as late as 1939 the famous Berlin playwright Bertolt Brecht sets his anti-war classic *Mother Courage and Her Children* in the Thirty Years War. Mother Courage is a sutler, pushing a barrow behind the armies, determined to make some money from the fighting, but in the process she loses all three of her children. Undaunted, she carries on and as the play ends she is still resolutely pushing her wares as her last child is shot.

The lesson for Berliners was that shown by Mother Courage: a need to get on with life whatever it throws at you and to try to rebuild. Physically the task was daunting. Brandenburg was still occupied by Swedish troops and Berlin itself was in ruins. Bodies had to be buried and streets cleared. In 2007 archaeologists found one of what must be many mass graves from the 1630s at Wittstock, one of several battles fought between the Swedes and Imperial troops on the north-west approaches to the city. The bodies of more than a hundred soldiers were found, showing terrible wounds from heavy blades and musket balls and all stripped of everything useable. But would Berlin be able to recover and would the Mark – 'then one frightful desert, which exhibited a lamentable spectacle of ruins, conflagrations, and of every scene of calamity that attends a long and furious war' – be able to survive?[49]

The Hohenzollerns had learned different lessons from the war to the Berliners but their interests would once again coincide in one of the most remarkable rulers Brandenburg Prussia has produced – and arguably one of the great monarchs of the seventeenth century – the Elector Frederick William, now always known as The Great Elector.

CHAPTER THREE

1640–1740

'It is necessary that you conduct yourself as a
good father to your people'

FREDERICK WILLIAM's letter to his son, 1667

Frederick William, The Great Elector or to the Berliners the *Große
Kurfürst*, was the first of four remarkable Hohenzollern electors and
then kings who ruled Brandenburg Prussia for the next 150 years.
Frederick William himself reigned from 1640 until 1688, being
succeeded as Elector by his son Frederick III. In 1701 Frederick
III made himself King in (not of) Prussia, as Frederick I, and was
succeeded in 1713 by his son King Frederick William I. In 1740
Frederick William was in turn succeeded by his son, Frederick II or,
as he is now always known, Frederick the Great. Confusingly, all
Hohenzollern monarchs after 1640 were christened either William
or Frederick or a combination of the two; one almost longs for
those classical surnames Frederick the Great found so silly. About
the only personal characteristic the Hohenzollerns would seem to
have shared is a loathing of their respective fathers, but they were
all united in their determination to make Brandenburg Prussia into
a European power and to ensure that Berlin provided a capital
commensurate with their status. For at least the first hundred years

of their combined reigns, their interests and Berlin's were consequently aligned.

Frederick William, The Great Elector, was a Berliner, born in the Berliner Schloss in 1620 to the irresolute George William and Elisabeth Charlotte, the Calvinist princess of the Palatine. His father died in 1640, with the war still raging. Given the instability in Brandenburg, Frederick William had been partly brought up at the Dutch court by his uncle, the Stadtholder Frederick Henry, whom he had accompanied on military operations. He had then been to university in Leiden, one of Europe's leading centres of Protestant learning. He was consequently strongly influenced by both the orderliness of Dutch culture and by the Calvinism that dominated Dutch life. He had scarcely lived in Berlin – his father's minister Schwarzenberg being keen to keep him at arm's length – and after Holland he had been sent to live in Königsberg. Besides, by the mid-1630s the Berliner Schloss was uninhabitable, with the roof caved in, and it was Prussian money that kept the Hohenzollern court afloat during the worst years of the war. Frederick William also had to secure Prussia from the Polish crown, which he succeeded in doing in October 1641 when he knelt in front of King Wladyslaw and – in exchange for a generous tribute, which he promised but did not have, and surrendering part of his customs dues – he was confirmed as Duke of Prussia.

It was also suggested that he might like to marry Wladyslaw's sister but he made little effort to secure her affections, appearing at a reception where she danced a 'graceful ballet to give him pleasure' in 'a dirty neckband and boots all worn one side and muddy half way up the leg, and altogether dressed with such negligence that the least observant could easily see that he had little heart for dancing in that company'.[1] There was always something direct and matter-of-fact about him – a pragmatic man who was expedient, unscrupulous even, and determined to secure the future of his dynasty. Queen Louise Maria of Poland, who seems to have had something of a soft spot for him, thought, noted her secretary, that he was 'a Prince of good height, well-built and with a determined appearance, a full face and large nose, fine eyes, very courteous, and he knows how to deal with people, to speak well about business and to grasp things quickly'.[2] The need to rebuild Berlin was something he grasped very quickly indeed.

With Prussia secure, Frederick William could turn his attention to Berlin and Brandenburg and to the overall state of his inheritance. It was a fairly wretched picture. 'Pomerania is lost, Jülich is lost, we hold Prussia like an eel by the tail, and we must mortgage the Mark,' complained one of his ministers.[3] Frederick William, however, had different ideas and realised that if he was to have any chance of wrestling some sort of state out of the ruins, he must make peace immediately. His overriding aim on assuming the throne was to end the war. This meant concluding a treaty with Sweden, which would be contrary to the Emperor's desire to continue fighting while the Swedes still occupied large parts of northern Germany.

Schwarzenberg, the arch Imperialist, still controlling Berlin, did his best to frustrate this. Frederick William realised he must confront him. He ordered him to dismiss the 4,000-odd mercenary troops he still controlled in the city, but Schwarzenberg refused, encouraging the mercenary colonels to declare for the Emperor and effectively mutiny against the new Elector. Frederick William had to face him down. In 1638 Schwarzenberg had sacked what was left of the Brandenburg Privy Council who met in Berlin. Frederick William now summoned them to Königsberg. Some were Calvinist, some Lutheran, but nearly all had turned against the Emperor's continuing war and wanted peace. He chose one of them, Konrad von Burgsdorff, a loyal army commander, to go to Berlin as his enforcer. Schwarzenberg realised he was beaten, dying in January 1641, but the governors of Spandau and Küstrin held out. Burgsdorff laid a trap for the governor of Spandau, Colonel Rochow, luring him outside the fortress's impressive fortifications. He duly obliged, was arrested and quickly executed. Berlin was now effectively back in the hands of the Hohenzollerns.

Burgsdorff became Frederick William's chief minister in the city, ruling alongside Margrave Ernst von Jägerndorf, the Elector's cousin. They concentrated first on re-establishing the Estates, the assembly of leading land-owning and commercial families of Brandenburg, heirs of an organisation originally encouraged by Joachim II when he had been (as usual) chronically short of money and that had increased in importance given the chaos of the war. Schwarzenberg had dismissed them, but their support would now be vital to rebuild both the city and the Mark.

In July 1641 a truce was signed with the Swedes, leading in September to a cessation of hostilities until the end of the war. At Regensburg the Emperor, outwitted by Frederick William, was forced to agree to an amnesty. 'On November 30th 1641, the imperial decree of amnesty was nailed up at Cölln on the Spree, in the Elector of Brandenburg's lands, but wind and rain reduced it to shreds in the night and buffeted the fragments contemptuously about the street',[4] encapsulating what most Berliners thought of the Emperor's sincerity. Yet somehow, as fighting continued on the Rhine, Berlin remained at peace. The Swedes had extracted tough terms from the Elector but at least they stuck to them. Swedish troops continued to occupy parts of Brandenburg, where their behaviour was not much improved and where they still helped themselves to what they wanted. Their general, Lilljehöök, thought that 'the Elector should not be allowed to recover'.[5] He would recover, but in his own time.

The Thirty Years War was finally ended through a series of complex negotiations that dragged on between 1645 and 1648 in the Westphalian cities of Osnabruck and Münster. Frederick William returned to Berlin from Königsberg in 1643 but spent the next five years occupied in establishing his position so that Brandenburg Prussia would emerge from these negotiations in a stronger position than the temporary situation he had achieved with Sweden. He had more or less secured his rights in Prussia but he now also had to ensure that he retained control of the wealthy western states that had come through his grandmother in 1609: Cleves, Mark and Ravensberg. He also wanted to try to regain control of Berg, which had been lost at Xanten. To enforce these claims, and mindful of how weak his father's position had been in 1627, he determined to start building a new army.

Once the mercenaries recruited by Schwarzenberg had been dismissed, the Brandenburg army stood at just over 2,000. The infantry was employed in garrisoning the fortresses and billeted in Berlin, with a tiny cavalry force given the fruitless job of policing the countryside. They did not have the trust of the Berliners – probably deservedly – and, as late as November 1641, the small cavalry force sent to protect the town of Brandenburg 'knocked down the walls of the few houses standing, tore out the lintels and beams, ripped up the floors, burnt the timber'.[6] This did not initially make Frederick William very popular in Berlin, where the last thing anyone wanted was yet more soldiers; neither was it well received in the western states, which each had their own powerful Estates who had a similar reaction. The Elector realised that in the short term at least he would have to secure his position through alliances instead.

He turned, surprisingly, first to Sweden and during the negotiations in Stockholm there was much discussion of him marrying his cousin, the seventeen-year-old Queen Christina. Although she was described as a 'headstrong bluestocking', marrying her would immediately remove the Swedish threat in Brandenburg and neighbouring Pomerania, and would make Frederick William one of the most powerful northern European monarchs. That was why the proposal came to nothing. Axel Oxenstierna, the over-mighty Swedish chancellor, did not want to share power with Berlin and the prospect was equally alarming to the Poles and the Hapsburgs.[7] Having failed in Warsaw and Stockholm, and complaining to his advisers that 'they will soon be suggesting a Tartar match', on 7 December 1646 Frederick William married another cousin, Louise Henrietta of Orange, the nineteen-year-old daughter of his uncle the Dutch Stadtholder and whom he had known as a child. The Dutch match helped him in several ways. It gave him a powerful ally in the peace talks, it strengthened his claims to his western states and, like him, Louise Henrietta was a strong Calvinist.[8] He even cleaned himself up for the occasion, which took place in a small room in the palace in The Hague, with Frederick William wearing a black and white satin suit 'set off with diamonds and gold embroidery'. All this had to be paid for by a loan of 50,000 thalers from the Berlin council. Although Louise Henrietta was rumoured to have been in love with someone else, it proved to be a happy and faithful marriage of twenty years and a union to which Berlin would come to owe much.

Despite a ham-fisted attempt to intervene in Berg in 1646, Frederick William's persistence paid off and Brandenburg Prussia emerged well from the final Peace of Westphalia. As well as retaining his three existing western states, he gained Minden, a poor state on the River Weser but strategically well positioned between Brandenburg and the Rhine, Magdeburg (or what was left of it after its dreadful sacking by Imperial troops) and Halberstadt, a rich former bishopric west of Magdeburg and again forming part of a link to the west. He lost Eastern Pomerania (that part across the Oder) to Sweden but retained control of Western Pomerania, which was richer. Righting what he saw as this historic wrong would dominate much of his reign. Perhaps as importantly for the Elector, the Peace of Westphalia also formalised the recognition of Calvinism. This, together with the limits placed on the powers of the Emperor, enhanced Frederick William's position as he determined to weld his fragmented possessions into a cohesive state. Brandenburg Prussia was now larger than Saxony and was the second-largest German state after the Hapsburgs. It was a remarkable achievement given the desperation of the 1630s and how low Brandenburg had been cast in the war. It now called for a proper capital.

There was nothing inevitable about Berlin becoming that capital. Königsberg had an ancient claim as the Prussian capital. It was much larger than Berlin, was an active port shipping Polish and Lithuanian amber, timber, corn and leather to western Europe and had a well-established university. It was, though, remote from Frederick William's western lands and it was still a Polish fiefdom. While he had been invested as its duke, and his relations with King Wladyslaw and his successor John Casimir were adequate, it would not be until the next century that the Hohenzollerns felt secure from Polish interference. Königsberg was also dominated by powerful tri-cameral 'Estates' made up of the regional governors, always from the major aristocratic families, the nobility and the towns. The Estates controlled the key policy areas, the military and taxation, and still looked to the King of Poland as their ultimate protector, regarding their dukes as something of an afterthought. They were also determined Lutherans who had no time for Calvinism, restricting Frederick William to hearing services only inside his own court. In 1642 he had to suffer the indignity of pleading with King Wladyslaw to pressurise the Estates to allow a Calvinist cleric to take his father's burial service, George William's body having remained embalmed since his death two years previously. Rich and vibrant city that it was, Frederick William must have felt somewhat relieved when he could return to Berlin where his cousin the Margrave Ernst had gone mad and died in October 1642.

The Brandenburg Estates, together with the Berlin burghers, would prove equally troublesome in the decades ahead, but in 1643 the priority was to rebuild and repopulate the shattered remnants of the city. As well as the loss caused by death and people fleeing during the war itself, the legacy of famine had left people physically weakened. Due to a lack of vitamin C, scurvy was common – and particularly bad in children. So too was rickets, due to lack of vitamin D, meningitis and lung infections. By 1648 the death rate among children was 45 per cent.[9] Much like Albert the Bear 400 years earlier, Frederick William turned first to Holland. Dutch farmers were given generous grants of land and tax incentives to resuscitate Brandenburg's deserted farmland. Wartime losses in Berlin were repeated across the Brandenburg countryside, with around 50 per cent of the population lost, and it would take several decades for farming to be re-established. The stock had all gone, buildings and farm implements wrecked and there was no labour to hire. One of the worst indignities noticed by a traveller, conscious of the prevailing social hierarchy in Brandenburg, was noble families having to work their own land 'with their children, their ploughs and harrows, they scrape a bare existence with their own hands, pushing wheel barrows, making their own bread and fetching their own water'.[10]

In 1652 – twelve years after the fighting had stopped – only about half the Elector's own farms near Brandenburg were being worked, while in the Ruppin district 13 per cent were still unoccupied as late as 1687. The larger towns of Frankfurt an der Oder and Brandenburg itself had both suffered heavily; Brandenburg had lost three quarters of its population and never really recovered. From the mid-seventeenth century onwards, Berlin would be the undisputed commercial and political centre of the Mark. Dutch craftsmen and artisans were welcomed to the city on generous terms, helped by a relative economic slump in the Low Countries in the 1650s. In the early years there was only a trickle and by 1654 still only a quarter of the houses were occupied. A few of those who settled did very well, such as the military reformer Benjamin Raule, the painter Jacques Vaillant (who became the court painter), the builder Michael Matthias Smids and a number of hydraulic engineers and shipbuilders but by 1680 still only around 4,000 had been tempted.

The Elector's resettlement and rebuilding work was interrupted by his own continuing wars. From 1655 to 1660 he fought the Swedes again, as Charles of Sweden invaded Prussia. Subsequently allying himself with the Swedes, he then took part in a joint attack on Poland that was bettered by King John Casimir, who retaliated by penetrating deep into Brandenburg. Berlin was directly threatened in the autumn of 1656 by the feared Polish cavalry; more seriously, in April 1658, after the Elector had again switched his allegiance, three separate Swedish armies closed in on the city. Just when it seemed as if they might be able to rebuild their lives, Berliners faced two unwelcome diversions. First, there was an imperative to provide men and money for the Elector's army – something they had so fiercely resisted just fifteen years previously. The Brandenburg Estates had not been convinced when the war started that they should pay anything towards the defence of Prussia, much as they had not seen the need to defend Jülich-Cleves in 1643. Their unhelpful advice then to Frederick William when he gathered them together in Berlin was to 'trust in God and wait patiently upon events'.[11] Frederick William's efforts to form an effective army would dominate his relationship with the Estates and, as he slowly prevailed and found the necessary funds, inevitably the burden of recruiting fell on Berliners and the already badly depopulated countryside. By 1660 the Elector's footguards, the *Leibregiment zu Fuss*, and the regiment of the Quartermaster General, Otto Christoph von Sparr, were billeted in the city. This was 1,500 soldiers in all, but when wives, children and servants were included it meant that Berliners were looking after 2,500 people. All new houses in Berlin and Cölln had now to include an attic so that troops could be billeted on the inhabitants, but the real complaint was that the citizens had to pay for their upkeep, which worked out at about 2.5 Reichsthalers a year per head.[12] Iron Tooth's few men at arms would have seemed a light burden compared to the 30,000 soldiers who comprised the Elector's army by the time he died, although of these there were never more than 2,000 actually in Berlin.

The second diversion was to rebuild Berlin's defences. The ancient wooden walls had been replaced in the late thirteenth century by a stone wall around both Berlin and Cölln, part of which still survives just behind the Klosterkirche. It had rather outlived its usefulness, demonstrated by how defenceless the city was in the Thirty Years War, and Frederick William now determined to replace it with the modern system of ravelins, moats and bastions being pioneered in France by Vauban that was becoming all the rage across Europe. The threatened Swedish attack of April 1658 led to a forced work party of 4,000 Berliners conducting hasty defences but, as the threat mercifully subsided when the Swedes' attention was diverted to Copenhagen, work started in earnest on the new system. Between 1658 and 1665 this quite remarkable set of fortifications was erected around Berlin and Cölln, directed by Johann Georg Memhardt, a military engineer and an accomplished architect. The outlying moat was 46 metres wide; the wall itself was only 9 metres high but 6 metres thick. There were thirteen bastions and six massive gates each with a drawbridge. In the end they were never put to the test and they would be demolished to make way for development a century later, but they would dominate the city for the next hundred years.

They may have made Berliners feel safer but, taken together with the new demands for military service, there was plenty of grumbling at the time. Designed and built by Dutch engineers, the total cost for Berlin's defences alone came to over 102,000 thalers – or 21 thalers per head, given the accurate census of 1654 that numbered Berlin's adult population at 3,599 and that of Cölln at 2,598. They were also largely built with forced labour. As with so much of Berlin's history, the accounts for the construction were kept meticulously, including compensation paid for houses knocked down to clear the ground, which gives a good idea of how cheap property had become. It also shows how agricultural Berlin still was as a city, with barns and farm buildings, orchards and small fields taken over to clear fields of fire. Expensive two-storey houses, of which there were very few standing, cost 400 thaler, while poor Frau Trotten only received 50 thaler for her barn, garden and 'bothy'.[13] Converting thalers (or, more correctly, Reichsthalers – the standard currency across north Germany and in Prussia until 1750) into modern prices is, as always with comparative currency calculations, problematic. Perhaps the best way of getting a feel for the sums involved is to compare them to contemporary average salaries in Berlin. Unskilled labourers and casual workers earned about 12 Reichsthalers a year, an infantry soldier earned 24, whereas a senior domestic servant received around 300. By way of contrast, Ludwig von Printzen, the Marshal of the Royal Court responsible for running the Berliner Schloss, got over 10,000. Based on those figures, which show the huge disparities in income in the seventeenth-century city, it would make one Reichsthaler worth about £100 today.[14]

Peace came in May 1660 at the Treaty of Oliva, when Frederick William was confirmed as Duke of Prussia. He would continue to fight against the Swedes until he had forced them from northern Germany at his great victory at Fehrbellin, on the Havel, in June 1675 and from threatening Prussia in 1678. Yet from the late 1650s he was able to spend more time in Berlin and to devote at least part of his formidable energy to rebuilding and, with the city's defences now nearing completion, he could look to its quality of life.

The Berliner Schloss was partly in ruins, so work started to renovate it. Frederick William never seems to have had the funds or inclination to do very much to it. That would be left to his son, but he borrowed money from one of the soldiers who had done very nicely out of the war, the Spandau garrison commander von Ribbeck, whose family had built the splendid palace in Breite Straße. Frederick William used a combination of Memhardt and the Italian architect Philippe de Chièze to do some basic work. Opposite the Berliner Schloss, in 1658 the Electress started laying out a Dutch-style garden in the Lustgarten, the area of open ground where John George had celebrated the birth of his eldest son. There had always been some sort of garden here – 'a fine, princely pleasure garden with beautiful fruit trees', according to a student who saw it in 1591 – and, through some complicated arrangement, it was worked by 'dissolute wives' who were 'entrusted with unskilled work to strengthen their moral rectitude and modesty'.[15] This, like everything else, had been devastated during the war, so the Electress now worked with Memhardt to erect a *Lusthaus* (pleasure pavilion) and a milk grotto. They designed a new kitchen garden, where she planted Berlin's first potatoes. Initially slow to catch on, once cropped properly potatoes would allow a cheap means of feeding the hundreds of thousands who would flock to the city in the industrial revolution. As in Ireland, potatoes were the cause of as much misery as they were of nourishment. Yet in the 1650s they were regarded as ornamental plants and, alongside 200 orange trees imported from Italy, under the guidance of the botanist Johann Sigismund Elsholtz, they became the basis of the first Berlin botanical garden – one that would soon include a *theatrum tulpinarum* with more than 126 varieties of tulips and also several greenhouses.

But both Frederick William and Louise Henrietta disliked the Schloss, which was still gloomy and damp despite its renovation and her gardens. It became more used as government offices while, in what was now emerging as the typical Hohenzollern pattern, the Electress concentrated on building herself a Dutch-style house north of Berlin in the village of Bötzow on the Havel. Renamed Oranienburg, after her family, and now the last stop north on the S-Bahn, it is still a charming and quiet refuge from Berlin despite insensitive later additions and its proximity to one of the darkest of Berlin's memorials at Sachsenhausen. It imparts a feeling of peace and yet it also has rather a sad air of homesickness as the poor young Electress tried to recreate the gardens and atmosphere of her Dutch homeland. The work was again given to Memhardt who built a tall, square Dutch-style country house and laid out a park alongside the river. The work was finished in 1655 and both she and Frederick William made frequent use of it until they started work on another house at Potsdam. Today it houses a good display of portraits and silver, much of it collected by Frederick William and Louise Henrietta. They were both avid collectors and loved 'things'.

That they found the time and the money to collect as much as they did is quite remarkable given the Elector's permanent shortage of cash. Joachim II's collections (except for his pictures, mercifully) had been lost after they were relocated during the war. Frederick William re-established the *Kuntskammer* (works of art room) in the Berliner Schloss and started to fill it. He particularly loved silver, much of which would be made in Berlin as the silver industry was gradually re-established, but he also loved ancient coins (of which his collections would soon boast 4,900) and curiosities. Many of these celebrated Prussia's magnificent Baltic amber, but he was also quite given to impulse buying. In 1648, when he was at his most stretched both politically and financially, he bought a jasper cup from Poland for 150,000 Polish gulden, 'which was more than the Prussian estates voted in taxes that year', and in 1661 he spent 8,000 Dutch gulden on a diamond ring for his mother-in-law, Princess Amelia, and held an enormous birthday banquet for her in Cleves 'at which he presented all the court servants with silver plate'.[16] He also loved books, amassing a collection of 90,000 volumes and 1,600 manuscripts housed in what was rapidly becoming an extensive library in the Berliner Schloss. Gradually, as his reign progressed, more attention was lavished on the gloomy structure as the international focus on Berlin increased and ambassadors needed to be impressed. His acquisitions started to form the basis of the Prussian Royal collections and, in time, of Berlin's museums. He also collected widely from South East

Asia, encouraged by his flirting with the idea that Brandenburg should develop overseas colonies, and bought artefacts from Japan, Ceylon and the Moluccas, again starting an international collection that would later make Berlin's museums so celebrated.

Yet, extravagant as he may have been when he could least afford it, the work in Berlin did generate income that helped get the city back on its feet and, as security and confidence improved, so did life for Berliners. Frederick William was a good delegator and, given that he was frequently away from Berlin, he left much of the detailed implementation of his policies to two remarkable men. The first, Otto von Schwerin, was an experienced and well-travelled Pomeranian nobleman, a dedicated Calvinist, poet and thinker who soon became a confidante of the Electress. In 1651 Frederick William sacked Burgsdorff from his Berlin offices and von Schwerin slowly took over his duties. In 1658 he became President of the Council, a post he occupied until his death in 1679. Although he would lead principally on foreign affairs and in relations between Berlin, Königsberg and Cleves, he would, working with the Electress, be responsible for many of the improvements in Berlin. The second was Friedrich Jena, who started life as one of the non-noble members of the Elector's council, often in opposition to von Schwerin, but through his financial and legal ability rose to be ennobled in 1663 and acquired large estates outside Berlin. Both families would continue to be closely associated with the city and with the Prussian establishment for generations. Kurt Christoph Graf von Schwerin would be one of Frederick the Great's field marshals and Gerhard Graf von Schwerin would narrowly avoid execution by the Gestapo for refusing to destroy Aachen on Hitler's orders in 1944. The von Jenas still live in West Berlin, also narrowly avoiding execution at the end of the war – this time from the Soviets.

The work they undertook to reinvigorate Berlin's trade and industry was a combination of some ambitious infrastructure projects and active trade promotion. They were helped by the imposition, in 1667, of government-appointed tax commissioners, effectively removing the authority to raise taxes in the city from the council – an early step in a process of centralisation that would be developed by later Hohenzollerns. Responsibility for Berlin's budget passed to the crown in 1714 and by the mid-eighteenth century even the city's magistrates' legal powers had been transferred to what were by then royal officials.[17] Berliners – so reduced and weakened by the war, and with the Brandenburg Estates already fighting Frederick William over the cost of his ongoing campaigns – submitted with little struggle; the spirit of Berlin *unwille* was temporarily in abeyance.[18]

In 1660 von Schwerin and von Jena, using soldiers not deployed on operations, started to dig the Frederick William canal, a 10-kilometre channel that ran through eleven locks to the south-east of Berlin and that joined the Spree to Müllrose Lake. Once open, it made a major difference to Berlin's trade, linking the Elbe and the Oder and reinvigorating Berlin as a port. In 1649 von Jena also overhauled the postal service, another vital link in co-ordinating the Elector's scattered territories. Under von Jena's direction this was so efficient that it took only five days for post to reach Königsberg from Berlin and six to Cleves. Later expanded to other north German states, by 1688 it was earning the Electoral coffers 40,000 thalers a year.[19] Proper schooling was also re-established with Zum Grauen Kloster reopened and a new Calvinist Gymnasium set up. In 1670 Frau Schmolz, the wife of one of the court officials, asked for permission to set up a school entirely for girls in the churchyard of the Nikolaikirche, and in 1674 a school for the children of soldiers was established, both quite revolutionary concepts in contemporary Germany.

Endless schemes were employed to reinvigorate manufacturing. Some were highly successful, others less so. Berlin's strength had always been as a trading city and investment in manufacturing – beyond the traditional guild-protected trades such as shoemaking – took some persuasion. Frederick William's understanding of trade was also slightly restrictive. His view was that he should try to prevent the import of foreign goods as this would ensure domestic production and prevent bullion from leaving the country, whereas the history of his capital city should have pointed him towards the advantages that active two-way trade gave in terms

of taxes, markets and profitability. Neither was he necessarily guided
to the domestic manufacture of goods for which Brandenburg could
provide the raw materials. One of his major projects was the establishment of a sugar cane factory – rapidly undercut by the English
and Dutch, who could import sugar cane more cheaply. An ambitious woollen industry project also failed, although arguably that
could have succeeded, both the city and its neighbouring villages
being well populated with hand looms much as they always had
been. A tobacco industry failed, but the production of silver did
start to succeed, as did a glass factory, the raw materials for both
being near at hand. A 'Monetary & Commercial College' set up in
1677 was not popular but its successor in 1684, a new Commercial
College, did better and would be developed over the coming decades.
Shipbuilding fared better, with new dockyards being established in
what is still today called Schiffbauerdamm, on the north bank of
the Spree just across the river from Friedrichstraße station. Today it
is famous for its theatre and restaurants.

Yet what was really needed was the skilled people both to make
these new enterprises work and to repopulate the still very empty
city where the population was still well below pre-war levels even
by 1670. This is where Frederick William's policy of religious tolerance would provide a real benefit to Berlin. Frederick William was
a Calvinist by conviction, as was his wife, but he was also, unlike
many of his contemporary European monarchs, remarkably tolerant
of other faiths. As with many of his family, there was a strongly
expedient element to this toleration; it would have been impossible
to try to prevent Lutheran worship in Prussia and Brandenburg and
nor did he have any interest in so doing. He did, however, believe
that the Lutheran Church must accept his religious authority as monarch, particularly after Calvinism had been endorsed at the Peace of
Westphalia. In Prussia he knew he must tread very carefully but in
Brandenburg he insisted that all Lutheran clergy must acknowledge,
in writing, the clause in the Westphalia protocol that acknowledged
Calvinism. Predictably, as with other monarchs who have tried to
insist on blanket acceptance of ideology, he found this difficult.

He was aided in this by both von Schwerin, who ran the process for him, and his fairly extreme Calvinist court preacher, Johann Bergius, a strong supporter of absolutism who argued that 'the worst tyranny is always better than a state without any sovereign at all'. Opposed to them was one of the more inspiring and talented Lutheran clerics of contemporary Germany. Paul Gerhardt was born in Wittenberg in 1607 and had been educated at the university there, still steeped in the purist Lutheran tradition. He had come first to Berlin in 1643, as the war was ending, and worked as tutor and chaplain for Andreas Berthold, a senior lawyer. There he met Johann Crüger, the organist of the Nikolaikirche, and between them they produced a book of eighteen hymns that quickly became popular among the city's Lutheran congregation. These hymns hit the public mood, celebrating the Peace of Westphalia, lamenting the destruction in the Mark, and warning of the trials to come as Berliners tried to rebuild their lives. Gathering in the Nikolaikirche, amid their shattered homes, Berliners found comfort in singing:

> Thank God it hath resounded,
> The blessed voice of joy and peace!
> And murder's reign is bounded,
> And spear and sword at last may cease.
> Arise, take down thy lyre,
> My country, and once more,
> Uplift in full-toned choir,
> Thy happy songs of yore.

In 1651 Gerhardt was ordained and became a pastor in Mittenwalde, outside the city, but in 1657 – now married to Berthold's daughter – he assumed the most prominent position in the Berlin church as pastor of the Nikolaikirche itself. Here he and Crüger continued to write and score the most beautiful hymns, many of which are still in daily use. By 1661 they had published the tenth edition of their hymnal, which now included ninety hymns including 'Awake My Heart With Gladness'. Perhaps one of his most famous was 'O *Haupt vol Blut und Wunden*', which Bach would score in his *St Matthew Passion*.[20] To Berliners, Gerhardt was the heir to Buchholzer and the acceptable, comfortable style of worship they wanted. Yet he was uncompromising and led the opposition to Frederick William's edict. The edict itself was not really extreme. Drawn up on 16 September 1664, it simply required mutual tolerance and for Lutheran ministers not to defame Calvinism, but Gerhard led the entrenched Lutherans who would not accept that Calvinism was a true religion. He was fairly offensive in his language, von Schwerin reporting that he called Calvinists 'Godless, thoughtless people ... and the devil's children'.[21] Consequently in February 1666 he was removed from office, but there was such a public outcry that he had to be restored. Schwerin then tried patiently to persuade him to relent but a year later he was permanently dismissed. The next year his adored wife Anna Maria died, having been predeceased by three of their four children, and a lonely, broken Gerhardt left Berlin for the more primitive pleasures of a parish in Lübben, where he died in 1676 having written a moving and sad testament to his sole surviving son.

Gerhardt's removal left an uncomfortable tension between the court and the city. Berliners, being tolerant themselves, were naturally inclined to be supportive of Frederick William's policy that the city should be open to any faith that he thought could benefit Berlin, yet his treatment of Gerhardt left a rift that would take a long time to heal. They were supportive when Frederick William allowed Catholics to hear Mass in private, although he drew the line at allowing the Jesuits to operate, expelling twenty of them in 1687. Yet the old anti-Semitism was still there and few, if any, Jews had returned since the terrible events of 1573. However, Frederick William had been quietly targeting successful Jews, especially bankers, to immigrate for some years. In 1665 he had employed a Polish Jew, Israel Aaron, as an army contractor, but in one of those curious moments of Hapsburg self-harm, in 1670 the Emperor expelled the Jews from Vienna. It was a move that would do immeasurable damage to the Imperial economy, but Frederick William was quick to offer fifty of the most prosperous and distinguished a *Schutzbrief* (guarantee of safety) if they would settle in Berlin. The first to accept was the family of the rabbinical scholar Model Ries, with his three sons. They were instructed to leave their families at the border while the men proceeded to Berlin to be interviewed by the Elector as to how rich they were, which must have been rather a demeaning experience. They were obviously persuasive: by 1672 all fifty families had migrated.[22] Others would follow later, with a further Hapsburg move against the Jews in 1683. In 1703 there was yet another Hapsburg persecution, when the Oppenheimer and Wertheim families (two families who would become famous in Berlin) had to leave Vienna; Samuel Oppenheimer was still owed 5 million gulden by the Imperial Court in Vienna when he died.[23]

The Berlin Estates complained bitterly to the Elector about these invitations but, strengthened by the Gerhardt affair, Frederick William held his ground, sensibly arguing that 'Jews do no harm to the country, but rather appear to be useful' and pointing out that 'it is known that cheating in trade takes place among Christians as well as Jews and with more impunity'.[24] By 1700 Jews made up 2 per cent of Berlin's population. It was not long before *Berlinerisch* had adopted some Yiddish words: *ische* for a young woman (now best avoided as it more literally translates as 'chick'), *meschugge* (crazy) or *tacheles* (meaning get to the point).

Frederick William's subsequent invitation to another set of immigrants was rather more difficult for them to object to. It was to be one of the turning points in the reconstruction of the city and one of the most famous legacies of this extraordinarily shrewd ruler. The Hapsburgs were only to be outdone in their short-sightedness by Louis XIV of France who – under the influence of his mistress Madame de Maintenon, a recent convert to Catholicism – on 19 October 1685 revoked the Edict of Nantes that had guaranteed rights to French Protestants, the Huguenots. They had been subject to persecution for some time, but the actual revocation was draconian. 'All remaining Protestant churches and schools were destroyed ... all Protestant assemblies and forms of worship were forbidden, all priests expelled. The possessions of all French Protestants abroad were confiscated.

Even the graveyard for foreign Protestants outside Paris ... was destroyed.'[25] Frederick William was naturally predisposed towards them (they being mostly Calvinists) and on 29 October he signed the Edict of Potsdam, which promised asylum and financial assistance to Huguenots who settled in his dominions. He then set up a refugee office through his ambassador in Paris, Ezechiel Spanheim, to process them and established staging posts to help them reach Brandenburg. In 1686 he opened a voluntary fund for their assistance, but when it received little support from his Lutheran subjects he made contributions compulsory. Whereas the Jewish immigration from Vienna was targeted and deliberate, there was a definite sense of moral purpose to the Edict of Potsdam but, as with all Hohenzollern policy, it also had its expedient side. At least 10,000 Huguenots settled in Brandenburg Prussia and the majority in Berlin. Soon after them came a further 7,000 from the Palatinate and a steady trickle from Switzerland. All brought a considerable contribution in terms of skills and trades that would provide the economic stimulus Berlin had been lacking since 1640. They also brought a determination to rebuild their lives and a Calvinist work ethic.

The impact the Huguenots had on Berlin was both important and immediate. By 1698 it is estimated there were 7,500 of them and they made up approximately a quarter of the population. They represented all levels of society. The most senior was the seventy-year-old Marshal Schomberg, one of Louis XIV's most trusted and successful generals, who was quickly recruited by the Elector to lead his own army. Schomberg brought hundreds of other Huguenot officers with him so that in 1687 Frederick William was able to form two companies of musketeers for his guard made entirely of Huguenot exiles. In total about 600 Huguenots became officers, including General de Forcade who would soon end up as the military governor in Berlin.[26] With the soldiers came people skilled in an estimated forty-six new trades so that new businesses and their workshops quickly sprouted around the city, readily taking advantage of Berlin's existing guild structure. About 90 per cent of those who came to Berlin were tradesmen. Jewellery manufacture, felt for hats, silk and fabric production all flourished, as did Berliners' liking for the French cuisine they brought with them. White bread (as opposed to the staple Berlin *Roggen*), cauliflowers, artichokes and asparagus (which would become a major feature of Berlin life) all rapidly became popular.[27] Berlin's famous meatballs are known as *Buletten* (*boulettes* in French) to this day. *Berlinerisch* of course adopted many other French expressions. Some Berlin streets are called *chaussee* and the pavement is a *trottoir*; *etepetete* means to be fussy and a *budike* is a small inn. *Bring ma nich in de Bredullje* (meaning 'Don't get me into trouble'), from the French *bredouille*, is still commonly used.

Other Huguenots established heavier industry, such as the Ravené family from Metz, who started what became a famous ironware business that would last for generations. Twenty-nine members of the Claude family also left Metz for Berlin in 1687, representing three generations. Establishing a leather business in Spandau and Berlin, they were still trading internationally in the twentieth century. France's loss was quickly turned to Berlin's gain. Frederick William gave the Huguenots grants of land for building, exempted them from military service, and allowed them to develop their own schools and churches. It is difficult to overestimate the contribution the Huguenots made to Berlin. Although these extensive privileges were understandably initially resented by the native Berliners – particularly the old guilds who saw their position threatened – the Huguenots' assimilation was remarkably quick. 'They have brought abundance and prosperity to the city and made it one of the finest in Europe,' wrote Karl Ludwig von Pöllnitz. 'To them we owe our factories, our police, our weekly markets and our cobbled streets. It was them who gave us the taste for arts and sciences, and by curbing our uncouth manners, they enabled us to stand comparison with the most enlightened nations.'[28] It was an exaggeration; in many ways the Huguenots just built on the old Berlin traditions established centuries before, but their impact at a time when the city was struggling to re-establish itself was hugely significant and long term. Initially, naturally enough, the Huguenots tended to marry within their own community but by the fourth generation 60 per cent of marriages were outside.[29]

All these new arrivals meant that, for the first time since the end of the war, Berlin needed to grow and to expand beyond the elaborate defence works that surrounded the Island with the Berliner Schloss, and the old centres of Berlin and Cölln. In 1662 Frederick William had started work to develop the one empty area within the walls, a strip opposite Cölln on the west bank of the Spree that immediately adjoined the Berliner Schloss. It was known as *Friedrich's Werder* (Frederick's Plot) but it wasn't really big enough for many houses, and many of the buildings were domestic offices linked to the palace, joined by the attractively named *Hundebrücke* (hounds bridge) that connected the Schloss to his kennels.

Louise Henrietta had died in 1667, leaving the Elector deeply depressed and with three small boys. Theirs had been a happy marriage, a meeting of minds from a shared childhood and helped by Calvinist conviction. Louise Henrietta had been close to von Schwerin and he took on responsibility for the children's education, but Frederick William felt the pressure to find another wife, partly to provide a mother for the boys. In 1668 he married a second time, to Dorothea, the widow of the Duke of Brunswick-Hanover. She was thirty-two and childless; the Elector was forty-eight. She was a very different personality to Louse Henrietta but agreed to convert to Calvinism from her native Lutheranism. In fact, she and Frederick William were very happy together and she proved to be more of the outdoor, hunting, partying, drinking type than her more reserved predecessor. She did, however, have a marked affinity for presents and money.

Frederick William gave her as a wedding present a large parcel of land outside the city walls, south of the river and bounded on the south by the road that led from the bridge in front of the Berliner Schloss to the Elector's hunting grounds, the *Tiergarten*, which in turn led on into the *Grunewald*. Dorothea set about developing her land with commercial acumen, dividing it up into building plots. To the south she planted rows of lime trees along the road, creating Berlin's best-known avenue, the *Unter den Linden*. Her new town,

Dorotheenstadt, flourished so that, with the flood of immigrants arriving, she then started work on a similar development to the south of the Unter den Linden, which would become *Friedrichsstadt*. Today the main street running parallel to the Unter den Linden to the north is Dorotheenstraße. These developments were, though, beyond the financial means of many new arrivals and instead they were given land further away from the city, north of the Spree and the Tiergarten, which they called Moab after the land where the Israelites had to wait before being allowed to enter the promised land of Canaan. It is still called Moabit today.

In 1679 Frederick William returned from his last major campaign. He had driven the Swedes out of Brandenburg at Ferhbellin in 1675; now he had driven them from Prussia in a campaign that included an extraordinarily swift winter offensive, immortalised as The Great Sleigh Drive. He had then taken Stettin. In 1680 he entered an alliance with France, securing his western territories, an alliance that survived his Edict of Potsdam. In 1683 the Hapsburgs had defeated the Turks outside Vienna and in 1686 Frederick William entered a formal alliance with the Emperor. In 1685 he had renewed his alliance with the Dutch. He was suffering heavily from gout – something that afflicted most Hohenzollerns – and he began to spend his time increasingly at Potsdam, Oranienburg holding too many memories of Louise Henrietta both for him and for Dorothea, who was keen to secure something for the four boys and two girls that she and Frederick William had together.

Frederick William's eldest son, the highly regarded Karl Emil, had died of disease while on campaign in 1674. His second son – Frederick, who now became the Crown Prince – was not well regarded, being described as 'reserved, sensitive, rather prickly and crippled from a fall as an infant'. Louise Henrietta had adored him, but Frederick William thought him 'good for nothing' and the English ambassador thought him 'low and something crooked, and does appear to want sense.'[30] Dorothea loathed him and he was convinced she was trying to poison him – a fear heightened when his youngest brother and the third of Louise Henrietta's boys, Louis,

died of scarlet fever in 1687. Frederick had been living away from
Berlin in the glorious setting of Köpenick. In 1683 his first wife died
and in 1684 he married Sophie-Charlotte of Brunswick-Hanover,
whom neither Frederick William nor Dorothea liked. Convinced
his evil stepmother was now about to poison them both, the couple
ran away to Hanover, with Sophie pregnant, prompting the unkind
remark by Frederick William 'but only God knew by whom'.
Relations were not patched up until 1688.

Frederick William and Dorothea started to work together on the
Potsdam hunting lodge originally built by Joachim I nearly 150 years
earlier. Again, Memhardt and Chièze were instructed and turned it
into a small palace, although the French ambassador sniffily thought
it no more than a farmhouse.[31] It would eventually grow into the
major town palace but for now it offered a retreat from Berlin.
Berliners, who had never liked Louise Henrietta because of her
uncompromising Calvinism, had treated her funeral disrespectfully,
thereby distancing the Elector even further from his capital. The
Berliner Schloss, even with the Elector himself only an occasional
visitor, was also becoming the centre of an elaborate and potentially
irritating court. When his nephew, the Prince of Orange, visited in
1680, he was greeted by twenty-four trumpeters and forty pages
and all the Elector's staff in new uniforms with gold braid. A French
visitor thought it was the most lavish court in Germany and 'royal
in all but name'. It could not compete with the glory of Versailles, of
course, and the poor hard-working von Schwerin had to double up
as both Lord High Chamberlain and Chief Minister, but it was very
different to the scene that had confronted Frederick William when
he had first returned to the roofless shell from Königsberg nearly
forty years previously.

He had set out to rebuild his capital and, although he still had a
long way to go, by the time he died in 1688 Berlin was unrecognis-
able. With its new fortifications, its old centres rebuilt, new gardens
laid out, avenues planted and with the settlements to the west, it
was now a city of around 20,000 people. Many of these were immigrants, some were Calvinist, many Lutheran, some Catholic and a

few Jewish. About a quarter were soldiers and their dependents, with the Elector's army now standing at 30,000 and including recruits from across Europe. The army did much else apart from fighting the Elector's wars; they were the police force, the nightwatchmen, the fire brigade, street cleaners and they were also used as a labour force for building projects.

Yet the core of the city's population were still those Berliners whose families had lived there before the war, the families of the old merchants, and the waves of immigrants who had come in the preceding two centuries. French was as widely spoken as German and would soon become the language of the court, and French culture was everywhere, but Dutch, Polish, English and Italian were all also heard. Berlin was a lot cleaner too. It had a governor, and citizens had to keep the street in front of their houses clear of rubbish (something that still applies today); if people came into the city with a full cart they had to take out a load of rubbish on their return journey. The penalty for leaving your rubbish on the street was to have it thrown back through your window. Farm animals were now forbidden on the streets. Dogs began to be seen not as scavengers and a nuisance but to be kept as domestic pets. People liked taking them for walks as it gave them an excuse to show off their 'accessories made from expensive materials' and it was common to see advertisements for lost dogs posted around the city. Typically, given Berlin's penchant for regulations, they soon had to be licensed and wear a tag but Berliners have since never lost their love for dogs.[32] Barns were no longer permitted alongside houses and had to be built outside, the origin of the *Scheunenviertel* (barn quarter) to the north-east of the old city. In 1680 street lighting was introduced, every third house being required to hoist a lantern on a pole on dark nights. Berlin was becoming a cosmopolitan city, and it was rapidly expanding into a successful city, but it was not necessarily a German city. Berliners would now enjoy a prolonged period of peace. The irony of the new defences was that they would never actually be used.

～

You cannot see much of The Great Elector's Berlin today other than the fact that it is a capital city at all; without him it would just be another Brandenburg town. His achievement was in saving Brandenburg and then creating the country around it that needed a capital, in giving it secure borders and an army and in rebuilding an economy that could support it. You get closest to him in Oranienburg, with its family portraits, and possibly walking on a spring evening under Dorothea's limes on the Unter den Linden, but he is missing from Potsdam (now too institutional) and from the Berliner Schloss. The impressive equestrian statue of him, commissioned from the Danzig sculptor Andreas Schlüter, that long stood on the bridge outside the Berliner Schloss now, for some obscure reason, stands in front of Charlottenburg, which was only the village of Lietzow in Frederick William's lifetime. Maybe he is best remembered by the establishment of Prussia as a nation, although it was his son, Frederick, whom he so despised, who would make the Hohenzollerns kings of Prussia rather than mere electors of Brandenburg. He should also be remembered in the character he returned to the city. By allowing the incomers the freedom to be themselves, ironically he made them into Berliners, into people who would adapt enthusiastically to the opportunity Berlin offered and help recreate the *Berliner Luft* that the Thirty Years War had so nearly destroyed.

Frederick William died in 1688. His was a good death, important to a Calvinist. 'Come, Lord Jesus, I am ready,' he said and with that he died. 'His family have been able to learn here, how one should die,' thought Otto von Schwerin's son, his father having predeceased his master.[33] Apart from instructing Frederick III (as he became) to protect the extended family (something he promptly ignored), his main injunction to him was to look after the Huguenots and to prevent fighting between the Lutherans and the Calvinists. In his 'Secret Letter' written way back in 1667, he had in fact already handed Frederick perhaps one of the most enlightened pieces of advice for an absolute monarch, uniquely emphasising the need to 'love your subjects regardless of religion' and 'try to promote their welfare at all times'. The monarch should 'work to promote trade everywhere and keep in mind the population increase of the Mark of Brandenburg'.[34] One cannot quite imagine Louis XIV having written something like that, nor a Hapsburg Emperor.

Frederick William was, Frederick the Great acknowledged, 'endowed with all the qualifications requisite to form a great man, and providence furnished him with the proper occasions of displaying them. This prince was kind, magnanimous, charitable, humane and naturally inclined to virtue'. He was also, which was a little rich coming from Frederick the Great, praised for being a constant and loving husband, qualities that were somewhat lacking in his great-grandson. Yet, much as Frederick the Great praised the father, so he equally castigated the son. He was 'violent by caprice, and mild thro' indolence; confounding trifles with grandeur; fond of the superficial, but neglectful of the solid; and more busy in the purchase of empty shew than of useful attainments'. And, he continued particularly stingingly, 'His embassies were as splendid as those of the Portuguese,' which was about as rude as he could be. Yet the problem with Frederick III is that he has always been judged by his grandson's bitter pen portrait, comprising several pages of vitriolic if amusing prose, and by his own son's rejection of so much of what he tried to achieve. Surprisingly and disappointingly, he lacks objective biography. Certainly he made some curious foreign-policy decisions, but he also made a major contribution to Berlin – arguably one of the greatest of any of the Hohenzollerns – and during his reign, from 1688 until 1713, the city's population trebled.

Now that the Hohenzollerns were important northern European rulers and second only to the Hapsburgs in the German-speaking world, Frederick believed they should become kings. Subsequently much mocked for his vanity (though it is of note that none of his successors choose to revert to being mere electors), he was not alone in his aspiration. The Elector of Hanover was to be King of Great Britain; Augustus the Strong, the Elector of Saxony, would become King of Poland and even convert to Catholicism to do so – something that deeply shocked his Lutheran subjects in Saxony. Europe had been at war for much of the first decade of Frederick's reign, the Nine Years War with France pitted against the Hapsburgs, Great Britain and Holland. It was a miserable time for northern Europe, coupled with bad weather, poor harvests, famine and plague. Berlin managed to avoid being directly affected but trade suffered. The fighting was concluded in 1697 at the Peace of Ryswick, but whereas France remained economically and militarily strong – or at least appeared so – the war had exhausted the Empire. Then in 1700 Charles II, the last Hapsburg king of Spain, died childless, sparking rival French and Hapsburg claims to his throne. The subsequent War of the Spanish Succession would condemn Europe to a further thirteen years of warfare.

In this chaos Frederick saw his opportunity. By offering the Emperor Leopold 10,000 fully equipped troops from the well-trained army The Great Elector had left him for the duration of the war, guaranteeing Brandenburg Prussia's political support for the Hapsburgs and to vote for Hapsburg sons in Imperial elections, Frederick was allowed to call himself King *in* Prussia. He could not be King *of* Prussia, as Prussia was still technically a fiefdom of Poland, although in reality The Great Elector's campaigns and treaty of 1654 had ensured Prussia was now indissoluble from Brandenburg. It was not a popular move. The Prussian Estates in Königsberg were predictably furious but Frederick the Great claimed that they were quietened by generous English subsidies, given England's need for allies against France. The Pope was also bitterly opposed, writing to Louis XIV that 'We cannot disregard this in silence. This deed runs counter to the precepts of the apostles ... a non-Catholic cannot assume the hallowed title of king.'[35] Yet such protest to a confirmed Calvinist like Frederick was meaningless and, despite the fact that Frederick made Louis XIV his idol (and would try to imitate in Berlin much of what he did at Versailles), the opportunity to advance the Hohenzollerns to monarchy was not one he would pass up.

The coronation had to take place in Königsberg and was predictably splendid. Frederick had appointed Johann von Besser as his master of ceremonies, a role in which von Besser, who loved nothing more than planning excessively detailed ceremonial, thrived. A brand-new coronation ceremony gave him the opportunity to develop the most elaborate rituals strongly supported by Frederick. The ceremonies started with the proclamation of the monarchy to a sceptical Königsberg public, followed by the founding of The Order of the Black Eagle, to be the senior Prussian order of chivalry. Von Besser surpassed himself in drawing up its constitution. It was to be limited to thirty members, who were to wear an orange sash and their insignia, an eight-pointed blue enamelled cross surrounding the initials FR for Fredericus Rex, every day; if they failed, they had to give 50 ducats to the Königsberg orphanage. After the ceremonies to found the order came the coronation itself, with Frederick placing the crown on his own head, thus becoming King Frederick I, and then crowning his wife Sophie-Charlotte as Queen. Arrogant as this may have seemed, it was partly because the Königsberg Estates had only reluctantly agreed to a Calvinist minister participating in what would traditionally have been a Lutheran service. A banquet and festivities in Konigsberg followed, before the now royal couple left for Berlin where they arrived in March 1701.

Von Besser arranged that they should first go to Oranienburg, where Frederick had been brought up by Henrietta Louise and where he probably felt happiest. There they were met by Count von Wartenberg, who had recently been made Lord High Chamberlain. Wartenberg had come to Berlin from Holland in 1688 and rapidly risen in Frederick's service. His wife, Katharine, was the daughter of a Rhine boatman and was later to be one of Frederick's mistresses. She caused considerable angst to von Besser by demanding 'that she should carry the train of the queen's dress. At first, carefully chosen words were employed to dissuade her. It was pointed out that she would get very tired, the procession would go on interminably, but to no avail. Her husband, who was terrified of her, got absolutely nowhere either with his pleas or threats.' He turned to his friend Christoph, Count von Dohna, one of the grandest Prussian nobles, but, as he complained, 'she started by sticking her hands on her hips and reviling me'. She was eventually persuaded that she might look ridiculous and gave way, for which von Dohna received 'the most effusive thanks' from both the King and Queen and Wartenberg himself.[36]

But for all these Ruritanian incidents, which so flustered poor von Besser, Berlin seems to have given the new monarchs a very friendly welcome. From Oranienburg they went to Schönhausen, where Frederick was then living, and on 6 May they processed into the centre of Berlin. It was a huge ceremonial procession: thirty-six coaches with courtiers and officials, eleven coaches of the royal family, sixteen more royal coaches, twenty of the King's horses being led, gendarmes, musketeers, twenty-four trumpeters, more guards, more coaches, the Countess of Wartenberg now safely in one of eight coaches with ladies-in-waiting, and so it went on. Von Besser was in ecstasy at the sight, and as they came into Berlin they passed under six ceremonial arches, on one of which 'two maidens in Roman garb standing on the pedestals of the two small side-arches sang a few rhymes to Their majesties ... and welcomed them in the name of Berlin as the oldest city.' The bells were rung and 205 canon, lining The Great Elector's ramparts, were fired while Bertram, a copper-smith, somehow 'positioned himself on the outermost spire of the high tower of St Mary's Church, with his six pieces, which he had miraculously planted on the highest peak of the tower, and fired three times whilst constantly waving a flag, and throwing down quantities of firecrackers'.[37] Eventually arriving at the Berliner Schloss, that night there was a magnificent firework display and the King and Queen took a night-time drive around the city, which was illuminated with 'lights, lanterns, torches and bonfires'. Berliners thronged the streets, parading with their guilds, dressed in their uniforms and finest clothes. Von Besser estimated there were at least 8,000 present.

Berlin had reason to be grateful to Frederick. While in Königsberg 'the public could not divest themselves of the prejudice they had conceived against this royalty', the reaction in Berlin was genu-inely different. Von Dohna, a hardbitten Prussian and unusually a Calvinist, and admittedly a strong supporter of Frederick, thought 'the inhabitants of Berlin felt nothing but joy at the accession of their good king and everyone vied one with the other to show him the pleasure caused by seeing him achieve his goal with such glory'.[38] And if we look at what Frederick was doing in Berlin, and the amount of work he was providing, it is an understandable reaction.

In 1702 an Englishman called John Toland visited Berlin. He had been sent to see what the German courts were like, something of particular interest to the British who had chosen the Electress Sophia of Hanover to succeed their childless Queen Anne. Her son would become George I while her daughter, Sophie-Charlotte, was married to Frederick with whom she had run away from Berlin to avoid being poisoned by her stepmother-in-law. The British were therefore very interested to learn about their potential royal family. There is, inevitably, a lot of flattery and humbug in Toland's account but, even allowing for that, he does seem to have been impressed by Frederick, saying there 'is no Prince at present in Europe, who has a nobler and greater soul'. Whereas he acknowledges that people criticise Frederick's 'conduct in some other matters', he argues that the enormous amount he has done for the arts and sciences would amaze the 'antient Romans' if 'they cou'd return again . . . to find barbarism overspread all their belov'd Italy while the Arts and Sciences flourish in the midst of Germany, which in their time was little else but immense Forests and Marshes'.[39]

Three things really impressed Toland. First, 'the great number of French refugees' and the economic contribution they were making; secondly, the 'intire Liberty of Conscience which all good Christians enjoy in this place', and that Lutherans and Calvinists were now living amicably together; and 'the third and last thing is the great number of Houses which His Majesty builds'.[40] It was an impressive record. Turning Berlin into a royal capital was making a lot of Berliners rich.

Frederick had started with the Berliner Schloss, which his parents had made habitable but not much more. As he and Sophie-Charlotte processed in on that glorious day in May 1701, they could see for the first time how Andreas Schlüter, who had started work in 1698, was transforming the medieval-cum-renaissance castle into a baroque palace. While preserving the hollow square shape, Schlüter had added stunning facades on the north facing the Lustgarten and on the west facing the river, with a main portal whose 'colossal columns even outshone Versailles' and a row of classical figures along the top. The courtyard was decorated with scenes from Greek mythology and behind the portal rose a giant staircase that was considered a masterpiece. Several future Hohenzollerns would modify and add to the Berliner Schloss, but it was Schlüter who gave it the style and shape that would dominate the centre of Berlin until 1950. Schlüter's association with his masterpiece was not, however, to have a happy ending. Frederick commissioned him to add the 'Mint Tower' on the north-west corner, where the bridge crossed the Spree at the junction of the Unter den Linden, but the foundations collapsed in the sandy soil and Schlüter was dismissed. Frederick replaced him with Johann Eosander von Göthe, who doubled the area of the palace by adding a second courtyard to the west of Schlüter's, so that the Berliner Schloss was now enormous and stretched from one side of the island to the other. Wisely he refrained from trying to add a tower, a dome eventually crowning the western facade a century and a half later. Arguably Eosander's work made the Schloss too big, almost disproportionate to its surroundings, impressive though just missing being elegant, but it was certainly not disproportionate to how Frederick saw Berlin as his new royal capital. Toland was also appreciative of the collections, already housed in the new apartments when he visited.

Schlüter also worked on the Armoury, principally designed by Johann Arnold Nering for Frederick, just west of the river so on the right as one progressed down the Unter den Linden. The *Zeughaus*, as it was known, was not Schlüter's alone but his most memorable contribution is the series of twenty-two heads of dying warriors, 'a very frank statement of the real foundations of Prussia's glory, of the human price that has to be paid for political greatness'.[41] Actually they were probably intended to represent the heads of Prussia's enemies but Berlin's subsequent suffering has made Berliners interpret them differently. The Armoury was used as its name suggests until the requirements of the Berlin garrison outstripped its usefulness, and it is now the excellent German History Museum.

Frederick himself spent much of his time at the idyllic small palace at Schönhausen, a then-beautiful estate to the north of Berlin in Pankow, taking its name from the River Panke that ran through the grounds. Schönhausen had been a country estate for the mighty von Dohna family but in 1691 Frederick bought it from them for 16,000 thalers. He then commissioned Nering to turn it into a palace, and Frederick lived there as Schlüter was working on the Schloss. Schönhausen will make several more appearances in the story of Berlin, but at the time the work was dwarfed by the project that Nering was completing for the then-Electress, soon-to-be queen, Sophie-Charlotte at Lietzow. Lietzenburg Palace, as it was then known, was on a much grander scale than Schönhausen, a long, two-storey baroque building with a central dome on a bend on the Spree as it looped its way west of Berlin towards its junction with the Havel at Spandau. Lietzenburg was perhaps the most ambitious of the Hohenzollern pleasure houses, designed to be both a palace and the ultimate summer house, in what was then a glorious woodland setting north of the Tiergarten, with theatres and pavilions, belvederes and temples in its gardens running down to the river. The emphasis was on light. The interiors were painted by the Flemish artist Jan Anthonie Coxie, but the most famous room was Schlüter's *Bernstein Zimmer* (amber room) with its walls covered in Baltic amber, which is sadly no longer there as it was given by Sophie-Charlotte's son to the Russian Czar as a present. Nering died before the palace was complete, and his place was taken by Schlüter.

Sophie-Charlotte was highly regarded in Berlin, not least because she refused to become a Calvinist, sticking to her Hanoverian Lutheranism. The shy princess who ran away from her parents-in-law when she was pregnant had emerged as a strong, cultured and energetic queen. Sent to report on her, Toland said that although she was 'somewhat too plump', she was otherwise 'the most beautiful Princess of her time'. She was 'very well read, cultured, played the harpsichord beautifully, sang sweetly, loving meeting strangers' and 'to inform her self of all that's worthy or remarkable in their several Countrys; and she has so just an Idea of Government, that in all Germany they call her the Republican Queen'.[42] She seems to have fallen out of love with Frederick relatively quickly. When she became ill she wrote, 'I am about to die, thereby doing everything for His majesty of which I am capable, in that I am not only lifting from his shoulders a burden that he always felt in my presence but also offering him the opportunity to mount a lavish funeral'.[43] Her bitterness was not unconnected to Frederick living openly with his mistress, the self-same Countess of Wartenberg who had made such a fuss at the coronation. He made matters worse by installing her in the Monbijou palace on the north bank of the Spree just opposite the northern tip of the island (now rather a scruffy park). His mother had a small palace here, where she had grown her potatoes, but Frederick had it extended by Eosander and then presented it to Wartenberg and his wife. Monbijou would subsequently be used by generations of Hohenzollern queens, but sadly it is now no more, having been so badly damaged in the Second World War that it was not thought worth rebuilding.

Sophie-Charlotte made Lietzenburg the centre of a cultural circle that Berlin had previously lacked. It was her patronage of Schlüter that led to the establishment of an Academy of Arts in 1696, and subsequently her friendship with and patronage of the scientist Gottfried Wilhelm Leibnitz that led to the foundation of its sister Academy of Sciences. 'Do not imagine,' she wrote to him, 'that I prefer this pageantry and pomp of crowns which are here too much esteemed, to the charms of the philosophical entertainments we enjoyed'.[44] Leibnitz in turn held her in high regard. 'Madam,' he replied, 'there is no possibility of satisfying you; you want to know the why and the wherefore.'[45] Both academies were housed beside the Schloss stables, leading some wit to remark that the sign over the gate should read *Musis et Mulis* (Muses and Mules).[46] Sophie-Charlotte died aged just thirty-six in 1705 and Frederick renamed Lietzenburg as Charlottenburg in her honour. It was badly bombed in the Second World War but it has now been well restored and you can still get a strong feel of Sophie-Charlotte and her circle walking in the gardens along the Spree or through the light-filled rooms that house an interesting, rather than accomplished, collection of Hohenzollern portraits.

The Berliner Schloss and Zeughaus, Schönhausen and Charlottenburg were by no means the limit of Frederick's building ambitions. Apart from Köpenick, where he had lived when he was first married, and Oranienburg, Toland also recorded royal houses at 'Faarlandt, Friedricsfeldt, Rosendaal, Rhudau, Blankenfeldt, Meyndershausen, Hoppengarden' and Belvedere quite apart from palaces in Tangermünde, Magdeburg, Cleves and Königsberg.[47] Frederick also spent much of his time at a small model farm he had set up near Oranienburg, Fridericsdaal, 'the King himself being the architect. To retire with a select Company, or to be alone among variety of Books, Fridericsdaal is the place I wou'd prefer before any other. Here the King is a Husbandsman, having a mighty pretty Farm and a neat dairy, manag'd by Suissers, who make as good butter and cheese as in their own mountains'.[48]

Berlin itself, with its growing population, was now expanding into the farmland south of the Unter den Linden, with Friedrichstadt, started by his stepmother but developed by Frederick, becoming an integral part of the city. The now well-travelled roads to Potsdam and Charlottenburg, Schönhausen and Oranienburg were also beginning to attract development. The merchants making money out of the building boom and increased trade tended to build smart new houses, unrestricted by the lack of space within The Great Elector's defences. 'The new houses are mostly built after the best Taste of Architecture,' Toland reported, 'being generally beautify'd on the outside, and not always ill-furnish'd within; the few old houses that remain being in respect of the others as ragged and deform'd Dwarfs compar'd with gentile and proper Men'.[49]

The city still lacked a university, although it did have Sophie-Charlotte's twin academies, and it enjoyed little cultural entertainment outside the court. There was some theatre but it was 'a monstrous mixture of bombast and buffoonery. It was a kind of low farce, contrary to all taste, politeness and morality,' according to Frederick the Great, and to be fair to him the Provost of the Nikolaikirche added that 'The players had ignored all warnings to moderate their language so there is no other way of dealing with this public nuisance and of retaining a sense of honour before God than by banning it outright.'[50] The Queen did, however, maintain a good small Italian opera, and touring French theatre companies were invited to Charlottenburg. The mood was that everything French was in good taste, a feeling created partly by Louis XIV's ostentatious court in the glory of Versailles and partly by the example of the Huguenots in Berlin itself, who still spoke French, ate French food and were rather obvious about missing French culture. It was a habit that would reach its apogee around 1710 before gradually wearing off over the next fifty years, and it was taken to some ridiculous extremes. One of the German poets whom was well regarded was von Canitz, whom Frederick the Great described as 'the Pope of Germany' (meaning Alexander Pope, the English poet, rather than the pontiff). Von Canitz's mother, though, was considered one of the most slavish devotees of French fashion, so much so that she was reputed to have 'commissioned a merchant to bring her a husband from France, who should be young, handsome, robust, witty, and of a good family, imagining this kind of merchandise was common'. The merchant, not wanting to miss out on a lucrative deal, produced the fifty-year-old 'M. de Brinboc, of a weak constitution and very sickly'. But so taken with all things French was Madame von Canitz that she married him all the same.[51]

One less attractive form of entertainment, which was nevertheless very popular, was the bear pit. Part of the entertainment after the marriage of Frederick's and Sophie-Charlotte's daughter Luise-Dorothea to Friedrich, Landgrave of Hessen-Kassel, in May 1700 – an occasion that allowed von Besser to hone his ceremonial skills before the coronation – was to drive out to 'the bear garden that lies within the ring wall to watch a fight among some wild beasts – bears, water buffalo and aurochs – which his Electoral Highness had brought from his distant provinces of Prussia and Kasubia for the spectacle'. One of the duties of the Chief Master of the Hunt, von Pannewitz, was to ensure that freshly captured animals were kept ready so that they 'were quite wild'.[52] It was a particularly gruesome form of entertainment that seems to have been popular across Germany. At both Schloss Grunewald and at Königs Wusterhausen there are paintings showing a large number of foxes corralled in a pen while spectators cheer on men beating them to death with clubs. It was obviously a major, if rather strange, contemporary source of entertainment.

One building that Frederick did not commission for Berlin was a cathedral. The Schloss chapel was technically called a cathedral, but it was not a cathedral in the tradition of the great German cities. Calvinism did not call for a beautifully decorated church and, besides, there weren't enough Calvinists in Berlin to fill it even if Frederick had built one. Neither was he likely to commission a Lutheran cathedral, and eventually it would be the Huguenots who would build their own church south of the Unter den Linden. Started in 1701 by Louis Gayard and finished four years later by Abraham Quesnay, the Französische Dom stood on what is still known as the Gendarmenmarkt, an open space so called because it used to house the barracks of a Huguenot regiment in the Prussian army and it doubled as the market for Friedrichstadt.

It is a plain, square building with a central hall and gallery, and now fittingly houses the Huguenot Museum. Opposite it, and to balance it, a Lutheran Neue Kirche was finished in 1708. Neither building was particularly striking until domes were added in 1785 by Carl von Gontard. Both are sometimes confusingly referred to as the French and German cathedrals but neither had a bishop. The Catholics would also have a cathedral before the Lutherans, and it was not until the bitter disputes between the Hohenzollerns' Calvinism and the Berliners' Lutheranism had died out that Berlin would actually get a Lutheran cathedral. Yet the influx of Huguenots, and The Great Elector's insistence on the Lutheran clergy in Berlin acknowledging Calvinism, had both served to start to reduce the heat in this bitter debate that was now more pronounced in Königsberg than in Berlin. This was also partly due to the increasing influence of Pietism, which was becoming a major movement in the early-eighteenth-century city.

Pietism was a movement that had its origins in Lutheranism, which advocated spiritual revitalisation. Its essence was that the individual should look more to their own conscience, rely less on the ministrations of the church hierarchy, and concentrate instead on their own spiritual purity and on good works. As with all church reform movements, it was unpopular as it was seen to threaten the Lutheran establishment that many, especially the Calvinists, thought was too similar to Catholicism with its bishops and its sacraments, its hymns and its decorated altars. Pietism came to Berlin from Saxony – as did so many other cultural movements – and in the form of Philipp Jakob Spener in March 1691 when he was offered the pastorship of the Nikolaikirche. Pietism was, understandably, respected by the Calvinists who saw in its teachings much of what they themselves believed, and it was welcomed by Frederick. In 1694 a new university was set up (again not in Berlin but in Halle) that was arranged on Pietist principles and would go on to have a major influence on the German enlightenment.

The practical effect in Berlin was twofold. First, Spener – in many ways the heir to Buchholzer and the early Berlin reformers – believed that Christian society should not allow poverty. In 1702, under his guidance, the government in Berlin set up a Poor Commission. The same year they opened an orphanage (the first of many, the majority of which would later be privately funded), and the Friedrich Hospital was established for the sick and the elderly. Secondly, it became difficult for Lutherans to oppose a movement born within their own church that was becoming respected and then popular among their more thoughtful adherents. It may be that Frederick was opportunist in moving so quickly to adopt Pietism; equally there is little evidence that, despite his love of ostentation and finery, he was not genuinely sincere in his religious belief. But whatever his motivation, Pietism gradually began to cool the passions between Lutherans and Calvinists so that they became less of an issue for Berliners. His son, Frederick William, would continue his policy so successfully that when his grandson declared himself an atheist, Berlin was more or less comfortable in its own faith.

Frederick's ambitious building plans and his sumptuous court may have given Berliners two comfortable and prosperous decades, but towards the end of his reign he predictably ran out of money. 'His court,' quipped Frederick the Great, 'was like to those great rivers, which swallow up the water of the little rivulets'. Lord Raby, the British ambassador, noted that his 'equipage, which in London was very fine, is nothing to those out her,' and, he added grumpily, 'I find I shall be no gainer by my embassy'.[53] Although fighting had continued throughout northern Europe for much of his reign, Frederick had managed to minimise Prussia's active engagement in the war, providing 'only' 30,000 troops. But from 1710 East Prussia started to suffer a severe outbreak of plague, purportedly introduced by Swedish troops, and a subsequent famine so that up to 250,000 people died. Badly served by some incompetent ministers (men like Wartenberg), Frederick became paralysed, not least because he relied heavily on the income from Prussian crown lands, which were among the worst affected. Wartenberg was sacked in 1710 – as were his co-ministers von Wittgenstein and von Wartensleben, known collectively as 'The Three Fold Grief' – and the Crown Prince's faction began to take control.[54] Von Besser who, among his many talents also turned his hand to writing opera, was a little wide of the mark when he had the Kingdom of Prussia sing 'Indeed tis my good fortune! I see peace and pleasure everywhere within my frontiers'.[55] By the end of Frederick's reign, content as Berlin was, that was certainly not the case in Prussia.

∼

Frederick William I came to the throne in 1713 – again, like his father, as King *in* rather than *of* Prussia. If he is remembered at all by Berliners, it is as a grumpy military martinet who concentrated on the army at the expense of their city but, as with his father, this is a superficial judgement that reflects how little they know about him. The things for which he is famous have had more profile than the things by which he should be remembered. He also tends to be judged through the words of his son, Frederick the Great (with whom he had an even worse relationship than was traditional between Hohenzollern monarchs and their heirs), and his eldest daughter, Wilhelmine, Margravine of Bayreuth (who seemed to have detested her childhood). It is odd that Frederick the Great is one of the most heavily written-about sovereigns in Europe whereas his father, who laid so many of the foundations for what he achieved, is scarcely recognised.

Frederick William was a complicated character. Whereas, for his many faults, Frederick I had been 'good natured, affable, generous, magnificent and charitable', Frederick William was brusque, rude and 'distrustful in the extreme and given to violent rages and attacks of acute melancholy'.[56] His focus was on the practical rather than the intellectual and on policies that would deliver an immediate effect but he did, like his grandfather The Great Elector, have that innate ability to govern and a burning passion for 'duty', and the overriding desire to see the dynasty and Brandenburg Prussia succeed that was so characteristic of the early Hohenzollerns. He could certainly be direct. On 19 November 1735 he wrote to his minister Kuhlwein, 'You filth don't interfere in my family or youll find there's a barrow waiting for you in Spandau fortress.' Two weeks before he had written on a report from the same Kuhlwein, 'Kuhlwein is an idiott he can kiss my arss.'[57]

His early life had been unsettled and left him distrustful of the Berlin court. When he was five he was 'found too intractable for Madame de Montbel, ... a French Protestant lady of great merit'[58] who was his governess and was sent away to Hanover to be educated alongside his cousin George who would become the British King George II. The two boys hated each other from the moment they met, and they fought so badly that Frederick William had to be brought back to Berlin and entrusted to the care of Count von Dohna. He was then sent to Holland (which, as with The Great Elector, gave him several ideas as to how to improve Berlin) and then to England. His first love was Caroline of Ansbach but she fell for Prince George of

Hanover, further increasing their mutual loathing. His mother died while he was away and he was subsequently married aged eighteen to Sophia-Dorothea of Hanover, sister of his hated rival and daughter of the Elector George who would become King George I. Their first son died soon after he was born; a second son, Frederick, who survived, arrived in 1712. He would succeed as Frederick II. Frederick William then spent his late teens campaigning with Marlborough and Prince Eugene in the Low Countries, being present with the Prussian troops at the battle of Malplaquet. He is often referred to as the soldier king who never fought a battle, evidence of how little is known about him. His experiences in the European wars of the early 1700s left a profound impression on him.

Berliners chiefly took against Frederick William because his first act as King, apart from refusing to take a coronation oath, was drastically to reduce Frederick I's extravagant court. Given that this was a major source of income in the city, it meant many tradesmen suffered badly. By 1713 Frederick I was spending 157,647 Reichsthaler on the court payroll; Frederick William cut this by two thirds so that in 1714 it was 54,086 Reichsthaler.[59] He also took an axe to his father's and von Besser's enormously long and complicated roll of court ranks and offices. These ranks numbered 131, ranging from the Lord High Chamberlain, through to the Chief Master of the Hunt at sixteen, the Grand Master of Ceremonies at twenty to the Court Pastry Cook at 122, and the Wine Clerks bringing up the rear. This list was reduced to twelve ranks, and those court officials who were left had their salaries cut by 75 per cent. Horses from the royal stables were sent to the cavalry and officials had to walk rather than use carriages, prompting Berlin wits to remark that their king had performed a miracle by making the lame walk again.[60] The distraught von Besser petitioned the King for another post but his letter was tossed into the fire and he fled to Dresden where the Saxon royal court still did things properly.

Perhaps more damaging for Berlin was that Frederick William also made severe cuts to the burgeoning cultural life in the capital. Donating the lions from his father's menagerie to the King of Poland was possibly a sensible economy but getting rid of Eosander von Göthe and disbanding the fledgling Berlin orchestra were unpopular moves, as was his donation of Schlüter's Amber Room in Charlottenburg to the Czar. He also neglected the twin academies established by his mother so that they became virtually ineffective. When Leibnitz died in 1716 he was replaced by a drunkard called Jacob Paul von Gundling, a ridiculous figure who had started life as an academic and was employed as the historian, researching the history of noble families, in von Besser's Chief Herald's office. This was predictably disbanded in 1713, after which Gundling's career degenerated and he took to the bottle, becoming Frederick William's *Hofnarr* (court jester). It was an unkind way to treat an academic but it also showed little respect for the academy, which was instructed to concentrate on improving medical care for the army. The Academy of Arts became more a school for portrait painters, practised in turning out a lot of not very good portraits of the royal family and the leading generals.

Frederick William did not like Berlin. Early in his reign he entertained the Russian Czar, Peter the Great, and was strongly influenced by hearing how he was building a new capital away from Moscow on the Gulf of Finland and how he lived in a simple cabin alongside the palace. It was a better visit for Frederick William than Sophia-Dorothea, who had generously but unwisely lent the Russian party Monbijou where she was then living in Berlin. As the Czar stepped off his boat on the Spree he tried to give her a passionate embrace, which she successfully parried. The Czarina then introduced 400 'ladies of her court'. These were each carrying a 'richly clad child in her arms and on being asked if it were her own replied, indulging in a long sequence of Russian bows and curtseys, that "His Majesty had done her the honour". This barbarian pageant moved on two days later. The Queen hurried back to Monbijou. There she encountered the Destruction of Jerusalem – I have never seen anything like it. Everything was ruined; the Queen had to have the entire palace renovated.'[61]

Frederick William's solution to his dislike of Berlin was, in true Hohenzollern fashion, to live outside it. The Berliner Schloss became government offices once again, with its important collections neglected so much that they started to be stolen. A Huguenot Goldsmith, Jeremie Payot, was rather surprised on 2 April 1718 to be presented with some very rare ancient Greek coins by Daniel Stieff, the court locksmith. He took them to Monsieur de la Croze, another Huguenot who was the Royal Librarian. Together they worked out that Stieff and the Schloss custodian, Valentin Runck, had been helping themselves to artefacts since Frederick William's accession and nobody seemed to have noticed. Stieff immediately denied any involvement and got his wife to nail a confession from two imaginary thieves to the gate of the Berliner Schloss. Sadly for Stieff, a schoolboy came forward, boasting that Stieff's wife had paid him 100 Reichsthalers to write it. Even Frederick William, with his disregard for his collections, appreciated this was going too far. Stieff and Runck were condemned to death by hanging 'after first being pinched with red-hot pincers' and, just in case that was an insufficient deterrent, they were also to have their limbs broken on the wheel. Their execution outside the Spandauer Tor on 8 June was attended by 60,000 prurient onlookers.[62]

Frederick William spent a certain amount of time at Potsdam and built a very attractive small hunting lodge there, the Jagdschloss Stern, which still stands as peacefully as it can just off the motorway east of Potsdam. But his main residence was a small *schloss* at Wusterhausen, a day's ride to the east of Berlin and now the last stop on the S-Bahn to the south-east. Königs Wusterhausen, as it came to be known, is chiefly recalled through Frederick the Great's and Wilhelmina's descriptions of how boring, cold and uncomfortable life there was. 'In Berlin,' wrote Wilhelmina, 'I had to endure only the pains of purgatory, but in Wusterhausen the torments of hell'. But Frederick William loved it and Wusterhausen offered him the opportunity to live like a country squire, engaged in hunting, drinking and praying while his family ran his household. The unfortunate Wilhelmina was put in charge of the linen cupboard and sewing.[63] The Queen was perhaps also a little disappointed to be given, as a special Christmas present in 1735, a 'gold hearth broom valued at 1600 dollars'.

After hunting, the King would retire to his *Tabakskollegium* (tobacco ministry), where he gathered in the upstairs hall of the *schloss* with his closest colleagues, most of whom were, predictably, army officers. It doesn't sound much fun to have been invited, great honour as it was. Smoking was mandatory, so the poor the old Prince of Dessau – the famous general known as the *Der Alte Dessauer*, the man largely responsible for reforming the Prussian army – had to hold an unlighted pipe in his mouth while the refined Count Seckendorf, the Imperial ambassador, had to light his and 'puffed and blew so as to have the appearance of a capital smoker.' Bread and cheese was brought in at 7 p.m. and conversation ranged from religion to politics to (inevitably) hunting.[64]

Hunting was something that Frederick William approached with the same passion for detail that he applied to the army. Perhaps even more bemusing for the poor Queen than to be presented with a gold hearth broom was to be told that her domestic allowance, from which she met the costs of running Wusterhausen, included powder and shot for partridge shooting, something the King was particularly fond of; in return she was allowed to sell the game. Given that the King insisted on killing 4,000 birds every autumn, and frequently fired 600 shots a day himself, this was an expensive item, although Frederick-William was 'so conscientious in fulfilling his contract with the queen, that, when he was confined by illness, he sent General Fauss, who was reputed to be the best marksman, to shoot partridges for him'. Then there was boar hunting with hounds, which provided a welcome service in the flat forests east of Berlin where the enormous number of boar did considerable damage. In 1729 no fewer than 3,600 were killed, some weighing up to 600 pounds.

Approaching Wusterhausen today, walking from the station through the attractive small town that escaped destruction in 1945 despite being on the route of the Soviet 5th Shock Army, you feel as if you are going to find that grim, dark *schloss* that Frederick and

Wilhelmine so hated. The reality is that as you cross the little river, a tributary of the Dahme and thence the Spree, you happen upon a mid-sized country house, not beautiful but charming in a rather upright Brandenburg sort of way. It has been very well preserved and is still full of the paintings and furniture from Frederick William's time. The *Tabakskollegium* hall has the table at which they met, together with an extraordinary painting by Georg Lisiewski from 1737 that shows them in session. The King sits at one end, facing Princes Frederick and Henry who both appear as absurdly miniature figures. At the far end von Gundling sits beside a hare, showing that he was not a brave soldier as were the others (hares being known as cowardly in German tradition). Wusterhausen also has a collection of Frederick William's own paintings. Later in life, when his gout, another hereditary Hohenzollern problem, meant he could not go hunting, the King would paint. His main subjects were to copy old masters, something he achieved with only a modicum of success. Typically of Frederick William, he decided that perhaps he should try to live on the proceeds of his art and, despite the wise advice of his *Tabakskollegium* colleagues, decided his pictures were worth a thaler for each day he spent on them. As an average painting took him five days, he approached a Berlin art dealer and asked him to make an offer. The dealer, sensing an opportunity, promptly offered him 100 thalers each and then put them on public display, much to the hilarity of Berliners and the King's embarrassment. Eventually the King had to pay him a very handsome profit to have them returned.

There are two other sets of paintings of interest at Wusterhausen. The first is a set of portraits of the officers of the Prussian army. It is more a catalogue of who was serving than painted for any artistic purpose but, covering a whole wall, as a historical reference point it is unique. Secondly, those hunting pictures with the extraordinary scene of spectators surrounding a small enclosure into which foxes have been driven and are being clubbed to death are still there. It doesn't seem as if that was the sort of 'hunting' that Frederick William would have enjoyed, but it leaves a strange taste. Not many people visit Königs Wusterhausen today, which is a pity; it is an easy and interesting journey from Berlin and it gives the best idea of Frederick William and court life in the early-eighteenth-century city.

But this is to paint the traditional picture of this strange king, and – idiosyncratic and dictatorial as he undoubtedly was, and amusing as we may find his odd life at Wusterhausen – such anecdotes mask what he was actually doing for Brandenburg Prussia in general and for his capital city in particular. A fairer testament to him is to look at how Berlin developed during his reign. Although he cut his father's court severely, this was not unusual in a Europe that had grown tired of the baroque excesses exemplified by Louis XIV's Versailles. This was not just because it was very expensive but it was becoming ineffective, and there was a Europe-wide reaction – from St Petersburg to London – that saw opulence as bad taste, almost effeminate.

There is a famous story of Frederick William, who habitually wore a soldier's uniform, welcoming the over-dressed French ambassador and his entourage to Berlin by dressing his military provost staff (those rough soldiers charged with administering discipline) in the same exaggerated fashion with 'great Hats, Feathers, their Hair in Bags, and the Cuffs of their Coat-Sleeves turned up with the same Stuff as their Waistcoats were made of. Count Rottenbourg [the Ambassador], who came in his coach with a Retinue of above thirty Persons, was surprised to see the Provosts dressed so like himself and his servants'.[65] By 1723 court expenditure (at 104,097 Reichsthalers, almost back to the level of 1713) was now being spent on guards and building projects rather than luxuries, but it still brought income to the capital and it is false to suggest that there was no formal court life in the city. The Queen escaped from Königs Wusterhausen as often as she could, running her own court, and there was also the need to entertain foreign ambassadors and visitors. Regular military reviews were instigated, the first of many that would variously entertain, impress, annoy and frighten Berliners as they made their way down the Unter den Linden, and the Annual General Review 'was the great spectacle in Berlin', with neighbouring monarchs like Augustus the Strong invited to witness Prussia's growing power.[66]

Frederick William also continued his father's work in improving Berlin's infrastructure. Frederick I's palaces and bear pits had undoubtedly given Berlin a very fine facade but, despite the early efforts at the relief of the poor, underneath visitors like Lady Mary Wortley Montagu found 'a sort of shabby finery' with 'a number of dirty people ... narrow nasty streets out of repair, wretchedly thin inhabitants, and over half of the common sort asking for alms ... How different from England.'[67] Frederick William embarked on two ambitious housing projects, one to extend Friedrichstadt and the other to build a new town in Potsdam, which he did in Dutch style – much to Frederick the Great's disappointment: 'we could have wished', he wrote, 'that the great sums which this prince laid out in buildings, had been directed by abler architects'.[68] He is, again, slightly unfair. These suburbs were certainly plain but also classical and elegant. They were not designed necessarily to accommodate new residents, who would have found them unaffordable, but for rich Berliners to invest. The Crown provided cash subsidies and building materials, even promising to ennoble families who reacted enthusiastically, but still the costs rocketed so that by 1735 even the frugal Frederick William was faced with a bill of 343,814 Reichsthaler – more than double the entire court budget. Both Potsdam and Friedrichstadt were designed with wide, straight streets planted with lime trees and planned to enhance the look of both cities.

Frederick William did also destroy part of the legacy of his parents and grandparents. The famous baroque garden in the Lustgarten was dug up and turned into a parade ground and, in 1733, with Berlin having been safe from attack for nearly a century, he authorised the destruction of The Great Elector's formidable defences. The city had long since outgrown them but until the 1730s they gave the old city centre a character and a robust sense of security. So solidly had they been built that dismantling them would take many years. The Hackesche Markt, built right on top of one of the bastions (and now one of Berlin's busiest S-Bahn stations and a restaurant and shopping area), was not developed until 1750 by Hans Christoph Friedrich von

Hacke. The wide curve the S-Bahn takes as it leaves the Hackesche Markt for Alexanderplatz is due to it following the line of the old ravelin, and the Märkisches Museum was built on what was also originally a bastion. Frederick William replaced the fortifications with a wall, Berlin's third. It was not a defensive wall as such and was known as the Excise Wall. It was 14.5 kilometres long, surrounding the new developments, and still enclosed plenty of open space that would soon be built over. Its purpose was to control the passage of goods through a series of fourteen gates manned by the military, although Berliners joked that the King had really built it to keep his soldiers inside the city and to stop them deserting. These gates have remained important Berlin landmarks and names to this day: the Brandenburger Tor controls the main east–west axis along the Unter den Linden and into the Tiergarten (although the famous gate itself would follow rather later); the Oranienburger Tor controls the road north; the Frankfurter Tor leads east and the Schlesisches Tor south-east; the Kottbusser Tor and the Hallesches Tor are respectively the roads to Kottbus and Halle.

Two famous Berlin streets, Friedrichstraße and Wilhelmstraße, were developed as part of this work, and Spandau-born Johann Philipp Gerlach was commissioned to design three elegant squares that linked the scheme together (see map on p. xv). Though much changed, these are still familiar parts of the city. The Pariser Platz was just inside the Brandenburger Tor. The Leipziger Platz was inside the Leipziger Tor, which was also called the Potsdamer Tor (Leipziger Platz today almost joins the Potsdamer Platz). The Rondell (Roundel) was inside the Hallesches Tor, and has since been called variously the Belle Alliance Platz (to commemorate the joint Anglo-Prussian victory at Waterloo) and is now the Mehringplatz. The Dutch Quarter of Potsdam is still much as it was, despite the attention of Allied bombers in 1945, although the area of southern Friedrichstadt has had to be substantially rebuilt. By the time Frederick William died in 1740, Potsdam had grown from a population of a few hundred to nearly 20,000. There is a helpful model in Berlin's excellent Märkisches Museum that shows what the city looked like as the wall was constructed, the neat new houses and gardens of Friedrichstadt and Dorotheenstadt contrasting with the medieval jumble of old Berlin and Cölln and the open spaces along the river.

Frederick William's other great investment was the army. Much has been made of his extraordinary predilection, almost a fetish, for recruiting very tall soldiers. He had one such special regiment – his *Lange Kerls,* the Potsdam Grenadiers – for whom he sought recruits all over Europe, paying absurd bounties to those who found them. Yet during his reign the rather ramshackle force that he had inherited underwent major reforms. He understood that Prussia was a disjointed nation, geographically incoherent with differing races and religions. The army was to be one of the forces that united the disparate kingdom, not just by ensuring it was safe in an age when other nations in northern Europe resented what Prussia had become but also by representing its spirit.

Mirabeau would write later that most states had an army whereas the Prussian army had a state, but it was Frederick William who developed the force that gave rise to that dictum. He inherited an army of about 35,000 but by the time he died in 1740 it had risen to 80,000. This was obviously very expensive but, again, military expenditure was structured so that it benefited the economy and particularly that of Berlin. In 1724 he banned the import of weapons. Arms factories in Spandau and Potsdam were set up and by 1730 were exporting weapons across Europe. In 1719 he also banned the import of foreign cloth and ordered all his colonels to reclothe their regiments every two years with locally manufactured textiles. It proved a boom to the Berlin woollen industry. A warehouse, the Berlin *lagerhaus* was set up for Berlin woven fabric, which paid a premium of 25 per cent for high-quality product so that Berlin wool production almost doubled between 1720 and 1730 and more than 5,000 weavers moved into the city. The bulk of the Prussian budget may have been now going to the army but much of that found its way back into Berlin households. Weaving – that old staple of Berlin – was now re-established so that it would form a major part of the city's economy until rendered irrelevant by the industrial revolution.

Perhaps Frederick William's most important military reform from Berliners' perspective, though, was his establishment of the canton system of recruitment. By 1713, Berlin was very used to living alongside its army, and by 1740 one quarter of the city was either in uniform or dependent on the military. However, the canton system, which concentrated army recruitment in the rural areas (with landowners providing the officers, and their estates and local areas the soldiers), meant that Berlin escaped the worst demands of a system that stripped out fit young men from the labour force and kept them in uniform for many years. The canton system also provided a reserve. It worked on the principle that all able-bodied men were liable for military service but, once they had been trained, they were released except for two or three months' refresher training each year and in time of war. Critically it exempted artisans and tradesmen from service so that, even during the bloodiest periods of fighting in the decades to come, Berlin would suffer less than rural Brandenburg. It was an effective but unpopular system. That Frederick William was able to introduce and enforce the canton system showed how completely the Hohenzollerns had consolidated power; that it endured would greatly benefit their capital.

It also placed landowners firmly under obligation to the state since service as an officer was equally mandatory, and a new cadet academy was established in Berlin to train them. 'The young nobility who were destined for the army' and who were trained there, may not have added greatly to Berlin's culture as they 'thought it a debasement to apply themselves to study' and 'they looked on ignorance as a title of merit, and learning as ridiculous pedantry',[69] but the ruling classes from across Prussia, and who were comprehensively snared in Frederick William's new system, would now all spend at least part of their formative years in Berlin. While the canton system may not have been popular across rural Prussia, the cadet academy was received better, allowing often struggling nobles to provide formal education for their sons at the state's expense. Whatever Frederick the Great's reservations, the cadets learned French, history, geography, logic, engineering, fencing, military drawing and, that odd adjunct of so many military syllabi, dancing. The system, effective though it was, would come at some cost. The Wedel family from Pomerania would lose seventy-two young men between 1740 and 1763, the von Kleists fifty-three, and the Belling family from Brandenburg twenty of thirty-three who served in the coming Seven Years War. Berlin was indeed fortunate.[70]

Apart from the benefits military spending brought to Berlin, Frederick William also introduced an effective programme to promote wider industry. He actively encouraged immigration, and one of his greatest services to Berlin was granting asylum to 20,000 Protestants driven out of Austria by the Archbishop of Salzburg in 1731, which would later give Goethe the material for his epic poem *Hermann und Dorothea*.[71] Most of these were destined for East Prussia, still depopulated after the outbreaks of plague in 1710 and 1712, but many ended up in Berlin. The city of immigrants once again justified its reputation. In 1734 a sweeping new set of city regulations was introduced, the various districts having been united under one municipal administration in 1709. The police force, which the Huguenots had originally started in their areas, was established city wide. A licensed hackney-carriage service was set up and there was one of Berlin's periodic clear-out of beggars. In 1740 the first city lottery was even started. Less successful was support for any trades that might be regarded as artistic. Bottcher, a successful chemist who was experimenting in porcelain manufacture, despaired of the lack of support and left Berlin to set himself up in Dresden, where he 'gave the king ... the secret of a kind of porcellane, which surpasses that of China, both for the elegance of the figures, and the fineness of the diapering'. It was to be one of the city's greatest losses.[72]

Lastly, Frederick William's reign saw the triumph of the Pietist approach. The King was himself a devout Pietist, strongly influenced by August Hermann Franke who had founded the famous Pietist school in Halle. It doesn't seem to have occurred to Frederick William that he could be anything else (though it is possible that his grief over the death of his first son may have inspired a deeper conviction), and because he was a Pietist, his somewhat individual logic ran, then so must everyone else be. Whether by conviction or coincidence, Pietism, with its ethos of service and obedience, was an approach that ideally suited the regime. In 1717 the government had introduced across Brandenburg Prussia a scheme for universal schooling along Pietist principles. The Cadet Academy was heavily influenced by Pietist pastors, and the army chaplains were mostly Pietists – a sensible move as soldiers facing battle generally prefer quiet reflection and spiritual guidance to tub-thumping sermons. Pietism would prove to be one of the Prussian army's greatest strengths in the trying decades to come.

One of the most touching examples of Pietism at work during his reign – and of how many well-off Berliners thought – is the story of Maria Rosina Schindler (who would not be the last German philanthropist to bear that name). Originally from Leipzig, in 1704 she married Severin Schindler who had established a very successful gold and silver manufactory in Berlin. He did so well that he was able to buy two estates to the east of the city, the attractively named Schöneiche (beautiful oaks) and Börnicke. Sadly Severin and Maria Rosina remained childless, so in 1730 she determined to turn Schöneiche into an orphanage. The first seven boys arrived on 6 May, and eventually the orphanage was caring for thirty at a time. When Maria-Rosina died in January 1746, the boys placed toys in her coffin as she was buried alongside Severin in the Nikolaikirche. They were discovered when it was disinterred in an archaeological dig in 1956. Her funeral sermon was based, as many contemporary Berlin funeral addresses were, on Luther's famous 1519 work *Sermon on Preparing for Death*. It was subsequently printed and distributed to friends and family, more it seems from a genuine spirit of remembrance than for any self-publicity. In 1748, Frederick the Great stepped in to fund the orphanage to ensure its continuity.

Frederick William was also a church builder, founding the garrison churches in both Berlin and Potsdam, sadly neither of which survived the Second World War but that were both destined to play a central role in Berlin's life over the next 200 years. He also rebuilt the Petrikirche after it burned down in 1730, all three churches now with spires topped by weathervanes with his 'FWR' mono-gram.[73] He also – again using Gerlach – completed the quiet and elegant Sophienkirche, which his father had originally intended to be dedicated to his third and mad wife, the 'helpless, mindless and melancholy' Sophie-Luise of Mecklkenburg-Schwerin (whom he had married after Sophie-Charlotte's death in 1708 and whom Frederick William could not abide). He had it renamed simply as the Spandauerkirche but it was later renamed yet again. Pietism had some interesting side effects. Dorothea Steffin, who was convicted of witchcraft in 1727, was not burned at the stake as she would have been in England or America but rather sent to Spandau for-tress where she was taught to spin.[74] Frederick William's Pietism did not, however, stretch to being tolerant of the Jews. By 1737 the number of Jewish families living in the city had grown to 180. Again, rather as in the dark days of the early sixteenth century, a trumped-up charge was laid against a Jew for stealing some silver. Frederick William appointed a *Judencommission* to investigate, with instructions to reduce the number of families to 120; subsequently 387 Jews were expelled. It was a strange move for a monarch who valued the commercial development of Berlin so highly and perhaps reflects that, as he entered his final years, he was becoming increas-ingly unbalanced.[75]

By the end he was, said his contemporaries, 'not only half-barbaric but also strange', 'exceptionally headstrong and bizarre',[76] and engaged in a vendetta against his eldest son, Frederick, who had tried to flee Prussia. Frederick was lucky to escape with his life, his companion von Katte being famously executed under his window in the fortress in Küstrin where he was imprisoned. Released in 1730, Frederick maintained a low profile as Crown Prince, living away from Berlin in Neuruppin and the attractive palace of Rheinsberg, surrounded by musicians and writing his study on kingship, *Anti Machiavel*, heavily subsidised by Seckendorf and the Hapsburg court and awaiting his opportunity. It came in 1740 when he was twenty-eight.

CHAPTER FOUR

1740–1786

*'Berlin is more a portion of the world
than a city'*

JEAN PAUL,
German romantic author, 1800

In 1740, the year Frederick the Great acceded, Berlin's population had grown to 98,000. The capital that the last three Hohenzollerns had worked so hard to create was now a substantial city, its population twenty times larger than it had been just seventy-five years earlier. It was beginning to sprawl beyond the neatly delineated suburbs but, despite Frederick I's palaces and Frederick William's fine streets, it was still not the equal of other European capitals. That would now change. In the next fifty years, during the immensely long reign of Frederick II, or Frederick the Great as he is always known, the population would nearly double and by the end of the eighteenth century the only German-speaking cities of a comparable size were Hamburg and Vienna. The accompanying development would shift the emphasis from the old city around the Berliner Schloss to the new streets stretching west and south. Of the 150,000-odd people living in Berlin when Frederick died, about a quarter were soldiers or their dependents, some now housed in eight new barracks that he had built for his guards, while the rest remained billeted with patient Berlin families. The others were the Jews and Huguenots, together with the many immigrants from German-speaking lands who had made up the population in 1740 but had since been joined by workers from France and Switzerland, from Holland, from Poland and waves from Saxony, from Thuringia and particularly from Silesia (which Frederick had annexed to Prussia). All these joined the original Berliners, those families who had survived since the Thirty Years War and who gave the city its original distinctive character – that rough, sharp, acerbic *Berliner Schnauze* that was both law-abiding and cynical of authority and that now adapted to accommodate this swell of new residents.

From Iron Tooth's brutal imposition of power in the mid-fifteenth century, through the trials of the Reformation and the terrible destruction of the Thirty Years War, Berlin had been little more than the Hohenzollerns' capital, their *Residenzstadt*. It was the electors and kings who had dictated the city's development, guided her reconstruction, and who, through the laws introduced by The Great Elector, ran her government. It is difficult to overestimate the catastrophic effect the Thirty Years War had on not just the physical shape of the city but also on its spirit and the confidence of Berliners; indeed, the same could be said for much of Germany. Recovery was slow – much slower than post-1945 but now, finally, just as the reign of Prussia's most celebrated monarch was starting, Berlin found itself strong enough, rich enough and diverse enough to start to re-establish its own identity. Frederick the Great has long been associated with this renaissance, and Berlin undoubtedly benefited considerably from some of his policies, much as it suffered from his interminable wars, but by the end of his reign the city's life was once again its own.

Frederick the Great was as enigmatic a character as his father, albeit very different in style and approach. He was driven by that same Hohenzollern determination to establish Prussia, although for him this did not mean just as a state but rather as the dominant German nation and as a rival to the Hapsburg Empire. He saw himself, genuinely, as a public servant, his famous maxim being 'The King of Prussia is the first servant of his state', but it was the state as he determined it. He may have been an enlightened absolute monarch but he was still absolute. He was celebrated as a liberal who did much to modernise Prussia's draconian legal system, abolishing torture and restricting the death penalty to murder; he insisted on signing off every capital sentence himself. He actively encouraged the development of the arts and sciences and is widely credited with the cultural renaissance in Berlin that followed his father's rather dull, militaristic approach and oversaw an impressive expansion of Berlin's commercial and industrial life. He was an atheist who tolerated all religions, provided that their religious practice suited Prussia's purposes. He was socially liberal and, being almost certainly homosexual himself, was happy for others to follow suit. He was also, at least to a point, tolerant of criticism. He believed, as Voltaire quipped, that in Prussia there should be 'freedom of conscience and the cock'.[1]

Yet Frederick's '"Enlightenment" should not be confused with democracy or liberalism'[2] as those concepts are understood today. The German word most commonly used for the Frederican renaissance is *Aufklärung* but (as with many German words) it is open to several interpretations, and there were two different movements in Berlin during his reign. First, Frederick surrounded himself with intellectuals at Potsdam, where he lived in a curiously old-fashioned world dominated by French thinkers and writers in a glorious baroque-style palace that was already outdated. This was certainly a cultural awakening after the sterile years of Wusterhausen but it was not really a renaissance as such. Berlin, on the other hand, was setting its own rather different agenda. Another of Frederick's well-known phrases referring to Berliners was that, 'They can say what they like as long as they let me do what I like,' and Berlin now developed its own cultural momentum, a genuine experimentation and with an increasing emphasis on things German, a Berliner *Aufklärung* as opposed to the outmoded, arguably obsolete, French circle around the king.

During his life Frederick was unchallengeable. This was for three reasons. First, he retained absolute power and a monopoly of force that he exercised with an efficient bureaucracy. This meant that Prussia was well governed and there was little appetite to change that. He was genuinely respected and there was no popular pressure for democratic representation as there was, for example, in France. Secondly, his liberal reputation gave him immense kudos internationally and particularly across Europe. He was renowned as the king who stood up for the underdog, the Protestant monarch daring to challenge the might of the Catholic Hapsburg Empire, of Russia and later of France. He was especially popular in England, a nation as intent on benefiting as much from the Seven Years War as Prussia and that subsidised much of his military expenditure. Bonfires were lit in London on his birthday and there were hundreds of English pubs called The King of Prussia (until, unsurprisingly, they were quickly renamed in 1914).

Thirdly, he was militarily competent and, as a king who successfully commanded his own armies and risked his own life on the battlefield, he gained immense prestige and an aura of invincibility that made him seem near-infallible. Despite coming very close to disaster, seeing Berlin occupied for the first time by the Russians and inflicting terrible damage on the economy he had worked so hard to build, and losing 200,000 men, he was still seen as a military genius and the Prussian army became the most feared and respected in Europe. In December 1740, months after he had succeeded, Frederick led the 81,792-strong and well-trained army he had inherited from his father into Hapsburg Silesia, the relatively developed and populous Catholic province along the River Oder south-east of Berlin. Although he concocted an elaborate claim, the invasion was an aggressive move to increase the size of Prussia at a time when the Hapsburg Empire was weak and unprepared, and to take the raw materials in which Silesia abounded. A series of victories at Mollwitz, where Frederick initially fled but then returned when he was told his army had in fact defeated the Austrians, and Chotusitz led to the peace treaties signed in Berlin and Breslau in June 1742

that effectively handed Silesia to Prussia. The Hapsburg Empress
Marie-Therese was, however, determined to recover it and a Second
Silesian War, in 1744–5, saw Frederick occupy Prague and then
Dresden, win the stunning victory of Hohenfriedenberg, and at the
Treaty of Dresden in December 1745 see his gains fully vindicated.

For Marie-Therese this was an unacceptable blow and she worked
in the coming decade to create a European alliance that sought to
marginalise Frederick and, crucially, included Russia. The resulting
Seven Years War – fought not only in Europe but also across the
colonies the European powers were contesting – brought Prussia very
close to disaster. Despite tactically brilliant actions at Rossbach, in
Saxony, and in 1757 in Leuthen, Silesia, Frederick found himself
increasingly on the defensive. In July 1760, in one of his most controversial actions, he again laid siege to Dresden, which a joint Austrian
and Saxon force had recovered in 1759. This time he brought up his
artillery and shelled the city indiscriminately, destroying at least
a third of it and killing 5 per cent of the population; altogether
100,000 Saxons would perish in the war, again 5 per cent of the
whole population. There was something in that old Berlin jealousy
of Saxony and the splendours of Dresden, dating back to medieval
times and the Reformation, that seems to have made Frederick particularly vindictive towards the Saxons. The city, with its beautiful
palaces and celebrated art collections, took many years to recover.
Frederick then destroyed the Elector's gardens at Pirna, an equally
vindictive and rather pointless act for an enlightened monarch.

By 1760 Frederick's position was desperate and he seriously considered abdicating in favour of his nephew. In 1757 an Austrian army
came very near to occupying Berlin and then in October 1760, while
he was manoeuvring around the Austrians in Silesia, a joint Russian,
Saxon and Austrian force actually did so. In the circumstances
and seeing what the Prussians had done to Dresden, it could have
been a far worse occupation than it was. The Russians only stayed
three days and behaved rather better than they might have done.
Charlottenburg and Schönhausen were badly damaged, and fifteen
Russian soldiers were killed trying to blow up a mill, but otherwise

casualties were light. For the Berliners, however, it was a humiliating business that aroused deep anger, although support for Frederick remained strong. It is also interesting because it gave rise to one of the first accounts we have by an ordinary Berliner – as opposed to a king, minister or churchman – about what life was like. The baker Johann Friedrich Heyde lived and had his bakery in Mittelstraße. He kept a diary that alternates between giving an account of Frederick's various wars and noting the price of rye and wheat. Like many tradesmen, he did well at the beginning of the war as the army's demands raised prices but suffered as the price of other food rose and the coinage was devalued five times. He was, though, a patriot and a strong supporter of the King, taking a keen interest in his victories. He was very critical of the Russian invasion, saying that Berlin was lucky not to have been burned to the ground by the Russian bombardment (though actually it seems to have done very little damage). The Schiffbauerdamm, the street just across the Spree from Friedrichstraße was completely plundered by the Cossacks while the Schloss was wrecked by being occupied by 1,000 soldiers. 'No one was safe on the street or in their houses' and 'you could buy a watch for a few Groschen and a gun for 3 Groschen,' Heyde complained. Potsdam suffered fire damage totalling 60,000 Reichsthalers and, he concluded bitterly, 'In summary we thought our Berlin had been given over to be a playground for the barbarians.'[3]

Perhaps more serious than the Russian occupation, high prices and a lack of food meant that by 1762 Berliners were suffering from malnutrition. A typical labourer's wage was 1–2 Reichsthaler per week, so 24 to 48 groschen (or about £100–200). Rye bread remained the staple food but prices had risen approximately four times during the war. In 1748 a pound of beef cost 1 groschen (about £4), a litre of beer was 6 pfennigs, and two and a half pounds of bread was also about 1 groschen. In 1748 you could eat out well for 1 groschen and 6 pfennigs (about £6). By the time the Russians left Berlin, 1 groschen only bought 8 ounces of bread, and a pound of meat now cost 8 groschen (about £32).[4] Leather had become almost unobtainable. A pair of shoes that had cost 1 thaler before the war now cost three times that. Although rural Prussia felt the huge loss of men most keenly, Berlin was not entirely exempt. Pfarrer Lüdicke, a pastor at the Nikolaikirche, noted sadly in the church records that year that 609 more parishioners had been killed than had been born, and that the number of men would continue to reduce while the terrible war 'eats countless people'.[5] Heyde had three sons serving, and noted with relief that when Johann Friedrich returned in 1761, he became a 'Master' the same year (so protected from further conscription), although Gottfried and Wilhelm Heinrich were both still serving, the latter in the artillery regiment then stationed in the new barracks in Oranienburger Straße.[6] Both boys in fact survived the war.

That Frederick, and Berlin, survived the Seven Years War at all is due to one of the most extraordinary accidents of history. In January 1762, just as it looked as if Prussia was finished and Russia would invade again, the Russian Empress Elizabeth – bitter enemy of Frederick and ally of Hapsburg Austria – died. Her successor, the unbalanced Czar Peter III, was not so much an ally of Frederick as someone with an 'inexpressible passion' for him, calling him 'one of the greatest heroes the world has ever seen' and habitually wearing the uniform of a Prussian major general. This was partly infatuation and partly because he was from Holstein (the eighteenth-century Russian Czars and Czarinas tended to be more German than Russian) and needed Prussian help in regaining Holstein territory from Denmark. The effect was that the Russian armies were ordered to stop attacking Prussia, and the Czar and Frederick concluded a peace treaty on 5 May 1762. The resulting Peace of Hubertusburg, signed in February 1763, confirmed Prussia in possession of Silesia. For many it merely sealed what had already been agreed at the treaties of Breslau and Berlin. Had the last seven years of war, asked the Danish minister Count von Bernstorff, just been 'for the very existence of the new monarchy which the King of Prussia has raised with a skill and speed that has astonished one part of Europe and fooled another?' Prussia, he continued, was a new sort of state: 'completely militarist and still possessing all the vigour, all the vitality and all the greed of a young and slender body'.[7]

Military and diplomatic success meant Berlin was in thrall to Frederick. The King had originally planned an ambitious new palace on the Unter den Linden, which would have been enormous and involved demolishing most of the existing buildings; Hitler would later plan something similar with his grandiose scheme for rebuilding the city centre. Given that the existing Berliner Schloss was already vast, Frederick's plans did seem a little unnecessary and he soon dropped them in favour of building at Potsdam. Disliking Berlin, which held unhappy memories for him, and handing Rheinsberg to his younger brother Prince Henry, he made Potsdam his home, living in the town palace in the winter and in Sanssouci (literally 'without care'), the charming, small, elegant palace he built on a hillside overlooking gardens and vineyards outside the town in the summer. The town palace was destroyed in the Second World War but it is Sanssouci that has come to identify Frederick. It has been mercifully very well preserved so it can be seen today much as Frederick would have known it, despite the GDR building some particularly unattractive high-rise blocks that spoil the original view.

Started in 1745, and designed by Frederick himself, although Georg Wenzeslaus von Knobelsdorff who had worked on Rheinsberg was the architect, Sanssouci is one of the most intimate and unlikely eighteenth-century royal residences. It was designed precisely as Frederick wanted to live in it, with no pretence to any state function or any allowance for his wife, the unfortunate Elisabeth-Christine of Brunswick Bevern whom he had been forced by his father to marry in 1733 and whom he almost completely ignored. The Queen lived in Berlin itself, principally at Schönhausen, while Frederick constructed the life he wanted at Potsdam. He was in fact actively unpleasant to her, calling her 'this incorrigibly sour subspecies of the female sex' and pointedly ignoring the poor woman for the fifty-three years they were married.[8] The design and lifestyle at Sanssouci suggests a strong preference for everything male. It was rumoured that Frederick was impotent, either as a result of his overly harsh treatment by his father or of a botched operation when he contracted syphilis from a courtesan in Dresden after a visit as a young man in 1728 (which, cynics infer, may have had something to do with the viciousness of his bombardment of the city). Certainly he had very close relationships with various members of his staff and court during his reign, from his valet Michael Gabriel Fredersdorf (who had been a musician in the army) and the Italian Francesco Algarotti (to whom Frederick sent endless not very good poems) to, as his critics would have us believe, a wide variety of pages and young officers. Interestingly Frederick's younger brother, Prince Henry, was also homosexual and – refreshingly in a contemporary Berlin society that was questioning if not actually hostile to homosexuality – he did not try to hide it.

The charm of Sanssouci is that it is easy to imagine Frederick's life there. He still seems to play his flute in the music room or to sit on the terrace with his dogs. It is built on one storey, with Frederick's library, bedroom and study at one end. Outside his study window is a Greek statue of 'the Praying Boy', dating from around 300 BC. It was known as Antinous, Emperor Hadrian's lover whom he subsequently made a god, and was clearly intended to make a homoerotic statement. Frederick's bedroom connected to his music room, where he gave flute concerts, to his dining room, where he ate with his circle of friends and famous visitors like Voltaire, speaking only in French, to a marble hall that is the only room with any pretence to grandeur. Beyond were a series of guest rooms. Every room opened directly on to the terrace and the glorious view over the stepped gardens and vineyards to the park and the woods beyond. Frederick's life there was a combination of work (something he never neglected), music, conversation and good food, surrounded by his dogs (he favoured whippets) and his friends. Later paintings by Adolph Menzel, the much-criticised mid-nineteenth-century Berlin artist, created an image of this relaxed and civilised life that has established the popular image of Sanssouci. Frederick later added a picture gallery and greenhouses to grow the exotic fruit he so enjoyed, and in 1763 he started work on the rather slab-like Neue Palais, a mile away from Sanssouci across the park and designed by Carl von Gontard, who did so much in Berlin, and Johann Gottfried Büring. This was designed to accommodate the increasing wider royal family and the inescapable requirements of protocol and entertaining that Frederick so detested. It is an easy and enjoyable walk from Sanssouci but it has none of the same charm or atmosphere.

Sanssouci was more to Frederick than merely an escape from Berlin. It was the place where he could gather around him like-minded thinkers, writers and musicians and where he could relax in their company. Attractive as that sounds, the Sanssouci idyll did not always work out quite as he might have hoped and – perfect though the setting was, and flattered as guests were to be entertained by so famous a host – there was always something a bit contrived about the intellectual circle he gathered. Perhaps his most famous visitor was the French writer, thinker and wit, Voltaire. He came first in 1750 for an extended stay, though he had originally met Frederick ten years before. Frederick was delighted by the attentions of such a well-known author, who flattered him outrageously, and he also wanted Voltaire's help with his writing. Frederick's work (much of which is still in print) and his fluency in French were impressive, but he seems to have realised that it was not as good as he thought it should be. Voltaire for his part liked the kudos of being associ-ated with the most famous monarch in Europe, 'the marks of his friendship which made my head spin', and was not averse to the large salary he drew as a royal chamberlain.[9] He was also probably hoping to pick up what useful intelligence he could to pass back to Versailles. Yet it was a relationship that was bound not to work out 'for, at bottom, however brilliant as intellectual sparring partners, Frederick and Voltaire were heartless old cynics between whom little love was lost'.[10]

Voltaire started making fun of Frederick's writing behind his back, and then got himself involved in a fraudulent deal involving war debt with a Berlin Jew called Abraham Hirschel. However, what he really objected to was that, once in Berlin, he was just one of Frederick's circle and found himself in competition with another French intellectual Frederick had imported, Pierre Louis Maupertuis, who had been made head of the re-energised Berlin Academy. Maupertuis was involved in a scientific dispute with a fellow scientist, Samuel König. Frederick supported Maupertuis, which he was really bound to do, and wrote an open letter to Voltaire to make his case. In retaliation Voltaire published a horrible counter-attack on Maupertuis and, by inference, Frederick, the *Diatribe of Doctor Akakia*. It was too much even for Frederick, who had the pamphlet burned by the public executioner in Berlin. In March 1753 Voltaire left, going first to Saxony where he republished his *Diatribe* and then to France. Frederick had him arrested in Frankfurt en route and held him for six weeks – illegally as Frankfurt was not part of Prussia – until he was sure Voltaire had surrendered all his copies of the King's unpublished work. They patched up their quarrel and later corresponded amicably again, but the spirit of what Sanssouci was meant to represent was badly tarnished.

Berliners watched all this with wry amusement. Frederick remained popular in the city and he also knew how to work a crowd when it suited him. Riding supposedly incognito through the town, he came across a large crowd 'laughing and cheering from a placard hanging from a rooftop. On hearing that it depicted His Majesty with a large coffee-grinder between his knees, Frederick rode up and ordered that the placard be hung lower so that the people could see it properly. The crowd was monstrously delighted and gave three rousing cheers for His majesty as he rode away.'[11] Coffee was highly taxed at the time, which was particularly unpopular with Berliners who had become coffee addicts, and they especially resented that there were official 'coffee sniffers' whose job was to denounce illegal coffee-drinking to the police.

But as popular as Frederick was (and these highly irrelevant rows were taking place when his reputation was at its height before the Seven Years War), the world of Sanssouci was seen by Berliners as remote and culturally condescending. Even Count Lehndorff, the Queen's loyal chamberlain who kept an attractively gossipy diary, wrote that 'the Berliners had been royally entertained,' adding sagely, 'all these great minds are bad characters'.[12] Frederick had a strange anathema to German culture and the German language, yet it was German – and the individual patois that Berliners developed as they assimilated so many new arrivals – that was one of the forces uniting the city. 'The German language,' Frederick wrote, 'branched out into an infinite number of dialects'. It 'wants proper rules to fix its true standard; besides we have no classic writers; and if we have some remains of our ancient republican liberty, 'tis only the barren privilege of mangling a rude and almost barbarous language according to our pleasure and fancy'.[13] He was also fairly damning of Berliners' aptitude for culture generally. He reckoned that only a tiny proportion of people – about one in a thousand – had any real interest the arts, and that in 'any age the number of philosophes will always be tiny, and the universe will be dominated by some form of superstition'.[14] 'The idiot public is born to vegetate,' he grumbled, 'and enslaved for life to its vacuous prejudices'.[15]

The Berlin that Frederick increasingly shunned (he visited just thirty-four times from 1750 to 1767 and then less than once a year during his remaining two decades) was struggling to manage the almost daily flow of immigrants while trying to establish the life that they sought. The centre was also, for much of Frederick's reign, a building site. Once he had abandoned plans for the vast palace on the Unter den Linden, he embarked on a lesser but arguably much more successful scheme incorporating four buildings that, though not actually designed as a sequence, work together remarkably well. The *Forum Fridericianum*, as it came to be known, filled the area just west of the Berliner Schloss and linked the Arsenal and Friedrichswerder to Friedrichstadt. It is now called the *Bebelplatz*, with the Unter den Linden running along its northern side. A quiet square, despite being favoured by skateboarders, it has retained much of its charm.

The first building Frederick commissioned – again from Knobelsdorff, and something that played directly to his tastes rather than the public's – was the opera house. A square, neat building with a strong portico, it was finished during the first Silesian War and the first performance was Carl Heinrich Graun's *Cesare e Cleopatra* just before Christmas 1742. It was something of a miracle that Knobelsdorff had managed to get it finished so quickly, the foundations being the same sandy soil along the Spree that had proved the undoing of poor Schlüter, and Frederick coming up with endless unhelpful alterations. It was entirely financed by Frederick, who continued to pay all its running costs and the salaries of the artists. The auditorium was segregated socially, so that the first two tiers were reserved for the court and ministers while the general public was allowed into the rear tiers, and the pit was kept for soldiers. The problem was that its capacity was rather larger than Berlin's ability to fill it, which, given Frederick's comments on Berliners' cultural tastes, should not have surprised him. His solution was to order all his senior officers and their staff to attend, which they duly did, standing behind the armchairs reserved for the King and his circle. Thereafter every regiment was given an allocation of tickets, and soldiers were generally quite happy to attend just to keep warm. Gradually its popularity grew and the availability of the free tickets became something of an issue. Gotthold Ephraim Lessing, the famous playwright, remarked sulkily that the King 'wants everybody, except those of the common masses, to be admitted to the theatre. Especially visitors to the city. But ... one sees the best boxes occupied by the degenerate trollopes whilst highly respectable folk are being turned away at the door with the most offensive of remarks.'[16]

As with everything in his life, Frederick had very clear views about what sort of operas he liked, and his taste was conservative. Graun, who had led his orchestra at Rheinsberg when he was Crown Prince, remained his trusted staple, frequently being ordered to rewrite his scores until the poor man refused, saying that his settings were already excellent. 'Music today has degenerated into a hullabaloo,' Frederick complained towards the end of his life. Mozart seems to have passed him by, although he would play for Frederick's successor in 1789. Haydn, he thought, wrote music that flayed the ears, and poor Johann Friedrich Reichardt, who became *Kapellmeister* in 1776, was told he could not write an opera to be performed in Berlin 'because he doesn't know how to do it or does everything wrong'.[17] Reichardt's career is in itself an example of how the city's musical tastes were changing. Originally from Königsberg, and widely travelled around Europe, he wanted to introduce not only his own works, which he had based on the powerful new operas then being staged in Paris, but also 'Concert Spirituels' that combined songs and music by him but also by composers like Handel. Frederick, whose idea was that opera was a 'static medium for vocal and visual display',[18] objected strongly. He lost interest, Reichardt concentrated on writing songs, and the opera became moribund. Yet Frederick had given Berlin an opera house, one of the first to be custom built, and started a tradition that would be developed over the next 200 years so that Berlin would produce some of the best opera in the world.

Frederick's approach to music was also driven by his own flute playing. He played mostly works written for him by Johann Joachim Quantz, who was his teacher and muse, but he also composed about a hundred of his own pieces, many of which impressed connoisseurs (despite Brahms's unkind comment about a rather later German court that one must 'never criticise the compositions of a Royal Highness; you never know who has written them').[19] Another composer who served Frederick for thirty years was Carl Phillip Emanuel Bach, second son of his famous father Johann Sebastian. Carl Phillip played the harpsichord at Potsdam before leaving in a huff in 1768, having failed in his frequent attempts to be paid the same generous salary as Quantz and Graun. His father did visit Sanssouci once, in 1747, where Frederick eagerly seized on him to listen to his own playing. Luckily the great composer was sufficiently tactful and subsequently dedicated works to the King.

The second part of the Forum Fridericianum was the Roman Catholic cathedral which was dedicated to St Hedwig, one-time Duchess of Silesia and Silesia's patron saint. Frederick enjoyed much praise for being so supportive of the Catholic church. In fact, most German cities had a Catholic cathedral, and St Hedwig's was as much a political gesture to consolidate Prussian rule in Catholic Silesia as it was any attempt at emancipation. Frederick also refused to pay for it, instead getting his rapidly increasing Catholic community (more than 8,000 by the end of the Seven Years War) to raise funds from across Europe. Unkindly described as an upside-down coffee cup, it was again designed by Knobelsdorff, who modelled it on the Pantheon in Rome. It took time to raise the money, and its construction was complicated by the war, so it was not opened until 1773. It was destroyed in 1943 during a bombing raid and rebuilt, not very well, by the GDR. It looks curiously uncomfortable as a building, rather squeezed into the corner of the Bebelplatz, between the Opera House and the luxurious Hotel de Rome. It is still, however, an active, welcoming church holding friendly family Masses (though it is due to close for major restoration work).

The third part of the scheme was a very large palace for Frederick's younger brother, Prince Henry, standing on the north side of the Unter den Linden and that is now the Humboldt University. There is something of a myth that, because Frederick lived his simple if comfortable life at Potsdam, the court in Berlin did not really function. Until she died in 1757, Frederick's mother maintained a substantial establishment at the Monbijou palace, something that must have given her considerable pleasure after the discomfort of Königs Wusterhausen. Meanwhile, the wretched Queen Elizabeth-Christine was ignored at Schönhausen; when Frederick did see her after returning from the Seven Years War, he is reputed to have greeted her with 'Madam has got fat.' 'I remain stuck in this old Chateau like a prisoner,' she complained, 'while the others have fun.'[20]

And the others did have fun, particularly Prince Henry in his new palace, which was finished in 1766 and where he employed no less than ninety staff. One evening Prince Henry and his friends all dressed up as Jews, which, tasteless as we find it today, was considered hilariously funny. Prince August-William, who came between Frederick and Henry and was, as Frederick had no children, the heir apparent (and who was not very bright), was then brought blindfolded into a room that looked like a synagogue, whereupon the Court Chamberlain appeared, dressed as a saint, and 'converted' them all back into Christians. But such high jinks went alongside the more serious side of court life. Ambassadors had to be entertained (something Frederick himself was offhand about), there were endless military parades to be reviewed and the Court played an important role in staging the annual Berlin carnival. The carnival was a week of music, dancing, fireworks and street fairs that was rapidly becoming a major part of Berlin's social life every winter and when the centre of court life moved back into the Berliner Schloss, which otherwise continued to serve mostly as government offices.

Apart from interminable military parades and the annual review, Berlin also staged the occasional set-piece event. One of the best was a *Carousel* to welcome Frederick's sister Wilhelmine in August 1750, which turned into a general celebration for the end of the Silesian Wars. There were three weeks of plays, concerts, banquets and even a mock 'tournament-cum-equestrian-ballet'[21] on the Lustgarten. The tournament was held at night, lit by 30,000 torches, with the court seated to watch Frederick's brothers variously command Roman, Carthaginian and Persian armies. Voltaire, who was in the grandstand, was particularly pleased by hearing the crowd murmur 'Voltaire! Voltaire!' as he appeared, and he obligingly wrote a glowing report for the Paris press.[22]

The last of the four Forum Fredricanum buildings was the Royal Library, occupying the west side of the square and, because of its curved shape, always known in Berlin as the *kommode*. Unsurprisingly Frederick did not rate the idea of having a library of German books, but he relented and in 1775 commissioned Georg Christian Unger to build the rather Viennese-looking building from plans originally drawn up by Johann Bernhard Fischer von Erlach. It provided a home for The Great Elector's collection and, again, formed the core of the famous Berlin State Library – today the pre-eminent research library in the German-speaking world and home to over 11 million books.

Frederick also gave Berlin one other legacy that showed, however much he may have protested against the trappings of monarchy and the court, that he realised they were essential pillars of his regime. In 1748 he founded a home for soldiers invalided in the Silesian Wars, the *Invalidenhof*. Situated near his father's hospital, the *Charité*, which had been originally set up to help plague victims in 1708 but, as the city was spared that disaster, had become a general hospital for Berlin's poor, the Invalidenhof soon became better known for the cemetery that was associated with it. This quickly became a national cemetery, the place where the powerful wanted to be buried. Its grassy paths are lined with those who fought Frederick's wars, their tombstones displaying the full honours that the Prussian monarchy conferred. The grave, for example, of Friedrich Wilhelm von Rohdich – who was General of Infantry and took part in most of Frederick's wars, was also War Minister and President of the War Commission – shows his many other honours and appointments, such as being Colonel of the Royal Guard, the King's *Leibgrenadier* battalions. Much later in the city's history, the Berlin Wall would run directly through the Invalidenhof.

These were grand, public buildings and institutions, but what Berlin now badly needed was mass housing for its rapidly expanding population, food for them to eat and industry to employ them. These were problems that Frederick confronted directly. The city was still controlled by the central government, and in 1742 Frederick removed responsibility for the city's administration from the War and Domains Chamber, the central government office under which his father had placed almost everything, and appointed a City Marshall. It was an office that would remain in charge of Berlin until 1876. He had 150 *bürgerhauser* (apartment blocks) constructed, really designed for the new officials in the various and multiplying government offices, though it would not be long before the principle of mass accommodation in one building was developed into the *Mietskaserne*, the large housing blocks that would become such a depressing part of Berlin life in the next century. His introduction of barracks was a welcome innovation for long-suffering Berliners who, by 1777, still had 21,334 actual soldiers, 11,301 of their wives and 14,334 of their children billeted on them and for whom they were still paying the 1720 *servisgeld* (service money). The soldiers were generally well behaved – and subject to ferocious discipline if they were not, with regular flogging and executions in the Molkenmarkt. Desertion, however, remained a constant problem, despite 1,000 soldiers being on guard duty around the city every day. So too did suicides: between 1781 and 1786, 132 soldiers took their own lives.

Between 1753 and 1782, thirteen large purpose-built barracks were constructed in the city and the suburbs, which went some way towards both easing family life for Berliners and improving the soldiers' lot.

Frederick was a strong advocate of eating potatoes, which would again cause major problems in the coming century, and of drinking beer; he was equally insistent that people should drink good Prussian beer rather than imported coffee. Berliners also drank an increasing amount of *Selters* (mineral water), which was produced in stone bottles and thought to be healthy. Smoking was common, from clay pipes, often sold with pre-loaded tobacco. The sculptor Johann Gottlieb Glume set up Berlin's first pipe manufactory on Köpenicker Straße in 1753, closely followed by a second started by Samuel Rhaue two years later. Chain-smokers, or people whose pipes never left their mouths, were a common site on the streets. Cooking was still done on open fires, however grand the house, but food imports eased up after the end of the wars and, while the poor would always go hungry, the city's markets were generally well stocked. Apart from the Berlin staples of cheese and sausage, the most common meat was mutton. On one day, the Schloss kitchens cooked 'mutton, followed by beef and veal, some venison (both roe and stag), 1 hare, 14 partridges, 49 skylarks, 1 capon, 52 chickens, 42 fat hens, one capon, 10 geese, 18 ducks, 46 pigeons on top of which there was also pike, carp, perch, crabs and 5 bratwurst sausages'.[23] Frederick's annual stay in the Schloss between mid-December 1748 and mid-January 1749 cost 1,400 Reichsthalers in food, 700 in patisserie and 312 Reichsthalers in wine, or about a quarter of a million pounds.[24]

Frederick concentrated in particular on developing industry in the city, especially after the end of the Seven Years War. He invested government money in textile mills, continuing his father's system of encouraging local weaving, clockmaking and arms manufacture including gunpowder. He also invested in some of the finer crafts, mostly run by Huguenots. Still smarting from losing Bottcher to Dresden, in 1761 he bought the Gotzkowsky porcelain works, which he renamed *Königliche Porzellanmanufaktur* or KPM, poached

workers back from Meissen (to the fury of the Saxons), and started
to export beautiful and high-quality porcelain around Europe. It
still has a successful shop on the junction of the Kurfürstendamm
and Uhlandstraße today. He hit on the novel, if discriminatory, idea
that Jews must purchase considerable amounts of expensive porcelain from the factory in exchange for extending their privileges. In
1755 he founded a silk factory and supported Pierre Mercier with
his tapestry works. He was, like his father, a protectionist, justifying
this by saying that 'I have poor soil; therefore I must give the trees
time to take root and grow strong before I can expect them to produce fruit',[25] although he did start the first effective state bank. His
acceptance of criticism from officials who criticised his policy only
went so far. In 1763 Erhard Ursinus, who held a senior finance post
in the General Directory, sent Frederick a detailed report that effectively damned this protectionist approach, saying it made Prussian
goods too expensive to export and encouraged poor quality at home.
Frederick flew into a rage and had poor Ursinus incarcerated in
Spandau for a year.

Life in the growing city attracted mixed reactions. The English
diarist James Boswell, visiting in 1764, thought it 'the most beautiful
city I have seen'[26] but was surprised to hear an officer he was having
dinner with openly criticise Frederick who, he said, 'had neither religion nor humanity' and was 'quite impotent'. He was also shocked
when watching soldiers drilling in Tiergarten to see that 'for the
least fault they were beaten like dogs'.[27] He visited a brothel, and
was challenged to a duel that fortunately, having drunk a bumper
of hock to calm his nerves, he managed to avoid by apologising.
Yet he reported that people found life in the city terribly boring,
that it felt too new and that you could not, according to the British
Ambassador, Sir Charles Hanbury Williams, 'dine or sup without an
informal invitation and that is a thing that very seldom happens'.[28]

Three contemporary German authors give us a perspective on
how they saw life in Berlin during Frederick's reign and how it
was changing. Friedrich Gedike arrived in the city in 1770 and
became co-editor of the *Berlinische Monatschrift*, one of the many

newspapers that were starting up. He noted that new arrivals commented on the deplorable state of the streets, the number of prostitutes and the large number of soldiers. They were also struck by how French the city seemed, the beauty of the Tiergarten and the surrounding countryside, and how outspoken the Berliners were. Much of that would have been true in the fifteenth century and much still applies today, as does Gedike's observation that most Berliners rented rather than owned their own houses: even 'the wealthiest merchants, the most respected officers of the king, even the high chancellor of the Prussian kingdom and other ministers and generals live in rented rooms in large houses and their neighbours are often manufacturers and tradesmen'.[29]

There was much in the city that was about outward show. Berlin residents were, he felt, a bit like their houses – 'splendour on the outside and deprivation within' – partly because rents and prices were constantly rising as immigrants arrived. The constant flow of new arrivals gave the impression of a temporary society. The court and the government were omnipresent and too opulent. They 'can think of no better way to while away their ever-so-tiresome leisure than to visit one another ... and to display their splendour'. Berlin was also a bourgeois city. In London, Paris and Vienna the aristocratic families maintained houses and spent much of the year in the political and social world of their capitals. That did not happen in Prussia, where the majority of Junkers could not afford such a luxury and were anyway bound to the army and their estates in much the same way as their workers. They would spend time at the Cadet Academy as young men but thereafter they tended only to come back to Berlin if they were offered a government or senior military post (though there were exceptions who maintained houses, such as the very grand East Prussian families like the von Dohnas). With the King and the court at arms' length, seventeenth-century Berlin society was still effectively led by merchants and businessmen as it always had been.

Gedike was also very critical of the number of immigrants, especially those from other parts of Germany. He was himself a proud Prussian, his grandfather having been Chaplain General to the army, and he remarked on 'the revolting chaos of the lower rabble which is without fatherland, faith, morals or principles, as well as the unnatural contrast between virtue and depravity, culture and barbarism, which one finds here in the highest degree'.[30] Others would take a more sympathetic, pan-German view.

In 1769 Friedrich Nicolai, an influential Berlin publisher and novelist, produced a three-volume *Description of the Royal Court Cities of Berlin and Potsdam*. It was a huge, expensively finished work that was part history, part guidebook, part gazetteer and part encyclopaedia; that it had to be re-published three times within twenty years showed both that it was popular and how rapidly Berlin was changing. Nicolai looks at 'the radical transformations that have shaped and reshaped the city since it came into existence'. He sets the history, inevitably, in the context of the Hohenzollerns but it is a history that is as concerned with the more middle-class concerns of finance, law and education than it is with dynasties and battles. He reckons that Berlin in 1786 had 7,000 houses, which shows how many people must have been living in each, and 7,000 manufactories. He also lists in detail some of the collections in the city, showing that the Hohenzollerns had not been idle collectors. Prince Henry seems to have had the best collection, with several Rubens, a Van Dyck, Rembrandts, a 'Breugel', and works by Teniers, Parmigianino, Watteau and many others, whereas the royal gallery had several Rembrandts, Caravaggios, Van Dycks, Rubens and a Poussin. The only other private collection of note was Baron von Schulenberg's, whose house on Wilhelmstraße had Italian works by Ricci, Tiepolo and Veronese.

Nicolai's work was eagerly read across Europe. Everyone now knew about the King of Prussia and his victorious army, but few had known much about his capital until Nicolai told them about it, and visitors now started to come in their thousands. But Nicolai also regretted that Berlin was not a national capital – a German capital in the same way that Paris was to France or London was to the British – and he felt this made it inferior. The *Description* was dedicated, tactfully, to Frederick but Nicolai's later work would be dedicated to furthering 'Germanness'. In 1773 he published *The Life and Times of Herr Magister Sebaldus Nothanker*, which tells the story of a rural pastor who is driven out of his parish for his advanced religious views by an orthodox superior and takes to the road. He approaches Berlin, which, he is warned by a Pietist, is 'a breeding ground for all forms of corruption and depravity ... where selfishness has reached new heights and all Christian love has been extinguished'.[31] Sebaldus argues that this cannot be right, for Berlin has become so prosperous, which could not happen if it contained so many terrible people. The Pietist, who is portrayed as one of the more extreme of his persuasion, retorts with 'O city ... you are like Sodom and Gomorrah, how soon God will rain his fire and brimstone upon you'. Sebaldus arrives to see for himself and visits the Tiergarten on Sunday, when Berliners turned out in their thousands to picnic. He avoids the fire and brimstone, greatly admires the trees and, in a typical Nicolai remark, notes that it is the parks that make Berlin superior to Vienna and Paris.

Nicolai, mindful of the Voltaire dispute with Maupertuis, has a good dig at intellectuals. 'I have noted,' says Sebaldus, 'that people who are considered quite famous at the university are totally unknown in Berlin,' and that 'the apocalypse has an even worse reputation in Berlin than philosophy'. Actually Berlin did not have a university then, but this is to nitpick. Importantly Sebaldus concludes that Berlin is a good and free city: 'the true land of freedom where everyman may speak his mind and where no man is denounced as a heretic'. In an interesting insight as to how the city will later polarise politically, Sebaldus notes how the suburbs are the most orthodox and it is the centre of the city itself that is more tolerant and free thinking.[32]

It was not the sort of book of which Frederick would approve. Nicolai was, through Sebaldus, introducing what he saw as the wholesome German rural values into Berlin. However cosmopolitan, Berlin for him must represent what the real Germany was. Sebaldus also became a bestseller, outperforming Goethe among others. Much as Frederick may have despised Sebaldus, he was very critical indeed of Nicolai's friend and fellow author, Gotthold Ephraim Lessing. Lessing was yet another Saxon who worked in Berlin, as well as Hamburg and Leipzig, during the 1750s and again briefly in the 1760s. Although he lived in the city for nearly ten years, he claimed to have never really liked it and he was as critical of the King as he was disapproving of Sanssouci. Prussia, he wrote to Nicolai, was the most slavish country in Europe and Berlin's alleged cultural freedom was illusory. He damned Frederick's now-famous religious tolerance as 'nothing more than the freedom to bring to market as many absurd arguments against religion as one likes and any honest man must quickly become ashamed of making use of this freedom'.[33]

There is a bitterness to Lessing's work (possibly influenced by the fact that he found it difficult to hold down a full-time job and was always short of money) that shows a very different side of contemporary Berlin in the immediate aftermath of the Seven Years War to common perception. Lessing's first great play, which has become one of the best known in the German language, was *Minna von Barnhelm*, first staged in 1767 although Lessing dated it 1763 to link it to the war. It was banned by Frederick's censors and had to be put on in Hamburg, but it soon became famous throughout Europe. It tells the story of the effects of war through the story of a discharged wounded officer, Major von Tellheim, and his intended, Minna von Barnhelm. Von Tellheim and his ex-sergeant, Werner, are the heroes – men who have given their service selflessly to Prussia but have been cast aside by Frederick's government as soon as they are no longer wanted. In 1764 Berlin's Poor Law Board 'estimated that 175 soldiers' wives and 160 soldiers' widows had to be supported with alms and free bread', so he certainly had a point.[34]

These authors were the public face of a deeper change that was taking place as the *Aufklärung*, in an increasingly rich and self-confident city, gathered its own momentum. Newspapers proliferated, there were numerous reading and debating societies, music groups with bookshops, coffee houses and an increasing number of salons after the model in Paris and London. Cultural life was now flourishing outside the court. In 1760 a new 1,000-seat theatre was opened in Spandau and just because Frederick did not like Mozart, that did not stop his operas being performed. While Frederick and Prince Henry collected old masters, a lively new group of artists was painting and drawing in Berlin. Some, like Anna Dorothea Therbusch – a rare example of a contemporary woman rising to the top of her profession – and Anton Graff, painted traditional portraits but of a quality that rather surpassed the offerings displayed at Wusterhausen. Incidentally, Therbusch actually had to spend her early years helping her husband run his Berlin *kneipe* (local inn), only really starting her artistic career in middle age. Others started to depict Berlin scenes so that we start to have a much better idea of what the city really looked like. Men like Jacob Philipp Hackert and Carl Traugott Fechhelm not only drew Berlin's buildings but also the people who inhabited them, the walkers in the Tiergarten, the soldiers on parade or the workers on the Spree. Perhaps the most revolutionary for his time was Daniel Chodowiecki, who came to Berlin from his native Danzig in 1743 and spent the rest of his life drawing and caricaturing the city and its people. He left more than 6,000 works – from pictures of Frederick reviewing his troops to his wonderfully comic *Family Outing*. He was also a prolific book illustrator who made Berlin the German centre for that art form. Frederick had reinvigorated the Academy of Arts early in his reign, as he had the Academy of Sciences, and in 1786, just before his death, it staged its first exhibition of contemporary painting. More than 300 were displayed, evidence of how far the *Aufklärung* had spread.

Music also thrived, partly in the many concerts now staged by the various musical societies, but also privately. There was an ever-increasing demand for musical instruments, for printed music and for music lessons as the idea caught on that everyone could enjoy music outside the confines of the court or opera. In 1783 Johann Carl Friedrich Rellstab opened the first music shop with a printing press and music lending library, and he sold a proliferation of harpsichords, clavichords, pianos, violins and, of course, flutes. With increasing wealth came the ability and desire to play, to listen and the time to do so. Leisure time was – at least for those who could afford it – something to be cherished. The restrictive, fussy dress styles that Berlin had copied from Paris at the beginning of the century, with absurdly high heels and an abundance of feathers and frills, had by the 1780s given way to clothes that people could enjoy wearing. Ladies' shoes became flatter and wider with low heels, and fashionable dresses were based on the 'English' style of a coat dress worn over a skirt.

Berliners did not necessarily see this cultural enjoyment as being in opposition to the formality of Frederick's French-dominated court but as something they could enjoy and develop in parallel. Some of the debate in the new societies and clubs was critical of Prussian absolutism, with the Monday Club – started in 1783 and numbering Lessing, Carl Philipp Bach and Nicolai among its members – being perhaps the most radical. Although it was quipped that Frederick preferred a worthless noble to a cultured bourgeois, it was not anti-monarchist in the same way as the Jacobin Clubs in France and still included state officials like Ernst Klein who would be so involved in reforming the Prussian legal system. The issues they debated were more about how government could be improved rather than over-thrown and how society could be made more inclusive. One of the principal subjects they debated was the 'On the Civic Improvement of the Jews', a paper by Christian Wilhelm von Dohm.

Frederick's legacy is that he supposedly encouraged Jewish set-tlement and emancipation; the reality is rather different. There is truth in Lessing's damning comment about the King's reputation as an atheist who tolerated and encouraged all religions. Frederick was not sympathetic to Catholics, but pragmatism demanded that he build them a cathedral to consolidate his hold on Silesia. Similarly, the partial Jewish emancipation that took place during his reign was more because the Jewish community had found leadership and a role. There were just over 2,000 Jews in Berlin by 1750 and on 17 April that year Frederick reissued *Revised General Privileges and Regulations for the Jews in the Kingdom of Prussia*, which was so restrictive that Mirabeau quipped that it was 'worthy of a canni-bal'.[35] All apart from the richest Jewish families were restricted to having one child, and those with the lowest incomes were prevented from marrying. It was anything but enlightened. But during the Seven Years War Frederick found himself increasingly dependent on Jewish finance, particularly from Veitel Heine Ephraim – builder of the luxurious Ephraim palace just beside the Mühlendamm, and the man who managed to reduce the amount of silver in royal coinage without the public losing confidence in it. The Ephraim Palace, though predictably destroyed under the Nazis, is still a major attraction in Berlin today and is used to house exhibitions.

Then in 1743 a young Jewish man from Dessau arrived in Berlin intent on continuing his Torah studies under the Rabbi David Fraenkel. Moses Mendelssohn lived in the city until he died in 1786, both pursuing a highly successful commercial career as the manager and then owner of a silk factory and as an articulate intellectual, friend of men like Lessing and Nicolai, and able to lead the debate on the inequity of singling out the Jewish community for persecution. He was building on foundations already laid by the prominent and successful Jewish families, like the Ephraims, Itzigs and Isaac-Fleiss, who between them ran nineteen important businesses in the city. Several Jewish women ran successful salons, like Henriette Herz (whose company included Wilhelm and later Alexander von Humboldt and the young dramatist and poet Heinrich von Kleist) and Rachel Levin, and Frederick's attitude was seen by many as reactionary. Mendelssohn's pre-eminence was boosted considerably when Lessing published his next play, Nathan the Wise, in 1779 (though it was not actually performed until 1783) in which the sympathetic and tolerant principal character was based on him. Johann Erich Biester, who ran the Monday Club, which he was continually trying to persuade Mendelssohn to join, wrote that Mendelssohn 'spoke with as much ease and clarity about the existence of God as about a new silk pattern, and with as much precision and accuracy about the silk as about the existence of God'.[36]

Taking von Bohm's paper, the Jewish community was able to start to argue its case intellectually in a way that they had previously found impossible. Men like Mendelssohn also tried to persuade his co-religionists that they should see themselves as Prussians who happened to be Jews rather than as Jews who happened to be living in Berlin. It did not have much effect on Frederick, who remained sceptical of the value of any organised religion. He described Christianity as 'an old metaphysical fiction, stuffed with wonders, contradictions and absurdities'[37] but was much ruder about the Jews who were, he wrote, 'the most dangerous because they do harm to the trade of the Christians and are of no use to the state. I have never persecuted them or indeed any other group for that matter but we need to keep an eye on them and make sure they do not increase.'[38] Mendelssohn was nevertheless a firm and vocal supporter of Frederick – even of his wars – but, despite twice being summoned to Potsdam, they never actually met and Frederick blocked his membership of the Academy of Sciences.

Unbending as the King may have been, the point was that Berlin as a society was beginning to re-establish itself as a more open and cosmopolitan community. There would be terrible anti-Jewish pogroms to come, but these would originate not within the city itself but rather from within the Prussian and later the German establishment. Berliners were also remarkably supportive of Freemasonry, with dozens of lodges by the end of the century. Lessing was a Mason and saw the development of the Masons as a natural extension of the *Aufklärung* and the establishment of the middle class. 'Freemasonry and the middle class are of the same age,' he wrote. 'Both originated side by side.'[39] Yet the major change was not in this spirit of tolerance – important as it was in establishing the culture of the city for the future – but in that Berlin now saw itself as a German city rather than just as the capital of Prussia. In 1773 the engraver Johann David Schleuen completed a map of Berlin. It was a very good map: detailed, accurate and including some miniature bird's-eye drawings of important buildings. It was, possibly less laudably, accompanied by some fairly dreadful verse, for example:

Was Paris zum Wunder macht
Ist auch in Berlin zu finden

This roughly translates as 'Everything that makes Paris so wonderful can also be found in Berlin'. Schleuen was articulating a feeling that for too long German culture had been considered inferior. Now that Berlin was a thriving, prosperous, diverse city, 'a capital city, a royal residence, a manufacturing centre, a trading city, a provincial city, a city with villages and farms all within a single city wall', it could justifiably claim to be the German equivalent of Paris, Rome and London.[40]

Frederick was to initiate one further great foreign-policy success (if you were a Prussian; it was a catastrophe if you were a Pole), when in 1772 he agreed with Russia and Austria to divide Poland. At a stroke the ancient 1,000-year monarchy was dissolved and Poland would not become a nation again until 1918. From Prussia's perspective it created a coherent nation, with East Prussia and Königsberg now joined physically to Pomerania and Brandenburg, and made Berlin an even more important capital. There is an image of Frederick – 'Old Fritz', as he was now known – riding into Berlin in his old age, his reins long, his back hunched as so well depicted by Chodowiecki, wearing a threadbare blue frock coat, a battered hat and his star of the Black Eagle, acknowledging the cheers as he rode along the Unter den Linden. Turning to an aide, he remarked that the people would as soon cheer a monkey if it appeared dressed as he was.

Goethe, the most famous German author of his day, visited Berlin in 1778. He was not that taken with Berlin as a city, finding it a coarse place and 'home to such an audacious set of men that you have to be a tough customer and a little rough around the edges now and then just to keep your head above water',[41] but he was fascinated by Frederick, and rulers like him, who determined the lives of his subjects down to the last detail. He found them especially interesting as 'they not only determine human destiny but also share it, thus becoming more interesting than the Gods themselves who indeed determine human destiny but are not involved in the consequences'.[42] Frederick, for his part, did not rate Goethe, not least because he actually wrote in German. 'Shakespeare can be forgiven,' he wrote to Voltaire, 'because he lived at a time when English culture had developed a little. However, there is no excuse for our contemporaries making the same mistakes – as has been done, for example, on Goethe's *Götz von Berlichingen*', which had just had its premiere in Berlin to wide applause and was, Frederick continued, 'an abominable imitation of those bad English plays'.[43]

Goethe saw a military parade while he was in Berlin and was appalled and fascinated to see such 'a monstrous piece of clockwork'. That military machine rotated around the old king, and once he was gone it would turn rather less smoothly. When he finally died in 1786, Berliners could not quite believe it. '17th August 1786. A mood of silence, though not of mourning; the people seem numbed rather than sorrowful. One scarcely sees a face that does not wear an expression of relief, even of hope. No voice of regret is to be heard; not a sigh, not a word of praise! Is this the sum of so many victorious battles, of such fame and glory? Is this the end of almost half a century of rule, a reign so rich in great deeds?' asked Mirabeau.[44] The doctor who tended the dying king answered with admirable sangfroid, when Frederick asked whether he had seen many men into the next world, 'not as many as Your Majesty'.

CHAPTER FIVE

1786–1840

'There was only one voice, one feeling, one anger and one love, to save the Fatherland and to free Germany'

ERNST MORITZ ARNDT, 1813

Strong though Frederick's influence had been, his legacy left many confused. Berlin, wrote the French *saloniste* and commentator Madame de Staël, 'offers a double face, like Janus, one of which is military, the other philosophical'.[1] Frederick's ghost still dominated the city, and a society that was so used to his authority seemed to have become paralysed. Three years after Frederick's death, revolution broke out in Paris but, despite many in Berlin thinking change to Prussian absolutism was inevitable, there was little appetite to initiate it. The government still worked tolerably well, even without Frederick, and while the Monday Club debated legal reform and Jewish emancipation, they stopped well short of advocating any more fundamental changes. Berlin remained the centre of the court, the bureaucracy and the army and it was also a city full of ideas and experimentation, but for the time being the two worlds avoided collision.

Otherwise the outspoken Anne-Louise-Germaine de Staël thought 'no spectacle in all Germany was equal to that which Berlin presented'. She commented that it felt like a modern city, but she disliked most of the major buildings being of Brandenburg brick rather than stone. Although she discovered 'no marks of the history of the country', she liked that 'at dinners, both ministerial and private, where the men meet together, the separation of ranks, so prejudicial to Germany, is not rigidly enforced, but people of talent of all classes are collected,' yet she deplored that 'the men rarely converse except with each other'. She blamed 'the military condition' for giving 'them a sort of rudeness, which prevents them from taking any trouble about the society of women'. But, having travelled widely around the German-speaking world, she also thought it was Berlin that was the centre of the German enlightenment, despite cities like Weimar (which had produced both Goethe and Schiller) having a strong counter claim. She remarked, in particular, how French was beginning to give way to German as the language spoken by the educated.[2] It was this focus on being a German as opposed to just a Prussian capital that would so strongly influence Berlin in the coming century.

Frederick's heir had been his brother August Wilhelm, whom he had bullied mercilessly, accused of cowardice and publicly disgraced in 1757 after the Prussian defeat at Kollin. August Wilhelm had never recovered, dying in 1758. The new King *of* Prussia, Frederick having got rid of the rather ridiculous '*in* Prussia' in 1772, was therefore August Wilhelm's eldest son, Frederick William II. He was a warm and relaxed man, 'genial, gregarious and recklessly heterosexual',[3] who had seven children with his wife and seven with his mistress. He was also a respected musician to whom Mozart sent scores. He had been born in the Berliner Schloss but, like so many of his family, he was happiest at Potsdam where he lived agreeably with his extensive family. One person who benefited directly from Frederick's death was his long-suffering wife, Queen Elisabeth Christine, who now found herself able to play a role in the court. She was close to the new king, who was also her sister's son and who treated her with respect. Schönhausen became something of a centre of court life and Elisabeth Christine started to enjoy herself. There is a very telling pair of portraits of her at Schönhausen, hanging side by side. In the first, painted by Frederic Reclam in 1764, the young queen, fashionably dressed in blue-grey silk, stares gloomily out of the frame, her expression one of infinite sadness. In the second, by Anton Graff, the old queen, dressed correctly in mourning for her late husband, beams happily and confidently, her black dress offset with luxurious fur. She outlived Frederick by eleven years, only dying in 1797.

One major change to the Berlin landscape came in 1788 when Friedrich Wilhelm II commissioned Carl Gotthard Langhans, a Silesian who was then the court architect, to design a gate for the Pariser Platz, where the Brandenburg Road, the continuation of the Unter den Linden, cut through the Excise Wall and led off into the Tiergarten. Langhans, who had not done much before other than some improvements to Charlottenburg and finishing the *Nationaltheater* on the Gendarmenmarkt between the two churches, surpassed himself, designing a simple, beautifully proportioned classical structure with twelve Doric columns and five passageways based on the Athenian *Propylaea,* the original gateway to the Acropolis. It was topped by a quadriga, the goddess of victory driving a chariot pulled by four horses, designed by Johann Gottfried Schadow, a native Berliner. Originally Schadow gave the goddess a staff with a laurel wreath. Over the next two centuries the story of the quadriga, and what the goddess carried, would become in itself a micro-history of the city. Originally called the *Friedenstor* (gate of peace), it quickly became known as the Brandenburg Gate and became, along with the Bear, the symbol of Berlin.

Partly because of where it was (in one of the most prominent spots in the city and on the main east–west route, that most important Berlin axis), partly because of its simple beauty, partly because it symbolised the idea of Berlin as the 'Athens on the Spree' (a concept dear to many of the proponents of the *Aufklärung*), and partly because it was soon to be so badly vandalised, the Brandenburg Gate came to represent both the spirit of Berlin and, especially, the city's freedom. This was emphasised when the Berlin Wall was built directly in front of it in 1961; when it was torn down in 1989 it was the Brandenburg Gate that became the world's focus at that historic moment. Today its image is everywhere, etched on the windows of every U-Bahn carriage, on every map and guidebook, and correctly on the cover of this book.

Frederick William II died the same year as his aunt, in 1797, being succeeded by his son, Frederick William III who would reign for forty-three years. A weak man, destined to be indecisive at a time when Berlin and Prussia called for the firm leadership of his great uncle Frederick or The Great Elector, Napoleon described him as 'no less false, than stupid'.[4] One of his better decisions was in 1793 to marry Luise of Mecklenburg-Strelitz. Luise would become a Berlin celebrity in a city unused to beautiful and approachable queens. Frederick William and Luise also had seven children. There is a nice story of the day she arrived in the city. As her carriage processed up the Unter den Linden, a small girl ran up to hand her a bunch of flowers. To the horror of her escort, Luise hugged the girl to her and kissed her, making Luise an instant Berlin heroine. Whereas Frederick the Great had been traditionally painted in uniform, glaring from the canvas, Luise had the royal family painted as a family group, very much a reflection of the bourgeois lifestyles that well-off Berliners were now embracing. Famous as Schadow is for his Quadriga, he has perhaps been rather overlooked for the beauty of some of his other work. Apart from quite a few statues of Frederick the Great and his commanders, one of his most beautiful and emotive works is his 1796 marble life-size statue of two of Frederick William and Luise's daughters, the Princesses Luise and Friederike as teenagers. Hidden away for many years as it was thought to be too suggestive, it is today in the Alte Nationalgalerie.

The Government did, however, in the aftermath of what happened in France in 1789, tighten Frederick's more liberal policies in some areas. Both the Lutheran and Calvinist churches had found Frederick's public atheism difficult and argued, with some justification, that ordinary people in the city were becoming confused. Why should they behave as God-fearing Christians, as their preachers and teachers insisted, when the King, their temporal master, clearly thought organised religion was laughable? Frederick had perhaps gone too far in inviting the extremist preacher Johann Christian Edelmann to live in Berlin. Edelmann preached against the sacraments, infuriating church leaders, and his books were burned in other German cities. God, in His various guises, was also the subject of much intellectual debate in Berlin. The works of the great Prussian thinker and philosopher Immanuel Kant, who lived and taught in Königsberg, were much debated. Kant had originally been thought rather helpful to the Prussian model of government, arguing that the 'convergence of sovereignty and enlightenment' in the same person, such as Frederick, transformed the relationship between politics and society.[5] However, in 1781 he had published his *Critique of Pure Reason*, which had annoyed the royal censors as much as it had excited discussion in the salons. The poet and wit Heinrich Heine compared Kant to the French revolutionary leader Robespierre. 'Nature,' he wrote, 'had destined them to weigh coffee and sugar, but Fate determined that they should weigh other things and placed on the scales of one a king, on the scales of the other a God.' Lessing, who had just died, was then scandalously accused of being an atheist, something hotly contested by his friend Moses Mendelssohn.

All this was in danger of being overplayed; it was a debate that remained obscure and of very limited interest to the average Berliner. It had shades of the row between Voltaire and Maupertuis that had afforded Berliners such hilarity and yet it was causing unease. In 1788 Johann Christoph Wöllmer, a man described by Frederick as a 'scheming, swindling parson', became Minister of Culture and that August he published an edict on religion to 'reverse the effect of rationalist speculation on the integrity of Christian doctrine'.[6] There were also measures to restrict public criticism of the government in the press. John Moore, an Englishman who visited in 1775, remarked that 'nothing surprised me more when I first came to Berlin than the freedom with which many people speak of the measures of government and the conduct of the king',[7] and there was the odd raised eyebrow that Frederick had put his entire revision of the legal code out for wide public consultation. The more perceptive Berliners also wondered whether it was wise to allow four of Berlin's burgeoning major newspapers to publicly praise what was happening in Paris. These measures, when compared to Vienna or London, were not oppressive but even so they caused Nicolai to pack up his business and move to Hamburg, railing against the restrictive new regime.

One area badly in need of reform but left untouched was the Prussian army. Frederick the Great's victories had given both his generals and the Prussian public the idea that their military were unrivalled and unbeatable. This is a dangerous assumption that afflicts many victorious powers in the aftermath of their success, and it meant that little had been done to modernise the army since the Seven Years War, more than forty years past by the time the army was needed again in earnest. Frederick's insistence on only recruiting officers from a narrow clique of noble families, the failure to observe the reforms that were making France's revolutionary armies successful and an over-reliance on Frederican tactics such as the 'attack in oblique order' (a complicated way of saying it's generally better to attack an enemy's weak spots than his strong ones) meant that by the early 1800s the Prussian army was outdated and much of its procedures, tactics and equipment obsolete. Berlin may have been full of soldiers, and the city's barracks may have been humming with life, but they were not the formidable military force that their forebears had been.

The army's weakness was also masked by a series of seemingly successful foreign ventures during the 1790s. The French Revolution meant that the old Prussian hostility to Hapsburg Austria was temporarily suspended. A joint Prussian and Austrian force had invaded France in 1792 only to be repulsed at Valmy, but it was a humiliation that was expunged by a successful if expedient reaction to Polish attempts to re-establish themselves as a separate nation. Poland was partitioned yet again in 1795, with Prussia now taking Danzig, or Gdansk, as well as Warsaw and swathes of territory that meant that Silesia and East Prussia were joined up, increasing the size of the country by one third and 3 million people. This process was formalised at the Treaty of Basle in 1795. Prussia agreed to withdraw from the coalition against France, known as the First Coalition, in return for French recognition of its gains in Poland. France also agreed to return all Prussian territory east of the Rhine in return for Prussia giving up territory to the west. Then, in 1803, the Imperial Diet met at Regensburg and, based on a plan agreed with France at the Treaty of Luneville, secularised seventy bishoprics and forty-five imperial cities across Germany and allocated them to new states. Prussia again increased significantly not just in size but in wealth, gaining Paderborn, Münster, Hildesheim, Erfurt and Essen and other towns. This *Reichsdeputationshauptschluss*, to give it its simple German name, made another half a million-odd Germans into Prussians. It was part of the process that would lead to the end of the Holy Roman Empire three years later and the Hapsburgs becoming instead emperors of Austria.

This policy of neutrality, much as the Elector John George had pursued at the outset of the Thirty Years War, served Berlin well until October 1806 when Frederick William – alarmed at growing French ambitions in Germany, and in alliance with Russia, Sweden, Saxony and Great Britain, the Fourth Coalition – declared war on Napoleonic France. It was an unwise move. The King had only to ponder what had happened to Austria and Russia less than a year earlier at Austerlitz to realise that the Napoleonic army was for-midable. Napoleon reacted by invading Prussia and defeating the Prussian army decisively at the twin battles of Jena and Auerstedt on 14 October. To make matters worse, those elements of the Prussian army that hadn't been defeated surrendered at Erfurt and Prenzlau two days later. On 25 October the French Marshal Davout led his victorious corps into Berlin and the next day Napoleon himself entered the city. The royal family fled to Königsberg and Prussia's humiliation was complete.

The ensuing French occupation of Berlin was not as violent or as marked by the atrocities that accompanied their presence in other parts of German territory. Davout's troops behaved despicably in some areas of Prussia, and in Hanover, causing tens of thousands

of local people to flee, many of whom ended up fighting France in
the British-trained and equipped King's German Legion. They also
aroused a deep resentment that Blücher and his army would be
intent on avenging when they occupied Paris after Waterloo nine
years later. It was, nonetheless, deeply shaming for Berliners and it
was fundamental in shaping the future attitudes of both Prussia and
later Germany to France. Berliners had not been greatly involved
in the battles themselves, which took place well to the south. The
canton system meant the army was again predominantly officered
by Junkers and manned from the rural areas, so when the news first
reached the city the reaction was one of stunned disbelief. Von der
Schulenberg, the city's Marshal, unable to bring himself to say that
the Prussian army had been defeated, issued a statement saying, 'The
King has lost a battle. The first duty of every citizen is to stay calm.'
Berliners did as they were told but by now there were two complete
French army corps in the city, together with two divisions of cavalry.
The Lustgarten had become a huge bivouac, where the soldiers sang,
danced and drank late into the night. Berliners watched mostly in
sullen silence as Napoleon paraded down the Unter den Linden on
27 October with his triumphant retinue, but 'In the pomp of his
generals and marshals, you would scarcely have recognised the
mighty one of the earth in his inconspicuous grey cloak – had not
the reverence shown by his entourage proved that it was he.' In front
of the Brandenburg Gate 'the earnestness of his face' was 'broken
by a smile ... a strange smile, quite peculiar to him' and he smiled
particularly when 'he heard not only his own troops shouting "Vive
l'empereur" but also a number of Berliners themselves'.[8]

There were certainly those who were not displeased to see
Napoleon, believing his arrival would mean an alleviation of
absolutist rule. Napoleon moved into the Schloss, sacked von der
Schulenberg and assembled 2,000 of Berlin's leading burghers, who
were told to elect a sixty-man city council. They met for the first
time in the Petrikirche on 29 October, the first time the city had been
governed by an elected body since Iron Tooth's days. He also formed
a police force from French Huguenots, smartly decked out in blue

French uniforms.[9] Napoleon then led his staff to the garrison church in Potsdam, where he raised his hat to Frederick the Great's tomb, saying, 'Hats off, gentlemen. We would not be here today if he was still alive.' Berlin was, with Fredrick William skulking in Königsberg, Napoleon's to lose but that is exactly what he did as the reality of French occupation became evident.

The French troops may have been quite well behaved but they were an unwelcome presence, always in evidence and lolling around on the streets, smoking (something Berliners were not allowed to do in public), and any initial enthusiasm soon waned. The most pressing problem was housing and feeding them. 'The excessive quartering with which the city was burdened caused food prices to rise unbelievably high,' wrote the bookseller Gustav Parthey, 'the bakers and butchers claim that the deliveries for the army took away all their flour and their meat. In the countryside they complain that the French army has taken so much that there is not enough left to feed themselves.'[10] Sophie, Countess Schwerin, wrote that 'Most of the generals live in our vicinity and from our windows I can stare into a surging sea of fiery-red hackles, plumes of feathers and hear the appallingly loud French commands echo up and down the long rows of soldiers, who lean negligently on their rifles,' smiling arrogantly and many of whom, she thought, were only fifteen years old.[11] She was furious that they used churches as supply depots and to stable their horses and even more incensed when General Jary, who had been billeted with her family, took fifty bottles of her husband's best wine when he left for Poland.[12] Many French officers took a liking to the city. Baron Percy, one of Napoleon's senior doctors, loved the 'ramrod straight' streets and the 'elegance of the architecture'. Berlin had, he thought, as much 'talent and taste' as Paris and he found it 'teeming with quick witted, artistic people' who were very sure of themselves but behaved to the French with brazen impertinence, always staring at them and showing their conquerors no respect.[13]

The French officers tried to socialise with Berlin society but it didn't really work. They organised balls at the Schauspielhaus but, remarked Countess Schwerin acidly, 'they were only attended by very few, and I only know of a few young ladies who went and they were foreigners themselves. Their attendance was never really forgiven and it had a bitter impact on their subsequent life in Berlin society.'[14] The French were also intent on making as many romantic conquests as they could and the Berlin expression *Fisimatenten* (which roughly translates as getting up to no good, and which is still in use) comes from the French *visitez ma tente* (visit my tent). The figures for illegitimate births in the city, which rose from 4 per cent in 1750 to 18.3 per cent by 1820, would suggest they had some success.[15] Rather worse was that Napoleon gave orders for Berlin's treasures to be stripped out and sent back to Paris, including Schadow's Quadriga. This was predictably deeply unpopular, earning Napoleon the nickname the 'Horse Thief of Berlin', but it was only the beginning.

In Napoleon's entourage was the art connoisseur Vivant Denon who had already arranged the treasures Napoleon had looted from his earlier campaigns in the Louvre. Denon arrived in Berlin on 5 November to survey the various collections and decide what he would have removed to Paris. Luckily Jean Henry, his Berlin counterpart, the Royal Librarian and Director of the Kunstkammer (a role that meant he was effectively in charge of all the royal collections), had been working on turning the Kunstkammer in the Schloss into a public museum. Consequently, he had carried out a complete inventory in 1805 and so knew where everything was. Concerned at the French invasion, he had already started to pack up the valuable coin and gem collection for evacuation. Driving his team of thirteen assistants mad with his incredibly slow and careful preparation, eventually they managed to ship most of the coins and gems to Memel but the bulk of the collection, particularly the statues and paintings, still had to be left behind. Denon helped himself to the 12,000 coins that remained, as well as the most important artworks. Among those taken, along with 116 paintings, were the statue of Antinous, 'the Praying Boy' that had stood outside Frederick the Great's study at Sanssouci and had been discreetly moved after his death, and 'the Knucklebone Player', which went on public view in Paris.[16]

More shaming than any of this was Napoleon's dismantling of Prussia at the Treaty of Tilsit in July 1807. After he had taken Berlin, he had moved on eastwards and defeated the Russians at the bloody battle of Friedland, near Königsberg, in June 1807. He subsequently met the Russian Czar Alexander on a barge moored in the middle of the Niemen River, between Russia and what had been East Prussia but that, as Napoleon's gesture made very clear, was now part of his empire. Prussia was stripped of most of her western territory, which became a separate kingdom of Westphalia under Napoleon's brother. Poland was re-established as the Duchy of Warsaw, Danzig made a free city, and Saxony and Russia given extensive Prussian land. Prussia's population was reduced by half, her state revenue savagely reduced, and Napoleon fixed a war indemnity on the now almost bankrupt nation of 120 million French francs – a huge sum roughly equivalent to seven times the annual government revenue.[17] The Prussian army was reduced to 42,000, with 16,000 of those being at Napoleon's disposal. Yet what perhaps hurt most was that, while Napoleon and Czar Alexander were bargaining away their country, Frederick William and Luise were kept waiting on the riverbank, not invited to participate. With Luise was her young son, the ten-year-old Wilhelm. It was a humiliation he would never forget and one that, sixty-four years later, he would amply avenge.

The French occupation of Berlin would last for eight long years, a period marked more by its inefficient administration and casual arrogance rather than by its actual brutality. The effect on Berliners of having Napoleon's soldiers billeted on them became progressively worse; a report sent to the King in 1807 said that it was not an exaggeration to say that 'many people, especially the poorer ones, have had to sell their furniture and their last bed and some of them even died of hunger and grief'.[18] The problem Napoleon had, given the speed and scope of his conquests, was that he did not have the resources, and probably lacked the inclination, to ensure that his new territories were properly governed in the manner he intended. Berlin was no exception, but with the court now far away in Königsberg, the city was left to govern itself. Its first major problem was its debt. Previously this had been covered by the Prussian government but Tilsit had made that impossible at a time when overseas trade, especially with Great Britain, came to a standstill because of Napoleon's Continental System and when the French were demanding their reparations. Secondly, in the early years Berlin definitely felt like an occupied city. Initially 25,000 French troops were stationed in Charlottenburg, but they were gradually reduced as they were needed elsewhere so that, after 1808, only a skeleton occupation force remained.

The one significant advantage of this idle French regime was that the Berlin reformers could now slowly begin to exercise control. Between 1806 and the final French expulsion from Prussia in 1814, Berlin was dominated by an extraordinarily able group of people – mostly men but some women – who would change not just the city but also Prussia and create the conditions that would lead to the founding of Germany as a nation rather than just a linguistic and geographical concept. The man who began to articulate this 'Germanness', and to turn the anti-French feeling into a movement, was a philosopher called Johann Gottlieb Fichte. Described as having 'something of Luther about him; Luther's massive intelligence, his rugged honesty, the mixture of professor and demagogue', Fichte was a pupil of Kant's. He arrived in Berlin soon after the debacle at Jena, and announced a series of public lectures.[19] Ostensibly philosophical lectures, the resulting *Speeches to the German Nation* were more of a rallying call to all Germans to appreciate their common racial heritage, to act as one nation and to seize the opportunity offered by what Fichte saw as the decline of the exhausted old European monarchies and their systems of government. The French seemed to have ignored him as some harmless old crank, and indeed French officers sat through his lectures, but Fichte was in fact arousing Berliners – and, through them, all Germany – to rise up against Napoleon and assert themselves not as Bavarians or Wurttembergers, Rhinelanders or Prussians but as Germans. He finished one of his lectures with the following words:

'If you continue in your dullness and helplessness, all the evils of serfdom are awaiting you; deprivations, humiliations, the scorn and arrogance of the conqueror; you will be driven and harried in every corner, because you are in the wrong and in the way everywhere; until, by the sacrifice of your nationality and your language, you have purchased for yourself some subordinate and petty place, and until in this way you gradually die out as a people. If, on the other hand, you bestir yourself and play the man, you will continue in a tolerable and honourable existence, and you will see growing up among and around you a generation that will be the promise for you and for the Germans of most illustrious renown. You will see in spirit the German name rising by means of this generation to be the most glorious among all peoples; you will see this nation the regenerator and recreator of the world'.[20]

From the tone of this it may not come as a surprise to learn that the Nazis lifted large parts of their ideology from his teaching, and unsurprisingly Fichte became rather unfashionable post-1945, but there is no denying his influence on his contemporaries or his importance in the creation of Germany.

He, in turn, drew on the interest in ancient and early-modern German history and its culture that had accompanied and inspired the *Aufklärung*. This Romanticism, as the movement became known (perhaps misleadingly), looked back to the age of heroes like Arminius, to the pure world offered by Germany's forests and mountains, to the language, stories and music that they had inspired, and to the cult of a physical, outdoor life of a pure people untainted with the softness of modern civilisation. It was an artistic movement but also one that emphasised the supposed values of old German lands, the sense of patriotism, the duty of obedience and that sense of victimhood, of being frustrated in fulfilling their national potential that had been so horrifically reinforced by the Thirty Years War and was now evident again in the shame and humiliation of Napoleon's easy victory. Romanticism would come to dominate German culture for the next century and in some instances well beyond. It formed the backdrop to the creation of the German nation and gave Berlin much of its nineteenth-century feel, the 'quaintness' of some of its building, its use of the almost indecipherable *fraktur* script from newspapers to railway signs, and the huge popularity of the city's surrounding woods and lakes. At its best it inspired poets like Heinrich von Kleist and works such as Grimm's fairy tales and Wagner's music; at its most extreme it inspired the mad, magical Bavarian castles of the mid-nineteenth century and allowed villains like Kohlhaas to become mythical heroes. At its worst it allowed an emphasis on racial purity and the historic wrongs suffered by the *Volk* (the German people) to be corrupted into Nazism.

In Berlin one of its best-known proponents was Heinrich von Kleist. Apart from dramatising Hans Kohlhaas's banditry, von Kleist's last and most famous work was his play *The Prince of Homburg*, in which the hero is a young prince who turned the tide in the Prussians' favour at The Great Elector's victory over the Swedes at Fehrbellin. However, in doing so he disobeyed his orders. Should his success, and the subsequent victory, stop his execution for disobeying orders? The Prince himself argues that it should not and prepares to die so that the overriding requirement for total obedience remains uncorrupted. The play contains such stirring lines as 'Death to all enemies of Brandenburg' and, of those who invaded his homeland, like the French, 'Kill them! History will not ask you why!' Von Kleist's prince seemed to many Berliners to be a model of a German hero and to encapsulate those patriotic qualities for which they were now searching. Von Kleist took his own life in 1811, before the French were defeated, and his grave quickly became a place of pilgrimage. It still is, and is easy to find, on the shore of the Wannsee, a reflective and rather beautiful spot to stop en route to Glienicke and Potsdam.

A rather different proponent of this new feeling of German values was the gymnast Friedrich Ludwig Jahn, who started a fitness movement called the *Turnverein*, which met on the charmingly named *Hasenheide* (hares' heath). There young men and boys conducted somewhat primitive gymnastic exercises 'in a cleared area ... screened by fir trees and surrounded by a moderately wide ditch'. Jahn divided the world into two categories. The *Turner*, his athletes, were forbidden every sort of alcohol as well as sweets and cakes and must not use any French expression. The rest were the 'pastry cooks', those Berliners who came out to watch and were made to sit on the far side of the ditch. Laugh as people did, Jahn's movement became increasingly popular and when Prussia finally started to stir against the French in 1813, the entire senior class at the prestigious *Graue Kloster* school, who were all members, volunteered for the army.

Three other areas of Berlin life were also being reformed. With the King absent, leadership of the government fell first to Heinrich Friedrich Karl Freiherr vom und zum Stein. Stein was an able and energetic career civil servant, originally from Franconia, who had come to Berlin in 1780. A social reformer as well as a capable administrator, he now worked to restructure the Prussian state. Together with his successor – Karl August Fürst von Hardenberg, with whom he is commonly associated – he abolished serfdom in Prussia, reformed the structure of land ownership so that land could now be freely traded, introduced a talent-based system of selection for the civil service and initiated local self-government. In 1808 Napoleon's instruction to give Berlin an elected council was codified in the *Städteordunung*. Berliners were given the right to vote for a city council, a magistrate and a mayor, a Bürgermeister, the latter responsible for the city's infrastructure. Less than 10 per cent of Berliners were eligible, but by contemporary standards it was still something of a new departure, even if key posts, such as *Polizeipräsident* (police chief), remained royal appointments. A national Council of State was formed and ministries modernised. There are, deservedly, twin statues of both Stein and Hardenberg, these joint heroes of reform, outside the Berlin Parliament building, the *Abgeordnetenhaus* in Niederkirchner Straße, as Prinz Albrecht Straße is now called.

Stein was also a dedicated patriot and very strongly anti-French. 'Napoleon,' he wrote, 'was a villain and enemy of the human race'. The French empire was 'a monstrous fabric cemented by the blood and tears of so many millions and reared by an insane and accursed tyranny.'[21] He ran a network dedicated to overthrowing the French in Berlin, but one of his letters was intercepted by Napoleon's agents and in early 1809 he had to flee. He did not actually like Berlin much, unfairly thinking Berliners lacked the drive to oppose the French. He blamed this on the capital being 'situated in the Electoral Mark. What impression,' he complained, 'can those flatlands make on the mind of the inhabitants ... What can you expect from the inhabitants of those sandy steppes, those smart, heartless woods, wooden half-educated people,' but in this he was very wrong, as events would soon prove.[22]

Hardenberg took over as the first minister, continuing with many of the reforms that Stein had initiated. The second area on which they concentrated was education and in 1809 Berlin finally got its own university. Prince Henry's great palace on the Unter den Linden, forming the northern side of the Forum Fridericianum, was handed over in September 1807 along with a budget of 150,000 Reichsthaler per annum to another outstanding Berlin reformer, Wilhelm von Humboldt. Together with his younger brother, the geographer and explorer Alexander, they would deservedly become two of Berlin's best-known intellectuals. Wilhelm was another career civil servant who had been an administrator and ambassador and had a lifelong interest in language, but it is his work in establishing the Friedrich Wilhelm University (subsequently renamed in his honour by the GDR in 1945) for which he is best known. Opening its doors in October 1810, and with Fichte as its first Rector, by 1840 the university had grown to 1,750 students and was well on its way to establishing its international reputation.

While his brother was reforming Berlin's education, Alexander was establishing himself as one of Europe's outstanding natural scientists. Born into a rich noble family in Berlin in 1769, he developed his fascination for the natural world in the woods around his childhood home at Schloss Tegel. Between 1800 and 1805 he travelled widely around both North and South America, the results of which he published in multiple volumes. He was particularly interested in why plants grow where they do, and in how the different parts of the natural world were interrelated. Later he would publish *Kosmos*, another multi-volume work, in which he drew his scientific findings together in an attempt to explain this. The range of his achievement is quite extraordinary. He became a European celebrity, in an age when that term had some meaning, and by the time he died in 1859 he would have a bay, a current, a glacier, a river, two lakes, four mountains and four mountain ranges, a waterfall, a forest, a sink hole, a lunar sea, two asteroids, nine schools and three universities named after him. What is so interesting about him from a Berlin perspective is not just that he was one of the city's most distinguished sons but that he was a product of that *Aufklärung* spirit of experimentation and exploration. He actually preferred living in Paris, and did not return finally to Berlin until 1827, settling into a house in Oranienburger Straße after the King insisted he did so if he wanted to retain his state pension; by that stage he had exhausted his own originally extensive personal fortune. He was as happy in French as in German, a close friend of Goethe and of Hardenberg and a man who represented both the rise of the German spirit and someone whose vision extended well beyond nationality.

It was Wilhelm von Humboldt who also left Berlin another remarkable legacy in his family house at Tegel. In 1766 Wilhelm and Alexander's father acquired the lease for Schloss Tegel and in 1820 Wilhelm engaged the architect Karl Friedrich Schinkel, a friend whom he had met in Rome, to reconstruct the house. Schinkel's brief was to build a house suitable for the von Humboldt family and in which they could show off the extensive art, books and collections that Wilhelm had accumulated. He designed an attractive, low white house with four corner towers, which not only met his brief but also fitted well into the surrounding countryside, then with vineyards as well as farmland. Miraculously the house survived the Second World War, but sadly Wilhelm's library, furniture and many of his other artworks, which had been moved for safety to Mecklenburg, disappeared in 1945. The sculptures that had been left in place were confiscated by the Soviets. They were eventually returned to the

GDR and most are now back in the places Schinkel designed for them so that when you visit today you can still get a very strong feel for this remarkable family.

Schloss Tegel, hard by its eponymous airport, still belongs to direct descendants of the von Humboldt family, who open the house and its surrounding park for visitors. It is one of those unexpected delights that both shows how rural Berlin once was and why it can celebrate today being the least densely populated capital in Europe. Wandering around the park, seeing the family cemetery that Schinkel designed, and where both Wilhelm and Alexander are buried, it is difficult to better the words of Theodore Fontane, who wrote extensively about the Mark later in the nineteenth century and who thought that 'a spirit of love and humanity hovers over it all'. Whereas the history of most old country houses in Brandenburg was dominated by religion, he wrote, being either 'strong fortresses of the Lutheran confession' or shrines of 'lax free thinking', Tegel was the only house that 'accommodated a third element ... that spirit which, equally distant from orthodoxy as from frivolity, nurtured itself slowly in classical antiquity and, smiling at the strife and feuding of both extremes, enjoys the present while placing its hopes in the mysterious hereafter'.[23]

A visit to Tegel encapsulates how much Berlin had changed by the early nineteenth century. Sanssouci has its own particular charm, but it is fussy, French and old-fashioned compared to the simple neoclassicism of Tegel. Although both houses celebrate the glorious countryside of the Spree and the Havel, the former speaks of an absolutist north European state while the latter is the product of an enlightened Berlin society. Schinkel would soon be able to work his magic on the much larger canvas of the city centre but first Berlin had to get rid of the French. Not all German states were as opposed to Napoleon as the Prussians, but then not all suffered so badly. Saxony, for example, although it had originally sided with Prussia in 1806, had quickly made its peace with Napoleon and its economy did very well when its manufacturing prospered as a result of the Continental Blockade. Goethe was even made a member of the French *Légion d'honneur*,[24] so it was in Berlin that the real German opposition began to take shape. Evidence of the inefficiency of the Napoleonic administration is that a group of Prussian military reformers, encouraged by Hardenberg, were able to reconstruct and modernise the Prussian army under the noses of their French occupiers.

In 1802 a Military Society had been set up in Berlin to debate the lessons learned from the successes of the French army as it became apparent to the more far-sighted Prussian officers that the military situation in Europe was changing rapidly. Yet the army – still dominated by veterans of Frederick the Great's campaigns, like the Duke of Brunswick and Field Marshal Möllendorf – did not see the need for change. It was not until after Jena that a military commission was officially established and charged with wholescale reform. It was dominated by men who were not necessarily either Prussian or aristocratic. Its leading light was Gerhard Johann David von Scharnhorst, a Hanoverian from a small landowning family, who had only joined the Prussian army in 1801 and become director of Berlin's cadet school. Together with August Wilhelm Neidhardt von Gneisenau (a Saxon) and Hermann von Boyen (the son of a Prussian officer), and against a framework of military doctrine provided by Karl von Clausewitz, they proceeded to restructure the Prussian army with extraordinary speed. Scharnhorst's vision was to base the regular army on a divisional and corps system, self-contained formations with their own integral cavalry, infantry, artillery and logistic support who could operate either independently or as an army. They would be backed up by a large part-time and territorially based reserve force, the *Landwehr*, that would combine providing a pool of manpower with uniting the Prussian nation behind the national effort. This would be overseen by a Ministry of War staffed by professional officers.

The old system of selecting officers based on their *Wappen* (coats of arms) was discontinued, there was a purge of senior officers as 103 of the 142 serving generals retired, and officer recruitment was theoretically opened to everyone, although in practice it would remain very much the preserve of the richer landowning and merchant classes. Soldiers would not now be recruited on Frederick William I's old canton system, which meant that the towns, and especially Berlin, that had not suffered as badly during Frederick the Great's wars as rural Prussia, were now included. Soldiers would be better treated, the more draconian forms of military corporal punishment were outlawed, and there was to be an emphasis on leadership as opposed to demanding blind obedience. Von Gneisenau's contribution was to create the Prussian general staff, a cadre of officers trained to run headquarters and able to plan operations and logistics in support of field commanders. The Chief of Staff (in a tradition that has lasted in the German army to this day) would have a much greater control over his operational commander than in other armies, a system that would soon be tested at Waterloo when von Gneisenau found himself in direct confrontation with Blücher. Clausewitz – who has possibly since been quoted rather more than he has been understood, and whose writings have occupied students at army staff colleges for many hours – provided the intellectual underpinning for the deployment and use of this new force. Von Boyen, who had been a pupil of Kant's in Königsberg and who wrote extensively, would become Minister of War in 1813.

The regular army had to remain small while the French were still in occupation but the creation of the Landwehr meant that, when the time came, it could be rapidly reinforced. Yet the French occupation seemed interminable and the King, who Napoleon directed to return to Berlin in 1809 so he could keep a closer eye on him, remained irresolute. In the spring of 1809 Austria had moved against France, the War of the Fifth Coalition, but the only real coalition partner was Great Britain, who mounted a desultory and badly managed expedition to Walcheren. Frederick William would not join the coalition and neither would Russia, but he was coming under considerable pressure to do something. In the autumn of 1808, a Prussian officer called Major Ferdinand Baptista von Schill, well known for his guerrilla tactics against the French in 1806, moved his regiment of irregulars into Berlin where he met with enormous popular support. Yet Napoleon ended the war with his decisive victory over the Austrians at Wagram, and when von Schill led his volunteers to fight the French he got as far as Straslund before he was comprehensively defeated and had his head cut off. Eleven of the officers who accompanied him were executed by the French for disobeying their oath to the King. Berlin was now subject to greater surveillance, and Napoleon finally got around to enquiring why the Prussian army had expanded quite so much. He threatened to send Davout back with his corps, an unpleasant threat as it was the appalling behaviour of Davout's troops in Brandenburg that had done much to make the French so hated. In the meantime, von Schill became something of a national hero. There is a statue of him in Potsdam, while the King was roundly criticised for not supporting him. Senior officers like Gerhard Leberecht von Blücher began to urge a widespread pan-Prussian campaign of sabotage and guerrilla attacks on the occupiers.

The opposition movement now moved underground. Von Schill, along with men like Scharnhorst, had been members of the *Tugendbund*. This was officially a 'moral and spiritual union for the revival of morality, religion and public spirit',[25] but it became a sort of clandestine anti-French society with branches across Germany. In Berlin it met in Reimer's bookshop on Koch Straße. Anti-French feeling was heightened by Napoleon now insisting on payment of the war indemnity, something Hardenberg co-ordinated with a call to people to contribute. Then in July 1810 Queen Luise died of an unidentified illness. Blücher blamed the French. 'Our saint,' he said, 'is now in heaven.'[26]

It was not until 1812, when Napoleon started to make his fatal moves against Russia, that any real opportunity to get rid of the French presented itself. The nadir of Frederick William's popularity came that spring as Napoleon concentrated his Grand Army in Prussia. Berlin was heavily occupied again as the army moved east and Napoleon insisted on Prussia contributing 20,000 men to his invasion. Frederick William agreed, to the fury of Scharnhorst and von Boyen, who resigned. The concentration of Napoleon's massive force in East Prussia prior to them crossing the River Niemen into

Russia caused widespread famine both there and in Lithuania, which the French stripped of food. 'The French,' said the Hanoverian diplomat Ludwig Ompteda, left the Prussians 'nothing but eyes to weep in their misery.' As the French began to suffer in Russia, the news was greeted with cheering in Berlin. The French diplomat Lecaro, who had been part of the Napoleonic administration for nearly four years, was shocked to see Berliners display 'such intense hatred and such open rage'. Berlin, he felt, 'no longer concealed its desire to join with the Russians in exterminating everything that belongs to the French system'.[27] Friedrich von Gentz, writing to the princes of the French-backed Confederation of the Rhine, summed up the popular mood when he said: 'This is Germany in its deepest humiliation. French remunerated generals, French customs officers and French officials of all kinds extort and squander the sweat of Germans and mock the unfortunate. He who is not outraged by this is no German – and no Prince.'[28]

The crisis of decision-making for Frederick William came with Napoleon's retreat from Moscow and the Russian advance during the winter of 1812–13. As what was left of the French Grand Army (approximately 30,000 of the nearly half a million men who had set out the previous June) fell back in the chaos, depression and the ignominy of defeat, they straggled through Berlin. Ludwig Rellstab saw the columns of starving, wounded men as they shuffled through the city: 'the appearance of the unfortunates was terrible,' he wrote,[29] and Stein, still in exile in Russia, wrote to his wife that he had seen a pyramid of corpses in the courtyard of a monastery 'as high as a third storey window and all frozen together'. As he travelled west his sledge trundled over the bodies of soldiers strewn along the road, many partly eaten by wolves.[30] Behind the fleeing French came the advancing Russian army and, in a most unusual turn of events for a Prussian general, General Graf Yorck von Wartenberg decided on his own initiative to defy the King and join the Russians against Napoleon. Such disobedience to orders was not something the Prussian army normally tolerated, but it would make Yorck a popular hero in Berlin. On 6 February 1813 an advance party of Cossacks entered the city and demanded that the 10,000-strong French garrison surrender. The French resisted but on 23 February the irresolute Frederick William, who was then in Breslau, strongly encouraged by Stein who had now arrived in Prussia, declared against Napoleon and made his famous speech *An Mein Volk* (to my people), appealing to Prussians to rise up against the French and volunteer for the army. The response was immediate. Some 6,500 Berliners joined up immediately, nearly 5 per cent of the city's population, proving Stein had been wrong when he said they had no appetite to fight the French. Schadow and Fichte joined the Landwehr, with its black uniform with red lapels and gold braid that would become the colours of German nationalism, although Fichte typically chose to wear a bizarre medieval uniform of his own. Berliners responded equally enthusiastically to a call for money by donating 1.2 million Reichsthalers in jewellery and plate. Prussia was now once again at war with France.

On 4 March the French garrison in Berlin finally surrendered, and on 17 March Yorck's corps marched into the city to enormous popular rejoicing. Frederick William returned the next week, announcing the creation of a new order, the *Eiserne Kreuz*, a simple iron cross designed by Schinkel, which, for the first time in the Prussian army, was to be awarded for valour regardless of rank. Previously Frederick the Great had awarded a medal for valour and exceptional service that he introduced in 1740, *Pour La Merité*, but that was only for officers and, besides, it had a French name. This was a German award, in solid German iron, and its first recipient was the late Queen Luise. Schinkel actually wanted to put a giant Iron Cross on top of the Brandenburg Gate but, perhaps fortunately, was dissuaded. Between 1812 and 1815, 5,041 were awarded – evidence of both the success of the idea and the intensity of the fighting still to come. The next year the King would also introduce the Order of Luise to be awarded, again regardless of rank, to 100 women who had made an exceptional contribution to Prussia.

The war, however, was far from over and Berlin was still threatened as Napoleon attempted to rebuild his armies. In August 1813

he instructed Marshal Oudinot to retake Berlin in an attempt
to knock Prussia out of the tripartite coalition with Russia and
Austria that was building against him. Oudinot divided his mixed
force of 60,000 French, Poles and Saxons into three columns,
advancing on Berlin from the south-west. Berlin was defended by
its reformed Prussian army, heavily reinforced with the Landwehr,
and also a strong Swedish contingent. Ironically the whole force
was under the command of one of Napoleon's former marshals
who had changed sides, Bernadotte, whose family had become, and
still are, the kings of Sweden. Luckily for Berlin it was a very wet
summer and the roads in the marshy area around the Havel were
almost impassable. Oudinot's force got badly delayed and when his
first corps, commanded by General Reynier, reached the village of
Großbeeren, just short of Potsdam on 23 August, he found himself
facing General Friedrich Wilhelm von Bulow's 3rd Prussian Corps.
He attacked immediately but was badly repulsed by von Bülow's
men. His two flanking formations were unable to come to his
aid and Reynier fell back, having taken 4,500 casualties and lost
most of his artillery. That evening Berliners, including Theodor
Fontane's mother, came out to treat the wounded. The Fontanes,
being Huguenot, still spoke French at home. Although his mother
was then still little more than a child, she helped a badly wounded
young Frenchman who was hardly able to breathe. She comforted
him in French and, she told her son, he sat up in amazement before
he died in her arms.

Großbeeren became a celebrated victory for Berlin not just
because it had saved the city but also because it was a victory for
Berliners, for the new Prussian army and for its citizen reserve, the
Landwehr. Given the plethora of other European battles that year, it
has now been slightly forgotten, although there is a memorial tower
there that was erected on its hundredth anniversary. Yet it did not
end the direct threat to Berlin. Napoleon now sent Marshal Ney to
supersede Oudinot and on 6 September a re-energised French, Saxon
and Bavarian army advanced on Berlin along the same route as they
had tried the previous month. This time they got as far as the village

of Dennewitz, where they were stopped again by von Bülow's corps. Von Bülow's men seized the key ground, which Ney failed to retake from them, and although the fighting continued all day with heavy casualties on both sides, when Bernadotte came up in the evening Ney's army broke. Dennewitz was the last French attack on Berlin. A grateful king made Bernadotte *Graf von Dennewitz*, and Schinkel designed a fitting memorial that is still on the battlefield, topped, of course, by an Iron Cross.

The fighting in Germany would not end until that autumn when Napoleon was defeated at Leipzig in the bloodiest battle of the whole Napoleonic wars. The Prussian army distinguished itself once more. Scharnhorst himself had been wounded in the battle of Lützen in May, dying the next month in Prague, but the army he had created had more than redeemed itself. When, in March 1815, Napoleon escaped from exile and again threatened Europe, it was the Prussian army with its strong Berlin contingent – fighting under Blücher, with von Gneisenau as his Chief of Staff and with von Bülow's corps to the fore, alongside the British and other German armies – that finally defeated him at Waterloo. Known as the battle of *La Belle Alliance* in Berlin, this final defeat of Napoleon was again widely celebrated. Frederick William I's Rondell inside the Hallesches Tor was renamed as Belle Alliance Platz. That area of Berlin was badly bombed in the Second World War and in 1947 it was renamed as the Mehring Platz after the revolutionary socialist Franz Mehring. Blücher's statue does, however, still stand proudly in the Forum Fridericianum, today's Bebel Platz. Scharnhorst was brought back from Prague and given the most prominent memorial in the Invalidenhof, which, ironically for a man who had done so much to bring Berlin and Germany together, ended up immediately under the Wall. It survived this ordeal and is still in the Invalidenhof today, topped by a sleeping lion and quietly dominating the graves of some other famous names of later Prussian history such as von Schlieffen and von Moltke.

~

The Quadriga had been returned to Berlin in 1814 when the Prussian army occupied Paris after the Battle of Leipzig. It took six huge wagons to transport it, each drawn by thirty-two horses, and Schinkel was tasked with replacing the goddess's staff with a Prussian eagle, the oak leaves of victory and an Iron Cross. On 7 August that year there was a victory parade with the King and his generals riding down the Unter den Linden and under the renovated gate, which now quite clearly celebrated victory rather than peace. The piazza to the east of the gate was renamed Pariser Platz and the Achteck, the eight-sided square just inside the Potsdamer Tor, was renamed as Leipziger Platz.

Much debate went into how else Berlin should commemorate its salvation. Schinkel proposed a cathedral and busied himself designing one based on Strasbourg Cathedral, which both he and Goethe believed represented the essence of the German spirit. It was to have been a massive building, with a 1,000-feet spire centred on the Leipziger Platz that 'would have overshadowed all else in the city and in the imagination of the nation. It would have been seen for miles across the Prussian plains and individuals would have been reduced to dust in its vastness.'[31] It was never built. Strasbourg was allocated to France at the Congress of Vienna, the European summit that met throughout 1814–15 to decide how to carve up Napoleon's empire, so it seemed inappropriate to model the centrepiece of the Prussian capital on its cathedral. This was maybe just as well. Schinkel's design would not only have changed Berlin's landscape fundamentally but it would probably have prevented him from executing the other buildings on which he was about to embark. Berlin would have to wait a few more decades for its cathedral. Schinkel's was not the only grand design that was never realised for the *Achteck*. In 1797 the young architect Friedrich Gilly had designed a similarly massive classical temple as a memorial and tomb for Frederick the Great for the square, which included a monumental Potsdamer Tor, but that had also foundered. Again, that may have been as well, not least for the repose of Frederick's soul, which would have been horrified at the pomp and the expense.[32]

The result of the debate was to be a rather more modest memorial, a cross on one of the slight mounds that passes for a hill in Berlin, which became known as Kreuzberg (cross hill), designed by Schinkel and unveiled in 1821. It was made of cast iron from the *Königliche Eisengießerei* (royal ironworks) that had been originally set up to produce armaments but became increasingly involved in producing decorative ironwork and made the Iron Crosses. Iron came increasingly to represent Berlin's spirit during the wars; the King ate with iron tableware and Berliners took pride in wearing iron jewellery engraved with phrases such as 'I gave gold for iron' or 'Exchanged for the welfare of the Fatherland' when they answered Hardenberg's and later the King's 1813 call for money. Iron was also seen as embodying the German character for which Fichte longed: the tough, uncompromising national spirit that refused to bend to the conqueror. Schinkel's cross is today in the Viktoriapark in Kreuzberg and a short walk from the Platz der Luftbrücke U-Bahn station.

The reaction in Berlin to the outcome of the Congress of Vienna was otherwise mixed. Apart from Strasbourg, and losing part of Poland to Russia, Prussia regained her former territory and was given more. Westphalia (parts of which had been Prussian anyway), Pomerania and a large part of Saxony, who had ill-advisedly sided with Napoleon, became Prussian. So too, most valuably, did the Rhineland with its iron and coal deposits in the Saarland and the Ruhrgebiet. Prussia now stretched from Lithuania in the east to the Netherlands in the west, and her population more than doubled so that Berlin became capital to a nation of over 10 million souls. There was, though, disappointment that Vienna had not delivered a German nation as such, and many of those who had volunteered in Berlin felt they had been fighting as much for Germany as they had for Prussia. Yet a German nation that would have threatened the supremacy of Hapsburg Austria was never going to happen while Metternich, the Austrian chancellor, controlled events in Vienna. Instead a Confederation of the Rhine was set up, replacing the arrangements made at Regensburg. It reduced the previous 300 German states to just thirty-nine, but they were only united via a relatively ineffective central Diet, or parliament, that would meet in Frankfurt. It was an artificial construct; Austria and Prussia, both with roughly similar populations and territory, dwarfed the next state, which was Bavaria at about one tenth of their size. Inevitably it premised a conflict between the two super-powers as to who would lead the 'German' nation if and when it materialised.

Yet, as well as disappointing those who saw 'Germany' as the logical outcome of the Wars of Liberation, Vienna also reinforced the powers of the German princes as absolute hereditary rulers, thus equally frustrating those who had hoped for a more liberal, democratic system after the failure of the monarchies against Napoleon. The spirit that had encouraged young men to volunteer to fight Napoleon now became polarised around the twin objectives of creating this German nation and making it a democracy. In June 1815 students at Jena University had started a *Burschenschaft* (student brotherhood) dedicated to 'Freedom, Honour, Fatherland'. They took as their colours the black, red and gold in which they had fought in the Landwehr. Between 17 and 19 October 1817, students from thirteen universities gathered at Wartburg castle in Saxe-Weimar to celebrate the 300th anniversary of Luther's *Ninety-Five Theses* and the fourth anniversary of the Battle of Leipzig. Wartburg was an emotive location. It was where medieval German minstrels were supposed to have gathered to compete against one another in a *Sängerkrieg* (song contest), and where Luther translated the Bible. There they listened to rousing nationalist speeches and burned the *Code Napoleon* and *The History of the German Empires* by the reactionary author August von Kotzebue. Two years later, in March 1819, one of the Burschenschaft, Karl Ludwig Sand, murdered Kotzebue in his home in Mannheim. Later that month, and as a direct result, Metternich steered the restrictive Carlsbad Decrees through the Confederation, which imposed severe restrictions on the press and banned nationalist societies like the Burschenschaft.

The nationalist movement was particularly prevalent in Berlin but Frederick William – his popularity restored after the successes of 1814 and 1815 – began to reject the reformers in favour of a more reactionary clique that became known as the 'Camarilla' and who now advised him. William de Wette, Professor of Theology at Berlin University was sacked for writing a letter to Sand's mother, saying what her son had done was 'a beautiful sign of the times',[33] and even poor old Jahn, the gymnast, was put on trial for being a member of the Burschenschaft and jailed for five years. Then in 1822 Frederick William reneged both on his promise that there would be a national Prussian parliament, replacing it instead with regional Diets, and that there would be a written constitution. The regional Diets would only meet every three years and would be divided into three houses: nobles, cities and commoners, but with the nobles' house having an effective power of veto. These arrangements were clearly ridiculous in areas like the Rhineland and Westphalia, which had strong traditions of self-government and had adopted (and still used) the Napoleonic legal code. In other areas, such as East Prussia, they actually worked quite well, suited as they were to a more archaic and semi-feudal social structure. Yet they left Berliners confused and angry, and Stein resigned in 1815. Hardenberg, who had negotiated for Prussia at Vienna, soldiered on until he too fell from favour, before dying in 1822. He had little time to enjoy the elegant, classical country house Schinkel had built for him at Neuhardenberg. Even the senior generals like von Gneisenau resigned, although he agreed to return to public life as Governor of Berlin in 1818 and subsequently commanded Prussian armies once more on the Polish frontier. He is, like Hardenberg, deservedly commemorated not just by a statue on the Unter den Linden but also in a street and, in the ultimate of Berlin honours, a U-Bahn station.

Berlin would show its reaction to this repression in two ways. First were those who bridled against it and would, in the spirit of *Berlin Unwille*, work for reform that, when it eventually came, would be violent. Secondly, there were those who realised that reform was still some way off and now just wanted to get on with their lives. The Napoleonic Wars had lasted for twenty-three years and killed nearly 7 million people; parts of Europe had been devastated and, while Berlin had not suffered as badly as it did in the Thirty Years

War, there was a young generation who had known nothing but the threat of war and invasion.[34] Coupled with the natural Prussian inclination not to upset the status quo and to obey orders, they now settled down to rebuild their lives. Consequently, there was something of a triumph of ordinariness about many Berliners in the ensuing decades. This has been typified as *Biedermeieresque*, a sort of German respectability that spread across central Europe and takes it name from *bieder* (a German term for being a bit boring or unadventurous) and *Meier* (a typical surname). These families concentrated on their homes and families, were generally religious, and followed respectable pursuits, taking walks in the Tiergarten and patronising Berlin's increasing number of shops and cafes. The richer ones had themselves painted by artists such as Johann Erdmann Hummel, who executed some almost photographic portraits of families at home, such as 'The Chess Match in the Voss Villa',[35] or Karl Begas's rigid but atmospheric portrait of himself with his own family,[36] and 'The Living Room of C.F.E Hausschild, Ironmaster' by Eduard Gaertner.[37] The living room of an ironmaster's house is not, perhaps, the most exciting subject for an artist, but the fact that such commissions were popular says much for the aspirations of Berliners like Hausschild at the time.

This Biedermeier art cannot be called dull in itself. As well as being often exquisitely executed, it offers a revealing insight into the lives of well-off Berliners and their families and tells us much more about contemporary Berlin than great war or allegorical scenes do. It follows very much in the tradition established by Queen Luise in the early nineteenth century of having the royal family depicted in semi-domestic settings as a sort of national role model. Berliners had loved her for this, as much as for holding hands with the King in public.

Architects like Schinkel were also giving Berlin the buildings and streets that Berliners of all persuasions could be proud of. Karl Friedrich Schinkel was born in Neuruppin, just north-west of Berlin, in 1781. His family moved to Berlin in 1794 and he was, as with so many prominent Berliners, educated at the Graue Kloster. He subsequently studied under David Gilly and his son, Friedrich, who designed the monumental tomb for Frederick the Great. Schinkel toured Italy in early 1803, returning determined to make his living as a painter. Turning gradually to architecture, despite producing some accomplished paintings, in May 1810 his talent was spotted by Wilhelm von Humboldt, who gave him a position within the Royal Building Authority. His first building in this new role was perhaps his most famous, the Neue Wache (new guardhouse) on the Unter den Linden just across the bridge from the Berliner Schloss and intended to house the royal guard.

It was inaugurated by the 1st Grenadier Guards in 1818 for the state visit of Czar Alexander and served its original purpose until 1919. In 1931 it became a national memorial for the dead of the First World War and continued to fulfil that role throughout the years of the Nazis. Under the GDR it became, predictably, a memorial to the 'Victims of Fascism', with an unknown soldier and concentration-camp victim interred beneath an eternal flame, guarded by smart GDR soldiers who performed ceremonial guard-changing ceremonies. It is today still a national memorial, now with a moving Pieta by Käthe Kollwitz as the focus for German mourning to the 'Victims of War and Dictatorship'. Many people would say that it is one of Schinkel's most satisfactory buildings, built like a Doric temple, in the slightly severe, unornamented Greek style that Schinkel favoured and that fits so well with the atmosphere of Berlin. Standing in the Neue Wache today takes you as close as you can get to understanding and sharing the terrible experiences Berlin has suffered since Schinkel designed it.

His other great classical buildings followed quickly thereafter. In 1817 Langhans's Royal National Theatre in the Gendarmenmarkt burned down and in 1818 Schinkel was commissioned to replace it. The result is the Schauspielhaus, which stands today (albeit heavily restored) between the Französische Dom and the Deutsche Dom. Next came the Schlossbrücke, the bridge connecting the island to the Unter den Linden, and then in 1822 he started work on a museum to house the artworks that Jean Henry had been cataloguing since the 1790s, including those now recovered from Paris. The resulting Altes

Museum (old Museum), with its Ionic colonnade on the opposite side of the Lustgarten to the Schloss, is one of his most famous and loved buildings and now almost as iconic an image of Berlin as the Brandenburg Gate. The only problem is that it was immediately too small to house the collections, and the then Crown Prince, Frederick William (who would become Frederick William IV in 1840), called for the whole of the northern part of the island behind Schinkel's new museum to become a museum quarter. When he became king he would begin to realise his dream.

Schinkel also designed much larger projects in Berlin. To him we owe much of the Unter den Linden, the Pariser Platz, and the feel of central Berlin with its restrained classical facades. What is so extraordinary about Schinkel is both the breadth of his talent and his extraordinary diversity. Not only did he paint, design buildings, conceive the Iron Cross and plan national memorials, but he was also an accomplished theatre designer, sculptor and furniture designer. He was a man who could build in brick as well as in stone and who was at ease designing Gothic revival churches like his unbuilt cathedral, or the Friedrichswerder Kirche, which is currently being restored, and the almost modernist brick Bauakademie (building academy), originally situated nearby but sadly destroyed in 1962 to make way for the GDR's Ministry of Foreign Affairs. He left his mark as much on Potsdam, where he designed the classical squares of the town centre and the Romantic castle of Babelsberg, part modelled on Windsor Castle, as he did on the Brandenburg countryside around the city with his country houses like Schloss Tegel.

Apart from Schinkel, Berlin in the early nineteenth century was rather lacking in artistic talent (considering what had been and what was to come). Many writers and musicians visited but few stayed. The poet and comic writer Heinrich Heine, who is often thought of as a Berliner because his wit seemed so *Berlinisch*, in fact only spent two years in the city from 1821 to 1823. He had been sacked from Göttingen University for duelling but was supported by a rich uncle so he could afford to spend his time in Berlin in the salon of Rahel Levin, where he became friends with Fichte and the von Humboldts. In 1822 he published his first collection of poems and a series of letters from Berlin. Heine found the contemporary political and social environment repressive. He was critical of nearly everything and everybody. Schinkel's buildings were 'long stretches of uniform houses, with long wide streets . . . but with no care given to the opinion of the masses',[38] and he reckoned that von Kleist's play *The Prince of Homburg* had not been performed because a 'certain noble lady, a descendant of Kleist's eponymous hero, felt personally insulted by the unheroic way the prince was portrayed in the play and had succeeded in having it supressed'.[39] His final word on the city was as he left in 1823:

> *Verlass Berlin, mit seinem dicken Sande*
> *Und dünnen Tee und überwitz'gen Leuten,*
> *Die Gott und Welt, und was sie selbst bedeuten,*
> *Begriffen längst mit Hegelschem Verstande*

This roughly translates as 'Farewell Berlin, with your thick sand and weak tea, where, due to Hegel's logic, you know everything there is to know about God and the world and are very aware of your own importance.'

Neither did Berlin produce the musical talent that was to be found in other German cities. The musical sensation of the 1820s was undoubtedly Felix Mendelssohn's performance of Bach's *St Matthew Passion* on 11 March 1829. Mendelssohn was Moses Mendelssohn's grandson. The Mendelssohn family had thrived during the past three decades, founding a bank while still closely involved in the city's intellectual and cultural life. Moses's daughter Dorothea had married the writer Felix Schlegel, who had taken young Felix to Weimar. There he had got to know Goethe – almost a rite of passage for any aspiring German man of culture – who had praised his compositions. Performed in the Opera with a choir of 400, the *St Matthew Passion* received rapturous applause despite the fact that Mendelssohn had altered Bach's original composition to suit what he thought a contemporary audience would want to hear. Mendelssohn was very much Berlin's own man and saw the city as both his home and his inspiration. Nevertheless, annoyed at being passed over as director of the prestigious music school, the *Singakademie*, he took himself off to Dresden where he died at the age of just thirty-eight in 1847.

Berlin's love of music remained as strong as ever and there was a continuing demand for performances. The Opera House and the Schauspielhaus were operated as one company under Count Brühl, who favoured German music and opera whereas the King, a keen musician himself, favoured French and Italian operas. It was almost an exact replay of the tussle between Frederick the Great and Reichardt. The two camps were represented by Gasparo Spontini, an Italian whom Frederick William had recruited and who was an accomplished and successful composer and conductor but never really succeeded in attracting Berlin audiences. By way of contrast, Carl Maria von Weber, whose work neatly encapsulated all the aspects of German romanticism that appealed to Berliners, was championed by Brühl. His *Der Freischütz*, which premiered on 18 June 1821 and was a *Singspiel* composition of the sort that so irritated Frederick the Great, contained a glorious mixture of ancient German mystery and myth. It was so popular that an Englishman, Julius Benedict, waiting for the doors to open, found himself 'literally carried into the pit by the surging human wave'. There were endless calls for repeats and 'of seventeen numbers fourteen were greeted with tumultuous applause'.[40] 'Even the gigantic mechanical owl which had behaved so disappointingly at the dress rehearsal, rose to the occasion and flapped its wings. The audience abandoned itself to the enchantment of this poetry of the German forest.'[41]

Visiting musicians also had a mixed experience. Ernst Theodor Amadeus Hoffman, always known as E.T.A. Hoffman, arrived in 1814 and quickly became a Berliner. He wrote romantic stories that verged on the bizarre and also composed music. Brühl staged his opera *Undine* in the Schauspielhaus in 1816 but he is probably rather better known as the author of the stories that Offenbach would later set to music. Hoffman died in Berlin from a combination of drink and syphilis in 1822, a tortured spirit who never quite seemed to fulfil his potential during his lifetime. Wagner, on the other hand, whose work should have appealed, came first in 1841 to conduct his *Fliegender Holländer* (flying Dutchman) in the Schauspielhaus. It was not a success. The first act did not receive any applause at all. The second and third acts aroused a polite reaction, while the second performance was greeted with as much hissing as clapping. This was, he was told, because the critic Ludwig Rellstab, who was also critical of Spontini, had delivered a damning review that morning and the Berlin audience was behaving as it thought it was expected to. Wagner never cracked it with Berlin audiences. On his next visit in 1847 he found he was overshadowed by Jenny Lind.

Liszt fared rather better. When he came for three months at Christmas in 1841 he was greeted with something like mass hysteria. After giving the obligatory royal performances, he staged twenty public concerts, donating the proceeds of half of them to charity, and 'elegant ladies displaying cameos with his likeness screamed and jumped up and down at his concerts in a display of mass hysteria worthy of a pop concert'.[42] Berlioz, who also visited in the early 1840s, came away saying that 'music is in the very air' of Berlin. 'One breathes it in theatres, in churches, in the street, in public parks – everywhere. For everyone respects music in Berlin, rich and poor alike, clerics and soldiers, the common people and the king.'[43] This popular appreciation and love of music had become a Berlin tradition – one that was advanced significantly when in 1826 a group of musicians formed themselves into the Berlin Philharmonic Society.

What Berlin may have lacked in authors and musicians it more than compensated for with its intellectual life. The city was slowly becoming a place where intellectuals gathered, partly because of the university and partly because, despite the censorship, it was an increasingly civilised city in which to live, with its music and parks and the plethora of cafes and restaurants opening in the 1820s. Berlin had long had plenty of taverns and a few restaurants; you can still eat today in the *Zur Letzen Instanz*, a restaurant that has served food from its premises in the Nikolaiviertiel since at least 1621. What changed in the 1820s was the opening of a different sort of establishment, coffee houses in the Viennese tradition such as Café Kranzler on the junction of the Unter den Linden and Friedrich Straße, which became an instant success. In the next decade more than a hundred similar coffee shops opened – often run by Swiss, Italian or Austrian immigrants – and they were followed by wine and beer cellars, which particularly appealed to the nationalist element. The most famous of these was the Lutter Keller in the wine merchants, Lutter und Wegner, in the Gendarmenmarkt, famous as the place where university students would debate late into the night. Two of these were Karl Marx and Friedrich Engels, the latter while doing his military service with the Household Artillery. Lutter und Wegner is today still selling wine and remains an excellent old-fashioned Berlin restaurant.

Von Humboldt's university also attracted many intellectuals to Berlin, not least because of the quality of its teaching. When he had set it up, von Humboldt had merged Sophie-Charlotte's old Academy of Sciences, the various medical schools in Berlin and other academic institutions while creating a new institution whose constitution enshrined three 'freedoms', that of research, of the individual and of nation. The university elected its own chancellor and its own deans. While the sciences formed the key faculties, the *primus inter pares* was the Faculty of Philosophy, which had originally been headed by Fichte. This semi-independent status was not proof against all royal interference – as demonstrated by the sacking of the unfortunate de Wette – but it did give the university a certain degree of freedom, which was important when it had to compete against the older established institutions like Göttingen and Jena with their long list of distinguished alumni. The philosopher Ludwig Feuerbach, who was a student there in 1826, described it as a very serious place. 'There is no question here of drinking, duelling and pleasant communal outings; in no other university can you find such a passion for work, such an interest for things that are not petty student intrigues, such an inclination for the sciences, such calm and such silence. Compared to this temple of work, the other universities appear like public houses.'[44]

Fichte had resigned from his chair in 1812 and, by a cruel irony, died of typhus contracted from his wife who had caught it while nursing the wounded. In 1818 Georg Wilhelm Friedrich Hegel was appointed as his successor. Hegel, originally from Stuttgart, was to prove enormously influential. He was also something of a gift for the government. In his first lecture he said that the Prussian state had 'now gathered me to itself'. Hegel believed the state represented the 'highest expression of the ethical substance of a people'. It was not simply there to administer its subjects' lives but it was also part of their very nature. Hegel was an indifferent lecturer; he mumbled and his pupils found him very difficult to understand. He said himself that he thought there was only one person who did actually understand him and 'even he did not'.[45] Yet he offered a helpful model that people should adhere to the state, which offered them a framework within which they could run their lives and develop politically. Hegel died of cholera in 1831 when Berlin suffered a bad outbreak and before Marx and Engels arrived at the university. Marx was nevertheless his disciple, and strongly influenced by his insistence on the authority and power of the state, although, as he said himself, 'I stood Hegel on his head and put him the right way up.' Marx's social and political model would, of course, look very different to the hierarchal society of early-nineteenth-century Berlin. Marx was less interested in interpreting the world as he found it; rather he wanted to change it. And the Berlin in which he arrived in October 1836 provided plenty of reasons why he thought he should do so.

CHAPTER SIX

1840–1871

'*What a change of Fortune, thanks to God's Providence*'

Banner hung on the Brandenburg Gate in 1870

At the end of the Napoleonic Wars Berlin had a population of around 200,000. By the 1840s this had doubled and by the 1870s it would reach one million. It was a huge increase and made Berlin the fastest-growing city in Europe. On the surface the city gave the impression of a calm, law-abiding capital with its neat houses and refined society. Berliners were proud of what they had achieved in defeating Napoleon, and many ordinary people wore their war medal with its ribbon in Prussian royal black, white and red with pride. Those who could afford it had themselves painted wearing it on their chest. The anarchist Bakunin, who visited in the 1840s, wrote that it was 'a fine town, excellent music, cheap living, very passable theatre, plenty of newspapers in the cafes ... In a word splendid, quite splendid – if only the Germans weren't so frightfully bourgeois. Yesterday I noticed a sign outside a shop: the Prussian Eagle above and below a tailor ironing. And underneath the following couplet:

Unter Deinen Flügeln
Kann ich ruhig bügeln'.[1]

This roughly translates as 'Under your wings I can peacefully iron'.[2] But while those who could afford it took advantage of peace and all the opportunities offered by the 'Biedermeier Years', two movements were growing in strength and impatience that would upset this world of comfortable respectability. The first was the Nationalists, heirs of the Burschenschaft and those who were frustrated that the Congress of Vienna had produced the clumsy compromise of the Confederation rather than a German nation. The second movement sought increased political representation and improved social conditions. The two were not discrete, and when the time came to take action they emerged as a joint force in opposition to the monarchy.

The Nationalists had been encouraged by a series of developments that played to their agenda. In 1818 Prussia had established a customs union to facilitate trade within its own borders. Previously goods travelling from, for example, Königsberg to the Rhine were liable to be inspected eighteen times, but now all internal duties were abolished and neighbouring states were invited to join. Many did so and by 1833 Berlin proposed a pan-German customs union, a *Zollverein*, within which goods could be traded freely. On New Year's Day in 1834 it was adopted by about 90 per cent of the Confederation, the notable exclusion being Austria where Metternich was suspicious of Prussian leadership. Later Sweden and Norway joined as well. The year before, in May 1832, 20,000 students from across Germany had gathered for the Hambach Festival in the Rhineland. Dressed again in what were now the accepted nationalist colours of black, red and gold (as opposed to the Prussian black, white and red), they demanded both political reform and national unity. Then in 1840 France repeated its historic demand that the Rhine should become its national frontier, which would have resulted in a significant loss of German territory. This led to an outbreak of patriotic fervour throughout the German states and repeated public renditions of a new song, '*Die Wacht am Rhein*', with its stirring first verse that roughly translates as:

The cry resounds like thunder's peal,
Like crashing waves and clang of steel,
The Rhine! The Rhine! Our German Rhine!
Who will defend our stream divine?

In 1841 August Heinrich Hoffman von Fallersleben wrote the
'*Deutschlandlied*' (song of Germany), which called for unity, justice
and freedom. Set to music that Haydn had originally written to celebrate the birthday of the Hapsburg Emperor Francis II, it became
an instant hit. With its famous opening lines of '*Deutschland,
Deutschland über alles*', it would become the German national
anthem after the First World War, although ironically Haydn's music
was used for the post-1806 Austrian national anthem as well. The
media was also becoming pan-German. Berlin had its own fifty-eight
weekly and thirty-two daily papers by the middle of the century,
but this did not stop demand for papers like the *Deutsche Zeitung*,
started in Heidelberg in 1846, or Marx's left-wing *Rheinische
Zeitung*, until it was banned in 1843.[3] The regimes in both Berlin and
Vienna were increasingly seen as an obstacle to a popular demand
that Germany should become a nation.

Yet the social pressures in Berlin were even stronger than the
nationalist ones. The extraordinarily rapid increase in population was caused by immigration largely from Poland and within
Germany. In 1830 the Poles rose up both against the Russians, which
resulted in heavy fighting that winter, and a flood of refugees. In
1846 the Poles rose once more, this time against the Russians and the
Prussians, again leading to more refugees. There was also a steady
stream of immigrants from Silesia, where economic conditions were
particularly hard in the 1830s and 1840s as new spinning machines
and factories replaced the old locally based weaving industry. In
1844 a group of 5,000 weavers revolted, smashing factory looms
and demanding jobs. The revolt was put down fairly brutally by the
Prussian army, causing Heine to write one of his best-known poems,
'*Die Schlesischen Weber*' (the Silesian weavers), which was quickly
banned in Berlin.

The draw of Berlin was not just that the army and the bureaucracy, the university and its traditional trades meant people had a
better chance of finding jobs there than in other parts of Prussia, but
that the industrial revolution was starting to create a mass demand
for workers to feed its factories. The speed and scale of the industrialisation in Berlin was to be the cause of both its hugely increased
prosperity and the creation of an underclass of workers whose conditions in the coming decades were among the worst in Europe. In
1815 Berlin did not have a single steam engine, whereas in countries
like Great Britain the industrial revolution had been energising
manufacturing for half a century. Berlin's industry by the end of the
Napoleonic Wars had not changed greatly since Frederick William I's
reforms and still relied heavily on its weaving and textiles, employing
28,000 workers, for which the army remained the largest customer,
while the iron foundries produced armaments. The luxury-goods
industry also remained strong but its businesses employed tens rather
than hundreds of people. However, Hardenberg was determined to
rectify this and in 1818 a Ministry of Trade and Industry was set up.
In 1821 a state technical college was opened, with officials charged
with learning what they could principally from their wartime ally
Great Britain. The key figure was another exceptional Prussian civil
servant, Peter Christian Beuth, who had fought in the war, received
the Iron Cross and now devoted himself to ensuring that Berlin
caught up economically. From 1830 he ran the Department of Trade
and Industry and it is to his energy and vision that Berlin owes much
of her industrial success.

The city's expansion was extraordinarily rapid, comparable to
the fastest-growing industrial towns in America. By 1847 there were
thirty-three factories spinning wool, thirty-five spinning silk, twenty-
two calico printers and seventeen chemical manufactories. The rapid
industrialisation reinforced the strong British links to Berlin that had
been evident during the coalitions against Napoleon. In 1816 the
Imperial Continental Gas Association of London installed the first
gasworks, which came with a twenty-one-year licence to provide
gas for the new streetlamps that started to appear in the 1820s, the

first set being installed on the Unter den Linden. British technology
and investment would also play a major part in modernising Berlin's
heavy industry. By 1830 the Cockerill brothers had fifteen steam
engines operating, running both woollen and paper mills. British
steamships started to operate on Berlin's waterways. Seventeen
steam vessels were operating by the mid-1840s, slowly replacing the
old barges powered by sail or towed by horses along the towpaths.
A steamboat service was introduced down the Elbe to Hamburg, a
journey that could now be made in a day. Another English company
introduced piped drinking water, though a universal sewer system
would not arrive until the 1870s.

The most significant change, however, came with the introduction of the railways. Berlin owed its early prosperity to its network
of waterways; now it would become the centre of the burgeoning German rail network. The first railway ran from Berlin to
Zehlendorf and then to Potsdam. It had six locomotives, which,
along with all the track, were built in England, but this was about
to change. One of the most impressive stories of the industrial revolution in Berlin is that of August Borsig, a carpenter from Breslau,
who had studied in Berlin and then worked with a British engineer
in his iron foundry. In 1837 Borsig left to start his own factory on
the Chausseestraße, where he first made plant for sugar refining but
subsequently switched to building locomotives. His first engine was
operational by 1840 and soon proved to be faster than a British one
built by George Stephenson. By 1844 he had twenty-four working on
three new railway lines. By the time he died in 1854 the 500th Borsig
locomotive rolled off his production lines and he was the major sup-
plier to the 3,400 miles of railway that had been laid in just twelve
years. More than 2,000 workers laboured in his factories. They were
well looked after with a sickness and an education fund, and the
business continued to grow after his death until it became the largest locomotive manufacturer in Europe. Borsig became immensely
rich, built himself a suitably luxurious house in Moabit and was
awarded the rank of *Geheimer Commerzienrat* (Commercial Privy
Councillor), a singular honour in a Prussian society still obsessed

with rank and title. A restless, driven man of extraordinary talent, possessed of much of the German soul, Borsig would stage traditional festivals to celebrate production milestones.

The old customs wall was still standing when the early stations were built. It would be demolished in the 1850s and 1860s once it was apparent it was restricting the city's expansion, but the original stations – the Potsdamer, Anhalter, Stettiner and Hamburger stations – had to be built outside it so that the lines they served were terminated. Berlin thus became a hub so that, as the rail network spread across Prussia, it would always be at its centre. In 1860 Berlin got its first *Stadt Bahn*, the overground city railway (later called the S-Bahn), which replaced the old horse-drawn buses and started to link the several termini.

Caring as Borsig may have been, significant problems arose as the new industries pulled in a huge number of immigrants, and the speed with which they arrived overwhelmed Berlin's existing infrastructure. There was insufficient housing, a lack of clean water, inadequate schools and hospitals, and many of Borsig's contemporaries were not as considerate as he was in providing care for their employees. As migrants arrived from Poland and Silesia, and increasingly from the further reaches of the Austrian empire, they had nowhere to live but in miserable shanty towns that grew up outside the wall and where disease, especially cholera, was quick to take hold. Berlin suffered bad cholera outbreaks in 1831 (the epidemic that killed Hegel) and 1866.

While the city that had celebrated their defeat of Napoleon so enthusiastically just twenty-five years earlier had been a mostly coherent and well-administered entity, with the majority of people adequately fed and in work, by 1840 Berlin offered an unappealing vision of life in two different worlds. In the centre, within the wall, was a comfortable and civilised existence with broad streets, good houses, coffee houses, shops, concerts and security, but on the outskirts, and particularly in the east where, unlike in the west which was protected by the Grunewald and the Tiergarten, migrant workers lived miserable lives. They had little shelter, no medical care and not much food, working in the increasing number of factories and not earning enough to feed their families. The problem was that they had little bargaining power, since the constant flow of immigrants meant there were always others wanting their meagre wages. The extreme part of this underclass was estimated to consist of '10,000 prostitutes, 12,000 criminals, 12,000 barge people, 18,000 serving maids and 20,000 weavers who cannot make ends meet through their work, 6,000 receivers of alms, 6,000 poor invalids, 3–4,000 beggars, 2,000 prisoners in jails, 2,000 illegitimate children, 2,000 children in care, 1,500 orphans,' and the list goes on – and these were the ones who were known about.[4] By 1843, wrote Gustav Kühne, 'street life has become louder, the middle class more lively. Luxury and opulence have risen but so has the misery that burrows and digs deep into the lower classes. The two classes now face each other, further and further apart. There is more aristocracy versus the mob, more perfumed haughtiness and more naked crime'.[5] A new Berlin was emerging.

Many of these poor were also wounded veterans, young men who had been badly disabled in the war and who now had to scrape a living on the streets. There was a famous ditty by a man called Fritz Werkmann who had lost both his legs at the Battle of Leipzig, where he had been awarded the Iron Cross, and who crawled around the Gendarmenmarkt on his stumps, his medals on his chest. He annoyed passing officers by singing a popular army song called 'I am a Prussian! Do you recognise my colours?' and a song he had composed himself that went something along the lines of:

> In the war that has just ended
> Both my legs were shaved away,
> But my manly chest was garnished
> By my king by way of pay.
>
> And he said 'My dearest Fritze,
> So that you may live at ease,
> We will grant a further favour:
> Crank an organ in the streets'.

So through the king's great mercy
I make a penny for a song,
Oh, it is too short for living,
And for dying it's too long.

Therefore this old freedom fighter
Lives today to do his thing,
Standing proudly to attention
Calling 'Three cheers for our king?'[6]

Various less sympathetic officers complained and Werkmann's licence to perform was withdrawn. Facing starvation, he tried to take his own life, but outraged Berliners started to raise money for him and installed him as a publican in Artelleriestraße.

Starvation was never far away from all Berlin's poor, and it is estimated that industrial workers had to spend 70 per cent of their wages on food. The staple and most affordable food was the potato, originally introduced by The Great Elector as a garden ornament and a delicacy, which now became the staple diet of the urban as well as the rural poor; although Berlin was rapidly industrialising, 70 per cent of Prussians in 1840 still lived off the land. Then in the 1840s the potato crop began to fail across Europe, the same outbreak that would eventually cause the terrible famine in Ireland. In 1847 there was a bad outbreak of potato blight, leading to starvation in Silesia and a subsequent outbreak of typhus fever; 16,000 died there. That year 400,000 peasants left the eastern provinces of Prussia. Many emigrated altogether but a significant number joined the already overflowing shanty towns around Berlin, where the workers found their food supply had virtually disappeared. In 1847 there were violent protests and rioting when starving workers charged food stalls in the city. These were put down by the still enormous military garrison (20,000 in the city alone with more in Potsdam) in the so-called Potato War. It was no wonder that Marx found more than adequate evidence on which to develop the social theories of his 1847 *Communist Manifesto*. Berlin, where the sale of indulgences had pushed Luther into launching the Reformation 300 years earlier, now gave rise to the second great social revolution in Europe: Marxism.

These twin revolutionary forces, of nationalism and social deprivation, combined to cause Berlin's second violent revolution. It would prove to be no more successful than the first but it was targeted at a similar perceived abuse of absolute power. Frederick William III died in 1840, actually mourned by many Berliners who felt that, though he may have deserted them in 1806, he had at least suffered with them under the occupation. He had also, after Queen Luise's death, married the attractive Auguste von Harrach, whom he had met in a spa in Bohemia. She was a Catholic so the marriage was kept quiet but in 1826 she became a Protestant and came to be liked and respected in the city.

His successor was his forty-five-year-old son, yet another Frederick William, who now became Frederick William IV. Bismarck would observe in his memoirs that the Hohenzollerns alternated between puritanism and a love of display. Whereas his father had been shy, almost taciturn, Frederick William IV definitely belonged to Bismarck's latter category. It was he who introduced to the Prussian army the *pickelhaube*, the famous but totally impractical spiked helmet that would become such an item of both status and ridicule. He is sometimes referred to as 'The Romantic' and he began his reign by making conciliatory gestures, with talk of a Diet and sacking the hated Berlin police chief, Karl Albert von Kamptz. Yet his mind was on other things. The Berliners nicknamed him Fatty Flounder. He would leave Berlin an important legacy in that he was the originator of developing 'the entire Spree island behind the museum [Schinkel's Altes Museum] into a sanctuary of the arts and sciences', yet he was not a reformer and neither he nor his government appreciated the pressures that were building in Berlin. Control remained with his hard-line advisers – men like von Gerlach and von Rochow – who saw pressure for reform as an attack on the sacred twin pillars of monarchy and Pietism.

In 1843 the composer and writer Bettina von Arnim published

Dies Buch Gehört dem König (This Book Belongs to the King), an attack on the government's complacency in tackling Berlin's growing social problems. She directly blamed the King's government. She included as an annex a report by a Swiss student who had lived in the slums of the area to the north of Berlin called the Vogtland, so called because many of its immigrants had come from the Vogtland in Southern Germany. His graphic account of the misery and abject poverty in which so many of its people survived gave the book its impact. The artist Heinrich Zille described his family's arrival in a Mietskaserne, one of Berlin's infamous apartment blocks, as a child: 'On the walls torn wallpaper, dirty contours, where a bed and furniture had been standing, looking almost like a pattern. In one corner a pile of straw, that was meant to be our bed'.[7]

Von Arnim was one of the Berlin glitterati. Born into a family of successful Italian merchants, she had married the romantic poet Achim von Arnim. Her brother was also a well-known composer and her brother-in-law was Friedrich Carl von Savigny, professor of law at Berlin University and a respected jurist after whom Berlin's Savignyplatz is named. She numbered Goethe (although she had a blistering row with Goethe's wife), Beethoven and Liszt among her friends as well as the King. She had worked in the slums during the 1831 cholera epidemic and emerged deeply shocked at just how quickly and far Berlin had fallen. Consequently, she represented not just the old Prussian aristocracy – there have been almost as many von Arnim Prussian generals as von Kleists – but also the intellectual world that centred around the university. She was not alone and in the aftermath of the 1830 revolution in Paris (which caused no direct reaction in Berlin), other writers and satirists began to join the call for reform. The Prussian establishment, closely grouped around the court and reliant on the acquiescence of the Berlin middle classes, were infuriated by men like Adolf Glassbrenner who wrote witty poems attacking the establishment like 'Logical Proof of the Necessity for Servants of the State'. One of his funniest was 'Lieutenants of the Guard':

Were there no Lieutenants of the Guard
There would be no honour;
Were there no honour –
How could dishonour ever be wiped out in blood?
If it could not be wiped out in blood,
There would be no challenges or duels;
But there must be challenges and duels so
There must always be Lieutenants of the Guard.[8]

The revolution, if it can be called that, came in 1848 as a result of a European-wide slump as the early gains from the industrial revolution wore off, creating unemployment in the towns that had rapidly industrialised. In January there had been a revolt in Sicily that was hardly noticed but in February Paris rose and the French monarchy was overthrown, being replaced by a republic, led (in what should perhaps have been a warning to Berlin) by Napoleon's nephew, Louis Napoleon. News from Paris was eagerly devoured in Berlin's coffee shops, and 'never were the restaurants, the pastry shops, the coffee shops so overcrowded as in those days. There was a real scarcity of news from Paris. As soon as a new paper came in whoever had it was forced to read it aloud so everyone else could hear. As soon as he had finished there was a lively debate.'[9] Then on 13 March Vienna rose, causing Metternich to flee, much to the satisfaction of Berliners who saw him as representing the arch-conservative forces that opposed both political reform and German nationalism. The same day troops charged a group of demonstrators returning from a peaceful protest in an area known as the Tents, where people could buy food and drink when walking in the Tiergarten, and which had become an unofficial rostrum for the reformers. The teenaged Carl Ludwig Zeitler had been in the habit of attending these speeches with his father, a cotton weaver, on Sunday mornings and noted how it was 'very strange, as the streets were cleared, to see the cavalry pressing forward, pushing the crowd back'.[10] The government, now thoroughly alarmed, published an order that 'parents, teachers and masters are to keep back their children, pupils and servants. The owners of factories are obliged to prevent their workers and apprentices from leaving their workshops.'[11]

In the face of this unrest, on 17 March Frederick William IV decided to call a Diet to draft reforms, although on the same day he also appointed Karl Ludwig von Prittwitz, the hard-line Colonel of the Life Guards, as commander of Berlin garrison. Berliners gathered on the Schloßplatz on 18 March to hear the King make a speech from the Schloss balcony in which he promised a draft constitution and to relax censorship. This all seemed to start quite well, with the crowd cheering the King, but then they began to object to the strong military presence that flanked them from the Lustgarten. Chanting for the soldiers to be removed caused von Prittwitz to order his soldiers to start clearing the square. The cavalry moved forward slowly but the crowd panicked, and the soldiers – unused to dealing with civil unrest – overreacted. One group of demonstrators was forced back by Major von Falkenstein's squadron into Breite Straße while a second group was forced over the Schloßbrucke into the Unter den Linden. The crowd started to form barricades, the first being in Friedrichstraße where they commandeered poor 'Mother Schmiddecke's fruit stall'[12] and another on the corner of Oberwallstraße and Jägerstraße. By the time the fighting stopped that evening the centre of Berlin was barricaded off and 230 people had been killed – mostly, but not all, civilians.

The events of 18 March were a muddle as much for the army as they were for the protesters. There was certainly some planning on the part of the latter. Zeitler was told by his school headmaster at 10.30 a.m. to 'Go home quickly, it's going to start today'. Zeitler was then sent by his mother to fetch his brother and to take lunch to his father in his shop, which involved crossing the Schloßplatz. He remembered seeing Frederick William, who 'stood, with his head covered, on the balcony above the first gate into the castle, having just addressed the group of citizens and officials, about 50 people who just wanted to thank their king ... but I saw that the square had been cleared from the jousting pitch out by a military column that stretched across the whole square'. Zeitler darted for cover, hiding in a doorway where

Breite Straße meets the Schloßplatz. The soldiers came right past him, and as they did so he saw two in the front rank knock their rifles against the pavement, Breite Straße having an elevated curb, so they went off accidentally. 'The soldiers looked as if they had been paralysed by the two shots. I heard the command "Stop" and saw an officer behind the front rank approaching the two soldiers' but those two accidental shots were 'the beginnings of the March revolution'.

Zeitler, who was now stuck in the centre of the action, recorded afterwards that most of the shooting only took place later that afternoon and evening and was at its worst when the 8th Infantry Regiment arrived from Frankfurt, storming up from the Frankfurter Tor to the Alexanderplatz. 'Most of those wounded or shot dead were just curious or shot by chance,' he recorded. 'A shoemaker was shot, having just come out of his shop at 26 Prenzlauer Straße in his leathers, wanting to see what was going on. He'd been shot the very moment he looked around the corner, wanting to see the Königsbrücke, which was occupied by soldiers. His wife held him tightly in her lap. She too was shot.'

Some soldiers lost control. Private Schadewinckel, having had his colleague shot beside him from behind the barricade in Breitstraße, admitted that he got into a 'state of agitation such as I have never been in before' and that he and his troop rushed into the neighbouring houses 'cutting down anyone who resisted'.[13] Most senior officers were out of their depth and unsure how to react. Alfred von Waldersee was a sixteen-year-old army cadet in the cadet school that day. His superiors, General von Below and Colonel Richter, were 'feeble old men – all elderly and most had taken part in the Wars of Liberation'. They could not make up their minds so von Waldersee and his fellow cadets decided that their honour demanded they defend the cadet school against the rioters until they realised that they had no ammunition for their rifles. On 19 March they were marched off to the Berliner Schloss. In the Königstraße 'most of the windows in the street were broken and all the houses showed marks of bullets' but they were relieved when on arrival they were ushered into the Schloss courtyard and given cups of coffee.[14]

The reason that young von Walderseee and his colleagues were stood down was because the King (against the strong advice of von Prittwitz and the hawks led by his brother Prince William, the Crown Prince – as Frederick William did not have any children – who wanted to bring up artillery to bombard the city) had now agreed to withdraw the troops to Potsdam. He distributed a letter to the city addressed to 'My Dear Berliners' in which he promised that the troops would be restricted to a few barracks. On 19 March he returned to the balcony of the Berliner Schloss to stand in respectful silence as the bodies of those killed the day before were paraded through the Schloßplatz. On 21 March he even marched behind the black, red and gold flag of the nationalist movement to the university, where he made another speech saying how much he regretted the loss of life of his beloved Berliners. Later he and his chief ministers also stood with bowed heads – again wearing black, red and gold sashes – as the funeral march for those killed processed through the city to their ceremonial interment in Friedrichshain cemetery. There was an immediate craze for black-red-gold. 'There were black-red-gold watch straps, tassels for walking sticks, notebooks, cigar cases, handkerchiefs, even gun stands. Everyone was expected to wear at least something even if it was only a cockade in their hat. In Rosenthalerstraße an enterprising tobacco shop gave away cockades when you bought cigars.'[15] Prince William became a popular hate figure and could not appear in public. He went into exile in England while the King went to Potsdam to explain his decision to an incredulous group of army commanders who banged their sword scabbards on the floor, about as close as the Prussian army would ever get to disagreeing with the sovereign.

Apart from what many perceive as an unlikely alliance between the nationalists and the socialists, what equally surprised about the 1848 uprising is that Berliners participated at all. This was not a revolt by the dispossessed but rather a middle-class protest led and supported by the very people who were assumed to be comfortable in their Biedermeieresque world, loyal to the Crown and exhibiting that peculiarly Prussian quality of obedience to authority. Many were like this – and they strongly disapproved of the revolt – but there were enough infused with the spirit of *Berlin Unwille* to take to the barricades. 'The locksmith journeymen Glaswaldt and Zinna,' for example, who 'defended a barricade on Jägerstraße. When a platoon of infantry approached from the direction of Friedrichstraße, Glaswaldt fought them off with an ancient rifle until he was hit by a bullet. Then Zinna, armed only with a rusty sabre, attacked the platoon alone, injured its officer; and then used paving stones against the soldiers until he was hit. He subsequently died of his wounds.'[16]

Zeitler saw his very tall headmaster, Herr Herter, 'arrest' the equally tall General von Möllendorf, who had gone 'all alone from the bridge to the Alexander Barracks' to negotiate with the rebels, and then take him away in a water cart. During the Napoleonic Wars the *Unwille* had been directed against the hated French; now, and for the coming decades, it would be directed at securing the democratic freedoms that Berliners saw as their right. Yet it was also an opportunity for Berliners to show how angry they were about the government's generally rather petty regulations. 'Dissatisfaction had become quite general among people in the pre-March period,' Zeitler added, 'and was fuelled by the foolish, arbitrary behaviour of the police, against whose abuses there was no justice.' One of the things that annoyed Berliners most was the rule against smoking in the street. Zeitler saw 'a man looking out of his window with a burning cigar in his mouth and who had that cigar ripped from his mouth'. He 'was then struck by the gendarmes. In addition, he had to pay a fine of two thalers as he had smoked on the street.' The result was that there were a series of 'smoking areas' just outside the city gates, where tobacco touts would do a good trade with those leaving the city desperate for a smoke.

For Zeitler, one of the main benefits of the March 'uprising' was that he and his friends managed to collect enough discarded gunpowder to make fireworks all summer. More seriously, the initial result seemed promising politically for the reformers. A tri-cameral assembly was duly established in Berlin and debated fairly inconsequentially that summer. Two prime ministers were appointed in succession. The second, von Pfuel, von Prittwitz's predecessor but less keen on bringing up the artillery, and a candidate who seemed capable of uniting the conservatives and the reformers, proved unable to reconcile the opposing factions. The fall of the assembly was sudden. To replace Pfuel, Frederick William appointed the hard-liner Friedrich Wilhelm von Brandenburg. On 9 November he told the assembly it was being prorogued. Directly after his announcement, and while the deputies were debating what they had just been told, General Friedrich von Wrangel, the new Military Governor of Berlin, and already something of a military hero, entered the city with 13,000 troops. Marching into the Gendarmenmarkt, where the assembly had been meeting, he instructed them to clear their building. They refused. Wrangel sat down on a chair outside Schinkel's Schauspielhaus where they met. A delegation from the assembly came out to tell him that they would 'only yield to superior force'. Wrangel smiled and replied, 'Superior force has arrived,' and he gave them fifteen minutes to get out, which they duly did. Martial law was proclaimed across the city, and the assembly was formally dissolved in December.[17] 'Papa' Wrangel himself entered Berlin legend – hated by the reformers but loved by the reactionaries. He remained military governor of Berlin until his death aged ninety-three in 1877, the embodiment of the Prussian army's power in the capital. He lived in a *schlösschen* (little castle or manor house), a handsome four-square classical house in Steglitz. It still stands today, known as *Das Wrangelschlösschen*, and can be hired out for parties, although what Wrangel's ghost may think about that is not clear.

Brave and inspired as Frederick William's actions in appealing to Berliners for calm may have been, his subsequent moves proved that whatever his personal feelings, his government was firmly under the control of the reactionary faction backed by the army, who felt that the events of the last months of 1848 had vindicated their position. There is a famous cartoon, *Zwischen mich und mein Volk soll sich kein Stück Papier drängen* (a piece of paper shall not come between me and my people), showing the reformers pushing at a door held shut by the portly King so they could present a petition. The King

in turn is being pushed from behind by a Prussian soldier in his new
pickelhaube, and between them they are keeping the door firmly
closed.[18] A new parliament was called but soon dismissed for voting
against the King. It was replaced by another bi-cameral assembly
in 1850 under a new constitution that gave the vote to all adult
men (but only for their own 'class' as determined by income, and
not to women) and included an aristocratic hereditary *Herrenhaus*
not unlike the British House of Lords. Slowly this new parliament
began to assert itself so that, by the time the government wanted it
to pass army reforms in the early 1860s, it was at least temporarily
able to refuse to do so. Another change was that the King himself
became increasingly divorced from daily politics, relying instead on a
Minister President, the first being from another of those great Junker
military dynasties, Otto von Manteuffel.

While these political storms were raging, the city itself still had to
come to terms with its extraordinarily rapid growth and the misery
and deprivation associated with it. It would – in common with so
many other cities that have a high level of immigration – remain a
city with a disproportionate number of poor and underprivileged
residents well into the twentieth century; even in 1900, 60 per
cent of Berlin's population were either first- or second-generation
immigrants. Gradually, however, during the middle decades of
the century, things would slowly improve and while the events of
March 1848 may have been unsuccessful in securing lasting political
change, they did at least draw attention to the terrible social conditions that so many Berliners endured.

The first requirement was for housing. The city that witnessed the
1848 uprising was essentially the old medieval area, centred on the
island and dominated by the Berliner Schloss, with the eighteenth-
century developments of Friedrichswerder, Friedrichstadt and
Dorotheenstadt, all within the Excise Wall that was in the process of
being demolished. This was the area beautified by Knobelsdorff and
Schinkel, up against which new developments were now pressing.
The Scheunenviertel – the original barn quarter where Berliners had
kept their animals – had become the Jewish Quarter after Frederick

William I had ordered them to live there, while mass immigration had led to sprawling development and a mixture of more upmarket homes in the west, particularly around the Tiergarten. To the east the shanty towns stretched out to Prenzlauer Berg in the north-east and to Friedrichshain and to Kreuzberg in the south-east. Moabit and the area north of the Spree was where the majority of the new factories were being built, while Charlottenburg, Tempelhof, Pankow and Schöneberg remained villages, albeit villages that would very soon be swallowed up. The man given responsibility for drawing up the plan for this was a surveyor called James Holbrecht who worked in the Royal Urban Planning Directorate. There had been previous attempts at a comprehensive plan for the city. In 1840 Frederick William IV had commissioned the landscape architect and garden designer Peter Joseph Lenné to prepare one, but not much had come of it. Holbrecht's brief was more expansive. He was to look at the city between the Customs Wall and the newly built S-Bahn ring. The plan he subsequently produced between 1858 and 1862 envisaged Berlin growing to between 1.5 and 2 million people. He advised the development of the areas within what became known as the Wilhelmine Ring, so that places like Wedding, Gesundbrunnen and Neukölln would also become part of the city. It was an imaginative and futuristic plan, but one that would soon be questioned because of how Holbrecht advised the developments should be carried out.

The actual layout of the new districts was to be with wide streets radiating from central points – similar to Frederick William I's original plans for Friedrichstadt – but what was controversial was the actual housing design Holbrecht envisaged. This was to build the infamous Berlin *Mietskaserne* (the rental 'barracks' or rather apartment blocks), which maximised the use of all available space and were reputed to take their name from the army barracks that Frederick the Great had built. The actual street frontage of the blocks was quite small, but each block was then to be built stretching back from the street around a series of courtyards, typically two or three but sometimes up to six. The regulation was that no block could be higher than 20 metres and each courtyard had to be a minimum of

5.34 metres square to allow a fire engine to reach the upper storeys and to turn, but otherwise developers had a free hand to cram in as many rooms as they could. The model saw the front, street-facing apartments being the more expensive ones, to be rented by the well-off, whereas the poor were forced further back without sunlight or ventilation.

Holbrecht's plan divided opinion. Many thought he had simply pandered to building developers, enabling them to maximise the number of families they could squeeze into each square metre and hence their profits; by 1910 the typical block housed seventy-six people, the highest concentration of people per square metre in Europe.[19] There was no attempt to provide decent and affordable working-class accommodation (as other European cities were considering), providing there was enough space to cram in the human fodder demanded by the rapidly industrialising city. The Mietskaserne were blamed for every social problem, the rapid spread of disease and were said to have exacerbated the vicious street fighting that would come in the 1920s. There was, however, an alternative view. The concept was a departure from the social norm where rich families lived in one neighbourhood and poor families in a less salubrious one. This certainly still happened in Berlin, but it was less marked than in London or Paris because the Mietskaserne principle lodged families from different income brackets in the same block. This meant that rich and poor families saw each other on a daily basis and their children inevitably played together. Consequently, a Mietskaserne block could develop its own sense of community. To be fair to Holbrecht, this is certainly what he envisaged, talking about 'Old Shoemaker Wilhelm in the attic' and 'Bedridden Mistress Schultz in the backyard tenement' being brought meals and warm clothing by their neighbours, and of the children from the basement flat walking along the same passages to their free school beside the children from the richer families en route to their grammar school. Many Berliners who have spent their lives in Mietskaserne would agree but others can say nothing good about them. Another side effect was to continue the Berlin tradition of families renting rather than owning their own property, something that continues today not just in Berlin but across Germany. Landlords were reluctant to break up blocks by allowing people to buy freeholds, so that the housing model was and is one based on renting. Whatever Berliners' views of living in them, the Mietskaserne have given Berlin much of its physical and spiritual character. From the outside, many of the blocks owed much to Schinkel, who had died only in 1842, with their restrained, classical facades.

Holbrecht's plan also led to the start of development in the villages around Berlin. In practice, several were already in that state of curious half-development – part old village centre and part suburb – but between 1860 and 1900 those within the Wilhelmine Ring became totally urbanised. Local farmers suddenly found themselves rich as developers were prepared to pay inflated prices for building plots, and due to the speed of development several were swallowed up more or less whole, which has led to the rather nice legacy of finding old village churches, mills and medieval houses within Berlin's outskirts. You can, for example, still make out the centres of the Wendish villages of Buckow (named after the Polabian for a beech tree) and Rudow, both now part of Neukölln and which have kept much of their charm, their churches and a mill. This rapid expansion also had another distinct legacy in that it has given Berliners a very strong sense of locality. Admittedly this exists in many large cities, but it was and still is particularly pronounced in a Berlin that was struggling to maintain its identity in the face of this period of mass building. This sense applied at a very local street level, where people, mostly men, would gather in their *Kneipen,* the small bars whose character so identified a street or square, to a whole neighbourhood. For a city that is today one of the easiest and most convenient in Europe to get around, Berliners are still often reluctant to move far from their neighbourhoods.

Housing would, however, remain a major problem in that the supply simply could not keep up with the demands of a population increasing by mid-century faster than in any other city in Europe. One solution was simply to overcrowd what rooms there were,

multiplying the public health risk. There was another cholera outbreak in 1868 and a smallpox epidemic in 1871 in which 6,478 died.
It was estimated that 5 per cent of the population were permanently
infected with venereal disease, a common result of how close people
were forced to live, but the biggest killer, given the poor air and
insanitary conditions, was tuberculosis, which accounted for 15
per cent of all fatalities in 1860.[20] The two half-yearly rent collection days, on 1 April and 1 October, were marked by large crowds
on the streets, turned out of their rooms, unable to pay their rent,
and wandering hopelessly in search of alternative accommodation.
Some ended up as *Schlafleute*, who hot-bedded where they could,
or others as *Trockenwohner*, who camped in new buildings as the
plaster dried.

Another significant development was in the canal system. Visitors
to Berlin may be forgiven for finding the city's waterways confusing:
water and bridges are seemingly everywhere and it is not immediately clear where they all flow or how they link up. The Oder-Spree
canal, completed by von Jena for The Great Elector, was enhanced
in 1845 by the digging of the Landwehrkanal. This joined the main
western river port on the Spree (the Westhafen) and the eastern port
(the Osthafen), thus avoiding the city centre so that river traffic
could pass quickly down to the Havel without negotiating the Spree's
narrow central stretches. Designed by Lenné, it ran for 10 kilometres
south of the central districts, cutting through the Tiergarten, where
it went through a lock, then via Kreuzberg to rejoin the river in
Friedrichshain. Now rather an attractive part of Berlin's life rather
than an economic artery, at the time it made a major difference
to shipping times. Lenné also designed the Hohenzollernkanal,
which created a direct link from the Westhafen to the Havel above
Spandau, thus making a quick link to the Oder. In 1848 he started
work on the short Charlottenburger Verbindungskanal, which
linked the Spree to the Hohenzollernkanal. Lastly he completed the
Luisenstadtkanal, which joined the Landwehrkanal and the Spree
by cutting through the city centre. This last one was hardly used and
was filled in during the 1920s.

Berlin also remained a city of barracks and military exercise areas. The Prussian army retained substantial garrisons at Potsdam, home to the Royal Guard and the King's Household Troops, and at Spandau. Despite Frederick William IV's assurances to the mob in 1848, when Wrangel returned with his troops they intended to stay and so nineteenth-century Berlin was as full of soldiers as it had ever been. Military parades along the Unter den Linden, and Changing the Guard at the Berliner Schloss were popular spectacles, even after the violence, but the difference now was that the soldiers were nearly all accommodated in barracks scattered across the city, many of which are still clearly visible even after wartime damage. There were also large training areas close to the city centre. The biggest was at Tempelhof, over 385 hectares, and the Tiergarten was also regularly used. Another substantial area was the Artillerie Feld, which stretched west of Heidestraße, beyond the Invalidenhof, towards Moabit. Today it is the Fritz-Schloss-Sportpark; probably few of those who now play football there realise how many generations of Prussian soldiers were drilled where they kick their balls.

Yet, increasingly, control in Berlin was passing from the army to the police. There had been a rather abortive attempt after March 1848 to set up a citizens' police force, the *Bürgherwehr* (literally the citizen force), but it had distinguished itself by laying down strict rules as to how little its citizen members should be expected to do, how they were not to be disturbed if off duty at home and how they should only be expected to wear uniform when in public. It had failed to prevent a major arms raid on the Zeughaus on 14 June 1848 and had spectacularly failed to appear when Wrangel had occupied the Gendarmenmarkt. Then in early 1849 a remarkable man, Karl Ludwig von Hinckeldey, was appointed as the city's police chief. The Burgherwehr were smartly reorganised and put into a military-style uniform complete with helmets. Von Hinckeldey had wide powers. As well as being responsible for law and order, he also licensed businesses, issued passports and could overrule the city council – something he had frequent recourse to do. He introduced a fire service, contracted a British company to lay a network of water pipes and fire hydrants, and also regulated the removal of human waste and rubbish; as late as 1900 only 8 per cent of Berlin houses had a loo. Yet Hinckeldey is probably best remembered for the *Litfaß* pillars, a Berlin institution still as much in use today as it was when he first introduced it. Annoyed by both the provocation and untidiness of the multiple posters plastered all over the city in 1848, Hinckeldey awarded a monopoly contract to Ernst Litfaß to erect 150 pillars around the city and the sole right to print and display posters on them; all other posters were banned. Known as *Dicke Damen* (fat ladies), their squat pillars are still in regular use today, having made the Litfaß family a large fortune.

One area where Hinckeldey failed to make an impression was in controlling duelling, which had become established as part of the honour code among the Junkers and army officers. Although it was lampooned by men like Glassbrenner, settling arguments, often about petty and irrelevant issues, by fighting with swords or pistols was ingrained in several of the older German universities whose student societies, the *corps*, made it a ritual. It was also ingrained in the army and condoned by both senior officers and the court. Having a duelling scar, preferably on one's face, was a mark of distinction. The problem was that this rather outdated concept of 'honour', which greatly appealed to the romantics, had become so widespread that it included even the most senior officials.

A quick look at the membership of the grander student corps, like the Borussian at Bonn, showed that it included many of the German royal families as well as senior ministers and officials – from the future Kaiser Wilhelm II to Bismarck. One of Berlin's most liberal and progressive mayors, and founder of the Progress Party, Max von Forckenbeck, was a member of the Corps Teutonia when he was at university in Giessen. General Edwin von Manteuffel, a cousin of the Minister President Otto von Manteuffel, wounded the liberal journalist Karl Twesten because he had insulted him in a pamphlet, which must have discouraged other journalists to follow suit. Karl Marx even fought a duel, and von Hinckeldey – one of the ablest public servants in Berlin – was challenged by a Junker whom he had upset by closing down his gambling den. One of his officials, Herr Nörner, tried to stop him but von Hinckeldey answered with the rather arrogant comment, 'Nörner, you don't understand these things.' They fought in the Jungfernheide park and 'an hour later he was dead'.[21] Berlin was soon to lose another of its great reformers in the same way. There is rather a nice memorial to von Hinckeldey in the Jungfernheide, a simple cross near the site of his death.

One community who benefited from the more liberal attitudes prevailing in the city were the Jews. One of Hardenberg's reforms had been to pass a Jewish Emancipation Edict in 1812, putting an end to the old practice of the city's Jews having to apply for a *Schutzjudenschaft* that made them subject to particular and restrictive measures. These included, for example, Frederick the Great's peculiarly discriminatory requirement that they buy a certain amount of porcelain from the state porcelain works. Hardenberg's action effectively made all Jews Prussian citizens and allowed them to serve in the army. There had been a significant Jewish response to the call to arms in 1813, with Jews commissioned as officers for the first time – something that would have had *Alte Fritz*, Old Frederick the Great, turning in his grave.

Already well established in commerce and playing a very full role in Berlin's cultural life through the salons of hostesses like Henriette Herz and through families like the Mendelssohns, the 10,000-strong Berlin Jewish community was beginning to feel that, possibly for the first time, they were both secure and valued. They tended no longer to see themselves as being defined by their Jewishness, as a community who huddled together for protection in a Prussian city, but rather as Prussians who happened to have a different faith. More than half the men worked in banking or commerce, and men like Joseph Liebermann took full advantage of the industrial revolution when it came. His textile works, pioneering new techniques, became the most successful in the city. He was known universally as *Der Liebermann* and, like Borsig, was paid the particular honour of being made a *Kommerzienrat*. Nearly half those honoured with this title in Berlin by the end of the century were Jews – Goldschmidts,

Meyers and Reichenbeims as well as Liebermann – a far higher percentage than in the rest of Prussia.[22]

However, there was still a strong undercurrent of anti-Semitism within Berlin's intellectual circles, in the military and on the streets. There was not, for example, a single Jew in the city administration prior to 1848, and even Achim von Arnim – poet and husband of the more famous Bettina – excluded 'all Jews, Frenchmen, Philistines and women' from membership of his intellectual Table Society.[23] Meno Burg, the most senior Jewish officer who served against Napoleon, never got promoted past Lieutenant, which he correctly put down to his refusal to convert. In September 1850 the composer Richard Wagner published his *Judaism in Music*, which was a bitter, almost hysterical polemic against German Jews. 'It is necessary for us to explain the involuntary repugnance we possess for the nature and personality of the Jews,' he wrote in a sad piece that would later have such an influence on the Nazis.[24]

It is therefore not surprising that there was a strong Jewish element manning the barricades of 1848 and Jewish names among the dead. The 1850 constitution did guarantee Jews full rights as citizens – a situation that would last until 1918, or effectively until the coming of the Nazis – but anti-Semitism remained prevalent among large parts of Berlin society.[25] Yet one very visible sign of the Jewish community's position was the opening on 5 September 1866 of the *Neue Synagogue* on Oranienburgerstraße. This was a large synagogue, with space for 3,000 worshippers, and it made a clear and very noticeable statement of emancipation and of confidence in the future of the Jewish community in the city. It was designed by Eduard Knoblauch and Friedrich August Stüler, who used an obviously Moorish style, a large dome, minarets and an interior modelled on the Alhambra. Ruined by the Nazis on Kristallnacht in 1938, it has been partially restored since 1989 and today the front looks much as it must have done when it was opened, though the building behind was too badly damaged to be reused.

Another major Berlin landmark completed around the same time, and also badly damaged in the Second World War but now fully restored, was the striking Rote Rathaus (red town hall), which occupies the same position on the south-east side of the Alexanderplatz as the old Berlin City Council. When Berlin and Cölln had merged their administrations in 1307 their joint town hall, on the Lange Brücke, had been painted red and so the idea of a 'red' town hall was part of Berlin's cult, but this new building was of typical Berlin brick so was very red indeed. Then, as Berlin became more and more socialist, it would also earn its name from its politics. The 1808 council that Napoleon had instituted was one of the few enduring legacies of the French occupation although the 1850 amendments to its constitution, which restricted the eligible franchise to those with an income of 1,200 marks, and the imposition of a tri-cameral system at the same time as it was applied to Prussia as a whole, meant that it was not exactly a democratic body. The power of officials like von Hinckeldey to override its decisions was also somewhat limiting. Nevertheless, the administration of the rapidly expanding city required rehousing. Designed by Hermann Friedrich Waesemann, based on an original concept by Schinckel, and completed in 1869, the Rote Rathaus has its supporters but also many detractors. It was, however, in itself a statement of how Berlin saw itself post-1848. Built in a very different style to the Berliner Schloss and its surrounding buildings, more like a *municipo* in an Italian city state, and with a tall tower facing the Schloßplatz, it was as strong a statement of civic autonomy as the new synagogue was of the Jewish community. One of its treasures, which is difficult to get access to, is a terracotta frieze that runs around the whole building depicting scenes from Berlin's history.

~

In 1861 Frederick William died. His successor was his brother, the hard-line Crown Prince William, who became King William I. A more considered king than the 'shrapnel prince' who had advocated shelling the mob on the Schloßplatz in 1848, he was also that small boy who had stood holding his mother's hand on the riverbank at Tilsit fifty-five years earlier as Napoleon had ritually humiliated

Prussia and the Hohenzollerns. In 1862 his War Minister, von Roon, persuaded him to appoint Otto von Bismarck as his Minister President. Bismarck is commonly characterised as a Prussian Junker of the old school, usually in uniform, making speeches about blood and iron, and as the man who enabled a militaristic Germany that invaded France three times in seventy years. He was indeed a Prussian Junker. 'I am,' he said, 'a Junker and I mean to take full advantage of that fact.'[26] He was born at Schönhausen on the Elbe in Brandenburg and then raised near Stettin on the Baltic coast. Yet, though he always professed to detest Berlin, he was as much a Berliner, educated at the Graue Kloster and, having removed himself from Göttingen, at Berlin University. He would repeatedly try to escape from the city but it would draw him back with equal persistence, and his legacy there is as evident in the developments he would make as it would be in the strategic decisions he made to create Germany.

Bismarck is perhaps the most powerful and absorbing character in the story of Berlin after The Great Elector. There was little in his early life to suggest that he would become the architect of the German nation. Fiercely traditional and a firm royalist while a young member of the Prussian Landtag, he advocated harsh measures after 1848 and opposed democratisation. In 1851 he was sent by Frederick William IV as the Prussian representative to the Frankfurt Diet, where he began to realise that the rivalry between Austria and Prussia had to be resolved if there was to be a unified state. In 1859 William I, who was acting as regent and saw Bismarck as an aggressive and destabilising force (the two men would never get on despite their long and successful association) recalled him from Frankfurt and sent him to Russia as Prussian Ambassador and then, briefly, in 1862 to France. Reluctantly recalled again by William I that autumn as being the only politician who could control the Prussian Landtag who were refusing to pass the King's military estimates, he was made Minister President of Prussia and Minister of Foreign Affairs. While his time in Frankfurt made him realise a denouement with Austria was inevitable, his time in St Petersburg and Paris taught him that

Prussia was vulnerable if it was ever threatened from east and west at the same time. It was a lesson that would guide his foreign policy for the next thirty-odd years. A devout Pietist, happier on his estates in Pomerania and usually portrayed in uniform as a Reservist officer, Bismarck was a more complex and contradictory character than his image as a typical Junker suggested.

From the outset of his time in power, Bismarck divorced the twin movements for a German national identity, which he championed, forged in blood and established, from political reform, to which he paid lip service. During his twenty-eight years in power – from his appointment in 1862 until his dismissal by Wilhelm II in 1890 – Berlin's destiny would be recast once more. Bismarck made it the capital of the German 'Empire' he created, and the seat of the German emperor. Yet as the power of the crown grew, Berliners would become increasingly the champions of political and social reform, first in their own city and later for the new nation. The spirit of *Berlin Unwille*, now often seen as 'Red Berlin', was articulated by reformers, writers, artists and socialists who would contend with the respectable, official, industrial, commercial and military Berlin, the Berlin of the government and the court that was consolidating its position as imperial capital.

An early if moderate personification of this *Berlin Unwille* was Ferdinand Lassalle, another product of Berlin University and strongly influenced by the work of Fichte and Hegel, though too young to have been taught by Hegel himself. Lassalle became a leading political agitator for reform in the aftermath of 1848. Despised by Marx and Engels for not being extreme enough in his political views, he advocated universal manhood suffrage but, despite being a socialist, he was also a nationalist and a monarchist. Consequently he and Bismarck established a rapport and, although they remained at different political poles, Bismarck would later admit to having been strongly influenced by him.[27] Lassalle's lasting achievement came in his founding on 23 May 1863 of the *Allgemeiner Deutscher Arbeiter Verein* (ADAV), a society committed to achieving universal suffrage by peaceful means. In 1890 the ADAV would become the

Social Democratic Party of Germany (SPD), who would play such a key role as the voice of the centre-left in the politics of Berlin and of Germany in the decades to come and as it still does today. Lassalle was, as with so many other talented men, killed in a duel in August 1864, although this time the argument was about love rather than politics. He was just thirty-nine.

Bismarck's skill was now to make himself the personification of the nationalist movement. In 1849 the Frankfurt Diet, that rather ineffective pan-German body established at Vienna in 1815, drew up a German constitution. They then sent a delegation to Berlin to offer Frederick William IV the German crown. He refused, sensing that he could not accept a crown from an elected assembly, which would be, he said, like picking 'up a crown in a gutter'.[28] His refusal was only partially based on pride, for Prussia was still not strong enough to face down Austria where, although Metternich had gone in the wake of 1848, a firm government under Prince Felix von Schwarzenberg was determined that Prussia should not dominate a German nation.

In November 1850 Schwarzenberg had forced a humiliating treaty on Prussia at Olmütz, which obliged her to withdraw from Schleswig-Holstein where her army had intervened to prevent the Danish occupation of Schleswig. Fourteen years later, in 1864 and with a stronger and better-equipped Prussian army, Bismarck determined to use the Schleswig-Holstein question to establish Prussian supremacy. The complications of the Schleswig-Holstein question are, fortunately, beyond the scope of this book. The British Prime Minister Lord Palmerston famously said of the Schleswig-Holstein question that 'it was so complicated that only three men in Europe have ever understood it. One was Prince Albert and he is dead. The second was a German professor who became mad. I am the third and I have forgotten all about it.' In the summer of 1864 Prussian and Austrian troops defeated Denmark in a bloody and unpleasant war that saw the unfortunate Danes outgunned and outmanoeuvred. Prussia emerged the winner at the subsequent peace made in Vienna in October 1864 but this was only a precursor to Bismarck's intention to remove Austria altogether as an obstacle to German unification.

On 18 June 1866 Bismarck had King William I issue a 'Summons to the Prussian People'. He declared the German Federation and the Frankfurt Diet dissolved and war on Austria. Within seven weeks Austria was decisively defeated by Prussia's army at Sadowa (or Könniggrätz) and, at the subsequent Treaty of Prague, Prussia assumed the leadership of the German world. The Emperor of Austria was forced to agree to 'the dissolution of the German Bund and gives his assent to a new form of Germany without the participation of the Austrian Empire'. The result was a North German Federation, established in 1867, but the four major southern German states – Bavaria, Baden, Württemberg and Hesse-Darmstadt – remained outside. It was a job half done.

Bismarck realised that, in order to finally persuade these states to join a German nation, he had to portray France rather than Prussia as the main threat to European peace. Through what has since been seen as either brilliant diplomacy or a cunning sleight of hand, he contrived to make Napoleon III appear as the aggressor through the Ems Telegram, whereby France was seen to have issued an ultimatum to Prussia over claims to the Spanish throne. France, obligingly, declared war on Prussia. The resulting Franco-Prussian War of 1870 was a triumph of military planning by a combination of the War Minister, von Roon, and the Chief of the Prussian General Staff, Helmuth von Moltke. Against strong opposition in Berlin, where the glorious tradition of the Landwehr and its victories against Napoleon still held considerable sway, they professionalised the Prussian army, increasing the length of regular service so that their formations were much better trained. Invading France through Alsace-Lorraine, within six weeks the French army and Emperor Napoleon III had been forced to surrender at Sedan. It was a stunning and complete victory. Paris was besieged and on 18 January 1871 William I was proclaimed as the first Emperor of Germany, the Kaiser, in the Hall of Mirrors at Versailles. It must have been a sweet moment to excise the ghosts of Tilsit. Berlin was now to be the imperial capital.

The well-known Berlin actress Caroline Bauer wrote in 1870:

'I loved the old Berlin that had a mere 193,000 inhabitants in 1824, no gas, no railways, no water supply, no sidewalks, and just two theatres and two newspapers. A cobbler's apprentice getting a hiding from his master, or a man flying a kite, or an overturned horse-and-cart to provide entertainment for hours ... But as for this second half of the century, this metropolis with its dazzling gas lamps in the streets, with its two dozen theatres, the roaring of steam engines, a feverish pursuit of riches, a philosophical nihilism and pessimism – it fills me with disgust.'[29]

Yet that was only the beginning. Berlin was about to undergo an even more major change. No longer just twin fishing and trading villages on the Spree, nor capital of the Mark of Brandenburg, nor even just the capital of the King of Prussia, Berlin had become the capital of first the German nation and soon thereafter the German 'empire'. It would also become the largest city in Europe.

CHAPTER SEVEN

1871–1918

'*You are crazy, my Child, you must go
to Berlin*'

FRANZ VON SUPPÉ, Austrian composer, 1876

Heinrich von Treitschke was a Berlin historian and, from 1871, a member of the Reichstag. Having started life as a liberal, he gradually came to espouse an extreme form of nationalism. Popular both as a lecturer at the university and as a demagogue until he died in 1896, Treitschke argued that what Bismarck had achieved was Germany's destiny. The English, Jews and socialists were all castigated. The English 'possess no redeeming qualities'; the Jews 'can be of no further use to the world', and socialists were obstructing the one pure form of government personified by the Hohenzollerns. War was a perfect state that was waged for the 'sublime moral good of the national honour'.[1] His extremist views represented one side of the polarised debate that came to dominate politics and thinking in Berlin in the fifty-odd years between 1871 and the end of the First World War. Behind Treitschke (though few were as extreme as he was) were the Court, the army and the government that Bismarck had constructed so as to preserve effective power with the Kaiser and his ministers. Opposing them were the socialists, who gradually extended their influence across the city. In 1871 socialist politicians were returned to the Reichstag in just two of Berlin's six electoral districts; by the turn of the century they controlled five. Men like Wilhelm Liebknecht, Paul Singer and August Bebel, heirs of Lassalle's legacy, merged their Social Democratic Workers Party with the ADAV at Gotha in 1875 and continued to articulate the case for political and social reform, although they themselves were challenged by those on the extreme left who drew their inspiration from Marx and Engels. While Germany, as it now was, became increasingly militaristic, Berlin became increasingly socialist.

The creation of Germany had two immediate effects on Berlin. First, it now found itself the home of the German parliament, the Reichstag, set up by Bismarck in the wake of that victorious proclamation in Versailles. Berlin was, of course, already home to the bi-cameral Prussian parliament, established under the 1850 constitution, with its *Herrenhaus* (a sort of House of Lords) and *Landtag* (the lower house elected on the rather curious three-tier franchise according to income). Now the united Germany of twenty-five states called for a pan-German assembly and, given that Prussia was the indisputable leader of Germany, this assembly was naturally going to be in Berlin. It was also to have two houses. The upper house was the *Bundesrat* and represented the reigning princes, while the lower house, the Reichstag, was elected by universal manhood suffrage from across Germany. On the face of it this was a fair attempt at giving the new nation a forward-looking democratic system, which was the effect Bismarck desired, yet the reality was that power stayed firmly with Prussia and, within Prussia, even more firmly with the Kaiser and his Minister President.

Once it had been set up, it only took fourteen votes in the Bundesrat to veto any proposed changes, and Prussia controlled seventeen. The state with the next-largest number was Bavaria, which only had six, whereas the once-mighty Saxony was reduced to four.[2] There was no cabinet as such, with all ministerial power vested in the Minister President who was both Chancellor of Germany and Prime Minister of Prussia, which meant that crucial areas such as foreign policy and the military remained out of the Reichstag's control. Neither did the constitution contain a bill of rights, as many had demanded. It was a system designed to preserve power in Bismarck's hands – 'an insurance against democracy', as Liebknecht termed it. This was all very well for Berlin and for Germany as long as Bismarck was in power; the problem would come once he was gone and had not been replaced by men of similar ability. For the next nineteen years, however, Bismarck was very much in the ascendant and Berlin would benefit directly from his vision. Having been opened in 1871, the Reichstag now decided that it needed a suitable building within which to meet. In 1872 a competition was launched for a design for a site on the Königsplatz, an area of open ground between the Brandenburg Gate and the Spree and on the edge of the Tiergarten. Because of arguments between the Kaiser, Bismarck and the members, it would take twenty-three years to decide, so in the meantime they met in Frederick the Great's old porcelain factory in Leipziger Straße.

The second effect of the creation of Germany was that Berlin now found itself very rich – or at least some Berliners did. This was partly because war indemnities imposed on a defeated France of 5 billion francs flowed into the city, partly because trade increased within the new barrier-free nation, and partly because the city now became the financial centre of Germany, taking over the position traditionally occupied by Frankfurt am Main. The major German banks – the Deutsche Bank, the Dresdner Bank and the Darmstädter Bank – all moved their head offices to Berlin, where Behrenstraße became the German equivalent of New York's Wall Street. In 1871 there was the beginning of an extraordinary economic boom that saw Berlin's already fairly frenetic development accelerate even faster, often called Berlin's *Gründerjahre* (foundation years). People continued to flow into the city so that, by 1875, its population was just under a million and by 1900 it had risen to 2 million, although these figures were artificially low as millions more lived in the outlying suburbs that were still not yet technically part of the city itself.

Development of the Mietskaserne spread east and north, beyond what had become the established industrial and working-class areas. Wedding (north of Moabit), Gesundbrunnen (meaning health springs), and Prenzlauer Berg (north and east of the Alexanderplatz) were engulfed. So too, beyond Prenzlauer Berg, was Pankow with its delightful park at Schönhausen. To the south Tempelhof and the outer reaches of Schöneberg provided more middle-class housing, while the better homes were built to the south and west of the Tiergarten and in Wilmersdorf. The very grandest moved even further out, bordering the Grunewald and in the villages towards Potsdam like Zehlendorf, and along the Havel and its lakes such as the beautiful Wannsee. There was a clear distinction between the misery and squalor of the 'one family to a room' apartment blocks, and the suburban 'villa', which became (and still is) as much a part of the western Berlin landscape as the Mietskaserne to the east. Some of these villas, built with the easy money that was now available, were designed 'in all known styles of expensive ugliness,' Christopher Isherwood commented[3]; *Geheimratsgotik* (officials gothic) became an accepted if pejorative term. Others, especially those along the lakes, offered a most attractive way of urban living for people who could afford them. While the older Berlin families tended to stay in their Schinkel terraces around Friedrichstraße, the nouveau riche preferred getting out of the city altogether.

Bismarck's personal relations with Berlin were strained. He had become something of a popular hero in 1866 when he survived an assassination attempt in the Unter den Linden. Walking back from an audience with the King, a young man fired three shots into his back. None of them penetrated very far through his thick coat. Bismarck grabbed the man by the arm and handed him over to the police before quietly resuming his journey to his office in Wilhelmstraße. His orchestration of the victories over Austria and France also made him a popular hero but he never liked the city much, telling his biographer that Berliners 'must always be in opposition and have their own ideas',[4] a feeling that would grow stronger as Berlin's socialism took deeper root. However, Bismarck did make a direct contribution to the city whose role, he felt, as imperial capital required it to be a little grander than it was. In 1873 an enormous victory column was erected on the Königsplatz, a few hundred yards from the Brandenburg Gate and just in front of where the Reichstag now stands. The *Siegessäule*, as it was called, was 67 metres high, based on a colonnade of red granite pillars and originally commissioned in 1864 to celebrate Prussia's not particularly edifying victory over the unfortunate Danes. However, by the time it was finished, Austria and France had also been defeated so those victories were incorporated by adding decorative bronze friezes showing the victorious Prussian army and their defeated neighbours, and a huge gold statue of victory on the top sculpted by Friedrich Drake. Known to Berliners as *Goldelse* (golden Else), it is meant to have been modelled on Drake's daughter.

The young Jewish Walter Benjamin found the *Siegessäule* both confusing, being unable to understand why the French had fought with the golden canons depicted on the reliefs, and very reassuring. 'With the defeat of the French, world history seemed to be safely interred in its glorious grave, and this column was the funerary stele.'[5] The Nazis had the Siegessäule moved in the 1930s as part of their plans for rebuilding the centre of Berlin, from the Königsplatz to where it now stands in the centre of the Tiergarten on *Großer Stern* where the main roads through the park meet. In 1945 the French had the reliefs showing their defeat removed but President Mitterand returned them in 1987 for the city's 750th birthday celebrations. During the Cold War it became something of a focal point for West Berlin, facing the Brandenburg Gate as it does and offering a wonderful view into East Berlin. It is well worth visiting today for the same view of the united city if you can cope with the 270 steps.

Bismarck also had a vision of a broad avenue linking the city to the Grunewald, rather along the lines of Paris's Champs-Élysées, with an upmarket housing colony at its western end bordering the forest. There had been a road there since Joachim II had one built to reach the Jagdschloss Grunewald and the charms of Anna Sydow more quickly. Now Bismarck wanted it turned into a wide and fashionable boulevard, with smart shops and houses interspaced with rows of plane trees. Work started on the resulting Kurfürstendamm in 1875. It was not exactly the grand avenue Bismarck envisaged but it quickly became the centre of the city's nightlife, its cafes and its main shopping centre. Starting by Zoo station, it runs 3.5 kilometres through Charlottenburg and Wilmersdorf to Halensee station, on the city ring and now close to the orbital autobahn. The Ku'damm, as it has always been known, suffered badly from the Nazi Jewish pogroms, many of its shops being Jewish owned, and from bombing in the Second World War but it was rebuilt after 1945, and when the Wall shut off Berlin's historic centre from the west the Kurfürstendamm became something of the main street for the west. It has, consequently, always occupied rather a special place in the city's heart, despite being the scene of some of the worst student protests in the 1960s.

With Bismarck's initiative the land north and south of the new boulevard was rapidly developed and Wilmersdorf quickly became one of the more fashionable areas to live, as it still is today. The major shops followed with the massive *Kaufhaus des Westens* opening on Tauentizenstraße, near the eastern end of the Ku'damm in 1907. Always known as the KaDeWe, it was comprehensively destroyed in the Second World War when an American bomber landed actually on it, but it has been rebuilt and still serves more than 40,000 customers each day from its original location. Other department stores, such as the equally famous Wertheim, opened in Leipzigerstraße but were later moved to the Ku'damm due to wartime damage.

The frenetic building and development masked the fact that Berlin in the 1870s was still a city of two halves. The continuing enormous influx of immigrants was driven by the industrial expansion, which tempted them with jobs and wages. Many of the original entrepreneurs of the 1830s and 1840s had thrived and the city was no longer reliant on imported British power and technology. The old English-provided power was now overtaken by two Berlin behemoths, a process aided by the Berlin Council reorganising itself in 1881 into two departments. The traditional council roles continued to be discharged by the *Magistrat*, headed by the Bürgermeister, but public utilities were hived off under the *Stadtverordnetvereinmeister*, who headed an elected body of 144 people that formed the *Stadtverordnetenversammlung*, whose job was simpler than its title, namely running public utilities. Berlin would soon become the centre of both the German and the European power and electricity industry. An artillery officer, Werner von Siemens, who started by developing a process for insulating wires so that they could be used along railways, had produced an electric telegraph that he had subsequently taken into successful production. Originally working from Schöneberger Straße, he had then built a substantial factory complex at what became known as Siemensstadt. In 1880 he introduced electric (rather than gas) street lighting in the city and linked up the first 200 telephones. By 1900 Siemens were employing 13,600 people and had 54 million marks of share capital.

Siemens's competition, and one of the city's most successful industrialists, was Emil Rathenau, who started by manufacturing Edison's light bulbs in Germany. Developing the business into a manufacturer of power-generation machinery, Rathenau started to build both power stations and electric trams. Quickly growing so that it overtook Siemens – and now called the *Allgemeine Elektrizitäts Gesellschaft* – AEG employed 17,300 Berliners, and by 1911 it was supplying 31 per cent of all electricity across Germany from 114 power stations.[6] Berlin itself was supplied by AEG's subsidiary, *Berliner Elektricitäts-Werke* (BEW), which opened its first generating stations in the city in 1885, and the subsequent electric lighting on the Unter den Linden and Pariser Platz 'was greeted by the whole city with joy'. BEW then started an extraordinarily rapid electrification programme, in huge demand from both the building developers and the 'lively nightlife of the city'. BEW were granted a monopoly on supplying power to the central districts by the council, and by 1895 Berlin was the most 'electrified' city in Germany, easily outstripping Hamburg and Munich. By 1914 power was also being distributed beyond the city out to a 30-kilometre radius. Berlin was consuming more power than either Chicago or London, but BEW were supplying it at a much lower cost per kilowatt. It was a remarkable feat of Berlin engineering, and for a time more households had access to electricity than they did inside plumbing.[7]

Engine manufacture and heavy industry remained a vital source of employment. Borsig had moved his factory out to Tegel and was being rivalled by Bethel Henry Strousberg, a Jew from East Prussia whose 'rags to riches and back to rags' story illustrated all the opportunities and prejudices of Berlin in the 1870s. Strousberg made a vast fortune building railway lines in East Prussia and then across Germany using a clever system whereby he paid his contractors in shares in the company that would operate along the lines they were constructing. This was fine so long as confidence in the operation was maintained, which it was until a project he was engaged on in Rumania went spectacularly wrong and he went bankrupt in 1872, losing a lot of money for well-connected Berlin investors. A fascinating man (a polymath who also owned ironworks as well as controlling Berlin's cattle market and being a member of the Reichstag), one of his major legacies was the Palais Strousberg, a large mansion he had built in Wilhelmstraße that the British government snapped up as their embassy when he was forced to sell. Damaged too badly in 1945 to be restored, the new British Embassy was built on the same site.

The initial rush of money in 1871 led to over-speculation and, predictably, after the boom came a severe financial crash in 1873. Equally predictably, the Jews were blamed and men like Strousberg excoriated. One of the leaders of this campaign, alongside Treitschke, was a man who should have known better, Adolf Stöcker, who was a Protestant clergyman and a chaplain at the Royal Court. Stöcker preached that money-lending and stock markets were evil and blamed the Jews for all the current financial woes. It was a simple and effective message but it was only heard because he was playing to an existing feeling of anti-Semitism. The party he founded, the Christian Socialist Workers Party, attracted large audiences after Stöcker made a particularly forthright attack on the Jews in a speech in 1879 ('Our Demands on Modern Jewry') that made headlines and made anti-Semitism seem respectable. Although Stöcker himself fell from grace at Court, his legacy was to be a terrible one.

Although the 1873 crash bankrupted some and caused a temporary rise in unemployment, the strength of Berlin's economy meant that the city soon recovered. Yet the social problems were still very much present, and homelessness was still running at around 5 per cent in the early 1870s. In July there were two days of rioting when the police cut down 159 people. Those who survived were then given long prison sentences. It was in many ways still the city of two halves, as it had been prior to 1848, with the comfortable and successful half in the west and south, and the poor industrial workers in the north and east. Again, as was common across Europe, there were thousands of domestic servants, and many of the daughters of immigrants who came in search of a better life found themselves condemned to the drudgery of working for middle-class families often in fairly dreadful conditions. By 1905 there were no less than 267 domestic employment agencies operating, and servants carried a *Gesindebuch* (servant book) with them with a record of their service and references. The main stations had Women's Missions where young girls arriving could get help and accommodation before they found a job, preventing many from disappearing into rather less salubrious employment in the Scheunenviertiel. One poor girl, just fifteen when she started, may have wished she had never come. She was a 'maid-of-all-work. I had to look after a small child, cook, do all the housework. In the afternoon I had to take the child out so all the housework had to be done in the evening. Then I had to do all the washing, usually overnight. And when one day my master came home at 3.00 a.m. and found me asleep he told me I was unreliable and lazy. When I dared to say that I hadn't had any sleep at all the night before they said "Such cheek! Such impertinence!"'[8]

Yet it is easy to overstate the poverty, which afflicted the majority of European cities at the time and sometimes masks the fact that many immigrants had taken the opportunity that the industrial revolution offered and were doing very well for themselves. Once the city council started to improve public utilities, conditions also began to improve so that by the turn of the century James Pollard, a city official from Edinburgh who was invited by Berlin Council to survey the state of the city's public services, reported very favourably.

After the major smallpox epidemic in 1871, which started among
French prisoners of war, the authorities had developed a large new
hospital at Moabit so that by 1900 there were three major hospitals
in addition to the venerable Charité founded by Frederick William
I (the other two being Friedrichshain and the Urban). Altogether
they provided 3,000 publicly funded beds and were administered
directly by a committee of the council. Schooling was compulsory
and Pollard estimated that 14 per cent of the city's population were
at school at any time, a higher proportion than in his home city of
Edinburgh (although, with the continuing immigrant numbers being
as high as they were, it is unlikely that this figure represents anything
approaching a totality). Pollard's report is in some ways a bit of a
whitewash. He was evidently invited out to produce something com-
plimentary, but his work was thorough and his figures do suggest
that improvements were being made.[9]

A steady improvement can also be seen in family diaries and letters
from the time, such as those of the Kirstaedter family, one of the few
Berlin families who seem to have managed to preserve their records.
Theodor Kirstaedter originally came to Berlin in 1844 aged twenty
and found work as a bricklayer. He married Anna, the daughter of
a locksmith called Störzer who lived by the Matthäikirche, built by
Stüler, in 1844 in the area being developed west of the Potsdamer
Platz and south of the Tiergarten. Anna could remember chatting
to Papa Wrangel as she walked to school one morning. The peppery
old general asked her to show him her drawings in her satchel and in
return he gave a small carved wooden box. They had eleven children
together, of whom five survived. Theodor thrived as a builder, benefiting from the 1871 boom, and there were at one time many houses
bearing his initials above their doors (though the area was very
badly bombed in the Second World War so none are known to have
survived). They did so well that they moved from the Matthäikirche
area to the smart new houses in Zietenstraße, by the Zwölf-Apostel
Kirche and near the Nollendforfplatz, another area that had been
recently developed. From Zietenstraße they made a short move to
the beautiful Motzstraße, where Theodor ended up owning three

houses, living in number 88 and renting out numbers 85 and 86. Theodor and Anna's son Johannes was born in 1866 and went on to become President of Berlin's Higher Administrative Court.

Carl Ludwig Zeitler, the weaver's son who wrote such a graphic account of the 1848 uprising, had, despite having been trained in his father's trade, also become a builder who had capitalised on the 1870s boom. He had been so successful that he was able to endow several foundations to support women in need and to educate girls. He had also built a fine family mausoleum in the Georgen-Parochial-Friedhof in Greifswalder Straße, which still stands as a proud record of his achievement with a fine mosaic of Carl Ludwig in his old age.[10]

A serious attempt was also made to improve workers' housing. A very well-preserved example is at Wildau in south-east Berlin, which you pass on the S-Bahn just before Wusterhausen. Schwartzkopff, a heavy engineering company who made locomotives, established a factory here in 1897 and built dedicated workers' housing with it, a sort of model industrial village. The neat rows of red-brick houses in a rural setting would have been a very welcome alternative to the cramped conditions of the inner city. The history of Wildau itself is typical of the villages around the city that became swallowed up in Berlin's various booms. Originally a fishing village on the River Dahme, the locals switched to producing bricks, which were shipped to the city centre down the Dahme and the Spree, then locomotives, causing its population to increase from 200 to 2,000 in just ten years. During the Second World War the factory switched to armament production then became part of the GDR's heavy-industry production with an engineering college. The village, which still feels like a village, is now home to business parks and a flourishing technical college.

Other aspects of Berlin's life were improving too. The number of visitors to the city was exploding as rapidly as its population; 350,000 foreigners came in 1883 but by 1906 that had increased to over a million.[11] These visitors needed places to eat and to stay, and the 1880s and 1890s saw the development of many of the city's famous restaurants and hotels. Berthold Kempinski had come to

Berlin from East Prussia in 1872 and started a successful wine merchant's business on Friedrichstraße. In 1889 he took the next step and opened a large new restaurant on Leipziger Straße that, both patriotically and astutely, he decorated with tiles made in a factory owned by the Kaiser. The Kaiser consequently came to his opening night, making his establishment instantly fashionable. The first grand hotel was the Kaiserhof, completed in 1875 on the Wilhelmplatz, but it burned down just after it was opened. Rebuilt, it was reopened by the Kaiser, who is said to have remarked, 'I have nothing like this in my own home', which was certainly true. The Schloss was well known for being very uncomfortable. In 1858 Queen Victoria's daughter Victoria, known as Vicky, married the then Crown Prince William's eldest son Frederick. She was only eighteen (he was twenty-seven) when she was brought to live in it, and she hated it. It had no bathrooms so if she wanted to bathe, hot water had to be brought from the Hotel de Rome in the Forum Fridericianum. She had to walk through Frederick William III's room to reach her apartments. It had been preserved exactly as he had left it, and she was convinced it was haunted. There were no cupboards and one room was full of thousands of dead bats. She did not like Berlin much either, writing to her mother that it was an 'awful hole, fearful pavements, awful smells'. Like all good Hohenzollerns, she and Frederick moved out to Potsdam as soon as they could. It was not surprising that the royal family came to favour the new and comfortable hotels.

The Kaiser would put his guests into the Adlon, which quickly became Berlin's leading hotel – a role it has maintained to this day. It was built on the site of one of Schinkel's finest houses on the Pariser Platz. In fact, the house had to be demolished to accommodate the new build, which was only authorised because the Kaiser backed the project. When it opened in 1907 the early guests were astounded that every room was not only soundproofed but had its own bathroom, and the staff could be summoned by electric signals instead of by bells. Others quickly followed so that Berlin became one of Europe's most comfortable cities to stay if you could afford it; by 1914 there were twelve five-star-equivalent hotels.[12] At the other end of the social scale there was an equal explosion of *Bierstuben* (beer halls). A chain called Aschinger ran around forty that became famous for also offering free rolls and sandwiches when you ordered a beer. They quickly became a Berlin institution.

Berlin in the late nineteenth century may have been the most densely packed city in Europe (if one takes the narrow definition of the city boundaries that prevailed until 1920), but in fact it has long enjoyed far more access to green spaces than many cities. Quite apart from the 22-square-kilometre Grunewald, which is as near a proper forest as is found close by any major city, and the 520-acre Tiergarten (210 hectares), there was the Volkspark Friedrichshain, founded in 1840 on Lenné's inspiration to commemorate the 100th anniversary of Frederick the Great's accession. Towards the east of the city, the 128-acre park became something of an oasis for the poorer areas of Prenzlauer Berg and Friedrichshain itself. It was genuinely a *Volkspark* (people's park) and one of its most charming features was the Märchenbrunnen (fountain of fairy tales). Berlin councillor Ludwig Hoffman had seen how many children from the surrounding Mietskaserne played in the park and he determined to do something to improve their experience.

Although the idea was originally put forward in 1893, the fountain was not actually finished until 1913 due to the Kaiser interfering with the plans, but during the First World War hundreds of poor Berlin children would have drawn a great deal of pleasure from the statues representing characters from nine of the Brothers Grimm fairy tales. Badly bombed in the Second World War, it was well restored but now seems to be undergoing another renovation. In another corner of the Volkspark is the graveyard for those who fell soon after it opened in March 1848, the *Friedhof der Märzgefallenen*. Bismarck hated it, thinking the inscription of 'Freedom and Justice' on the graves was a 'mockery to God',[13] but the graveyard became a revered national memorial to freedom fighters from various revolutions. Each of the 1848 graves also says very pointedly what labouring trade the person buried there pursued or, in a few sad cases, they simply state *lehrling* for the young apprentices. It is a peaceful and rather dignified place, despite the traffic on the nearby Landsberger Allee, and well planted with spring flowers. The approach road is named Ernst-Zinna-Weg after the locksmith who was killed on the barricades, and there are also memorials to those who died in 1918–19. The GDR later erected a memorial plaque there to all those who lost their lives in the cause of 'freedom'. Interestingly no victim of the 1953 Berlin uprising against the communists was ever included. Freedom remains, of course, a subjective notion.

Another public attraction was the Zoologischer Garten, Berlin Zoo. Frederick William III had been very fond of his menagerie, which he kept on Pfaueninsel (peacock island), an island on the Havel near Potsdam. His father had used the island as a love nest and had a small folly built there, but in the 1820s Frederick William III commissioned Schinkel and Lenné to lay out a park and gardens with buildings for his animals with a palm house and an aviary. It was a sort of exotic retreat for him and Auguste von Harrach, but he allowed Berliners to visit three days a week to look at his growing collection of wild species. Frederick William IV did not share his father's passion, so in 1841 Martin Hinrich Lichtenstein (a professor at Berlin University and friend of Alexander von Humboldt) persuaded him to turn over his pheasant house in the Tiergarten so that he could found a proper zoo. Lenné was again asked to design it, and in 1844 Berlin Zoo opened its gates for the first time. After a slow start, a new management team in the 1860s raised funds and erected new and striking oriental-style buildings and worked to increase the collection, so that by 1900 what had started as a small private menagerie had become the zoo with the greatest variety of species in Europe and was pursuing ambitious breeding programmes. Berliners became very proud of their zoo, and some of the animals became household names. By 1939 there would be 4,000 of them, although by 1945 considerably fewer. Pfaueninsel continued its life as a retreat for Berliners. It's an attractive if sometimes rather crowded sanctuary from the summer heat of the city centre, served by a regular ferry service with connections to Wannsee S-Bahn, and with the mini *schloss* and Schinkel's aviary and Lenné's gardens all well preserved.

Another major improvement to Berliners' lives came with the introduction of the *Untergrundbahn* (the underground railway, always called the U-Bahn). Berlin by the 1890s was, with now nearly 2 million people, facing a major transport problem. The S-Bahn had been continually improved and the existing Berlin Ring line was operating by 1882. Siemens suggested another overground railway, but AEG argued that the S-Bahn already provided that and instead they should go underground. In 1902 the first short line opened, linking Stralauer Tor in Friedrichshain with the Zoo (the Zoo would become one of the city's major transport hubs, as it still is) with a branch to Potsdamer Platz. In fact, most of this line, called the *Stammstrecke* (literally the original line), was in fact overground and built by Siemens but the extensions that rapidly followed went underground, to Warschauer Straße and to Ernst Reuter Platz, which was then called the Knie. Stralauer Tor is no more, being one of two U-Bahn stations that were so badly damaged in the Second World War that it was not worth reopening.

The U-Bahn was continuously developed for the next fifty years, albeit interrupted by the First World War, with some of the stations being gloriously designed by the Swede Alfred Grennander. The first one he built was Ernst Reuter Platz but altogether he was responsible for about fifty. The early ones are in art nouveau style, and make generous use of tiles and decorated columns, good examples of which are the U2 line platforms at the Alexanderplatz and Sophie-Charlotte-Platz. His later stations, completed in the late 1920s, like Jannowitzbrücke and Gesundbrunnen, were more modernist. Many have survived more or less intact, protected from the bombing though suffering from the post-1945 division of the city. In fact, Berlin had been digging for some time. The loose, sandy soil of the Spree valley was easy to dig in but, as poor Schlüter had discovered when his tower at the Schloss collapsed, it was unstable and the water table was high. This water was, however, very useful as it gave the city a clean and accessible supply, now piped widely throughout the various districts, helping to reduce disease and improve public health. It also had other uses, such as brewing, and many of Berlin's many breweries started life underground.

~

Berlin in the last decades of the nineteenth century was now a *weltstadt* (world city), a metropolis, the fastest-growing major city in Germany and Europe, although some of the smaller German industrial cities on the Ruhr did grow even faster. It now had its schools and its hospitals, its power and water, its transportation systems and its parks, its hotels and restaurants. It was a city with a far better standard of social care than just fifty years earlier but it remained that city of two halves, not just divided by income and lifestyle (which could be said of most major European cities around the turn of the nineteenth and twentieth centuries) but more strongly by political persuasion and aspiration. One half saw Berlin as the capital of Germany, the residence of the Kaiser, the seat of government, the financial and manufacturing centre, the headquarters of the army, a self-confident, successful city that had achieved great things. The other half saw it as a city ruled by an intolerant and repressive regime, dominated by the military, with false democratic institutions, inadequate social care and culturally restricted. Many of this latter group may have shared in Berlin's success – indeed many had helped to create it, and they were not by any means the dispossessed. Rather they were the heirs to that spirit of *Berlin Unwille*, those who saw the Hohenzollerns still as autocrats and, however much they have applauded the creation of the German nation, it was a country they wished to see as democratic and free.

This tension was brought into sharp relief when the old Kaiser, William I, died in 1888 aged ninety-one. No longer the shrapnel prince who had wanted to shell the protesters in 1848, he was now the father of Prussia, the creator of Germany and its first emperor. Cheered as he drove along the Unter den Linden – an avuncular, comfortable figurehead, who would be revered and much sculpted by his grandson – he represented stability and tradition to a nation who valued those qualities perhaps more than many countries. He was succeeded briefly by his son, the liberally minded, fifty-seven-year-old Frederick III who was married to the British Princess Victoria but he died from cancer within ninety-nine days, leaving the throne to his eldest son, the twenty-nine-year-old William II. Frederick III was mourned by those who thought he would have been able to moderate Bismarck's policies and champion reform. It is one of those much-debated if futile questions as to how Europe may have developed had he lived. He did leave a particular legacy to Berlin in that he founded the museums of *Völkerkunde* (ethnology) and *Kunstgewerbe* (artistic crafts), which both started to develop important collections. As it was, Berlin, Germany and Europe had in William II the most unstable, almost paranoid, egocentric, aggressive and ultimately destructive prince the Hohenzollerns had produced. In thirty short years he would bring crashing down everything that his family had worked towards for 500 years. He was, thought Gertrude Bell, who had an audience with him in 1897, 'disappointing when one sees him close; he looks puffy and ill and I never saw anyone so jumpy. He is never still a second while he is talking.'[14]

There have been many attempts to psychoanalyse William II. Born with a withered arm, he suffered from a lack of self-confidence as a child and hated his mother to whom he hardly spoke. As Kaiser this lack of self-confidence turned into aggression, so that he seemed to encapsulate in his personality the sense of victimhood that many thought had so affected Germany since the Thirty Years War. Three things made this particularly concerning and would contribute to the Hohenzollerns' downfall. First, the machinery of government that Bismarck had created left overall control over the military and foreign affairs in his hands. Secondly, he seemed genuinely to believe that he had been endowed with extraordinary political, military and cultural judgement. Instead of appreciating that he was a man who had been born into a privileged position in which he must behave pragmatically to further the national good and protect his own dynasty (as Frederick the Great had so capably achieved), William

II appeared to think he was a genius. Thirdly, he was backed by a military who had enjoyed extraordinary power and prestige since Bismarck deployed them so effectively in the 1860s and who thought it was their destiny to be used. All these unsatisfactory traits were to cause Berlin untold suffering and misery.

The first issue began to surface while William I was alive. Once Germany was established as a nation, and Bismarck had convincingly established Prussian dominance, he turned his attention to the socialists. A failed assassination attempt on the Kaiser in 1878 had been used as a reason to clamp down on them. The SPD and the Progress Party were banned, many working men's clubs and associations were closed, and forty-five newspapers were shut down. At the same time Bismarck moved against the Roman Catholic Church, the so-called *Kulturkampf*, believing that the Catholics were acting against Prussian interests in southern Germany and in Poland. It was a counter-productive policy. There was immediate sympathy for the socialists, with supporters 'lining up along the platform to salute the elderly August Bebel as he was led to prison accompanied by his pet canary and a cartload of books'.[15]

The SPD – previously broadly supportive of the system – now became strongly anti-establishment. Bismarck's repression only increased the SPD's popularity so that in 1890 the party polled 1.5 million votes in the Reichstag elections and emerged as the largest single political party; its heartland was in the working-class districts of north and east Berlin. Bismarck attempted to modify his stance with what was actually a far-sighted social insurance package in the late 1880s, introducing health insurance (which covered 14 million people by 1914), accident insurance and comprehensive factory legislation, but it did little to blunt the appeal of socialism.[16] The measures against the Catholic Church were similarly unsuccessful. Although the Jesuits were banned in 1873 and a quarter of German parishes were without a priest by 1881, Bismarck had no effective way of enforcing his measures and he reckoned without the strength of Catholicism, which had, after all, weathered many worse storms.[17] All he did was once more play into the hands of those who criticised his government for being repressive and drove the centrist liberal deputies in the Reichstag towards the socialists.

What these measures had shown was that the Reichstag, with all its limitations, was powerless to stop a determined chancellor and Kaiser. Bismarck was losing his magic touch by the time William I died, but he still represented the authoritative voice in foreign policy and, muddled as his domestic agenda had become, he had proved adept at preserving Germany's position in Europe and in maintaining peace after 1871. In 1878 he had placed Berlin at the centre of the European diplomatic world by hosting the Congress that was called to resolve the outstanding issues in the Balkans. Much as many Berliners detested him, they were alarmed when William II forced him to resign in 1890 and he was followed by a succession of inadequate sycophants whose chief merit seems to have been their ability to praise the Kaiser. None of the men who served in that immensely powerful position from 1890 until 1918 had Bismarck's ability or determination, leaving the running of Germany's foreign policy in the unstable hands of the Kaiser himself.

That was, of course, a problem that affected Germany as a whole, while the manifestations of William II's character defects were felt closer to home in Berlin itself – and nowhere more so than in the design of the buildings and statues he had erected. His first priority was to honour his grandfather and the chancellor he had just dismissed. In 1894 he had the buildings west of the Berliner Schloss cleared to put up a massive memorial to Kaiser William I. A competition was organised and eight architects submitted designs but William II then insisted that his favourite architect, Rheinhold Begas, be added to the list. Four of the original architects resigned and Begas predictably won. His work was unveiled in 1897, to rather limited acclaim. The statue was badly damaged in the Second World War and subsequently demolished by the GDR. But it was not the only memorial. One of Berlin's more bizarre churches is the Kaiser-Wilhelm Gedächtniskirche at the eastern end of the Ku'damm. A Romanesque-style building completed against a commission placed by the Kaiser in 1895, it is famous more for its dominant position than its artistic merit. Yet it is also famous for being a really good example of how Berlin faces its past and incorporates it in its buildings and its life rather than trying to hide it. The church was very badly bombed, as was all that eastern end of the Ku'damm, but rather than be demolished, the ruin has been preserved as a museum with a new mostly blue-glass church built alongside. Whatever one may think of the replacement (and opinions are divided), here is a place of worship that commemorates.

The fashion for commemorating the old Kaiser did go rather too far. A bemused French visitor, the journalist Jules Huret, noted in 1907 that 'there are two things that strike a visitor the moment he leaves the station [in Berlin]. One is the huge number of electric street cars speeding along the streets. The other is a statue of Kaiser Wilhelm I or Bismarck. At the beginning I used to keep count of these statues and keep post cards of them, in spite of the fact that there was little difference between one blackened figure and another. But I soon gave up. There are too many.'[18]

Berlin had never had a proper cathedral. There had been the chapel in the Berliner Schloss, which was called a cathedral, and there was the Deutsche Dom balancing the Französischer Dom in the Gendarmenmarkt. The Nikolaikirche still represented for many the heart of the Church in the city but, with Schinkel's original designs for his massive gothic cathedral having never come to anything, these churches were nothing on the scale of London or Paris, which the Kaiser felt made Berlin somehow inferior. The Pietist tradition, which had so successfully melded Lutheranism and Calvinism, did not really need any huge and ostentatious building to give it substance, of course, but that was not the point. Now the Catholics had their cathedral in the Forum Fridericianum, and the Jews had their Neue Synagogue, there must be a cathedral for the Protestants. Frederick William IV had toyed with the idea and identified the site but nothing had happened other than endless designs, prompting Berliners to refer to the area east of the Lustgarten as the most expensive turf in the city. But in 1894 work started on a substantial building designed by Julius Carl Raschdorff that would cover what

Hohenzollern graves had been under the old Berliner Schloss chapel. It stands there today, massive rather than beautiful, looking faintly vulgar beside Schlüter's rebuilt Berliner Schloss facade to its south and Schinkel's Altes Museum to its north, but it is well worth a visit for two reasons. First, whatever it may lack in being a physical manifestation of Berlin Protestantism, it more than amply compensates for by the summation of its spirit, manifest particularly in the beauty of its music; Sunday evening services there are not to be missed.

Secondly, William II intended it to be as much a Hohenzollern mausoleum as a place of worship, and he gathered around ninety sarcophagi together in the crypt (which can also be visited). Tombs are not especially interesting in themselves but there is something quite impressive, if decidedly gloomy, in finding so many Hohenzollerns together, although those such as The Great Elector and John Cicero must have objected to being uprooted and reinterred. The Great Elector lies in a massive sarcophagus of red marble with his two wives either side of him. Frederick I, his son, lies in a simple marble tomb chapel to his left, with Sophie-Charlotte beside him, although he may have been annoyed not to have made more use of two quite magnificently vulgar gold sarcophagi, almost the last works executed for him by Schlüter, and which stand empty in the chapel at the top of the crypt stairs.

William II's obsession with his family's origins is perhaps yet another sign of his insecurity. Parvenus as they may have been considered in 1415, by 1905 when the Berliner Dom finally opened, the Hohenzollerns had been on their throne for nearly 500 years and had outlasted most other European dynasties. Yet in Schloss Charlottenburg, where there is a very good permanent exhibition about the Hohenzollern family, you can look at absurd portraits that purport to show their ancestry back to the heroes of classical antiquity. William II's most ill-judged attempt to demonstrate the antiquity and legitimacy of his dynasty – and one that met with almost universal derision – was, however, the *Siegesallee*. This was a series of thirty-two statues of the rulers of Brandenburg, starting with Albert the Bear and ending with Kaiser William I, arranged along a 500-metre avenue that cut through the Tiergarten from the Siegessäule, then on the Königsplatz, parallel with the Brandenburg Gate, to finish on the southern edge of the park near the Potsdamerplatz. Were it still standing today, it would bisect the Soviet War Memorial. Each ruler was flanked by two notable characters who had contributed to that monarch's reign, one in war and the other in peace, positioned to look up respectfully at their master. Frederick William III, for example, was flanked by Blücher and vom Stein. It was not only the vulgarity of the idea that irritated but also the clumsy execution. It was known derisorily in Berlin as the *Puppenallee* (avenue of dolls). Begas was again in charge of commissioning and produced a series of undistinguished sculptures in supposedly classical pose. Each statue had a park bench in front so that passers-by could contemplate the figures' greatness in comfort, and schoolchildren were especially encouraged to use the avenue for their history lessons.

The Kaiser was delighted with it, however, remarking complacently that through it he could 'show the world that the most satisfactory means of fulfilling an artistic purpose is not by forming committees or announcing competitions but, in the manner tried and tested by antiquity, and in the Middle Ages, by direct contact between patron and artist'.[19] Others were less convinced, and one enterprising company used it in an advertisement for toothpaste. The avenue was not that badly damaged despite the fierce fighting around the Tiergarten in the Second World War, but the Allied Powers occupying West Berlin thought the statues too reminiscent of the martial Germany they had just defeated so they prepared to cart them off to the Teufelsberg rubble mountain. Hinnerk Schaper – responsible for Berlin's monuments in the aftermath of the war – intervened and asked that they be kept. The twenty-six remaining ones were consequently buried in the gardens of the nearby Schloss Bellevue and, after a roundabout journey, they have ended up in Spandau Citadel where you can see them today.

Poor Reinhold Begas! His work seemed destined to be subject to the Kaiser's whim in its execution and then subsequently destroyed.

He was not alone. The reason that it took Hoffman so long to erect the Märchenbrunnen in the Volkspark Friedrichshain is because the Kaiser even interfered with that, insisting that it incorporated his own view of the famous fairy stories. One commission Begas managed to carry out successfully, and which today is seen daily by thousands, is his Neptune Fountain in the Alexanderplatz, just in front of the Marienkirche. This was actually commissioned by the city council as a gift for William II, so he could not interfere much in its design. It shows Neptune sitting in the middle of four river goddesses representing the great German rivers – the Rhine, the Elbe, the Oder and – then – the Vistula. It is an effective piece and forms a central point for the open space where so many people congregate in central Berlin. Begas also executed the statue of Bismarck that originally stood on Königsplatz and is now on Großer Stern, and that of Alexander von Humboldt at the entrance to his university on the Unter den Linden.

The most famous and symbolic of all Berlin's buildings built at the turn of the nineteenth century was, however, the Reichstag. Since 1871 the members had been meeting in their temporary accommodation in Leipzigerstraße while interminable arguments raged about the design of their new home on the Königsplatz. Many Berliners are dismayed today at how long it has taken to build and operate their new airport, but they should take comfort from the fact that the rows about the Reichstag show that an inability to execute a major project is not exactly new in the city's history. First there was a disagreement about the location, with members arguing that the Königsplatz – until recently just another parade ground for the city's garrison – was too remote from the old centre. Once they were persuaded, in 1872 a design competition was launched, which was won by an architect from Gotha, Ludwig Bohnstedt. However, the government then discovered they could not actually acquire the Königsplatz site. This took a further ten years to sort out, by which time the original competition was obsolete so it had to be rerun. This time it was won by the previously little-known Paul Wallot from Frankfurt, who now faced the near-impossible task of satisfying the

Kaiser (still the old Kaiser William I in 1882), the Reichstag members and Bismarck. He had to produce a building that was both a symbol of the new German nation and of democracy within it.

His product, finally finished in 1894, could not have been expected to please everybody; nor did it. The new Kaiser predictably said it was 'the height of tastelessness', while others said it was a building that could not decide what it wanted, that it 'presented a different appearance on nearly every façade and yet another different one in the cupola'. Instead of symbolising German unity, it was an example 'of the deep division in the German empire and of a parliament's powerlessness to become a master in its own house'.[20] Whatever people thought, the Reichstag became, perhaps more than any other building in Berlin with the possible exception of the Brandenburg Gate, the face of the city and of Germany, a fame only strengthened by the Soviet army deciding that its fall in May 1945 symbolised the final defeat of the Nazis. The famous inscription written above its entrance *Dem Deutschen Volke* (to the German people), which became one of the building's best-known features, was added in 1916 rather than by Wallot.

~

William II's belief in his own cultural infallibility, and the weakness of his ministers after Bismarck, also led to tension between the government and what was fast becoming an artistic renaissance of a different kind in Berlin. Whereas the middle decades of the nineteenth century had been culturally a bit dry (especially when compared to the richness of the early years), by the time William II acceded, literature and the theatre were being influenced by a younger group of talented writers who saw the world very differently than the uniformed officials in Potsdam and who enjoyed a press through which they could communicate. By 1872 Berlin had its first daily paper that can be said to have had a real national impact, Rudolf Mosse's *Berliner Tageblatt*.

This was not necessarily a sudden transition. Writers like the novelist Theodore Fontane were realistic rather than controversial.

Fontane was a chemist's son, born in Neuruppin in 1819. A Huguenot who spoke fluent French despite it being 200 years since the Edict of Potsdam, it was Berlin and Brandenburg that defined him as much as he defined them; they are the thread that links all his writing. He spent his early life as a journalist, participated half-heartedly in the 1848 uprising, partly because the firearm he was issued was so antique it posed more danger to him than any soldier he might discharge it at, and partly because he was not sure that he supported upsetting the established order. He then spent a spell in London, and covered all Bismarck's wars, nearly getting himself shot as a spy in France when he got lost behind French lines. He excused himself by saying that he was searching for Joan of Arc's village of Domrémy, whereupon his patriotic French captors gave him a guided tour. His best-known book, *Wanderungen durch die Mark Brandenburg* (Wanderings through the Mark of Brandenburg), was not a novel at all but a loving description of walking around his home country. Published in five volumes between 1862 and 1889, it covers the history, the nature, the landscape and local stories and was a bestseller, inspiring thousands of young Berliners to walk in the countryside. Heirs of those gymnasts who followed Jahn to Leipzig, this love of nature and the countryside, and of walking, became a strong tradition across Germany as a whole and in Berlin in particular. The *Wandervogel* movement, an increasingly popular expression of this, was a peculiar mixture of a desire to get out of the city (its motto was *Los von Berlin*, away from Berlin), to find ancient roots in the Brandenburg countryside and to take physical activity. Members greeted each other with a raised right-arm salute and the word *Heil*. National Socialism would build on the foundations it and its mentor, Karl Fischer, laid.

Fontane's detractors said that he was too deferential to the nobility in his descriptions of their castles and estates but Fontane's focus was on the people themselves rather than on social commentary. He started writing novels in the 1870s and produced fourteen. His stories are about people, generally well-off people, who behave rationally and his focus is on them as characters rather than the social issues they must resolve. His best known are probably *Effi Briest* (considered by literary critics to be the equal of *Madame Bovary* or *Anna Karenina*), and *Irrungen, Wirrungen*, which has been translated as *A Suitable Match*. In *Effi Briest*, Effi's happy marriage is destroyed when her husband discovers that she has committed adultery years before. He doesn't feel angry with Effi but honour demands that he challenge her lover to a duel in which he kills him. It is all rather pointless, two families are destroyed all for a concept that none of the characters really understand. In *Irrungen, Wirrungen*, Botho von Rienäcker becomes the lover of Lene Nimptsch, a working-class girl who lives on the junction of the Ku'damm and Kurfürstenstraße. They adore each other but cannot marry as she is not a suitable match for a lieutenant in the Imperial Cuirassiers. Both end up marrying people who are more suitable but neither is happy. There is no dramatic ending, no murders or suicides, but just rather a sad commentary on social stratification in late-nineteenth-century Berlin.

Fontane was a liberal who believed in reform but his commentary on his characters is more objective and pitying than it is damning. Later he would be directly critical of the Prussian obsession with nobility, to which he had been accused of pandering, and of the Kaiser's government; he particularly disliked the colonisation programme on which William II was embarking. His great contribution is more in the view he gives us of Berlin society than as a social reformer. Gerhart Hauptmann, however, took a very different view that allowed him the distinction of becoming the Kaiser's most hated author. Hauptmann, who was a Silesian, came to Berlin in 1884. He was a prolific writer of almost everything from novels to poetry, but it is as a playwright that he is best known and for which, to the Kaiser's abject fury, he won the Nobel Prize for literature in 1912. Whereas Fontane observed what was wrong, Hauptmann attacked it directly. Hauptmann's success was in large part due to the theatre manager Otto Brahm. In 1889 Brahm and a group of friends had opened the *Freie Bühne*, a theatre designed specifically to stage plays that challenged. Their first performance was Ibsen's *Ghosts*, banned in Berlin when it had previously opened two years earlier but able to be staged through an ingenious scheme of Brahm's whereby he made the theatre a club. It was at the *Freie Bühne* that Hauptmann's first play, *Vor Sonnenaufgang* (Before Sunrise), was put on. Cast in a small Silesian mining community, it was a story of unremitting gloom with characters who 'stand for adultery, cruelty, alcoholism, attempted incest and suicide'.[21] Berlin had seen nothing like it before. Half the audience hated it but the other half loved it.

'Theatre is not just theatre,' said Brahm afterwards, 'but a vehicle of literary agitation and the most powerful there is'. Hauptmann's best-known play, *Die Weber* (The Weavers), about Silesian weavers during the famine in 1844, was banned when it opened in the Deutsches Theatre in 1892 and the police tried to bring charges against him for sedition. Again Brahm made the theatre a private club. *Die Weber* quickly became a European success, but in 1896 the Kaiser intervened to stop Hauptmann being awarded the prestigious Schiller Prize for literature, insisting instead that it went to a bizarre man called Ernst von Wildenbruch who was renowned for writing boring historical plays about the Hohenzollerns that sent his audiences to sleep. The Kaiser, who had a curious mixture of admiration and hatred for all things English, also loved trying to outperform London with Shakespeare productions. He told the bemused Gertrude Bell one evening during a performance of *Henry IV* that 'no plays of Shakespeare were ever acted in London and that we must have heard tell that it was only the Germans who had really studied or really understood Shakespeare'.[22] It was perhaps another iteration of Berlin's love for The Bard.

While *Die Weber* revolutionised the Berlin theatre, another of Hauptmann's great plays, *Die Ratten* (The Rats), is about Berlin and specifically life in a Mietskaserne in 1884, although the play was not actually produced until 1911. *Die Ratten* is a bitter attack on the poverty, desperation, alcoholism and misery of the life of Berlin's poor. Hauptmann casts the main character, a drama student called Spitta, as his spokesman. Spitta is taking lessons from a retired and ultra-conservative theatre director, Hasenreuter, who has fallen on hard times and who lives in a rat-infested apartment with a motley cast of Berlin characters. Hasenreuter is furious when Spitta suggests that 'Before art, as before the law, all men are equal', and demands to know why his student thinks a Berlin cleaning woman might be as suitable a subject for a drama as King Lear or Lady Macbeth. He tells Spitta that he is a rat who is working to undermine the Reich and that he wants to drag the imperial crown down into the dust. Of the other characters in the house, one is murdered, one has been abandoned by an army officer, one is a vile criminal, and one – Frau John, whom Spitta has suggested might be the subject of a play – takes her own life. The real rats are those who permit such misery to exist.

The more conservative elements of Berlin continued to loathe Hauptmann. Prince Chlodwig zu Hohenloe-Schillingfürst wrote after seeing one of his plays: 'A monstrous, wretched piece of work ... in general abominable. Afterwards went to Borchardt's, to get ourselves back into a human frame of mind with champagne and caviar'.[23] Hauptmann never seemed to achieve the recognition outside Germany that he enjoyed at home, possibly because in his old age he was equivocal about and even supportive of the Nazis, but *Die Ratten*, like *Die Weber*, came to define the Berlin theatre as a vibrant and effective force for change.

Theatre of all types was becoming increasingly popular in Berlin and new ones were opening all the time. The Theater des Westens was opened in 1896, the Schiller Theater in 1906 and by 1907 there were thirty venues putting on dramas. Not all Berlin theatre was highbrow and there was also an active music-hall culture that became increasingly popular in the decade before 1914. Impromptu cabaret was taking off in the numerous *kneipen*, and the director of the *Wintergarten*, Julius Baron, put on shows where he used *Berlinerisch*, giving it a sort of bourgeois respectability and making it widely known as the language of quick-witted Berliners. The Wintergarten – then in Mitte although now in Potsdamer Straße – was also the first theatre ever to show a film.[24]

The city also maintained its deep enthusiasm for music. This

ranged from the popularity of the endless military-band concerts –
where regimental bands in their smart uniforms played not just
rousing and patriotic songs but also serious pieces – to an increasing interest in classical music and opera. One enterprising military
bandsman, Benjamin Bilse, had left the army and set up a travelling
light orchestra. He rented a venue in Leipziger Straße and started
regular weekend concerts that proved immensely popular, not least
because concert-goers could bring their children and order food
and drink during the performances. Unsurprisingly this began to
irritate the musicians and in 1882 most of them left to set up their
own Berlin Philharmonie, the Philharmonic Orchestra. Around the
same time, the conductor Hans von Bülow was in Berlin conducting
Brahms and causing a sensation by the intensity of his performances.
Five years later von Bülow returned and became the Philharmonic's
conductor. A new concert hall was acquired in an old skating rink
and perhaps Berlin's most famous musical legacy was forged. The
Berlin Philharmonic would go on to attract some of the world's
greatest conductors and musicians of the next century including
Artur Nikisch, Wilhelm Furtwängler and Herbert von Karajan. In
their wake came numerous other concert halls so that, by the turn
of the century, there were hundreds of public concerts annually.

Opera was also in increasing demand. Whereas even the Kaiser's
censors found it difficult to interfere too deeply with purely musical
performances, they were more active in trying to ensure that opera
met their sovereign's view as to what constituted art. Countless very
boring performances were commissioned 'By Royal Command',
most of which had the glory of the house of Hohenzollern or the
necessity of firm government as their central theme. The Kaiser intervened directly to commission the Italian Leoncavallo to turn Alexis's
novel *Der Roland von Berlin* into an opera, which was an instant
flop, as were *Agnes von Hohenstaufen* and *Feldlager in Schlesien*.
Nevertheless, one man did protect opera at least a little from the
dead hand of the court, the charismatic Botho von Hülsen, who
was *General Intendant der Königlichen Schauspiele* (which roughly
translates as chamberlain of the Theatre Royal) for thirty years. A

young Guards Officer with a passion for acting, although criticised by some for being too heavy-handed in what performances he allowed, von Hülsen did manage to make opera more accessible so that by 1905 the *Komische Oper* had opened in Friedrichstraße and by 1914 it had seen 500 performances of Offenbach's *Tales of Hoffman*. In 1912 the *Deutsche Oper* had also opened in Charlottenburg. Then in 1898 Richard Strauss was appointed as musical director of the State Opera, a post he would occupy for fifteen years. After a tremendous start, with popular performances of *Tristan und Isolde* and *Die Fledermaus*, he had the inevitable fall-out with the Kaiser who thought that his own *Feuersnot* opera was 'insulting to Prussian morality'. Strauss was, William announced, a serpent who he had been sucking to his breast. From then on Berliners referred to Strauss as the 'Imperial Breast Serpent'.

There is an ironic twist to the story of Botho von Hülsen. The post of *Intendant der Königlichen Schauspiele* was taken over by another von Hülsen, General Georg von Hülsen-Haesler, whose performance in the role earned him a place in the Invalidenhof. He was given a splendid grave there surrounded by wrought-iron railings incorporating the family's ilex leaf motif. In the 1960s the Wall ran very close to the graveyard and at some stage during the Cold War the Hülsen railings disappeared from his grave only to reappear round the famous *Zum Nussbaum* cafe near the Nikolaikirche. A sharp-eyed member of the family spotted this after 1989 and the railings are now restored and back where they belong. Lying beside Hülsen-Haeseler's ornate grave lies the simple unremarkable grey granite slab of Helmuth von Moltke.

If the Kaiser's interference in theatre and opera was damaging, the art form where his views clashed most directly with the modernists was in painting. Adolf Menzel, a tiny man born in Breslau in 1815 and who came to Berlin in 1830, was to Berlin art what Fontane was to its literature. He was an artist who brooked the transition from classical to modern, a man who could paint extraordinarily vivid and atmospheric scenes from life in a way that the Biedermeieresque artists had never achieved, but whose art was more objective than it was revolutionary. Consequently, he found himself criticised by both camps. The Kaiser felt that his representation of industrial scenes, such as 'The Rolling Mill' painted in 1872, showed too much hardship and some of his war scenes were stark and morbid. On the other hand, the modernists laughed at his cosy scenes of court life such as his famous 'Tafelrunde' (Frederick the Great's round table at Sanssouci) and his even more well-known 'Flötenkonzert' of Frederick playing the flute. Menzel ended his life revered in Berlin, ennobled as von Menzel and the Kaiser himself attended his funeral. In March 1905 the National Gallery put on a memorial exhibition of his work, funded by the Kaiser, and a special fund was set up to allow the nation to buy much of his enormous product; he produced nearly 7,000 different paintings and drawings during his long life.

The experience of his contemporaries was to be very different. The conservative school, of whom the Kaiser strongly approved, was best represented by Anton von Werner, whom he made director of the Royal Academy. It is to him we owe the great pictures of the proclamation of William I as emperor at Versailles and William II opening the Reichstag. The true modernists and the early impressionists were, however, heavily criticised. In 1892 the Norwegian artist Edvard Munch was invited by the Association of Berlin Artists to exhibit in Berlin, but his work was so badly received by the critics that his exhibition closed after two days. Munch's rejection prompted what became known as the *Sezession* movement, led by painters like Max Liebermann, Walter Leistikow and Käthe Kollwitz to mount their own exhibition. Housed originally in the Theater des Westens, it first ran through the summer of 1898, moving to the Ku'damm in 1905 and becoming both a permanent fixture in the city and a major artistic movement. The Kaiser called it 'the art from the gutter' and he ordered officers who wished to visit such a degenerate exhibition not to wear uniform. He particularly disliked Leistikow, whose painting of the *Der Grunewaldersee* had, he said, for ever ruined his enjoyment of the forest. Impressionism as a whole was not encouraged. James Huneker, a visitor to Berlin, wrote that 'A visit to the National

Gallery of Berlin makes me gnash my teeth. The sight of so much misspent labour, of acres of canvas deluged with dirty, bad paint, raises my bile.' What Impressionist works the gallery had bought, against the Kaiser's express wishes, were hidden away in an attic, and the artists who had 'fallen under the ban of official displeasure included Monet, Manet, Pissaro, Renoir, Sisley and Cézanne'.[25]

Max Liebermann, who became the leader of the Sezessionist movement, was a Berliner through and through, born in the city, a scion of the famous manufacturing and banking family, and dividing his time between his studio on the Pariser Platz and his delightful lakeside villa on the Wannsee. He liked to speak in *Berlinerisch*, and rejoiced in quick, sharp Berliner comments that frequently disarmed his clients. A rich banker whose portrait he had just completed was admiring it in his studio. 'What a wonderful likeness!' he declared. 'Yes indeed,' replied Liebermann, 'nauseatingly so.'[26] His paintings – from the realism of 'Women Plucking Geese', painted in 1871, and 'Flax Spinners', completed in 1887, to the later impressionist studies – offer an incomparable view of contemporary German and Berlin life. Any visit to Berlin is incomplete without seeing his villa, garden and paintings at Wannsee, which is preserved as a charming small museum. It also displays works by Lesser Ury (Liebermann's one-time pupil, although they later had a major falling-out), whose impressionist paintings of Berlin by night capture the atmosphere of the early-twentieth-century city so brilliantly.

Käthe Kollwitz's work was, by contrast, more emotional. Kollwitz has deservedly become something of an icon for the very difficult years Germany was to suffer in the early twentieth century, and it is her drawings and sculpture that so starkly illustrate the torment Berlin endured. Kollwitz came from a socialist and very religious background in East Prussia. She married a Berlin doctor and they lived in Prenzlauer Berg, where he ministered to Berlin's poor. Her drawings for *Die Weber*, which she finished in 1896, prompted Menzel to nominate her for the prestigious gold medal of the *Große Deutsche Kunstausstellung*. Predictably the Kaiser intervened, partly because he hated her work and partly, as he told Menzel, 'medals and honours belonged on the breasts of worthy men' not women.[27] Kollwitz's next series was on the sixteenth-century Peasants' War, again illustrating the suffering of the dispossessed. It is her moving 'Mutter mit totem Sohn' that is the centre of Germany's National Memorial in the Neue Wache on the Unter den Linden today.

One other artist who portrayed Berlin's life as the imperial city drifted towards 1914 was Heinrich Zille. Zille was really a cartoonist, capturing the humour and absurdities of daily life in the city but also its grittiness. His pictures of life in the Mietskaserne, of Berlin's prostitutes and of the harshness of poverty are funny but do not hide any of the nastiness. It was a world he knew only too well, having been brought up in a rancid Mietskaserne apartment himself. He described his first encounters with art: 'The oil print had just been invented ... the "oil paintings" of the poor. The pictures were cheap and "decorated" the flat and at the same time they served as a "bug-trap". I still see before my mind's eye, in a pitiful room, in which 7 people were housed, that portrait of Kaiser Wilhelm I was gently moving ... so many bugs were crawling behind that picture.'[28] Zille was much influenced by his friend Dr Ebelin, who told him that '70 per cent of Berlin children have no idea of what a sunrise looks like, 76 per cent don't know what dew is, 82 per cent have never seen a lark, half have never heard of a frog'.[29] Zille intended to shock, and drawings like his Hurengespräche, of a young girl performing oral sex on an old man, and his scene of a prostitute having sex on one bed while an old woman lies dying in the next-door one, are scathing. Some of his other work, such as his Berlin beach scenes, are more comic. Zille was tremendously popular and became a Berlin institution during his lifetime. Liebermann brought him into the Sezession, even though Zille would protest that he was not a proper artist, and there is a small museum to his work in the Nikolaiviertiel.

Reflecting art of a very different genre, another man who made a significant contribution to Berlin was Wilhelm von Bode, appointed in 1872 as an assistant curator in the Altes Museum aged just twenty-seven. Bode thought museums should give the visitor an insight to what life was like at a particular time, and he objected strongly to the contemporary habit of showing objects out of context and with no explanation of their background. What museums should do, he argued, was give the visitor an overall impression of a particular lifestyle or epoch, combining pictures, furniture and sculpture in rooms designed to reflect certain historical styles. After protracted negotiations, in 1898 he managed to secure the necessary permission and funding to build a new museum on the northern tip of the Island, the northern half of which was now becoming referred to as Museumsinsel (Museums Island), the result of which was the Kaiser-Friedrich-Museum, which in 1956 was renamed as the Bode Museum in his honour. Berlin's loose sand made construction as difficult as ever, particularly on the point where the two arms of the Spree reunite, but the resulting building, with its low dome and curved facade facing out downstream, with a piazza at the island's very tip, is one of Berlin's most satisfactory. Just opposite was the site of the now-destroyed Monbijou Palace where Frederick I had so enjoyed himself and after which the connecting bridge is named.

Bode went on to be the Director General of Berlin's Museums in 1906, a feared and effective fundraiser who would use his friendship with the Kaiser to extract money from potential benefactors. He was also a discerning collector so that many of Berlin's treasures today owe their provenance to him. With increasing competition from emerging American collectors, Bode still managed to buy works by Rembrandt, Dürer and Hals, as well as the famous head of Nefertiti, now in the Neues Museum. When Bode started his long tenure, Museumsinsel north of the Lustgarten consisted of Schinkel's original Altes Museum, Stüler's Neues Museum behind it and the Nationalgalerie, a building designed as a Greek temple, which had been opened in 1876. By the time he stepped down in 1920, not only was the Kaiser-Friedrich-Museum complete but work was well underway on the nearby Pergamonmuseum. This last was built to house the many treasures that flooded into Berlin from the various German archaeologists digging up the ancient cities of the Near and Middle East. From Carl Richard Lepsius, who dug in Egypt in the 1840s, to Carl Humann, who spent eight years excavating in the ancient city state of Pergamon in the eastern Aegean and after which the museum is named, to Heinrich Schliemann, the discoverer of the so-called Priam's treasure at Troy, to Robert Koldewey who worked in what is now Iraq, Berlin found itself the recipient of the most extraordinary number of ancient objects. The Pergamon became home both to a remarkable reconstruction of Babylon's Ishtar Gate and to the Roman Market Gate of Miletus, both of which make it today Germany's most visited museum. Supplemented by Bode's astute acquisition, by 1914 Berlin was becoming the museum capital of Europe. Despite extensive wartime damage, and quite a bit of Russian looting in 1945 including Priam's Treasure, which Schliemann had controversially brought back from Troy, most of what Bode achieved is still there. After an extensive and ongoing restoration programme post-1989, Museumsinseln once again constitutes one of the world's unique cultural collections.

~

What was so concerning about the Kaiser's attitude to art was that he genuinely believed he should be the arbiter of it. In one speech he said that 'An art which transgresses the laws and barriers outlined by Me [his capital M], ceases to be art; it is merely a factory product, a trade'. He then went on to say that 'To us, to the German people, ideals have become permanent possessions, whereas amongst other peoples they have been more or less lost. Only the German nation is left, and we are called upon to preserve, cultivate, and continue these great ideals.'[30] Such personal and national self-belief was particularly dangerous when it was unchecked by ministers or parliament and backed by a military who believed that they had forged the German nation in the 1860s and 1870s and that they had a key role to play in its future. Just in case anyone forgot, on 2 September 1895 they staged a major parade to celebrate the twenty-fifth anniversary of the capitulation of the French army at Sedan, with the Brandenburg Gate festooned with a banner that read *Welch Eine Wendung Durch Gottes Fuhrung* (a great event by God's grace). Silver medals were issued to all the campaign veterans with a portrait of the Kaiser.

Sedantag (Sedan day) became a public holiday. Berlin society put the military on a pedestal and, though the power of rank and uniform was scorned by the socialists, many Berliners both envied it and aspired to it.

There is a famous Berlin story of a petty criminal called Wilhelm Voigt who came to Berlin in 1906 in search of acquiring a residence permit but was denied it because of his criminal record. In desperation he stole the uniform of an army captain, presented himself at one of the many Guards' barracks in Berlin and ordered ten soldiers to accompany him on the train to Köpenick. On arrival he marched his detachment to the town hall, where he arrested the mayor and the police inspector, although he then released the latter as he was in the act of having a bath. Voigt then told the mayor that he had been sent to investigate various irregularities in the town's books, and ordered him to hand over the available cash, 4,000 marks, which the mayor promptly did. Voigt and his small squad returned to Berlin, where he dismissed them before he disappeared with the money. The incident only came to light some time later when Voigt boasted about it while in prison for some other petty crime. The story quickly became public, making a laughing stock not just of the unfortunate mayor but also of Berlin's obsession with the authority of a uniform; the Kaiser was unamused and the army referred to the incident as a 'Second Jena'. It was later made into a play by Carl Zuckmayer that was hugely popular in Berlin not least because it used quite a lot of *Berlinerisch,* including that well-known expression '*Nachtijall icke hör dir trapsen*'. Commissions in the army reserve were very highly prized, allowing the recipients to continue working but also to enjoy the privileges and trappings of rank. Officers were served first in shops, took the best tickets at theatres, and many considered themselves above the law.

Despite the success of the SPD, in 1900 many Berliners were still generally nationalist and monarchist. A poll taken by the *Berliner Illustrierte Zeitung* in 1898 asked Berliners twenty-seven questions about the century just passing. The results were reassuring for the Kaiser. The greatest German was Bismarck; the most important woman was Queen Luise of Prussia; Kaiser William I was the greatest Berliner, tying with Alexander von Humboldt. Menzel was the greatest artist and – to the Kaiser's delight and the modernists' chagrin – Begas was the greatest sculptor, which given that the poll included all European artists was a little surprising. Perhaps the strangest answer of all, however, was that the greatest thinker was Moltke rather than Kant or Hegel. Only one Berliner answered the question 'Who was the greatest Berliner?' in typical Berlin fashion when he replied, 'There is no such thing as a great Berliner.'[31]

Middle-class life was comfortable and stable. Walter Benjamin describes growing up in a well-off family around 1900. It was a childhood full of security and excitement, of solid houses, his grandmother's 'a giant bloom of plush', their holiday home in Potsdam where he learned to bicycle, of swimming lessons, of reassuring sounds of home such as a carpet being beaten in a courtyard, of walks, meals and all that Biedermeieresque cosiness, which the German language sums up so well as *gemütlichkeit*. The Benjamin family were Jewish, and the world he describes reflects that the early twentieth century was a period when Berlin's Jewish community was at its most secure and when many had successfully achieved the aim of being Germans who were Jewish rather than Jews who happened to live in Germany. There was, admittedly, still a certain snobbishness that excluded them from some positions, but the success of businessmen like Rathenau and Liebermann had given them cachet. Neither could the Jewish community be spoken of as a single entity by 1900. There were the rich and well-established families like the Benjamins but there was also a continuous stream of *Ostjuden*, Jews immigrating from eastern Europe, of whom 12,955 had arrived by 1900. They were blamed by some for keeping alive Berliners' negative image of Jews and tended to live in areas like the Scheunenviertiel, which was still regarded as a sink of petty crime and prostitution. What makes Walter's memoir so poignant is that he was writing long after that reassuring and certain world had been destroyed.

Benjamin's memoir and the results of the 1898 *Berliner Illustrierte*

Zeitung show a Berlin that was, at least among the middle classes, supportive and indeed partly reliant on the stability provided by the monarchy and the government. Such adulation required in its turn the Kaiser, his court and the military to behave as the Berlin bourgeoisie thought they should. This was not always the case. In 1907 Maximilian Harden, the editor of a socialist-leaning Berlin weekly *Die Zukunft* (The Future), published an article that effectively accused two of the Kaiser's key advisers, Prince Philip von Eulenburg and the commander of the Berlin Garrison, Count Kuno von Moltke, of having a homosexual affair and holding orgies with soldiers from the Guards regiments. Despite the Kaiser's urging, Eulenburg refused to sue Harden and resigned but von Moltke took him to court. Homosexuality was then illegal in Germany, and although Berlin was always more tolerant of sexual inclinations than most European cities, what was so damaging was that this affair implicated the Crown. From October Berliners were variously entertained and shocked by stories of gay parties among the military elite. Even worse was that von Moltke's ex-wife testified that she thought he was homosexual and the court refused to convict Harden of libel. Von Moltke also had to retire from public life. Then the next year General Count Dietrich Hülsen-Haeseler, from the same family as the Schauspiele directors, collapsed and died while staying in a shooting party with the Kaiser. Not unusual perhaps in itself, but it transpired that the general, who headed the Kaiser's military cabinet, had collapsed after the exertions of dancing in front of the monarch while wearing nothing but a pink tutu.

Revelations like these, humorous as they appeared to many Berliners, were making the court and government seem hypocritical and out of touch. Neither was Germany's foreign policy going well. In 1907 Britain, France and Russia had signed the Triple Entente, which, while not a military alliance as such, committed signatories not to conclude a separate agreement with Germany without the consent of the other parties. It was a reaction to Germany's Triple Alliance, with Austria and Italy, but in Berlin it gave the feeling of encirclement. There was also strong criticism of German colonial policy, the Kaiser being determined that Germany should have a similar share of overseas possessions to other European nations. Attitudes in the city began to change and the socialists slowly gained more influence. In 1900 Jens Birkholm painted a stirring painting that he called 'The Gospel of the Poor'. A speaker talks to a rapt audience about socialism. In the background is a bust of Marx, while two policemen look on. In 1911, 150,000 Berliners demonstrated in Treptow park over German intervention in Morocco. That same year two workers were killed and 150 injured in clashes with police, and when a protester called Paul Singe was killed more than a million people turned out for his funeral, lining the seven-mile route from his house to the cemetery in Friedrichsfelde. In 1912 the SPD won 35 per cent of the vote in the Reichstag elections, dwarfing the centrist parties and doubling their number of seats. The population of Berlin, nudging 4 million, was becoming increasingly politically active and increasingly socialist.

It is beyond the scope of this story to explain in detail the cascade of events of the summer of 1914 that would lead Europe into the First World War. To many it seemed as if no one really knew why it had started. The English-born Princess Blücher von Wahlstatt, who was living in Berlin, wrote 'Exactly what was the real cause of the war no one seems to know.'[32] Yet the declaration of war caused a huge public outpouring of support in Berlin and, at least temporarily, relegated these political differences to the side lines. At 5 p.m. on 31 July a young lieutenant of the Guards stood by Frederick the Great's statue on the Unter den Linden and read out a declaration of martial law. Civil rights were suspended. Berlin was now under the actual as well as the moral control of the army.

On 1 August – the day war was declared against Russia, France and Belgium – the Kaiser appeared on the balcony of the Berliner Schloss (the same spot from where his great-uncle had addressed the protesters in 1848) and received rapturous applause when he announced that 'In the battle now lying ahead of us, I recognise in my people no more parties. Among us there are only Germans ... all that now matters is that we stand together like brothers, and then

God will help the German sword to victory.' 'One thing grows clearer to me every day,' Princess Blücher continued, 'neither the people here nor there wished for war, but here they are now being carried off their legs with patriotism, at seeing so many enemies on every side.'[33] There was even more celebrating when war was declared against England on 4 August. Tilla Durieux was an actress living in Berlin. 'We found the city in roaring excitement,' she wrote in her memoirs:

> 'Everywhere there were crowds of people and columns of soldiers marching at whom people were throwing flowers. Every face was beaming with joy: we have war! In the cafés the bands were incessantly playing *Heil Dir im Siegkranz* and *Die Wacht am Rhein*. Everyone stood up to sing along; meanwhile the food got cold and the beer got warm. People were queuing to register their cars for an emergency service ... the soldiers at the stations received mountains of bread with butter, sausages and chocolate. There was an abundance of people, of food, of enthusiasm.'[34]

Walter Rathenau, son of Emil who founded AEG, and who was put in charge of war materials in 1914, thought the socialists cheered as loud as anyone. A particular enmity had developed between Germany and England in the preceding decade, strange when the two countries had been close allies. 'The people will bless Germany's decision to enter upon the defensive war against Britain and win the freedom of the seas,' said the famous historian Friedrich Meinecke, after whom the eponymous street off the Ku'damm is now named. 'England', said Professor Erich Marks, 'is our true mortal enemy.'[35] There was a popular song called the *Hasslied*, a 'Chant of hate against England' sung all over Berlin, which contained the lines 'We have one foe and one alone – England!'

Many of those who might have opposed the war now backed it. Ninety-three artists and writers signed a manifesto in October 1914 publicly supporting Germany's actions. Given German troops had been accused of atrocities in Belgium, this was considered ill advised by some. There were some surprising names on the list, including

Gerhart Hauptmann, Max Liebermann, Wilhelm von Bode, Max Klinger and the theatre director Max Reinhardt.[36] One man who did oppose it was August Bebel, leader of the SPD. He was jeered when he stood up in the Reichstag and declared, 'There will be a catastrophe ... 16 to 18 million men, the flower of different nations, will march against each other, equipped with lethal weapons ... I am convinced that this great march will be followed by the great collapse ... What is the result? After this war we shall have mass bankruptcy, mass misery, mass unemployment and great famine.' A voice shouted back at him, 'Herr Bebel, things only get better after every war,' a throwback to the era of Bismarck, but Bismarck would never have allowed Germany to fight a war on two fronts simultaneously.[37] The Forum Fridericianum was renamed as the Bebelplatz in honour of this doughty political fighter in 1947.

Most nations have a strange habit of celebrating when their young men are about to be sacrificed. Berlin that summer seems to have been excessively enthusiastic, that old fear of thinking they were preventing invasion, that ancient sense of victimhood re-emerging now in an era when technology had transformed soldiers' ability to kill without giving them the communications or means to target the dreadful new power they now possessed. A thirteen-year-old girl from Schöneberg called Marlene Dietrich, a promising violinist, wrote that she remembered 'soldiers marching through the streets, flowers on top of their rifles, laughing, singing, kissing the women, flags hanging from windows ... Barbarians celebrating the outbreak of war'.[38]

Käthe Kollwitz tried in vain to stop her adored son Peter from signing up but even she did not feel she could break with the prevailing public mood. She kept a detailed diary throughout the war, the entries for that summer recording the celebrations in Berlin as Liège fell on 7 and Alsace on 11 August. On 21 August the Germans entered Brussels. She supported the war financially; a district meeting called by the mayor in Prenzlauer Berg on 14 August subscribed 6,000 marks to the war effort. People went round the streets singing *'Jeder Schuß – ein Russ; jeder Stoß – ein Franzos; jeder Tritt – ein*

Brit' (Every shot a Russian; every stab a Frenchman; every kick a Brit).[39] The Kirstaedter family had been on holiday in Greifswald that July. They returned the day before war was declared. 'The enthusiasm was tremendous,' wrote Gerda Kirstaedter in her memoirs, 'everyone thought the war would end quickly and no one guessed its terrible consequences. My father, a captain in the Reserve immediately called in to the war clothing depot in Spandau.' Helmut and Werner, two brothers, volunteered for the 35th Infantry Regiment. 'They were trained and moved into the field two and a half months later. The farewell was very sad. I can still hear how Werner said to me "Gerda we will not meet again".'[40]

In late September the news began to dry up. Nothing was reported from the Western Front for several days, although there were positive reports from Hindenburg in the east. In early October, his training completed, Käthe Kollwitz waved Peter off to join his regiment in Belgium. He suffered from arthritis in his knee and had been delayed. He wrote when he could, and she received a letter from him on 24 October saying all was well but he could now hear gunfire. On 30 her diary has a one-line entry: 'Ihr Sohn ist gefallen' (Your son has fallen). In fact, Peter had been killed on 22 October and was already dead when his last letter arrived home. The diary assumes a flatter tone thereafter. Peter's room was kept untouched, preserved just as he had left it, and Kollwitz said his death was a wound that would never heal. She drew one of her starkest pieces, 'Killed in Action', showing a mother's horrified reaction on being told of a death at the front. It is one of her most moving and frightening works. Later she would sculpt an equally emotive memorial for his grave in a Belgian war cemetery. 'The Grieving Parents' is stark, frightening and compassionate, and if anything good can come from Peter's wasted life it is that Kollwitz found the feelings that would allow her to articulate so movingly in stone the bereavement so many Berlin families were feeling and that would lead to her 'Pieta' in the Neue Wache.[41]

Peter's death came at a time when the initial euphoria in Berlin had begun to wear off. Paris had not fallen and, although Hindenburg duly defeated the Russians at Tannenberg in late August, the famed

Schlieffen Plan (which the General Staff were so insistent would bring quick victory in the west) had led to the German army retreating from Paris and now being bogged down in Flanders as they struggled for the Channel ports. October was the beginning of four long, hard, bitter years as Berliners came to terms with just what the war they had cheered so enthusiastically actually meant. One of the first British actions had been to blockade Germany's ports so that not only could food and raw materials not be imported but also Berlin's factories lost their markets. The British naval blockade is one of those little discussed campaigns of the First World War but it was arguably the most critical in Germany's defeat. The first war casualty lists had been posted in Dorotheenstraße on 9 August and they surprised and depressed people by how long they were. By October Käthe Kollwitz noted that one family she knew had already lost five sons. Soon after Peter was killed, Werner Kirstaedter was hit in the head by a French bullet as he was digging a trench on the Western Front. He lived for ten days, partially conscious, but could not pull through. His brother Helmut was with him and had a nervous breakdown. He was sent back to an asylum at Erkner. Then unemployment soared to 20 per cent as factories could not sell their product; many workers found themselves drafted into five new infantry regiments being raised in the city. Soup kitchens were set up in September for families without wages, and that winter food supplies started to reduce. Bread rationing was introduced in February 1915 and there was a chronic shortage of fuel for heat and transport. But, said the mayor, Adolf Wermuth, 'the Reich capital must and will take the lead in terms of discipline and willingness for sacrifice'. Wermuth was in office from 1912 until 1920 and, despite his exhortations not appealing to everyone, he must take the credit for keeping the city administration functioning during the difficult war years.[42]

Berlin found itself in a slightly strange place as the war stagnated that winter. For the rest of Germany, it became somewhere they were suspicious of and then actively disliked. It was, for many Germans, the centre of the government that was causing so much hardship and, as men like Rathenau worked to direct the war economy, inevitably

more and more decision-making was centralised. Then there was
the vexed issue of industrial workers' recall. As the war economy
ground into life, skilled workers who had been recruited into the
army were recalled to their previous jobs and, Berlin being one of
the great manufacturing centres, this applied to more Berliners than
other Germans. More than 90,000 benefited from recall during the
war, and overall Berlin mobilised only 60 per cent of its eligible men
(the figure for the rest of the country was nearer 80 per cent). It did
not, however, make Berliners feel any better off, and the demands the
war placed on the city were heavy. Industrial recalls notwithstand-
ing, Berlin still fielded a considerable number of soldiers. Apart from
the 44,000-strong Guards Corps – based in Berlin and Potsdam in
peacetime and recruited from across Germany but inevitably including a large proportion of Berliners – many joined the locally recruited
5th and 6th Divisions. They fought on the Western Front before
being moved east in 1917 to combat the Russian Kerensky offensive,
then south to Italy before being sent back to France again in 1918.

In the spring of 1915 a dummy trench was built in Reichkanzlerplatz
in an attempt to boost morale. 'A major interest,' ran an article about
it in *Vorwärts* magazine, 'will be the dugouts. There is a dugout
for the company of 50 men, furnished with all modern comforts.
Of course, the dugouts for the officers are even more elegant, with
tables and proper furnishings. The sergeant's quarters could not be
better furnished, even in peace time, and even an inkpot is present.'
Yet it was propaganda. The pain felt by Kathe Kollwitz would be
often repeated. One of Berlin's more extraordinary and little-visited
memorials to those who fell in the war is the *Langemarckhalle* at the
Olympiastadion, the sporting complex built for the 1936 Olympic
Games. Hidden from public view, the Nazis built a memorial hall to
the 10,000 Germans who fell at the Battle of Langemarck in October
1914, called First Ypres by the British. The story – often called the
Langemarck myth – is that young German Reserve Divisions, hastily
mobilised and containing a high proportion of Berlin students and
schoolboys, flung themselves with heroic if senseless bravery at the
Allied lines in a desperate attempt to break through to the Channel,

singing patriotic songs as they did so. The truth is more prosaic. Von Falkenhayn, then German Chief of Staff, wanted to find a better story to tell than that his last attempt to break through in the first stage of the war had failed. One of those boys was Werner Pfaffenberger, the eighteen-year-old son of a government official who had volunteered alongside most of his fellow pupils in his class at his gymnasium. He had dreamed of becoming a priest in a small village living in a house surrounded by flowers loved by a sweet girl. His teacher edited his letters and poems, alongside those of his fellow pupils, producing a book entitled *Letters From Heroes*, romanticising the glory of dying for the Fatherland. His mother, although deeply shocked by his death, strongly approved.[43]

For the Nazis the idea of Langemarck offered both a propaganda opportunity and also a chance to celebrate that strange part-medieval, part-Prussian, part-romantic, part-physical cult that they so perverted. The idea was that the hall remembered those who should have been competing in the Olympic Games but instead had given their lives for the Fatherland. It is a classic example of Nazi architecture: grey stone, with black iron shields commemorating the formations who took part, their names picked out in silver. There are no windows towards the stadium itself; this was not to be seen by an unsuspecting world at the Olympics. On the Wall are inscribed words by Walter Flex, the nationalist poet killed in 1917 and Hitler's favourite author, who wrote the much-quoted Prussian Military Oath 'He who swears on the Prussian flag has nothing left that belongs to himself'.[44]

It is difficult to think of Langemarck as a memorial to all those young Berliners who died rather than as a piece of Nazi propaganda. Another memorial is in a song. On the night of 3 April 1915, Hans Leip of the Fusilier Guards was on guard duty at his regimental barracks in Chausseestraße, *Die Maikäferkaserne* (the Cockchafers Barracks), so called because of the Fusilier Guards' regimental symbol. He was annoyed as it was his last night in Berlin before being sent to the Carpathian front. He would have preferred to have spent it with the girl he adored, Betty Marleen, known as Lilly, and the daughter of the greengrocers with whom Leip lived. As he stood by the barrack gate, Lilly appeared and stood under the lantern so he could see her. The song he wrote about it, 'Lily Marleen', became a sad reminder to generations of soldiers of all nationalities of the cost of war and separation.

> Vor der Kaserne, vor dem großen Tor,
> Stand eine Laterne, und steht sie noch davor,
> So wolln wir uns da wiedersehen
> Bei der lanterne wolln wir stehn,
> Wie einst Lili Marleen

The Maikäferkaserne was destroyed but its location, just on the corner of Chausseestraße and Habersaathstraße, is now the site of a large anonymous building euphemistically referred to as the *Bundesnachrichtendienst Hauptquartier*, or the headquarters of the Federal News Service.

By 1917 life in Berlin was beginning to get very difficult. Food was becoming very short indeed and then the potato crop, on which so many of Berlin's poor still depended, failed. There were food riots to get hold of turnips and the ersatz K (Krieg – black bread made out of potatoes or, as many thought, cardboard). By 1918 meat consumption was down to 12 per cent of 1914 levels, fish down to 5 per cent and eggs at 13 per cent. 'There is,' wrote Princess Blücher, 'intense cold here, such as has not been known for more than half a century. There are shivering throngs of hungry care-worn people picking their way through snowy streets ... We are all gaunt and bony now, and have dark shadows around our eyes. Our thoughts are chiefly taken up with wondering what our next meal will be, and dreaming of the good things that once existed.'[45] Many schools were closed, partly because 3,600 Berlin teachers had been drafted and partly because there was no coal to heat them. Schoolchildren were sent instead to gather acorns and berries in the Grunewald. Marlene Dietrich, whose family had moved to Dessau for much of the war, recalled girls conducting 'charcoal and potato drives' and spending 'their evenings at railroad stations singing ever younger soldiers off to war or at military hospitals singing them to a final peace'.

Women were increasingly drafted in to do industrial work as well as filling the lighter roles in service industries. Berlin was becoming a 'women's world, a 'world without men'.[46] Berlin had been a lot less oppressive to women than many European cities. Women had practised as doctors since 1876, when Franziska Tiburtius set up her women's clinic, and women had studied at the university since 1908, but this was different; this was women now moving into areas that had previously been a solely male preserve. The actress Tilla Durieux was working as a nurse in a military hospital. 'It took a huge effort for me to do the work without crying, without trying to run away from all that misery,' she wrote. 'It was very hard. By the evening I fell dead tired into bed. My feet swelled so much that at night I had to wrap them in wet towels. There were far too few nurses. It was one sister and an assistant for 30 badly injured men. The first time I took part in an operation I nearly fainted. I was given a leg that had been sawed off to dispose of. With all my power I pulled myself together, but I still feel the weight of that leg today.'[47] Gerda Kirstaedter also worked in a hospital. Her first job was to 'disentangle cats' guts and pack them in small bags for sewing wounds'. Later she was moved to the military hospital on Eisenacherstraße, where she did the laundry of wounded soldiers returned from the front and also had to prepare lunch. 'I still think of it,' she wrote later, 'with absolute horror.'[48] In 1915 she became engaged to her cousin Helmut as he slowly recovered from his shell shock but there could be no question of them getting married in wartime.

Martha Kups, who was doing industrial work, received a food allocation from her factory – 'horse sausage, horse meat and margarine' – but what really affected her was the cold:

'The public transport conditions on the S-Bahn were dreadful. Only when the carriages were totally packed did you get a bit warm. But often the train got stuck and then we were freezing again. In the factory there was no coal. You had to do your work

with numb fingers and so earned less. Once in a while there was a
coal wagon at Weißensee station. I was in the fortunate position
of owning a hand cart. I would take the biggest sack I could find
and rush there. There was always a major fight to get onto the
wagon and it took an enormous amount of strength to lift a full
sack; anyone who faltered doing so was ruthlessly pushed aside.'[49]

What irritated was that those with money could still eat well, and
hotels like the Adlon kept going throughout. This inevitably led to
indignation, particularly among soldiers home on leave who saw, on
the surface, some enjoying a high life on war profits while large parts
of the east and north were starving. One wounded soldier, who made
his first visit in October 1916, was not impressed. Adolf Hitler would
never like Berlin. It was, he wrote, a city of 'a thousand superficial
impressions – cheap neon advertising, sham politics everywhere you
look'.[50] The anti-war feelings began to become more public. 'For
four years I have given my all for this insane war and have lost, lost,
lost,' wrote Walter Gropius of Bauhaus fame, 'what a gloomy fate
to have to sacrifice everything that makes life worthwhile for an
even more doubtful patriotic ideal!'[51] Troops in Berlin on Sedan Day
were heard to sing the Marseillaise. Walter Rappolt, a lieutenant in
the Guards Artillery who was training recruits at Döberitz Camp,
wrote that he 'always wore civilian clothes when I went to Berlin,
because as a commissioned officer you were in danger of your epaulettes being torn off'.[52] A 'haves and have-nots' mentality affected
the city. The 'haves' were seen as war profiteers and nicknamed the
'English at Home'. 'The English abroad have made life very difficult
for us,' stormed the socialist daily *Vorwärts*, 'the English at home
have done the rest.'[53]

Anger was directed at the SPD, who were felt to be doing very
little either to help the people or to put pressure on the government
to stop the war. From 1916 various splinter groups started to form in
the Reichstag. These ranged from the extreme-left Spartakusbund –
led by Karl Liebknecht (son of the well-known socialist Wilhelm)
and the Polish socialist Rosa Luxemburg – to an Independent SPD,

the USPD, which in 1917 advocated taking a stronger anti-war line, to the right-wing Fatherland Party. In practice, though, there was little they could do. Effective control was with the army, with Hindenburg and Ludendorff, the two victors of Tannenberg, whose position was – at least until the middle of 1918 – unassailable. The Kaiser spent the war at his forward headquarters, which had moved by early 1918 to Spa in Belgium. His absence weakened support for the war in Berlin. William himself seems to have existed in a world of make-believe, that after the war was over Europe would revert to the dynastic cosiness of pre-1914. In 1894 he had been made Honorary Colonel of a British cavalry regiment, the Royal Dragoons, by Queen Victoria. When officers from that regiment were captured he instructed his staff that he was to be informed immediately. He then had them measured for new 'mess kits', the elaborate uniform worn by officers for dinner, and invited them to dine with him. He was surprised and offended when none of them accepted.

Spirits rose with the April revolution in Russia in 1917 but it failed to take Russia out of the war despite a peace initiative by the Catholic centrist politician Matthias Erzberger. He anyway had little political support. Hindenburg and Ludendorff retained the confidence of the Kaiser, and they controlled the levers of power. A huge wooden statue of Hindenburg was erected outside the Reichstag so that patriotic people could buy nails for a mark and bang them into him to help the war effort, but Hindenburg's reputation was now tarnished. 'Why is Hindenburg like the nation's sun?' ran a popular Berlin joke. 'Because he rises in the east and sets in the west.' Armed groups of deserters, many of them Spartacist supporters, holed up around the city. One group, the *Der Gruppe Kelmer*, fought a pitched battle with the police in October 1917. They beat the police and took their weapons. At night they would put up anti-war and pro-Spartacist posters. More and more deserters joined them that winter.

On 27 January 1918 there was, as normal, a service in the cathedral to celebrate the Kaiser's birthday. It would be the last time that the Lustgarten and the Schloßplatz were filled with 'gold-embroidered uniforms, decorations and glistening stars'.[54] After accepting the good wishes of his subjects, the Kaiser left for the front. Then, on 28 January, 3,000 workers went on strike. On 31 January 20,000 gathered to protest in Treptower Park. There was a firefight with police in Moabit and a policeman was killed. The strike did not, however, grow into the mass movement its organisers had hoped for, and its impact was – for the time being – limited. The government was still very much in control and able to move swiftly to suppress it. By 2 February, 150 of the ringleaders were in prison and most of the affected factories were back at work. Any worker who had been allowed home on recall was immediately returned to the front and soldiers patrolled the streets. It was, however, a warning. 'Those who are in the know,' wrote a young diplomat, Albrecht Graf von Bernstorff, 'are very worried. That the strike was badly organised and badly run was a matter of chance but we are in the territory of a Putsch, and we will, unless there is great and significant change, see one.'[55]

The Treaty of Brest-Litovsk in March 1918 did finally remove the threat from the east but the renewed offensive in the west stalled and, with the Americans now fighting in France as well, it was clear even to the army high command that the war was unwinnable. As the news from the now-critical Western Front became desperate, and German forces fell back in the face of Allied advances, Berliners revolted.

CHAPTER EIGHT

1918–1933

*'The horizons of Berliners imaginations have
for some time been narrower than those of
their city'*

KURT TUCHOLSKY, Berlin journalist,
author and satirist, 1919

On 27 September 1918 the Berlin papers reported that the war was
won. Despite all the hardship, the starvation, the loss of life, even
the hardened socialists clung to a belief that Germany would –
must – win in the end; Germany always won wars. It was a cruel
piece of false news. Once Ludendorff's Spring Offensive had faltered,
on 8 August, a day that Ludendorff described as a 'Black Day'
for Germany, the Allies had counter-attacked. The German army
was unable to stem the ensuing '100 Days' offensive and was now
retreating. On 29 September British and French forces assaulted the
once-impregnable Hindenburg Line of fortifications. The same day
Hindenburg and Ludendorff told the Kaiser they thought the war
was in fact now unwinnable, and on 30 September they told the
Reichstag. The Chancellor, Georg von Hertling, and his government resigned and an obscure cousin of the Kaiser's, Prince Max
of Baden, was appointed Chancellor. Baden was a strange choice.

The Kaiser – who still nurtured the idea that family links mattered, despite the carnage of the past four years – thought he would be a good person to negotiate as he was a descendant of Napoleon. The SPD felt he was among the least militaristic of the possible candidates and his administration included both SPD Party Chairman Philipp Scheidemann and the Trade Unionist Gustav Bauer. Hindenburg and Ludendorff, keen to shift the blame for the coming debacle to the politicians, accepted him at least initially. As the war dragged on, and casualties continued to mount, Baden attempted to negotiate with the Allies. They were sceptical of Germany's real intentions, fears heightened when Ludendorff changed his mind in mid-October and advised that the army must fight on. He was finally dismissed by the Kaiser on 26 October.

Events then began to move quickly and beyond the control of both Baden and the army's high command. The German navy had spent most of the war – apart from a brief period of action at Jutland – tied up alongside in Kiel. Morale was consequently low and when, in the last week of October, they thought they were being prepared for a last-ditch and clearly suicidal operation against the British, several ships refused to obey orders. On 3 November their crews demonstrated publicly in Kiel, demanding 'peace and bread'. By 4 November they had taken over control of the town, and troops sent to deal with them were either overpowered or joined them. They formed 'Sailors and Soldiers Councils' and drew up a list of fourteen points demanding largely military rather than political reform, which quickly circulated around Germany.

By November 1918 normal life in Berlin was close to collapse. The average daily food intake was now around half of what was required to stay healthy, and half the deaths in the city's hospitals were due to malnutrition. Apart from 44,000 disabled veterans, there were 34,000 war widows and 50,000 orphans to be cared for and, with the naval blockade still firmly in place, there was no chance of quick relief; in fact, the blockade was not lifted for a further nine months. The only foods available in the shops were cabbages and turnips, although the black market was flourishing for those able to afford it.

The Blankenfelde painting in the Marienkirche. Thomas is to the fore on the left (as we look) – his long-suffering wife to the right – with their twenty-one children. Behind Thomas is Johann, who financed Tetzel's indulgence scandal. Katharina, Joachim I's mistress, is the last of the girls.

The Nikolaikirche – the oldest church in Berlin and the centre of the city's spiritual life until the nineteenth century.

The Dance of Death in the Marienkirche – restored by the GDR in 1987 when the Communists decided they approved of its message of equality.

Joachim I and Joachim II by Cranach. These portraits hang in Jagdschloss Grunewald where Joachim II's mistress was reputedly walled up by his son.

The Great Elector and Louise Henrietta with their three sons.

Frederick I King *in* Prussia.

Frederick William I at his *Tabakskollegium*. Gundling is at the far end with his hare. The miniature figures to the left of the King are Frederick the Great and his brother.

Frederick II – Frederick the Great.

Berliner Schloss – built on the site of the Zwingburg – as it looked in the sixteenth and seventeenth centuries.

And in the eighteenth and nineteenth centuries.

Jagdschloss Grunewald. Only a short bus ride from the Ku'damm but surrounded by the forest. Berlin has more open space than any other European capital.

Oranienburg – designed by Louise Henrietta to remind her of Holland.

Königs Wusterhausen – 'In Berlin I only had to endure the pains of purgatory but in Wusterhausen the torments of hell', wrote Frederick William's daughter Wilhelmina, but the King loved the place.

Sophie-Charlotte, 'the most beautiful princess of her time' but 'somewhat too plump'.

Charlottenburg Palace, built for her by Nering in the last decade of the seventeenth century.

Daniel Chodowiecki's *Family Outing*. Chodowiecki portrayed and satirised Berlin life in over 6,000 works during the reign of Frederick the Great.

Schleuen's map of Berlin designed to show off the growing splendour of the Prussian capital.

Frederick the Great was horrible to his wife Elisabeth-Christine who led a miserable life at Schönhausen, as portrayed by Reclam in 1764.

But she cheered up considerably after his death, so well captured by Anton Graff.

Moses Mendelssohn and Gotthold Lessing debating. Both prominent leaders of Berlin's *Aufklärung*, Mendelssohn was responsible for changing the city's attitude to its increasing Jewish population.

Unter den Linden in 1770 by Carl Fechhelm showing the growing sophistication of both the city's appearance and its citizens.

Queen Luise, married to Frederick William III, was responsible for having the royal family portrayed as a homely family as opposed to in the previously formal military style. This charming sculpture of Princesses Luise and Friederike is by Schadow, famous for the Quadriga on the Brandenburg Gate.

Karl Friedrich Schinkel, painter, sculptor, furniture maker, but above all architect as well as the designer of the Iron Cross.

Berlin's appearance owes more to Schinkel than any other architect.

Schinkel's Neue Wache, the guardhouse on the Unter den Linden that became Germany's National Memorial.

Alexander von Humboldt, explorer, geographer, scientist, educationalist, and after whom, with his equally distinguished brother William, Berlin's university is now named.

Hegel, who headed the school of philosophy at the new university. He said that only one person understood his lectures and 'even he couald not'.

Sans Souci – Frederick the Great's charming and intimate rococo refuge at Potsdam designed by the King and Knobelsdorff in a style that was already becoming unfashionable in eighteenth-century Berlin.

While Schinkel's Schloss Tegel, built for the von Humboldts, represented what many saw as a more refined, Germanic taste.

Scenes of life in Berlin from the Biedermeier years. Eduard Gaertner's *Parochialstraße* shows a typical residential street.

While Johann Hummel's *Chess Match in the Voss Villa* summarises the settled domestic life to which many aspired.

The 'Revolution' of March 1848 – troops firing on the barricades. The uprising was more restricted than later commentators would have us believe.

'A piece of paper will not come between me and my people'. How the cartoonists interpreted King Frederick William IV's infamous promise of a constitution.

A Berlin cityscape. Schinkel's Altes Museum is on the far left, then the cathedral. The empty space in front of the cathedral is where the Palast der Republik has been demolished and where the Humboldt Forum now stands. In the foreground are the twin spires of the Nikolaikirche; the Marienkirche is in the middle ground on the right, just behind the Rote Rathaus.

Mietskaserne – the controversial nineteenth-century apartment blocks which still dominate Berlin today.

Life in a Mietskaserne. By the mid-nineteenth century Berlin was desperately short of accommodation.

Heinrich Zille's cartoon of street life in East Berlin. Zille lived in a cramped and rundown Mietskaserne block when his family first arrived in the city.

The Kaiser hated Max Liebermann's work, such as his *Flax Spinners*, and the *Sezession* movement he championed.

Artists like Ernst Henseler were more to the Kaiser's taste, as in his painting of *Bismarck addressing the Reichstag.*

More realistic depictions of Berlin life in the early-twentieth century were Jens Birkholm's *Gospel of the Poor*

And Leon Ury's atmospheric *Nollendorfplatz By Night.*

The Kaiser thought his *Siegesallee*, an avenue of statues of the Hohenzollern rulers in the Tiergarten, was an artistic triumph. Berliners were less sure.

But his declaration of war in 1914 from the Schloss balcony united the city behind the government, although not for very long.

By 1917 Berlin was angry, starving, full of wounded soldiers and on the verge of revolution. *There is no food and no work in Berlin* says the poster encouraging ex-soldiers to leave the city, but there was, allegedly, plenty of both outside.

Revolution came on 9 November 1918. A squad of revolutionary sailors march through the Brandenburg Gate decorated to celebrate the Armistice.

Käthe Kollwitz's *Pieta*, inspired by the loss of her son in 1914, is now the focus of the German National Memorial in Schinkel's Neue Wache.

George Grosz's view of the Nazis, which explains why he had to leave Berlin quickly as they seized power in 1933.

Hitler hated Berlin and thought it was not grand enough to be the capital of his Thousand Year Reich. He and Speer designed a new capital, *Germania*, which would have led to the destruction of much of the old city but which was mercifully never built.

'Where they burn books, one day they will also burn people'. Heine accurately predicted the direction Nazism would take after Goebbels' public book burning in the Forum Fridericianum (Bebelplatz) on 10 May 1933.

The early days of the Nazis in Berlin –
a parade on the Lustgarten.

And the last days. Many of Berlin's
defenders in 1945 were boys. Only a
few of those taken prisoner returned
from Soviet captivity.

May 1945. Soviet tanks enter the city
centre. A Berliner looks on holding
her shoes – leather had been strictly
rationed.

The Soviet flag flies over the Reichstag.
The Soviets saw the Reichstag as the
symbolic heart of the city.

German defenders emerge from the
cellars.

While the Soviets helped themselves
to what they wanted, bicycles and
watches being particularly popular.

Central Berlin in ruins.

A Soviet soldier, wearing the Order of the Red Star, sits on Hitler's sofa in the 'Führerbunker'.

Trümmerfrauen. Berlin's women bore the brunt of clearing the city of debris, mostly using their bare hands.

The Berlin Airlift. During the Soviet blockade from June 1948 to May 1949 the Allies supplied Berlin entirely by air.

Berliners try to stop Soviet tanks during the East Berlin uprising on 17 June 1953. They were brutally suppressed.

Walter Ulbricht and his wife en route to Moscow. The GDR elite looked after themselves very well.

Whereas Ernst Reuter, in his hallmark black beret, became the international face of West Berlin.

The Berlin Wall was first erected in a well-planned operation on 13 August 1961.

In the first few days it was just coils of wire and relatively easy to escape to the West. Conrad Schumann makes his iconic jump. His story would have a sad ending.

East Berlin guards and West Berliners. There was little that the Western Allies could do as the Wall went up but West Berliners mounted furious demonstrations.

Kennedy, Brandt and Adenauer on the occasion of Kennedy's famous speech in 1963 when he inadvertently said he was a jam doughnut – 'Ich bin ein Berliner'. Adenauer hated Berlin, saying it reminded him of Asia.

Tanks face each other down Friedrichstraße as the Wall made Berlin the focus of the Cold War.

Alexanderplatz – the centre of the GDR's 'socialist consumer paradise' and the Fernsehturm. Much to the irritation of the anti-Christian Ulbricht, a cross appears on its revolving dome when the sun shines.

The Humboldt Forum, a clever reconstruction of the Berliner Schloss which unites Schluter's original work with a contemporary eastern façade.

There was hardly any coal for fuel and the first bout of Spanish flu
had hit that summer, claiming 40,000 lives. The hospitals – already
caring for 250,000 war wounded – had been overwhelmed. Infant
mortality was at a medieval level, with 6,380 children dying before
their first birthday.

Whatever else was going wrong, the Berlin habit of very detailed
record-keeping was alive and well. The authorities had been trying
to get people to leave the city, and posters covered the Litfaß pillars
showing a picture of a hungry, miserable veteran in Berlin opposite
a smiling, well-fed one in the country. 'There is little food and no
work in Berlin,' ran the caption, 'therefore no pay and bad humour.
There's plenty of good food and work outside Berlin, therefore good
pay and good humour. Ask at the nearest employment office.'[1] By
the end of 1918 they were paying out 220 million marks in welfare
payments, a figure approaching a quarter of their entire budget, and
the city was 875 million marks in debt. Berliners were miserable,
angry and they also wanted peace and bread; the sailors message
found a ready audience. 'A bitter distrust gradually began to grip
the population,' wrote novelist Stefan Zweig, 'distrust of money,
which was losing more and more of its value, distrust of Generals,
the officers, the diplomats, distrust of every public statement by
the government and General staff, distrust of newspapers and their
news, distrust of the very war itself and its necessity.'[2] 'I was back
in Berlin,' wrote the artist and satirist George Grosz, who had been
drafted to the Western Front, 'and the city looked like a stony grey
corpse. The houses were cracked, paint and plaster had crumbled
away, and in the dull, grimy eye-sockets of the windows you could
see the caked traces of tears.'[3]

The divisions in the socialist movement had deepened since 1916.
The SPD remained the largest party in the Reichstag and now, with
Baden and Scheidemann in government, it was seen by many as
the best alternative to the existing regime. Its leader was Friedrich
Ebert, a politician from humble origins who had taken over from
August Bebel in 1913. Ebert was a socialist but a moderate one and
he remained strongly supportive of the war effort. He had taken

much of the criticism for the SPD being thought ineffective in 1916. He was deeply suspicious of the USPD, the breakaway left-leaning faction, and even more so of the far-left Spartacist League led by Liebknecht and Luxemburg.

Yet events in Berlin in 1917 had inadvertently strengthened the Spartacists. The Kaiser's government had, in pursuit of their overriding priority to get Russia out of the war and disappointed that Kerensky's April revolution had not done so, financed Lenin and enabled him to return to St Petersburg. On 11 April a special train carrying the Bolshevik high command had steamed quietly into the Potsdamer Platz station. Transferred in the hours of darkness to Stettiner station, Lenin and his party were moved secretly onwards into Russia. A year later, having successfully seized power in the Bolshevik November revolution, Lenin duly obliged by signing Brest-Litovsk. On the face of it, this gave Germany huge concessions and stripped Russia of much of her European resources and population. However, Lenin knew that Germany was powerless to enforce it and bided his time. Berlin – inspiration of Marx and Engels, with its huge, restless and increasingly militant proletariat, and which Lenin knew well from having lived in the city in the 1890s – was earmarked as a city ripe for a communist overthrow. Throughout 1918 he poured in money and agents, controlled through the Russian Embassy on Unter den Linden under the compelling figure of the ambassador, Adolph Abramovich Joffe, a committed revolutionary from a rich Jewish merchant family and the man who had negotiated Brest-Litovsk. He had caused considerable offence by erecting a huge hammer and sickle over the embassy and a communist banner urging the workers of the world to unite. The result was that, although Liebknecht and Luxemburg had spent much of the last years of the war in prison, their Spartacist League was now a much more formidable force than the rather inconsequential group they had been, while the USPD appeared unable to muster sufficient support to mount a serious challenge.

So, when Berlin caught alight as the embers of the Kiel mutiny were blown south, the flames were fanned by two opposing groups:

by the SPD controlling the Reichstag and by the Spartacists as they attempted to control the streets. Matters came to a head on 9 November 1918, which must rank as one of the most extraordinary days in Berlin's history. On the evening of 8 November revolutionary groups issued a call for a general strike and mass protest march the next day. The Kaiser had left the city for the last time on 29 October, a move that damaged his authority; it would be the last day a Hohenzollern monarch resided in Berlin. The Allies were demanding his removal as a precondition for an armistice, and on 1 November Baden gained the consent of the Bundesrat for his abdication. The Kaiser, forward in his military headquarters was not, however, inclined to go, miscalculating his support both across Germany and in the army. He appeared to be unaware of the chaos enveloping the country and that the revolution had spread to Munich, Hamburg and the Ruhr. Now, with Berlin becoming ungovernable, and with a mass protest and a general strike looming, Baden decided he would announce the abdication himself and then resigned as chancellor. It eventually took Hindenburg to persuade a furious Kaiser that he had no other choice, and on 10 November he boarded his train in Spa and steamed into exile in Holland. He would never return to Germany.

Five hundred and three years after they had arrived in Berlin to such popular approval, the last Hohenzollern skulked away, leaving his capital city in the worst state it had been in since the 1630s. This great dynasty – a family that had produced a series of the most capable rulers Europe had known – had been destroyed by its most catastrophic son. Their passing was much regretted by some Berliners, mostly (but not exclusively) the better off, who saw the monarchy as one of the pillars of the prosperity they had enjoyed for the last century and which seemed to them to be the embodiment of the German nation which as Prussians they so proudly led. Yet for the majority – and especially those who were now hungry and cold, bereaved or wounded – he was well gone.

There was anyway little time to mourn him. The army had been mobilised to prevent the protest march and by 3 a.m. on 9 November troops were posted around the city. At 6 a.m. revolutionary councils

were distributing leaflets at factory gates and issuing arms, lots of
ex-military weapons being available. Anna Rehme was one of those
who then went to the barracks in central Berlin. 'We disarmed the
officers ... then we went to the company rooms and debated with
the soldiers. We demanded that they renounce the war and join our
movement. We asked them to gather in the barrack yards where
we addressed them. Many gave us their guns. I was given a belt of
machine gun ammunition and went with a colleague to take up a
position in Scharnhorststraße.'[4] By 8 a.m. they had persuaded the
army not to use force against the marchers. At 9 a.m. the march
converged on the centre of the city, on the Schloßplatz. Banners
demanded the end of the war, the abolition of the monarchy and
carried slogans such as 'Justice & Freedom' and 'Brothers Don't
Shoot'. At 11 a.m. disgruntled soldiers staged a protest demanding
their back pay in front of Blücher barracks and set up barricades in
Alexanderplatz. By noon the march had reached the Reichstag and
spilled over into the surrounding streets. Then three marchers were
shot by army officers in front of the Maikäfer Barracks, where Hans
Leib had sung to Lili Marleen. The first casualty was a twenty-four-
year-old machine tool worker, Erich Habersaath, who had been in
the front rank. He was followed by Franz Schwengler, a mechanic
and Richard Glathe, a screw maker. They became instant heroes.

   The shooting changed the marchers' mood and they began to get
more violent. At 1 p.m. they broke into gaols around the city and
freed the prisoners. Then at 2 p.m. Scheidemann came out onto the
balcony of the Reichstag and announced the end of the war and the
creation of a republic. It seems as if he did this as an almost off-the-
cuff reaction. He had been having lunch with Ebert in the Reichstag
dining room as the protesters arrived. However ill-prepared, his
words '*Seid einig, treu und pflichtbewusst! Das Alte und Morsche,
die Monarchie ist zusammengebrochen. Es lebe das Neue! Es lebe
die Deutsche Republik!*' (which translates as 'Let us be as one,
faithful and dutiful. The old rotten order, the monarchy, has gone.
Long live the new! Long live the German Republic!')[5] have become
justifiably famous. At 4 p.m., not to be outdone by Scheidemann's

announcement, Karl Liebknecht, only recently released from prison, forced his way onto the balcony of the Berliner Schloss and announced a '*Freie, Sozialistische Republik Deutschland*' (a free socialist German Republic) and that he would create '*eine Regierung der Arbeiter und Soldaten*' and '*eine neue Staatliche Ordnung des Proletariats*' (a government of workers and soldiers and a new proletarian order). By 5 p.m. the marchers had taken over the offices of the *Berliner Lokal-Anzeiger* newspaper and printed the first edition of the revolutionary paper *Die Rote Fahne* (The Red Flag), the Spartacist League paper. At 6 p.m. a firefight started in the Schloßplatz and firing continued through the night, with about twenty people killed. Harry Count Kessler, a publisher, diplomat, soldier and cosmopolitan diarist, thought it did not amount to much and was 'like a quiet night at the front'.[6] This 'tremendous world-shaking revolution went through Berlin's everyday life in a flash like a detective film'.[7]

Martha Globig, a young Spartacist volunteer, a stenographer and a member of USPD, remembered the excitement and the emotion that evening. 'There were countless people on the streets. Soldiers tore off their badges and medals. There were no officers to be seen. Red flags appeared everywhere, often strips torn off the red part of the old Reich flag. Complete strangers hugged each other. We heard that they needed help at the Police Headquarters. We received red armbands and about 10 of us, young girls and lads, set off. We were ordered to take over the telephone exchange. Calls came in non-stop. It was very lively,' and then, in a scene that could only have happened in a city where adherence to the rules is so highly valued, 'a squad was sent off because we had a call saying that someone was trying to enter one of the state museums' without a ticket.[8] Perhaps more telling was that a vegetable cart was stolen and a grocery store broken into.

The next morning Berlin found itself with two rival parties claiming to be in government, with no Kaiser but with fighting continuing on the Western Front. Between March and November 1918 Germany lost approximately 900,000 soldiers, at least a third of whom were killed in action, and for many Berliners the priority was the armistice. It finally came the next day, 11 November. For some in the German army who, although in retreat, were not actually defeated, the events in Berlin were a *Dolchstoß* (a stab in the back) that would become part of the Nazi ideology. For the majority it was more just a relief that the fighting was finally over. For Berlin the next two months were a period of violence and confusion. On 10 November 3,000 'workers and soldiers' met near the Hackescher Markt in the Circus Busch, one of the few buildings that could take that number. Liebknecht had planned the meeting to upstage the government that Scheidemann and Ebert were in the process of setting up, but in the event the huge assembly endorsed ending militarism and creating a socialist Germany, both of which were SPD aims. On 11 November the 'dreadful armistice terms'[9] were signed and the fighting on the Western Front finally stopped.

Meanwhile, both the SPD and the Spartacists were organising demonstrations, the latter making the funerals of those killed on 9 November into a major political rally, with huge crowds following their coffins on 20 November as they were carried to Friedrichshain Cemetery to join the dead from 1848. Another factor was also now coming into play: the army was beginning to return from the Western Front, many of them bitter, demoralised and angry at what was taking place. The key Berlin regiments remained intact, loyal to their officers and still well armed. Ebert had made a pact with the de facto head of the army, General Wilhelm Groener. Groener committed the military to work with Ebert's administration – a novelty for an army that had previously worked directly to the Kaiser – in return for Ebert's commitment to disperse the Workers and Soldiers Councils and to restore order. As the Spartacists became politically marginalised, and as they planned a more violent revolution, they found themselves facing army units on the streets. These came to be known as the *Freikorps*, taking their name from the volunteers who had fought Napoleon. Ebert put the Freikorps under the hard-line Gustav Noske, later his defence minister. On 6 December, again outside Leip's *Maikäfer* barracks, the Fusilier Guards shot sixteen protesters; that these incidents always seemed to take place outside the *Maikäfer* was because it was next door to the large armament factories at the northern end of Chausseestraße.

Politically frustrated, Liebknecht again tried to seize the initiative from Ebert when he convened an assembly in the Prussian Landtag. On 15 December 512 delegates from across Germany met but once more they voted in favour of the SPD agenda, supporting parliamentary democracy and elections to a national assembly. Furthermore, they rejected both the Kiel sailors' fourteen points and Liebknecht's call to nationalise key industries. 'What,' demanded SPD Deputy Max Cohen, 'has Bolshevism achieved in Russia? What has the dictatorship of the proletariat accomplished? In my view nothing that does credit to Socialism.'[10] Things were not going according to the Spartacists and Lenin's plans, added to which Ebert's government had sent Joffe back to Russia as an undesirable.

Kessler, who had been on a diplomatic mission in Warsaw, returned to Berlin on 17 December and commented 'not a red flag to be seen; nothing but black-white-red, black-white and here and there a black-red-gold. The majority of soldiers and officers are wearing badges and epaulettes again.'[11] On Christmas Eve Freikorps units used artillery to break up a mass demonstration by sailors protesting about their conditions in front of the Berliner Schloss's stables, but Christmas festivities for many continued much as normal. 'The blood-letting Hurdy-Gurdies played in Friedrichstraße while street-vendors sold indoor fireworks, and silver tinsel. Jewellers' shops in Unter den Linden remained unconcernedly open, their windows brightly lit and glittering. In Leipziger Straße the usual Christmas crowds thronged the big stores. In thousands of homes the Christmas tree was lit ... In the Imperial Stables lay the dead, and the wounds freshly inflicted on the Palace and on Germany gaped into the Christmas night.'[12]

The Spartacists' next move came on 1 January 1919 when, in the ballroom of the Prussian Landtag, Liebknecht and Luxemburg founded the KPD, the German Communist Party. This effectively swallowed up the USPD, although many Berliners retained their

USPD credentials for some months to come. Then on 4 January Ebert tried to sack Emil Eichorn, the left-wing Berlin police chief. Eichorn refused to leave, barricaded himself inside his headquarters and issued arms to his supporters. On 5 January 100,000 protesters marched in his support. For the next four days Berlin was in open revolt, with pitched battles in the streets as Spartacists fought it out with the Freikorps, but it was a revolt that had broken out spontaneously and it was not well planned. Few of the revolutionary regiments in the military turned out, and gradually the better-organised Freikorps established their authority. By 11 January, Major Franz von Stephani and his Potsdam Regiment had cleared the last Spartacist positions and Liebknecht and Luxemburg went into hiding. A Freikorps unit under an ultra-conservative Austrian officer, Waldemar Pabst, arrested them on 15 January and dragged them to the Guards Cavalry barracks in the Eden Hotel near the zoo. Arrested with them was a young communist, William Pieck, who would go on to be the first (and only) president of the GDR. He managed to talk his way out but Liebknecht and Luxemburg were interrogated by Pabst. As they were being taken away, allegedly to prison in Moabit, a soldier hit them over the head with a rifle butt. They were then taken to the Tiergarten and shot. Liebknecht's body was thrown into the Neue See, the pond in the Tiergarten, while Luxemburg was dumped in the Landwehrkanal.

That was not the end for either of them. In death they became symbols of the revolution and the KPD. Mies van der Rohe was commissioned by the KPD to build a memorial on the site of their murder. This was unveiled on 13 June 1926 and became a popular meeting point for KPD rallies and pilgrimages as well as a grave-yard for those who would be killed in subsequent fighting with the Nazis. Unsurprisingly, after the Nazis came to power they razed it to the ground, labelling the November revolutionaries the *Novemberverbrecher* (November criminals), responsible for the loss of the monarchy and the 1918 armistice. After 1945 the GDR, equally unsurprisingly, turned both Liebknecht and Luxemburg into heroes. A medal was issued to those who, like Pieck, had taken part in the fighting, the 'Medal for Participation in the Revolutionary Struggles of the German Working Class 1918–1923', which bore the proud inscription *Kämpfer Gegen Die Reaktion* (fighter against the reactionaries). From 1946 Ulbricht organised annual marches to commemorate their death. The western end of Prenzlauer Allee, the main route north-east out of Berlin, was renamed Karl-Liebknecht-Straße, as it still is today. Bülow Platz, which had become Horst-Wessel-Platz under the Nazis, was renamed Rosa Luxemburg Platz after 1945. Rosa-Luxemburg-Straße now runs through her eponymous square to join Schönhauser Allee.

The worst of the street fighting was still to come. Fearing the increasing militarisation of the city as the Freikorps expanded their control, the KPD called a general strike in early March 1919, which led to some of the most savage fighting between Freikorps units loyal to the government and the revolutionary units such as the *Volksmarinedivision* (the peoples' marine division) and the Spartacist militias. Most of the fighting was in East Berlin, around Friedrichshain, where the *Volksmarinedivision* built barricades. The Freikorps brought up tanks and artillery, and by the time the violence ended on 13 March some 1,200 people had been killed; only seventy-five of these were Freikorps. Many of them were Spartacists executed after they had surrendered. On 12 March eleven prisoners were shot in the cemetery in Möllendorf, including Johann Karl Rudolf and Walter Poemann, both aged eighteen, for having held a belt of machine-gun ammunition; the site is marked today by a plaque to their memory.

~

By March 1919 Berlin had steadied into an uneasy but generally more settled period. National elections had been held in January, the first in Germany in which women could vote and with the eligible voting age reduced to twenty. The Assembly met in Weimar rather than Berlin, hence the term Weimar Republic, which is used to describe the republic until the coming of the Nazis. Ebert is reputed to have thought an association with Weimar – home to Goethe and Schiller – would improve Germany's post-war image but realistically the violence and street fighting in Berlin made holding the Assembly there difficult. Whatever was going through Ebert's mind, it made little difference to the subsequent harshness of the Treaty of Versailles. Germany had to accept severe restrictions on its armed forces, huge financial reparations, and the loss of all her colonies (although, of all the Versailles conditions, this last actually saved Germany going through the later decolonisation agonies suffered by Britain and France). Versailles also included a clause on 'War Guilt', which blamed Germany as the sole aggressor in 1914 and caused huge resentment in Berlin. Not only had the German army been forced to agree to an armistice when it felt it had not been defeated, but now it was also shouldering all the blame for the war. It was these two issues that would deepen the hatred for France and would play so strongly to the Nazis' future agenda.

Ebert's government, advised by Groener, accepted these conditions; in practice there was little else he could do. On 22 June the High Seas Fleet scuttled their ships in Scapa Flow rather than hand them over to the British. The next morning Berlin students burned French flags in front of Frederick the Great's statue. On 9 July the Assembly accepted the Versailles conditions and on 21 August Ebert's government was sworn in under the terms of the new constitution. Kessler, who was present, thought there was 'something tragic about it. This petty drama as conclusion to the tremendous events of the war and the revolution. Pondering the deeper significance of it can bring tears very close.'[13]

For the next four years Berlin was the setting for continued fighting between the Spartacists (or what was left of them) and the Freikorps, who now used a swastika as their symbol. After the brutal suppression of the March general strike, the city was officially placed in a state of siege and was very much under the Freikorps' control. In December, thirty-three of the sailors who had led the Spartacist violence were executed, a move described as 'motivated by that spirit of unnatural inhumanity which can only inspire the most extreme abhorrence'.[14]

In early 1920 the Versailles conditions were officially ratified in Paris, leading to rioting outside the Reichstag (which had returned to Berlin from Weimar earlier that year) that left thirty dead and 400 injured. In March Wolfgang Kapp, a former civil servant and proponent of the *Dolchstoß*, and General Walther von Lüttwitz, the regular army commander in Berlin, staged a coup against the government after Ebert and Noske tried to force them to disband an extreme group in the Freikorps, the Ehrhardt Brigade. The Ehrhardt were stationed near Berlin and were held responsible for much of the violence in the city. For six days Berlin was paralysed by a retaliatory general strike mounted by the left. It caused considerable hardship. By 22 March, complained Käthe Kollwitz in her diary, it had been going on a whole week. 'For the whole area there is no light, no water, no coal, no means of transport, no supplies, no vegetables.'[15] The strike forced the Erhardt Brigade to withdraw and it was eventually disbanded. Although the right remained very much in the ascendancy, there were those heirs of Liebknecht and Luxemburg who were pondering the future of communist Berlin. The revolution may have failed but that merely called for a reappraisal. Walter Ulbricht, a former soldier from Leipzig, and a group of disgruntled former USPD and Spartacist supporters joined the fledgling KPD, the German Communist Party. Ulbricht himself was described as 'incredibly hard-working, always willing to take the initiative, extremely solid; he had no vices and no obvious weaknesses. He didn't smoke, he did not drink and he had no personal associates.'[16] Taken to Moscow for training, Berlin would get to see a lot more of Walter Ulbricht.

In June 1922 Berlin awoke to the news that the Foreign Minister, Walther Rathenau, had been assassinated as he drove from his house in the Grunewald to the Foreign Ministry in Wilhelmstraße. Rathenau was Jewish, immensely able, and the son of Emil Rathenau, the founder of AEG. He was one of those successful middle-class businessmen who were so representative of Berlin, people who 'moved like fiery meteors in a frigid world of horsehair furniture'.[17] He had become the face of Ebert's government abroad, creating a striking impression and helping to strengthen the idea that Germany had moved on. 'The elegance of his tall figure,' wrote the Hungarian minister and novelist Miklos Banffy, 'was accentuated by clothes of such high quality as to give him an almost exaggerated distinction. With his small, tapering beard, he was like a half-Mongol, half-Jewish Mephistopheles. He seemed to be able to speak all languages ... He made a most moving speech, describing Germany's poverty in the darkest terms. It was indeed a beautiful and affecting oration.'[18]

His success in promoting the Republic incurred the envy and anger of the far right. Rathenau was murdered by an extremist, anti-communist, anti-Jewish group called Organisation Consul whose members were largely drawn from the Ehrhardt Brigade. They said they had killed him because he had recently signed the Treaty of Rapallo with Soviet Russia. Most Berliners believed he had been killed because he was a successful Jewish minister who was doing his best to make the Weimar government work. His death, however, had an enormous impact in Berlin. Organisation Consul had already murdered Matthias Erzberger, the Finance Minister and the man who had made peace overtures in 1917. Altogether they would kill several hundred of their political opponents, but it was the death of a man whom Berliners saw as one of their own that caused such an outrage. On Sunday 25 June more than 200,000 people protested in the Lustgarten to hear speeches defending the Republic and condemning the killers. It was a sea of black-red-gold flags as opposed to the Freikorps' black and white. On 27 June Rathenau's funeral service took place in the Reichstag and even the Nationalist members attended. Rathenau's mother was seated in what had previously been the imperial box, which was still decorated with large letter 'W's from the Kaiser's last appearance. The coffin was then borne away in state with a military escort. 'Lassalle's dream of passing through Brandenburger Tor as President of a Republic of Germany was,' Kessler wrote in his diary, 'today fulfilled by the Jew Rathenau because of his martyrdom in the service of the German people.'[19] As the tension between the far left and the far right intensified in the coming decade, Berlin looked to men like Rathenau as an example of how the republic, however fragile, could have worked.

~

Berlin was also trying to come to terms with the shattering impact of the hyperinflation that hit Germany as the government devalued the mark in an attempt to pay reparations. In 1914 the mark had been 4 to the US dollar; by 1921 it was trading at 75. By February 1923 it was 48,000, by October 440 million, and by November 4.2 billion, by which time it had ceased to have any real value. A loaf of bread went from 17 million marks in September to 140 million by November. Pictures of Berliners taking wheelbarrows full of money to buy a loaf of bread were commonplace. Inevitably some people – the so-called *Raffke* – did very well out of exploiting the system, using dollars to set up businesses and then paying their workers in the worthless marks. Hugo Stinnes built up a vast coal-mining empire by doing so, although predictably he went bust when the currency was eventually stabilised.

The people who really suffered were the old and the poor, those who had built up savings or were on fixed incomes. Suicides were common as it became impossible to pay bills and feed families. In 1914, five people had been registered as dying of starvation; in 1923 that had risen to more than a hundred, with many more unrecorded. More than 100,000 Berliners were being fed by public soup kitchens by the end of the year.[20] Companies had to pay workers every day; otherwise by the end of the week their wages would have become worthless. To make matters worse, foreigners were able to live extremely well on very modest incomes, reinforcing to many Berliners the unfairness of Versailles. While Berliners starved, the high life continued, much as it had done in the last years of the war. Kessler attended a dinner party in late November 1922 with the very rich ex-head of the Security Police who lived in Roonstraße. They ate a 'millionaires' meal, attended by a mixture of politicians like Gustav Stresemann, a Berliner from Kreuzberg who would soon become Chancellor, 'remnants of the old court society' like Count Platen,

and 'the gem of the evening ... Frau von Wassilko, the Ukrainian
Minister's wife. Small and thin she seemed to consist entirely of
brilliantly dyed red hair and diamonds, with quantities of paint and
enamel where the face usually is. The diamonds on her fingers were
the size of pigeon's eggs and of the finest water. Rows upon rows
of them, intermingled with strands of large pearls. My first notion
was that, representing a Soviet republic, she was wearing the entire
Ukrainian aristocracy's confiscated jewellery.'[21]

On the other hand, the diarist Christabel Bielenberg had a more
sobering conversation with her gardener, Herr Neisse. He had been
saving for years to have enough to buy a little bit of land and marry
his sweetheart Hilde, but everything he had was now worthless:
'The inflation, you see, Frau Doctor; suddenly we had nothing.
With my savings I was able to buy just one cup and saucer which I
gave to Hilde instead of her marriage lines. Funny, wasn't it, that
I should be so keen on the saucer?' Bielenberg recalled: 'His voice
shook with emotion, and the usual concise movements of his hands
became nervous and erratic. The loss of his little bank account had
not only shattered whatever faith he might have had in constitution
or government, but also struck at the root of his very being, his self-
respect, and his right to be respected. The saucer, perhaps there was
something respectable about a saucer.'[22] The aged and successful
author Maximilian Bern concluded he was too old to start again.
He withdrew all his substantial savings from his bank, blew it all on
one U-Bahn ticket and then locked himself away in his flat. He was
found dead from starvation some weeks later.[23]

The actress Lotte Lenya was trying to launch her career in Berlin.
She thought she was lucky in that 'I still had my jewellery I could
sell'. She lived in a tiny corner room on the top floor of a house in
Lützowstraße. She had one light bulb and a picture of Nijinsky that
she had cut out of a magazine and framed. Her landlady was meant
to feed her. 'Many times I tried to figure out what I was eating. It
looked like "Königsberger Klopse", a dish [like meatballs] I had
eaten before in Switzerland, but they sure tasted different there. I
once asked her what it was in those Klopses and she said in that

inimitable Berlin dialect: "'s ist keene Katze, die Sie da essen, und vajessen Sie nicht, Fräulein, wir haben den Krieg valoren" (It ain't a cat you're eating, and don't forget, lady, we lost the war). I never asked her again and ate her Klopse without a murmur.'[24]

Inflation was at its height in 1923, a year made worse economically by the French occupation of the Ruhr on the pretext that Germany was falling behind with its reparation payments, and by further coup attempts such as the Nazis' Beer Hall Putsch in Munich that November. Although Hitler was jailed, he was released in 1924. November also saw the Berlin unemployment rate climb to nearly 300,000, when the city was only set up to provide relief for half that number. 'Everything just gets worse,' lamented Käthe Kollwitz in November. 'There is looting, attempted murder and hunger! A loaf of bread 140 Billion then "reduced" to 80 billion. Hans Prengel without work. Alexander was dismissed. Hunger! Hunger everywhere. The streets are swarming with the unemployed.'[25] Predictably people started to look for scapegoats and, in true Berlin fashion, they blamed the Jews, who were said to be speculating and hoarding. There was bad rioting in the Scheunenviertel, with Jews beaten up and some murdered and – again predictably – the police slow to react. It was a terrible comment on Berlin. Some 50,000 German Jews had fought in the war; of those, 4,000 became officers, something that would not have happened a few decades earlier, and 1,200 were awarded the Iron Cross; 12,000 were killed. Altogether, 1923 was a miserable year for Berlin.

The next year would be better. Stresemann did manage to introduce a new currency, the rentenmark, which held its value. A decision was taken not to try to oppose the French in the Ruhr and in 1925 they left. The Dawes Plan, introduced in 1924 by the American Charles Dawes, also brought some sort of order to reparation payments. By that spring Berlin was beginning to breathe more easily. Despite the turmoil, the city had seen some important changes. In 1920 Adolf Wermuth, who had proved a popular and successful mayor during the war years when his office had arranged the efficient distribution of ration cards, masterminded the unification of Berlin's boroughs. The existing six boroughs, Mitte (the area around the Berliner Schloss and Unter den Linden), Tiergarten, Friedrichshain, Kreuzberg, Prenzlauer Berg and Wedding were merged with the previously independent boroughs of Charlottenburg (which had been the second most prosperous city in Prussia after Berlin), Köpenick, Lichtenberg, Pankow, Neukölln, Schöneberg, Wilmersdorf and Spandau, together with nearly sixty small rural communities, into Greater Berlin. The new mega-city was divided into twenty districts, each with its own mayor and local district council but all subordinate to Wermuth and the main city council in the Rote Rathaus. This made Berlin enormous, over 878 square kilometres, or the size of the Ruhr industrial area. Municipal reorganisations might be of limited historical interest to the general reader but Wermuth's was to assume a greater significance as it was the districts and boundaries he established that would come to define the boundaries of the free world.

Over 350 square kilometres of this new city were woods, parks and lakes, making Berlin the largest capital in Europe but also the most sparsely populated, something that still holds true today. The city had always had a rather attractive rural feel (the French having sniped at The Great Elector when he asked them how his capital compared to Paris that in Paris they did not graze cows in the streets). Now, as the villages became an even more integral part of Berlin's life, after the pattern established by Rudow and Buckow, more and more Berliners – or at least those who could afford to – lived in the suburbs and commuted in on the S-Bahn and U-Bahn. Berlin's names today still give that feeling of space: Ahrensfelde; Jungfernheide; Grunewald; Schöneweide; Lichterfelde; Weißensee; Gesundbrunnen and the list goes on. This union also enhanced Berliners' already very strong sense of locality and of loyalty to their own district.

And, despite all the hardships of the war and its aftermath, immigrants were still coming. Many in the early 1920s were Russians, especially white Russians who had held on hoping that the Bolsheviks might have just been some passing phase but who were now realising the perils of living under the communist system. In 1918 there were 50,000 Russians in the city, the majority living in Charlottenburg (jokingly referred to as Charlottengrad). By 1922 there were 100,000 and by 1924 more than 300,000. Some of these were rich and princes like the Obolensky family; some were poor; others were cultural exiles like the painter Kandinsky and the pianist Vladimir Horowitz. Several distinguished Russian writers also came, such as Gorky, Pasternak, and Vladimir Nabokov who started a Russian-language newspaper, the *Rul* (rudder), which was an instant success. Many were also Soviet agents and in the febrile, suspicious atmosphere of the streets the areas around Charlottenburg and Nollendorfplatz where they congregated had an air of intrigue and suspicion.

~

The 1920s are sometimes referred to as Berlin's golden years but it is hard to see why. For most Berliners it was at best a short break in their continuity of misery from 1914, a period in which they had either suffered for four years at the front, or someone in their family had, endured hunger, illness, cold, unemployment, revolution, savage repression and then a terrible inflation that destroyed what savings and aspirations they may have had. Their nation had gone from being among the proudest and most successful in Europe to something of an international pariah. The war, said Walter Gropius, 'is more than just a lost war. A world has come to an end.'[26] It is, however, fair to say that it was something of a golden age in terms of the cultural diversity that it spawned, when Berliners could experiment without the disapproval of the ever-present royal censors and when people were searching widely for an alternative to a system that had failed so catastrophically. But it is important to remember that this cultural freedom had very little effect on the vast majority of the city's now 4 million population. Dada artists like the satirist George Grosz depicted ordinary Berliners bewildered by contemporary painting, sculpture and architecture that was to them both incomprehensible and irrelevant. The Dada movement, of which Grosz was one of the leading exponents, questioned all traditional culture. 'If that word, "Dada", meant anything at all,' wrote Grosz, 'it meant seething discontent, dissatisfaction and cynicism.'[27] They mounted an exhibition in 1920 which appalled both the right and the left; one of its posters read 'Dilettantes Rise Up Against Art!'[28] Although Grosz's drawings would become very popular in their own right, Dada never really caught on as a movement – but then that was really its point.

The city's cultural freedom was in many ways a by-product of what had become, by 1918, a much looser social structure. Not only had the respect for the military influence been greatly reduced (though it was always there under the surface, as the Nazis would demonstrate), but society had become less ordered, more carefree, almost desperate and even licentious as people tried to make sense of the enormity of the catastrophe. Berlin had long been more socially liberal than many other world cities but the 1920s saw this taken to new limits. This was reflected in how the city approached sex. Berliners are refreshingly unembarrassed about sex, which they regard more as a basic human need to be enjoyed like food, and certainly in the post-war years everything was on the menu in a way that would have been unthinkable in London. 'All moral restraints seemed to have melted away,' noted Grosz. 'A flood of vice, pornography and prostitution swept the entire country.'[29]

The artist Francis Bacon, who arrived from a stuffy Dublin in 1927, found 'there was something extraordinarily open about the whole place ... You had this feeling that sexually you could get absolutely anything you wanted.'[30] What Bacon wanted was gay sex, which was openly on offer while homosexuality was still illegal in Britain; actually, it still was technically illegal in Germany, although only between men, not women. There is a story, which seems to have been rather exaggerated in the telling, that his father had sent him to Berlin with a strict uncle as he had been showing homosexual tendencies at home but instead Bacon ended up sharing a bed with him in the Adlon Hotel. 'Berlin is a bugger's daydream,' wrote W.H. Auden, who visited in late 1928. 'There are 170 male brothels under police control.'

Gay men came to the city in their hundreds, some taking unattractive advantage of young Berlin boys who resorted to prostitution out of financial desperation, and others because they could find the freedom and acceptance that was denied them at home. The most famous of them was Christopher Isherwood, who saw in Berlin an opportunity to 'unchain his desires and hurl reason and sanity into prison'.[31] He first came in 1929, frequenting a gay bar called The Cosy Corner in Kreuzberg. 'It was heated by a big old-fashioned iron stove. Partly because of the great heat of this stove and partly because they knew it excited their clients, the boys stripped off their sweaters or leather jackets and sat around with their shirts unbuttoned to the navel and their sleeves rolled up to the armpits.'[32] Later Isherwood moved in with his boyfriend, whom he calls Otto Nowak and who lived in a Mietskaserne in Kreuzberg. They shared a tiny room in a cramped apartment with Otto's parents, elder brother and younger sister. It was rough and uncomfortable, 'a leaky stuffy attic which smelt of cooking and bad drains. When the living room stove was alight, we could hardly breathe; when it wasn't we froze.' The only washing facility was a small kitchen sink. His first rent payment to Frau Nowak caused her to splash out on an 'immense meal of lung hash, black bread, malt coffee and boiled potatoes' and at night he would lie awake listening to the sounds of the Mietskaserne as people fought, cried, banged doors so that it was 'like sleeping out in the jungle'.[33] What was more extraordinary for Isherwood was that Otto's parents did not see anything strange in their son sharing a bed in their tiny flat with another man – something that would have been inconceivable in London.

Later Isherwood moved into the more salubrious surroundings of the Nollendorfplatz, renting a room from a landlady he calls Fräulein Schroeder (her real name was Meta Thurau) who called him 'Herr Issyvoo'. When she heard Isherwood and his male lovers enjoying themselves she would sigh, 'How sweet love must be!' Nollendorfplatz then was a rather shabby area, known for its station (which Lesser Ury painted so effectively at night, illuminated by car headlights) and for its two solidly impressive Berlin brick churches: Die Zwölf-Apostel and the St Matthias Kirche. Nollendorfstraße is now quite grand, lined with lime trees and large terraced houses. The heart of Berlin's gay district is in Motzstraße, which leads off the Nollendorfplatz and where Berlin's refreshingly open attitude to sex is demonstrated by one of the city's very smart hat shops being next door to one that specialises in male leather wear. Motzstraße ends in the charming Viktoria-Luise-Platz, one of Berlin's more peaceful and upmarket places to live. There is today a plaque outside Fräulein Schroeder's house at number 17 Nollendorfstraße.

There was, however, a degree of sadness to some of this very overt sex. The Russian writer Ilya Ehrenberg, who came to Berlin in 1921, recalled being invited to a new 'club'. Having travelled miles out into the suburbs, and walked seemingly for ever down muddy, dark streets, they came to a respectable flat where they were given 'champagne', being lemonade laced with spirits. Their guide's two daughters then appeared stark naked and started to dance for them, their mother wondering whether Ehrenberg and his friend would like to pay for the girls in foreign currency. When they declined she sighed 'Is this life? It is the end of the world.'[34] Berlin theatre was also putting on shows where girls performed naked or semi-naked. The black American singer Josephine Baker, who wore little apart from her famous banana skirt, took the city by storm with her travelling show *La Revue Nègre*, which opened on the Ku'damm in 1925, but there was a strong sense of the racism in some of the reviews. 'In her the wildness of her forefathers, who were transplanted from the Congo to the Mississippi, is preserved most authentically,' commented the *Berliner Tageblatt*.[35]

For many, 1920s Berlin – with all its sexual freedom, fun, loucheness and underlying sadness – is encapsulated by the musical *Cabaret*. Based on Isherwood's novels, it tells the story of the actress and singer Sally Bowles, a character drawn from Jean Ross who also lived with Fräulein Schroeder. In fact, she was not very successful, securing a fairly minor part as one of a pair of lovers carried onto the stage in litters in Max Reinhardt's production of Offenbach's *Tales of Hoffman* where, she claimed, she had sex on stage with her partner every night. Isherwood, who sat in the audience with binoculars trying to verify her claim, did not believe her. Yet Sally Bowles, although English, came to symbolise this world that seemed to offer an escape from the depressing reality of life for so many Berliners.

Reinhardt (the assumed name of Max Goldmann) was a major influence in Berlin theatre. He had started as an actor in the 1894 Deutsche Theater production of *Die Räuber* and subsequently bought that theatre and the Theater am Schiffbauerdamm. In 1919 he built the Große Schauspielhaus, which would last until 1980 and was one of Berlin's biggest venues. By 1930 he ran a total of eleven Berlin theatres and had also founded the Salzburg Festival, along with Strauss and Hofmannsthal. He had signed the 1914 Declaration of Ninety-Three, which he later said he regretted. It was on 31 August 1928, in his Theater am Schiffbauerdamm, that Bertolt Brecht's *Die Dreigroschenoper* opened. Based on an old English play, *The Beggars' Opera*, Brecht's production – usually referred to as 'the Threepenny Opera' – was styled a play with music. It was a blistering attack on capitalism and within a week of opening had been hooked by fifty theatres across Germany. Its line '*Erst kommt das Fressen, dann kommt die Moral*' ('Food first, then morality') became a catchphrase for the Berlin left. Brecht, who came from Bavaria, was another of those whose life and work became part of Berlin. He was a controversial character, and the success of the Threepenny Opera made him more 'cocky, rich and more Communist-oriented than ever',[36] but he was one of the most important inspirations and voices of the left in the years ahead.

Many of Berlin's leading writers contributed to *Die Weltbühne* (the World Stage), a magazine edited from 1926 by Kurt Tucholsky, a Berliner, a Jew and a member of the USPD. One of the decade's most influential journalists, he would use the pages of his famous small red publication to warn of the rise of the Nazis. Another author, and perhaps even more famous than Brecht, was Alfred Döblin whose 1929 novel *Berlin Alexanderplatz* tells the story of the vicious criminal world that centred around Alexanderplatz, a world without hope and from where it seemed impossible to escape; again, he warned of the coming of National Socialism. *Berlin Alexanderplatz* came to symbolise 1920s Berlin in much the same way as *Cabaret* or the

Threepenny Opera did. Döblin was not a native Berliner, coming from Stettin, but as with so many others, he never left until forced into exile by the Nazis. 'I belong to Berlin,' he said.[37] Others who wrote regularly for Tucholsky were the Mann brothers, the more conservative Thomas and his more radical brother Heinrich.

It was Heinrich's attack on the old Imperial system, his novel *Professor Unrat* (which probably translates best as Small-Town Tyrant), that was made into one of Berlin's great early films, *The Blue Angel*, which gave that aspiring violinist-cum-actress from Schöneberg, Marlene Dietrich, her big break. Then there was the extraordinary story of Hans Ditzen. Ditzen made a suicide pact with a friend, Hans Dietrich von Necker, with whom he was having a homosexual affair, when they were both aged just eighteen. They planned it as a duel. Von Necker missed Ditzen but was himself killed by Ditzen's bullet. Ditzen was so distraught that he then shot himself in the chest but survived. After being treated in a mental asylum, he slowly recovered and started to write. He took as his pen name Hans Fallada, after the horse in the Brothers Grimm fairy tale that keeps on speaking the truth even after it has died. His 1932 novel *Kleiner Mann, was nun?* (What now, Little Man?) was an instant success, touching so many Berliners because its story of a middle-class, aspiring sales clerk called Johannes Pinneberg shows that the events of the 1920s have left the middle class in much the same position as the working class, with their dignity and dreams shattered. It was the frustration and bitterness of men like Pinneberg that would allow the Nazis to seize power. Later Fallada would be at his most articulate in his criticism of that Nazi regime.

One area where Berliners could relax rather than being constantly challenged was in music, and through all the really difficult years the city's obsession with both playing and listening continued uninterrupted. The most popular works in both the Staatsoper and the Schauspielhaus on Gendarmenmarkt were by Strauss and Puccini. In 1922 Wilhelm Furtwängler took over as conductor of the Berlin Philharmonic, a position he would occupy for twenty-three years, leading them, not uncontroversially, through the tough times to come. In 1929 Strauss and Toscanini both performed at the first Berlin Music Festival, staged when the city was entering the misery of the Depression. Music was strangely conservative when compared to the theatre and to writing. The Kroll Opera, which had been started in 1841 and then merged with the Staatsoper in 1895, was revived after the war and staged a variety of more modern pieces but it never seemed to catch the enthusiasm of the music-going public whose tastes were more traditional. In 1931 it closed, and in due course its 2,300-seat auditorium, which faced the Reichstag across the Königsplatz, was taken over by an emasculated Assembly.

Physically Berlin changed little in the 1920s but the changes that were made were important. In 1919 Walter Gropius, fresh back from the Western Front, founded the Bauhaus School in Weimar. The Bauhaus principle was to combine simplicity of design with beauty and utility of purpose and to allow for mass manufacture. Although the Berlin branch of the school would not open until 1930, when it was started by Ludwig Mies van der Rohe, Bauhaus still had a profound impact on Berlin's architects. Finally free of the heavy and ornate buildings that had marked imperial Berlin, such as the Berliner Dom and the Reichstag, men like Bruno Taut, Martin Wagner and Erich Mendelssohn (another member of that extraordinarily talented family) could experiment.

There were modernist buildings being erected prior to 1918, such as the AEG turbine factory built by Peter Behrens in 1909, but one of the most satisfying buildings from the 1920s is the Hufeisensiedlung (the Horseshoe Estate) in Britz, designed by Taut and Wagner. Britz, in Neukölln, was another of those villages incorporated into the city when it had expanded so rapidly in the mid-nineteenth century. The Horseshoe was a semi-circular development of workers' houses designed around a garden and pond to create a community; it was, in some ways, a modern and more enlightened Mietskaserne but built using modern techniques. It survived the war and is well worth a visit. Construction of the traditional Mietskaserne was banned in 1925. Another remarkable building is the Einsteinturm (the Einstein Tower) in the Einstein Science park in Potsdam. It was designed by

Mendelssohn in 1924 and contains a telescope designed to prove Einstein's theory of relativity. Einstein, who had lived in Berlin since the beginning of the war and who was a close friend of Kessler's, did not actually work there and was reportedly guarded in his comments on the building that would bear his name. Mendelssohn said it had emerged from 'the mystique around Einstein's universe' and it certainly made him instantly famous.[38] Shortage of houses would, though, remain a serious problem throughout the 1920s. The number of homeless had risen sharply from 13,000 in 1918 to 78,200 in 1922; it would settle lower from 1923 until 1929 but then rise sharply again.

~

By 1929 Berliners could look back on the last five years and think they had at least been a lot better than the decade that preceded them. Despite having sixteen governments in fourteen years, the Republic had worked – after a fashion – but the earlier wounds to the city had cut deep. Berlin was still 'like a seething cauldron. It could not be seen who was fanning the flames; all one knew was that the cauldron was growing hotter all the time ... It all added up to an orgy of execration, and the forces of the new republic were too weak to prevent the impending collapse,' wrote Grosz.[39] Berlin had been acquiescent if not actually supportive of the Republic, but in the 1928 Reichstag elections, in which the SPD were returned as the largest party nationally with 30 per cent of the vote, the communist KPD increased their share of the city's vote by 130,000. Interestingly the Nationalists, who only received 3 per cent of the national vote, hardly showed at all. Red Berlin seemed to be increasingly living up to its name, yet the tension between left and right remained raw. Then there was the huge sense of unfairness that pervaded almost every class, the idea that they were the undefeated capital of an undefeated nation and that Versailles – and especially its clause on war guilt – had been vindictive. Harry Kessler was amused, chatting to his barber while having his hair cut, that he thought all the talk in the press about treaties with Russia must be the prelude to Germany reinvading France.

The extensive Berlin criminal networks were also strong and disruptive at a time when the city's police were at their most inefficient. There were sixty-two of these *Ringvereine* (criminal societies) operating across the city, strongest in the poorer north and east but present everywhere. They controlled the lucrative drugs trade, which had spiralled well outside the government's control, as well as the equally enormous market for male and female prostitution. Originally started as organisations to help rehabilitate ex-prisoners, these societies had ironically become their main employers. Well-connected internationally, and with their own complicated rules and codes, by 1929 two of the most powerful – the *Immentreu* and the *Nordpiraten* – staged a pitched battle in which more than a hundred shots were fired. At the subsequent trial in Moabit nobody could be found to give evidence. It was not until 1934 that the societies were finally eradicated by the Nazis, with many of their more hardened members dying in concentration camps.

In the end it was the economy rather than politics, crime or the cynicism of authors and playwrights that caused the Berlin cauldron finally to boil over. In October 1929 the American markets on Wall Street collapsed and the resulting Great Depression hit the fragile Germany economy harder than most. Berlin – the country's economic as well as its political capital – was hit the hardest. Business after business collapsed so that by 1931 there were 5 million unemployed across the country and 636,000 in Berlin. Even Borsig would eventually close his factory, posting a notice on the factory gate shortly before Christmas 1931 to tell all his staff that they no longer had jobs. The effects were felt across all sectors, with thousands of houses and apartments left empty despite the number of homeless, and, for once, the city suffered from net emigration as many of the first to suffer were inevitably the last who had arrived. The Russian community was especially badly hit, with many Russians moving to France or the USA and some even braving returning to Russia itself. Cafes and shops closed, newspapers were shut down, and thousands queued daily for the street soup kitchens. Suicides were so commonplace they weren't even reported. It was as if the nightmare of the

1922–3 hyperinflation years had never gone away and those who had recovered from that first disaster now found themselves ruined again.

The novelist Erich Kästner, famous for his children's story *Emil and the Detectives*, summed up the anger and frustration of the Depression in his novel *Fabian* in which his central character is the highly educated Jacob Fabian, 'aged thirty-two, profession variable, at present advertising copywriter, 17, Schaperstraße, weak heart, brown hair'. Despite his ability and his wry but broad outlook on the world, Fabian 'is condemned to a menial and low-paid job, and even that lacks security'.[40] In Fabian's world everything that makes life worth living has become too expensive or is forbidden, and his 'ironic pessimism' turns to something darker.

It was against this unhappy and volatile backdrop that the Nazis began to build their strength. The Nazi party's power base was in the south of Germany, in Munich rather than Berlin, but after their failed 1923 putsch Hitler realised he had to control the capital if he was to establish his authority nationally. It is impossible to define Nazism because it was 'both an irrational belief and a chance combination of social forces which hoped to profit from Adolf Hitler's demagogy',[41] but much of the warped ideology that the Nazis developed was based on ideas and movements that had originated in Berlin. First was its links to the Prussian state and to Prussian militarism, both traditions that the Nazis would exploit. Then Berlin was the city that had defied Napoleon, the cultural capital of a unified Germany and the place where nationalism and the concept of *das Volk* had been nurtured. Fichte's lectures, Hegel's concept of the supremacy of the state, von Treitschke's ramblings, and the *Wandervogel* movement with their raised-hand salute all played their part in Nazi thinking. Even Heinrich von Kleist, so celebrated by the Romantics, had written in his *Catechism for Germans* 'Dost thou love thine Fatherland, my son? Yes father, I do. And why dost thou love it? Because it is my Fatherland.'[42]

More practically, it now had a disillusioned population who were politically febrile, had regularly mounted anti-Jewish pogroms and had recently shown a capacity for violence. In November 1926

Hitler appointed Joseph Goebbels as the Nazi gauleiter in the city. Goebbels's task was a formidable one. In the 1925 local elections the Nazis had done best in Spandau, but they had only managed 137 votes against 604,696 for the SPD and 347,381 for the communist KPD; the Nazis would always do better in Berlin's suburbs than in the city itself. Goebbels, a Rhinelander educated by the Jesuits, was as able as he was evil, and if he lacked the morals of his mentors he had certainly learned from them the importance of singled-mindedness. He began to build the party apparatus in Berlin. Moving the headquarters into Lützowstraße, he used what he described as Berlin's 'pitilessness', which he thought had 'found expression in its people. The motto here is: "Eat up bird or starve!" and anyone who has not learned to use his elbows will go down' to provoke confrontation with the communists.[43] He was helped by having the organisation of Ernst Röhm's *Sturmabteilung* – the SA, or the Nazi militia – behind him and he now built up their numbers as he increasingly orchestrated street fights with the KPD and their Red Banner fighters. Gradually the Nazi hold increased; in the 1928 elections they won ten seats, and Goebbels was allocated one.

Effective as Goebbels was, what really swelled Nazi support was the recession. There was a feeling in Berlin that, as everything else had failed, the Nazis might just offer a solution. Nazism was clever in that it offered all things to all people; it was socialist in that it was certainly not a party of the old monarchists, yet it was also nationalist in that it promoted German values and social order. It was patriotic, it seemed to have the quality so admired in the city of being able to get things done and it appealed to the nascent militarism that was never far from the surface. Most importantly, the SPD, the Republic, was seen to have failed, leaving hundreds of thousands of able and aspiring people without jobs or savings. Communism, which the city had flirted with in 1919, had been shown merely to promote violence and strikes. What the Nazis offered was an alternative.

Goebbels was also a master of propaganda and he seized on an incident in 1930 to give the party an image that he knew would appeal. A young SA street fighter called Horst Wessel was shot by a communist Red Banner agitator called Albrecht Höhler. Wessel, whose father was a pastor at the Nikolaikirche, was a thoroughly unattractive thug and pimp who had an argument with the prostitute he was living with over rent. His landlady called in some local Red Banner vigilantes led by Höhler, who came round and shot him. Höhler, who was equally unattractive and just out of prison, did not do a very good job and Wessel took six weeks to die. It was a gift for Goebbels whose propaganda machine quickly made Wessel a martyr not just for the Nazis but for Germany, a young 'socialist Christ who had chosen to live among those who scorned and spat upon him'.[44] His funeral became a huge public event with an agreeable amount of fighting between the SA and Red Banner gangs, but Goebbels's master stroke was to come up with some lyrics, allegedly written by Wessel, and turn them into a Nazi marching song. The 'Horst Wessel Song' became the Nazis' anthem and was soon as popular as *Die Wacht am Rhein*. It would be treated as an alternative national anthem when Hitler finally achieved power.

As Nazi strength grew, and as jobs became scarcer and disillusionment increased, Berlin found itself plunged into a similar level of street violence to that suffered at the beginning of the decade. Christopher Isherwood was still living in Berlin in the winter of 1932–3, just before the Nazis actually came to power, and he wrote about the gang warfare between the SA and Red Banner gangs. He recalled overhearing a conversation in a cafe between a young Nazi and his girlfriend discussing the future. 'Oh, I know we shall win, all right,' he exclaims impatiently, 'but that's not enough!' He thumps the table with his fist: 'Blood must flow!' The girl strokes his arm reassuringly ... 'But, of course, it's going to flow, darling ... the Leader's promised that.'[45] Later he was walking up Bülowstraße:

'Walking along the pavement ahead of me were three SA men. They all carried Nazi banners on their shoulders, like rifles, rolled up tight around the staves – the banner-staves had sharp metal points, shaped into arrow heads ... All at once they came head to head with a youth of seventeen or eighteen, dressed in civilian

clothes who was hurrying along in the opposite direction. I heard
one of the Nazis shout: "That's him!" and immediately all three of
them flung themselves upon the young man. He uttered a scream
and tried to dodge but they were too quick for him, kicking him
and stabling him with the sharp metal points of their banners.'

Once the beating had finished, Isherwood found the young man lying
in a doorway, his left eye poked half out and blood gushing from his
head. 'By this time dozens of people were looking on. They seemed
surprised, but not particularly shocked – this sort of thing happened
too often, nowadays.'[46]
Much of this violence was, of course, directed against the Jews
and as the Nazis gained strength so did their anti-Jewish rhetoric.
There were 160,000 Jews living in Berlin by 1933, making up about
4 per cent of the population. That latent anti-Semitism, which had
been so evident in 1919–22, was now apparent again as new scapegoats were sought for the recession. Isherwood was surprised, soon
after his arrival, to hear Fräulein Mayr, who also lived with Fräulein
Schroeder, celebrate the Nazis having smashed up Jewish-owned
shops on Leipziger Straße. 'Serves them right!' she exclaimed. 'This
town is sick with Jews. Turn over any stone and a couple of them
will crawl out. They're poisoning the very water we drink. They're
strangling us, they're robbing us, they're sucking our life-blood.'[47]
Yet, while the rest of Germany succumbed to the false promise of
National Socialism, Berlin held back. The Nazis believed that 'virtue
resides in the unspoilt child of nature, in this case the hardy peasantry
of the Bavarian Alps'.[48] It did not reside in a city like Berlin, with its
population of immigrants, Jews and intellectuals who seemed to miss
the finer points of their creed. In the 1930 elections, while the Nazis
increased their Reichstag seats to 107, 27 per cent of Berliners voted
for the KPD and only 14 per cent for Hitler. By November 1932 the
KPD Berlin vote had increased to 31 per cent, overtaking the SPD
and making them the largest party in the city, against the Nazis' 28
per cent, although the Nazis were the largest party nationally. Even
after Hitler had seized power in January 1933, and with considerable

bullying and election rigging, the subsequent March 1933 elections still only gave the Nazis 34 per cent of the Berlin vote, with 24 per cent still voting KPD. Goebbels may have tried to win Berlin but he had failed and the next eleven years would see the city – although cowed, subdued and eventually crucified – as the least Nazi part of Germany. The spirit of *Berlin Unwille* was as alive as ever.

Looking at the city he had grown to like and enjoy, if not love, as Isherwood prepared to leave in 1933, the hardness of Berlin seemed to have got to him.

'Berlin is a city with two centres – the cluster of expensive hotels, bars, cinemas, shops round the Memorial Church, a sparkling nucleus of light, like a sham diamond, in the shabby twilight of the town; and the self-conscious civic centre of buildings round the Unter den Linden, carefully arranged. In grand international style, copies of copies, they assert our dignity as a capital city – a parliament, a couple of museums, a State Bank, a cathedral, an opera, a dozen embassies; nothing has been forgotten. And they are all so pompous, so very correct ... But the real heart of Berlin is a small damp black wood – the Tiergarten. At this time of year, the cold begins to drive the peasant boys out of their tiny unprotected villages into the city, to look for food and work. But the city, which glowed so brightly and so invitingly in the night sky above the plains, is cold and cruel and dead. Its warmth is an illusion, a mirage of the winter desert. It will not receive these boys. It has nothing to give. The cold drives them out of its streets, into the wood which is its cruel heart. And there they cower on benches, to starve and freeze, and dream of their far-away cottage stoves.'[49]

As Isherwood left, Berlin was about to embark on the hardest decade of all.

CHAPTER NINE

1933–1945

'Berlin – a melting pot of everything that is evil'

JOSEPH GOEBBELS, 1938

On 21 March 1933, Goebbels orchestrated a parade at the Garrison Church in Potsdam, burial place of Frederick the Great. The Day of Potsdam, as it came to be called, was a shameless attempt to associate Hitler and the Nazi party with *Alte Fritz* and the heady days of Prussian military success. Hitler swapped his normal drab Nazi uniform for a morning coat and top hat. The aged Hindenburg, still president, attended in his full uniform with rows of stars and medals and his *pickelhaube*. All available army units marched past with their bands, accompanied inevitably by the Nazi SA and SS militias, and Hitler swore to maintain the honour and tradition represented by those who lay in the Garrison Church. Hindenburg was reported to have been so overcome that he burst into tears, but then the old man was becoming increasingly muddled. He would comment when another large Nazi parade passed under his windows in Wilhelmstraße, 'I had no idea that we took so many prisoners at Tannenberg.' That evening there was a performance of Wagner's *Die Meistersinger von Nürnberg* at the Staatsoper, which Hitler attended.

The day was officially the opening of the new Reichstag, in which Hitler did not have an absolute majority. The elections in March 1933 had given him only 43.9 per cent of the national vote but on 23 March he managed – with a great deal of intimidation – to pass his Enabling Act. This was achieved by stopping any KPD and many SPD members from attending and by pressurising the other right-wing parties. By passing this act, the Reichstag effectively handed absolute power to Hitler and wrote itself out of the next eleven years of Berlin's story. The members had to meet in the Kroll Opera House, the Reichstag building itself having been gutted by fire on Göring's orders on 27 February. Göring, Hitler's flamboyant deputy, unconvincingly blamed a Dutch simpleton called Marinus van der Lubbe who was, he maintained, part of a communist ring. 'This twenty-year-old simpleton,' wrote Kessler, 'is supposed to have stowed inflammable material at thirty different spots in the Reichstag and to have kindled it without either his presence, his activity or his bestowal of this enormous quantity of material being observed by anyone. And finally, he ran straight into the arms of the police, having carefully taken off all his clothes except for his trousers.'[1] It was not the first time in Berlin's history that a fire had been blamed on a convenient scapegoat. That night 4,000 communists and political opponents of the Nazi party were arrested across Berlin, including Carl von Ossietzky, editor of *Die Weltbühne*.

Nazi repression in the city now intensified. On 10 May Goebbels arranged a book-burning across Germany, an almost medieval event where gangs of SA men threw books considered anti-regime, written by Jews or thought in some other way decadent, into public bonfires. In Berlin it took place outside the National Library, the Kommode, on the Forum Fridericianum. Goebbels may not have been aware of Heine's famous line in his 1821 play *Almansor*, 'Where they burn books, one day they will also burn people,' but as volumes by Einstein, Mann, Brecht, Grosz, Döblin and many more authors who were living in the city were chucked into the flames, those writers realised they must leave. The only author who was actually present to see his own books go up in flames was Erich Kästner, whose

Fabian was thought offensive by the Nazis as it was rather too candid about contemporary morals. The site of Goebbels's book-burning is marked today by an effective, simple memorial let into the cobbles of Bebelplatz (as the Forum Fridericianum is now known). A glass cover looks into a room lined with empty bookshelves, beside it Heine's famous lines are engraved on a plaque. Students at the nearby Humboldt University hold a book sale annually on 10 May to commemorate the event.

Until now, Berlin's story has been chiefly about immigration, and why hundreds of thousands of people had been attracted to the city, many of them artists, authors and thinkers who, although born elsewhere, felt it was the place where they could best develop, practise and live. The events of 1933 changed this, and two significant groups – the artistic and the Jewish communities – now started to emigrate or, more accurately, to be exiled. It was a difficult decision for writers and artists to take. 'Once you had Berlin, you had the world,' wrote the playwright Carl Zuckmayer, 'and once you lost Berlin, you lost the world.' At first it was not clear that the Nazis would survive. As he left in 1933 Alfred Döblin told people they would just have to wait for the storm to blow over. But, after the arrests following the Reichstag fire and the book-burning, the literary community became nervous – not helped by Göring's comment that whenever he heard the word 'culture' he reached for his revolver. Between 1933 and 1939 it is estimated that around 1,300 writers left, some for other European countries, many for the USA. Erich Kästner, who was in Switzerland in 1933, actually came back to Berlin as he was determined to write a novel about the Nazis. It is probably as well that he never did so and he managed to survive the war.

The big, international names – men like Brecht, the Mann brothers and George Grosz – found that they were well enough known to be welcomed elsewhere. Others such as 'small-town' journalists, critics and freelance writers 'lost their livelihood when freedom of expression died'. An example of an author whose career was ruined by the Nazis was Gabriele Tergit. Originally a court-room reporter, in 1931 she had published a successful first novel, *Käsebier erobert den Kurfürstendamm*, which has been translated into English as *Käsebier Takes Berlin*. Tergit, her pen name – she was born Gabriele Hirschmann – satirises a Berlin that takes a remarkably untalented and mediocre entertainer, the 'small-time crooner' Käsebier (literally 'Cheese Beer'), and makes him into a sensation. It was a clever, witty exposure of how fake the Berlin cultural world could be, but it was seen as sending up traditional German values, and Tergit was Jewish. She fled first to Czechoslovakia then London but her writing career never really recovered.[2] Even poor Harry Kessler was told he was liable to be arrested and so he fled to Paris, never returning to Berlin. And it was not just writers. The architects Walter Gropius and Mies van der Rohe left; Freud and Einstein fled; the Berlin theatre lost Reinhardt; music lost Schoenberg, Weill, Eisler, Walter, Klemperer and Kleiber.[3] Käthe Kollwitz, who had recently started to work in wood, was expelled from the Prussian Academy of Arts and was no longer allowed to exhibit.

Lining the first-floor corridor of the Humboldt University's main building on Unter den Linden (Prince Henry's former palace) are photographic portraits of some of their most distinguished alumni, winners of Nobel Prizes and the like. Walking along them is a sobering and sad experience that shows how deep Nazi intolerance went and how much Germany lost. Gertrude Kornfeld, senior lecturer in physical chemistry – the first woman to hold such a post – had her teaching credentials revoked because of her Jewish background and was forced to emigrate. The brilliant economist Charlotte Leubuscher, the first woman to complete her qualification for a professor's chair outside the natural sciences, was forced out in 1933. The historian Hedwig Hintze, sacked for her Jewish ancestry in 1933, went to the USA. Rahel Hirsch, the first female professor of medicine in Prussia, was forced out in 1933. The scientist and expert in cell research Rhoda Erdmann was denounced and sacked in 1935. Gertrude Bäumer, who headed the schools department in the Ministry of Interior, was sacked in 1933. It is a long list and, looking at this sad and distinguished group, one cannot help but think just how irrational it was of the Nazis to believe they could strip Germany of its intellectual talent and still build their 1,000 Year Reich. Perhaps the saddest photograph of all is that of the scientist Liselotte Hermann, sacked in 1933 for signing a 'Call to defend democratic rights and freedoms at the University of Berlin', who was subsequently executed in Plötzensee in 1938.

Controversially, several of those who might have left stayed and were, if not actually sympathetic to the regime, then not actively opposed to it. Perhaps the most famous example is the Berlin Philharmonic under Wilhelm Furtwängler. By 1933 the orchestra was in serious trouble financially. Furtwängler, who became a friend of Goebbels and whom he seems to have admired, saw an opportunity to sort out its finances and to retain his musicians. However, this came at a price. Goebbels interfered in almost every detail of the orchestra's life. In 1935 they played 178 times; Beethoven appeared on the programme eighty-five times, Brahms forty-five, Bach twenty-eight, Handel sixteen, Pfitzner fifteen, Robert Schumann twenty, Richard Strauss twenty-nine, Wagner sixteen, Weber nineteen, Bruckner sixteen, Haydn twenty-six, Mozart thirty-eight and Schubert twenty. Only one non-German composer, Tchaikovsky, made it into double digits. More sinister was that by 1935 there were no Jewish musicians left in the ensemble, and Goebbels's apparatchiks were pursuing those Germans who had Jewish wives. Furtwängler's subsequent air of injured musical pride when international Jewish musicians rejected requests to play with them was difficult to take seriously.

Richard Strauss also remained and in 1933 took over from Toscanini as Director of the *Reichsmusikkammer* and of the Bayreuth Festival. Subsequently accused of being a Nazi sympathiser, Strauss argued that he supported Jewish musicians like Stefan Zweig and did what he did in an attempt to protect the Jewish members of his family. More controversial was Gerhard Hauptmann, who actually applied to join the Nazi party. He was lionised by Goebbels as one of the great German writers and his eightieth birthday in 1942 was used to stage celebratory performances of his plays. It has done much

to tarnish his reputation today. Strangely, Hitler – like the Elector
John Sigismund and Kaiser Wilhelm II – had an unshakeable belief
that the Germans understood Shakespeare better than the English.
Shakespeare's plays were frequently performed during the 1930s and
Hitler remarked that 'in no other country is Shakespeare performed
as badly as in England'.[4]

The second group who realised they must leave were Berlin's
Jews. Again, many of them believed that Hitler's anti-Semitic rav-
ings were just electoral tactics and hoped that, once in power, he
would moderate his views. It was not to be and anti-Jewish measures
were implemented almost immediately. Jews were excluded from
all official positions and the 'Aryanisation' of business began. On
1 April 1933 Jewish shops including the huge Wertheim, KaDeWe
and Karstadt were boycotted. Worse was to come after the 1935
Nuremberg Race Laws, which made marriage between Germans
and Jews illegal. The Reich Citizenship Law deprived Jews of basic
civil rights, including forbidding Jewish doctors, lawyers and other
professionals to practise. The Nazi policy at that time was to get all
Jews to leave Berlin. Goebbels wrote in his diary on 10 June 1938,
'I actually goad them. Not a trace of sentimentality. The law is not
important. What is important is harassment. The Jews must leave
Berlin. The police will help me to this end.'[5] On 16 June 1938 thousands of Jews were rounded up and accused of drug-dealing, but
much worse was to come on Kristallnacht (the night of broken glass)
on 9 November. Synagogues, Jewish shops and businesses had their
windows smashed, were looted and many set on fire. Some 12,000
Jews were subsequently arrested, many blamed for the damage to
their own property.

Ruth Andreas-Friedrich was in her apartment on 10 November
when at 7 a.m. her doorbell was rung ten times in succession 'as
if someone was beating a tattoo on it'. It was a lawyer friend, Dr
Weissman. '"Hide me, they're after me!" he pants. Who? What? I
don't understand,' she replied. '"Are you living on the moon?" he
asks bitterly. "The devil is walking in Berlin! The synagogues are on
fire. Jewish blood is flowing from the knife. The storm troops are on

the march, smashing windows ... They're hunting us like rabbits. They made me run halfway down the Ku'damm, and yelled after me 'Jewish swine, mass murderer, drop dead' ... the police just looked on."[6] Later that day she witnessed a gang smashing up a Jewish shop in Hausvogteiplatz. 'Five fellows in crumpled civilian clothes, wearing peaked caps, their faces distorted with exertion' as they knocked out the windows. 'There is,' she thought, 'neither hatred in them nor indignation, neither frenzy nor anger.' The onlooking crowd was silent and unemotional. 'Is this the spontaneous rage of the people finding vent?' she asked herself. 'No, nothing of the kind. But if those five were ordered tomorrow to kill all the chimney sweeps in Germany with flails, they would go to it, and leave no one alive. They would be without passion and without mercy, not because they hated chimney sweeps but because they loved obedience – loved it so much that even the soul stood at attention before it.'[7]

From November 1938 the repression continued in an unending stream of bitterness and extraordinary pettiness. On 12 November Berlin's Jews were forced to pay for the damage inflicted on Kristallnacht. On 15 November Jewish children were banned from public schools; on 3 December Jewish driving licences were rescinded, while on 5 December pensions of Jewish officials were withdrawn. The same day Jews were banned from visiting theatres and cinemas and from the city centre.

By 1939 half of Berlin's Jews had left but 75,344 remained. The problem was that it was not easy for the poorer families, especially the *Ostjuden* in areas like the Scheunenvieriel, to emigrate nor for them to find countries willing to take them. The richer and better-connected Jews had left early either because, like Walter Benjamin who fled to France, they could see what would happen or, like Alfred Kerr, a well-known, fiercely anti-Nazi theatre critic, because he had to if he was to avoid arrest. Kerr's daughter, Judith, the famous children's author, recorded the fear of growing up as a young Jewish girl in 1930s Berlin in *When Hitler Stole Pink Rabbit*. She had been given the choice of taking just one toy into exile and so selected a stuffed dog, having to leave her equally beloved pink rabbit behind.

She recorded one of the most venal of Nazi persecutions, that Jewish families may not keep pets. The Kerr family came to England, as did many other Jewish children from Berlin. After Kristallnacht the British government, along with the governments of France, Belgium and Holland, organised a scheme to resettle Jewish children from across Nazi-occupied countries in Great Britain, the so-called *Kindertransport*. The redoubtable Florence Nankivell took herself to Berlin to organise the evacuation of Berliners and, despite considerable harassment from the Nazis, she organised the first train, with 196 children, to depart on 1 December 1938. The scheme ran until the invasion of Poland and the declaration of war made it impossible, but altogether 10,000 children were rescued. It was to prove a bittersweet experience for many of them who ended up being the sole surviving members of their families. They had to cope with terrible personal loss as well as making a new life in a strange country and learning a new language. It is a testament to the resourcefulness of Berlin's Jewish community that so many made such a success of their lives – men like the painter Frank Auerbach – as it is to the perhaps slightly unusual open-mindedness of the British government and the kindness of the families who took them in.

Another group who were 'exiled' from Berlin were those Berliner children evacuated to the countryside under the *Kinderlandverschickung* scheme (the KLV, as it was known). Started in September 1940, by November 189,543 children had been evacuated, largely driven by their parents' fear of bombing. Although some children loved country life, many found it alien and hated being expected to join in farmwork. Many too were sent to East Prussia, Silesia and Saxony, the areas that would suffer worst in 1945, and would never see their parents again.[8] Ilse Koehn, whose grandmother was Jewish, was sent with her school to a small village in Bohemia. 'We looked out of the window, breathed the fresh air and enjoyed the wonderful smell of the fir trees – and suddenly we are deeply depressed. We feel that we are in a trap, alone and far away from home.'[9]

Then there were the communists. In June 1933, in Köpenick

where there had been communist protests against Hitler, the SA arrested more than 500 people and threw them into camps. Ninety-one of their mutilated bodies were later found floating in the River Dahme. Press censorship was already in place. Berlin had enjoyed 147 independent newspapers in 1927, but by the end of 1933 there were none. The socialists and communists had lost their leaders and their voice. Moscow had, however, already made arrangements for men like Walter Ulbricht and William Pieck. The future leaders of the GDR would spend the Nazi years in exile, planning and waiting for what they saw as the inevitable downfall of the right and the triumph of communism in the city they had come, they thought, so close to taking in 1919.

Today Berlin is about to open a Museum of Exile. The brain-child of the well-known art collector Bernd Schultz, and directed by Christoph Stölzl, *Stiftung Exil* will be housed appropriately in Anhalter Bahnhof, the station from which so many started their journeys away from the city. It will address, for the first time, the lives and stories of those who were forced out and whose loss so weakened Berlin. What was so hard for many exiles was not just the cruelty and injustice of having to leave but the loss of their very being. This was particularly true of so many Jews who, in the Mendelssohn tradition, had always seen themselves as Germans who were Jews rather than Jews who happened to be living in Germany. Many had fought through the First World War and given so much to their country but that country had then rejected them. 'Nobody,' said the film director Georg Stefan Troller, 'has ever asked me about, or apologised for, that deeper meaning of exile – which is, in fact, a bit like losing your life's centre, its binding thread.'[10]

With this level of violence, it may seem as if Berlin in the 1930s was a dangerous and difficult place to live, but that only applied if you were Jewish, communist or victimised by the regime in some other way. For many Berliners, even though 70 per cent of them had not voted for Hitler, the years between 1933 and 1939 would be relatively stable and happy. 'The 1930s were beautiful,' noted Gerda Kirstaedter. Her father's spirits business had been a victim of the

recession so that the family had to sell their furniture and silver that
she remembered so well from her wedding. Now the Nazis seemed
to offer some stability. Unemployment was vastly reduced, the mark
remained stable, and petty crime disappeared from Berlin's streets.
The Nazis seemed to have given a new self-confidence to a city that
had suffered so much. Goebbels, as gauleiter, also did quite a bit to
clean up the seamier side of Berlin's sex trade so that 'no longer did
male prostitutes display their charms openly on the Tauentzienstraße
and the Ku'damm'.[11] Yet much of the fun and the nightlife remained.
The theatre and the concerts may have been more limited but tourists
still flocked in and the hotels were booming.

The Nazis did not like Berlin, however, and Hitler would never
forgive Berliners for rejecting him in 1933. The huge set-piece annual
rallies after the Nazis took power were still held in Nuremberg,
where people could be expected to turn out and cheer enthusiastically, rather than in the capital with its sceptical population. But
Hitler felt that, as the Reich's capital, Berlin needed aggrandisement.
It was, he thought, 'an unregulated accumulation of buildings. The
only monumental parts are Unter den Linden, the palace and their
immediate surroundings.' It did not compare with Paris or Vienna.
Berlin 'must be raised to such a high level of urban planning and
culture that it may compete with the other capital cities of the
world.'[12] Having closed down Gropius's Bauhaus, and rejected Mies
van der Rohe's plans for a new Reichsbank building in favour of
a solid, block-like structure designed by Heinrich Wolff (which is
now part of the German Foreign Ministry), Hitler planned his new
capital with a Rhinelander called Albert Speer. Speer had come to
his attention for his design of the huge sets and back-drops for the
Nuremberg rallies, illuminated by torchlight, flaming lanterns and
searchlights playing on the black, red and white of the party insignia.

Hitler and Speer now came up with a scheme for *Germania*, a new
name that would remove the distasteful legacy of Berlin. It was to be
a city for 10 million people based on airports. A broad ceremonial
avenue was to be built from Tempelhof airport in the south of the
city, running 3 miles to the eastern side of the Reichstag. Anhalter

and Potsdamer stations were to be moved and at the northern end, dwarfing the Reichstag itself and the Brandenburg Gate, Hitler (who fancied his skills as an architect) designed a massive hall, sixteen times bigger than St Peter's in Rome. It was to be the biggest building in the world, with seating for 150,000 people. At the southern end of the avenue would be an equally massive ceremonial arch on which would be engraved the names of the 1.8 million Germans killed in the First World War, although the Jews were to be left off. Germania, along with several other major Berlin projects such as Schinkel's cathedral, was fortunately never built although the Nazis did busy themselves turning the area around Wilhelmstraße into their administrative centre.

In 1933, Ernst Sagebiel started a new aviation ministry for Göring who, among his other appointments and sinecures, was Reich Aviation Minister. When completed in 1935, it was the largest office building in Europe, with 2,000 rooms. On the corner of Wilhelmstraße and Leipziger Straße – on the site of the old Prussian Ministry of War, and directly beside the Bundesrat, the old Prussian Upper House – what is remarkable about this monolithic building is that it has survived more or less intact. Under the GDR it became the Ministry of Ministries, a wonderfully Orwellian title reflective of communism's love of bureaucracy. Now it houses the Federal Ministry of Finance, although the GDR murals of happy East Germans going about their daily socialist lives have been preserved on Leipziger Straße. Now called Detlev-Rohwedder-Haus, after the SPD politician murdered by the Red Army Faction in 1991, it is the best example of Nazi-style building left in the centre of the city. Behind the Aviation Ministry, orientated east–west and facing onto Wilhelmstraße, was Hitler's Chancellery. Every visitor to Berlin seems intent on finding the Chancellery and the spot where Hitler would later take his own life, but it has all been destroyed, flattened after the war by the Russians. The site of its entrance is now a Chinese restaurant and the closest you can get to it is to see the red marble taken from the rubble to rebuild nearby Mohrenstraße U-Bahn station that was very badly damaged in 1945.

Another famous and sinister Nazi building was the SS headquarters in Prinz-Albrecht-Straße, renamed Niederkirchnerstraße by the
GDR in 1951. The SS gradually came to replace the SA as the Nazis'
official militia. Under the direction of Heinrich Himmler, on 30
June 1934 Hitler, apparently fearful that Ernst Röhm would mount
a putsch against him and wanting to consolidate the army leadership
behind the Reich, authorised the SS to murder Röhm and disband
the SA. Known as the Night of the Long Knives, hundreds of SA men
were killed in three bloody days. From 1934 the SS, the *Schutzstaffel*,
became the main instrument of Nazi security. They took over the
Prinz Albrecht Hotel, facing onto the eponymous street, and brought
the Gestapo and the RHSA (the *Reichssicherheitshauptampt*,
the Nazi security office) under one roof answering to Reinhardt
Heydrich. Christabel Bielenberg found it a terrifying place when she
went in the winter of 1944 to plead for her husband who was incarcerated in Ravensbrück concentration camp. 'My coat was made of
synthetic wool, a new discovery since the war, material made from
wood and felt like wool and might have been cotton netting for all
the warmth it provided. I began to shiver a little as I paused at the
top of those wide stone steps. This was it. It was here that the green
padlocked vans drew up daily and disgorged their victims ... They
had all mounted those stairs, hoping – hoping, hoping against hope.
The atmosphere of the place was horrifying, silent, echoing and cold,
deathly cold.'[13] The building was destroyed in the war and is now the
site of the *Topografie des Terrors*, a moving and important exhibition
of the Nazi terror and another example of how Berlin refuses to hide
its past. Opposite the Chancellery was Goebbels's so-called Ministry
of Enlightenment, the propaganda ministry, from where he also ruled
Berlin, and close by was the office of Hitler's deputy Rudolf Hess.

Hitler and Speer were also conscious, despite their plans for a
grand north–south avenue, that the main Berlin axis had long been
east–west, along Unter den Linden, through the Brandenburg Gate
and the Tiergarten. They now moved the Siegessäule from its site on
the Königsplatz opposite the Reichstag and put it in the middle of the
Tiergarten on the main road, the Charlottenburger Straße (what is

now called Straße des 17 Juni). Beyond the Tiergarten they widened and improved Heerstraße (Army Road), built in the 1870s to move troops quickly from Spandau. It would soon have another important purpose because in 1936 Berlin hosted the Olympic Games, which took place in a newly built stadium at Spandau.

The 1936 Summer Olympics were awarded to Berlin, which had been intended as the site of the 1916 Games (cancelled for obvious reasons). Hitler now determined to make the Games a showpiece for the Nazi regime, and Werner March was commissioned to work with Speer to rebuild the old Deutsche Stadion in Spandau. March produced a three-part complex: the actual stadium itself, which seated more than 100,000 and had a special VIP section for Hitler and the party hierarchy; the *Maifeld*, a 28-acre field for athletic events that was subsequently used for Nazi rallies; and the *Waldbühne*, a 25,000-seater amphitheatre. At the entrance was the famous bell tower. The complex was not badly damaged in the Second World War Two, apart from the bell tower, which the Russians demolished but has now been rebuilt. For many years it was the headquarters of the British forces stationed in Berlin in the Cold War, who were largely based in Spandau.

Goebbels then milked the Games for all he could. On 1 August 29,000 Hitler Youths greeted the Olympic flame in the Lustgarten. This was not an ancient Olympic tradition but something dreamed up by Goebbels for dramatic effect. The flaming torch was then borne the 11 kilometres to the stadium along the route through the Tiergarten and along Heerstraße, guarded by 40,000 SS men. Hitler followed in a ceremonial procession, standing upright in his car, unsmiling and with his hand raised in the Nazi salute. On his arrival he was escorted to his box as the bands played Wagner's *Homage March*. The Nazi high command was on a charm offensive. Göring hosted endless parties. 'He was fun,' recalled the American swimmer Eleanor Holm. 'I enjoyed the parties, the "Heil Hitlers", the uniforms, the flags.' Even the sceptical British diplomat Robert Vansittart was temporarily taken in by Goebbels. 'I found much charm in him – a limping, eloquent slip of a Jacobin, quick as a whip, and often, I doubt not, as cutting,' he reported. 'These tense, intense people are going to make us look like a C class nation.' Goebbels himself used his diary to vent his disgust at some of his Nazi peers. Joachim von Ribbentrop, whom he loathed, had 'bought his name, married his money and cheated his way into a job,' but Ribbentrop was also charming the world. It didn't work with the British politician Chips Canon, who remarked even more bitchily that Frau von Ribbentrop was wearing 'appalling khaki coloured clothes ... is it because their women are so unattractive that the German race is largely homosexual?' The Nazi film-maker Leni Riefenstahl, an active propagandist who would later excuse her work as art, incurred the fury of the foreign press by stopping anyone else apart from her crews from filming.

But there was little Hitler could do to stop the black American athlete Jesse Owens from winning four gold medals, although Hitler did refuse to present any of them to him, saying, 'I am not shaking hands with this Negro.' Otherwise an attempt was made to hide the regime's anti-Jewish policies. A Jewish woman, Helene Mayer, was allowed to participate in the German fencing team and won a silver medal, and the virulently anti-Semitic newspaper *Der Stürmer* was suspended during the Games. Yet it was all a front. The stadium hid the Langemarckhalle and as Goebbels wrote as the Games drew to a conclusion, 'After the Olympics we will get ruthless. Then there will be some shooting.' Captain Wolfgang Fürstner, the officer responsible for running the Olympic Village, had a Jewish grandfather. During the Games some bigot displayed a banner saying, 'Down with the Jew Fürstner'. 'Two days after the end of the games ... Fürstner dons his best uniform, replete with medals, and marches through the Olympic Village towards the lake in the woods, he draws his pistol, puts the barrel to his forehead and pulls the trigger.'[14]

~

In March 1936, in direct contravention of Versailles, Hitler had reoccupied the Rhineland; neither France nor Great Britain had intervened. In March 1938 German forces moved into Austria, the *Anschluss*, annexing it to the Reich. In September 1938 Hitler had outmanoeuvred France and the British again at Munich, leading to his occupation of the Czech Sudetenland that October. In March 1939 German forces had invaded the rest of Czechoslovakia. While this terror was going on abroad, the Gestapo were, as Goebbels had promised, doing the same thing at home and especially in Berlin. Berlin had several prisons in the 1930s, the main ones being in Moabit, Spandau and at Plötzensee in Charlottenburg. Judicial executions were, under the stringent German legal code, carried out in a strangely medieval way by beheading with an axe. The main execution site was at Plötzensee. From 1890 to 1932, thirty-six people were put to death there, almost all for murder. By contrast, from 1933 when the Nazis came to power until 1945 that figure was 2,891, with the last person executed as the Russians were about to take the area. Nazi executions were initially also carried out with an axe in the prison yard but later a guillotine was used or prisoners were hanged. It was in the execution shed at Plötzensee that many of the 20 July 1944 bomb plotters against Hitler were murdered. Others were innocent victims of the regime, such as Hans Dobroszcyk, a ticket-taker at the Ufa Cinema on Nollendorfplatz. He picked up a handbag from the ruins of a bombed building and handed it in to the police. He was accused of looting, tried by Special Court II of the Berlin Regional Court and sentenced to death. On 3 March 1943 he was guillotined in Plötzensee. His last letter to his wife and daughter reads: 'Dear wife and daughter, I have been sentenced to death although innocent. I cannot say why. Stay healthy and happy. Yours, Papa.'[15] In a particularly morbid and unpleasant twist, the victim's families had to pay the executioner's fee of 300 marks before they were allowed to reclaim their possessions. There is now a sad and moving memorial there to all the men and women who died.

These prisons were insufficient to cope with the mass arrests and detentions that the Nazis had instigated. In 1933 they took over an old military prison on the northern edge of Tempelhof Airfield, Columbia House, which would serve until 1945 as an overflow for the Gestapo's victims in Prinz-Albrecht-Straße. From 1934 it became a concentration camp within the city and was mainly used to house political prisoners, but Berlin's main concentration camp was the feared Sachsenhausen at Oranienburg. Oranienburg was strongly pro Nazi, as were several of Berlin's outlying suburbs. The local party was one of the first branches to be founded in Prussia and by 1933 Nazi voters easily outnumbered both SPD and KPD. In March 1933 the Nazis won fifteen seats on the local council against seven for the SPD and six for the KPD. Some of the first inmates of the concentration camp were the recently elected KPD councillors. Established on the site of an old brewery by the SA in 1933, Sachsenhausen was initially used to incarcerate the Nazis' political opponents like these, sixteen of whom were executed there. Being on the main road into Berlin, however, it was thought to be too public. The executed corpses were taken into Berlin for disposal but on one occasion fell out of the lorry onto the street. In 1936 the SS occupied the site, which was laid out as a 'model' concentration camp, and the concentration camps' overall administrative staff were transferred there.

From 1936 until 1945, 200,000 people were imprisoned in Sachsenhausen, tens of thousands of whom died of malnourishment, disease or were executed by shooting or in the gas chamber. In 1945 thousands more died on 'death marches' as the camp was evacuated so that, when the Russians arrived in April 1945, they found just 3,000 sick. The Russians then used it as a prison camp in their turn, operating it until 1950. During this time, 60,000 were detained, of whom 12,000 died. It is a sad and sinister place to visit. Preserved almost as it was – with its prison huts, its kitchens, workshops, parade ground and gallows – and with an excellent museum, it seems extraordinary that it should have been operating so close to Berlin itself and strange that such an enormous number of people could have suffered and died there without it being noticed locally. Visiting Sachsenhausen is something one does for education – the last stop on the northern S1 S-Bahn line is Oranienburg and you can visit the Schloss at the same time – but, again, here is

Berlin putting its history on public view with no attempt to hide what happened.

Berliners had generally accepted the Nazis' early victories, the Rhineland and the *Anschluss*, seeing them as a re-establishment of German national pride. The possible invasion of Czechoslovakia had, however, been something rather different. On 27 September 1938 columns of troops passing through Berlin were greeted in silence by people on their way to work, and when Hitler appeared on the Chancellery balcony to review them he found there was no crowd to cheer him. Berliners did subsequently turn out to cheer the Munich Agreement with 'delirious joy', said the American correspondent William Shirer who was working in Berlin, because they thought Germany had won a bloodless victory and war had been avoided.[16] Neither did many of them react well to Kristallnacht that November. Some did and their behaviour, wrote the *Daily Telegraph*'s correspondent, was 'nauseating ... Racial hatred and hysteria seem to have taken complete control of otherwise decent people'. But many were shocked and upset. Hans Werner Lobeck recorded that as drunken Nazi storm troopers emerged from the wreck of a Hungarian Jewish-owned restaurant on the Ku'damm near the burning synagogue on Fasanenstraße, carrying bottles of looted wine that they offered to those watching, 'a shudder went through the crowd and it fell back. The people dispersed leaving the SA men alone on the sidewalk.'[17] They looked on, many with amused scepticism, at Hitler's fiftieth birthday celebrations on 20 April 1939, when he drove in state along the length of the east–west axis to the Olympiastadion, the whole route decorated with new flagpoles. They listened respectfully as he was serenaded by the SS choir and they enjoyed, as Berliners do, a mass military parade of 40,000 men the next day, accompanied by an equally impressive fly-past by the Luftwaffe.

However, by August the constant talk of war made people nervous. They turned out to cheer loudly once again on 24 August 1939 after Foreign Minister Ribbentrop signed a pact with his Soviet counterpart, Molotov; as with Munich, the cheering was because a city that could so clearly remember 1914–18 thought they had again avoided war. Yet the news the last week of that hot, humid month became progressively worse and there was talk of war being imminent. The media was full of stories of alleged Polish atrocities, and as Shirer sat in his room at the Adlon he saw soldiers installing anti-aircraft guns. They started to spring up all over the city, and the streets were full of passing army vehicles and troops marching. On 31 August there was a practice air-raid alert, something that was new and frightening. The streets were cleared as people were herded into cellars and U-Bahn stations.

Then in the early hours of 1 September 1939 Hitler announced that Germany had that morning invaded Poland. At 10 a.m. he drove to the Reichstag, still meeting in the Circus Busch, to make a statement. The Nazi hierarchy were surprised and annoyed to find the streets empty. There were no cheering crowds, no flower-throwing or general mood of excitement and celebration as there had been twenty-five years earlier. This time Berlin was a city full of quiet, resigned, anxious people. A diplomat in the American embassy noticed that workmen on a nearby building site did not even bother to stop work to listen; as Hitler's car returned to the Chancellery it was greeted by an 'eerie silence'. There was 'no enthusiasm, no joy, no cheering. Everywhere one encountered an oppressive calm, not to say depression. The entire German people seemed seized by a paralysing horror,' wrote the Nazi Karl Wahl.[18] Dorothea von Schwanenflügel recalled her father turning to her mother and saying, 'My God! Wasn't one war enough in our lifetime?' When Britain declared war two days later, on 3 September, the mood deepened. 'I remember,' wrote Else Diederichs, a seventeen-year-old schoolgirl as she caught her train, 'that we all sat there with these frightfully serious faces. We were depressed. We had the feeling that something quite terrible was coming.'[19]

Poland was quickly overrun and, although a few Polish aircraft did fly over Berlin, there was no air raid. By the second week of October it was all over and, while the Poles never actually surrendered, they were now an occupied country. Berliners clustered around their radios on 10 October as Hitler made a much-publicised speech in which everyone assumed he would announce that they were now at peace. The American diplomat William Russell joined a crowd outside a radio shop that had a loudspeaker. Hitler spoke for forty minutes. He 'finished and the sound of rousing *Sieg Heil! Sieg Heil!* came through the noisy loud-speaker. There was no mention of the new peace in any sentence ... The crowd was bewildered and disappointed.'[20] When France fell the following July, public reaction was again muted albeit more enthusiastic. Shirer – still working in Berlin as America was not at that stage at war with Germany – wrote that the words 'Germans capture Paris are magic words to so many here,' and there was a huge traditional victory parade on the Pariser Platz and down Unter den Linden. This time there were flowers, cheering and a festive mood. Berliners' enthusiasm, though, was rather because they again thought victory would bring peace and because they were pleased to have their husbands and sons back. Many of the 60,000 German soldiers killed in the first year of the war were Berliners. It was not to be. Britain fought on and any chance of an early settlement faded. In February 1941 Hitler sent troops to bolster the failing Italian effort against the British in North Africa. In April 1941 Germany invaded Yugoslavia and Greece and then in June Germany invaded Russia. Berliners realised they must resign themselves to a long war.

For the next four years, until April 1945 brought about their city's destruction, Berliners experienced the war through hunger, through the increasing terror unleashed by the Gestapo and the police, through bereavement and perhaps most directly through British and American bombing. Rationing was introduced immediately, and there was a rush to stock up with supplies despite harsh penalties for hoarding. Christmas 1939 offered a foretaste of what was to come, with little let-up and people questioning just how efficient the Reich's supply system was. Just as in the First World War, the issue was the naval blockade, and once war with Russia shut off supplies from the east, and the enormous military machine had been fed, food and fuel became scarce. The rationing system was complicated, being divided into different categories depending on what work people were doing. Manual workers got the most, office workers the average and there were special scales for children, but people felt it was a system open to abuse. Milk and the Berlin staple, the potato, were always in short supply – a situation made worse by the lack of transport to bring them into the city. Coal was also always scarce and heating was a luxury. Petrol became increasingly hard to come by as the war progressed, so taxis and private cars virtually disappeared from the streets. Clothing was rationed and people were only allowed two pairs of shoes. Inevitably, as in the First World War, a thriving black market developed and those with money seemed able to live much better than their poorer counterparts. Even in the last year of the war, the smart restaurants had 'hors d'oeuvres, fried fish and plenty to drink,' noted the journalist Ursula von Kardorff who, illegally, kept a diary from 1942 to 1945. She also remembered the absolute bliss of being temporarily accommodated in the basement of Speer's Munitions Ministry in Pariser Platz as it meant she had hot water.[21] What Berliners remembered was the misery of being perpetually hungry, cold, always tired and mostly frightened, partly from the fear of the police but mostly from the bombing.

That terror got progressively worse as the war started to go badly for Germany, and particularly so for the Jews. By 1943 there were about 75,000 left in Berlin – those who had nowhere to go or no means of getting there, and many of whom believed things could get no worse. Still the repressive measures continued. In September 1941, in a sort of macabre medieval throwback, all Jews were forced to wear a yellow star. Their ration cards were stamped with a 'J' that meant they were entitled to less food, and they were segregated in air-raid shelters. Then in January 1942 the senior Nazi leadership met in the exquisite surroundings of the Villa Marlier, a lakeside lodge built on the Wannsee in 1914 for one of Germany's richest men, and sold to the coal baron Friedrich Minoux. Wannsee had been developed as a colony for rich Berliners in the late nineteenth century and enjoyed an idyllic position on a wooded peninsula on the southern end of the eponymous lake created by the Havel's meanderings north of Potsdam. Several rich Berliners had villas here, including Max Liebermann whose particularly attractive and peaceful house and garden stretched down to the water's edge. Wannsee had, like Oranienburg, long been a strongly Nazi area. As early as 1933 a notice had gone up on the lido, banning Jews from swimming there, a particularly horrible move since the area had a significant Jewish population whose children often bathed in the lake. In 1941 the SS had acquired the Villa Marlier and, in one of those terrible ironies of history, they now chose this most beautiful of natural locations to plan the 'Final Solution' to what they saw as the problem posed by Europe's 11 million Jews. It was as a result of this conference, chaired by Heydrich, that the mass murder of Jews in the concentration camps was planned. The minutes were taken by Adolf Eichmann. Today the Villa Marlier is preserved as a museum and study centre.

By January 1942 10,000 of Berlin's remaining Jews had been sent to camps mostly in the Baltics and Western Russia. In February 1943 the rate was rapidly increased by the 'Factory Action', when Jews working in the armaments factories were also rounded up. They made the sad journey, having been first taken to be 'processed' at the centres on Große Hamburger Straße near the Sophienkirche (originally a Jewish old people's home) or to the synagogue on Levetzowstraße, then from the Anhalter and Potsdamer stations to the concentration camps, to Theresienstadt in Czechoslovakia, to Auschwitz and to other camps in Poland. The Berlin resistance organiser and diarist Ruth Andreas-Friedrich recorded watching one of the Factory Action operations. 'Since six o'clock this morning trucks have been driving through Berlin escorted by armed SS men. They stop at factory gates, in front of private houses; they load in human cargo – men, women, children. Distracted faces are crowded together under the grey canvas covers. Figures of misery, penned in and jostled about like cattle going to the stock-yards. More and more new ones arrive, and are thrust into the overcrowded trucks with blows of gun butts.'[22]

By 1945 more than 50,000 of Berlin's remaining Jews had been

shipped to their deaths in 122 consignments, each carefully recorded
with grim efficiency by the SS. Of the remaining 25,000, it is estimated that 7,000 took their own life and about 5,000 managed to
hide. Some, though perhaps not as many as should have been, were
hidden by brave Berlin neighbours. Others went into hiding around
the city, including one group who hid in huts on Reiswerder Island
in the Tegeler See. The island had been a popular Berlin weekend
retreat but was hardly used during the war, when it was leased by
a couple called Harry and Margarete Bonus. They hid five Jews in
the holiday huts: Gerhard and Erna Fleck who had been tipped off
about the 'Factory Action'; Hermann Dietz, a shop assistant whose
store had been bombed and who had a Jewish mother and a Catholic
father; Lotte Basch who had seen her parents arrested in 1942; and
an eighteen-year old girl called Gerda Lesser. Eventually betrayed,
the Gestapo rowed over and arrested them all. The Bonuses seem
to have been allowed to stay but Gerda Lesser was deported to
Auschwitz, where she was murdered on arrival.[23]

There were very few exceptions. A few privileged people like the
conductor Leo Blech, whom Göring arranged to have smuggled out
to Sweden, did escape but the vast majority did not, including members of the leading German commercial families. In January 1944 the
Gestapo arrived to arrest ninety-four-year-old Fritz Springer of the
famous publishing family at his Wannsee villa. His daughter managed
to hold them back for a few minutes, which gave him time to take
poison. He died the next day but his kinsman, the eighty-four-year-old
Ernst Springer, was sent to Theresienstadt where he was murdered.
Max Liebermann had – mercifully for him – died in 1935. His wife,
Martha, had been forced to sell their beloved villa on Wannsee in
1940. On 5 March 1943, bedridden and very ill in the house on
Pariser Platz, she was told she was going to be sent to Theresienstadt;
again, she managed to take her own life just before the police arrived.
There is now a *Stolperstein* outside her house, a nice Berlin custom of
marking the houses from which Jews were deported.

In many cases families agreed to take their own lives rather than
face what was coming. Helmuth von Moltke wrote to his wife that

he had 'Yesterday said goodbye to a once famous Jewish lawyer who has the Iron Cross First and Second Class, the Order of the House of Hohenzollern, the Golden Badge of the Wounded and who will kill himself with his wife today, because he is to be picked up tonight.'[24] The Jewish husbands of non-Jewish women were segregated after the Factory Action for 'special screening' but, in a most unusual event for wartime Berlin, on Sunday 7 March 1943, thousands of their Aryan wives mounted a mass demonstration in front of the building in Rosenstraße where they were being held. They stayed there all night and the next day so that at noon on Monday the SS announced that these men were to have special status as 'Privileged Ones' and be allowed to stay.[25]

The terror was, of course, not only directed against the Jews. Tens of thousands of ordinary Berliners were also victimised. Communists, intellectuals, religious leaders, homosexuals and anyone who spoke out against the regime were all likely to find themselves despatched to the camps, and many Berliners ended up in Sachsenhausen. There were several resistance groups operating in the city, some communist and with links to Russia, like *Gruppe Ernst* and *Rote Kapelle*, and some groups like Ruth Andreas-Friedrich's *Onkel Emil*, which existed mostly to shelter those in hiding from the Gestapo; she hid people in her cellar in Steglitz. *Onkel Emil* was a band of about twenty mostly professional people, and there were others like it – many of which, given the destruction of 1945, have never been properly credited for their bravery. A question often asked of Berliners was why they did not do more to oppose the Nazis. In response most Berliners, if not Germans, will not quote the rather tired 'sense of duty' argument but say instead that by the time they realised the true nature of the beast it was too late. The Reich's security apparatus had a complete monopoly on violence and such a tight grip on the city, much as the Stasi would a few years later, that active resistance was virtually impossible. They would also point out that the July 1944 plot to assassinate Hitler involved a lot of very brave people who suffered horribly for their courage.

The best way to experience that is to visit the *Gedenkstätte*

Deutscher Widerstand (the Memorial to the German Resistance) housed in the Bendler Block at the back of the German Ministry of Defence, the *Das Bundesministerium der Verteidigung*, off the aptly named Stauffenbergstraße. On 20 July 1944, Colonel Claus von Stauffenberg placed a bomb beside Hitler in the Führer's briefing room at his military headquarters in East Prussia. It was moved behind a solid table leg before it exploded so that Hitler was protected and he escaped with minor injuries. What might have happened had Hitler been killed has prompted many hours of debate, but the conspirators' plan was to overthrow the government and talk to the Allied Powers, who by then had staged the successful D-Day landings in France. Instead Stauffenberg and his immediate accomplices were rounded up and shot that evening in the Bendler Block courtyard, hence the location of the memorial museum (there is a plaque at the spot where he fell). Over the coming months more than 7,000 people – even those only vaguely connected with the plotters – were arrested, tried by a 'People's Court' under one of the worst sort of Nazi apparatchiks called Roland Freisler and about 5,000 executed, many in the execution shed at Plötzensee. What the memorial museum does is show how wide the opposition to Hitler in fact was. Not all those featured were Berliners but many were.

What is of particular interest is the attitude of the church in Berlin. The churches have been criticised for not opposing the Nazis more strongly, excusing themselves on the basis of the Calvinist tradition of loyalty to their rulers and the Pietist belief that religion is for internal guidance rather than external action. Pietism may have served Prussia well but now, when a moral challenge was needed, it was found wanting. The Martin Luther memorial church in Mariendorf even had a portrait of Hitler alongside Luther in its side chapel, and its new pulpit was supported by sculpted figures of a Hitler youth, a storm trooper and a soldier.[26] Yet some church leaders had always been open in their defiance of what Hitler stood for. Dietrich Bonhoeffer was a 'typical Berliner' in that he was born in Breslau but completed his doctorate at Berlin University, taught theology there and was ordained in the city. Although he frequently taught and preached abroad, he always returned to Berlin until he was banned from entering by the regime in 1938. He was executed in Flossenburg concentration camp just before the end of the war for alleged involvement in the 1944 plot, as was one of his brothers and two of his brothers-in-law.

The Bendler Block memorial also records the resistance of the Roman Catholic Bishop of Berlin, the simply named Johann Konrad Maria Augustin Felix Graf von Preysing Lichtenegg-Moos. Bishop von Preysing, as he was more helpfully known, had been made Bishop of Berlin in 1935. He opposed the Nazis from the start, saying when they were elected in 1933 that Berlin had 'fallen into the hands of criminals and fools,'[27] and remained outspoken in his criticism throughout the war. He commanded considerable respect across Germany, and the Gestapo did not dare arrest him despite him also encouraging other Catholic prelates to be more active in their opposition. Church attendance in Berlin predictably increased during the war years, with people remarking that the Roman Catholic Act of Holy Communion was a more comforting fulfilment of divine worship than a Calvinist sermon.[28] The city did not, though, lose its traditional scepticism of organised religion. The Anonymous Woman – the unknown author of *A Woman in Berlin*, one of the most moving and horrifying accounts of Berlin in 1945 – thought that 'Here in Berlin, in this motley mix of five story tenements, you'd be hard pressed to find a group of people willing to come together and say the Lord's Prayer.'[29]

Preysing was particularly critical of Cardinal Adolf Bertram, and the senior Roman Catholic hierarchy in Germany for being appeasers, and said of his cousin, the equally splendidly named Clemens August Graf von Galen, the Bishop of Münster, when, having initially been supportive of Hitler's wars, he finally preached against the Nazis euthanasia programme: 'He had a very average mind but this time the Holy Spirit has enlightened him.'[30] He survived the war and was made a Cardinal by the Pope for his resistance. On being told his red hat would be suspended from the roof of his cathedral, as was the custom, he remarked that he had no roof as St Hedwig's Cathedral in the Forum Fridericianum had been destroyed in a bombing raid. It was only after the war that the full extent of his anti-Nazi activities materialised, including infiltrating agents into the Reich ministries. He blessed von Stauffenberg before the July 44 plot and was, in his final years, as critical of the communists as he had been of the Nazis.

~

What enthusiasm there had been for the Nazis among Berliners was rapidly disappearing as the war dragged into its fourth year. In the early war years Goebbels had been determined that life would continue as normally as possible, with sporting events still being staged, and cinemas, theatres and most restaurants and cafes staying open. That became increasingly difficult as rationing tightened and bombing started, but it was really Stalingrad that was the turning point. The war in the East had started well for Germany, with her armies in 1941 poised to take both Moscow and Leningrad (as St Petersburg was then known). Then a combination of inadequate preparation for the Russian winter, a lack of proper Luftwaffe support, a stoical Soviet reorganisation and the sheer scale of what they were attempting caused their advance to falter. They were halted at Stalingrad in the winter of 1942–3, causing their southern flank to collapse. Approximately 850,000 German and Axis powers soldiers became casualties, at least 250,000 of them killed. From the spring of 1943, despite major German counter-attacks at Kursk, the direction of the war changed so that during the remainder of 1943 and 1944 Hitler's armies were pushed back into Poland and then East Prussia. Stalingrad led to the declaration of 'Total War' in Berlin. This meant that 'with a stroke of a pen Goebbels had abolished almost everything enjoyable. No theatres, no variety, no dance clubs, no wine bars. Berlin had become the most boring capital in the world,' complained the Norwegian reporter Theo Findahl.[31]

Berliners sensed that, despite Hitler and Goebbels's unceasing propaganda about imminent Soviet collapse, ultimately, the Soviets would come for them. It was the war in the air and in the east, rather than the Western Front in Europe, that preoccupied Berliners. 'Our

fate,' wrote the anonymous author of *A Woman in Berlin*, 'is rolling in from the East and it will transform the climate like another
Ice Age.'[32] 'The pessimism that prevails in Berlin puts them off and
sometimes infuriates them,' noted von Kardorff of men returning
from the front.[33] She herself found that, though the streets were
filthy, 'the people are more polite to one another than they were and
face their destiny with a show of good manners. I heard a woman
in the tram say "I don't worry any more now. When the alert goes I
get down into the cellar. At first I used to go out into the woods and
spend the night there, but now what I say is, if you're going to get
hit you're going to be hit, and that's the end of it. You can't escape
from fate."'[34] Families had got used to expecting that awful visit
from the postman, 'the one with the black border on the envelope
and the military markings ... The mail carrier,' wrote a neighbour
on seeing one being delivered, 'had tossed the letter into the mailbox
in the door and raced down the steps so she would not have to hear
Frau Müller's screams. She was not fast enough though.'[35]

On 9 November 1942 Ursula said goodbye to her much-loved
twenty-three-year-old brother, Jürgen von Kardorff. On 13 February
1943 she was told he was dead. The formal notice in the papers read
'Killed in action during the heavy fighting on the Donetz, on 2nd
February, Jürgen von Kardorff our beloved younger son and brother,
Lieutenant and Company Commander in an armoured regiment. He
died, as he had lived, a brave man and a faithful Christian.' Ursula
felt she had always known it would end like that.[36] The next spring
she spent a weekend staying with friends outside Berlin. 'In the
evening we sat under a lime tree which must have been centuries old.
The eldest son of the house is returning to the Eastern Front in a few
days' time. And suddenly he leant close to me and said softly, so that
the others could not hear, "I know I shan't come back. This is the last
time I shall sit here." And then, with typical Prussian nonchalance,
"Still, I'll be able to watch the radishes growing from underneath."'[37]

What made life most difficult of all for Berliners was the Allied air
raids. Berlin had been concerned about air raids from the beginning
of the war and, despite Göring's unwise and often-repeated promise

that no enemy bomber would ever get through, a strict blackout had been maintained since September 1939 that made night-time movement difficult and time-consuming. The feared Polish raids had never materialised and, although there had been a British raid by ninety-five aircraft on 25 August 1940 that hit targets at Tempelhof and Siemensstadt, it was more a psychological than a physical shock for the city. Its chief benefit was to infuriate Hitler, who returned from his Bavarian retreat, the Berghof, shaming Göring and leading Goebbels to think, falsely, that all Berliners would now feel they were engaged in the war. The German reaction was to improve significantly Berlin's air defences. Göring appointed General Hubert Weise (who had commanded German air defence in France) to establish *Luftgaukommando III*, charged with the defence of the capital. Weise sent Colonel Josef Kammhuber to work to organise a co-ordinated system that came to be known to the British Royal Air Force as the Kammhuber Line. This consisted of an 'illuminated zone' stretching from occupied Denmark across to northern France through which any aircraft attacking Berlin would have to fly. This zone was covered by the Germans' effective Freya Radars and by sound-detection devices and observer posts. They in turn alerted the Luftwaffe's night fighters, who would be scrambled to intercept. The only problem was that the Luftwaffe did not have any, Göring having deemed night fighters unnecessary, so they had to re-role their day fighters and the JU-88 medium bomber, although both actually proved most effective.

Around the city itself, Kammhuber grouped searchlights and large numbers of the Nazis' very effective anti-aircraft guns. Hitler had a thing about searchlights, imagining Berliners had to actually see attacking aircraft being shot down to believe the Reich was defending them. Berlin began to bristle with ant-aircraft batteries, and Hitler also insisted on the construction of three huge flak towers. These were massive concrete structures, with walls 3.5 metres thick that could withstand all known Allied ordnance. Equipped with Würzburg radars, each tower also had a formidable range of armament with eight 128 mm guns and thirty-two 20 mm cannon so they could fire 8,000 rounds a minute. They were built in pairs – one pair at Friedrichshain, one at the zoo, and the third (still partly intact) at Humboldthain by Gesundbrunnen station. The idea was that working together they could cover the city centre, and Humboldthain could protect the industrial areas of Moabit and Wedding.

Kammhuber's system was so effective that Berlin was spared Allied raids throughout 1940 and 1941, added to which the RAF's existing fleet of twin-engine bombers was operating at the limit of its range. A mass raid of 160 bombers on 7 November 1941 was again fairly ineffective and twenty aircraft were lost, but it proved to be a turning point. Air Chief Marshal Sir Arthur Harris, subsequently known as 'Bomber Harris', took over Bomber Command and the RAF started to introduce its large four-engine Lancaster bombers with a much-improved pathfinder system of targeting. The primary objective of Harris's command was to destroy the morale of the 'enemy civil population and in particular of the industrial workers'.[38] During the rest of 1942, however, his attention was on the U-boat pens on the French coast and on the ports of Hamburg, Bremen and Wilhelmshaven, so it was not until 1943 that he could start to implement his policy in earnest and to work to destroy the Reich capital.

The first major raid on Berlin was on the night of 16/17 January 1943, when 190 of the new Lancasters bombed fairly ineffectively, their only major success being the complete destruction of the Deutschlandhalle where a circus performance was in full swing. In fact, casualties were fairly low and once again Harris's attention switched to the industrial areas of the Ruhr and Hamburg. By November, however, Berlin was back in his sights. Between November 1943 and March 1944, the RAF mounted sixteen major raids on Berlin, using up to 900 aircraft each time and inflicting significant damage. Some 4,000 people were killed, 10,000 injured and nearly half a million made homeless. Again Kammhuber – now promoted to Major-General – saw his defence system work well, with the RAF losing more than 500 aircraft, a loss rate of nearly 6 per cent, which was considered unacceptably high. However, large parts of Berlin now lay in ruins. The area around the Kaiser-Wilhelm-Gedächtniskirche and the eastern end of the Ku'damm was largely destroyed, the church itself having burned 'like a blazing torch' and, added Ursula von Kardorff, 'for the first time in history it looked vaguely romantic'.[39] Christabel Bielenberg, who had been out of Berlin, walked through the area some time afterwards. 'When I reached the truncated Gedächtniskirche, I was surrounded by a frozen sea of shattered ruins. I had never seen bombing like it before. In Budapester Straße house after house was an empty shell, not one single building had survived. The centre of Berlin, capital of Hitler's mighty empire which, he had boasted, would last a thousand years, and I was alone in a silent ghost town.'[40] The zoo and Charlottenburg had been badly hit, and the palace partially destroyed. The zoo lost one third of its animals, including seven elephants, whose meat was much appreciated. Its surviving animals became major Berlin celebrities, with the city following their survival with rapt interest. The Ministry of Munitions and the Waffen SS College had gone, as had the British, French, Italian and Japanese embassy buildings in the Chancellery district. Spandau, with its barracks and armaments factories, had been very badly hit. The centre of Potsdam, again with its multiple barracks, was hit late on in April 1945 and also devastated. Around all these sites, street upon street of ordinary houses and apartment blocks lay blackened and uninhabitable.

RAF attention was diverted in the spring of 1944 to preparing for D-Day but, if Berlin thought it had been spared any more night raids, it now suffered from the American 8th and 15th Air Forces with their massive B-17 Flying Fortresses and B-24 Liberators. American tactics differed from the RAF in two important aspects. First, they preferred daylight raids in which they could keep tight formation and, secondly, they favoured attacking industrial rather than civilian targets. Added to this, they had also introduced the very effective P-51 Mustang Fighter, something Hitler and Göring failed to take seriously. Their tactic was therefore to send mass daytime bombing fleets to Berlin, which would draw the Luftwaffe's day fighters up. The Mustangs, which outperformed the German machines, would then destroy them while the bombers proceeded to attack the city.

The first American raid on 6 March 1944 consisted of 600 aircraft that dropped 1,600 tons of bombs, and their fighter escort shot down 20 per cent of the Luftwaffe interceptors. By 1945 the 8th Air Force under its dynamic commander, General Doolittle, was mounting 1,000 bomber raids protected by more than 500 Mustangs. On 3 February 1945 they attacked the Berlin railway system; by this stage in the war the German defences were so weak that only thirty-six aircraft were lost and the resulting fires raged for four days. A subsequent raid on 26 February left a further 80,000 people homeless. In March and April, the Soviets were also mounting bombing raids but theirs tended to be launched more in support of their ground forces than for any strategic intent.

It is often said that the bombing raids had little impact either on morale in Berlin or on its industrial capacity, but many of those who lived through it took rather a different view. The psychological effect was very real and presented Goebbels with a problem. He could no longer laugh off the British attacks as ineffective, so he now portrayed them as cowardly, 'terrorist' attacks on harmless civilians, German media having never let on that the Luftwaffe had bombed civilian targets in the London Blitz. It also caused a problem for the overall Nazi propaganda about the war. If it was going so well for Germany, as the population were constantly told, how could these mass fleets of sophisticated bombers penetrate deep into the Reich night after night? It rather gave the lie to the idea that the British were about to surrender. William Shirer wrote that 'the main effect of a week of constant British night bombings has been to spread great disillusionment among the people here and to sow doubt in their minds. One said to me to-day: "I'll never believe another thing they say. If they've lied to me about the raids in the rest of Germany as they have about the ones on Berlin, then it must have been pretty bad there."'[41] What also irritated people was the regime's condescending habit of handing out extra rations after a heavy raid, 'cigarettes, coffee, meat. As Dostoevsky's Grand Inquisitor said "Give them bread and they will back you up."'[42]

The attacks also badly disrupted Berlin's industrial capacity.

By 1944 the twenty-seven main aircraft factories in Germany had been broken down into 729 smaller units. Engine plants were split into 249 from fifty-one, putting a huge strain on the transport and logistic systems. Berlin's factories virtually all failed to meet their production quotas that year. Albert Speer, Hitler's architect and now also Reich Minister for War Production, wrote after the war:

'I drove to those districts of the city where important factories were situated. We drove over streets strewn with rubble, lined by burning houses. Bombed-out families stood in front of the houses. A few pieces of rescued furniture and other possessions lay about on the sidewalks. There was a sinister atmosphere full of biting smoke, soot, flames. Sometimes the people displayed that curious hysterical merriment that is often observed in the midst of disasters. Above the city hung a cloud of smoke that probably reached twenty thousand feet in height. Even by day it made the macabre scene as dark as night. I kept trying to describe my impressions to Hitler. But he would interrupt me every time, almost as soon as I began: "Incidentally Speer, how many tanks can you deliver next month".'[43]

Inevitably Berliners started to live part of their lives underground. Night-time activity had virtually stopped anyway, the black-out making movement dangerous and every street being patrolled by the officious police and security services. Life in the air-raid shelters began to assume its own pattern, communities forming in the cellars and stations where people spent most nights

'Shuffling feet. Suitcases banging into things. Lutz Lehmann screaming "Mutti!" [Mummy]. To get to the basement shelter we have to cross the street to the side-entrance, climb down some stairs, then go along a corridor and across a square courtyard with stars overhead and aircraft buzzing like hornets. Then down some more stairs, through more doors and corridors. Finally, we're in our shelter, behind an iron door that weighs a hundred pounds.

The official term is air-raid shelter. We call it cave, underworld, catacomb of fear, mass grave.[44]

The shelters were initially well organised but became, in themselves, something of a demonstration of how the regime began to fail as the war progressed. Many were extensions to the U-Bahn stations. They were all meant to have 2 metres of concrete and be steel-lined, but most only had a single metre despite Goebbels's assurances. The allocation was meant to be one person per square metre but again, as the bombing increased and the pressure of numbers grew, most became badly overcrowded. No provision was made for the hundreds of thousands of slave labourers imported into the city to work on the defence systems and in the factories; they were expendable. It is estimated that 12,000 German companies used slave labour in some form, many of the slave workers being Russian prisoners who after the war were told by the Soviets they should never have allowed themselves to be taken and were marched off to the Gulags. Ventilation systems were introduced so that capacity could be increased but they too were often inadequate.

In January 1946 schoolgirls in Prenzlauer Berg were asked to write an essay about their experiences in an air-raid shelter. 'The room is full of chatter and laughter,' wrote one:

'But over everything lies a nerve-shattering tension. There, a close hit! The anti-aircraft guns begin to fire. The shocks become stronger and stronger. The chatter grows softer, and the laughter stops altogether. Suddenly, a deafening bang! The lights flicker, the room sways. Frightened, we all flinch. The old woman across from me begins praying softly. Sobbing, a child buries its head in its mother's lap. Its whining hangs in the air like the embodiment of our fear. Hit after hit! Each of us feels the nearness of death. Perhaps in three minutes, perhaps two, perhaps only one! The young woman next to me stares with dull eyes into the emptiness. Like all of us, she has given up on life.'[45]

Life in the flak towers also assumed a strange atmosphere, slightly removed from reality. They were designed so that, as well as being air-defence installations, they could be used as above-ground shelters. Each had room for 10,000 civilians and was equipped with a hospital. During the final battle for the city they were sheltering up to 30,000 people each, and the Soviets found them difficult to take, eventually giving up and talking them into surrendering. The Allied pilots tended to avoid them but nevertheless they were occasionally hit. Speer was in one during the November 1943 raid: 'In spite of the tower's stout concrete walls, heavy hits nearby were shaking it; injured antiaircraft gunners crowded down the stairs behind me; the air pressure from the exploding bombs had hurled them into the walls. When the rain of bombs ceased I ventured out onto the platform. My nearby ministry was one gigantic conflagration.'[46]

One peculiarly nasty feature of the flak towers, and of the whole Berlin air-defence system, was that it was largely crewed by boys, the *Flakhelfer*. On 7 January 1943, the Nazis ordered that, so as to free adult soldiers for frontline duty, all boys in secondary schools born in 1926 and 1927, so sixteen- and seventeen-year-olds, were to be drafted into anti-aircraft service across Germany. After one year's service they were subsequently to be drafted into the armed forces and be replaced by boys born in 1928. In practice many were only fifteen when they were conscripted, and many went to their deaths in the crumbling armies facing the Soviets. Altogether about 200,000 boys were taken, allegedly continuing with their studies in the daytime and manning the anti-aircraft guns by night, but in practice they mostly became full-time auxiliaries. They wore dark-grey Luftwaffe fatigues with a Hitler Youth armband, which many resented as this had a swastika that could lead to summary execution by the Soviets and were discarded where possible. Within fourteen days of it being established, the first six boys were killed in the Berlin raid on 1 March 1943.

For the boys themselves it was an obviously terrifying experience, any initial excitement rapidly being subsumed by the sheer horror of the bombing. 'Suddenly, around the northern part of the city,

heavy Flak opened up ... over the anti-aircraft fire, we heard the
dull rumble of the approaching bomber fleet. All of a sudden, cas-
cades of red light appeared in the *Leichentuch*, pall, above the city,
descending very slowly,' which were the marker flares dropped by
the pathfinders. '"*Gruppenfeuer*" [group fire], the chief shouted. I
hurried obediently to a position under the barrel. The explosion hit
me like a tumbling wall. I thought my eardrums had burst. Over the
crashing gun I heard another sound, the terrible roar of many explo-
sions that seemed to make the earth shake,' recorded Karl Heinz
Schlesier.[47] Another *Flakhelfer* was Peter Schmidt, who crewed one
of the guns on the zoo flak tower and who helped out at Berlin Zoo
in his spare time. When the zoo was badly hit for a second time,
on 30 January 1944, Peter and his colleagues rushed to help save a
baby hippo called Knautschke. Although he was badly burned, they
managed to clear a big enough space for him to escape from his
shelter and jump into his pool, which saved him. Knautschke lived
until 1988, fathering thirty-five children and considered a Berlin
hero to the end. There is a life-size bronze statue of him outside the
hippo house today.

~

A sense of tired resignation verging on despair affected Berlin during
the winter of 1944–5. In April 1945 Ursula von Kardorff summed
up what many people felt when she wrote, 'The things I loved have
ceased to exist, my ideals have been besmirched, my friends have
been killed in action or hanged, churches, cities, all the places of
which I had my happiest memories, have been burned down. What
should one wish for now, what should one believe, what should one
strive for?'[48] The shortage of food and fuel was made worse as the
city became more crowded; as well as 800,000 slave labourers and
'foreign workers', refugees had been arriving from Poland and East
Prussia in front of the advancing Soviet armies. But if Berliners had
found life tough, it was now set to become unimaginably worse.

By April 1945 Soviet forces were on the River Oder within 50
miles of Berlin. At the Yalta Conference of the Allied Powers – USA,

Britain and the Soviet Union – in February 1945 it was agreed that, regardless of whether the Western Allies or the Soviets reached Berlin first, it would be divided into three, later four sectors: Russian, American and British with the subsequent addition of a French sector. In February 1945 it was still not clear that the Soviets would necessarily get to Berlin before the Allies but a curious decision by General Eisenhower – who favoured a broad attack through central Germany, with no special provision for Berlin – left the capital open to the Russians. Eisenhower's decision, deeply unpopular in London, which was communicated to Stalin on 28 March 1945, was received with undisguised satisfaction in Moscow. Not only would taking the Reich capital, the 'lair of the Fascist Beast', be a huge psychological victory for the Soviets after all that Russia had suffered, but Stalin realised it would enhance his ability to establish post-war communist control over central and eastern Europe. It would also allow him to seize the German nuclear research facility, the *Kaiser-Wilhelm-Institute* in south-west Berlin. He told the Allies that he would only make Berlin a secondary objective and that he would plan attacks to commence in late May; in fact, he set his *Stavka* (the Soviet high command) to work immediately to plan his offensive. On 1 April the two senior Soviet commanders who would lead the assault, Marshals Zhukov and Koniev, were called back to Moscow for a planning conference. Both had assumed they would be given time to reorganise and resupply their forces, but Stalin gave them just forty-eight hours to come up with their plans.

By April 1945 Soviet forces were ranged against Germany in three 'fronts'. To the north Marshal Rokossovsky commanded the 2nd Belorussian Front facing the Baltic. To his south was Marshal Georgi Zhukov's 1st Belorussian Front, directly opposite Berlin; to his south was Marshal Koniev's 1st Ukrainian Front, well south of Berlin but able to swing north and attack the capital from the south-east.[49] Well to the south again were 4th then the 2nd Ukrainian Fronts, which would attack into Czechoslovakia while the 3rd Ukrainian Front would drive into Hungary and Austria. Yet the *Stavka*'s focus was on Berlin and in taking it before the British or Americans could get there. Two of these enormous fronts, each numbering millions of soldiers, would converge on the city. Both Zhukov and Koniev were to attack together, Stalin knowing that the rivalry between the two marshals would ensure they would compete to be first into the city. Zhukov had the advantage in that he was closer, just 50 miles east of Berlin, and in March 1945 had already got some of his troops west of the River Oder north of Küstrin so that he would not have to start his assault by fighting his way across the wide, fast-flowing river. His disadvantage was that he faced the Seelow Heights, a range of low hills immediately west of his positions, which dominated the Oder Plain. Koniev would start from further to the east but then faced easier terrain.

German plans to defend Berlin were chaotic and demonstrate just how worn down the *Wehrmacht* (the German armed forces) were after six years of constant fighting. Formations were at a fraction of their proper strength, logistics were haphazard at best, and air support was almost non-existent. Soviet forces numbered around 6 million men – probably the largest army ever assembled – against what on paper should have been 2 million Germans and their allies but what in reality was far less. The Soviets also enjoyed a massive advantage in equipment. Soviet industry had recovered from the losses of 1941 and was now producing crude but effective tanks, guns and aircraft, added to which they benefited considerably from the Allied lend-lease programme that gave them soft-skinned vehicles, clothing and food. Zhukov, for example, would use one artillery piece for every 13 feet of their assault frontage. The Germans could not hope to match this. German industry was not only exhausted and badly hampered by the bombing campaign so that production of all military equipment was well below its target. It also suffered from the added disadvantage of Hitler's insistence on 'wonder weapons' that meant resources were devoted to producing a small number of technologically advanced weapons, like jet fighters and the Tiger tank, rather than on numbers.

In February 1945 Hitler had declared Berlin was to be a *Festung* (a fortress) that was to be defended to the last. Should the Soviets get into the city, then the logic – if it can be called that – was to fight them to the last man, an idea that may have appealed to the Nazi hierarchy but was hardly convincing to Berliners. But Hitler, still convinced he was on the point of defeating the Soviets, had not allocated any troops to its defence. The officer in charge of defending the city was General Helmuth Reymann, who now found himself facing the full weight of the Soviet onslaught with what forces he could cobble together, on top of having to deal with the whole charade of Nazi organisations in the city who each controlled their own men. As well as what regular troops he could muster, he had to deal with the Hitler Youth, whose boys would be made to fight, the SS, the Army Reserve and the local Nazi party, which ran the *Volkssturm* (the local Home Guard). Some of the Hitler Youth were only in their early teens. 'I went over to him,' wrote Dorothea von Schwanenflügel when she saw a child-soldier crying in the street, 'and found him a mere child in a uniform many sizes too large for him, with an anti-tank grenade lying beside him. Tears were running down his face and he was obviously very frightened of everyone. ... He had been ordered to lie in wait here, and when a Soviet tank approached he was to run under it and explode the grenade. I asked how that would work, but he didn't know.'[50]

From his headquarters in the Zeughaus on Unter den Linden, Reymann attempted to put together a plan. There would be a line of forward defences close to the Oder, using natural obstacles, then an outer defence ring around the city's boundaries. Further in would be an inner ring, roughly corresponding to the S-Bahn ring, and then a final *Zitadelle* in the centre with bastions around the Alexanderplatz and the Knie, or what is now Ernst-Reuter Platz. Impressive as this sounded, there was a chronic shortage of trained troops and equipment to make it work, many of the defenders being those in the *Volkssturm* who were too old for military service or the boys in the Hitler Youth. Soviet intelligence calculated they might face up to a million regular soldiers, together with 200,000 Hitler Youth and *Volksturm*, with 10,000 guns, 1,500 tanks and 3,500 aircraft. This turned out to be an enormous overestimate. Post-war they judged the total figure had been much smaller, at least from those they encountered once they entered the city centre.

On 9 March Reymann put out what was meant to be a stirring call to the city: 'The Reich capital will be defended to the last man and the last cartridge.' The enemy 'who must not know a minute of peace, must burn and bleed to death'. It was 'not important that every defender of the Reich capital have a perfect grasp of the techniques of military science but every fighter be inspired and permeated by the fanatical Will to WANT TO FIGHT'. But by now Berliners had seen enough fanatical Nazi literature, and his oration was received with weary resignation. Reymann finished by saying that the 'Battle for Berlin may decide the outcome of the war' but to Berliners who had heard the menacing rumble of Soviet guns, their priority was to survive.[51]

Zhukov's and Koniev's assault began on 16 April (see map on p. xvi). Zhukov's armies took four days to clear the Seelow Heights and open the road west. German resistance here was tougher than expected, helped by the commanding ground and some spirited tactical leadership. German troops were rushed out to Seelow and fed into the battle piecemeal, but Soviet numbers began to tell and the German positions collapsed. Zhukov's original plan had been to rush two tank armies straight into the city centre but he now changed his mind, instead assaulting the city from the north and north-east and south and south-east, the latter move also designed to prevent Koniev's men looping around from the south and beating him to the prize. At 11 a.m. on 20 April (which, in one of those rather neat historical twists of fate, was Hitler's 56th birthday) and while he was entertaining the remaining Nazi high command in his bunker under the Chancellery, Zhukov's artillery opened up on the city for the first time. The Soviets would always maintain that their artillery would do more damage to Berlin in the next ten days than the Allies had done with their bombing in four years; whatever, it was a new, terrifying and horribly destructive experience for Berliners. As Zhukov raced his men in from the east, Koniev's leading formations had reached the outskirts in the south, despite

being held up by taking the massive German headquarters complex
at Zossen and the concentration camp at Babelsberg. On 23 April
Koniev's leading formation, General Rybalko's 3rd Guards Tank
Army had linked up with General Chuikov's 8th Guards Army,
leading Zhukov's advance, at Schönefeld, where Berlin's ill-fated new
airport is located. Stalin now agreed a boundary between the two
fronts, running from Mariendorf along the railway line to Anhalter
Bahnhof, placing the Reichstag just within Zhukov's boundary. He
told his forward troops to take it at all costs.

On 28 April, as Rybalko's men turned west, Chuikov's troops
made their final attack into the *Zitadelle*. Hitler had, character-
istically, sacked Reymann, and on 22 April he replaced him with
General Helmuth Weidling, an artillery officer who was commanding LVI Corps; Hitler had in fact summoned Weidling to the bunker
to demand to know why he had allegedly withdrawn without orders.
Weidling emerged from his interview tasked with trying to restore
some order into the defence. He estimated that, by that stage in the
battle, he had elements of five divisions, plus 40,000 *Volkssturm*,
the Hitler Youth, the Reich Labour Service and the police. Hitler
kept the area around the Chancellery – under SS General Mohnke
with about 2,000 SS men, many from Hitler's own *Leibstandarte SS
Adolf Hitler Division* – under his own direct command. Weidling
moved his headquarters into the Bendler Block, from where he
was reasonably well placed to control the battle for the city centre,
although he would find that the area he controlled was rapidly reducing. Hitler had also flown into a rage because German formations
outside Berlin, which he had instructed to attack into the city, had
not moved. Although some of them did succeed in counter-attacking
Koniev's forces, others decided to head west so they could surrender
to the Americans. The Soviets surrounded a German force of nearly
200,000 men near Cottbus, and although some managed to break
out, the majority of this enormous group were either killed or went
into captivity in Russia, most never to return.

The Berlin operation posed quite a challenge to Soviet troops
with little experience of attacking cities, the battles of Leningrad

and Stalingrad both being very much defensive. Since early 1943 the Soviet formations had mostly been used to fighting in open countryside. The tactics they now adopted were crude but effective and relied on using their overwhelming advantage in numbers and in artillery. This meant the destruction Berlin suffered was disproportionately worse than that suffered by cities taken by the Western Allies. A street would be allocated to a regiment, so approximately between 1,000 and 1,500 men. Each regiment had three battalions of about 4–500 men; two would take one side of a street each while the third was kept in reserve. This meant that there could be up to 1,500 men on a frontage of just 200–250 metres, which, when they were backed by tanks, artillery and assault guns, gave them enormous firepower. In addition, they had engineers with explosive charges and flamethrowers to clear cellars. Above the regimental level, the parent formation would mass its artillery. A Soviet army had more than 800 guns in support, which were positioned wheel to wheel. From 24 April they would fire for an hour at first light on the army's objectives for that day. The artillery was backed by the feared *Katyusha* rocket launchers that fired phosphorus. Once the artillery had finished, tanks would roll forward, destroying each building piecemeal to eliminate snipers. Consequently, much of the heavily fought-over areas were not just destroyed but literally turned into rubble.

By 27 April the area under German control had shrunk to about 16 kilometres east–west and 6 kilometres north–south centred on Charlottenburg. The final battle began on 28 April. While Chuikov and Rybalko had been battling in from the north-east and south-east respectively, two of Zhukov's other armies (Berzarin's 5th Shock Army and Kutznetsov's 3rd Shock Army) had been looping north. As Berzarin's men fought their way through Kreuzberg, Kutznetsov's leading units had swept in from the north-east via Prenzlauer Berg into Mitte. His most forward formation, Major General Perevertkin's 79th Rifle Corps, found itself now just a few hundred metres north of the Reichstag. Kutznetsov told Perevertkin the commander of the first unit to hoist its flag over the Reichstag would be made a hero of the Soviet Union. First, Perevertkin's men had to seize the Moltke Bridge over the Spree, still in the same place today on Willy-Brandt-Straße. The Germans tried to destroy it but, after savage hand-to-hand fighting, the Soviets managed to get across in the early morning of 30 April. By the time it was light they had taken the Ministry of Interior, Himmler's headquarters, although Himmler himself was well away from Berlin, having left on 22 April on the excuse of talking to the Swedes about surrender terms. By midday two entire Soviet Divisions were formed and ready to assault the Reichstag. They were rather concerned that there appeared to be a huge anti-tank ditch in between them and their objective, until they realised it was a U-Bahn extension under construction. At 1 p.m. eighty-nine guns opened up on the Reichstag at a range of just a few hundred metres so that the building disappeared in a pall of dust and smoke; under cover of the barrage the infantry of 756th Rifle Regiment moved forward. Captain Neustroyev's 1st Battalion led (he was in the van with his reconnaissance unit). They brought up artillery to blast open the doors and, as the German defenders retreated into the building's ample basements, Neustroyev sent Sergeants Yegorov and Kantariya to plant the red flag on the roof. The subsequent famous photograph was in fact taken the next day when the event was restaged, and fierce fighting continued in the building until midnight. By the end of 1 May Kutznetsov's, Chuikov's and Berzarin's troops had linked up and at 3 p.m. on 2 May they ceased fire.

The Germans had in fact tried to surrender beforehand. Hitler, believing in miracles to the last, had continued raving and issuing orders to imaginary formations until 30 April. Göring had (like Himmler) got out while he could but had unwisely signalled to Hitler that, should he not hear from him, he would assume the worst and take over the government. He was promptly sacked by the enraged Führer, who replaced him as head of the Luftwaffe with the charismatic Generaloberst Robert Ritter von Greim. Von Greim was summoned to the Führer Bunker to be given his orders – not the easiest journey to undertake when it was being encircled by three Soviet armies. Undeterred, von Greim (accompanied by his equally charismatic mistress, the flying ace Hanna Reitsch) took a Focke-Wulf 190 fighter, von Greim in the pilot's seat and Reitsch lying full length in the fuselage behind him, and managed to land in Gatow. Here they swapped to a light Fieseler Storch liaison aircraft, which they somehow managed to land on the east–west Axis in the Tiergarten. They made it safely to the Bunker only to be lectured by a deranged Hitler about mythical fleets of jet aircraft.

On 30 April, having finally accepted that he was defeated, Hitler married Eva Braun, his secretary, and then they both killed themselves, their bodies being subsequently burned in the Chancellery garden. Goebbels seemed to have formed the notion that the Soviets might negotiate a surrender with him. In the early morning of 1 May he sent General Krebs with a white flag to Chuikov's headquarters at Tempelhof in an attempt to discuss terms. Krebs was given a predictably frosty welcome and told the only acceptable move now was unconditional surrender. He returned to Goebbels, who authorised hostilities to continue. Every Soviet gun in the city opened up in response. SS General Wilhelm Mohnke had made his headquarters near the Chancellery in Mohrenstraße U-Bahn station and he and his remaining SS men continued to resist. It took the Russians some very heavy fighting to dislodge him. Mohnke, a Hitler loyalist, survived, and was a Soviet prisoner for ten years. He returned to Germany, became a car dealer and only died in 2001.

Weidling meanwhile took matters into his own hands and sent a message to Chuikov that he wished to surrender the Berlin area. At 6 a.m. on 2 May he presented himself to the Soviets on Potsdam Bridge. On arrival in Tempelhof he found yet another emissary from Goebbels, Dr Fritzsche, who haughtily explained that it was his job to offer to surrender the city. Chuikov, in true Soviet style, would not trust a civilian and accepted Weidling's word.

It was time to count the cost, which was truly terrible. The Russians had lost 304,887 killed or wounded in the space of twelve days. In purely military terms, the Soviets had destroyed ninety-three German divisions and taken 480,000 prisoners; of these

134,000 were taken in Berlin itself. In addition, the Germans had lost 1,500 tanks and 10,000 guns. It is likely that more than 100,000 Germans – both military and civilians – were killed in Berlin in those final days, far more than from the bombing; because of the complete breakdown of any record-keeping it is impossible to give an accurate figure. A large proportion of those who died were old men who had been drafted into the *Volkssturm* or young boys in the Hitler Youth. Those who had still enjoyed a home in March 1945 were now on the streets, although some of those suburbs that had not been badly fought over had survived remarkably unscathed. A sizeable proportion of the German army did manage to break out west and surrender to the British and the Americans on the Elbe; they were fortunate as, after a short period in captivity, they were repatriated. Those taken by the Soviets were less fortunate and vast numbers perished in Gulags and the labour camps.

Most Berliners – or at least those who had not been drafted into one of the makeshift units to defend the capital – tried to spend those last weeks of April underground. All those who could got away. Most could not because they simply did not have the means or places to go. The roads and railways were already packed with refugees; the police and the SS – in vengeful mood as they sensed they would soon be on the receiving end – took a perverse delight in arresting and frequently executing anyone they thought was running away. On 22 April, with the Soviet attack well underway, the SS took out the remaining sixteen political prisoners in Moabit Prison and shot them, including Dietrich Bonhoeffer's brother Klaus. Tens of thousands sheltering in their 'caves' were simply killed by the Soviet attack, blasted or buried alive, but for those who survived it was a terrifying ordeal of waiting for the unknown. With no radios and only occasional very limited party newspapers, information was at a premium. For others there was just the absolute necessity of survival. 'She just stormed in,' wrote the Anonymous Woman of the 'widow' with whom she shared a house, 'all worked up. A shell hit outside Hefter's meat market, right in the middle of the queue. Three dead and ten wounded but they're already queueing up again. The widow demonstrated how people were using their sleeves to wipe the blood off their meat coupons. "Any way only three people died," she said. "What's that compared to an air raid?"[52]

The Anonymous Woman in Berlin found her first meeting with the Soviets quite reassuring. She lived in East Berlin so her area was one of the early parts of the city to be taken. 'They had set up a field-kitchen in the garage across the street. And for the first time we could make out faces, features, individuals – sturdy, broad foreheads, close-cropped hair, well-fed, carefree. Not a civilian in sight. The Russians have the streets entirely to themselves. But under every building people are whispering, quaking.'[53] Later she would tell a very different story.

A seventeen-year-old girl, Lieselotte, had a very different experience. She kept a diary from 30 April that ran:

'30.4: I was at the top of the stairs when the bomb hit. The Russians are here. They are completely drunk. Rapes at night. Not me. But mother. Some people 5–20 times. 1.5: The Russians are coming and going. All the clocks are gone. The horses are lying on our beds in the courtyard. The cellars have been broken into. We have fled to Stubenraucherstraße. 2.5: The first night of peace. From Hell to Heaven. We cried when we discovered the lilac blooming in the courtyard. All wireless sets must be turned in. 3.5: Still in Stubenraucherstr. Can't go to the window in case a Russian sees me. They say there are rapes everywhere. 4.5: In Derfflingerstr. No news of Papa. 5.5: Back to Kaiserallee. Chaos! 6.5: Our house was hit 21 times! Cleared and packed all day. I crawled under the bed for fear that the Russians were coming. But the house was only rattling so because of the shelling. 8.5: Shovelled the street clear. Queued for bread. News that Papa is alive. 9.5: Armistice.'[54]

Among all the other hardships, it would be the rapes that would prove the most frightening for Berliners in the coming weeks. As with the casualty figures, it is impossible to know how many women

were raped by the Soviets in those early months of the occupation.
'Estimates from the two main Berlin hospitals ranged from 95,000 to
100,000 rape victims. One doctor deduced that out of approximately
100,000 women raped in Berlin some 10,000 died as a result, mostly
from suicide,' wrote Antony Beevor who also records one woman
being raped by twenty-three soldiers one after another and who subsequently had to be stitched up in hospital. 'Three in one night for a
virgin of sixteen. Seven in an hour for a mother of two, the last one
a Mongol who had the daughter next. A war widow endured twenty-
three before slitting her own throat ... a girl of fourteen, a girl of
twelve. A girl of seven,' ran another account.[55] There were those who
sought to excuse the Soviets' behaviour as normal when an army of
millions of young men have been without female companionship for
two years; others said it was justifiable revenge for what the Germans
had done to Russia. 'Apparently Stalin has declared that "this kind
of thing" is not to happen,' noted the Anonymous Woman, 'but it
happens anyway.' She records an officer reprimanding two soldiers
about to rape her. 'One of the two men being reprimanded voices
his objection, his face twisted in anger: "What do you mean? What
did the Germans do to our women?" He is screaming. "They took
my sister and" ... so on. I can't understand all the words, only the
sense.' The man rapes her anyway. Berlin women tried different
ways of coping. Some took senior officers as 'protectors'; others
bartered for food, but nearly all were psychologically damaged and
Berlin's hospitals had to deal with a mass increase in abortions, with
an explosion of venereal diseases and with abandoned babies; few
Soviet rape children were taken home and cherished, particularly if
a woman was waiting for her husband to return. One estimate puts
the number of these 'Russian babies' as high as 150,000.[56]

Rape was not the only problem Berliners faced. Peter von Jena,
whose ancestor had been The Great Elector's minister, had lived
with his family in Berlin throughout the war and was too young to
be conscripted. Their house in Halensee had escaped bomb damage
but that was to change. Drunk Soviet soldiers arrived searching for
valuables and found the family's hunting rifles. Peter and his parents

were, luckily for them, away at the time but the staff who were in the house were taken out and shot and the house burned down. Drink played a large part in how the Soviets behaved. Sober and with officers present, they could be responsible, even polite, but once drunk they were unpredictable.

The subsequent behaviour of the Soviet Union in eastern Europe, and of Soviet soldiers themselves in Berlin, has meant that today we do not always give those young Russian men and women the credit for their bravery or for the fundamental part they played in defeating Nazism. Their losses were staggering and many had seen their families butchered and homes destroyed in Hitler's extraordinarily brutal and ultimately pointless occupation of western Russia. There are two Soviet memorials in Berlin. The first is easy to see as it lies just inside the Tiergarten, west of the Brandenburg Gate and exactly on the line of William II's vulgar *Siegesallee*. Erected soon after the end of the war, a statue of a Soviet soldier, his hand extended in an act of suppression, tops a portico made from marble taken from Hitler's ruined Chancellery. Behind him, across the trees, is the Reichstag. An inscription reads 'Eternal Glory to the Heroes who Fell in Battle with the German Fascist Invaders for the Freedom and Independence of the Soviet Union'. Two thousand Soviet soldiers are buried there. It is flanked by two Soviet 152 mm guns and two T-34 tanks. The tanks are interesting. The T-34 was the mass-produced tank that was the workhorse of the Soviet armies. Originally it was produced with a 76 mm gun, although later, and in the battle for Berlin, most had been upgraded to an 85 mm one. These two tanks, numbered 200 and 300, are both the older model with the smaller gun. They were battalion commanders' tanks, so not in the front line, hence not having the larger gun. Also, if you look carefully at the front of the one on the left, you can see a hole where the frontal armour plate, the glacis plate, has been hit by a 50 mm German anti-tank gun that probably put it out of action. Some Berliners, reeling from the behaviour of Soviet soldiers in the summer of 1945, nicknamed the memorial 'The Tomb of the Unknown Rapist'.

The main Soviet memorial is in Treptower Park, a bit of a journey

from the city centre. It is a moving, peaceful place, both a cemetery for 7,000 soldiers and a memorial. It is somewhere valued by
Berliners, particularly those who lived in the GDR; when it was
vandalised post-1989, crowds turned out to help restore it. Two
Soviet flags built from the same red marble from the Chancellery
flank an avenue that leads past sarcophagi representing each of the
then sixteen Soviet Republics, to a huge statue of Sergeant Nikolai
Masalov, cradling a baby girl. Masalov was a real hero, who ran
forward under fire across a bridge to rescue the girl whose mother
had been killed. The bridge is the one on Potsdamer Straße, across
the Landwehrkanal, beside the National Gallery. Both Masalov and
the girl survived, he only dying in 2001. He leans on a sword, the
fighting done, with a crushed swastika beneath his feet. Around the
memorial are rows of Russian trees, weeping for Mother Russia but
upright to commemorate her soldiers.

CHAPTER TEN

1945–1961

'The freedom-loving Berlin population will
build a dam against which the red tide will
break in vain'

ERNST REUTER, 29 September 1948

Berlin, the most anti-Nazi city in the Reich, had suffered horribly. Mitte, Charlottenburg and Tiergarten were almost completely destroyed. Large parts of Friedrichshain, Kreuzberg, Prenzlauer Berg, Wedding, Moabit, Wilmersdorf and Schöneberg were in ruins. No one knew the exact population figures but it is estimated that it was now about 2 million (as opposed to 4 million in 1939), of whom two thirds were women; a quarter of the population was over sixty.[1] You could tell the main Soviet avenues of advance from the corresponding damage to the buildings. In the south, where Chuikov's 8th Guards Army had used Martin-Luther-Straße and then An der Urania (the wide street that covers the Urania Stream) as their main axis, and where 1st Guards Tank Army had used Potsdamer Straße, there were wide corridors of ruins up to the Landwehrkanal. In the east, along Große Frankfurter Straße (now Karl Marx Allee after a short period as Stalinallee), which had formed Kutznetsov's main axis, the devastation was complete. You can still see bullet holes and shell damage to many of the buildings towards its eastern end today. More than half a million homes had been destroyed, with hundreds of thousands more badly damaged. The water mains had been broken in more than 3,000 places; the hospitals had stopped functioning and the stench from bodies decomposing under the rubble was horrible. The canals were full of slowly rotting corpses. The streets, otherwise quiet at night, were punctuated by agonising screams as the rapes continued.

On 24 April, before the city had fallen, Stalin had selected General Nikolai Berzarin, who had led 5th Shock Army in the assault, as Berlin's commander. He moved the Soviet headquarters from the old German barracks at Karlshorst, in Lichtenberg in south-east Berlin, where Zhukov had taken the final, formal German surrender, to Luisenstraße in Mitte. Berzarin had two priorities. His first was to try to restore some sort of administration and to feed not only the 2 million-odd people who remained in Berlin but also the 2 million Soviet soldiers who now had little to do. Hunger was the overriding problem and most of the city's population were verging on starving. The Nazi rationing system had worked tolerably well while there was food to distribute, but the fighting during the last month meant hardly any supplies had reached beyond the suburbs. The Soviets had taken the food reserves the Nazis had stockpiled in the Westhafen warehouses and had raided the surrounding farms. The situation by the middle of May was desperate. The Anonymous Woman recorded that, even after she had managed to find something to eat, 'the hunger is gnawing away at me like a savage beast'. She read a novel that included the words, 'She cast a fleeting glance at her untouched meal then rose and left the table.' She found herself 'magnetically drawn back to that sentence. I must have read it a dozen times before I caught myself scratching my nails across the print, as if the untouched meal – which had just been described in detail – was really there and I could physically scrape it out of the book.'[2] Should a horse collapse, which many did from overwork and undernourishment (and the Soviet army was, as the German army had been, heavily dependent on horses for transport), it would immediately be fallen upon by eager housewives with their knives, as described by Beatrice Collins:

'The cart horse swayed and sank forward to its knees. The boy with the reins in his hands and the sob in his voice started to shout, "Come on ... gee up! ... Move! Why have you stopped? Move! Please move?" He hit the horse's ridged brown back with his whip once, twice, three times. The horse flinched, showed the whites of its eyes, and then with a small moan, a letting out of breath, of steam, of life, it slumped and collapsed into a heap of angular bone and sagging skin ... No sooner had its head hit the cobbles than a dozen women appeared from doorways and alleyways armed with knives and bowls and cups. They ignored the boy's cries, his tears, his laments, and began to butcher the carcass, sawing through bone and slicing through veins to let the spurt of warm blood flow into their bowls.'[3]

The few remaining animals in the zoo, which included the sole surviving elephant, a bull called Siam, who had lent a hand to transport work, Knautschke the hippo and a female chimp called Suse, all of whom were minor celebrities, had to have an armed guard. Berzarin brought Soviet rations into the city and honoured the existing ration cards. At first Berliners did not believe him. What shops were thought still to have supplies had already been raided. The ration was barely adequate – 14 ounces of potatoes, 7 ounces of bread, 0.8 ounces of meat, 0.35 ounces of salt and 0.7 ounces of coffee – but at least it was something and the Soviet distribution system worked in that basic but effective Russian way. Disease was also a major issue, the decaying bodies spreading infection and there being very little medicine available. Dysentery was understandably widespread, but typhoid, diphtheria and tuberculosis also spread extensively; by mid-summer 4,000 people were dying daily. Many of these were the old. Only 10 per cent of the population were under thirty and of these more than 50,000 were homeless orphans. Women outnumbered men, and those men taken in uniform were rounded up and shipped eastwards, including many of the boys who had been forced into the fighting in those closing weeks. The Soviets would continue to arrest and deport Germans at random well into 1946; Hans-Jürgen Kirstaedter was abducted by a group of Russians on a Berlin station in 1946 and was never seen again.

Berzarin slowly began to clamp down on the rape too, actually executing some of the worst offenders, although it did not stop what had become an epidemic. Looting was seen as less of a problem, with the Soviets helping themselves to most of what they wanted in those early weeks. Bicycles were particularly popular, even if many did not know how to ride them, but the most prized possession was watches; Soviet soldiers wearing four or five up their arm was a common sight. It says much for Berzarin, as it does for Berliners' willingness to follow orders, that something that passed for normal life in the skeleton of the city returned remarkably quickly, albeit on Moscow time (two hours ahead of Berlin time), which the Soviets insisted on imposing. In fact it made little difference, most Berliners having had their watches stolen and now living more by the hours of daylight.

On 25 May Berzarin authorised a municipal police force and reopened the public prosecutors' office and the courts. The U-Bahn had been less affected by the fighting than surface transport, and the first U-Bahn train was running again by 14 May. The first edition of the *Berliner Zeitung* was on sale on 20 May. On 26 May the Berlin Philharmonic gave their first post-war concert, in the Titania-Palast in Steglitz, which had not been badly damaged. Predictably, the programme was still heavily biased in favour of German composers but it now included, significantly, Mendelssohn's Overture to *Ein Sommernachtstraum* (A Midsummer Night's Dream) – Mendelssohn's works, as a Jew, having been banned by the Nazis – and Tchaikovsky's Symphony Number 4. By the end of the month the most pro-Nazi members of the orchestra had been sacked. Wilhelm Furtwängler, latterly suspected by the Gestapo of involvement in the July plot, had already fled to Switzerland. Later, because of his earlier flirtation with the regime, he would be put on trial for pro-Nazi activities but acquitted.

'It is astonishing how fast everything happens,' noted Margaret
Boveri in her diary on 13 May. 'The removal of heaps of debris from
the streets organised by the citizens themselves, many of them also
conscripted for much more extensive clearing work; the public utilities taken in hand by their clerks and workers, who became skilled
at repair during the air raids. In Friedenau some streets already have
water and electricity ... there has already been water in our cellar
twice for an hour at a time. In Friedenau,' she added, 'people are
also getting special rations because Friedenau surrendered without a
fight.'[4] The rubble clearing would become one of the most celebrated
achievements of Berliners that year. Mostly done by women, there
being few men to help and those there were taken by the Soviets for
other labouring tasks, these *Trümmerfrauen* (rubble women) cleared
away the debris from the destroyed houses, freeing the streets, and
recovering and cleaning bricks for future reconstruction work. There
were around 50,000 of them. They were paid a very small basic
wage and they did get better ration cards, but they had virtually no
tools or machinery to help them, most using handcarts, old prams,
sacks and anything they could lay their hands on. Rubble was taken
away to various collection sites. The main one, out to the west in the
Grunewald, was the *Teufelsberg*, an artificial hill 400 feet (roughly
120 metres) high that covers 18 million cubic metres of rubble; it is
now a popular weekend spot for walking. There were several other
dumps too, in Pankow, at Schöneberg and in Friedrichshain. Pictures
of the *Trümmerfrauen*, often with their very small children, patiently
confronting their massive task, have become one of the enduring
images of Berlin. They are a comment on the waste and stupidity of
war as well as on the quiet resilience of Berliners.

Another issue to confront the city was the number of political
prisoners, foreign forced labourers and prisoners of war who were
now free – or at least at liberty. This turned into a significant logis-
tical problem. There were several categories. First were the Allied
prisoners of war. There were several PoW camps around Berlin and
these were quite easy to deal with – the British, American, French,
Dutch and Scandinavians were sent on home. More complicated

were the Soviet and Polish prisoners who knew that returning home could mean exchanging one prison camp for another, as was liable to happen to anyone accused of fraternising with the Germans. The Soviet definition of fraternisation included allowing yourself to be captured. Then there were the inmates of the huge number of forced labour camps who had served Berlin's war industries; there were 666 camps registered, housing hundreds of thousands of labourers, again many Russian or Polish. The concentration camps at Sachsenhausen and Babelsberg had been liberated, although the Soviets would continue to use Sachsenhausen for their own prisoners for several years. Perhaps most serious for Berlin was the very large number of refugees from East Prussia and Poland who had fled in front of the Soviet armies and who crowded into the capital. It was estimated that 500,000 arrived each month over the winter of 1944–5. The Nazis had forbidden them to enter the city and most had already been moved on but from April many, especially German-speaking Poles, took advantage of the collapse in government to squat in the ruins. The solution was to establish transit camps and forty-eight had been set up across the city by July. The Jewish community, of which there were under 10,000 still left, ran seven camps. The Americans were still running six major installations in what was by then their sector as late as December 1945. Many of those exiled Berlin schoolchildren were forgotten in the chaos. Joachim Ziedler, sent with his school to Bohemia, was simply left to his own devices. Together with a classmate he started to walk to Berlin, begging food from farmers and sleeping in barns. Eventually they made it back to their bombed-out homes.[5]

Berzarin, who quickly established himself as a relatively popular figure among Berliners, also had other priorities. It had been agreed at Yalta that whoever reached Berlin first, the city would be divided post-war into those three sectors between Russia, Britain and the USA, but in May the American and British troops were still many miles away on the Elbe. Stalin sensed that he now had an opportunity both to establish strict communist control on Berlin, and to help himself to what he regarded as Russia's rightful reparations, before the Allied Powers arrived. Berzarin was instructed to do whatever he could to delay the Allies in the west, including saying that the city still needed to be de-mined before it was safe for them to arrive.

The Soviets had a bizarre approach to this looting, which seems to have been driven partly by wanting to make the Germans pay for what they had done to Russia, partly by wanting to steal whatever technological advantage they could (such as taking over Berlin's nuclear research programme), and partly by an almost childish desire to take anything they did not have at home. Their first moves were predictable. On 15 May Major Feodor Novikov appeared at the Reichsbank and took what was left; it did not amount to much – ninety gold bars, $4.5 million in coin and $400 million in bonds – most of the other reserves having been long since removed because of the bombing. Then all the typewriters were confiscated on the basis that they could not then be used to write any anti-communist material. More strangely, all Berlin's telephones were collected, before the city's industry was systematically stripped of everything portable. Train after train departed eastwards carrying the machinery and equipment from the great Berlin factories. Siemen's electrical installations were stripped out but in such a way that they were unusable thereafter even if Soviet engineers could have puzzled out what to do with them. This wholescale dismantling of Berlin's factories, which included much of the rolling stock on the railways and 11,800 kilometres of track, marked the end of the city's primacy as Germany's industrial capital. With the isolation it would soon suffer, although the GDR would rebuild industrial plants in what would become East Berlin, the commercial future for Berliners would be more in finance and services than manufacturing.

The Soviets also used those weeks to help themselves to Berlin's art treasures. The museums had sensibly started to move their collections from as early as 1940 after the very early air raids. Some were taken outside Berlin but most were moved into the cellars under the Molkenmarkt, into the cellars on Museum Island itself or into the flak towers in Friedrichshain and the zoo. The Pergamon Altar was dismantled and taken to the zoo flak tower but the market gate from Miletus was left in place and protected with sandbags. There was some opposition from the Nazis to this evacuation, which suggested all was not normal. Two exhibitions were mounted in the National Gallery to support the war effort. The first, in March 1940, was called *Greater Germany's Struggle for Freedom*, about the Napoleonic Wars, and a second, which Goebbels came to regret, was on the Prussian alliance with Russia, which was quickly discontinued after 1941.

Yet from 1943 the evacuation of art treasures was speeded up, with the National Gallery's collection being sent to a salt mine at Grasleben and the remaining portable items moved from the museums. In November 1943 the Neues Museum had suffered a direct hit and was gutted by fire. The raid on 3 February 1945 caused widespread damage to the Pergamon Museum and superficial damage to the Kaiser Friedrich-Museum (now the Bode Museum); part of the Miletus Gate was hit. In the fighting in April 1945 the Altes Museum was also badly damaged, as was the National Gallery, which had the misfortune to find itself on one of the main Soviet approaches to the Tiergarten. During those final days thousands sheltered in the Pergamon Museum. The Soviets, ranging at this stage across the whole city before the Allies arrived, therefore found that a lot of what they wanted to take was already packaged up. Much of it – including Schliemann's Troy hoard, which had been in the zoo flak tower – found its way back to Russia. Some was subsequently returned to Berlin under the GDR but many items remained in Russia as they do to this day, something regularly raised by German leaders as a diplomatic issue. Less important and smaller items were looted by individual Soviet soldiers and ended up being sold on the black market, from where they still make the odd reappearance.

More sinister was the political manoeuvring that was designed to consolidate communist control of the city before the Allies finally got there. Berzarin may have been in command militarily, but as early as 1 May two aircraft (ironically supplied by the US under lend-lease) had taken off from Moscow carrying Walter Ulbricht and the key Berlin communist leadership, or at least those who had survived Stalin's purges; just because you were a foreign communist you were not necessarily saved from the cellars of the Lubyanka. Ulbricht was sent with very clear orders that he was to establish a government obedient to Moscow and he was to answer not to Berzarin but directly to Stalin through the NKVD (later the KGB). Berzarin was unexpectedly killed on 16 June in a traffic accident; there were rumours that he was murdered as he was achieving too high a profile but it seems unlikely. Ulbricht was already well in control by then. A functioning city administration was in place by 17 May under a figurehead mayor, Dr Arthur Werner, whose deputy, Kurt Maron, was one of Ulbricht's inner circle. District mayors were selected throughout Berlin on the same basis, with even relatively centrist men being chosen for some of the more affluent western districts, but always with a hard-core communist deputy who wielded effective power. One of Ulbricht's circle was a young communist who had fled to Moscow in his teens, Wolfgang Leonhard, who would subsequently escape to the West and write a damning indictment of Ulbricht's methods in those early years. 'It has to look democratic,' Ulbricht told him, 'but we must have control of everything.'[6]

~

At the Yalta conference the three Allied Powers had agreed that all Germany, not just Berlin, would be divided into occupation zones, with the French being invited to take over a zone as well should they wish to do so. The zones would all come under an Allied Control Commission headquartered in Berlin. No boundaries were agreed at Yalta. At that stage the Allies did not know who would be where when the war ended, which is why a separate agreement existed for the capital to be similarly divided, again with the French taking a sector if minded to do so. Berlin, being so far east, would most likely fall well inside the Soviet zone but in February 1945 that was still not inevitable. The British subsequently took the northern part of Germany, including Hamburg and the Ruhr, while the Americans took the south and the French would come in on the south-west. However, it was not at all clear in May 1945 whether Stalin would stick to the terms he had agreed at Yalta. Given his policy of total communist control of the central and eastern European countries his armies now occupied, would he try to do the same in Germany? He could not hope to control Germany west of the Elbe, but he could create a solid communist block east of the Elbe in which having US and British forces in Berlin would be an unwelcome irritant. Almost immediately Soviet forces had arrived they were instructed to frustrate Allied efforts to reach the city, hence Berzarin's line that the streets were too badly mined to allow Western forces to come.

This prevarication lasted for six weeks until, on 23 June, an American reconnaissance party under Colonel Frank Howley started off and got as far as Babelsberg before they were turned back. On 30 June Eisenhower's deputy, General Lucius Clay and General Sir Ronald Weeks for the British flew in to see the Soviets. They negotiated directly with Zhukov. They made two agreements, both of which would subsequently cause serious problems. First, they agreed to the Soviet demand that future Allied access could only be via one main road, one railway line and two air corridors. Secondly, they agreed that decisions taken in the Allied Control Commission required unanimous agreement, in other words by the Soviets as well as the British and the Americans and subsequently the French. What Clay and Weeks's visit did, though, was allow US and British troops to move up from the Elbe. On 1 July Howley's column set off again and this time gained access, albeit passing a series of very reluctant Soviet checkpoints. The next day the British arrived. There was one sad consequence of the Allies forcing the Soviets' hands. American forces had, before the ceasefire came into effect across Europe on 7 May, exploited well east of the Elbe in northern Germany and in central Germany had pushed through Thuringia as far as Leipzig. The Soviets now insisted on them withdrawing. German families who had celebrated life under the benign American military government now realised they would be living instead under Soviet control. Many packed up and fled west with the withdrawing US forces. They would not come back for forty-four years.

The division of Berlin into sectors was done exactly according to the district boundaries laid down by Mayor Adolf Wermuth in 1920. The Soviets took the centre, Mitte with Prenzlauer Berg and Friedrichshain, and the outlying districts of Treptow, Köpenick, Lichtenberg, which included the Soviet military headquarters at Karlshorst, Weißensee and up to Pankow in the north. The British took the west and north-west, Tiergarten, Charlottenburg, Spandau and Wilmersdorf. The British boundary with the Soviets was consequently the boundary between Mitte and Tiergarten, which is why the Berlin Wall later ran directly in front of the Brandenburg Gate. They also originally had Wedding and Reinickendorf but these two northern districts were subsequently handed over to the French on 12 August. The Americans took the south-west, Kreuzberg, Schöneberg and Neukölln, Tempelhof, Steglitz and Zehlendorf. The Allied Control Commission set itself up in the *Kammergericht* (the Court House) in Schöneberg with responsibility for the Allied controlled zones across Germany, while the four sector commandants in Berlin would meet in Dahlem to run the city itself.

These developments were keenly watched by Berliners and it was rather a surprise to British troops, arriving in smartly repainted vehicles and new uniforms rather than the medley of comfortable clothes they had worn as they fought across Europe, to find themselves warmly greeted as they arrived. 'Hundreds of Germans' turned out to meet them, 'by no means sullen or resentful, as some of the papers will report tomorrow for greater effect; they gaze fixedly, but many smile and some wave, a few almost cheer. It is indeed more like a sober liberation than a triumphant entry into a conquered city.'[7] Ruth Andreas-Friedrich was similarly pleased to see the Americans, as if they were protection against the Soviets. 'The Americans are here ... The victors from the West for whom we have waited since the beginning of April. More and more eagerly each day and more and more urgently each night.'[8] Others found the British very correct but slightly reserved. Karla Höcker had what was left of her house in Charlottenburg requisitioned. 'A British officer, intelligent, superior, speaking very good German, chairs the meeting. Next to him a very young colonel, stolid, blond, earnest, with the typical Anglo-Saxon upper lip. Both have lists in front of them and read out the conditions under which we must vacate the building. The English are polite, firm and completely impersonal.'[9] The British reaction on taking over a recently vacated barracks in Spandau was a little less positive. The barrack rooms, cupboards and cellars were full of 'the defilement of personal excreta', the plumbing system having not worked for several months, and the Russians had taken everything movable including every stick of furniture. The British soldiers were amazed to find slot machines in all the washrooms full of contraceptives, provided by the German army at 20 pfennigs a shot, and tellingly completely ignored by the Soviets.

That summer was dominated for the Allies by the Potsdam Conference, which started on 17 July between Stalin, Harry Truman (who had, as Vice President, succeeded as American President after Roosevelt had died in office on 12 April) and Churchill (who lost the British General Election that month). They met in the Cecilienhof Palace in Potsdam, a bizarre building constructed for the last Crown Prince and modelled on a mock-Tudor suburban English villa. It enjoys a glorious setting on the shores of one of the Havel's many lakes, set in a peaceful park and garden but strangely incongruous in Brandenburg. Around the palace Potsdam was a heap of ruins, the April bombing raid having destroyed the town centre, although mercifully Sanssouci was untouched. Today it has regained some of its former feel, and – just as elsewhere in the city and its relationship with the past – there is a well-laid-out exhibition about the conference.

The Potsdam Conference came to some important conclusions that would have a direct bearing on what now happened in Berlin. First, it said its purpose was to 'convince the German people that they have suffered a total military defeat and they cannot escape responsibility for what they have brought upon themselves, since their own ruthless warfare and fanatical Nazi resistance have destroyed the German economy and made chaos and suffering inevitable'.[10] This was, as the Allied leaders surveyed the ruins of Berlin, possibly a statement of the obvious. The Allies then went on

to say that local self-government should be re-established throughout Germany on democratic principles and particularly through
elective councils as rapidly as possible; that all democratic political
parties should be allowed and that Germany should be treated as a
single economic unit, although it stopped short of restoring a central
German government. The Soviets were authorised to extract reparations both from the sector they controlled and also 15 per cent from
the American and British sectors, although this was a formalisation
of what had already happened.

While they were in Berlin the Allied leaders took every opportunity to stage victory parades. On 21 July Churchill took the salute at
a British parade on the Charlottenburger Straße, the east–west axis
through the Tiergarten. When he was later opening the Winston
Club for British forces on the Ku'damm, he was rather taken aback
to be met by the cheers of a German crowd. Churchill 'seemed
nonplussed, raised his arm as if to acknowledge the applause, but
let it drop'. 'He looks good, the old man,' one German said, and
another muttered, as if he could scarcely believe his eyes, 'So that
is supposed to be a tyrant, is it?'[11] The major Allied parade was on
7 September and was taken by Zhukov, 'a glittering figure wearing
medals on both sides of his tunic down to the navel. Even Göring
could never have displayed so many and, according to the Berliners,
would not have attempted to do so, but would have borne only one,
inscribed 'See list'. General George Patton was there, the American
82nd Airborne Division took part, the British Brigade of Guards and
the French Spahi Bugle Band 'immaculate in scarlet suede and white
kid gloves'. But the soldiers who made the greatest impression were
the Soviet infantry, 'the dense ranks of their companies ... so closely
dressed that they seem to overlap each other'. They had a 'boundless
strength' about them, 'a terribly vivid air of menace' rather like a
massive medieval army.[12]

Once the conferences and parades had passed, Berlin returned to
the grim reality of the winter to come. Food was still very scarce,
and everyone who could grew their own vegetables. 'Field theft' was
common. Karla Höcker went to water her garden in Lindenallee one

evening in September to find it had been 'ransacked and plundered with indescribable brutality. Tiny bulbs, doll potatoes were strewn all around; it was a bit like child murder. I was devastated. All the effort it had cost us to find seed-potatoes! They would have yielded two hundred pounds, salvation for the winter!'[13]

'So this is Berlin – fascinating and depressing,' Ursula von Kardorff noted in her diary on 20 September. 'All the people look half out of their minds, utterly worn out by the struggle for existence. In spite of everything they are kind, touchingly hospitable and amusing. But the whole thing is ghastly. We are sleeping in Bärchen's old flat in Savignyplatz, in a room with no outer wall.'[14] The black market was rife with Russian black marketeers moving in, although Soviet troops had it fairly well covered; the British military police found themselves arresting a Soviet major general for selling stolen goods in their sector. There was a semi-official black market in the Tiergarten near the Reichstag. Although the old Reichsmarks were still officially in use, cigarettes became the favoured currency, especially imported American and British brands. A new Berlin profession started, the *Kippensammler*, boys who gathered cigarette ends discarded near barracks and clubs and reprocessed them to make whole cigarettes. Many Berlin heirlooms, either looted or saved during the war, now changed hands for Allied rations, especially chocolate, white bread and coffee or for the price of a few cigarette butts.

De-Nazification committees were formed, and anyone associated with the former regime (the list of organisations ran to forty-two different bodies from the Nazi party itself to the *Reichsfilmkammer* and the *Deutsche Christen Bewegung*, the German Christian Fellowship, which was considered to have been supportive of the Nazis) were investigated. It had been decided at Potsdam to put the major Nazi figures on trial but the issue was what to do about the hundreds of thousands of minor officials who had worked for the party in some way or other. Many of them were essential to restore the services so badly needed as the city slowly came back to life, and in the west many found themselves re-employed. It was rather different in the Soviet zone, and the newly established *Deutsche Verwaltung des*

Innern or DVdI (the Communists' own police force modelled on the NKVD) rounded up anyone suspected of Nazi links as well as quite a few liberals and others they felt were in some way opposed to the regime. These were interned in the camps so recently vacated by the Nazis, with Sachsenhausen entering a new and grim chapter in its already bloody history. It is estimated that in total more than 150,000 Germans were interned by the Soviets. Many never came back. One man, on arrival back at the same camp in which he had been imprisoned under the Nazis, simply showed the tattoo on his wrist and asked, 'Shall I keep the same number?'

The winter of 1945–6 was predicted to be a very cold one, and many Berliners would be facing it living in houses with no walls, let alone windows, doors or fireplaces. In fact, the winter was not as bad as had been expected and somehow the city struggled through, despite receiving thousands more Germans from what had been East Prussia and was now partly Poland and partly Russia (it is estimated that nearly 3 million were expelled to Germany between 1945 and 1950). But the winter of 1946–7 was terrible, and thousands died of cold and hunger. The British troops stationed in Spandau near the Grunewald were slightly alarmed to see signs posted along the edge of the forest telling them to beware of wolves. Normality still seemed a very long way off. 'My most striking first impression,' wrote George Clare that winter:

'was not visual but aural. The 1938 Berlin had assaulted one's ears with lively and strident crescendos, harsh, atonal, high-decibel; a medley of blaring car horns, squeaking brakes, snorting buses, clanging trams, shouting newspaper sellers. But now – like slow eerie drum-beats of a *danse macabre* – each sound rose and remained alone, the clip-clop of often wooden-soled footsteps, the rattle of a hand-cart or an occasional tram, the chugging of a wood-fuelled bus, the gear-clash of an Allied army lorry. This absence of the constant roar of city life was more unsettling than the sight of broken masonry framing bits of blue sky ... Yet Berlin was not a lifeless moon-scape. It lived – albeit in something of

a zombied trance – mirrored in the dazed looks of many of the
people I passed, more often noticeable in men than in women. But
the men were mostly old or elderly, bowed and bitter faced; the few
young ones who were about – emaciated shadows of the soldiers
who had almost conquered an entire continent – looked pathetic
and downtrodden in the tattered remnants of their Wehrmacht
uniforms.'[15]

Amazingly, the Jewish community began to re-establish itself. On 6
May 1945, as the city was surrendering, the Polish chief rabbi who had
entered with the Soviet army, blew a shofar (a Hebrew musical instrument used in religious ceremonies) at a service held in Kantstraße. On
11 May Martin Riesenburger, a preacher, held another service in a
tiny synagogue on Lothringer Straße. 'Several people came,' he wrote,
'who were emerging for the first time from the underground – into
the daylight – where they had hidden for so many years.' Slowly about
8,000 would emerge, thinking sadly of their 56,000 relatives who
had been murdered. The pogroms in Poland that accompanied the
mass deportation of Germans later that year increased the population
considerably. They were helped on arrival by a Jewish American aid
organisation, known as the 'Joint', which became a welcome source
of food, fuel and cigarettes. 'Judaism,' wrote one official crossly, 'is
now not seen as a source of spiritual nourishment but as a way of
obtaining the greatly desired "Joint" parcels.'[16]

In accordance with what had been decided at Potsdam, in October
1946 Berlin went to the polls for the first time in eleven years to
elect members to the new city council, the *Magistrat*. Political parties had been reformed, the three main ones in June 1945 ahead of
Potsdam: the Communists (the KPD), the Socialists (the SPD) and the
more right-wing Christian Democrats (the CDU). Ulbricht, mindful of the lessons of 1918–19, was determined that this time there
should be one united left-wing party, and in April 1946 he forced
a merger between the KPD and the SPD to form the *Sozialistische
Einheitspartei* (Socialist unity party, the SED). To his immense irritation, the SPD in west Berlin refused to go along with his plan and

remained independent. Fighting the election on their own ticket, they took sixty-three seats in the 120-seat assembly, with the CDU winning twenty-nine but Ulbricht's SED only twenty-six, a clear rejection of Soviet domination. When the *Magistrat* assembled they chose the SPD leader, Otto Ostrowski, as mayor but the Soviets insisted that he run the city jointly with Ulbricht's candidate, Otto Grotewhol. When Ostrowski agreed to compromise he was forced from office and the assembly replaced him with an ex-Communist but now dedicated Social Democrat, Ernst Reuter. Ulbricht – who loathed Reuter, viewing him as a turncoat from the communist cause – refused to work with him.

In June 1947, after the terrible winter that Europe had suffered, General George Marshall (wartime chief of the US Army Staff and now Truman's Secretary of State) announced the development of the Marshall Plan, which envisaged the USA giving generous assistance to try to revitalise European economies. Assistance was also offered to the Soviets, who rejected it both for themselves and the eastern European countries they controlled. A critical part of returning Germany to some sort of normality was the need for a respected currency. Berlin was still using the old unstable Reichsmarks, which attracted little confidence (hence trade taking place in cigarettes). In parallel with the Marshall Plan, a new currency, the Deutschmark, was introduced in the British, American and French zones of West Germany, and to Berlin on 23 June 1948 where the crisp new notes were stamped with red 'B'. Sixty old, worthless Reichsmarks were exchanged at a very advantageous rate for the new currency per head, effectively handing everyone a free cash sum of 60 Deutschmarks. The effect was almost instantaneous, with goods appearing in the shops almost overnight. The British and the Americans had already concluded that their zones in West Germany, as opposed to Berlin, should be self-governing under a new German constitution. As a preliminary step they had agreed to merge their economic administrations, creating an area known as 'Bizonia', which the French – always troubled at Germany regaining her strength too quickly – reluctantly joined as well to form 'Trizonia'.

Now with a new currency, the Soviets realised they were losing economic and political control. They tried to block its introduction, saying it required the agreement of all four powers. For five days they attempted to introduce their own alternative in Berlin – in fact old Reichsmark notes with a small sticker attached not very skilfully with potato-starch glue – called Ostmarks. Predictably it failed, with Berliners almost universally using the Deutschmark. The Allied generals, now without the Soviet Marshal Sokolovsky who had walked out on 16 June, declared that the Soviet order imposing their currency did not apply to their sectors. A subsequent vote in the *Magistrat* upheld their decision despite intense intimidation by Ulbricht's thugs, and Reuter announced that both currencies would remain in use in their respective sectors. Stalin and Ulbricht's plans were not going well. Any thoughts of forcing the Allies out of Berlin, and then subduing the West Berliners under SED leadership, had to be reassessed. Unwilling, and probably unable, to face the risk of war, Stalin tried another method of forcing the Western Allies out.

On 24 June the Soviets closed off all road, rail and water access to Berlin, imposing a blockade with the intention of literally starving West Berlin and the Allies into submission. Food supplies were cut off, as were electricity and gas, most of which was sourced from the Soviet sector, the Soviets having comprehensively stripped out the power station in the British sector. The Allies faced a considerable dilemma. Forcing supplies through by land faced the likelihood of having to confront the Soviet military, something that could easily escalate. On the other hand, they could not simply let the 2.5 million-odd Berliners living in their sectors starve, the city's population having swelled in the past three years with so many arrivals from Poland and East Prussia. This was precisely why Stalin had calculated he could force them to abandon the city altogether. However, he reckoned without two things. The first was the military power of the USA and Britain, both of which had severely reduced their armed forces since the end of the war but who still held sizeable air transport fleets. The second was Berliners' determination not to be bullied into submission.

The only way into Berlin now was by air and, at the inspiration of General Lucius Clay, who calculated correctly that resupplying the city by air could be achieved without causing a war, President Truman was persuaded to authorise the first Skymasters to deliver supplies to Tempelhof on 25 June. It was a significant challenge. Berlin needed about 8,000 tons of supplies a day, requiring around 1,000 flights so three Skymasters hardly met the requirement. Those Berliners who had known what happened at Stalingrad would hardly have been encouraged after the Luftwaffe's dismal failure to resupply von Paulus's army. The Americans, however, had two people who understood large-scale air supply. The first, who happened to be in Germany, was Albert Wedemeyer, the man who had resupplied Chiang Kai Shek's armies in China over the 'Hump' from India in 1944–5 and who, coincidentally, had attended war college in Berlin in the 1930s. The second, and the man who directed the airlift from Wiesbaden, was an air-transport specialist called Lieutenant General William Tunner, who also had extensive experience in China. By stripping out US airbases around the world (at one time it was estimated that three quarters of all US military transport aircraft were dedicated to the Berlin operation) and with significant support from the British Royal Air Force, who provided a quarter of the aircraft, Tunner achieved the near-impossible: by the spring of 1949 he achieved 1,383 flights a day, delivering 12,849 tons. This meant that an aircraft was landing in Berlin every sixty seconds, with the Berliner ground crews taking just twenty or thirty minutes to unload them.

It was a dangerous and costly operation. Altogether thirty-nine British and thirty-one American aircrew were lost, together with thirteen German civilian lives. There is a touching memorial to them at Tempelhof. Short of actually shooting down an aircraft, the Soviets did all they could to disrupt the operation. Soviet fighters 'buzzed' the incoming flights, forcing the pilots to take sudden evasive action. The sheer number of aircraft landing and taking off in such a tight timetable, the limited space on the airfields and the weather all combined to make conditions really difficult. Tunner wrote afterwards of the very foggy Friday 13 August 1948, one of the most difficult days, when a Skymaster had overshot the runway at Tempelhof: 'As their planes bucked around like grey monsters in the murk the pilots filled the air with chatter, calling in near panic to find out what was going on. On the ground a traffic jam was building as planes came off the unloading line to climb on the homeward-bound three minute conveyor belt, but were refused permission to take off for fear of collision with the planes milling around overhead.'[17] Fortunately Tunner was able to direct all the circling aircraft to return to their bases.

Another problem was the lack of airfields. The main Berlin airport, recently developed by the Nazis, was Tempelhof in the American sector but its runways were inadequate and had to be rebuilt in the summer of 1948. The British-run airfield at Gatow lacked capacity and was a long way from the city centre on the west bank of the Havel. A plan was therefore made to build a third airport at Tegel in the French sector. By November 1948 a 5,500-foot runway was completed by 17,000 Berlin volunteers, using bricks and rubble from the city's ample supplies, which involved demolishing a radio mast used by the Soviets. Although the French did not actually participate in the airlift, General Ganéval, the French commandant at the time, deserves a place in history for his put-down to the Russian General Kotikov. Expressing outrage that his radio mast had been demolished, Kotikov raged: 'How could you do such a thing?' Ganéval replied: 'With French engineers and dynamite.' The three airports would continue to function right up until the 1990s, although ironically it is Tegel that is now the city's main hub, at least until the new Schönefeld Airport fully opens.

The other factor that Stalin and Ulbricht failed to appreciate was just how deeply antagonistic Berliners – especially those living in the western zones – had become towards the Soviet domination of the east. Berliners were prepared to put up with this fresh round of deprivation despite all the hardship involved because they knew that if they did not, and the Allies were forced out, their future would be under communist dictat. Life was tough, particularly in the early months. Power supplies were limited to an average of two hours per household. They were limited to 25 pounds of coal per month, and a calorie intake just above starvation levels, although as the efficiency of the airlift improved, by April 1949 they were receiving 2,300 calories a day, which was more than Londoners still on wartime rationing were getting. One of the most telling facts about the airlift was that, while there was nothing to stop Berliners moving into the Soviet sector where fresh food was imported daily from the Soviet-controlled zone, only 4 per cent did so and they tended to be those who lived in the west but worked in the east or SED party members. Many East Berliners smuggled food across the border. Gisela Bilski did so regularly, taking food and lumps of coal to her aunt who lived near the zoo. Everything went well for the first couple of trips but on her third trip the police decided to search everyone on her train in Friedrichstraße station. She had a basket of apples, which she just managed to throw out of the train window, but she had aroused suspicions. On her next journey she was caught with a pound of butter and five lumps of coal. Despite being only thirteen years old, she was hauled off to prison. She was soon released – on the strict condition that she never talked about what she had done – but from then on she was branded as an 'economic criminal'.[18]

This spirit of resistance and determination was articulated by Ernst Reuter, who became both the political and emotional leader of Berlin's resistance. Reuter was a typical Berliner in that he came from Schleswig-Holstein but made Berlin his home. He had served on the Eastern Front in the First World War, been captured by the Russians and converted to communism while a prisoner. He had got to know Lenin, who appears to have rated him so that in 1918 Reuter had been sent to Berlin and quickly rose through the ranks of the KPD. Yet he fought with rivals in the party and came to see the drawbacks of communism, switching to the SPD and then never wavering from it. He was Mayor of Magdeburg and a member of the 1933 Reichstag when the Nazis came to power. Interned briefly in a concentration camp, he was released and spent the war years in Turkey. Back in Berlin he was elected to the *Magistrat* in 1946 and then chosen as mayor. He would come to grace the cover of *Time* magazine with the simple caption '*Herr Berlin*' and he was, in his trademark black beret pulled well down over his head, the international symbol of Berlin's resistance.

Predictably he had to contend with considerable Soviet opposition. On 26 August 1948 the *Magistrat* met to condemn the blockade, only to be harassed by an SED mob accusing them of crimes against humanity. The SED were particularly irritated because, due to the Soviet-backed police's partisan behaviour under their unpleasant ex-Nazi boss, Paul Markgraf, especially in arresting liberals even in West Berlin, the *Magistrat* had earlier that month sanctioned establishing a separate West Berlin police force under Johannes Stumm. This had immediately attracted three quarters of serving officers. At the 26 August meeting a motion was moved by CDU members, who felt threatened by Ulbricht's mob, for the *Magistrat* to leave the Rote Rathaus and meet in the West. This was initially resisted by the SPD but on 6 September, at their next meeting, members were again assaulted and then barricaded in their offices by SED-hired thugs and East Berlin police. When members tried to leave they found the building surrounded by police and Soviet soldiers. Eventually freed after the Allies intervened with Kotikov, the council split with western members henceforth meeting in Schöneberg town hall. The real impact came three days later. Some 300,000 Berliners gathered in Königsplatz, now renamed Platz der Republik, to hear Reuter speak in front of the burned-out hulk of the Reichstag. Reuter told them that Berlin would say 'No' to communism, and that the 'freedom-loving Berlin population will build a dam against which the red tide will break in vain'. He finished, as Allied aircraft landed and took off overhead, by saying, 'People of this world, look upon this city, and see that you should not, cannot abandon this city and this people.'

Fired up by his words, the crowd spilled beyond the Brandenburg Gate into the Pariser Platz, where they were instantly rounded on by the East Berlin police. Fifteen-year-old Wolfgang Scheunemann was shot dead trying to shield a young woman. Twelve people were wounded and the British rushed to protect the Soviet War Memorial a short distance away in the Tiergarten in case the now-infuriated mob should attack it. That December Berlin went to the polls again to elect a *Magistrat* for the West. It was a freezing, grey, horrible winter's day, everyone hungry and cold but 86 per cent of eligible voters turned out, and 64.5 per cent voted for Reuter and the SPD, 19.4 per cent for the CDU and 16 per cent for the Liberal Democrats. The SED did not participate. Berlin was now very clearly politically divided between east and west.

Whereas Reuter became the figurehead for Berlin, the city's dogged determination made it internationally much better known and respected. Previously it had been seen as 'the Lair of the Fascist Beast', the world being unaware at that stage how anti-Nazi it had been. Now it was seen as the front line of democracy standing up to Soviet totalitarianism. The aircrews who were landing every minute laden with food and fuel were the same men who only four years earlier had been dropping a more deadly cargo. A real empathy developed for Berliners, especially the children, and a US pilot called Gail Halvorsen started the habit of dropping sweets for them as his plane was coming in to land at Tempelhof. The practice immediately caught on so that the crews prepared mini-parachutes with sweets that they let go as they approached. The children called the planes *Rosinenbomber* (raisin bombers), which became the icons of the air lift and of American and British friendship. Halvorsen started to dip the wings of his aircraft as he approached, warning the children to be ready and earning him the nickname *Onkel Wackelflügel* (Uncle Waggle Wings). The dignity of Berlin children made a deep impression on him. 'These kids didn't have chocolate and they really craved it but wouldn't beg for it,' he told *Der Tagesspiegel* years later, 'If they had we would have just given them the two sticks of chewing gum I had. But these children wanted nothing more than freedom.'[19]

In September 1946 the Americans had set up Radio Berlin, *Rundfunk im Amerikanischen Sektor* (RIAS, or Radio In the American Sector), in Schöneberg. Its strong transmitter enabled it to broadcast twenty-four hours a day. During the airlift it attracted both a very large group of listeners and, despite being government-owned, a wide variety of German talent. Its show *Die Insulaner* (the Islanders), first broadcast at Christmas 1948, became its flag-ship programme and it is estimated that, despite the shortage of power, nearly three quarters of Berliners listened to it during that dark winter.

By May 1949 it was clear to the Soviets that the blockade had failed. It had also begun to cause them problems as retaliatory measures by the west had severely limited the supply of the resources from West Germany that the East Germany economy needed after the Soviet looting. On 11 May the road and rail links were quietly reopened. Since 24 June 1948, a total of 277,804 flights had delivered 400,000 tons of food and fuel; in addition, 83,000 tons of cargo had been flown out of Berlin so that at least some of the factories could sell their products, and 68,000 people taken for medical or personal reasons.[20] It was a hugely impressive achievement but it still left a divided city deep inside the Soviet zone while the rest of those parts of Germany that the Allies controlled now became organised as a separate state. Just after the blockade finished, the British, American and French zones became the Federal Republic of Germany, the FRG. Fairly obviously, Berlin could not be the capital of the new state, so this instead went to Bonn.

Many Berliners saw this as a positive signal; surely had the new state wanted a permanent capital they would have chosen Frankfurt am Main or Hamburg? Choosing a relatively obscure Rhineland city must mean that in the deep recesses of their hearts they saw Berlin eventually reassuming its role? The first elections were held on 14 August and resulted in Konrad Adenauer forming a coalition govern-ment in which his CDU party had a narrow majority. That October the Soviets founded the *Deutsche Demokratische Republik* (the DDR in German, or the German Democratic Republic, the GDR, as it was known in English). Its capital certainly was Berlin, where its 2,000-strong assembly met, whose members were overwhelmingly from the SED. This was not altogether surprising given that there had only been one choice of party on the ballot paper. Wilhelm Pieck, the veteran communist who had narrowly escaped execution with Liebknecht and Luxemburg in 1919, became its first president and

Otto Grotewohl its first prime minister but power still lay with the First Secretary of the KPD, Walter Ulbricht. Both new countries took the old nationalist colours of 1848 – red, black and gold – for their flags but the GDR superimposed a compass, a hammer and a sheaf of grain on to theirs to represent industry, science and agriculture. They also integrated the party police force, the DVdI, into the state as the *Staatsicherheitsdienst*, abbreviated to Stasi.

The economy in West Berlin recovered only slowly after the end of the blockade. Unemployment remained, at over 30 per cent, far higher than in the newly established FRG, where it was 11.5 per cent.[21] Factory output had suffered from a combination of Soviet looting, the lingering effects of the destruction in the war, and the blockade itself. While the FRG looked to establish itself as a nation, Berlin found itself slightly isolated. Adenauer had never liked the city, famously remarking that he pulled down the blinds in his railway carriage when he crossed the Elbe as the landscape reminded him of the Asian steppes. A deeply Catholic Rhinelander, he remarked that 'Although the Berliners have some valuable qualities, I've always had the feeling in Berlin that I was in a pagan city.'[22] Berlin was governed by its Allied Kommandatura who worked increasingly closely with Reuter and the *Magistrat* but they only sent observers to the parliament in Bonn and were, at least officially, not part of the FRG. Adenauer took some persuading to help but – under pressure from the USA – Bonn did start to give the city direct financial assistance. The USA gave nearly $3 billion in aid and slowly some sort of parity was achieved with the FRG economy, which grew at 8 per cent per annum on average during the 1950s, the fastest rate in Europe and the so-called German 'economic miracle'.

Yet while life in West Berlin began to stabilise and slowly improve from 1950, life in East Berlin, which had been materially little different to that in the west since 1945, gradually began to deteriorate. Margit Hosseini, who lived in the west but made frequent visits to family in the east in the 1950s, described how 'even as a child one immediately sensed and saw how quickly the atmosphere changed' once she walked out of the S-Bahn:

'When one travelled Friedrichstraße, there were big posters advertising socialism and the greatness of it. As you then moved further
into East Berlin, away from the centre of town, it became grim;
there were less colourful posters and everything was grey ... in
many places the city was in ruins, and whole streets and buildings were reduced to rubble ... I do recall in my mind's eye the
endless grey shuffling of people along the street, not talking to
each other. Whilst in the West, we were talking and laughing or
making gestures.'[23]

The GDR was considered economically one of the fastest developing
states in the Communist bloc, but compared to the FRG its growth
was poor. 'It was not nice in the GDR, and we were constantly told
what to do at work – to join organisations like Free German Youth
and so on – but I didn't join any of them,' said Hardy Firl, a young
driver from East Berlin. 'You faced a lot of disadvantages if you
didn't want to join the party. Everyone had work, but we earned very
little and there wasn't much, unlike West Berlin that had everything.
From the end of the war to the early 1950s, it all got worse. There
was hardly anything to buy any more. My parents wanted a few
nails, and even those were not available.'[24]

Ulbricht took as predictably a hard-line view on economics as
he did on security, so that growth was slowed by his and the SED's
insistence on collectivisation in agriculture and cumbersome state
planning in industry. Heavy industry was favoured over the production of consumer goods, meaning there was little in the shops
to cheer otherwise drab lives. By 1953 approximately 750,000
hectares of otherwise productive arable land were uncultivated
due to incompetent state planning. The GDR government was also
becoming increasingly alarmed by the number of East Germans who
were crossing over to live in the West. Life in the East was becoming very obviously less attractive than in the West. In 1952 Stalin
had made a surprising offer to the Allies. He proposed a reunified
Germany with free elections providing the reunited country did not
join any military alliance. The catch was that the border of this new

Germany would be along the Oder–Neisse line, in other words the old East Prussian territories would be signed away for ever to Russia and Poland. This made the offer toxic in Bonn, where the Eastern refugee organisations were strong, and was inevitably going to be unpopular in France, which would remain resolutely opposed to any form of reunification for some decades, pointing out – with some justification – that since Germany had been united she had invaded France on average every twenty-three years. Adenauer never seems to have taken Stalin's offer seriously, believing that Germany east of the Elbe was anyway part of Asia and favouring the close relationships he was now successfully building with the West. The result was that Ulbricht was able to persuade Stalin that he should now protect the GDR by isolating it and that same year he started to fortify the border between the two Germanies.

A strip 5 kilometres wide was cleared of residents – usually at short notice and fairly brutally – and a barbed-wire fence erected along the actual border line. Special permission was required to enter the 5 kilometre area and later the barbed wire would be replaced by a virtually impenetrable fence, set about with mines, trip-wires, searchlights and machine guns all manned by a well-trained and officious 47,000-strong guard force, the *Grenztruppen* (usually known as the *Grenzer*). The Inner German Border (usually shortened to IGB) became the visible symbol of the Iron Curtain, a phrase coined originally by Churchill in a speech in Missouri in March 1946 to refer to the border between the free world in the West and the Communist bloc in the East. Stretching 1,400 kilometres from the Baltic Sea to the border with Czechoslovakia, the IGB would become all too familiar to the Germans who lived on both sides of it as well as to generations of American and British soldiers who spent long hours patrolling it. Ulbricht also moved against West Berliners who owned allotments or plots in the East, confiscating all western-owned property, a venal move particularly when so many Berliners relied on their smallholdings for those extra potatoes and vegetables that were still in such short supply.

The problem for Ulbricht was that, although he had shut off the border between the GDR and the FRG, Berlin remained an open city. He could now stop his people crossing direct into the FRG, but he could not stop them entering Berlin, their capital, then crossing over the open boundary between the Soviet and Allied sectors and then on to West Germany. As conditions in the GDR gradually worsened, and as it became clear that political and cultural restrictions would get tougher rather than ease off, more and more citizens of the GDR chose to leave: 197,788 in 1950, 165,648 in 1951 and 182,393 in 1952. The majority of these were the younger, more ambitious types, the sort of people a society trying to rebuild itself and its economy could not afford to lose. Ulbricht was only too aware of this, and in late 1952 he managed to persuade Stalin, who seems always to have had a soft spot for this dour Saxon, that he should be allowed to police the border in Berlin as well. Fate intervened to prevent him. First, in March 1953 Stalin died, throwing the Soviet Union into temporary political paralysis. The curious oligarchy who assumed interim power in Moscow – Molotov, Beria, Khrushchev and Gromyko – believed Ulbricht was too hard-line. Marshal Chuikov, who had commanded 8th Guards Army in 1945 and to whom Weidling had surrendered – and who was now the commander of what the Soviets termed the Group of Soviet Forces Germany (known to the west as GSFG) – was instructed to talk to the German communists. His instruction was to advise them to make life a little easier for their people so that, the Politburo argued rather reasonably, fewer of them might want to leave.

Ulbricht was now in a potentially dangerous place. He had lost his protector, things were going badly domestically, he was facing criticism among his own ministers who were beginning to take a more openly reformist line, and now his Soviet mentors were turning against him. Yet Ulbricht seemed impervious to criticism, believing, in his uncompromising traditional communist way, that the answer was tougher social policies, more collectivisation and more heavy industry. He moved to tighten the regulations against any private businesses, removing ration cards from many 'bourgeois' elements who still owned property, refused to ease his moves against the churches, and, most controversially, increased the 'work norms' (the amount of work labourers had to fulfil to receive the same wage) by 10 per cent. In June 1953 he was summoned to Moscow for talks on how the GDR could be reformed so that people actually wanted to live there. It must have been a galling experience for him. On his return he was forced to issue, on 11 June, a statement in Berlin that mistakes had been made – something that was both previously unheard of and very popular.

It showed Ulbricht to be vulnerable. In early June there had also been trouble in Czechoslovakia, with workers rioting in protest against their own repressive government. In East Berlin, with Berliners possibly reading too much into the 11 June announcements and in light of the ever-present contrast with their western neighbours just a few blocks away, it seemed to many that there was an opportunity. On 16 June a group of builders working on the Stalinallee (the new development along the shattered Große Frankfurter Straße that was to be Ulbricht's way of showcasing the wonders of East Berlin) decided they would march in protest to demand from Otto Grotewohl that the increase in work norms be abandoned. Starting in Strausbergerplatz, with its vast bronze statue of Stalin presented to Berlin by the Soviets in 1951, they marched down Stalinallee, through the Alexanderplatz and along the Leipziger Straße to the Prime Minister's office in Göring's old Aviation Ministry, singing the old 1918 revolutionary marching song *'Brüder, zur Sonne, zur Freiheit'* ('Brother, Forward to the Sun, Forward to Freedom'), whose last verse goes something like 'Cast off slavery and fight the last holy battle'. They gathered considerable support along the way so that it was a crowd of thousands who demanded that Grotewohl come out and talk to them. Predictably he refused, cowering inside while the SED Party Secretary, Heinz Brandt, was sent out to promise that the work norm increases would be rescinded. It was not enough; the crowd sensed they had the government on the run.

A general strike was called for the next day, 17 June, broadcast around the GDR not by the state-controlled official media but by RIAS broadcasting from West Berlin, which most people in the

GDR listened to. The next day nearly half a million people gathered across the GDR in protest. In Berlin they met in Strausbergerplatz, in Friedrichshain, again marching into the city centre, down the Unter den Linden, past the Soviet Embassy, where they sang and chanted ant Russian slogans. The teenaged Joachim Rudolph joined in. 'We passed a shoe factory,' he recalled, 'Many women were leaning out of the windows, looking and waving and cheering ... we called "Come down! Join us! You can see and you know that the national strike is today." And they said: "Yes, we would like to but the management has locked all the doors and gates. We can't get out." Then someone climbed over the steel gate and managed to break the gate open ... Many women came down and joined the march in their work aprons.'[25] The red flag was torn down from the Brandenburg Gate. They surged into Leipziger Straße, shouting anti-Ulbricht chants such as 'The Goatee must go!' (referring to Ulbricht's habitual goatee beard) and 'Goatee, Belly and Glasses are not the will of the masses,' the last two referring to the corpulent Pieck and Grotewohl.[26] Their more serious chanting, however, was still about the new work norms. Again, there appeared to be paralysis on the government's side. Bruno Leuschner, Chairman of State Planning Commission, collapsed with a heart attack. The police seemed equally bewildered as more and more demonstrators arrived. Joachim Rudolph was with a group trying to get into a building belonging to the SED:

> 'It was locked of course. We went up some stairs and knocked on one of the window-panes ... And there was a roller shutter, which you couldn't tear out or break open. In front of these bars, there was a disabled ex-serviceman who had lost a leg in the war. He was beside himself with anger and ranted on the steps and stabbed with his crutches through the roller shutter and smashed all the glass panes ... I could see the outlines of men's faces behind the net curtains in some of the windows. It was the SED-party bigwigs, also afraid.'[27]

Overnight, however, Ulbricht had planned an uncompromising response. Talking to both the new Soviet military commandant in Berlin, General Pyotr Akimovich Dibrova, and the Soviet Commissioner Vladimir Semyonov, they had agreed to use the Soviet army. Late in the morning, as part of the crowd attempted to storm the Ministry building, Soviet T-34 tanks started to roll down Leipziger Straße. Initially the tanks did not get very far, being surrounded by crowds shouting at the crews and chalking words like 'Shame' on their sides. Their Russian crews also seemed to waver but this was not what Dibrova had in mind. The endless loudspeaker demands to the crowd to disperse being impossible to hear, Dibrova gave a signal to the tanks to advance. 'We could just see from the movement of his mouth that he was shouting, making threats and waving his fist. Then, at a distance of 10 or 15 metres, the next tank followed around the corner. And they just drove into the crowds.'[28] Emboldened, the police made truncheon charges. Unsurprisingly most of the crowd began to run, but groups of youths stood firm, pelting them with stones in scenes witnessed by West Berliners watching from the Potsdamer Platz. By the evening more than fifty demonstrators were dead (the exact number is difficult to determine) and a further eighteen summarily executed around the city, including one unfortunate West Berliner, Willi Göttling, who just happened to be passing through but was rounded up and shot against a wall as a provocateur. The revolt had spread across the GDR and, although the world's attention was on Berlin, where it was so visible, there were countless other brave demonstrations throughout the country. All were suppressed with the same brutality.

Even sadder was the inevitable round of subsequent arrests and executions, with 1,500 imprisoned and an indeterminate number executed. Twelve of these were Russian soldiers, mostly tank crews, who had refused to fire on unarmed demonstrators, although Dibrova would insist in the usual Soviet style that the crowd had been armed and funded by the Western Allies. The area immediately in front of the Aviation Ministry – framed by the socialist murals depicting the world of joy and plenty that existed only in Ulbricht's mind, and

where many of the demonstrators were shot – was renamed after
1989 as the Platz des Volksaufstandes von 1953 (Square of the 1953
Popular Uprising). There is a most effective memorial there, a photograph of the demonstrators with linked arms set into the pavement.
Hardy Firl was rounded up as he was trying to get away. He dropped
his banner and was thrown into the back of an army truck. He was
taken to the Stasi prison at Hohenschönhausen and was interviewed
by a senior policeman who told him he was working with the CIA
because he was wearing American jeans. He denied that but was
then shown a photograph of himself at the demonstration and so
had to admit to taking part. He was told to plead guilty or he would
be beaten with a truncheon, so he did. He was sentenced to three
years in the *Zuchthaus*, a tougher type of prison. On arrival he was
made to strip completely, had his head shaved and was issued with a
striped prison uniform. He was put in a cell with four men and two
wooden bunk-beds, one blanket and some straw.

The West protested but it did little good. Reuter did what he
could. In West Berlin 17 June became a public holiday, and the
Charlottenburger Straße – from where it enters the Tiergarten west
of the Brandenburg Gate to what would later become Ernst-Reuter-
Platz in tribute to this great man who died of a heart attack shortly
afterwards – was renamed Straße des 17 Juni. It ran directly past
the Soviet War Memorial. In 1956 the Hungarians rose against
the Soviets, only to meet a similarly savage repression, but it is yet
another honourable first for Berliners that they were the first to rebel
against Soviet totalitarian rule. The more immediate effect was that
Ulbricht, far from being weakened, was able to persuade Khrushchev
(who was by then establishing himself in power in Moscow) that
only his strict, unbending interpretation of socialism would succeed
in the GDR. The two politburo members who had been trying to
have him removed, Wilhelm Zaisser and Rudolf Herrnstadt, were
sacked. While he and his politburo colleagues took themselves out
of Pankow, where they had been living, to the claustrophobic safety
of a newly built protected compound – the Waldsiedlung (the Forest
Colony), 30 kilometres north of Berlin near Wandlitz, surrounded

by its own high security fence – East Berlin faced the prospect of a grim, grey future. Hundreds of thousands of Berliners, mostly the young, decided that was not for them.

~

It is perhaps unsurprising that cultural life in East Berlin in the 1950s was limited. Bertolt Brecht, having spent the war years in the USA, where he produced some of his strongest anti-war literature such as his *Kriegsfibel* (*War Primer*), returned to Berlin via Switzerland in 1949. Predictably given his communist sympathies, he settled in the East where he founded his Berliner Ensemble theatre company in the renovated theatre on Schiffbauerdamm (still there and just over the bridge from Friedrichstraße). Brecht's plays, especially *Mother Courage*, appealed greatly to the Communist authorities but Brecht himself began to drift away from the regime and now wrote little new. But he did not support the 1953 revolt and was thought to be rather too supportive of Ulbricht's repression. However, several months later Brecht wrote a damning poem sparked by Kurt Bartel, the secretary of the GDR Writers' Union, who had published a horribly obsequious pamphlet saying how ashamed he was, as a good socialist, of the demonstrators' actions. Brecht's response was '*Die Lösung*' (the solution), which included the damning lines:

> After the uprising of 17th June
> The Secretary of the Writers' Union
> Had pamphlets distributed in the Stalin Allee
> Stating that the people
> Had forfeited the confidence of the government,
> And could win it back only
> By redoubled efforts. Would it not be easier
> In that case, for the government
> To dissolve the people
> And elect another?

It was not published until *Die Welt* got hold of it in the West in 1959.

The Opera House reopened in 1951 but was predictably restricted in what productions it could stage, and a new *Komische Oper* was opened in Behrenstraße, the old building in Friedrichstraße being too badly damaged to repair. With the Berlin Philharmonic firmly in the West, in 1952 the East restarted the Berlin Symphony Orchestra, which was originally founded in 1924. Although it would never reach the same standard or have the international appeal of its rival, it would give hours of pleasure and escapism to many East Berliners. East Berlin's music and opera would inevitably suffer, given the regime's dictat that 'Music in our republic exists against a background of socialist realism,' but it still produced very highly regarded performances.[29] Berliners' long love affair with music would sustain those fated to remain in East Berlin during the dark days to come and there was always a feeling that, especially in the 1960s, however socially realistic their score, musicians were sympathising with their audience in their difficult and sad lives.

A major issue facing Ulbricht and his politburo was how to approach rebuilding East Berlin, which, now that Mitte was the proud centre of the capital of their new socialist republic, could not really remain in ruins. Added to that was the problem that the legacy of many of its finest buildings, built by an authoritarian Prussian regime, were inimical to them as good communists. The future of some buildings were relatively easy to decide. The Opera House – in many ways redolent of everything royal and privileged – was too well known to be left in ruins and could be used to stage wholesome socialist performances, hence its reopening in 1951. The university was renamed after the von Humboldts and that too was quickly opened, albeit with a very different curriculum and choice of courses to what had gone before. The Neue Wache – used since 1931 as a memorial to the dead of the First World War – could continue in the same office; badly damaged by bombing it was rebuilt and opened in 1960 as a 'Memorial to the Victims of Fascism and Militarism'. Later a glass pyramid in the centre housed an 'eternal flame' and an unknown soldier and concentration camp victim were interred beneath it. Two soldiers from the GDR's Guards Regiment (the

Frederick Engels' Guards) mounted sentry duty there, performing a smart ceremony when they changed reliefs. It was something the GDR did rather well.

A bigger problem was the brooding hulk of the Berliner Schloss, which had been heavily bombed on 3 February 1945 and burned for several days. Although most of the interior was destroyed, the damage was not catastrophic and the outer walls were still more or less intact, leaving it as a darkened skeleton dominating the centre of the city. Actually, it had not been much occupied since 1918, the Nazis having used it as an art gallery and as a backdrop for their enormous flags when they held seemingly endless military parades on the Lustgarten. At the end of the war an enterprising coal merchant had taken over some of its useable rooms but in 1946 it reverted to being a rather impromptu exhibition centre; an exhibition of French Impressionists was staged there and the famous White Hall was patched up enough for the city to mount a small but rather optimistic display entitled '*Berliner Plant*' (plans for Berlin). In 1948 there was an exhibition to celebrate the centenary of 1848, what the communists called the 'revolution'. For many, the Berliner Schloss was very much the symbol of Berlin's history, its centre and its heart, but not for Ulbricht. He thought the Schloss represented everything bad about Berlin. He saw the Schloßplatz and the Lustgarten as becoming 'a grand square for demonstrations, upon which our people's will for struggle and for progress can find expression', although admittedly he said that in 1950, before the trouble of 1953. Despite considerable protest, he had the Schloss itself demolished in four months at the end of 1950, the public line being that it had been too badly damaged by Anglo-American 'terrorist' bombing to be left standing. Most of it is now in the rubble hill in the Volkspark Friedrichshain. The empty space it had occupied became a giant car park but that, again, was felt not to show the GDR off to its best effect.

The only piece of the old Schloss to be saved was the balcony facing out across the Lustgarten because allegedly it was where Karl Liebknecht – now a hero in the GDR's pantheon of revolutionaries – had declared his ill-fated socialist republic on 9 November 1918.

Ironically it was, of course, the very same balcony from which the
Kaiser had announced the declaration of war in 1914. The problem
was how to fill the space behind it, now renamed Marx-Engels-Platz,
and this would involve considerable socialist soul-searching. In 1948
a delegation from East Berlin went to Moscow and returned duly
impressed with the huge 'Stalinist Gothic' skyscrapers that were
being erected there. A scheme was prepared to build something
comparable and sketches were drawn up showing a similar building
dominating the Lustgarten, where troops of happy socialist youth
paraded and danced. Luckily it was not to be and the area was left
empty apart from a rather forlorn reviewing stand put up for the
GDR politburo to take the salute at May Day parades. Framed by
the rather absurd fragment of Schluter's facade with the Liebknecht
portal, and the equally badly damaged skeleton of the Berliner Dom,
it looked faintly ridiculous.

Ulbricht, who had a particular loathing for the Church as an institution, had also wanted to blow up what was left of the Berliner Dom
but had been persuaded to leave it standing because of the bad pub-
licity its destruction would cause internationally. Ultimately it was
decided that the area would be redeveloped as a sort of government
piazza, the so-called 'East German U-shaped political centre'. The
first building to be started was the *Staatsratsgebäude*, the GDR State
Council building that occupied the south side of the square and into
which Ulbricht ordered the Liebknecht portal to be incorporated. Yet
it was so full of bullet holes, both from 1918 and 1945, that it fell to
bits as it was moved; the neighbouring portal, which had also been
preserved, was used instead and duly assumed the function of sacred
socialist relic. Ulbricht also objected to the Prussian crown and eagle
above the main window so these were removed. The other two buildings that would complete the 'U' would follow some years later.[30]

On Museumsinsel, the Pergamon, the now renamed Bode and
Alte Museums were all eventually reopened. Artefacts that had
been stored for safety during the war in the west tended to end up
in the new West Berlin museums when they were brought back from
Wiesbaden and Celle in 1956, while some of those taken by the

Soviets were eventually returned to Museumsinsel in 1958. The fate of the Neues Museum, which had been very badly damaged, hung in the balance. It was still a shell when in 1963 the First Secretary of the Berlin SED, Paul Verner, suggested it be demolished and replaced with a wholesome socialist building. In one of his rare constructive acts, Ulbricht blocked that idea and so the old building was slowly restored, although it only finally reopened in 2009 when Nefertiti's head, which had been stored in the West and kept there after 1945, was returned.

The Brandenburg Gate, which now stood exactly on the boundary between the Soviet and British sectors, also presented a problem. Even Goebbels had not dared to remove the Quadriga, fearing that to do so would be seen as giving in to the Allied bombing. It was subsequently badly damaged in a raid but the Nazis had taken the precaution of having a plaster cast made. It was decided, in one of the very few incidents of East–West cooperation, that the East would have the gate itself repaired while the West would recast the Quadriga. This they duly did, leaving it for the East to erect in 1958. Before they put it up, and to the fury of the West, the Easterners cut off the Prussian Eagle from the goddess's staff and the Iron Cross out of the wreath; depiction of the Iron Cross had been banned in the GDR. From 1958 the goddess therefore presided over the renovated gate minus both eagle and Iron Cross. She was, the GDR announced, now a symbol of world peace.

There was some other limited restoration of Prussian royal monuments. Wilhelm Pieck installed himself in Schönhausen, as president, living in the charming rooms used by Frederick the Great's wife, Elisabeth Christine, in her happy widowhood. Rather incongruously with the beautiful eighteenth-century wallpapers and sweet portraits of her young ladies-in-waiting, he introduced heavy, garish, neo-rococo decoration and furniture that was so beloved of totalitarian regimes. He used the panelled Cedar Room as his personal cinema, which may explain the origin of the GDR's obsession with the heavy panelling they would replicate in so many of their official buildings. There was also a suite for visiting VIPs, heavily bugged and with some very uncomfortable rooms and a quite horrible purple bathroom. Once Pieck died in 1960, Ulbricht took over the role of president himself, so Schönhausen's main function was as official guest house. Initially the other GDR leaders lived clustered around Schönhausen in Pankow until, badly frightened in 1953, they removed themselves to the safety of the Waldsiedlung colony.

The GDR also had to confront the mass destruction on the city's outskirts and particularly the lack of housing. Ulbricht conceived the idea of rebuilding the Große Frankfurter Straße – still in ruins after serving as 3rd Shock Army's main axis – as a showpiece of the new republic. Two kilometres long, and renamed as Stalin Allee (later tactfully changed to Karl-Marx-Allee after Khrushchev's denunciation of Stalin), it was on this project that the 1953 workers were employed when they downed tools over the revised work norms. The result was a wide road, the main highway to the east, lined with seven- to ten-storey blocks, inspired by the Stalinist style in Moscow – featureless, massive, utilitarian but still strangely impressive as they ran in a straight line down to the Frankfurter Tor. Construction, which started in the east and worked west, took ten years, but by 1960 Ulbricht's scheme was complete. As much a political as an architectural statement, it was nevertheless functional. Driving along it today, perhaps what is most noticeable is that where the great blocks finish and the remains of the old buildings start, most still have visible 1945 bullet holes.

The problem West Berlin had with its rebuilding was that it had no centre. Isherwood had remarked that in the 1930s Berlin had two centres: the old political centre in Mitte and the artistic centre at the eastern end of the Ku'damm around the Gedächtniskirche. With the politicians now installed in the rather faceless Schöneberg town hall, it was this second area that came as close to a centre as the West could muster. The Reichstag presented a similar problem to the West as the Berliner Schloss had to the East. It could not revert to its original purpose, with the German Parliament, the Bundestag, meeting far to the west, in Bonn, yet it could not really just be left as a ruin. That was, however, exactly what happened. In 1961 limited restoration work was undertaken, and the building later became a permanent exhibition of German history, *Fragen an die deutsche Geschichte,* which was well constructed but included little on the GDR. Opposite, the very badly damaged Kroll Opera House was pulled down in 1951.

Part of its vacated site would be used for one of West Berlin's most eye-catching projects, the Kongresshalle. The airlift, and the fact that Berlin was now the front line in the Cold War, meant a special bond was developing between the city and the USA. The Americans marked this by giving Berliners a 1,200-seat hall, designed by Hugh Stubbins, which was opened in 1957. Known as the 'Pregnant Oyster' because of its shape, it was a landmark building funded largely due to the efforts of John Foster Dulles, US Secretary of State from 1953 to 1959, and his sister Eleanor, both of whom formed a particular attachment to the city. The main road on which the hall was built, the old An den Zelten (to the tents), was renamed John-Foster-Dulles-Allee, which is rather a pity as the old link to the tents where Berliners bought refreshments in the Tiergarten was lost. The building was designed so it could be seen from the east and, when in the 1960s the Bonn Bundestag did meet in Berlin, to undisguised Soviet fury they did so in the Kongresshalle. There was a minor mishap when its roof collapsed in 1980 but, now fully repaired, it is called the Haus de Kulturen der Welt and is used for events and exhibitions. The Americans had also substantially helped to open the Free University of Berlin in Dahlem, as early as 1948, persuaded by students who could not face the Soviet control at the Humboldt, while the British facilitated converting the *Technische Hochschule* (the technical high school) in Charlottenburg into the Technical University.

A new complex of buildings associated with the arts, the *Kulturforum*, also began to take shape immediately west of Potsdamer Platz, which, in the 1950s was something of a no man's land bordering so closely on the Soviet zone. The idea of the Kulturforum was that it would be West Berlin's answer to Museumsinsel, and a whole range of venues was planned. Hans

Scharoun's Philharmonie building was started in 1960 and became for many a symbol of a new and forward-looking city. It wasn't to everyone's taste. Gerda Kirstaedter, whose great-grandparents had originally built their house beside the Matthäus-Kirche regretted that, although the church was rebuilt after the war, Scharoun's building made the 'area look bleak' as all the old houses were demolished and she thought that the 'newly built Philharmonie' was 'a strange building that looks like a tent'. Music lovers, however, pointed to its superb acoustics, and Herbert von Karajan opened it in October 1963 conducting Beethoven's Ninth. Von Karajan – like Furtwängler, whom he had succeeded as the Philharmonic's principal conductor in 1956 – was accused of supporting the Nazis to further his musical career. Again, like Furtwängler, he was acquitted by a tribunal and soon the quality of his music would make people concentrate on what he was now doing with Berlin's primary orchestra rather than on his past. He would remain the principal conductor until 1989, his name always associated with his adopted city. The Deutsche Oper west of the Tiergarten was rebuilt too, opening in 1961 so that West Berlin also had an opera house. Mies van der Rohe's new national gallery was opened in 1968. Other buildings would take longer but by the 1980s the Kulturforum would include, among others, the Gemäldegalerie, the Kunstgewerbe Museum and the Staatsbibliothek.

The priority in the West, as in the East, was housing. The Hansaviertel – the old Hanseatic Quarter in the bend in the Spree north of the Tiergarten – had been almost completely destroyed by bombing in 1943. In 1952 the city announced an international competition to rebuild it so that by 1957, when the *Interbau* exhibition was held, they were able to show off the results: an impressive range of buildings by a collection of the world's leading architects. It was a clever and novel way of shaping the city's development and, as in the 1870s, this surge in construction served to accelerate other economic activity. The same year, 1957, the 100,000th government-funded new apartment was opened.

A British visitor to Berlin in 1945 thought the city smelled of 'death and dust'. Returning in 1949, he thought 'a real Berlin essence had re-established itself, a mixture of stale diesel oil, cheap cigars, the unwashed and the sauerkrautish odour of thousands of tenements, soot, pungent perfume, beer and, oddly enough, leather.' In 1945–6 he could scarcely recall a flower, but by 1949 there were flowers everywhere: in the Tiergarten, among the still-gutted houses, in countless window boxes, in front of shops, 'in brilliant finery on roof-gardens. In truth there were far fewer flowers in Berlin than in Paris or Rome then, but they were so much more welcome' as they were a sign of hope. By 1960 confidence in the future, however weak it may have been in the dark days after the war, had been at least in part redeemed but only for West Berliners. For those in the East the next three decades would still be purgatory.[31]

CHAPTER ELEVEN

1961–1989

*'All free men, wherever they may live, are
citizens of Berlin, and therefore, as a free man,
I take pride in the words Ich bin ein Berliner'*

JOHN F. KENNEDY, President of USA, 1963

By 1958 Ulbricht was feeling secure. The Soviets had suppressed the 1956 revolt in Hungary with a similar brutality to that which they had used in East Berlin, and Nikita Khrushchev was firmly in control in Moscow. On 27 October 1958 Ulbricht made a speech strongly attacking the West and described the whole of Berlin as part of the GDR. The West must now, he insisted, recognise and sign a treaty with the GDR. On 10 November Khrushchev took up the refrain in Moscow, making another attempt to force the Allies to leave. He gave the USA, Britain and France an ultimatum to evacuate their forces within six months. The reaction in West Berlin was, in the 7 December elections, to choose the strongly anti-Soviet Willy Brandt as mayor by a huge majority. Brandt's SPD won seventy-eight seats to the CDU's fifty-five; the Free Democrats, who advocated a softer line, were wiped out. Brandt then formed a coalition with the CDU so that there was in effect no opposition. Brandt himself would go on to become, in the tradition established by Reuter, one of West Berlin's two great post-war leaders.

Brandt, whose real name was Herbert Karl Frahm, was from an impoverished background in Lübeck. Joining the small and subsequently politically irrelevant Socialist Workers Party, which pitched its message somewhere between the SPD and the KPD, the young Brandt was soon attracting attention for his outspoken political speeches particularly attacking the Nazis. Fearing arrest, in 1933 he was smuggled across the Baltic to Norway, where he learned Norwegian and joined the Norwegian army, taking the name Brandt to avoid detection. When the Nazis invaded Norway, he was smuggled out again, this time to Sweden. When the war ended he returned to Germany as a reporter to cover the Nuremberg trials and then, as a major in the Norwegian army, was posted to Berlin as a military press officer. Re-establishing himself as a German, in the face of some criticism for his wartime behaviour, he allied himself closely to Reuter and the SPD and was seen by many as Reuter's heir presumptive. He did not succeed him directly but in August 1957 he became mayor. Brandt was good-looking, charming, charismatic and, much as Reuter had done, came to be seen as the personification of West Berlin's struggle during the difficult years ahead.

And they were going to be very difficult years indeed. Through the mediation of British Prime Minister Harold Macmillan, President Eisenhower managed to calm Khrushchev down and get him to the USA for talks in 1959, but the crisis remained unresolved when a new American president, John F. Kennedy, was elected in 1960. Allied forces remained in the city but the Soviets were still demanding their removal. In June 1961 – two months after the Bay of Pigs, when the USA had tried and failed to get rid of Castro's regime in Cuba and which had not gone well for Kennedy – he met Khrushchev in Vienna. Khrushchev appears to have thought he could bully the new president into submission. The summit went badly and when Khrushchev returned home he announced a treaty with the GDR effectively terminating any third-party occupation rights in Berlin. Kennedy retaliated by saying that anything interfering with

American access to West Berlin would be regarded as an act of war. He announced a $3.25 billion increase in defence spending and the addition of a further 200,000 troops to the US armed forces, at the same time encouraging NATO allies to do the same thing. 'Berlin', Kennedy said, 'had now become – as never before – the great testing place of Western courage and will, a focal point where our solemn commitments stretching back over the years since 1945, and Soviet ambitions now meet in basic confrontation.'[1] There was thought to be a genuine risk of war.

The real problem, unstated by Khrushchev and Ulbricht, was that the GDR continued to haemorrhage people, particularly the able young generation who were vital to the country's future. It is estimated that at least 2.5 million East Germans had emigrated west by 1961, a sixth of the entire population, and it is possible that the actual figure was considerably higher; upper estimates are nearer 3.5 million. The aftermath of 1953 had led to a huge exodus of 400,000, dropping to 290,000 in 1954 but rising again in 1955–7. By 1959 it had 'stabilised' at around 250,000.[2] At the SED congress in 1958 Ulbricht had boasted that the GDR would overtake the FRG in the production of food and consumer goods, and Khrushchev had declared that the USSR's economy would overtake the USA's. Ulbricht's claim could hardly be fulfilled with no skilled workforce. The exodus was also a very visible sign of the GDR's weakness. The SED could say that *Republikflucht* 'leaving the GDR is an act of political and moral backwardness and depravity' but, with life becoming evidently more attractive in the West by the day, that is exactly what people did. Having failed to call the Allies' bluff, and unwilling to risk war over Berlin, Khrushchev and Ulbricht had to think of an alternative.

On 15 June 1961 Ulbricht made another speech in which he said the GDR had no intention of blocking off the border between East and West Berlin. '*Nieman,*' he said, '*hat ein Absicht ein Mauer zu errichte*' (no one has any intention of building a wall).[3] However, he went on to say that when the treaty with the USSR was signed, the GDR would assume control of all land and air routes into his envisaged 'free Berlin'. Berliners now being wise to Ulbricht, this caused an immediate increase in refugees: 19,000 left that month and 30,415 in July. More than half of these were under twenty-five. Ulbricht introduced new restrictions on East Germans travelling into East Berlin and tough new measures on the boundary itself but it did little good. A further 21,828 followed in the first twelve days of August. It was clear the GDR had to do something, and Ulbricht was finalising exactly what that would be.

Operation Rose (as sealing the Berlin border and building the Berlin Wall was called) was planned very efficiently by Erich Honecker, a forty-nine-year-old Saarlander who was Secretary for Security in the GDR politburo. Honecker was a lifelong communist, as his coal miner father had been before him. A member of the KPD in the 1920s, he had been imprisoned by the Nazis in 1937 for treason in the notorious Görden prison near Berlin and was lucky to survive. He was quickly released by the Soviets and pointed out to Ulbricht as a reliable official, so that he was promoted to head of the SED youth committee and became a member of the SED Party Committee while still relatively young. Honecker was close to Ulbricht and was seen very much as his first lieutenant in the same way as Brandt was to Reuter.

Operation Rose would be Honecker's big test and one he passed so successfully that his position as heir apparent became unquestioned. It was not easy to seal off half of a large modern city, especially one where significant parts were still in ruins. The preparation for Operation Rose was complex, involving co-ordinating the Soviet army, the GDR's own *Nationale Volksarmee* (the National People's Army), the *Volkspolizei* (the police), the *Grenzers* (the border guards), the *Betriebskampfgruppen* (factory fighting units – a strange group of organisations peculiar to the GDR), and the *Freie Deutsche Jugend* (the GDR Youth Movement), all while maintaining strict secrecy. Had plans leaked, the likelihood is there would have been a mass border-crossing attempt. Inevitably, though, the movement of so many men and so much building material (which required 400 lorries) drew attention, and the usual Soviet excuse that it was just an exercise seemed a little hollow. GDR units would be engaged in the actual construction of the Wall while two Soviet divisions, the 1st and 8th Motor Rifle divisions would form a second line behind the construction task force to ensure there was no chance of the events of 1953 repeating themselves.

Careful as Honecker was, the warning signs should have been more obvious to the West. Kennedy himself had said in July that he was certain Ulbricht would seal off the border. Ulbricht had been to Moscow in early August to get final approval from Khrushchev, and the liaison officers from the American, British and French headquarters to the GSFG (the Group of Soviet Forces Germany) were surprised when they paid a routine call to GSFG headquarters at Wünsdorf on 10 August to be met not by General Yaubovski as normal but by one of the conquerors of Berlin in 1945, Marshal Koniev. He had been brought out of retirement to make the point that the Soviets were taking things seriously. Koniev appeared to be much enjoying his new role and the impact his appearance had on the confused allies – even more so when he assured them that, despite considerable GSFG activity, there was no threat to West Berlin. In East Berlin Ulbricht and Honecker had restricted the knowledge of what he was planning to the politburo and on 12 August Ulbricht summoned other senior government officials to a garden party in a house that had once belonged to Göring's huntsman, *Haus zu den Birken* (the Birch House), at Döllnsee beyond Wandlitz. After supper had been served, Ulbricht gathered his guests together and explained what was about to happen but no one was allowed to leave until the border closure had actually started. No one demurred.

The first sign visible to Berliners that something was happening was when, early on 13 August 1961, the S-Bahn trains from East to West Berlin stopped and the passengers were turned out. West Berliners were allowed to continue by foot but all East Berliners were sent back. As they walked back they saw long columns of *Nationale Volksarmee* vehicles, lorries loaded with wire and concrete posts. At 1 a.m. the sealing operation began so that by 4 a.m. a line of barbed-wire coils supported on concrete posts ran for 43 kilometres from Waltersdorfer Chaussee in the south, where Neukölln in the American sector bordered Treptow in the Soviet sector, to the point where French-controlled Reinickendorf and Soviet Pankow joined the GDR border in the north.

The reaction in the West was initially muted. Willy Brandt was on a train between Nuremberg and Kiel, where he was campaigning to be elected as Chancellor in Bonn, when he heard. Flying directly to Berlin, he demanded that the Allies immediately deploy troops along the Wall but they hesitated. To be fair, there was very little they could do and there was some relief that the routes between West Berlin and the FRG had not been blocked off as well, as they had in the past and as had been implied by Khrushchev's initial threat. Brandt was furious, admonishing the western military commanders, and writing a very strong letter to President Kennedy demanding American troop reinforcement. Berliners, he said, now doubted the Three Powers' ability to act resolutely, and their inactivity and defensiveness would lead to a crisis of confidence. Kennedy was initially put out. 'Who does he think he is?' he demanded, but the following weekend he sent Vice President Lyndon Johnson and the Berliners' favourite American General, the hero of the airlift Lucius Clay, to welcome publicly a 1,500-strong American Battle Group that was driven up in full operational mode from the FRG. The Soviets did all they could to delay it, and it seemed at one point that it might be taken as a hostile act, but the choice of a battle group was a clever one. Far too small to be taken as a serious military threat, it soon became clear that it was a symbolic reinforcement, and its commander, Colonel Johns – having been driven mad by obfuscating Soviet officers all day – finally drove his vehicles into the Dreilinden Checkpoint (Checkpoint Bravo as it would come to be known), where the autobahn from Helmstedt entered the West Berlin perimeter, and made his public rendezvous with the Vice President.

West Berliners, furious at the GDR's action, were more active. Groups had been demonstrating at the Wall for several days, throwing stones at the construction teams and shouting at watching East Berliners to make a run for it before it was too late. Many did and were not, at that stage, shot at. The sudden closure of the border had, though, left many families divided and people's lives dramatically altered. Adolf Knackstedt, a German American working for US intelligence in Berlin, remembered that:

'Never have I seen so many tears flowing down the cheeks of grown-up men and women as I saw in those days. Mothers, fathers, grandparents, kids, as well as curiosity seekers stood at the border, looking over the newly constructed fences and barriers in the hope of seeing or being able to communicate with a relative or friend. Somewhere along the southeastern border of the city, in the borough of Neukölln, I ran across a young couple who had just gotten married, with the bride still in her white wedding gown, standing to the west side of the fence and waving to her mother and father, who were standing approximately one hundred metres on the other side of the barriers, guarded by indifferent and aggressive-looking border guards ... The parents were hindered from attending the wedding of their daughter ... A little boy standing to our side asked an East German border guard to give the flowers he was holding to his grandmother who was standing approximately fifty metres from the fence in the east. An East German officer took the flowers and, instead of passing them to the old grandmother who was leaning against a building and sobbing, he dropped them on the ground and stomped on them.'[4]

Berliners generally hated the Saxons who had been brought in as border guards to replace the native Berliners, who had proved too soft and sympathetic to their own kind. The Saxons were considered politically reliable but Berliners found them rude and aggressive. Gisela Bilski recalled that she and her friends used to call them the 'Fifth Occupying Power'. They thought they were 'mouthy' and came specifically to take it out on Berliners. Ancient hatreds died hard.

There were also East Berliners, happy living in the Soviet Zone, who now found themselves trapped in the West. Nineteen-year-old Doris Kohn lived in the East but went to school in the West. On

Saturday 12 August she had gone to a family party in the West at her sister's. The U-Bahn was shut while they were there so they could not get home. They were taken to a refugee camp, much to the distress of her mother who had already lost everything once when she had been bombed out in the war, although Doris was quite happy as she knew that her exam results from her West Berlin school would not have been recognised in the GDR.[5]

Now that access was becoming impossible, East Berliners who had been working in the West lost their jobs. Initially West Berliners were still able to cross to the East, although many were understandably reluctant to do so, but on 23 August Ulbricht announced that in future they would need visas issued by the GDR and that he would set up two visa agencies in West Berlin to that end. Brandt rejected that out of hand. He had no choice. To do so would have been to have accepted the legitimacy not only of the GDR regime but also of the erection of the Wall. The result was that no West Berliners could then visit the East either, causing further misery to families. Then on 24 August came the first fatality, a twenty-four-year-old tailor called Günter Litfin who had been living in Weißensee in the East but working in the West. He had bought a flat in the West and was on the point of moving when the border was sealed. Determined still to go ahead, he had identified what he thought was a weak point in the Wall, on the Humboldthafen, the basin where the Berlin Spandau Canal joins the Spree. Spotted as he was about to cross the railway bridge, he dived into the water but was shot as he swam across. Five days later Roland Hoff was shot trying to swim across the Teltow canal. They were the first of sixteen deaths that year.

The most tense period that autumn came on 22 October when an American diplomat called Lightner was stopped by the VoPos, the *Volkspolizei*, who demanded to see his papers as he was crossing at Checkpoint Charlie to go to the opera. This was something he was entitled to do but, as an American, he could only be stopped by the Soviets, not the East Germans. It was a classic trial of strength by the VoPos but they had reckoned without the determination of Lightner and General Clay. When the officers insisted on seeing his papers, Lightner reversed back to the checkpoint and found Clay had mobilised a full platoon of US soldiers. The VoPos stood aside. Emboldened with his new escort, Lightner drove around the Soviet sector not once but twice, complete with some rather nervous American soldiers. The Soviets predictably complained strongly but Clay wanted to prove his point. He now sent two US officers in civilian clothes across and, when the VoPos again demanded their papers, he responded by deploying not only infantry but a squadron of battle tanks that sat ostentatiously at Checkpoint Charlie, their barrels pointing down Friedrichstraße directly at the GDR check-point. In response the Soviets deployed their own tanks so that by the next day there were two columns of armour facing each other. The situation was now dangerous and Kennedy and Khrushchev were both briefed. The Americans were not sure whether the T-34s they were facing were Soviet or East German. In an act of astonish-ing bravery, two US officers drove across the border, climbed into one of the tanks while the crew had been dismounted for a briefing, and brought back a copy of a Soviet newspaper to prove they were indeed Russian. On 28 October – after background talks between Washington and Moscow – Koniev, who was still in command of GSFG, started to withdraw his tanks one by one; the Americans did the same. Gradually the situation was diffused but it had been close. From that moment until 1989, the Allies refused to show their papers when the VoPos demanded to see them.

During the autumn of 1961, what had started as a simple line of barbed wire became a much more sophisticated and sinister obs-tacle belt, so that crossing it became increasingly difficult. In August 25,605 people still managed to cross – many of them soldiers, border guards and VoPos – but that had reduced to 2,420 by December; soon thereafter it would reduce to a trickle. Seen from the West, the Wall looked like a high concrete barricade with a pipe running along the top to make it difficult to climb over. The Wall itself was built just behind the actual border so that a narrow strip of footpath in front of it was technically East German territory, allowing the border guards to clean off the inevitable graffiti. Behind it, on the eastern side, there was a floodlit 'death strip', a cleared area with concrete watchtowers and behind them rows of 'Czech Hedgehogs', anti-vehicle caltrops. Behind them again were one or two high electric fences and another wall. Work on the Wall went on almost constantly, making it more impenetrable year by year, and it was still being worked on in 1989. It cut off sixty-two streets and 131 roads, twelve S-Bahn and U-Bahn lines, canals, rivers and sewers.

In places Honecker's plan had to compromise where the district boundaries ran close to houses, so that in Bernauer Straße (the border between Wedding and Mitte) the houses formed the eastern boundary while their pavement outside was the western. Consequently, Honecker's men blocked off the doorways and ground-floor windows, thus trapping the residents in the East; they then discovered that people were lowering themselves from the upstairs windows. Two people died trying to do so. On 19 August Rudolf Urban fell as he was trying to climb down and on 22 August, fifty-nine-year-old Ida Siekermann jumped and fell. Soon the upstairs windows were bricked up too, as was the west door of the Versöhnungskirche (the Church of the Reconciliation), which bridged the border line with its main door in the West but is chancel door in the East. The GDR border guards used the spire as an observation post until they finally blew it up in 1985. There is now a rather effective modern chapel on the site, built of clay but incorporating much of the rubble from the old church and forming part of the Bernauer Straße Visitors' Centre. In Neukölln the opposite applied; there was a street with houses in the West but the pavement in the East, so the Wall was built directly in front of the houses and blocking their light. That traditional Berlin attention to detail was never far away.

Among the outrage in West Berlin, there was particular anger at Honecker's walling-off the Brandenburg Gate, which now looked ugly and threatening. From the West you could see the top and the Quadriga but facing you was a blank wall of concrete blocks. The great Berlin vista from the Tiergarten through the Gate and down the Unter den Linden was now interrupted both psychologically and physically by this slab-like excrescence. The frustration people felt at this interruption was expressed in a bronze named *'Der Rufer'* (the crier) by the sculptor Gerhard Marcks. The bronze figure stands almost opposite the Soviet War Memorial from where he could look over the Wall, his hands raised to his mouth, shouting 'Peace'. The inspiration came from Petrarch, who wrote that he wandered the world crying 'Peace, Peace, Peace'. *Der Rufer* stands there still. At least the Wall in front of the Brandenburg Gate could be moved in the future; Honecker's bulldozing of the Potsdamer Platz could not be so easily made good. Schinkel's colonnade for the Potsdamer Tor, and what was left of Kempinski's *Haus Vaterland* were bulldozed, as was a large area including the Leipziger Platz. What had been very much a popular centre was now an open, barren space framed on the east side by the Wall. It looked horrible and became for many Berliners the place in their city that symbolised the desolation the Wall had caused. It would also become the place where busloads of foreign tourists would come to gaze at the barrier between the free world and the Communist bloc; it was also the place that took them as near as they could get to the site of Hitler's bunker. There was a common myth that it was still there.

Initially Honecker had planned twelve border crossing points but this was soon reduced to seven. Four of these could, in theory, be used by West Berliners. Running from south to north, these were Sonnenallee between Neukölln and Treptow; Oberbaumbrücke between Kreuzberg and Mitte; Invalidenstraße between Tiergarten and Mitte; and the nearby Chausseestraße. Two were reserved for West German citizens, in Prinzenstraße and Bornholmerstraße, although this latter crossing could also be used by West Berliners, while Allied military personnel, diplomats and foreigners had to use the infamous Checkpoint Charlie on Friedrichstraße. There was also a crossing point at Friedrichstraße station, a complicated rail hub where S-Bahn and U-Bahn lines intersected normal rail services. The checkpoint there was known as the *Tränenpalast,* the palace of tears, after the many sad farewells that took place there as East Berliners said goodbye to their Western families. It would become well known as it featured in so many spy stories. The Wall had also cut West

Berlin off from the GDR. A further 112 kilometres encircled the Allied sectors; as important for the Western Allies, and for West Germans visiting West Berlin, was that the three autobahn transit routes, to Hamburg, Helmstedt and the south were kept open as were the rail transit routes that entered West Berlin at Griebnitzsee near Potsdam and Spandau.

The escapes over the Wall have become a Berlin legend in themselves. Many were dramatic, clever, daring and caught the imagination of the international press, which should not disguise the fact that they were nearly all driven by desperately sad circumstances or ended in serious injury or death. Despite Honecker's elaborate precautions and the veritable fortification that the Wall became, there were 5,043 successful escapees of whom 565 were members of the security services or armed forces. Approximately 5,000 more were arrested in the attempt and at least eighty lost their lives. The GDR later admitted to its security services having fired on escapees more than 1,500 times. There is an active museum by Checkpoint Charlie that shows how some of these escape attempts were set up. The ingenuity is extraordinary, from mini submarines to fake coffins to several tunnels; all have their share of pathos. One of the most famous early successful attempts was by an eighteen-year-old GDR soldier, Conrad Schumann, who found himself on duty on 15 August guarding the workers constructing the Wall in Bernauer Straße. He hesitated for an hour, debating whether to make a run for it or not, watched by a photographer on the western side called Peter Leibing. Leibing had called up a West German police car and kept shouting to Schumann to go for it. Finally, Schumann decided to do just that. 'My nerves were at breaking point,' he said afterwards. 'I was very afraid. I took off, jumped, and into the car . . . in three, four seconds, it was all over.' Leibing's photograph became instantly famous. Afterwards the Stasi went after Schumann's family, trying to lure him back so he could be punished. It was a story that would have a very unhappy ending, as we will see later.

A more brutal episode, and one that caused widespread international revulsion, took place in Kreuzberg on 17 August 1962. Two

young construction workers with family in the West had been talking
about escaping for some time, and decided to attempt to cross by
hiding in an upstairs room then jumping down into the 'death strip'
while the border guards' attention was diverted. Helmut Kulbeik
made it but Peter Fechter was hit in the hip and fell wounded into
the death strip immediately in front of the Wall. Despite there being
lots of GDR security personnel about, no one went to his assistance
and after an hour he bled to death, crying for help as they watched.
The dreadful scene was well recorded by media in the West.

For those who did make it across – and for the many deported
because the GDR didn't want them, including many pensioners –
the first they saw of their new home was the refugee centre at
Marienfelde in Tempelhof, originally opened to cope with the mass
outflow after 17 June 1953. Marienfelde's job was to take the refugees in, look after them, try to screen out the endless GDR spies,
issue them with their prized West German identity card, and then
process people as quickly as possible on to the FRG. They managed
this with considerable efficiency given that at peak times they were
dealing with well over 1,000 per day. One of their busiest days
ever was on 12 August 1961, the day before the border was closed,
when they handled 2,662. Many refugees wanted to stay in Berlin,
their home, but they were usually only allowed to do so if they were
from the city itself. Those from the wider GDR were pressurised
to move on to the FRG. However well the West Berlin economy
may have been doing, it simply could not absorb numbers on that
scale. Exceptions were made for various skilled trades, and several
ingenious East Berliners found themselves claiming to be expert
technicians in crafts they knew very little about.

By 1962 the Berlin Wall had become the international recognised
symbol of the Cold War, and as the United States and the Soviet
Union faced off against each other around the world, it was Berlin
that epitomised for many just what the loss of freedom meant.
Kennedy visited in 1963, escorted by 'a smiling Brandt and a sour-
faced Adenauer',[6] and on 26 June in front of Schöneberg town
hall he made his famous speech to a crowd estimated at 300,000

to show American solidarity with Berliners. It was a very strong speech. 'There are many people in the world,' Kennedy said, 'who really don't understand, or say they don't, what is the great issue between the free world and the Communist world. Let them come to Berlin ... All free men, wherever they may live, are citizens of Berlin, and, therefore, as a free man, I take pride in the words *Ich bin ein Berliner*.' He received rapturous applause. The oration was only slightly spoiled by his concluding words, which some interpreted as 'I am a jam doughnut' ('*ein Berliner*' being what outsiders called a *Pfannkuchen*, a Berlin doughnut speciality) rather than '*Ich bin Berliner*'. But it didn't really matter and his gesture of solidarity was immensely popular.[7] Khrushchev visited East Berlin a week later and made a worthy speech about creating a single socialist state in Germany; it failed to have quite the same impact.

~

From Ulbricht's perspective, the erection of the Wall, however flat Khrushchev's reception may have been, was a major success. There had been very little unrest in East Berlin and certainly no mass protests. Secure behind his new barrier, he could now concentrate on building the GDR'S economy, safe in the knowledge that his workers could no longer flee west – or at least if they did they would be shot or arrested. The escapes did continue, one of the most spectacular being in October 1964 when fifty-seven people tunnelled their way under the Wall from Strelitzer Straße. Ulbricht attempted to turn this into a propaganda coup as a young border guard, Egon Schultz, was shot when trying to stop them; it later transpired that he was shot by one of his colleagues by accident. Miserable as the Wall made life for so many of his subjects, it did mean he was free to develop his vision of what a socialist state should be, but he could only do so if he had absolute control. For this he relied on the Stasi, possibly one of the most invasive and omnipresent internal state security services ever, though curiously rather less efficient and not quite as deadly as they liked to imagine. It was as much an organisation that spied by bureaucracy as it did by more sinister means, although it certainly employed those too. At its height the Stasi employed 91,015 full-time staff, who drew on a network of 174,000 informants embedded throughout the GDR. By 1989 they had amassed an archive that stretched for 178 kilometres and held files on 6 million people, so about a third of the GDR population. They even, rather bizarrely, held thousands of jars containing human scents. It was alleged to have been the most intensive surveillance operation of a whole population in history. What made it so unpleasant is that the Stasi placed agents in families, encouraging family members to spy on one another, in offices, factories, the army, the arts and in the government itself. They expended vast resources trying to destabilise the FRG and West Berlin in particular. It is estimated that at one time they had 3,000 agents in the West and were adept at kidnapping people even after they had fled across the border.

A favoured Stasi trick in the West was to use the 'Romeo' technique, whereby a Stasi agent would befriend a lonely female employee. One of their most successful agents at doing this was Herbert Schröter, who was sent on a language course in Paris in 1964. His brief was to pick up a West German woman who might be employed by the government in Bonn. He was remarkably successful, first seducing a young lady called Gerda who ended up working in the FRG Foreign Ministry and became a prolific Stasi spy. They lived together for nine years until she got fed up with him and turned herself in. Schröter fled back to East Berlin then went on holiday to Bulgaria and promptly tried again, this time with Karin who subsequently managed to get herself a job in the Chancellor's office in Bonn. She was eventually discovered in 1977 and imprisoned. Gerda and Karin were but two of many vulnerable young women whose lives the Stasi ruined. The Stasi's most spectacular success came in 1974 when it was revealed that Günter Guillaume, an aide who worked in Willy Brandt's office when he was Chancellor in Bonn, was also a long-standing Stasi spy. Brandt had to resign and Guillaume was sent to prison, although he was later returned to East Berlin in a spy swap. Senior Stasi members would later question whether it had been worth losing Brandt, who knew Berlin so well, and argued that the whole affair had been a mistake, but the fact that they had managed to infiltrate an agent into the highest political office in the FRG was seen by many as a significant success.

When compared to other state security services, the Stasi was enormous; even the Gestapo at its height only employed 31,000 people across all Nazi-occupied territories. The KGB in the 1960s had one officer for every 600 citizens while their Polish equivalent had one for every 1,575. Yet the Stasi were certainly not as deadly as either the Gestapo or KGB. It is estimated that 208 people were executed for political crimes in the life of the GDR – a horrific figure but small when compared to Nazi Germany or Soviet repression. It is often said that the Nazis left behind a mountain of corpses while the Stasi left behind a mountain of files and not a few broken hearts.[8]

The Stasi were not just a secret police force. They also carried out a wide range of other security duties, such as running prisons, controlling the border, issuing passports and conducting their own investigations. The organisation was run by Erich Mielke, another long-serving Communist who had joined the party in 1927. Mielke was a Berliner, born into a poor labouring family in Wedding in 1907. In 1931, probably on Ulbricht's orders, he had shot and killed two Berlin policemen, Paul Anlauf and Franz Lenck, who Ulbricht maintained had been harassing the KPD. Mielke was subsequently spirited away by the KPD to Moscow to save him from prosecution. Educated by the Soviet security establishment, he was sent to Spain during the civil war, where his job was to root out 'counter revolutionaries' from the Communist ranks. He was in France in 1939, where he was interned, and he spent an inglorious war in various labour organisations. Returning to Berlin in 1945, he worked his way rapidly to a senior position in the KPD, heading their internal policing department, and (like Honecker) was taken into Ulbricht's trusted inner circle. The Soviets were a bit suspicious of his wartime record and so took time to accept him back, but by 1957 he was confirmed as Minister of State Security, a post he occupied until 1989. Mielke, who lived a luxurious private life on a large estate where he could indulge his passion for deer stalking, saw his mission as the protection of the GDR in general and of the SED in particular.

The Stasi's two main bases in Berlin (they had more than 4,200 separate locations in the city) were their headquarters in Ruschestraße in Friedrichshain and their prison at Hohenschönhausen, both of which are now preserved as museums. The headquarters is revealing in that it shows the real banality of spying. It was, in effect, a massive filing cabinet, now well arranged to show the dirty tricks the Stasi employed. Equally absorbing is seeing Mielke's private office and quarters, which show how senior GDR functionaries were not averse to looking after themselves and are a classic example of the heavy 1960s Soviet imperialist style typical of the Eastern bloc. Hohenschönhausen is more sinister and it is, fittingly, both a museum and a memorial to those who suffered here. Most of the victims at Hohenschönhausen were political prisoners. Originally a Soviet NKVD prison set up on the site of an old Nazi factory in 1945, it was subsequently taken over by the Stasi, who cleared and cordoned off the local area as an operating base; it did not appear on maps, and was conveniently far from the centre of Berlin and therefore unobtrusive. It was where they took their victims for initial questioning and to get them to confess by using a range of violent mental and physical torture. Preserved with its cells and interrogation rooms, it is a sinister and depressing place; some of the guides who show visitors around the exhibition are former inmates.

The treatment of Walter Janka was typical of how the regime dealt with opposition. Janka was no stranger to prisons. He had been incarcerated in both Bautzen and Sachsenhausen by the Nazis for being a member of the KPD, and in France after having fought in the Spanish Civil War. After 1945 he ran a film production company and publishing house in East Berlin. When life in the USSR marginally began to relax after Stalin died, he demanded the corresponding reform of Ulbricht's strict socialist model in the GDR. Arrested by the Stasi in December 1956, after the Hungarian uprising, he spent six months in Hohenschönhausen before being convicted of forming a counter-revolutionary group and being sentenced to five years' imprisonment. He was sent to Bautzen again, but his health had been so badly damaged in Hohenschönhausen that he was granted early release and in fact survived to witness 1989. Another high-profile prisoner was Max Fechner, who had been the GDR's Minister for Justice but was sacked for announcing immunity for those who went on strike on 17 June 1953. Arrested by the Stasi, he was given an eight-year sentence for 'boycott agitation'. The actor Heinrich George, one of Berlin's best-known pre-war actors who had been in *Berlin Alexanderplatz*, was arrested by the Soviets in 1945 because he had made an anti-Semitic film, *Jud Süß*, and had allegedly appealed to Berliners to stay the course towards the end of the war. He was so badly treated and starved in Hohenschönhausen, where he lost 83 pounds, that he died a year later. Another inmate who died was the theologian Rudolf Vogel whose crime was to have baptised fifty of the Russian forced labourers he ministered to in wartime Berlin, something the Soviets viewed as a serious offence. Arrested in 1949, he died in Hohenschönhausen in 1951.

The Stasi did not regard the borders of the GDR as necessarily applying to themselves. In 1950 they lured Kurt Müller, a member of the Bundestag, to East Berlin and arrested him on suspicion of having been a Gestapo officer and of planning terrorist attacks against the USSR. Mielke himself led his brutal interrogation in Hohenschönhausen. He was subsequently convicted by a Soviet tribunal and sent to a labour camp for twenty-five years, although international pressure forced his release in 1955. Their most brazen arrest, however, was of the West Berlin lawyer Walter Linse. Linse had been investigating human rights abuses in the Soviet sector. At 7.30 a.m. on 8 July 1952 he was kidnapped by the Stasi from outside his front door in Gerichtsstraße, in the American sector, and taken to Hohenschönhausen. Handed over to the Soviets, he was sent to Moscow and executed. There is a Walter-Linse-Straße in Lichterfelde in his memory. Less well-known people also suffered there.

Wolfgang Göbel was the son of a senior Communist but had become very disillusioned with the GDR. Once he had finished his military service, where he had refused to join the SED and so could not become an officer, Göbel took himself off to live with his girlfriend's family in West Germany for three months. He returned voluntarily but was arrested and put in Hohenschönhausen. He was kept there for over two months in a shared cell with a simple wooden bench. There was 'no access to daylight, neither was there a toilet', just a bucket. 'It was very embarrassing when you had to relieve yourself, then everyone had to watch, listen, smell. It was a very severe time,' he recalled. 'I had to endure night-time interrogations, which were very hard, brutal. You were picked up at 9 p.m., then questioned all night and early in the morning you were released again, and then you were back in the cell where you were not allowed to sleep all day. If you do that for three weeks, you don't know where you are anymore. But I had the advantage that I hadn't really done anything.' Luckily he had not been through the West German refugee system so he had not been interrogated by any intelligence services. This meant he could not be convicted of military espionage, which was what the Stasi wanted and would have earned him five years in prison. Once he was released, Göbel escaped to West Berlin and did not come back. His job there, ironically, was to run the *Studio am Stacheldraht* (the barbed-wire studio), neon signs along the Wall started by West Berlin radio to try to influence the *Grenzers*, telling them they would be held to account in the future should they shoot anyone.[9]

It is important, however, not to be two-dimensional about the Stasi. Many of its officers were decent, patriotic people who saw service in its ranks as a way of improving their families' lives. Mikael Adam's father was a Stasi officer in Potsdam. Growing up in a Stasi household was difficult, he said, as everyone locally knew your father was a Stasi officer and they tended to be suspicious of you. 'When we needed to move to a new house my father went to the municipality for help but they just said, "Well, why don't you ask the Stasi to sort it out for you?" My father refused, saying it was an abuse of privilege, and ended up building a house himself. Credit for building materials then was on a ninety-nine-year payback but it was still a huge expense and undertaking.'[10] Neither were all the border guards on the Wall vindictive Saxons. Many would pass notes across to their western counterparts, usually asking for favours or money. 'Could you be so good as to pass me a pair of seamless socks over the Wall? Size nine and a half and not too bright?' was one of the stranger ones; more usual were requests for cigarettes.[11]

In the 1960s Berlin would, as the meeting point of the East and West, become the spy capital of Europe; Hollywood would also make both Friedrichstraße station and the Glienicker Brücke famous as the Bridge of Spies. The Glienicker Brücke carries the main Berlin-to-Potsdam road as it crosses the Havel between Wannsee (in the American sector) and Potsdam (in the GDR). It took its name from the attractive Glienicker Palast, on the Berlin side, built by Schinkel as a country retreat for Prince Carl, a younger son of Frederick William III. Nearby is Schloss Babelsberg, the mini Windsor Castle also built by Schinkel for William I and where Princess Vicky felt so much more at home than in the gloomy old Berliner Schloss. The border of Berlin ran down the middle of the Havel so the border between East and West was a line drawn across the centre of the bridge. In films it always appears dark and misty, conveying the prevailing atmosphere, but in fact it is one of the most beautiful places on the city's outskirts. The reason it was used for spy swaps is that Eastern checkpoint was always manned by the Soviets rather than the VoPos. The first swap was on 10 February 1962, when Gary Powers – the pilot of the U2 spy plane shot down by the Russians in 1960 – was swapped for the Soviet spy Rudolf Abel. In June 1985 it was the scene of a major swap when twenty-three American agents were released, but perhaps it was most famously used for the 1986 exchange of the human rights campaigner Anatoly Shcharansky.

Kennedy was assassinated in November 1963 and a year later Khrushchev was deposed by the more hard-line Leonid Brezhnev. As the Cold War intensified around the world, Berlin continued as the uneasy front line. The Wall was an uncomfortable fait accompli, its future now part of what happened on a wider political stage. Ulbricht was also determined to make his capital city a showcase for his socialist republic. He had been forced to conform when

Khrushchev had denounced Stalin, ordering the giant bronze of his hero in Strausberger Platz to be demolished and Stalinallee to be renamed Karl-Marx-Allee. He now also directed resources to more peaceful building projects than the Wall. The most striking example of this was the Fernsehturm (the television tower) on Alexanderplatz. The Alexanderplatz had been famous as an area of petty crime and prostitution, immortalised in Döblin's book, but Ulbricht saw it as the centrepiece of his new capital.

Demolition of war-damaged buildings had in fact created a far bigger open space, and in 1965 one of Berlin's few remaining medieval quarters, the neighbouring Fischerkiez (fishermen's quarter), had been cleared as well (which, to be fair to Ulbricht's planners, was difficult to avoid given the extent of the bomb damage). The Fernsehturm, built just behind the venerable Marienkirche, was designed to show the world what an advanced nation the GDR was. Built in the rocket style so beloved of the Soviets, at 368 metres it was the second-tallest TV tower in the world, tactfully just shorter than the Ostankino Tower in Moscow. It had a rotating restaurant with a view across 80 kilometres on a clear day. When it was opened in October 1969, however, it presented a problem for Ulbricht: its rotunda, which housed the restaurant below the spire, was constructed of stainless-steel tiles that, on sunny days, reflected the sunlight into the form of a cross. Given Ulbricht's hatred for the church, the tower was quickly nick-named 'the Pope's Revenge' or 'St Walters'. Painting the tiles failed to solve the problem, so the cross remained. Around it, where the Fischerkiez had stood, six new apartment blocks were built, together with restaurants, shops and a leisure complex creating what was, by East Berlin standards, a very desirable area. The *Centrum Warenhaus* department store became the fashionable place to shop in the GDR, a sort of East Berlin Harrods.

Ulbricht did not have long to enjoy looking at the TV tower. By 1971 he was losing the confidence of Moscow where Brezhnev was moving, admittedly slowly, towards detente and a less confronta-tional policy with the West. His economic reforms were not working, despite having now trapped his labour force, and he was seen as increasingly out of touch. On 3 May 1971 he was forced to resign by an impatient Honecker. He was allowed to live out his days with more dignity than Brezhnev had permitted Khrushchev, remaining as Chairman of the State Council and being awarded a state funeral when he died after a stroke in 1973. In September 1971 Honecker and Brandt (now Chancellor of the FRG, having handed over as Mayor of West Berlin in 1966) prepared the Four Power Agreement on Berlin, signed by the Soviets, Americans, British and French. This did not make any major changes to the overall situation but it did allow some relaxation. West Berliners and East Berliners could now telephone each other, albeit paying international rates, and access for West Berliners and West Germans to the East was made easier. The next year a treaty between the FRG and the GDR allowed each country to recognise the other and to exchange ambassadors. In 1973 the GDR subsequently took its seat at the United Nations as a nation in its own right. This was even more reason for East Berlin to be seen as a proper capital.

Honecker's main focus on building was on meeting the still serious shortage of basic housing. West Berlin had completed its 250,000th new apartment by 1964 and East Berlin was lagging far behind. Honecker prioritised building blocks from prefabricated concrete panels in the outskirts, not just in Berlin but across the GDR; they still dominate the approaches to many East German towns today. They were ugly and the apartments were very small but they were practical and they met East Berlin's need. By 1989 a third of East Berlin's population lived in three satellite cities: in Hohenschönhausen in the north-east, and Marzahn and Hellersdorf in the east. Marzahn alone had 56,000 apartments. By 1975, the city council proudly declared with its bureaucratic obsession with figures, there were 489,659 houses available and 82.2 per cent had flushing loos while 62.7 per cent had a bath or a shower, although only 20.2 per cent had central heating. Despite calls for the Honecker blocks to be flattened after 1989 because they were said to be poorly constructed and unsightly, it is hard to know how Berlin would meet its housing needs today without them.

By the early 1970s Honecker had to decide what to put in the large open space where the Berliner Schloss had stood, now a curious void in the city's heart. The *Staatsratsgebäude* (the state council building) already occupied the southern side and in 1964 a monolithic Ministry of Foreign Affairs had been put up on the western side of the river, which infuriated many as it involved demolishing what was left of Schinkel's Bauakademie. In 1973 construction started on the major Palast der Republik on the eastern side, opposite the cathedral. It was finished three years later, a rectangular, flat-roofed building in the functional communist style that had superseded Stalinist Gothic as the preferred architectural style of the Soviet bloc. It housed the People's Chamber, the rubber-stamping parliament that Ulbricht and Honecker used as pretence at democracy, a cultural centre, a restaurant, bowling alleys and a concert hall. It was said by East Berliners to be the only place that the telephones worked because they were bugged by the Stasi as was everything else, including the salts and peppers in the restaurant. It also incorporated, as did so many buildings of the early 1970s, a large amount of asbestos. The Schloßplatz itself, now the open middle of what was called 'East Germany's U-shaped political centre',[12] became a parade ground, looking across to the Lustgarten.

Life in East Berlin during the early Honecker years was not all bad, just as life in West Berlin was far from all good. Travel outside the Eastern bloc was still very difficult, almost impossible for working-age people, and those trying to escape were still being shot – another forty-nine would die before the Wall came down – but there was a realisation in the SED regime that they had to try to make the GDR a more attractive place to live and that Berlin should be the exemplar of that. 'East Berlin,' went the official line, 'is a showcase for socialism in the GDR.' It was 'a socialist consumer paradise' and 'the luxury goods shops introduced by the GDR offer high-quality clothing, cosmetics and food'. This was only partly true. There was a chain of shops selling supposedly luxury goods called *Exquisit* but they never seemed to have anything in them. A well-known Berlin joke went, 'A man walks into an Exquisit shop and asks for a pair of shoes. The shopkeeper answers "Sorry, you are in the wrong place. No shoes are available next door." [13]

'The government', the official line continued, 'also gives special attention to culture. Numerous theatres, cinemas and museums turn East Berlin into the cultural capital of the GDR.' [14] This may have been wishful thinking but many in the GDR believed it. For those East Berliners born in the 1930s and 1940s, life by the 1970s was as stable as they had known it. They had jobs, enough food and most had houses. They were no longer hungry, there was an adequate medical system in place and, though life may have been dull, they had not known anything else. 'In 1971 my parents, who had just fallen in love, travelled from Thuringia to East Berlin,' wrote Babette Stäbler-Kirsten:

'It was shortly after their *Abitur* examinations [roughly the German equivalent of A-Levels in the UK] and my father had a job interview with *Interflug* [the GDR's airline]. Together they enthusiastically explored the capital. The highlight was a visit to the restaurant in the recently opened Television Tower (Fernsehturm). They had to reserve seats for the Tele-Café in advance, and their stay 207 meters in the air was limited to exactly one hour. During that time the restaurant revolved 360 degrees, circling a piano player who provided musical accompaniment.'

The visit was the high point of their lives; they kept the menu as a souvenir and gave it to Babette in 2017. [15]

The Berlin staples of football, pubs and music were all as available in the East as the West. Football rivalry in the GDR was fierce and the competition between teams in the *Oberliga* (the league) was intense. The teams' names may have been a bit socialist, but the rivalry between BFC Dynamo and Number 1 FC Union often resulted in hooligan-led violence of which the VoPos seemed surprisingly tolerant. Of all the crimes laid at Mielke's door, the one for which he was never forgiven was that, furious that Dynamo Dresden had beaten his beloved BFC Dynamo to win the national championships for a third time in 1978, he was alleged to have sent Stasi agents to infiltrate the Dresden team and come up with charges against three of their key players. BFC Dynamo then won the next ten championships. East Berlin pub culture, and loyalty to the local *Kneipe*, was also not something the Stasi, who generally acted against family businesses, interfered with. Many of Berlin's oldest pubs, like the *Metzer Eck* in Prenzlauer Berg, continued to be managed by the families who owned them; the *Metzer Eck* is still run by the Falkner family today. The East also built up its own zoo, in Friedrichsfelde. Three Berlin bears – Nante, Jette und Julchen who lived in a special bear pit in Köllnischer Park from 1953 right up until 1979 – became the popular symbols of the city, seen as fellow sufferers, and found themselves made into endless souvenirs as toys and chocolates.

Intellectual life and the arts were more difficult and that was an area in which the Stasi took a particular interest. They would have liked all artistic talent to be channelled through the *Haus der jungen Talente* (the house of young talents) at the Podewil Palace, which, despite its socialist name, attracted a range of able musicians and performers but was never going to lure those who could not stomach contributing to something so obviously under government control. The real cultural life in East Berlin took place in private, where authors and artists could express their revulsion at the regime. Once West Berliners were allowed to visit, many groups of friends formed who met in what they remember as a highly charged atmosphere, made all the more exciting given the ever-present Stasi threat. Irene Kempff, the daughter of a West German diplomat and therefore of interest to the Stasi, thought she was often followed when she would travel over regularly to play music, read aloud, drink and talk with a wide group of friends. 'Sitting on the floor, drinking every last drop of beer out of cans, it was an exciting atmosphere,' she recalls. 'There was something in that atmosphere of oppression and stupidity of authority that brought people together and made them value things, the written word, a piece of music, each other so much more than in West Berlin which we found degenerate by contrast. People had it too easy there.'[16]

Groups like these later produced the extraordinarily influential satirical *Mikado* magazine. It never ran to more than 100 copies for each of its twelve editions produced between 1983 and 1987, but they were seen and circulated widely. It had striking covers drawn by well-known artists and its content was focused on life in a dictatorship. There was a sense of deep friendship, of shared values, of honesty and truth in adversity among many such groups in East Berlin; many who participated find they miss that very special atmosphere in the reunited city today. Yet the Stasi penetrated several of these informal cultural groups by using their informant network. One of the most active groups was in Prenzlauer Berg into which the Stasi managed to infiltrate two informants, Sascha Anderson and Rainer Schedlinski, during the 1980s. Their brief was to exploit quarrels and differences of opinion, to persuade the 'hostile groups', as the Stasi termed them, to write less about politics and to report back on individuals. How effective these operations were is open to question. The Prenzlauer Group was in fact considered not to be very political but that may have been as much a matter of choice as of clandestine Stasi influence, several of them believing a more subtle way to influence events was via more mainstream writing. It is perhaps another example of the Stasi going to great lengths but achieving very little.[17]

The Church was also a strong supporter of freedom of thought. Churches looked after those written off by the regime, those who had tried to leave the country, or 'punks' – who were beyond the comprehension of the authorities – by giving them jobs and shelter. The Erlöserkirche (The Church of the Redeemer) in Mitte became particularly well known for its defiant approach and for holding services that included music and sermons that stretched the limits of what was allowed. Pietism, which had served Berlin so well in the eighteenth and nineteenth centuries but had arguably failed Berliners in the first half of the twentieth century, now seemed to come back into its own.

Irene Kempff's view of West Berlin was widely shared. Despite what angry and envious young East Berliners thought, the Wall created almost as many problems for the West as it did for the East.

First, it made West Berlin even more of an island than it had been. However much it may have been the focus of the international community, have benefited from the presence of American, British and French troops, and enjoyed a greater focus from Bonn once Brandt had taken over as federal Chancellor, it had become a difficult place to live. Young people would not stay when other parts of the FRG offered better careers and an easier way of life. Andreas Austilat, born in 1957 in the undivided city, was brought up in the American sector. He remembers being terribly proud when an American soldier's son from California said he preferred Berlin to Los Angeles. Austilat recalled that the Americans soldiers 'were bewildered. They couldn't understand it at all. But we thought "He's our boy." He preferred it here. It was his home. And many people couldn't understand that because there was this perception of Berlin from the outside, that it was a divided city, an island so we must somehow be badly off but that was not how we felt. Our feeling was that we had things alright. Sometimes it was a bit tiresome when you wanted to go on holiday but basically it was okay.'[18]

Whatever Austilat's feelings, by 1971, 25 per cent of the population were over sixty-five whereas in the wider FRG that figure was 15 per cent. Only 15 per cent of West Berliners were under fifteen, again comparing unfavourably with 23 per cent for the FRG. Some saw the fact that young West Berliners were excused military service as an advantage, but at a time when many young West Germans looked at the Soviet bloc and regarded service in the Bundeswehr as something they had a duty to do, it was only a marginal attraction. Bonn introduced *Zittergeld* (literally 'jitter money'), special payments to people to persuade them to stay in the city. Immigration from outside Germany continued, ironically facilitated by the GDR. In 1961 there were only 20,000 non-Germans in West Berlin but by 1975 there were 190,000, many of them immigrants to the GDR whom the Communist authorities quickly shipped over the Wall wholescale so that West Berlin had to look after them. By 1989 that figure had risen to nearly 300,000, and Turks made up 6 per cent of the population; by contrast, by 1989

East Berlin only had 20,000 non-Germans. Berlin was still as much a city of immigrants as ever.

West Berlin benefited from having an extraordinarily wide-ranging and liberal cultural life. This seemed as if it had to be even more hedonistic because just across the Wall life was so controlled and grey. There was an almost desperate need to enjoy the freedoms you had. It was as sexually free in the Wall years as it had ever been in the 1920s, although the GDR did legitimise homosexuality rather earlier than some western countries. Berlin nightlife was as active as its theatres, its music and its art. International figures like David Bowie came to live there because, much as in the 1920s, you could be and do what you wanted in West Berlin without anyone else judging you. Bowie lived in Schöneberg and, rather like Isherwood writing his novels inspired by Berlin life, so he recorded his Berlin Trilogy of albums there. He found the city a warm and inspiring place where he and Iggy Pop could experiment without interference. At a time when London was still quite restrictive and judgemental, Berlin offered artistic freedom. It was, Bowie said, 'the greatest cultural extravaganza that one could imagine'.[19]

West Berlin also became the focus for groups who objected to its rather obvious capitalist lifestyle. One of the most fascinating and seemingly contradictory leaders of this movement was Rudi Dutschke. Born into a religious family in Brandenburg, he initially joined the *Freie Deutsche Jugend*, was a promising athlete and seemed set to follow a good communist career. However, the brutal Soviet repression of the Hungarian uprising in 1956 made him change his views. He refused to do military service in the GDR and was consequently not allowed to attend university, but he managed to cross the border three days before the Wall went up and instead attended the new Free University in West Berlin. Having refined his views, when he left he became the leading figure in the German Student Movement and in what is sometimes called the APO, the *Außer Parlamentarische Opposition* (opposition outside Parliament). He called for radical change in politics and society, based on a combination of Christian and socialist principles,

remaining a committed Christian all his life, which slightly fazed
his many critics. He also called for change in the Third World, in
the Soviet bloc and in the West at the same time, and in June 1967
organised mass protests against the Vietnam war and at the Shah of
Iran's visit to West Berlin, during which the police shot and killed a
student called Benno Ohnesorg. Ohnesorg's death lead to a growing
number of protests, which Dutschke led, but in April 1968 he was
approached in the Ku'damm by a young anti-communist called Josef
Bachmann who shot him in the head. Dutschke survived but only
just and took himself to England, where he continued studying until
he was thrown out, and then Denmark. He eventually died from
the wounds he had received. There is a plaque to his memory in the
pavement where Joachim-Friedrich-Straße joins the Ku'damm on the
spot where Bachmann shot him and a street named after him that
runs between Friedrichstraße and Oranienstraße. Berlin is good at
remembering all its sons, however alternative.

Dutschke's greatest significance was in his legacy, which developed
in a way he probably would not have wanted. His supporters claimed
the Axel Springer publishing empire had demonised him, and that it
was their newspapers that had encouraged Bachmann. The Springer
publishing house, originally from Hamburg, had been influential
in post-war Berlin since buying the *Berliner Morgenpost* in 1959.
Fiercely anti-communist, they had built their offices hard against
the Wall as an act of defiance to the GDR, and they certainly took a
hard-right line against the APO and the student movement. Whereas
Dutschke was a thinker and worked to an agenda, his successors
in the opposition movement he created verged on the anarchic.
The same year that Dutschke was shot, a pacifist journalist called
Ulrike Meinhof moved to Berlin where she met Andreas Baader,
a violent revolutionary about to be jailed for fire-bombing shops.
She helped spring him from prison and they both went to Palestine
where they were trained as terrorists. Returning to Germany, their
Red Army Faction, known to western media as the RAF, mounted a
campaign of terror against the German establishment. When Baader
and Meinhof were arrested, their followers continued to carry out

killings right up until 1988, including the hijack of a Lufthansa jet that ended up at Mogadishu. To many old West Berliners, those who had lived through the war and its aftermath, this was a betrayal of everything they had tried to achieve. Younger Berliners, however, understood the anger that had led to the RAF's actions and, although very few condoned it, many sympathised.

The RAF were but one of the issues that West Berliners were finding difficult to reconcile in the 1970s and 1980s. A more fundamental question was what would happen to their city in the decades ahead and what, now that detente was in the air, was going to happen in the GDR. Were the Soviets still determined to wipe West Berlin from the map? And if so, would Bonn and the FRG, now part of NATO, stand by them? In practice there would be little that the Allied forces in the city (which numbered thousands against the GSFG's hundreds of thousands) could do. They would be quickly overrun in the event of an attack and were only there as a deterrent; by attacking West Berlin the Soviets would in effect be declaring war on the USA, Britain and France, but would the Allies risk a war that could easily escalate to nuclear conflict for the isolated island of a city in the sand? Or was the Soviet Union really serious about detente? Would the Honecker regime continue to soften and maybe even think about some sort of reunification of the two Germanies?

On the face of it, the Soviet threat in the late 1970s and early 1980s seemed as real as ever. The Allies maintained military liaison missions in Berlin whose job was to penetrate beyond the Wall and try to find out what the GSFG were up to. The Soviets maintained a similar mission in the FRG. Originally set up between the British and the Soviets in 1946 to help find prisoners of war, locate missing people and war graves, a model later emulated by the Americans and the French, by the 1970s both BRIXMIS, as the British mission was known, and SOXMIS its Soviet equivalent, had become 'official' military spying missions. They would access the GDR via the Glienicker Brücke, given that it was always manned by the Soviet army rather than East German border guards, and then try to avoid being followed as they tried to find out what the Soviet forces were

up to. It was exciting and dangerous work, which the Soviets and the
GDR did their best to frustrate, leading to casualties.

Having crossed the bridge in their up-armoured cars, equipped
with high-spec cameras, the missions' teams were invariably tailed
by the Stasi, who would note in typical detail exactly where they
went. Getaway driving skills and strong nerves were required to lose
them. Frequently they would try to ambush them, especially if the
teams were near any site they thought particularly sensitive. Peter
Williams – then a captain in the British mission – found himself inadvertently passing a radar site near the border at Athenstedt. A 10-ton
East German air force truck rammed them as they passed the gate,
trying to kill him and his passenger, the recently appointed British
brigade commander in Berlin. The armour in their car saved them,
as did a small fruit tree that caught the car and stopped it rolling.
The truck driver, interviewed long after Germany was reunited, told
Williams that he was awarded two weeks extra leave for what he
did but if he had succeeded in killing them he would have received
four weeks and 1,000 marks. On 23 March 1985 the Soviets did kill
Major Arthur Nicholson of the US mission while he was photograph-
ing Soviet tanks near Schwerin.

The information that the missions gained was one way NATO
knew that the Soviet army in the GDR (the GSFG) was maintained
at a state of readiness, which – despite many of their soldiers being
bored conscripts who drank the alcohol-based brake fluid from their
tanks to get a high – indicated they were poised to attack western
Europe. NATO nations consequently maintained huge armies facing
the border between the FRG and the GDR, who spent their days
rehearsing for a mass Soviet assault. Year on year the army groups
would exercise against various possible scenarios. Would GSFG
loop north, heading first for Hamburg and Denmark, or would they
drive straight for the Ruhr? Should they be stopped on the border or
allowed to penetrate deep into the FRG and then counter-attacked?
The latter course was predictably more popular with Allied military
planners than it was with Bonn. And when would the conflict 'go
nuclear'? Was it permissible to use the tactical nuclear weapons the

Allies possessed to stop the expected legions of Soviet armour, or would that lead to a strategic nuclear exchange? Such questions, which occupied western planners throughout the 1970s and 1980s and required maintaining large numbers of troops in the FRG, seemed very real to those involved. In all these scenarios, West Berlin was written off.

Travelling up the corridors from the FRG to West Berlin was to experience the strange atmosphere of menace created by both the border between the two Germanies, the IGB and the Wall, and the presence of so many Soviet troops. As a young officer, fresh from university and naive as to the realities of the Cold War, the author found himself commanding the regular British Military Train that ran from Braunschweig, Brunswick, via Helmstedt (where the rail corridor crossed the IGB) to Griebnitzsee in Berlin, where it crossed through the Wall into the American sector (see map on p. xvii). The journey was a rigmarole of protocol. We had to wear our smartest uniforms so that we created a good impression. The train left Braunschweig at precisely 15:50. German trains in the 1980s were punctual, a habit the Deutsche Bahn has sadly lost. On arrival at Helmstedt twenty-seven minutes later, the engine was taken off and replaced with a GDR one and a GDR crew. It then stopped at Marienborn, where I had to get off, together with an interpreter, and present a list of all the passengers to the duty Soviet officer who had been similarly ordered to be in his Sunday best. This was the first time I had encountered one of the fearsome 'Russians'; he was very pleasant, rather geeky and asked for cigarettes. From Marienborn the train entered a corridor of concrete, barbed wire, lookout towers, minefields and tank traps, something that brought home the reality of what the Cold War meant. The train then headed for Magdeburg, where it crossed the Elbe, and then went via Brandenburg, past the old engine sheds at Werder where the Kaiser's personal train once lived, until it arrived in Potsdam.

At various points we were ostentatiously served large meals in the dining car, the idea being to show any East Germans who chanced to glance in how comfortable our lives were. At Potsdam the process was reversed. The GDR engine and crew were taken off, replaced with a Berlin one, and the VoPos made a great show of searching the train for illegal border crossers. Again, we crossed through that grim world of concrete, wire and watchtowers before rolling into Charlottenburg station at 19:59, exactly four hours and nine minutes after we had left. For any young person making that extraordinary journey, the impression was of being on the brink of war. By contrast, West Berlin seemed quite incongruous, like some sort of artificial light amid a sea of darkness, but one that would almost inevitably be extinguished.

Crossing into East Berlin via Checkpoint Charlie, which was relatively easy to do as an Allied officer, again took one into a world that seemed surreal. The immediate impression one got after crossing through the Wall – again in best uniform to make a good impression, and avoiding showing any papers to the VoPos – was one of grey emptiness. After the bustle, noise and traffic of the West, East Berlin's streets seemed deserted. Even as one turned into Friedrichstraße and looked north past Checkpoint Charlie up towards the station, there never seemed to be anyone about. Many of the buildings, as soon as one was away from the centre, were still pockmarked with bullet holes.

The official exchange rate was one East mark to one Deutschmark but no one stuck to that. Before any trip the first stop was the zoo in West Berlin, where you could get anything from 5 to 10 East for one Deutschmark. Thus equipped, the shops in East Berlin became ridiculously cheap, and one could buy the few things that the GDR made really well, like binoculars and optics, for a fraction of their nominal value. The *Centrum Warenhaus* on the Alexanderplatz always seemed to have as many Allied personnel in its cavernous aisles as East Germans. Restaurants were also very cheap. One of the best was the Ganymed on Schiffbauerdamm. Originally a *Kneipe* for shipworkers, in the 1930s it was taken over and done up as a fashionable restaurant with a striking interior for the *haut monde*. Renovated after the war by the same architect who built the Stalinallee, Hermann Henselmann, it became a favoured haunt of the East Berlin elite. Serving good food by East Berlin standards, what made it so sad was the quartet of old men who played while you ate. They had played there during the war, and now in their seventies they played on, occasionally something lively but mostly slow, poignant music that seemed to speak of wasted lives. Eating there became horribly embarrassing; for a pittance one was enjoying what would have cost East Berliners a week's wages, and the quartet sensed that. The Ganymed is still there today and thriving as an upmarket brasserie.

It was perhaps music that gave some comfort to East Berlin. Music is the most difficult of the arts for totalitarian regimes to control. The Berlin Symphony Orchestra may not have been quite as good as the Philharmonic in the West, but it still staged excellent performances, as did several other orchestras. Sitting in its concerts, the feeling one got was that the audience felt temporarily safe to think and dream what they wanted without anyone interfering or the Stasi spying on them. Concerts offered rare moments of privacy and escapism, as did the great Berlin tradition of musicians studying and playing in private that was as popular in the East Berlin of the 1970s and 1980s as it had been two hundred years before.

In the many days I spent exploring East Berlin, the overwhelming feeling was one of sadness, of frustrated lives, of those wasted opportunities and of anger. It was to us absurd that people should have to save for years to be able to afford a Trabi, the little car made of plastic with a two-stroke engine like a mowing machine that came to be seen as a symbol of the GDR. They were horribly polluting and gave East Berlin its distinctive smell of plasticine. Why, we wondered, should the East Berliners have to put up with this? It was a question that many who had the misfortune to live in the Soviet bloc were asking with more confidence in the early 1980s. Real as the threat of further Soviet aggression undoubtedly was, as much from miscalculation as from deliberate policy choices, it appeared to be reducing, as if some sort of status quo had been established from which things were unlikely to regress. Berliners seemed to sense this.

Honecker himself did appear in some ways to be softening. In 1975 he had signed the Helsinki Accords, which nominally committed the GDR to greater respect for human rights. Although the GDR's observance of the Helsinki wording was always marginal, the Accords did at least give the regime's opponents a certain legitimacy. There was increasing co-operation with West Berlin in some areas, helped by the CDU politician Richard von Weizsäcker becoming Mayor of West Berlin in 1981 and actually paying a visit across the Wall. West Berlin agreed to pay for work to stop East Berlin's effluent polluting its waterways, and an agreement was reached to lay a gas pipeline from the USSR into West Berlin. West Berlin also agreed to take over the S-Bahn system, which had been run by the East and was beginning to fall to pieces. Now that the GDR was regarded as an international state in its own right, Honecker also revised his view of German history. Previously anything 'Prussian' had been considered militaristic and best forgotten about but now, if the GDR was Germany, then surely German history was important? Christian Daniel Rauch's great equestrian statue of Frederick the Great, which had been unceremoniously removed from outside the university in the Unter den Linden and carted off to Potsdam, was now reinstated, and an exhibition was held entitled 'Prussia – An attempt at a complete picture'.

Honecker was planning to make Berlin's 750th birthday, in 1987, into an opportunity for the GDR to claim to be the true Germany and East Berlin its proper capital, not a particularly difficult argument to make when his opposition was Bonn. Between 1981 and 1987 reconstruction work started on the war-damaged central areas that had remained unrepaired. The Nikolaiviertel was largely rebuilt. Subsequently there has been much criticism of how architect Günter Stahn approached this but, given that he was in many cases having to rebuild from scratch, he did not do a bad job. He managed to preserve both the medieval city's original layout and its concept of the church as the focus of shops, markets and housing. The West's contribution to the city's 750th birthday was to erect a bell tower, the Carillon (often called the Black Bell Tower), near the Haus der Kulturen der Welt. It contains a peal of ringing bells that can be played electronically; musically it is very successful.

For all Honecker's apparent softening, however, he had made three bad miscalculations. First his economic planning had gone badly wrong, a situation worsened by the economic crisis of the early 1980s caused by the rise in the price of oil. Ironically the GDR thought it could benefit from this by buying oil and gas cheaply across the Soviet bloc, refining it and then selling it on at a profit to the West. In theory that was sound, but the plan involved investing in expensive refining equipment that the state could only afford if it cut back on other key infrastructure. As the oil price dropped, the GDR found itself laden with massive debts in western currencies and with a lowering standard of living as money used to buy imports dried up. Honecker had to turn to the West, and between 1982 and 1984 he negotiated loans totalling 2 billion Deutschmarks from the FRG. In exchange he agreed to 'release' people so that in 1984 35,000 East Germans were given permission to cross the border. In practice this 'cash for souls' had been going on for some time, but the economic crisis took it new levels and showed that the GDR was economically unsustainable.

Honecker's second miscalculation was that he misread the friendly approaches from the FRG as some sort of genuine acceptance of him and his regime, forming the idea that a future Germany would have to include his unreformed socialist state. In 1987, after Moscow had finally given him permission, he had paid an official visit to the FRG, holding talks in Bonn, visiting his Saar homeland and being feted in Munich. It had come as something of a shock to him when, on 12 June that year, President Reagan speaking in front of the Brandenburg Gate at West Berlin's 750th birthday celebrations said that 'As long as this gate is closed, as long as this scar of a wall is permitted to stand ... it is not the German question alone that remains open but the question of freedom for all mankind,' finishing with: 'Mr Gorbachev, tear down this wall.' He was followed by Chancellor Helmut Kohl saying of the Wall that 'this division will not stand the test of time.'[20] As a result, Honecker withdrew his invitation for West Berlin's mayor Eberhard Diepgen to attend East Berlin's corresponding party.

Yet his most serious miscalculation was that, rather like Ulbricht before him, he failed to read what was happening in Moscow correctly. Brezhnev had died in 1982 and been succeeded by Yuri Andropov, who died after two years in office and was followed by Konstantin Chernenko. Chernenko only lasted a year and in 1985 he was succeeded by Mikhail Gorbachev. The 1980s were a difficult time for the USSR. Their 1979 invasion of Afghanistan had seen them involved in a costly guerrilla war from which, as with other interventions in Afghanistan, it was difficult to extract themselves. In President Reagan they had found a Western leader who would not compromise and who had both launched his Star Wars programme (which threatened to undermine the nuclear balance) and in 1983 deployed Pershing 2 medium-range missiles to Europe. The Soviet economy was doing badly, and demands for reform across the Soviet bloc were growing louder. While Gorbachev started to confront these problems with his policy of *perestroika* (meaning restructuring) and *glasnost* (meaning openness), Honecker maintained his commitment to totalitarian socialism. Those attempting to escape across the Wall were still being shot – Lutz Smith in 1987, Ingolf Diederichs, Chris Gueffroy and Winifred Freudenberg in 1988 – although now their deaths were hushed up and their families simply told they had left for the West.

In 1988 strikes and demonstrations swept Poland so that in early 1989 the Polish government collapsed. Honecker publicly supported the Chinese government's crushing of the Tiananmen Square protests in June 1989 (in many ways similar to what had happened in East Berlin in 1953), while Gorbachev – who had visited Beijing in May while the protest was going on – remained circumspect. The same month Gorbachev was mobbed by cheering crowds when he visited Bonn. Then on 27 June Hungary opened its border with Austria, saying it would allow East Germans to travel across; by September 25,000 East Germans had done precisely that. On 6 October Gorbachev visited East Berlin for the celebrations for the fortieth anniversary of the founding of the GDR. He did not like Honecker. He had told the GDR leadership in 1985 that 'the kindergarten was over. No one would lead them by the hand. They were responsible for their own people.'[21] Now he reiterated his message but Honecker chose to ignore him, saying the GDR would sort out its problems by its own socialist means. Hundreds of students cheering Gorbachev outside were brutally dispersed by the police. Even if Honecker did really believe he could change, he had left it too late. With thousands now leaving via Hungary, the Wall was anyway in danger of becoming obsolete. On 18 October the GDR politburo voted unanimously to replace him, even Mielke voting against him. Officially he resigned 'for health reasons'. He was replaced by his deputy, Egon Krenz, universally known in East Berlin as Horse Face. News of his election was broadcast as East Berliners were watching a favourite TV programme called *Everyone Dreams of a Horse*, which caused much hilarity. Krenz could do little better.

On 4 November the biggest demonstration ever held in East Berlin took place on Alexanderplatz. Hundreds of thousands chanted anti-government slogans and demanded reform. This time the Vol'os looked on and did nothing. Pressure was now building on the GDR from other Soviet bloc countries to do something to stem the flow of refugees – particularly the Czechs, who reported that they were being overwhelmed by East Germans flooding their cities. Krenz had no new solutions other than to consider issuing passports, which might slow the exodus and allow the government to control it. On 7 November the SED politburo, effectively the government, resigned but then reappointed itself; there was not exactly an alternative. On the evening of 9 November the party spokesman in Berlin, Günter Schabowski, was holding a routine press briefing to announce which minister was now going to do what job in the politburo musical chairs. He was asked by a journalist what the government was going to do about the Czech request and the future travel regulations. Schabowski, who had in his hand a politburo note about travel that was meant to be embargoed until the next day and which provided for some controlled emigration, replied that the government would now issue passports on demand and that people could use the border crossings between the two Germanies. 'When would this take effect?' he was asked. 'Immediately,' he replied, an assumption he made not having been briefed differently. He made that statement at 6.57 p.m. Within minutes fleets of Trabis were converging on the border crossing points, particularly at Checkpoint Charlie and on the Glienicker Brücke, demanding to be allowed into West Berlin. The border guards had received no instructions but several of them had heard Schabowski's announcement. With the crowds and the pressure building, at 11.30 p.m. the Stasi officer on duty at Bornholmer Straße, Harald Jäger, finally gave the order to lift the barriers. Hooting and cheering, the Trabis drove across. Berlin, and the world, had just changed for ever.

CHAPTER TWELVE

AFTER 1989

'Berlin is condemned only ever to become and never to be'

KARL SCHEFFLER, Berlin art historian, 1910

'This new Berlin with its language, which is not a dialect, but a whole new city language, the city of migration, the city of intelligence, this laboratory of irony, the only really cosmopolitan German city; this city, which, according to the unavoidable quote from Karl Scheffler, "is cursed to be forever going forward and never arriving"' was founded on 9 November 1989.[1] Ironically, the GDR, the German socialist state, began to fall apart on the very same day that Karl Liebknecht had tried and failed to establish it in 1918, and the same day on which the Republic was founded. It was also the date that Hitler had mounted his failed putsch in Munich in 1923 and the date of Kristallnacht.

Berlin's reaction to the extraordinary, unexpected and bewildering events of that night was mixed. At first there was an air of real excitement. East Berliners milled through the West, claiming their 100 Deutschmarks welcome money, singing, dancing, drinking, partying. Hundreds had climbed on top of the Wall, helping each other up from East and West. 'This is really a scene of happiness,' reported ABC News, 'the Wall is still standing, as you can see, but the Wall is political rubble.' People started making it literal rubble as well, attacking it with hammers from both sides. 'They crossed the border with incredible joy, amazement, tears and good humour. They sang and sparkled, above, below and beside the Berlin Wall. It was one of those very rare, absolutely electrifying, moments when the ordinary lay people take over and all the professionals – from prognosticators to border guards – get quietly out of the way,' recorded the *Guardian*,[2] which was not quite true as some of the more dutiful border guards sprayed water cannon at the crowd although they soon gave up. More sinister was a Stasi crisis meeting on 10 November to decide whether to mobilise the army and reclose the crossings. Mercifully they appreciated that things had gone too far. Scenes of people celebrating on the Brandenburg Gate dominated the world media that weekend, iconic images of a free Berlin. The Brandenburg Gate really was now the Gate of Peace but not quite in the manner in which Ulbricht had originally intended. The next morning the SED party newspaper *Neues Deutschland* felt it had to say something but could not quite bring itself to report the truth. It summed up the events of that tumultuous night with: 'Lots of traffic at the border crossing.'[3]

Annemarie Reffert, an anaesthetist, claims to have been the first East German actually to cross. She had heard Schabowski's press conference and said to herself that she did not believe him so she and her daughter climbed into their Trabi and drove to the border from Gommern where they lived. As they passed a sign saying 'Last Turning for Citizens of the GDR', her daughter said, 'Mum, what happens if they won't let us back in?' Annemarie 'got shit-scared then and wanted to just turn around and go back'. The guard at their checkpoint hadn't heard anything. He let them proceed but there were more checks to come. Then she felt 'real fear. The wait at the last control point felt like an eternity.' Would they be arrested or turned back? Eventually they were told they could drive on and they duly arrived in the West, where they were besieged by camera crews. She wanted to buy a can of beer for her husband but it was far too expensive so she turned around and drove back. 'You have a completely different society,' she told the waiting media, and anyway she had to be in her operating theatre first thing in the morning. The border guards were rather surprised to see them return. They were home by 10.30 p.m.[4]

As the excitement subsided, and the hangovers began to clear, the question was what would happen next. Willy Brandt summed up what many were feeling when he said on 10 November, 'Now what belongs together will grow together.'[5] FRG Chancellor Helmut Kohl took Europe rather by surprise on 28 November when he presented a ten-point plan for the reunification of the two Germanies. Both France and the United Kingdom were not sure what they thought about that. Yet the momentum came as much from the GDR, and from East Berliners, as it did from Bonn. In March 1990 the GDR held its first free elections – the first time voters had a choice other than to rubber-stamp the SED candidate. The SED received 16 per cent of the vote, the SPD only 22 per cent, and Kohl's CDU won easily with 40 per cent. By July 1990 the Deutschmark had replaced the worthless GDR Ostmarks and FRG laws had replaced the GDR's legal code. In September 1990 the four occupying powers in Berlin – the British, American, French and Soviets – gave their formal agreement to a new pan-German settlement, Moscow only agreeing if the FRG picked up the huge bill for dismantling and repatriating their forces stationed in the GDR. On 3 October 1990, less than a year after the Wall was first breached, the GDR was dissolved and its territories absorbed into Germany. Berlin was now formally reunited.

Berliners called that year *die Wende* (the turning point). It was a turn that had happened very quickly and, although it would lead to many exciting opportunities (what many East Berliners valued above all was now being able to travel outside the Soviet bloc), it would also lead to considerable hardship and disillusionment. Colonel Frithjof Banisch was a senior border guard on duty the night the Wall came down. He felt only contempt for all the East Berliners massing to cross. 'Quite honestly, I was embarrassed for these people,' he said.

'It still causes me pain. Just to think that everything we undertook in the GDR ... it hurts me that in the end all these things were just trampled underfoot.' Banisch was brought up among wounded veterans whom he watched trickle back from captivity in the USSR; his grandfather only had one lung and one eye. On Friday nights the family would play cards, using stands as two of his uncles had lost their arms, he told *The Times*. 'They all kept saying: never again, never again,' and he thought the GDR was a way of ensuring that peace would last. He was angry that the GDR chain of command appeared to have broken down on the night of 9 November. The crowds kept growing but he still could not get any orders. He decided he had no choice, having heard Schabowski's broadcast, than to allow people to cross.[6]

'People were convinced that socialism was the right thing,' said Wolfgang Hübner, editor of *Neues Deutschland*. 'There were only very few – and I was not one of them – who said at the time: this is not going in the right direction. Things should be different.'[7] Katharina Hermann summed up the feelings of many East Berliners when she said: 'I was quite taken aback when very soon there was talk about unification. I was born a very long time after the war and the building of the Wall. I didn't really consider myself as part of a larger Germany; I didn't have a lot in common with a lot of West Germans ... Being reunited was an alien idea to me. I would have thought and hoped that there would be a getting-closer process as part of being in the European Community – that was the process I would have liked much better.'[8] Mikael Adam, whose father was a Stasi officer in Potsdam, remembers being frightened. 'Many of us wanted the GDR to change but we didn't want to give it up. 1989 turned out to be a miracle, on both sides. It could so easily have gone wrong. Then we saw what happened in Rumania in December [when Ceausescu and his wife were summarily tried and executed] and we thought that the mood in Berlin could still change. It was, for us as a Stasi family, a very difficult time.'[9]

'There was an assumption,' continued Katharina Herrmann, 'that if you were in or from the East and you weren't an active dissident, you were automatically a Stasi member, or somebody who had totally wrong or undemocratic ideas. There was an assumption that you would immediately accept West was good, East was bad. There was a lot of negative propaganda about people like my parents, for instance, who had spent their lives trying to build on something very worthwhile and positive – an egalitarian social experiment, no matter how flawed.'[10] 'You had the feeling of being a nothing,' added Elisabeth Heller. 'You always had the feeling of having to justify yourself to other people who didn't understand why you were unemployed and had no job. It was an exasperating state, which lasted until I reached pensionable age.'[11] It was, perhaps, that feeling of wasted lives that East Berliners found most difficult to accept, especially those like Heller for whom adaptation was so troublesome. Some East Berliners did feel that their lives had not been as full as they could have been, but many – perhaps the majority – did not and resented the inference from the more tactless in the West that somehow they did. Berlin may have been reunited physically but it would take another generation before Berliners would begin to feel united in equality of opportunity.

Some of the actions taken by the new Germany, and the new Berlin, seemed vindictive but were probably inevitable. Honecker was treated roughly. Thrown out of the Waldsiedlung Colony, he took shelter with the Soviets and was spirited away to Moscow. When the Soviet Union was dissolved in December 1991 he sought refuge in the Chilean embassy in Moscow, reasoning that he had given sanctuary to Chileans after the Pinochet coup, and his daughter was married to a Chilean. However, they ejected him and he was returned to Berlin and detained in Moabit. He was put on trial in Berlin in 1992, accused of erecting the Wall and for the shoot-to-kill policy that he had instigated and encouraged. During the criminal investigation he was found to have authorised many more deaths than those shot trying to escape. He was, by now, seriously ill with liver cancer and, after endless legal arguments, he was released despite strong objections from the families of the Wall's victims. He was flown to Chile, where he died in 1994. Mielke was put on trial with him for the deaths on the Wall and for a catalogue of other crimes. He was also charged with the murders of Captains Anlauf and Lenck back in 1931. He was convicted and sentenced to six years but was released in 1995 aged eighty-seven, it being claimed that he was too mentally disturbed to remain incarcerated. He died in Berlin in 2000 in the comfort of a nursing home. His humiliation was in many ways more complete than Honecker's. In November 1989 he had been summoned to appear in front of the GDR parliament, reinvigorated after the resignation of the government and now beginning to exercise some authority. Asked to justify his position and his conduct, Mielke gave a rambling and incoherent speech using the typically meaningless platitudes that had become so customary for SED officials. When challenged, he went to pieces. His final words were: 'I love all – all humanity. I really do. I set myself before you.' The assembled members collapsed in laughter. There is still residual anger that Mielke got off lightly, and the ex-prisoners who now act as guides at the Stasi prison comment bitterly that he was moved to a West Berlin prison as he complained that the conditions in Hohenschönhausen were too uncomfortable.

Lower-level Stasi officers were also charged. The two border guards who killed Peter Fechter, for example, were convicted of manslaughter rather than murder and given relatively short sentences. This was felt by many to be unfair as they had only been obeying orders, that age-old plea with echoes of the controversial Nazi trials. GDR officials were also incensed that they received lower pensions, in real terms, than their FRG counterparts; the Stasi, who had previously received more generous pensions than other officials in the GDR, had their rate reduced so that it was the same as the VoPos. Other officials felt equally discriminated against. Only one of the GDR's diplomats was taken on by the German Foreign Ministry, the man who happened to be running the Strategic Arms Limitation Talks.

Discriminated against as they may have felt, the experience of those on whom the Stasi had preyed was perhaps more disturbing. The Stasi had burned and shredded as many of their files as they could in 1989, but the sheer volume of paper and the lack of shredders meant they could only do a partial job; ironically, cars were despatched to buy more shredders in the West. Consequently, a great number of files were left when, in January 1990, a large crowd stormed the headquarters building in Lichtenberg. After a protracted debate it was decided that individuals could apply for access to their files. Irene Kempff went to read hers. What surprised her was just how much pointless detail had been amassed on her visits to her literary evenings in East Berlin. For her the file was a matter of passing interest, but what she found more difficult was watching others as they read and discovered that so many parents and siblings, friends, relations and colleagues had been Stasi informants. The trust that had bound many lives was shattered.

The decision to open the files has remained controversial. Some former East Germans see it as a way of destroying the careers of former GDR officials so that former West Germans would not face competition for jobs, and some restrictions were later introduced. Neither was the collapse of the Wall necessarily a happy reunion for those who had successfully fled to the West. Conrad Schumann, the young soldier who jumped over the wire back in August 1961, had ended up working for twenty-seven years in the Audi factory in Ingolstadt in Bavaria. When he was finally reunited with his family and friends, they found reconciliation difficult. The Stasi had persecuted his family and several people treated him as a traitor. In 1998 Schumann was found hanged in a wood near his home. He never earned any money from the iconic photograph that came to symbolise the Wall for so many.

These were some of the negative consequences of reunification but they should not cloud the enormous sense of excitement and opportunity that the collapse of the Wall offered. If life in the GDR had been so wonderful why had millions been so desperate to leave? Berlin had not been this free politically for fifty-six years, since 1933. Arguably the after-effects of the First World War, of hyperinflation and recession meant the city had not really been 'free' in the full sense since 1914. It was, said veteran CDU politician Wolfgang Schäuble, 'the high point of my political life' and the majority of Germans would have agreed with him.[12] The government of the city was relatively easy to sort out. Elections were held across Berlin in December 1990. The CDU, led by Eberhard Diepgen, the ruling mayor of West Berlin, received the most votes but with just 101 seats they could only form an administration in coalition with the SPD, which is what they did. The SED had been disbanded but its remaining supporters fought the election as the *Partei des Demokratischen Sozialismus* (the Party of Democratic Socialism). They won just under 10 per cent of the vote, demonstrating that not everyone supported reunification.

Having signed away any residual powers in 1990, the Allies' military role was now finished. Apart from being present to act as a 'trip-wire' to prevent Soviet aggression, which had worked well, they had also been fulfilling other tasks. Until 1987 the four powers had been guarding Rudolf Hess, Hitler's deputy sentenced to life imprisonment at the post-war Nuremberg trials, in Spandau Gaol. Originally one of seven who were incarcerated there (Albert Speer and the others having been released), Hess lived on until he was ninety-three, a pathetic figure alone in a massive nineteenth-century prison designed for 600. It was demolished as soon as he died so that it did not become a neo-Nazi shrine. Thirty-seven soldiers – rotating between the British, Soviets, Americans and French – guarded Hess. Together with a massive administrative staff, this cost the West German tax payer $670,000 per annum. Any suggestion that he be released or moved was immediately vetoed by the Soviets who, it was felt, were not just being vindictive but liked their access to West Berlin.

In September 1994 the city said a formal, and warm, farewell to the Allied troops, in much the same manner as they had arrived in 1945, with a parade through the Brandenburg Gate. 'Today, as you leave Berlin,' said Chancellor Kohl, 'we can definitely say: Freedom has won.' Soldiers who had come to police the Lair of the Fascist Beast had quickly realised that Berliners were different, that the majority loathed Hitler and they now had a common cause in opposing communism. The Allied legacy in Berlin is strong. The

Free University, the Technical University, the Kongresshalle, and Tegel Airport are all part of it, although some parts of this legacy are more esoteric. The Berliner passion for Currywurst is a case in point. The British army, with its strong Indian influence, ate endless curry. In the hungry years, a British quartermaster gave away some curry powder, which enterprising Berliners used to cheer up their fare by sprinkling it over their sausages. The habit caught on.

The more difficult question, as we have seen, was whether Berlin should once again become the capital of Germany. After that narrow vote in favour by 338 votes to 320 on 20 June 1991 in the Bundestag, the German parliament in Bonn, Berlin now had to prepare itself once more to be the national capital of the most prosperous and economically powerful nation in Europe. The physical aspects of this were to prove as challenging as the spiritual. A new range of government offices was required and the decision was taken to locate these in the loop in the Spree immediately north of the Reichstag. Berlin architect Axel Schultes was the clear winner of the competition to design them, and his 'Spree Arc' (which joins Mitte, Tiergarten and Moabit) seems to draw the city together. The best way to see it is from one of the many Spree river cruises or, even better, from the Reichstag. The President of Germany, the Head of State, was given the nearby Bellevue Palace as their official residence, thus creating a convenient government area of the city.

A similarly awkward decision was what to do with the Reichstag, which should correctly become the Bundestag's new home now that Berlin had been chosen over Bonn. There was opposition to this from several quarters. For those on the left, the Reichstag represented Imperial Germany and it was unsuitable as the focus for the new democratic Germany. For those on the right it would always be a symbol of Germany's shame and defeat. For some time, an American artist called Christo, originally from Bulgaria, and his wife, Jeanne-Claude, had been lobbying to 'wrap' the building, something they specialised in doing to public buildings. They first suggested the idea during the Cold War but made no progress despite lobbying for twenty-four years. The decision to move the capital back to Berlin changed all that, and the politicians who had argued that it was an undignified way to treat such an iconic Berlin landmark saw that 'wrapping' could be a useful way of marking the transformation they were seeking. Christo was finally given the go-ahead in 1994, and on 24 June 1995, a hundred professional climbers abseiled down the face of the building, unrolling aluminium fabric that was then fastened in place with blue rope. The wrap lasted for two weeks and was seen by an estimated 5 million people. Some senior German politicians remained unconvinced, saying it would polarise people rather than unite them and that it trivialised Berlin's history. Looking back, however, Christo's plan is generally judged to have been a success, not least because it was funded by selling models and photographs of the wrap in place and so no public money was spent.

What it did do was focus international attention on the Reichstag and on the competition to renovate it, which posed the competing architects as many problems as Wallot had faced in the 1880s. It had to be a working assembly for Bundestag members, while symbolising the hopes and aspirations of the new Germany, and all within an existing structure that could not be fundamentally altered. The competition was won by the British architect Sir Norman Foster whose plans included a spectacular central glass dome with a core of mirrors that would let light flood down into the chamber. Work was completed in 1999. His design, which involved gutting everything from the inside of the building so that only its shell remained, met with almost universal praise, unlike poor Wallot's. Foster succeeded in making the new Bundestag both important and approachable. His plans were environmentally ahead of their time, including using the hot air generated internally for the heating; Berliners quickly noted that hot air was a commodity the members generated in abundance. The whole point of the project was to make the Bundestag open and transparent – hence the dome and the treatment of light – and in that spirit the building is open to visitors. The walk up the dome is spectacular, offering a wonderful view of the city's landmarks.

On the other hand, there was the question of what to do with Ulbricht's 'U-shaped political centre', the hollow square of not very lovely – but, to many East Berliners, important – buildings that occupied the area where the Berliner Schloss once stood. Again, there were opposing views. To the traditionalists, the destruction of the Berliner Schloss in the 1950s had been a crime, compounded by flattening Schinkel's Bauakademie just west of the river for the Ministry of Foreign Affairs building. The Palast der Republik was, they argued, an ugly symbol of an evil regime and should be demolished. Together the buildings represented an 'insult to urban development'[13] and must go. Others argued that at least the Palast der Republik, if not the other buildings, now spoke for a period of Berlin's history and should thus be preserved. They lost the argument, not least because the Fernsehturm was thought to be a better symbol of the GDR and because the Palast was found to be riddled with asbestos (although its supporters would say that was an excuse to speed its demolition). The decision was ultimately taken that it should go and it stood, empty and forlorn, for nearly fourteen years while the debate raged about what should replace it. Given that this was the central space of one of Europe's great capitals, it is not surprising that the argument was intense. Those who had favoured preserving the Palast der Republik had already lost, so it came down to a debate between those who thought the Berliner Schloss should never have been torn down and should therefore be replaced, and those who argued the new Germany needed a futuristic building that portrayed opportunity and unity.

The debate polarised Berlin but it tended to matter more to the older generation; younger Berliners seemed slightly disinterested in it and more worked up about the failure of the Schönefeld airport project. The traditionalists were led by a Hamburg businessman called Wilhelm von Boddien who in 1993 formed the *Förderverein Berliner Schloss* (Berlin Schloss Association), dedicated to rebuilding the Schloss as it had been. 'I have had,' he said, 'a passion for the Schloss since the age of nineteen.'[14] His plan involved erecting a reconstruction painted on canvas over a scaffolding framework so Berliners could see what it would look like. Opposition was strong and immediate both from contemporary architects and from politicians and journalists who saw the Berliner Schloss representing a reactionary era from which Germany had moved on. Meanwhile von Boddien's supporters started to raise large amounts of money; for a period it was not unusual to receive one of the formal funeral notices that some German families still put out asking for donations to the Berliner Schloss appeal rather than for flowers. In 2000 the German and Berlin governments formed a committee of seventeen international experts to try to resolve the matter. Fifteen of them decided that – given the surrounding buildings, the Berliner Dom and the Altes Museum across the Lustgarten – the new building should be of the same size as the original Schloss and occupy the same ground plan. Eight voted in favour of recreating the baroque outer facades and Schlüter's courtyard. The east-facing facade, overlooking the river towards Alexanderplatz, which had never had a baroque facade, would be modern. The Schloss had always represented a synthesis of styles and this modern facade would link the new buildings to its east with the older ones along the Unter den Linden. The scheme was finally approved by the Bundestag on 4 July 2002. They contributed 478 million Euros to the project, Berlin contributed 32 million and von Boddien's society contributed 105 million, which covered the cost of reconstructing the exterior facades.

The new building, due to be completed in October 2020, is to be called the Humboldt Forum and will become a shared forum for Humboldt University, the city of Berlin and the Prussian Cultural Heritage Foundation. Items from Berlin's exceptional Asiatic and ethnographic collections are planned to find a permanent home here, although, as Paul Spies (the art historian and director of the *Stiftung Stadtmuseum Berlin*) says, its 'purpose is to show how the world is present in Berlin and Berlin is present in the world.'[15] Rude as people are about the Humboldt Forum, one critic describing it as 'Chernobyl – concrete on top of a problem',[16] and with arguments still running as to whether western museums should exhibit the cultural heritage of nations previously subdued and colonised, the Humboldt Forum offers Berlin an exciting new venue that will create an open and accessible focus for the city and can be put to multiple uses. 'It is not a museum,' explains Hartmut Dorgerloh, a former East Berliner and its new director, 'it's not a palace. It's a forum, an accessible place where various parties congregate to engage with different ideas.'[17] Neil MacGregor, former director of the British Museum and who has written extensively on Germany, was one of three directors charged by the German government with bringing the project to fruition. It will be, he says, 'an amazing opportunity to attract new audiences' and to turn 'museums that have been the preserve of the highly educated into places where the curious can come.' He also persuaded the authorities that, unusually for Berlin, entrance should be free.[18]

Whether Berliners are supporters of the way the Humboldt Forum has been conceived, or whether they belong to the modernist camp, most would agree that what the project has done is to recreate a centre for their city. When the scaffolding is finally cleared away from the Berliner Schloss and its surrounding area, Berlin will have a focus that it has lacked for seventy five years. With the renovation work completed on the museums, Berlin and Germany will have a visual, cultural and historic heart that it has so badly needed.

'Berlin,' continues MacGregor, 'remembers through its buildings', and the clearest examples of that are how, since 1989, Berlin has chosen to acknowledge Germany's guilt in the Second World War and, in particular, the Holocaust. Few cities would make such a public statement of national guilt as Berlin has chosen to make in its *Holocaust Mahnmal* (the Memorial to the Murdered Jews of Europe). This is not hidden away in embarrassment in a suburb but absolutely in the heart of Berlin where the Wall ran between the Brandenburg Gate and Potsdamer Platz. On the surface, facing the Tiergarten, is a wave of 2,710 stelae, or concrete blocks, with no obvious purpose or way in or out. They represent many different things to different people; they are random, tomb-like, apparently without reason, like the Holocaust itself. Underneath is a Holocaust Museum that tells the appalling story of the murder of 6 million people honestly and without sparing the visitor. It receives more than half a million visitors each year. Some Berliners do not think the memorial works, arguing that too often families are picnicking on the stelae or children rushing through them playing. Others find it moving and successful in what it is trying to achieve. Whatever people's views, there is no denying its centrality to Berlin nor the statement it makes.

Berlin, the most un-Nazi of German cities, has to pay a heavy price for having been the capital of Hitler's Reich. Another shocking and extraordinarily effective Second World War museum is the *Topographie des Terrors*, an exhibition of the Nazi terror housed in a new building on the site of the old Gestapo headquarters in what was then Prinz-Albrecht-Straße but is now Niederkirchner Straße. Again, told without any concession to the squeamish, it is as fascinating an exhibition as it is horrifying.

One particular advantage of the collapse of the GDR was that the Quadriga goddess on the Brandenburg Gate could be returned to her original state. This poor deity and symbol of Berlin – who had been cast, stolen, hauled back, copied, bombed and had her staff chopped up – was now returned to how she had been in 1815 when Schinkel gave her an Iron Cross and a Prussian eagle. There was an inevitable debate as to whether she should be seen to carry these symbols of Prussian militarism, until it was pointed out that the Iron Cross was designed for those who fought the French tyranny in the Napoleonic wars and that it was Ulbricht who had removed both it and the eagle. She quickly had them both returned and she was rededicated on 6 August 1991. A similar problem was what to do with the Neue Wache now that the rather smart Frederick Engels Guards had been consigned to the history books. Chancellor Kohl felt Germany needed a national memorial. Yet again he entered a political minefield. Who was it a memorial to? Those Germans killed? Or those they had killed? And how could you commemorate both together? And why choose a building with militaristic Prussian heritage that had so recently been guarded by goose-stepping communists? The Neue Wache was, Kohl argued, a building that dated from Germany's 'honourable past' and could reasonably honour all Germans. How, chanted demonstrators, could

Hitler's sadistic hanging judge Roland Freisler, killed in a bombing raid, be remembered alongside his victims? Kohl nevertheless saw his plans to completion, compromising on a plaque outside the Neue Wache that records who is, and who is not, being remembered. He also replaced Heinrich Tessenow's granite block and silver wreath memorial, originally dedicated to those lost in the First World War, with an enlarged version of Käthe Kollwitz's 'Pieta'. Even this did not satisfy everyone. Some now argued the Pieta conveyed a sense of hopeless grief; others said it honoured the necessity of suffering and sacrifice. Most visitors today, standing in respectful silence in the quiet of the temple after the noise of the Unter den Linden, think only of the loss that Germany in general, but Berlin in particular, has endured.[19]

There was much work to do to restore those parts of Berlin's heritage that the GDR hadn't quite got around to repairing, either from lack of funds or lack of enthusiasm. Much of East Berlin in 1989 still looked as it had in 1945; I remember standing outside the Pergamon Museum one day waiting for a colleague and counting the bullet holes. Even today very smart buildings, such as the charming houses in the short mall leading to the Sophienkirche, just north of Hackescher Markt, are riddled with them. A particular issue was what to do with the bulldozed Potsdamer Platz. Arguably this is a test Berlin failed. Potsdamer Platz, with its gate and station, and with Leipziger Straße leading east towards the centre, had long been seen as one of the city's focal points; it was also the intended site of Frederick the Great's monumental tomb and Schinkel's most German cathedral. Sadly, the city allowed commercial companies to buy up and develop sites after 1989 without any overall aesthetic plan. The result is that, although there are some striking skyscrapers, as a whole Potsdamer Platz feels a mess that lacks an overall vision, not helped by having become one of Berlin's busiest traffic hubs.

There was also the perennial Berlin problem of whose statue was in and whose was out, whose name could continue to be honoured in a street name and whose must go. Stalin had obviously gone from the Strausberger Platz, but the old Stalinallee kept its name as

Karl-Marx-Allee as Marx was a Berliner, or at least had been for long enough to be counted as such. But what about Lenin? In 1992 the Berlin government established a commission to advise on which monuments should be kept and which should be got rid of. In 1970 Ulbricht had dedicated a 62-foot statue of Lenin in red granite that stood, appropriately, in Leninplatz, a square surrounded by new housing in Friedrichshain. Despite it being a listed monument and having been sculpted by Nikolai Tomsky (president of the Soviet Academy of Arts), Diepgen said that Lenin was a 'despot and murderer' and that he must go. His statue was destroyed in 1991 and its rubble carted away to the Müggelberg. However, some time later his head re-emerged from its sandy grave and was taken back to join the gallery of unwanted Berlin statues in Spandau.[20]

More complicated was the monument to Ernst Thälmann in Prenzlauer Berg. Thälmann was leader of the KPD from 1925 until his arrest by the Nazis in 1933 and his subsequent death in Buchenwald, yet he was also a strong supporter of Stalin. In 1986 Honecker had unveiled a massive bust of him, fist clenched and red flag flying behind him, which was again the centrepiece of a new housing development. He had a heating system incorporated into his nose so that it wouldn't freeze in winter. Despite the Commission recommending that Thälmann should go, there was a certain amount of local support for keeping him, added to which it was going to be so expensive to get rid of him that eventually he was given the benefit of the doubt; he is still in Prenzlauer Berg today. The joint statue of Marx sitting and Engels standing, which originally stood in front of the Palast der Republik, fared better and the Commission recommended keeping it. It had always attracted a fair amount of Berliner humour, being known as 'Next time we promise we will do better' or 'Applicants waiting to emigrate'. Marx's lap is a popular place for people to sit and have their photograph taken.[21]

A similar issue was whether to preserve any parts of the Wall, both because Berlin does not hide its history and because it had also been a major tourist attraction while it was standing. It was something visitors associated with the city, even post-1989, and people wanted to see what it had been like. Given how much of the Wall was chipped away and kept as souvenirs or sold in Berlin's markets, it is a wonder there is any left at all. Obviously the main stretches all had to go as the city came together, but some parts were kept. The best place to experience what it was like is in Bernauer Straße, the street where the Wall ran down the back of the houses and where the GDR destroyed the Church of the Reconciliation. There is a memorial here, with iron stakes and new trees that trace the actual course of the Wall, and a good museum. A 1,300-metre stretch has also been kept in Mühlenstraße, running along the river between Kreuzberg, which used to be the American sector, and Friedrichshain, which was Soviet. Originally covered in graffiti, as was so much of the Wall, in 1990 it became a sort of impromptu open-air art gallery as artists celebrated the collapse of the Iron Curtain and communism. Now called the East Side Gallery, it is both the best place to see what the Wall looked like and to see some wonderful spontaneous art. The most famous scenes are Brezhnev and Honecker kissing in 1979, and a death mask of Andrei Sakharov, the Russian human rights activist. In many places in the city, such as east of the Reichstag and in front of the Brandenburg Gate, there is also a double line of stones let into the road to show the Wall's exact course.

In 2006 Germany hosted the World Cup. The final was played in the Olympic Stadium in Berlin. By 2006 this seemed to be a natural choice. Although the German team were beaten by Italy in the semi-finals, the competition was seen as a major success for Germany. Germans cheering on a German team, waving German flags and playing the final in the same stadium where Hitler had staged his pre-war Olympic Games was symbolic of a new German order. The qualifying games had been played in stadia in the former GDR as well as the FRG, and it seemed as if, seventeen years after the Wall had come down, that Germany was genuinely uniting and that Berlin was its natural as well as its political capital.

Yet contemporary Berlin is still home to as many conflicting tribes as it has ever been. There is the hard-core socialist group, those who regret the passing of the GDR and the failure of what they believed was a worthwhile experiment, however flawed. They still suffer from (or celebrate) *Ostalgie*, read *Neues Deutschland* and vote for *Die Linke* (The Left: the party that is the heir to both the SED and the PDS, the post-unification Party for Democratic Socialism). They have twenty-seven seats of the 160 in the *Abgeordnetenhaus*, the post-unification Berlin assembly, but their agenda is becoming increasingly unfamiliar to the old-school communists. That traditional right-wing element in the city is still around 15 per cent; the *Alternative für Deutschland* party have twenty-five seats. The majority of Berliners still, however, vote for either the CDU or the SPD. A difference – as is common across Germany but particularly so in Berlin – is the rise of *Bündnis 90-Die Grünen* (the Greens), who have twenty-seven seats.

Once again, there is a strong Jewish community – including many who have returned despite losing family in the Holocaust – and, in a sad comment on the present state of the Middle East, a growing number of young Israelis. Many Soviet Jews also made Berlin their home after the collapse of the USSR. Jews have been encouraged by how open the city has been about the terrible events in the past. Apart from the Holocaust Memorial, there is the acclaimed and much-visited Jewish Museum designed by Daniel Libeskind and the Neue Synagogue has been restored, at least in part, so that its striking gold dome again dominates the skyline to the north of the city centre. The charming villa where the Wannsee Conference was held has also been made into a memorial museum. Yet it is more than that. The Hungarian novelist Imre Kertész, who survived Auschwitz, moved back to Berlin in 2000 in his eighties, despite the fact that many of his family had been murdered by the Nazis. In 2009 he wrote an essay entitled 'Why Berlin, of all places'. He explained that he missed 'the many languages you hear spoken on the street, the fact that few people care where you come from, the acceptance he feels, how Berlin has long read and supported obscure writers from beyond its own borders'. Berlin, he felt, was a city where he could be himself, and a city that, he continued, 'embraces me and peels away the leaden airs of melancholy, leaving no traces behind, like crisp winds shearing the morning haze in the air'.[22]

While the Jewish community is smaller than it has been historically, the Muslim population – largely Turk but also Middle Eastern and North African – is now somewhere over 6 per cent. Germany no longer keeps records of its citizens' religions so it is hard to be exact. There have long been strong German–Turkish links, dating back to the First World War, and Turks started coming in numbers in the 1960s to help rebuild the economy. Many settled in Kreuzberg and Neukölln because they were cheaper areas to live, close to the Wall and less popular with Berliners. Then there is a sizeable Vietnamese community. The Vietnamese were originally invited to the GDR as contract workers to fill the gaps left by all those East Germans who had left for the West. Many of them were women who worked in the clothing industry. The GDR policy was to rotate them so that they would not settle permanently, and they were discouraged from intermingling with the locals – as were contract workers from Mozambique and Cuba. It was an unpleasant and discriminatory policy but many Vietnamese found ways of staying. There is also a strong Russian presence. The old 1920s joke about Charlottenburg being Charlottengrad still holds true today, but these Russians have very different priorities to their forebears. Then there are the endless Berlin cliques and pressure groups, political and cultural, and one of the strongest LGBT movements in Europe. Berlin has always prided itself on its sexual toleration and the LGBT rainbow colours are displayed across the city through conviction rather than conscience.

Like so many regional dialects, *Berlinerisch* is spoken less and less, and for some time it has been heard more in the eastern districts than the west, but it has developed something of a cult following. There is a daily column in the *Berliner Morgenpost* called *Kasupke sagt*. Kasupke is a taxi driver, a 'typical' Berliner, who comments on current events in *Berlinerisch*. Most taxi drivers in Berlin now actually don't speak *Berlinerisch* – for many of them, German is a second language – but a younger generation is commendably trying to preserve a unique part of Berlin's culture.

There is, however, an assumption among some elements in the city that it is being strangled by immigration. Berlin's traditional strength in opening its arms to incomers and quickly assimilating them has, they maintain, gone too far and is now in danger of strangling the city's life. Children should be held back from school until they can speak German, according to Carsten Linnemann, a CDU member of the Bundestag. He is concerned that 'parallel societies' are springing up across Germany.[23] A quick look at the facts shows this argument to be wrong at least as far as Berlin is concerned. Berlin has not grown in the last twenty-five years; in 1995 its population was 3.6 million, much as it is today. Only 15 per cent of those were born outside Germany (6 per cent in Europe and 9 per cent outside). By way of contrast, the corresponding figures for Brussels in 2016 were nearly 35 per cent, with 12 per cent born outside Europe. Berlin also has a much lower unemployment rate, at 8 per cent, which is higher than the German average but still lower than 17 per cent in Brussels.

What have, however, changed in Berlin are property prices. Between 2015 and 2018 Berlin property went up by about 40 per cent. The city now boasts about 1.7 million apartments but they are getting more and more expensive. In a 2018 survey, 80 per cent of Berliners polled said it was really difficult to find affordable housing. What is happening is not that immigration is excessive but that Berlin is becoming 'gentrified'. Precisely because it is such a nice place to live, lots of people want to live there, with many rich Germans and foreigners maintaining second homes.[24] It remains, perhaps unexpectedly for a great capital city, one of the least densely populated in Europe, a huge attraction in a world where access to open space is becoming so highly prized. Not many other capitals can claim 5,000 wild boar among their population. The boar thrive in the Grunewald and, having become wise to the dangers of traffic, can be seen, in best Berliner tradition, forming an orderly queue to use pedestrian crossings. The problem is not Angela Merkel allowing in Syrian immigrants – something many Berliners responded to with warmth and kindness, nearly 1,000 households welcoming families to live with them – but rather that too much money is chasing too few dwellings.

When *Times* correspondent David Charter left Berlin in 2018, he recorded being woken at night by his admittedly eccentric neighbour smashing up his Prenzlauer Berg apartment with a sledgehammer. Once he had been calmed down, the reason he gave was sad. He had lived there on a cheap rent since reunification but now, as property prices soared, apartments in Prenzlauer Berg were becoming very sought after. Prenzlauer Berg (which was in the East) and Kreuzberg are the two Berlin districts that have become the most fashionable, with the strongly Turkish and Middle Eastern Neukölln not far behind. Consequently, he had been pressurised to vacate the flat he had loved for thirty years by his investor landlord. He had been paid €20,000 to leave but by doing so he had increased the value of his now-vacant property by double that amount.[25]

Will that change Berlin? It would be sad if it did. The character established by those merchants and fishermen nearly 800 years ago has proved remarkably resilient: a diverse, open community, law-abiding but independent of authority, in a city that geography never really intended to be there but that has forced its way onto the world stage by using the talents of its people. The Hohenzollerns are still in the wings. The current head of the family, George Friedrich, great-great-grandson of the last Kaiser, is taking the German government to court, arguing that they have appropriated palaces and art collections that belong to his family not the state. He is taking advantage of a law that allows restitution to Germans who had their property confiscated by the Soviets and the GDR. There is, however, a clause in the law that says it does not apply to families who made substantial contributions to the Nazis. It is an interesting case, with major collections in Berlin and Potsdam at stake.

There is an interesting line in the preamble to the Weimar Constitution: 'The Germans, united in their tribes, and inspired by the will to renew and strengthen the Reich in liberty and justice, to preserve peace at home and abroad and to foster social progress'.[26]

It's a pretty good summary of what many democracies would aspire to. It took Germany seventy-odd years to achieve that goal, but in 1989–90 it did so convincingly with the triumph of the democracy to which the Weimar politicians aspired. The period of autocracy and militarism that had interrupted German national progress was finally defeated in 1945 in the West and in 1989 in the East. There is much talk in Germany today of political polarisation, of both the left and the right becoming more radical at the expense of the centre – much as happened in the late 1920s – and of the East and the West beginning to drift apart. It is even more important, then, to focus on what Berlin represents now, much as it did back in the thirteenth century: a place that is 'united in its tribes'. Slavs or Romans, Christian or pagan, Catholic or Protestant, Calvinist or Lutheran, monarchist or republican, enlightened or reactionary, militaristic or peaceful, Marxist or Fascist, Socialist or Conservative, native-born or immigrant – they were or are all Berliners. Germany has long had in its capital city the model to which it aspires as a nation.

Notes

Prologue

1 Professor Doktor Christoph Stölzl in conversation with the author, 9 October 2019, and also quoting his lecture 'Reflections on Prussia'.
2 *Völkischer Beobachter*, 1928.
3 Read & Fisher, *Berlin: The Biography of a City*, p.3.
4 Neil MacGregor talking to the author, 6 August 2019.

Chapter One:

1237–1500

1 *Memoirs of the House of Brandenburg*, p.211.
2 Richie, *Faust's Metropolis*, p.20.
3 Read & Fisher, p.9.
4 St Mary's Church Berlin Visitors' Guide: *St.Petri-St.Marien mitten in Berlin*.
5 The library, the *Marienkirchebibliothek*, is now housed in the *Landeskirchlichen Archiv*.
6 Nachama, Schoeps & Simon, *Jews in Berlin*, p.11.
7 Taken from *Reisebericht des Jacobus von Brugge,* an account of 13th Century Berlin assembled from various sources by Adriaan von Müller 1987.
8 Müller, Jacobus von Brugge, p.36.
9 *Memoirs of the House of Brandenburg*, p.214, quoting Loxelius in 1364.
10 *Memoirs of the House of Brandenburg*, p.215.
11 Richie, pp.29–30.
12 Mander, *Eagle & Bear*, p.7.
13 *Memoirs of the House of Brandenburg*, p.215.
14 Quoted by Richie, p.32.

15 This translation comes from the English version published by the
    Marienkirche, taken from Peter Walther's *Der Berliner Totendanz zu St.
    Marien*, Berlin 1997, p.69.

16 *Memoirs of the House of Brandenburg*, p.20.

17 Mander, p.6.

18 The *Stadtbuch* was found in the possession of a magistrate in 1728. It
    then went missing before turning up in Bremen City Library in 1812. In
    1836 Bremen presented it to Berlin, where it is now in the Landesarchiv.

19 Schneider, *Berlin: Eine Kulturgeschichte*, p.42.

20 Richie, p.29 quoting *Stadt Buch*.

21 Nikolaikirche commentary on his portrait.

22 Luxusordnung of 1334 quoted by Werner, *Berlin 1000 Jahre Geschichte*,
    p.27.

23 Werner, p.42.

24 *Jews in Berlin*, p.12.

Chapter Two:

1500–1640

1 Figures taken from Paul Hohenberg & Lyn Lees, *The Making of Urban
   Europe 1000–1950*, CUP 1985.

2 *Memoirs of the House of Brandenburg*, p.216.

3 Taylor, *Berlin and its Culture*, p.14.

4 *Memoirs of the House of Brandenburg*, p.218.

5 Wolf Jobst Siedler, *Das Schloss lag nicht in Berlin – Berlin war das
   Schloss*, reproduced in Palace City Berlin Stadtmuseum Berlin 2016, p.9.

6 Ibid.

7 For a full description of the Desecration of the Host scandal see *Jews in
   Berlin*, p.12.

8 Snyder, *Documents of German History*, pp.63–6.

9 George Ganss, *Martin Luther und die Ablass*, p.540.

10 This only came to light in the archives at Marburg in 1883.

11 Stegmann, *The Reformation in Berlin-Cölln*, p.22.

12 Much of this information is gleaned from Sträßner, *Elisabeth von
    Dänemark*.

13 Stegmann, p.22.

14 Johannes Agricola's work has been analysed by Sander Gillman of Cornell
    University in *The Sixteenth Century Journal*, Vol.8 No.1 April 1977,
    'Johannes Agricola of Eisleben's Proverb Collection'.

15 *Jews in Berlin*, p.13.

16 Taylor, *Berlin and its Culture*, pp.23–4.

17 Taylor, *Berlin and its Culture*, p.30.

18 See Ribbe, Geschichte Berlins 1, pp.300–302, or for a more detailed study Agathe Lasch, *History of Written Language in Berlin*, Dortmund 1910, particularly Ch.7.

19 *Memoirs of the House of Brandenburg*, p.219.

20 *Memoirs of the House of Brandenburg*, p.220.

21 *Memoirs of the House of Brandenburg*, p.220.

22 Eikermann & Kaiser, *Die Post in Berlin 1576*.

23 Clark, *Iron Kingdom*, p.4.

24 *Verordnung zur Sauberhaltung von Berlin-Cölln*, 1583.

25 Ribbe, *Geschichte Berlins 1*, 1600.

26 Strohmaier-Wiederanders, *Glaubenskonflikte und Toleranz im Berlin 17. Jahrhunderts*, p.34.

27 Wedgwood, *The Thirty Years War*, p.44.

28 See Lisa-Gerda Henkel Stiftung Lecture No. 5302, *Anna von Preussen*.

29 Wedgwood, p.47.

30 *Memoirs of the House of Brandenburg*, p.40.

31 George William to the Emperor, quoted in *Memoirs of the House of Brandenburg*, p.48.

32 For a good explanation of the Kipper und Wipper Zeit see *Smithsonian Magazine*, 29 March 2012, '*Kipper und Wippe*: Rogue Traders, Rogue Princes and Rogue Bishops: The German Financial Meltdown 1621–1623' by Mike Dash.

33 Medick & Marschke, *Experiencing the Thirty Years War*, pp.105–9.

34 Quoted by Schiller, *The Thirty Years War*, p.87.

35 Reichsthalers were the standard currency across the Holy Roman Empire from 1566 and were widely used in Brandenburg and Prussia until 1750 when Prussia minted its own thalers. It is impossible to calculate accurately what 30,000 thalers would be today given the fluctuations in currency values caused by the Thirty Years War but, very roughly, it is probably about £10–15 million, a huge price for a devastated Brandenburg.

36 This and following quotes from Peter Thiele are from Mortimer, *Eyewitness Accounts of The Thirty Years War*, p.165.

37 Mortimer, Illustration No.5 from the original in the Bodleian Library, Oxford.

38 Mortimer, p.165.

39 Richie, p.47.

40 Mortimer, p.166.

41 Richie, p.47.

42 Mortimer, p.165.

43 *Memoirs of the House of Brandenburg*, p.39.

44 Schiller, p.84.

45 Green, *Reluctant Meister*, p.7.

46 Stephen Green's translation, *Reluctant Meister*, p.6.
47 Mortimer, p.178.
48 Schiller, p.4.
49 *Memoirs of the House of Brandenburg*, p.226.

Chapter Three:

1640–1740

1 McKay, *The Great Elector*, p.22.
2 Des Noyers, Secretary to Queen Louise Maria of Poland. Quoted by McKay, p.96.
3 Wedgwood, p.439.
4 Wedgwood, p.441.
5 McKay, p.21.
6 McKay, p.20.
7 McKay, p.30.
8 McKay, p.35.
9 'Sheds and Bones: Fragments of Everyday Life from Baroque Berlin' by Julia Heeb, quoting Jungklaus *Kindersterblichkeit und Lebensbedingungen* in *Palace. City. Berlin*, Stadtmuseum Berlin 2016.
10 McKay, p.52.
11 McKay, p.62.
12 This system of paying a tax to the 'Service Treasury' for soldiers' billeting charges was not changed until 1720.
13 Johannes Schultze, *Der Ausbau Berlins zur Festung*, Verein für die Geschichte Berlins Jahrbuch, 1951.
14 The figures for court employees come from 'Smart, Clean & Neat: The Baroque Palace and its Domestic Staff' by Jan Mende published in *Palace. City. Berlin: The Residence Shifts to the Centre*, Stadtmuseum Berlin 2016.
15 Zorn & Hanus, *Museum Island*, p.17.
16 McKay, p.74.
17 For a more detailed analysis see Clark, p.149.
18 In 1650 the Brandenburg Estates in Berlin submitted a formal protest to the Elector at the heavy tax burden imposed by the ongoing war. For the full text see *Documents of German History*, p.91.
19 McKay, p.183.
20 Taylor, *Berlin and its Culture*, p.37.
21 Beeskow, *Paul Gerhard 1607–1676*, p.64.
22 *Jews in Berlin*, p.16.
23 Jewish Museum Vienna, *Samuel Oppenheimer*.
24 McKay, p.186.

25 Mansel, *King of the World*, p.308.
26 Mansel, p.316.
27 Read & Fisher, p.20.
28 Taylor, *Berlin and its Culture*, p.35.
29 'Refugees Welcome: Population Policies and the Intake of Refugees as the Foundation of Berlin's Urban Development in the Wake of the Thirty Years War' by Brenda Spiesbach in *Palace. City. Berlin*, Stadtmuseum Berlin 2016.
30 McKay, p.238.
31 McKay, p.235.
32 See 'Sheds and Bones: Fragments of Everyday Life from Baroque Berlin' by Julia Heeb reproduced in *Palace. City. Berlin*, Stadtmuseum Berlin 2016, p.38.
33 McKay, p.261.
34 *Documents of German History*, p.94.
35 Pope to Louis XIV, 16 April 1701, quoted in *Documents of German History*, p.98.
36 Friedrich & Smart, *The Cultivation of Monarchy and the Rise of Berlin*, p.389.
37 Von Besser, *History of the Prussian Coronation*, quoted in Friedrich & Smart, pp.148–51.
38 Christoph von Dohna, *The Original Memoirs on the Reign and Court of Friedrich I*, quoted by Friedrich & Smart, p.395.
39 Toland, *An Account of the Courts of Prussia and Hanover*, p.21.
40 Toland, pp.24–7.
41 Mander, p.19.
42 Toland, p.33.
43 Taylor, *Berlin and its Culture*, p.38.
44 *Memoirs of the House of Brandenburg*, pp.171–2.
45 *Memoirs of the House of Brandenburg*, p.180.
46 Mander, p.19.
47 Toland, p.31.
48 Toland, p.31.
49 Toland, p.17.
50 Philipp Jakob Spener to Frederick I, quoted by Taylor, *Berlin and its Culture*, p.48.
51 *Memoirs of the House of Brandenburg*, p.241.
52 Friedrich & Smart, p.155.
53 Clark, p.71.
54 Friedrich & Smart, p.390.
55 Friedrich & Smart, p.362.
56 Clark, p.78.
57 Clark, p.78.

58 Förster, *Friedrich-Wilhelm I König von Preussen.*
59 Marschke, *A Conspicuous Lack of Consumption*, p.98.
60 Read & Fisher, p.30.
61 Princess Wilhelmina quoted by Mander, p.17.
62 Museum Island, p.22.
63 Blanning, *Frederick the Great*, p.28.
64 All quotes in this paragraph are from Förster.
65 Marschke, *Le Charactère Bizarre*, p.52.
66 Marschke, *Le Charactère Bizarre*, p.53.
67 Richie, p.62.
68 *Memoirs of the House of Brandenburg*, p.245.
69 *Memoirs of the House of Brandenburg*, p.247.
70 Figures from Clark, p.157.
71 Taylor, *Berlin and its Culture*, p.54.
72 *Memoirs of the House of Brandenburg*, p.248.
73 Marschke, *A Conspicuous Lack of Consumption*, p.107.
74 Richie, p.64.
75 *Jews in Berlin*, p.33.
76 Marschke, *Le Charactère Bizarre*, p.49.

Chapter Four:

1740–1786

1   Blanning, p.371.
2   Mander, p.24.
3   Heyde, *Der Roggenpreis*, p.83.
4   Prices taken from Heyde p.93 and from *How the Electoral Capital Became Prussia's Largest Garrison City* by Uwe Winkler, reproduced in *Palace. City. Berlin*, Stadtmuseum Berlin 2016, p.50.
5   Heyde, p.72.
6   Heyde, p.35.
7   Blanning, p.258.
8   Blanning, p. 60
9   Voltaire to Duc de Richelieu, quoted by Blanning, p.332.
10 Mander, p.31.
11 Mander, p.25.
12 Blanning, p.334.
13 *Memoirs of the House of Brandenburg*, p.223.
14 Frederick to d'Alembert, quoted by Blanning, p.336.
15 Blanning, p.336.
16 Taylor, *Berlin and its Culture*, p.70.
17 Blanning, p.137.

18 Taylor, *Berlin and its Culture*, p.72.
19 Taylor, *Berlin and its Culture*, p.74.
20 Blanning, p.59.
21 Blanning, p.434.
22 Blanning, p.434.
23 'Smart, Clean & Neat: The Baroque Palace and its Domestic Staff' by Jan Mende, reproduced in *Palace. City. Berlin*, Stadtmuseum Berlin 2016, p.70.
24 Ibid., p.71.
25 Frederick to de la Haye de Launay, quoted by Richie, p.70.
26 Richie, p.74.
27 Boswell, *Boswell on The Grand Tour*, pp.70–97.
28 Richie, p.5.
29 Erlin, *Berlin's Forgotten Future*, p.45.
30 Erlin, p.101.
31 Erlin, p.82.
32 All quotes from *The Life & Times of Herr Magister Sebaldus Nothanker* are from Erlin, pp.82–90.
33 Erlin, p.97.
34 'How the Electoral Capital Became Prussia's Largest Garrison City' by Uwe Winkler, reproduced in *City. Palace. Berlin*, Stadtmuseum Berlin 2016, p.49.
35 Schoeps etc, p.33.
36 Erlin, p.132.
37 Blanning, p.371.
38 Blanning, pp.379–80.
39 Richie, p.81.
40 All these quotes are from Erlin, pp.160–69.
41 Goethe, 1823.
42 Mander, p.38.
43 Blanning, p.343.
44 Mander, p.39.

Chapter Five:

1786–1840

1 De Staël, *Germany*, p.114.
2 De Staël, pp.114–16.
3 Clark, p.267.
4 Balfour, *Berlin: The Politics of Order 1737–1989*, p.30.
5 Clark, p.255.
6 Clark, p.269.
7 Clark, p.256.

8   Mander, p.47.
9   There is a good picture of some of them in their uniforms in the
    Märkische Museum.
10 Parthey, *Tagebücher*, p.111.
11 Schwerin, *Vor hundert Jahren*, p.112.
12 Schwerin, p.111.
13 *Journal des Campagnes du Baron Percy*, Tallandier, 1986, p.95
14 Schwerin, p.165.
15 Figures quoted by Richie, p.166.
16 For a fuller list see *Staatliche Museen zu Berlin* Museum Island, pp.28–35.
17 Clark, p.313.
18 Schwerin, *Vor hundert Jahren*, p.162.
19 Mander, p.50.
20 Johann Gottlieb Fichte, *Addresses to the German Nation*, Harper & Row
    1968, p.215. Originally quoted by Balfour, p.30.
21 From an article in *Encyclopaedia Britannica* vol.25, p.872 by Rose, John
    Holland.
22 Richie, p.114.
23 Quoted in the Schloss Tegel guidebook (p.8) DKV Art Guide No.150
    English Edition.
24 There is a portrait of him wearing this decoration by Gerhard von
    Kügelen in the German History Museum in Berlin.
25 Richie, p.109.
26 Sarah Knowles Bolton, *Famous Types of Womanhood*, 1892 Thomas
    Crowell & Co. New York, p.57.
27 These quotes are reproduced by Clark, p.356.
28 Deutsches Historisches Museum Display.
29 Ludwig Rellstab, *Aus Meinem Leben*, Berlin 1861 vol.1 p.165, quoted by
    Richie, p.111.
30 Quoted by Richie, p.113.
31 Balfour, p.35.
32 Sketches survive for both Schinkel's and Gilly's plans. See Balfour, pp.21
    and 35.
33 Clark, p.401.
34 For an explanation of these figures see White-Spunner, *Of Living Valour*,
    pp.xviii–xix.
35 In the *Niedersächsische Landesmuseum*.
36 Wallraf-Richartz-Museum, Köln.
37 Stadtmuseum, Berlin.
38 Quoted by Richie, p.122.
39 Taylor, *Berlin and its Culture*, p.135.
40 Taylor, p.143.
41 Mander, p.62.

42 Taylor, *Berlin and its Culture*, p.150.
43 Berlioz in his memoirs, quoted by Taylor, *Berlin and its Culture*, p.150.
44 McLellan, *Karl Marx: A Biography*, p.15.
45 Richie, p.154.

Chapter Six:
1840–1871

1 Mander, p.76.
2 Translated by Sabine Scherek, January 2020.
3 Figures taken from Richie, p.125.
4 Read & Fisher, p.84.
5 Dr. Gustav Kühne, *Carneval in Berlin*, Reproduced in *The Foreign & Quarterly* Volume 2 Article XVII p. 283 London 1843.
6 This is reproduced verbatim from Read & Fisher, pp.68–9, who translated it from the original.
7 Südekum, *Großstädtisches Wohnungselend*, p.12.
8 Taken from Mander, p.77 and his translation and lyrics.
9 Streckfuss, *Berlin in 19. Jahrhundert*, p.341.
10 All quotes from Carl Ludwig Zeitler are taken from *Angeschossen sein, soll wehe tun: Errinerungen eines Zeitzeugen*, published in *Berliner Geschichte Ausgabe 13* and edited by Doris Tüsselmann.
11 Order given on 14 March in Berlin by von Pfuel and quoted by Geist & Kürvers in *Das Berliner Mietshaus 1740–1862*, p.347.
12 Richie, p.128.
13 Clark, p.473.
14 Field Marshal Alfred von Waldersee, *A Field Marshal's Memoirs*.
15 Taken from the Verein fur Geschichte Berlin, *Bär* 16 Jg. 1889 s. 570.
16 From H.W. Koch, *A History of Prussia*, quoted by Sullivan & Krueger, *Berlin: A Literary Guide for Travellers*, p.70.
17 Mander, p.89.
18 Reproduced in *Berlin Geschichte Ausgabe 13*, p.35.
19 Ladd, *Ghosts of Berlin*, p.101.
20 Figures taken from Richie, p.164.
21 Theodore Fontane, *Wanderings in the Mark of Brandenburg* quoted by Read & Fisher, p.96.
22 Richie, p.151.
23 *Jews in Berlin*, p.80.
24 See *Documents of German History*, p.192 for extracts from the text.
25 Article 12 of the 1850 Constitution guaranteed freedom of religion.
26 Crankshaw, *Bismarck*, p.9.
27 Bismarck to August Bebel in the Reichstag 1878.

28 *Documents of German History*, p.186.

29 Bauer, *Berlin: Illustrierte Chronik bis 1870*, Berlin 1988 and quoted by Taylor, *Berlin and its Culture*, p.161.

Chapter Seven:

1871–1918

1 *Documents of German History*, p.262.

2 For a full version of the 1871 Constitution see *Documents of German History*, p.226.

3 Isherwood, *The Berlin Novels*, p. 259.

4 Read & Fisher, p.103.

5 Benjamin, *Berlin Childhood*, p.46.

6 The figures and details in this and the preceding paragraph come from Hughes, *Networks of Power*, Chapter VII.

7 Hughes, pp.181–200.

8 Schultz, *In Berlin in Stellung*, p.72 and Glatzer, *Berliner Leben 1870–1900*, p.270.

9 Pollard, *A Study in Municipal Government*.

10 From Zeitler, *Angeschossen sein soll wehe tun*.

11 The Berlin police kept exact records of visitors who all had to complete a registration card. These figures are taken from Masur, *Imperial Berlin*, p.136.

12 Figures taken from Masur, p.139.

13 Bismarck to his wife, 16 September 1849. From Bismarck's Letters Stuttgart 1919, edited by Herbert von Bismarck.

14 Gertrude Bell, *The Letters of Gertrude Bell*, 12 February 1897, quoted by City-Lit, *Berlin*, p.105.

15 Richie, p.178.

16 Figures taken from Richie, p.178.

17 Figure taken from Clark, p.569.

18 Quoted by Taylor, *Berlin and its Culture*, p.169.

19 Quoted by Taylor, *Berlin and its Culture*, p.169.

20 Quoted by Ladd, pp.86–7.

21 Taylor, *Berlin and its Culture*, p.200.

22 Gertrude Bell, *The Letters of Gertrude Bell*, quoted by City-Lit, *Berlin*, p.104.

23 Richie, p.182.

24 Peter Jelavich, *Berlin Cabaret*, p.22.

25 James Huneker, 'Max Liebermann and some phases of German Art' published in *Ivory, Apes & Peacocks*, New York 1917, p.173 and reproduced by Masur, p.226.

26 Quoted by Masur, p.148.

27 Herbert Bittner, *Käthe Kollwitz*, Thomas Yoseloff 1959, p.1.

28 Fischer, *Zille*, p.22.

29 Richie, p.186.

30 Ernst Johann Editor, *Reden des Kaisers*, Munich 1966, p.102, translation by Gerhard Masur.

31 This questionnaire was published in *Berliner Illustrierte Zeitung* No.52 on Christmas Day 1898.

32 Blücher, *Princess Blucher.*

33 Sullivan & Krueger, p.10.

34 Durieux, *Meine Ersten 90 Jahre*, p.212.

35 Both quotes are from *Documents of German History*, p.344.

36 The Manifesto of the Ninety-Three, as it was called, was published on 4 October 1914 'To the Civilised World from the Professors of Germany'.

37 Translation of Bebel's speech taken from Richie, p.255.

38 Steven Bach, *Marlene Dietrich*, p.24.

39 Durieux, p.216.

40 From *Errinerungen von Gerda Kirstaedter*, private family manuscript shared with the author.

41 These quotes are taken from Kollwitz, *Die Tagebücher 1908–1943*, Entries for August to October 1914.

42 Quoted by Clay Large, *Berlin: A Modern History*, p.109, although he refers to Wermuth as Anton.

43 Letter from Professor Wolfgang Pfaffenberger to the author 8 May 2020.

44 I am much indebted to Nigel Dunkley for explaining the Langemarck Memorial to me.

45 Blücher, p.161.

46 Bach, p.25.

47 Durieux, p.215.

48 *Errinerungen von Gerda Kirstaedter.*

49 Glatzer, *Berliner Leben 1914–1918*, p.299.

50 *Hitler's Berlin* by Thomas Friedrich, translated by Stewart Spencer.

51 Walter Gropius, quoted by Richie, p.295.

52 Peter Hart, *The Last Battle*, p.325.

53 Altenhöner, *Vor der Revolution.*

54 Altenhöner.

55 Altenhöner.

Chapter Eight:

1918–1933

1 All these figures and quotes are taken from the Märkische Museum's excellent exhibition on the 1918–19 Revolution mounted in 2018. The poster was designed by Joe Lowenstein.

2 Quoted by Steven Bach, *Marlene Dietrich*, p.29.

3 Grosz, *A Small Yes and a Big No*, p.91.

4 Anna Rehme, quoted in *Berliner Tageblatt* 9.11.18, p.436.

5 Taken from Juchler, *Die Deutsche Revolution*.

6 Kessler, *The Diaries of a Cosmopolitan*, p.6.

7 Kessler, *The Diaries of a Cosmopolitan*, p.632.

8 Martha Globig, *Weiße haben hier nichts zu suchen*, Berliner Leben 1914–18, p.460.

9 Kessler, *The Diaries of a Cosmopolitan*, p.6.

10 Juchler.

11 Kessler, *The Diaries of a Cosmopolitan*, p.36.

12 Kessler, *The Diaries of a Cosmopolitan*, p.42.

13 Kessler, *The Diaries of a Cosmopolitan*, p.109.

14 Kessler, *The Diaries of a Cosmopolitan*, p.114.

15 Kollwitz, *Tagebuch* 22nd March 1920.

16 Ernst Wollweber, KPD Official, quoted by Taylor, *The Berlin Wall*, p.25.

17 Kessler, *Walther Rathenau*, p.4.

18 Bánffy, *Transylvanian Trilogy*, p.xiiii.

19 Kessler, *The Diaries of a Cosmopolitan*, p.186.

20 Dr Jürgen Wetzel, *Die Inflation in Berlin 1923*, Berliner Geschichte Ausgabe 20. The figures above for the increase in the price of bread are taken from the same source.

21 Kessler, *The Diaries of a Cosmopolitan*, p.199.

22 Bielenberg, *The Past is Myself*, p.56.

23 This story is told by Walter Henry Nelson in *The Berliners*, p.107.

24 Lenya, *Speak Low*, pp.21–2.

25 Kollwitz, *Tagebuch* End of November 1923.

26 Taylor, *Berlin and its Culture*, p.210.

27 Grosz, p.103.

28 Clay Large, p.200.

29 Grosz, p.94.

30 Quoted by Clay Large, p.222.

31 Christopher Isherwood, *Christopher and his Kind*.

32 Isherwood, *The Berlin Novels*, p.363.

33 All these quotes are from Isherwood, *The Berlin Novels*, pp.362–87.

34 Read & Fisher, p.170.

35 Quoted by Clay Large, p.211.

36 Nelson, p.108.
37 Taylor, *Berlin and its Culture*, p.234.
38 Wolf von Eckardt, *Erich Mendelssohn*.
39 Grosz, p.115.
40 Kästner, *Fabian*, Introduction by Rodney Livingstone, p.xiv.
41 Mander, p.129.
42 Quoted by Mander, p.130.
43 Goebbels diaries, quoted by Read & Fisher, p.188.
44 Read & Fisher, p.188.
45 Isherwood, *Berlin Novels*, p.479.
46 Isherwood, *Berlin Novels*, p.482.
47 Isherwood, *Berlin Novels*, p.409.
48 Mander, p.129.
49 Isherwood, *Berlin Novels*, p.465.

Chapter Nine:

1933–1945

1 Kessler, *Diaries*, p.448.
2 Tergit died in 1982 and it is heartening that she now has a Berlin street named after her, Gabriele Tergit Promenade that runs from the Landwehrkanal to Leipziger Platz. *Käsebier Takes Berlin* was published in English in 2019 by the *New York Review of Books* and Dr Elke-Vera Kotowski at the Mendelssohn Institute is doing much good work to establish her legacy.
3 Taylor, *Berlin and its Culture*, p.263.
4 Stargardt, *The German War*, p.120.
5 *Jews in Berlin*, p.192.
6 Andreas-Friedrich, *Berlin Underground*, p.18.
7 Andreas-Friedrich, p.23.
8 For a fuller coverage of the KLV scheme see Stargardt, pp.114–16.
9 Ilse Koehn, *Mischling zweiten Grades*, p. 111.
10 Stiftung Exil website, January 2020.
11 Mander, p.133.
12 Read & Fisher, p.204.
13 Bielenberg, p.229.
14 All these quotes come from Hilmes, *Sixteen Days in August*.
15 From the Plötzensee Memorial exhibition.
16 Shirer, *Berlin Diary*.
17 Both these quotes are from stories told by Read & Fisher, p.217.
18 Quoted by Moorhouse, *Berlin at War*, p.18.
19 Moorhouse, p.20.

20 Russell, *Berlin Embassy*, p.76.
21 Kardorff, *Diary of a Nightmare*, pp.84 and 92.
22 Andreas-Friedrich, *Berlin Underground*, p.90.
23 This story is taken from an article in *The Times*, 25 January 2020, about Christiane Carsten's book on Reiswerder.
24 Quoted by Moorhouse, p.179.
25 Andreas-Friedrich, p.92.
26 Detailed in Stargardt, p.29.
27 *Time* magazine, 7 January 1946.
28 Kardorff, p.18.
29 Anonymous, *A Woman in Berlin*, p. 51.
30 Quoted to the author by Dr Eckerhardt Klausa, Director *Gedenkstätte Deutscher Widerstand* in an interview, 20 November 2019.
31 Theo Findahl, quoted by Moorhouse, p.347.
32 *A Woman in Berlin*, p.18.
33 Kardorff, p.13.
34 Kardorff, p.63.
35 Moorhouse, p.252.
36 Kardorff, p.31.
37 Kardorff, p.111.
38 Middlebrook & Everitt, *The Bomber Command War Diaries*, p.92.
39 Kardorff, p.70.
40 Bielenberg, p.207.
41 Shirer, p.387.
42 Kardorff, p.92.
43 Speer, *Inside the Third Reich*, pp.393–5.
44 *A Woman in Berlin*, p.23.
45 *1945: A Documentation*, Text 4.
46 Speer, pp.393–5.
47 Karl Heinz Schlesier, *Flakhelfer to Grenadier*, p.37. Schlesier was actually writing about his experiences in Dusseldorf rather than Berlin but the guns, drills and effect were the same.
48 Kardorff, p.180.
49 Marshall Ivan Stepanovich Koniev is sometimes spelled as Konev but he is the same person.
50 Quoted by Moorhouse, p.363.
51 *1945 A Documentation*, Text 8 Bengt von zur Mühlen *Der Todeskampf der Reichshauptstadt* Kleinmachnow 1994.
52 *A Woman in Berlin*, p.45.
53 *A Woman in Berlin*, p.66.
54 *1945: A Documentation*, Text 114.
55 From Dan Vyleta, *Pavel and I*, quoted in CityLit Berlin, p.137.
56 Taylor, *The Berlin Wall*, p.32.

Chapter Ten:

1945–1961

1 Taylor, *The Berlin Wall*, p.287.
2 *A Woman in Berlin*, p.20.
3 Beatrice Collins, *The Luminous Life of Lily Aphrodite*, quoted in Sullivan & Krueger, p.207.
4 *1945: A Documentation*, Text 115.
5 Pfaffenberger, *50 Jahre Zentralstelle für Auslandsschulwesen – Bundesverwaltungsamt 2018*. Ziedler later became a teacher in Steglitz and Director of the German Schools Abroad Scheme.
6 Leonhard, *Die Revolution entlässt ihre Kinder*, p.294.
7 Richard Brett-Smith, *Berlin '45 The Grey City*, pp.43–4.
8 Ruth Andreas-Friedrich, quoted by Clay Large, p.384.
9 *1945: A Documentation*, Text 106.
10 *Documents of German History No.160*.
11 *Guardian*, 17 July 1945.
12 All the quotes in this paragraph are taken from Brett-Smith, pp.58–66.
13 *1945: A Documentation*, Text 117.
14 Kardorff, p.213.
15 Clare, *Berlin Days 1946–47*, p.16.
16 *Jews in Berlin*, p.228.
17 Tunner, *Over the Hump*, p.161.
18 Gisela Bilski interview with Sabrine Schereck, 2016, and also quoted by Kendall, *The Cold War: A New Oral History*, p.67.
19 Gail Halvorsen interviewed by *Der Tagesspiegel* in 2013 and reported by Oliver Moody in *The Times*, 21 February 2019. Halvorsen returned to Berlin on the seventieth anniversary of the airlift.
20 Facts and figures on the Berlin Airlift are taken from the Archive of the Royal Air Force Museum.
21 *Trading Economics*, German Unemployment rates from 1949: see also Barry Eichengreen & Albrecht Ritschl, *Understanding West German Economic Growth in the 1950s*, Humboldt University SFB Series 649.
22 Quoted by Clay Large, p.412.
23 Margit Hosseini, interviewed by Iain MacGregor in *Checkpoint Charlie*, p.18.
24 Hardy Firl, quoted in Kendall, p.159.
25 Kendall, p.164.
26 Quoted by Clay Large, p.426.
27 Kendall, p.166.
28 Kendall, p.167.
29 Ernst Hermann Meyer, East German composer, writing in 1987 and quoted by Taylor, *The Berlin Wall*, p.377.

30 Most of the detail in this paragraph is taken from the author's conversation with Marc Metzger and from his pamphlet *Das Berliner Schloss*.

31 Brett-Smith, p.xi.

Chapter Eleven:

1961–1989

1 Quoted by Frederick Taylor, *The Berlin Wall*, p.133.

2 Figures taken from German Centre for Higher Education and Research Conference Paper, November 2016, *Between Deterrence & Welcome*.

3 Walter Ulbricht, 15 June 1961.

4 Quoted by Iain Macgregor in *Checkpoint Charlie*, p.53.

5 Related by Doris Kohn, now Tüsselmann, to Professor Wolfgang Pfaffenberger and passed to the author 11 May 2020.

6 Read & Fisher, p.284.

7 Quoted by MacGregor, p.99.

8 This quote and the figures above are taken from Karl William Friche, *Bedrückende Mf S-Erforschung*, Deutschland Archive 33, 6 (2000): 1026 and quoted in Department of History Amherst College Paper, *The Stasi*.

9 Wolfgang Göbel interviewed by Sabine Schereck 2018. Transcript with the author.

10 Mikael Adam conversation with author, July 2019.

11 Notes included in Stadt Museum Berlin exhibition, *East Berlin*, Ephraim Palace, 2019.

12 Metzger, *Das Berliner Schloß*, p.45.

13 Told to the author by Professor Wolfgang Pfaffenberger, 11 May 2020.

14 Stadt Museum, *East Berlin* exhibition.

15 Stadt Museum, *East Berlin* exhibition.

16 Irene Dunkley in conversation with the author, 22 November 2019.

17 For a fuller account of these Stasi operations see Lewis, *Die Kunst die Verrats*.

18 Andreas Austilat, interviewed by Sabine Schereck 2018. Transcript with the author.

19 David Bowie, 1978, quoted in Märkische Museum.

20 From YouTube, *Reagan Library*.

21 Rice & Zelikow, *Germany Unified and Europe Transformed: A Study in Statecraft*, p.35.

Chapter Twelve:

After 1989

1 Professor Dr Christoph Stölzl, *Nachdenken über Preussen*, lecture notes shared with the author 2019.
2 *Guardian* editorial, 10 November 1989.
3 Quoted in interview by Wolfgang Hübner, Editor of *Neues Deutschland* and Tobias Buck, *Financial Times*, 2 November 2019.
4 Annemarie Reffert, interviewed in the *Financial Times* by Guy Chazan, 9 November 2019.
5 Willy Brandt, 10 November 1989, quoted by Frederick Taylor, p.430.
6 Frithjof Banisch, interviewed by Oliver Moody in *The Times*, 9 November 2019.
7 Quoted in interview with Wolfgang Hübner by Tobias Buck, *Financial Times*, 2 November 2019.
8 Quoted by Kendall, p.547.
9 Mikael Adam interview with author, 2019.
10 Quoted by Kendall, p.553.
11 Quoted by Kendall, p.554.
12 Wolfgang Schäuble interviewed by Guy Chazan in the *Financial Times*, 23 March 2019.
13 Metzger, p.47.
14 Wilhelm von Boddien interviewed by Frederick Studemann in the *FT Weekend* magazine, 14 September 2019.
15 Paul Spies interview with author, 22 November 2019.
16 Quoted by Paul Spies, 22 November 2019.
17 Hartmut Dorgerloh interviewed by Frederick Studemann in the *FT Weekend* magazine, 14 September 2019.
18 Neil MacGregor interview with author, 6 August 2019.
19 For more detail see Ladd, pp.217–24.
20 For more detail see Ladd, pp.196–7.
21 Quotes from Ladd, p.205.
22 Taken from Braun, *City of Exiles*, p.29.
23 Quoted in *The Times*, 8 August 2019.
24 Figures taken from the *Financial Times*, 15 June 2019, drawing on *The Statistical Office of Berlin-Brandenburg CBRE; Berlin Hyp.Statbel*.
25 Taken from David Charter's 'From Our Correspondent' in *The Times*, 23 July 2018.
26 Translated from *Die Verfassung des Deutschen Reiches* vom 11 August 1919.

FURTHER READING
AND NOTES ON SOURCES

This book has been written from a great variety of sources. First, I am much indebted to Sabine Schereck for her research work in a range of Berlin libraries and archives and for the richness of the original material she discovered. I am also most grateful to her for the many interviews she conducted for me, and for making available those she had completed earlier for both Bridget Kendall's *The Cold War: A New Oral History* (a most valuable book) and for Iain MacGregor's much-acclaimed *Checkpoint Charlie*. Where I have taken quotes from these interviews that have already been used in either of those books, they have been fully accredited in the text. Secondly, I am equally grateful to *Verein für die Geschichte Berlins* (the Berlin History Society), founded in 1865, which is a formidably impressive institution and to the ever-helpful Professor Wolfgang Pfaffenberger. The Society has an excellent library and archive in the Neuer Marstall, the old royal stables across from the Berliner Schloss, run by a most accommodating team of volunteers, and publish a regular magazine, *Berliner Geschichte*, each edition examining an aspect of the city's history in detail. They also publish a yearbook, appropriately entitled *Der Bär von Berlin* (The Berlin Bear), as well as regular *Mitteilungen* on a wide variety of subjects. I have relied heavily on their work and assistance. Thirdly, I was very fortunate to have access, via Professor Pfaffenberger, to the Kirstaedter family papers, unusual and valuable in being the story of an ordinary Berlin family as opposed to the normal records of the great and the good. There are two Berlin history societies. There is also a British Berlin Historical Association, which tends to look at more recent history and who also stage some excellent lectures and visits.

It will come as no surprise that a lot of history has been written about Berlin as well as much fiction; inevitably in a book of this scope, I have drawn heavily on previously published works. I have listed most of these in the bibliography below although, with so much available, it is far from being exhaustive. There is not, however, much history in English and very little on the earlier years. There is only one in-depth history that starts with the city's origins, Alexandra Richie's magisterial *Faust's Metropolis*. A very full and immaculately researched book, at just short of 1,000 pages, it remains a seminal work though it is fuller on the nineteenth and twentieth centuries than on the earlier years and doesn't cover the Reformation. John Mander's *The Eagle and The Bear* is an excellent if brief study of the twin characters of the city, both as a cosmopolitan, independently minded trading community and the Hohenzollern capital. Anthony Read's and David Fisher's *Berlin: The Biography of a City* is an entertaining and very readable short history, albeit annoyingly without source notes. Then Rory MacLean's *Berlin*, which tells the city's story through the real and imagined experiences of twenty-three Berliners and visitors, is a wonderful book that goes a long way towards capturing Berlin's atmosphere over the ages. Brian Ladd's *The Ghosts of Berlin* is, by contrast, an excellent survey of the built city and its architecture, as is Alan Balfour's *Berlin: The Politics of Order 1737–1989*, while Paul Sullivan and Marcel Krueger's *Berlin: A Literary Guide for Travellers* and Heather Reyes and Katy Derbyshire's City-Lit edition, *Berlin*, are both really good anthologies of Berlin literature. An exceptional book – and essential reading for anyone interested in Berlin, although it deals with a wider landscape – is Professor Christopher Clark's *Iron Kingdom: The Rise and Downfall of Prussia 1600–1947*, which, unusually, is as widely read in Germany as it is in the English-speaking world. Another wonderful book on the wider German nation (written in English but that again Germany interprets as its own) is Neil MacGregor's *Germany: Memories of a Nation*, the written version of his immensely popular talks on BBC Radio 4.

Four other books I have found particularly helpful that cover the whole story are, first, *Berlin: Geschichte in Daten*, an entertaining list of what happened in the city by date. It starts, optimistically, in 60,000 BC but becomes fuller when it reaches 1237! Secondly, *Jews in Berlin*, edited by Andreas Nachama, Julius Schoeps and Hermann Simon. Professor Dr Julius Schoeps is a descendant of Moses Mendelssohn and Chairman of the Board of Directors of *Moses Mendelssohn Stiftung*, the eponymous institute in Berlin. Thirdly, *Berlin and its Culture* by Professor Ronald Taylor, one-time professor of German at the University of Sussex and a man who understood German culture in general – and that of Berlin in particular – better than most Englishmen. Sadly he died in 2013. Lastly, *Documents of German History*, edited by Professor Louis L. Snyder in New York and published in 1958, is an excellent compendium of some of the key documents that have affected Berlin, together with a helpful commentary.

Annoyingly, there are few particularly good guidebooks that combine history with cultural and practical information. An early Cadogan Guide, published in 1991, is now very out of date, and other contemporary guides tend to be in the 'top ten things to do in Mitte' category. The best currently available is Joseph Pearson's *Cityscope Berlin* (2017), which has a good introductory history as well as amusing essays on different aspects of Berlin life.

Please refer to the bibliography for a more detailed list, but I have noted below some English sources that may be of particular interest. (Obviously there is a lot more in German, and I have included the odd German book below as well.)

EARLY YEARS

Apart from Richie, there is really very little in English, so for those who want to explore in more depth it is a question of brushing up your German. *Berliner Geschichte* has run several useful editions on medieval Berlin, which are particularly helpful on the early Church, the development of the city's trading routes and the Reformation: *Ausgabe 4, 8, 9* and *14*. Adolph Streckfuss published his four-volume *Berlin seit 500 Jahren – von Fischerdorf zur Weltstadt* in 1864, of which Volume One is helpful, even more so if you can find an edition that is not printed in *Fraktur*. Frederick the Great's *Memoirs of the House of Brandenburg* is in English (it was written in French originally) and is pithy, amusing and mostly correct. However, one must bear in mind that even Frederick suffered from the chronic Hohenzollern sense of insecurity and he wrote the book as much to prove the antiquity and legitimacy of his family as he did for a historical record. Then the fictional account *The Travels of Jacobus von Brügge*, written from a clever use of original manuscripts, gives a good idea of what life was like in thirteenth-century Berlin.

SIXTEENTH AND SEVENTEENTH CENTURIES

It is strange, given the huge contemporary interest in written history and the richness of the subject matter, how little has been written in either German or English about the great events in Brandenburg-Prussia in the lead-up to the Thirty Years War and its aftermath, particularly as the war has been so instrumental in forming the current shape and psyche of the modern German nation. Karin Friedrich's *Brandenburg-Prussia 1466–1806* is very good, albeit intended more for an academic audience, and Derek McKay's *The Great Elector* in the Pearson 'Profiles in Power' series is equally excellent. For the Thirty Years War, there is nothing comparable with C.V. Wedgwood's *The Thirty Years War* as a general history. Friedrich Schiller's *The Thirty Years War* gives a very good summary of the German experience, and Hans Medick and Benjamin Marschke's *Experiencing the Thirty Years War* is an excellent brief history with documents recording first-hand experiences. For braver souls *Berlin im Dreißigjährigen Kriege* by Eberhard Faden, published in 1927, contains considerable detail.

Eighteenth century

There is an equal dearth of biography about Frederick I and Frederick William I. Luckily there are some good first-hand accounts of Berlin at the time, many included in Karin Friedrich and Sara Smart's *The Cultivation of Monarchy and the Rise of Berlin*, and John Toland's personal account of his embassy in 1702. There is a three-volume biography of Frederick William I by Dr Frederick Förster, published in Berlin in 1835, but fortunately we may soon be treated to a modern appraisal by Professor Benjamin Marschke, who has written extensively on early-eighteenth-century Berlin and the Prussian Court. Helga Schultz's *Berlin 1650–1800* is a most helpful, largely empirical, survey. If there is a shortage of material before 1740, then with the accession of Frederick II, The Great, the floodgates are opened. He must have enjoyed more biographies than almost any other European monarch. By far the best is Professor Tim Blanning's *Frederick The Great*, published in 2015. From the 1750s onwards we get more writing specifically about Berlin itself as the city establishes its own identity separate to that of the Hohenzollern Court. A most interesting study is Professor Matt Erlin's *Berlin's Forgotten Future* on which I have relied heavily for information about Berlin's literary and cultural life in this period. For those who are interested in more detail on how Frederick's system of government worked in Berlin, there is Hubert Johnson's *Frederick the Great and his Officials* while Master Baker Johann Friedrich Heyde's account of everyday life during the Seven Years War, *Der Roggenpreis*, gives a street-level view but I cannot find a an English edition. I will not repeat here the great works of German literature that are discussed in the main body of the book and need no further explanation, but there are some informative late-eighteenth-century travelogues that should be mentioned. James Boswell's *Grand Tour* in 1764 gives a good and entertaining idea of how Berlin appeared to a British visitor. Madame de Staël's *Germany*, first published in 1810, has a lot about Berlin and the author – an early revolutionary intellectual who realised sooner than many the true nature of Napoleon's ambition – is fluent and informative. Nicolai's famous description of Berlin and Potsdam is still in print in German and French but probably only of interest to those who would like a more detailed description of what the city was like at the time.

Nineteenth century

The Napoleonic era has been well covered in the hundreds, if not thousands, of histories of Napoleon's campaigns. David Chandler's *Jena 1806* is a good short study of the invasion of Prussia. For devotees of the industrial revolution Thomas Hughes's *Networks of Power* (1983) is a fascinating study of the effects of electrification. Gerhard Masur's *Imperial Berlin* (1971) is an equally excellent study of the city from mid-century, while Gordon Craig's *Germany 1866–1945* (1978) is a comprehensive wider history. Bismarck has enjoyed almost as many biographies as Frederick the Great; Edward Crankshaw's 1981 *Bismarck* is one of the most approachable and Jonathan Steinberg's 2011 *Bismarck* one of the most complete. Alistair Horne's *The Fall of Paris* remains one of the best accounts of 1870. Walter Benjamin's *Berlin Childhood* is a charming and evocative portrait of comfortable bourgeois life in Berlin before the First World War. For first-hand accounts of life in Berlin in the 1890s and 1900s, try Evelyn Princess Blücher's diaries, *A Private Memoir*.

Twentieth century

David Clay Large's *Berlin: A Modern History* is a good and entertaining account of the city from 1870 to 1989. For a gossipy account of the 1920s there is little to beat Harry Kessler's *Diaries of a Cosmopolitan* or his very good biography of *Walter Rathenau*. Christopher Isherwood's *Berlin Novels* are technically fiction but in reality they provide an absorbing account of life just before the Nazis seized power. William Shirer's *Berlin Diary* is a frenzied account by an American correspondent of Berlin in the 1930s until he was forced to leave in 1941. Christabel Bielenberg's *The Past is Myself* has justifiably become a classic, while Ruth Andreas-Friedrich's *Berlin Underground 1938–1945* and Ursula von Kardorff's *Diary of a Nightmare* are but two examples of first-hand accounts by those who hated the Nazis. Roger Moorhouse's *Berlin At War* is a very well-researched account of everyday life in Berlin 1939–45, while Nicholas Stargardt's *The German War* is an exceptional look at how Germany as a whole reacted to Hitler's wars. Three books stand out on 1945 and the city's fall. Antony Beevor's *Berlin* is now justifiably a classic; Beevor also edited the anonymous *A Woman in Berlin*, the story by an unknown Berliner of her life and multiple rapes by the Soviets. The second is John Erickson's *Road to Berlin*. Another evocative, sad but charming book is Thomas Harding's *The House by the Lake*, the story of a house and the families who lived in it at Glienicke.

Frederick Taylor's *The Berlin Wall* and Iain MacGregor's *Checkpoint Charlie* are two exceptional accounts of the era of the Wall, while Anna Funder's *Stasiland* and Bridget Kendall's *The Cold War* both portray vividly what life was like behind it. Stephen Green's books *Reluctant Meister* and *Dear Germany* offer a thoughtful look at modern Germany from someone who knows Berlin well. Stuart Braun's *City of Exiles* is a moving study of those who have come and gone from Berlin during the last century.

Space prevents me from offering but a short list here. By far the best way to learn more about this most absorbing and exciting of European capitals is to go there. Start in the incomparable *Märkische Museum*, which tells the city's story so well, and then begin walking. If you are anything like me, you will still be walking forty years later.

BIBLIOGRAPHY

PUBLISHED BOOKS

Alexis, Willibald, *Der Roland von Berlin* (Rütten & Loening, 1987)

Andreas-Friedrich, Ruth, *Berlin Underground 1938–1945* (Paragon, 1989)

Anonymous, *A Woman in Berlin* (Virago, 2011)

Antill, Peter, *Berlin 1945: End of the Thousand Year Reich* (Osprey, 2005)

Arenhövel, Willmuth, *Berlin 1945* (Verlag, 1995)

Arnold, Benjamin, *Princes and Territories in Medieval Germany* (CUP, 1991)

Aster, Misha, *The Reich's Orchestra: The Berlin Philharmonic 1933–1945* (Souvenir, 2010)

Bach, Steven, *Marlene Dietrich* (Harper Collins, 1993)

Balfour, Alan, *Berlin: The Politics of Order 1737–1989* (Rizzoli, 1990)

Bánffy, Miklós, *Transylvanian Trilogy* (Arcadia, 1999)

Barraclough, Geoffrey, *The Origins of Modern Germany* (Blackwell, 1979)

Bath, Matthias, *Berlin – eine Biografie: Menschen und Schicksale* (Nünnerich-Asmus Verlag, 2016)

Bauer, Frank, *Napoleon in Berlin: Preußens Haupstadt unter Französischer Besetzung 1806–1808* (Story, 2006)

Beeskow, Hans-Joachim, *Paul Gerhardt 1607–1676* (Heimat-
Verlag Lübben, 2006)

Beevor, Antony, *Berlin: The Downfall 1945* (Viking, 2002)

Benjamin, Walter, *Berlin Childhood*, trans. Howard Eiland
(Harvard, 2006)

Bielenberg, Christabel, *The Past is Myself* (Corgi, 1993)

Blanning, Tim, *Frederick The Great, King of Prussia* (Penguin, 2016)

Blücher, Fürstin Evelyn von Whalstatt, *Princess Blucher, English
Wife in Berlin: a private memoir of events, politics and
daily life in Germany throughout the War and the social
revolution of 1918* (Constable, 1920)

Böhme, Helmut, *An Introduction to the Social and
Economic History of Germany*, trans. W.R. Lee
(Blackwell, 1978)

Boie, Heinrich Christian, *Briefe aus Berlin 1769–70*
(Gerstenberg, 1970)

Boswell, James, *Boswell on the Grand Tour 1764*, ed. Frederick A.
Pottle (Heinemann, 1953)

Braun, Stuart, *City of Exiles: Berlin From Outside In*
(Noctua, 2015)

Brett-Smith, Richard, *Berlin 1945: The Grey City*
(Macmillan, 1966)

Bunsen, Marie von, *A Winter in Berlin*, trans. Mrs Dugdale
(Edward Arnold, 1899)

——*The World I Used to Know*, trans. Oakley Williams
(Butterworth, 1930)

Citino, Robert M., *The German Way of War* (University Press of
Kansas, 2005)

Clare, George, *Berlin Days 1946–47* (Pan, 1989)

Clark, Christopher, *The Iron Kingdom: The Rise and Downfall of
Prussia 1600–1947* (Penguin, 2006)

Clay Large, David, *Berlin: A Modern History* (Penguin, 2000)

Craig, Gordon, *Germany 1866–1945* (OUP, 1978)

Crankshaw, Edward, *Bismarck* (Papermac, 1981)

——*The Fall of the House of Hapsburg* (Papermac, 1963)

Danyel, Jürgen, *Ost-Berlin 30 Erkundungen* (Christoph Links, 2019)

Dietrich, Marlene, *Gott Sei Dank, Bin Ich Berlinerin* (Ullstein, 1990)

Donath, Matthias, *Architecture in Berlin 1933–1945: A Guide Through Nazi Berlin* (Lukas Verlag, 2006)

Durieux, Tilla, *Meine ersten 90 Jahre* (Ullstein, 1991)

Duwe, Georg, *Berlin in fremder Hand* (Osnabrück, 1991)

Eckardt, Wolf von, *Masters of World Architecture: Erich Mendelssohn* (Mayflower, 1960)

Eikermann, Diethelm & Kaiser, Gabriele, *Die Pest in Berlin 1576* (Basiliken Presse, 2012)

Erickson, John, *The Road to Berlin* (Grafton, 1985)

Erlin, Matt, *Berlin's Forgotten Future: City, History and Enlightenment in Eighteenth Century Germany* (University of North Carolina Press, 2004)

Evans, Richard J., *The Third Reich in History & Memory* (Little Brown, 2015)

Faden, Eberhard, *Berlin im Dreißigjährigen Kriege* (Deutsche Berlagsgefellschaft für Politik und Geschichte Berlin, 1927)

Fallada, Hans, *Alone in Berlin*, trans. Michael Hofman (Penguin, 2010)

Fehring, Günter, *The Archaeology of Medieval Germany* (Routledge, 1991)

Fischer, Gerhard, *Hugenotten in Berlin* (Union, 1988)

Fischer, Lothar, *Zille* (Rowholt, 1979)

Fontane, Theodore, *Effi Briest* (Penguin, 1967)

——*Irrungen, Wirrungen* (Reclam, 1991)

——*Wanderungen durch die Mark Brandenburg: 5 Vols. 1. Die Grafschaft Ruppin; 2. Das Oderland; 3. Havelland; 4. Spreeland; 5. Fünf Schlösser* (Inselverlag, 1993)

Förster, Dr Frederick, *Friedrich-Wilhelm I – König von Preussen*, 3 vols (Berlin, 1835)

Fraser, David, *Frederick The Great* (Penguin, 2000)

Friedrich, Karin, *Brandenburg-Prussia 1466–1806* (Palgrave Macmillan, 2012)

——with Smart, Sara, *The Cultivation of Monarchy and the Rise of Berlin* (Ashgate, 2010)

Friedrich, Ruth-Andreas, *Der Schattenmann* (Suhrkamp, 2000)

Friedrich, Thomas, *Hitler's Berlin: Abused City*, trans. Stewart Spencer (Yale UP, 2016)

Funder, Anna, *Stasiland: Stories from Behind the Berlin Wall* (Granta, 2003)

Ganss, Henry George, *Johann Tetzel* (Robert Appleton, 1912)

Geist, Johann Friedrich & Kürvers, Klaus, *Das Berliner Mietshaus 1740–1862* (München, 1980)

Gerard, James W., *My Four Years in Germany* (Hodder & Stoughton, 1917)

Giebel, Wieland, *Die Franzosen in Berlin 1806–1808* (Story, 2006)

Glatzer, Ruth, *Berliner Leben 1870–1900 Errinerungen und Berichte* (Rütten & Loening, 1983)

——*Berliner Leben 1914–1918* (Rütten & Loening, 1983)

Green, Stephen, *Dear Germany; Liebeserklärung an ein Land mit Vergangenheit* (Theiss 2017)

——*Reluctant Meister* (Haus, 2016)

Grosz, George, *A Small Yes and a Big No*, trans. Arnold J. Pomerans (Zenith, 1982)

Gutt, Barbara, *Frauen in Berlin* (Arani, 2017)

Hagen, William, *Ordinary Prussians: Brandenburg Junkers and Villagers 1500–1840* (CUP, 2002)

Harding, Thomas, *The House by the Lake* (Windmill, 2015)

Haverkamp, Alfred, *Medieval Germany* (OUP, 1988)

(insert above Harverkamp)

Hart, Peter, *The Last Battle: Endgame on the Western Front 1918* (Profile, 2018)

Heine, Heinrich, *Briefe aus Berlin* (Hofenberg, 2017)

Heinrich, Prof. Dr Gerd, *Kulturatlas Brandenburg* (Bäßler, 2015)

Henkys, Albrecht, *Berlin's Nikolaikirche Stadtmuseum* (Berlin, 2015)

Hessel, Franz, *Walking in Berlin* (Scribe, 2018)

Heyde, Johann Friedrich, *Der Roggenpreis* (Akademie-Verlag
    Berlin, 1988)

Hilmes, Oliver, *Sixteen Days in August*, trans. Jefferson Chase
    (Bodley Head, 2018)

Hinterkeuser, Guido, *Berlin Palace* (Schnell & Steiner, 2014)

Hubatsch, Walter, *Frederick The Great: Absolutism and
    Administration* (Thames & Hudson, 1973)

Hughes, Thomas P., *Networks of Power* (Johns Hopkins
    University Press, 1983)

Hugues, Pascal, *Ruhige Strasse in guter Wohnlage* (Rowohlt, 2019)

Hürliman, Martin, *Berlin: Königsresidenz; Reichshaupstadt;
    Neubeginn* (Atlantis, 1981)

Ingrid, Heinrich-Jost, *Adolf Glassbrenner* (Stapp, 1981)

Isherwood, Christopher, *The Berlin Novels* (Vintage, 1999)

Isherwood, Christopher, *Christopher and his Kind*
    (Littlehampton, 1978)

Janetzki, Ulrich, *Henriette Herz – Berliner Salon. Erinnerungen
    und Portraits* (Ullstein, 1984)

Jelavich, Peter, *Berlin Cabaret*, (Harvard, 1996)

Johnson, Hubert C., *Frederick The Great and His Officials*
    (Yale, 1975)

Jones, Dan, *Crusaders* (Head of Zeus, 2019)

Kähler, Susanne, with Krogel, Wolfgang & Uhlitz, Manfred, *150
    Jahre Metropole Berlin* (Elsengold, 2015)

Kardorff, Ursula von, *Diary of a Nightmare: Berlin 1942–1945*,
    trans. Ewan Butler (Hart-Davis, 1965)

Kästner, Erich, *Fabian*, trans. as *Going to the Dogs: The Story of a
    Moralist*. Introduction by Rodney Livingstone (NYRB, 1990)

——*Emil & The Detectives* (Red Fox, 1995)

——*Das Blaue Buch: Geheimes Kriegstagebuch 1941–1945*
    (Atrium, 2018)

Kendall, Bridget, *The Cold War: A New Oral History* (BBC
    Books, 2018)

Kerr, Alfred, *Aus dem Tagebuch eines Berliners* (Paperview, 2008)

Kerr, Judith, *When Hitler Stole Pink Rabbit* (HarperCollins, 1974)

Kessler, Harry Graf, *The Diaries of a Cosmopolitan 1918–1937*
  (Phoenix, 2000)
——*Walther Rathenau* (Fertig, 1969)
Keun, Irmgard, *Gilgi – Eine von Uns* (Ullstein, 2005)
Kiaulehn, Walther, *Berlin: Schicksal Einer Weltstadt* (Beck, 1976)
(insert above Kollwitz)
Koehn, Ilse, *Mischling zweiten Grades: Kindheit in der Nazizeit*
  (Rowohlt, 1987)
Kollwitz, Käthe, *Die Tagebucher 1908–1943* (BTB Random
  House, 2007)
Kotowski, Elke-Vera, *Gabriele Tergit: Großstadtchronistin der
  Weimarer Republik* (Hentrich, 2017)
Kühne, Gustav, *Carneval in Berlin* (Braunschweig George
  Westermann, 1880)
Ladd, Brian, *The Ghosts of Berlin* (University of Chicago Press, 1997)
Lange, Friedrich, *Großberliner Tagebuch 1920–1933* (Westkreuz
  Verlag, 1982)
Lange, Helene, *Lebenserinnerungen* (Herbig, 1921)
——*Briefe: Was ich hier geliebt* (Wunderlich, 1957)
Legg, J.W., *An Account of the Anointing of the First King
  of Prussia in 1701* (Harrison, 1899); reprinted from
  Archaeological Journal, June 1899
Lehndorff, Ernst Ahasverus Heinrich von, *Dreissig Jahre Am Hoffe
  Friedrichs Des Grossen* (Friedrich Andreas Berthes, 1907)
Lenya, Lotte, *Speak Low – The Letters of Kurt Weill and Lotte
  Lenya* (University of California Press, 1996)
Leonhard, Wolfgang, *Die Revolution entlässt ihre Kinder*
  (Ullstein, 1970)
Lewis, Alison, *Die Kunst des Verrats* (Würzburg, 2003)
Leydecker, Karl, *German Novelists of the Weimar Republic*
  (Camden House, 2006)
Löhken, Wilfried, *Die Revolution 1848: Berlin und Berlinerinnen
  aud den Barrikaden* (Hentrich, 1990)
MacGregor, Iain, *Checkpoint Charlie: The Cold War, the Berlin
  Wall and the Most Dangerous Place on Earth* (Constable, 2019)

MacGregor, Neil, *Germany: Memories of a Nation*
    (Penguin, 2014)

MacLean, Rory, *Berlin* (Weidenfeld & Nicolson, 2014)

Mander, John, *Berlin: The Eagle & The Bear* (Barrie &
    Rockcliff, 1959)

Mann, Golo, *The History of Germany Since 1789* (Chatto &
    Windus, 1972)

Mann, Thomas, *Royal Highness*, trans. A. Cecil Curtis
    (Minerva, 1997)

Mansel, Dr Philip, *King of the World: The Life of Louis XIV*
    (Allen Lane, 2019)

Masur, Gerhard, *Imperial Berlin* (Routledge & Kegan Paul, 1971)

Materna, Ingo & Ribbe, Wolfgang, *Geschichte in Daten Berlin*
    (Koehler & Amelang, 1997)

McKay, Derek, *The Great Elector* (Longman, 2001)

McLellan, David, *Karl Marx: A Biography* (Paladin, 1977)

Meckel, Christoph, with Weisner, Ulrich & Kollwitz, Hans, *Käthe
    Kollwitz* (Inter Nationes – Bad Godesberg, 1967)

Medick, Hans & Marschke, Benjamin, *Experiencing the Thirty
    Years War: A Brief History with Documents* (Bedford Series
    in History, 2013)

Meier, Norbert W.F., *Berlin im Mittelalter* (Story, 2012)

Metzger, Marc, *Das Berliner Schloss* (Story, 2018)

Meyer-Abich, Adolf, *Alexander von Humboldt* (Rowohlt, 1967)

Meyerbeer, Giacomo, *Briefwechsel und Tagebücher 1860–64*
    (Gruyter, 1959)

Middlebrook, Mathew & Everitt, C., *The Bomber Command War
    Diaries* (Viking, 1985)

Mirabeau, Comte Honoré Gabriel, *Secret Memories of The Court
    of Berlin* (M. Walter Dunne, 1901)

Mitford, Nancy, *Frederick The Great* (Hamish Hamilton, 1970)

Moorhouse, Roger, *Berlin at War: Life and Death in Hitler's
    Capital 1939–1945* (Vintage, 2011)

Mortimer, Geoff, *Eyewitness Accounts of the Thirty Years War
    1618–1648* (Palgrave, 2002)

Müller, Adriaan von, *Edelmann, Bürger, Bauer, Bettelman* (Harde & Spener, 1979)

——*Berlin Vor 800 Jahren: Städte, Dörfer, Wüstungen von der Gründung bis zu, 14. Jh.* (Bruno Hesling, 1968)

——*Reisebericht des Jacobus von Brugge 1220* (SMPK Staatliche Museum, 1987)

Müller-Mertens, Eckhardt, *Berlin im Mittelalter* (Druckerei Schweriner Volkszeitung, 1987)

Nachama, Andreas, with Schoeps, Julius & Simon, Hermann, *Jews in Berlin* (Henschel, 2002)

Nelson, Walter Henry, *The Berliners: Portrait of a People and a City* (Longmans, 1969)

Nentwig, Franziska, with Bartmann, Dominik, *West: Berlin – Eine Insel auf der Suche nach Festland* (Stadt Museum Berlin, 2015)

Neudegger, Johannes OSB, *Die Vergessene Generation: Aus dem Alltag eines Flakhelfers 1944–45* (EOS, 2010)

Nicolai, Friedrich, *Description De Villes De Berlin Et De Potsdam* (Berlin, 1769; reproduced by Wentworth Press, 2018)

——*Das Leben und die Meinungen des Herrn Magister Sebaldus Nothanker* (Reclam Leipzig, 1938)

Parthey, Lili, *Tagebücher aus Berliner Biedermeierzeit* (Leipzig, 1926)

Percy, Pierre-François, *Journal des Campagnes du Baron Percy* (Tallandier, 1986)

Pollard, James, *A Study in Municipal Government: The Corporation of Berlin* (Forgotten Books, 2017; reprint of original 1894 edition)

Rachel, Hugo, Papritz, Johannes & Wallich, Paul, *Berliner Großkaufleute und Kapitalisten. Erste Band: Bis zum Ende des Dreißjährigen Krieges* (Gesillius, 1934)

Read, Anthony & Fisher, David, *Berlin: The Biography of a City* (Pimlico, 1994)

Reis, Friedhelm, *Berlin – Geschichten und Anekdoten* (Berlin Flair, 2017)

Reissner, Alexander, *Berlin 1675–1945* (Oswald Wolff, 1984)

Ribbe, Wolfgang & Schmädeke, Jürgen, *Kleine Berlin Geschichte* (Historischen Kommission zu Berlin, 1988)

Ribbe, Wolfgang, *Schloß und Schloßbezirk in der Mitte Berlins* (BWV Berlin, 2005)

——*Geschichte Berlins 1 – von der Frühgeschichte bis zur Undustrialisierung* (C. Beck, 1988)

——*Geschichte Berlins 2 – von der Märzrevolution bis zur Gegenwart* (C. Beck, 1988)

——*Berlin – Geschichte in Daten* (Koehler & Amelang, 1997)

Rice, Condoleezza & Zelikow, Philip, *Germany United and Europe Transformed: A Study in Statecraft* (Harvard University Press, 1995)

Richie, Alexandra, *Faust's Metropolis* (Carroll & Graf, 1998)

Rürup, Reinhard (ed.), *Berlin 1945: A Documentation* (Landesarchiv Berlin, Arenhövel, 1995)

Russell, William, *Berlin Embassy* (MacFadden, 1962)

Saherwala, Geraldine, *Bürger, Baurer, Edelmann   Berlin im Mittelalter* (Nicolai, 1987)

Schäche, Barbara & Thamer, Hans-Ulrich, *Alltag in Berlin: das 19.Jh* (Elsengold, 2017)

Schiller, Frederick, *The Thirty Years War* (Jefferson Publications, 2016)

Schlesier, Karl-Heinz, *Flakhelfer to Grenadier: Memoir of a Boy Soldier* (Helion, 2014)

Schneider, Rolf, *Ritter, Ketzer, Handelsleute – Brandenburg und Berlin im Mittelalter* (Bebra, 2012)

Schneider, Wolfgang, *Berlin: Eine Kulturgeschichte in Bildern und Dokumenten* (Kiepenheuer, 1980)

Schoeps, Professor Doktor Julius, *Das Erbe Der Mendelssohns: Biografie einer Familie* (Fischer, 2013)

Schultz, Helga, *Berlin 1650–1800: Sozialgeschichte Einer Residenz* (Akademie-Verlag Berlin, 1987)

Schultz, Violet, *In Berlin in Stellung* (Hentrich, 2000)

Schwerin, Gräfin Sophie von, *Vor hundert Jahren: Errinerungen der Gräfin Sophie Schwerin* (Stargardt, 1909)

Seldeneck, Lucia Jay von, Huder, Carolin & Eidel, Verena, *111 Orten in Berlin die Geschichte Erzählen* (Emons, 2018)

Shirer, William, *Berlin Diary* (Sphere, 1970)

Sidgwick, Mrs Alfred, *Home Life in Germany* (Lightning Source, 2019)

Snyder, Louis L. (ed.), *Documents of German History* (Rutgers University Press, 1958)

Speer, Albert, *Inside the Third Reich* (Sphere, 1971)

Staël, De, Madame Anne-Louise Germaine, *Germany*, 2 vols (Hurd & Houghton, 1844)

Stargardt, Nicholas, *The German War* (Vintage, 2015)

Steegmann, Eva Rieger, *Göttliche Stimmen: Lebensberichte berühmter Sängerinnen von Elisabeth Mara bis Maria Callas* (Insel, 2002)

Steinitz, Regina & Neumärker, Uwe, *A Childhood and Youth Destroyed: My Life and Survival in Berlin* (Foundation Memorial to the Murdered Jews of Europe, 2017)

Stöver, Bernd, *Berlin: A Short History*, trans. Donna Stonecipher (C.H. Beck, 2012)

Streckfuss, Adolph, *Von Fischerdorf Zur Weltstadt: Berlin Seit 500 Jahren* (Berlin Seidel, 1864)

——*Berlin in 19. Jahrhundert* (Berlin Seidel, 1867)

——*1848 die Märzrevolution in Berlin: ein Augenzeuge Erzählt* (Köln, 1983)

(Insert above Sullivan)

Südekum, Albert, *Großstädtisches Wohnungselend* (Verl, 1908)

Sullivan, Paul & Krueger, Marcel, *Berlin: A Literary Guide for Travellers* (I.B. Tauris, 2016)

Sutcliffe, Anthony (ed.), *Metropolis 1890–1940* (Mansell, 1984)

Taylor, Frederick, *The Berlin Wall* (Bloomsbury, 2006)

Taylor, Ronald, *Berlin and its Culture* (Yale, 1997)

Tergit, Gabriele, *Käsebier Takes Berlin* (New York Review of Books, 2019)

Toland, John, *An Account of the Courts of Prussia and Hanover* (first published 1705; this edn Manuscript Publishers, 2013)

Tunner, William, *Over the Hump* (Duell, Sloane & Pierce, 1964)

Unger, Helene Friederike, *Briefe über Berlin: aus den Briefen einer reisenden Dame an ihren Bruder in H. 1798* (Aldus, 1930)

Varnhagen, Rahel, *Jeder wunsch wird Frivolität gennant* (Luchterhand, 1983)

——*Briefe au Aufzeichnungen* (Luchterhand, 1983)

Veigel, Hans Joachim, *Die mittelalterliche Handelsstadt Berlin – Cölln* (Märkisches Museum, 1987)

Virchow, Rudolf, *Briefe an seine Eltern 1839 bis 1864* (Wentworth, 2018)

Volks, Sybil, *Torstraße 1* (dtv, 2014)

Warnecke, Heinz, *Barrikadenstandorte 1848* (Luisenstädt, 1999)

Wassiltschikow, Marie, *Die Berliner Tagebücher der Marie 'Missie' Wassiltschikow* (Btb, 1990)

Watson, Alexander, *Ring of Steel: Germany and Austria-Hungary at War 1914–1918* (Allen Lane, 2014)

Webber, Andrew J., *The Cambridge Companion to the Literature of Berlin* (CUP, 2017)

Wedgwood, C.V., *The Thirty Years War* (Methuen, 1981)

Werner, Henry, *Berlin 1000 Jahre Geschichte* (Elsengold, 2014)

Wernicke, Kurt, *Vormärz – März – Nachmärz: Studien zur Berliner Politik und Sozialgeschichte 1843–1853* (Luisenstädt, 1999)

White-Spunner, Barney, *Of Living Valour* (Simon & Schuster, 2015)

Wilson, Peter H., *German Armies 1648–1806* (UCL Press, 1998)

Winteroll, Michael, *Die Geschichte Berlins* (Nicolai, 2012)

Wirth, Irmgard, *Berliner Biedermeier* (Rembrandt, 1972)

Zorn, Olivia, with Hanus, Christina, *Museum Island: History & Stories* (Elsengold, 2019)

Catalogues and exhibitions

Fragen an die deutsche Geshichte: Ideen, Kräfte, Entscheidungen Von 1800 bis zur Gegenwart (Berlin Bundestag Press, 1984)

The East German Handbook: Art & Artefacts from the GDR (Wende Museum Produced by Benedikt Taschen, 2014)

Berlin 18/19: Das Lange Leben Der Novemerrevolution
(Märkisches Museum, 2018–2019)

ACADEMIC PAPERS AND ARTICLES

Altenhöner, Florian, *Vor der Revolution: Berlin in der
Endphase des Krieges Zwischen Januarstreik und
Waffenstillstandersuchen* (Berliner Geschichte Ausgabe 15)

Asche, Matthias, *Wie tolerant waren die Hohenzollern?* (Berliner
Geschichte Ausgabe 19)

Börsch-Supan, Helmut, *Neues Kunstleben Nach Der Kriegs-
Katastrophe: Der Grosse Kurfürst Als Mäzen* (v Juli 2015)

British Army Public Information, Berlin, *Fotoreihe von den 49
Jahren der Anwesenheit des Britischen Militärs in Berlin*
(Army Public Information Berlin 1994)

Brumme, Carina, *Stiftung, Sühne, Konkurrenz – die mittelalterliche
Kirche Berlin-Cöllns* (Berliner Geschichte Ausgabe 8)

Deuschle, Matthias A., *Reformations-gedenken im Berlin des 19.
Und 20. Jahrhunderts* (Berliner Geschichte Ausgabe 8)

Escher, Felix, *Mittelalterliche Herrschaft in Berlin und
Brandenburg* (Berliner Geschichte Ausgabe 14)

Feuerstein-Praßer, Karin, *Königin Elisabeth Christines Leben am
Preußischen Hof* (Berliner Geschichte Ausgabe 16)

Finkelnburg, Klaus, *Die preußischen Verfassung von 1848 und
1850* (Berliner Geschichte Ausgabe 13)

Fischbacher, Thomas, *Mythos Grosser Kurfürst* (Berliner
Geschichte Ausgabe Juli 2015)

Juchler, Ingo, *Die deutsche Revolution 1918–19 in Berlin* (Berliner
Geschichte Ausgabe 15)

Kaiser, Dr Michael, *Anna von Preussen: Der Gewinn des
Niederrheinischen Erbes* (Lisa-Gerda-Henkel-
Stiftung 5302)

Kirstaedter, Gerda, *Errinerungen von Gerda Kirstaedter*

Krogel, Wolfgang, *Totendanz und Elendgilden – Kirchen, Klöster
und Hospitale* (Berliner Geschichte Ausgabe 14)

Krosigk, Klaus-Henning von, *Lenné und sein grünes Erbe in Berlin* (Berliner Geschichte Ausgabe 10)

Lange, Markus, *Fer 18. März und due Folgen* (Berliner Geschichte Ausgabe 13)

Marschke, Professor Benjamin, *Vater und Sohn: Die Gefahr vom Kronprinzen. Friedrich der Große und die Dynastie der Hohenzollern* (Stiftung Preußische Schlösser und Gärten, Potsdam 29 September 2011)

——*A Court Society without a Court: Power, Communication and Monarchical Self-Representation in King Frederick William I's Prussia (1713–1740)* (Forschungskolloquium, Geschichte der Frühen Neuziet, Friedrich Meineke Institute, Freie Universität, Berlin. 15 June 2010)

——'*Hard Working, Sincere & Frugal': Changes and Continuity in Monarchy and Political Culture in the Eighteenth Century: The Case of Frederick William I of Prussia (1713–1740)* (University of Oregon, Eugene, 5 May 2009)

——'*Le Caractère Bizarre: Princes' Power, Aristocratic Norms and Personal Eccentricities: The Case of Frederick William I of Prussia (1713–1740)*' (German Studies Association Annual Conference, San Diego, 4 October 2007)

——'*Von dem am Königl. Preußischen Hofe abgeschafften Ceremoniel': Monarchical Representation and Court Ceremony in Frederick William I's Prussia* (Frühe Neuzeit Interdisziplinär International Conference, Duke University, Durham, 7 April 2005)

Melisch, Claudia & Garlisch, Ines, *Die Gründung Berlins und seine ersten Bewohner* (Berliner Geschichte Ausgabe 14)

Schultz, Kurt, *Wagenschott und Berliner Roggen – Handel und Handwerk* (Berliner Geschichte Ausgabe 14)

Seelow Scholar: British Army Berlin Battlefield Study Guide 2019

Stegmann, Andreas, *Die Reformation in Berlin-Cölln* (Berliner Geschichte Ausgabe 8)

Stolpe, Manfred, *Der Fromme Kurfürst: Friedrich Wilhelms Religionspolitik* (Berliner Geschichte Ausgabe Juli 2015)

Stölzl, Prof. Dr Christoph, *Nachdenken uber Preussen*
(Lecture Berlin)

Sträßner, Ulrike, *Elisabeth von Dänemark und die Reformation in
Brandenburg 1485–1555* (Lisa-Gerda-Henkel Stiftung 5305)

Strohmaier-Wiederanders, Gerlinde, *Glaubenskonflikte und
Toleranz im Berlin 17. Jahrhunderts* (Berliner Geschichte
Ausgabe 8)

Studemann, Frederick, *Berlin's Memory Palace* (*Financial Times*
magazine, 14–15 September 2019)

Uhlitz, Manfred, *Die Hugenotten in Berlin* (Berliner Geschichte
Ausgabe 19)

——*Der Aufstieg Brandenburgs Unter Dem Grossen Kurfürsten*
(Berliner Geschichte Ausgabe Juli 2015)

——*Die Hugenotten und die Berliner Wirtschaft* (Berliner
Geschichte Ausgabe 19)

Violet, Robert, *Globalisierung vor 200 Jahren – Das weltweite
Netzwerk einer Refugié-Familie* (Berliner Geschichte
Ausgabe 19)

Wagner, Volker, *Juden im mittelalterlichen Berlin* (Berliner
Geschichte Ausgabe 14)

Welz, Joachim, *Biedermeier auf dem Vulkan* (Berliner Geschichte
Ausgabe 13)

Wendebourg, Dorothea, *Die Reformation im Heiligen Römischen
Reich Deutscher Nation* (Berliner Geschichte Ausgabe 8)

Wetzel, Jürgen, *Die Französische Gemeinde in Berlin* (Berliner
Geschichte Ausgabe 19)

——*Zwischen Königstreue und Bürgerinteressen* (Berliner
Geschichte Ausgabe 13)

Wimmer, Clemens, '*Nach Der Heutigen Art Ein Ganz New
Werck*': *Der Berliner Lustgarten Unter Dem Grossen
Kurfürsten* (Berliner Geschichte Ausgabe Juli 2015)

Zeitler, Carl Ludwig, '*Angeschossen sein, soll wehe tun!*' (Berliner
Geschichte Ausgabe 13)

ACKNOWLEDGEMENTS

A lot of people have very kindly helped me write this book and, as ever, it is difficult to know how to thank them all. I must, however, start with the late Michael Sissons, my agent at Peters Fraser & Dunlop, who very sadly died between commissioning it and publication. This was the last book Michael sold and I hope I have been able to do him justice. Along with many other authors, most far more distinguished than me, I owe him a huge debt for his encouragement, friendship and inspiration. I am most grateful to Fiona Petheram, who has taken on Michael's mantle and who saw the book through to its birth. I am also deeply grateful to Iain MacGregor, then heading the non-fiction side of Simon & Schuster, who knows Berlin well and who gave me so much support in getting this project started. Many thanks also to Ian Marshall, Iain's successor, to Louise Davies and to everyone else at Simon & Schuster for all their continuing help.

I could not have written the book without the help of Sabine Schereck – researcher, translator, mentor and friend – who has spent long days trawling Berlin's archives, nor without Conrad Deverell and Jonathan Barr's accurate translation; very many thanks to them all. Neither could I have written it without the unstinting help and advice of Professor Wolfgang Pfaffenberger and the ever-helpful staff of the Verein für Geschichte Berlins (the Berlin History Society), particularly their archivists in the Neuer Marstall.

In the UK my deepest thanks to Dr Philip Mansel, both for his help and for introducing me to Marie-Louise von Plessen, who gave me so much encouragement; to Lord Green for his generous advice and to Tim Church for connecting us; to Emma Treichl for all her introductions from her seemingly inexhaustible address book and to my business partner, George Busby, for his forbearance and his introductions. A particular thank you to Neil MacGregor, who knows Berlin far better than most, for his kind introductions, advice and his time.

In Berlin I am particularly indebted to Nigel Dunkley for his endless help and for so kindly spending long hours guiding me around twentieth-century Berlin and following the Soviet 1945 advance. Many thanks also to Irene Dunkley for her time and reminiscences of East Berlin; to Astrid von Deichmann for her wisdom and advice; to Peter and Isabel von Jena, representatives of one of Berlin's oldest and most distinguished families; to Falk Alexander and Christina, Freiherr und Freifrau von Oeynhausen and Professor Dr Friedrich-Carl Wachs for their advice and hospitality; to Mikael Adam for his memories of 1989; to Professor Dr Julius Schoeps and Dr Elke-Vera Kotowski of the Mendelssohn Institute; to Dr Ekkehard Klausa of the Gedenkstätte Deutscher Widerstand; and special thanks to Dr Paul Spies, Vorstand und Direktor des Stadtmuseums Berlin, and to Professor Doktor Christoph Stölzl, Founding Director of Stiftung Exil Berlin, the new Museum of Exile planned to open beside the old Anhalter Bahnhof.

From wider Germany special thanks to Professor Benjamin Marschke, Professor of History at the Humboldt University, for his enormous help in bringing early-eighteenth-century Berlin to life; to Dr Adam Storring of Tubingen University for his endless wise advice; to Busso Freise, Charlotte von Saldern and Irmgard von Puttkamer-Moog for all their help and leading me to such interesting material.

Lastly, a very big thank you to my family, and dogs, who have put up with me closeted for long hours devouring Berlin's history when I ought more properly to have been spending time with them.

INDEX